Methodology in Language Teaching

An Anthology of Current Practice

Edited by

Jack C. Richards
Willy A. Renandya

CAMBRIDGE
UNIVERSITY PRESS

CAMBRIDGE UNIVERSITY PRESS

Cambridge, New York, Melbourne, Madrid, Cape Town, Singapore,
São Paulo, New Delhi, Dubai, Tokyo

Cambridge University Press
c/o Cambridge University Press India Pvt. Ltd.
Cambridge House
4381/4, Ansari Road, Daryaganj
New Delhi 110002
India

www.cambridge.org
Information on this title: www.cambridge.org/9780521004404

First published 2002
First South Asian edition 2010

Reprinted 2011

This South Asian edition is based on Jack C. Richards and Willy A.
Renandya / Methodology in Language Teaching / 9780521004404 / 2002

Printed in India at Shree Maitrey Printech Pvt. Ltd., Noida – 201301

A catalogue record for this publication is available from the British Library

Library of Congress Cataloging in Publication Data

Methodology in language teaching : an anthology of current practice / edited by Jack
C. Richards and Willy A. Renandya.
p. cm.
Includes bibliographical references and indexes.
ISBN 978-0-521-00440-4 (pbk.) ISBN 978-0-521-80829-3 (hbk.)
1. Language and languages - Study and teaching. 2. English language - Study and
teaching - Foreign speakers. I. Richards, Jack C. II. Renandya, Willy A.
P51.M44 2001
418'0071 - dc21 2001025746

ISBN-13 978-0-521-15203-7 (paperback)

CONTENTS

ACKNOWLEDGMENTS

We are grateful to the contributors to this volume for allowing us to include their papers in this anthology. All royalties generated from the sale of this book payable to the editors and to the contributors are being donated to the South East Asian Ministers of Education Organization (SEAMEO) Regional Language Centre (RELC), Singapore, to support scholarships for English language teachers from SEAMEO member countries to attend in-service courses offered at RELC.

Introduction

This book seeks to provide an overview of current approaches, issues, and practices in the teaching of English to speakers of other languages (TESOL). It has the following goals:

- to provide a comprehensive overview of the field of second and foreign language teaching, with a particular focus on issues related to the teaching of English
- to provide a source of teaching principles and classroom activities which teachers can refer to in their work
- to provide a source of readings and activities that can be used in TESOL teacher-education programs, for both preservice and in-service courses

The articles in this anthology offer a comprehensive picture of approaches to the teaching of English and illustrate the complexity underlying many of the practical planning and instructional activities it involves. These activities include teaching English at elementary, secondary, and tertiary levels, teacher training, language testing, curriculum and materials development, the use of computers and other technology in teaching, as well as research on different aspects of second language learning. The issues that form the focus of attention in TESOL around the world reflect the contexts in which English is taught and used. English in different parts of the world where it is not a native language may have the status of either a "second" or a "foreign" language. In the former case, it is a language that is widely used in society and learners need to acquire English in order to survive in society. In the latter case, it may be taught as a school subject but has restricted uses in society at large. Learners of English may be studying American, Canadian, Australian, British, or some other variety of English. They may be learning it for educational, occupational, or social purposes. They may be in a formal classroom setting or studying independently, using a variety of media and resources. The teachers of English may be native speakers of English or those for whom it is a second or foreign language.

The issues seen to be important at any particular point in time and the approaches to teaching that are followed in different parts of the world reflect contextual factors such as those just mentioned, current understanding of the nature of second language learning, educational trends and practices in different parts of the world, and the priorities the profession accords to specific issues and practices. In the last 30 years or so, the field of Teaching English as a Second or Foreign Language has developed into a dynamic worldwide community of language teaching professionals that seeks to improve the quality of language teaching and learning through addressing the key issues that shape the design and delivery of language teaching. These issues center on

- understanding learners and their roles, rights, needs, motivations, strategies, and the processes they employ in second language learning
- understanding the nature of language teaching and learning and the roles teachers, teaching methods, and teaching materials play in facilitating successful learning
- understanding how English functions in the lives of learners, the way the English language works, the particular difficulties it poses for second language learners, and how learners can best achieve their goals in learning English
- understanding how schools, classrooms, communities, and the language teaching profession can best support the teaching and learning of English

It is this view of teaching that has guided the selection of articles for this anthology. The anthology brings together articles which have been published in journals in many different parts of the world but which deal with issues that are of importance no matter where English is being taught. (Only three articles in the collection – those by Farrell, Lewis, and Renandya and Jacobs – have not been published previously.) The goal of the collection is to bring together in one volume articles which treat the range of issues normally included in TESOL methodology courses. We have sought to include only recent articles or articles that present perspectives that are still current. Most of the articles in the collection, therefore, have been published within the last 5 years. Nearly 70% of the articles have been published since 1996, and of the rest, none was published before 1992. The following topics are included:

- *the nature of teaching* – methods, teaching skills
- *classroom interaction and management* – lesson planning, grouping, classroom dynamics
- *teaching the skills* – reading, writing, listening, speaking
- *understanding learner variables* – learning strategies, motivation, age
- *addressing linguistic competence* – grammar, vocabulary, and pronunciation
- *curriculum factors* – syllabus design, materials development
- *assessment of learning* – alternative assessment, proficiency tests
- *the role of technology* – video, computers, the Internet
- *teacher development* – evaluating teaching, classroom research, action research

The book is organized into sixteen sections that reflect these topics. Each section includes a balance of articles that address both theory and practice. Key issues in relevant theory and research are presented. At the same time, classroom practitioners show not only how theory can inform classroom practice, but also how the practical realities of teaching can inform theory and research.

Two sets of discussion questions are included. One set serves as prereading questions and seeks to explore some of the background knowledge, beliefs, and practical experience that student teachers and teachers in training possess and that can provide a source of reference when reading each article. The second set of questions is designed to be used after the section has been read and seeks to engage the readers in critical reflection on the issues discussed, as well as to provide application to teaching practice. We hope that student teachers, teachers, and teacher educators will find the collection a useful resource for the understanding of current approaches and practices in the teaching of English as a second or foreign language.

SECTION I

APPROACHES TO TEACHING

INTRODUCTION

The two papers in this section reexamine the notion of methods of teaching and offer complementary perspectives on how the nature of teaching can be understood. Although for much of the twentieth century a primary concern of the language teaching profession was to find more effective methods of language teaching, by the twenty-first century there has been a movement away from a preoccupation with generic teaching methods toward a more complex view of language teaching which encompasses a multifaceted understanding of the teaching and learning processes. Brown traces this movement from a preoccupation with "methods" to a focus on "pedagogy."

The notion of teaching methods has had a long history in language teaching, as is witnessed by the rise and fall of a variety of methods throughout the recent history of language teaching. Some, such as Audiolingualism, became the orthodox teaching methods of the 1970s in many parts of the world. Other guru-led methods such as the Silent Way attracted small but devoted followers in the 1980s and beyond, but attract little attention today. Many teachers have found the notion of methods attractive over the last one hundred or so years, since they offer apparently foolproof systems for classroom instruction and are hence sometimes embraced enthusiastically as a panacea for the "language teaching problem." The 1970s and 1980s were perhaps the years of greatest enthusiasm for methods. In what has been called the "post-methods era," attention has shifted to teaching and learning processes and the contributions of the individual teacher to language teaching pedagogy.

Brown discusses a number of reasons for the decline of the methods syndrome in contemporary discussions of language teaching. As he and others have commented, the notion of all-purpose "designer methods" that will work anywhere and for everyone raises a number of problems:

- Methods are typically top-down impositions of experts' views of teaching. The role of the individual teacher is minimized. His or her role is to apply the method and adapt his or her teaching style to make it conform to the method. Methods are hence prescriptive.

- Methods fail to address the broader contexts of teaching and learning and focus on only one small part of a more complex set of elements. Brown describes what may be called a "curriculum development" approach to teaching, which begins with diagnosis (i.e., needs analysis, syllabus, and materials development), then moves to treatment (i.e., instruction and pedagogy), and involves issues of assessment (i.e., testing and evaluation).

For Brown, the term *method* is best replaced by the term *pedagogy*. The former implies a static set of procedures, whereas the latter suggests the dynamic interplay between teachers, learners, and instructional materials during the process of teaching and learning. Brown characterizes the basis of language teaching pedagogy in terms of twelve principles that reflect current research and theory about second language acquisition.

Richards seeks to show how three different conceptions of teaching in the recent history of language teaching have led to different understandings of the essential skills of teachers and to different approaches to teacher training and teacher development. *Science-research conceptions* of teaching seek to develop teaching methods from applications of research, and see improvements in teaching as dependent on research into learning, motivation, memory, and related factors. Good teaching is a question of applying the findings of research. Task-Based Language Teaching and attempts to apply brain research to teaching are current examples of this approach. *Theory-philosophy conceptions* of teaching derive from rational "commonsense" understandings of teaching or from one's ideology or value system, rather than from research. Communicative Language Teaching (CLT) is a good example of this approach, since it is based on an ideology rather than a research agenda, as are such movements as Critical Theory and Critical Pedagogy. Advocates of these movements see their mission as to convince teachers of the correctness of the theory, to review their teaching to see to what extent it matches their values, and to seek to incorporate the relevant principles or values into their teaching. *Art-craft conceptions* of teaching, by comparison, see good teaching as something unique and personal to teachers. A teaching theory is viewed as something that is constructed by individual teachers. From this perspective, teaching is viewed as driven by teachers' attempts to integrate theory and practice. Teacher-education programs give teachers a grounding in academic theory and research, which they test out against the practical realities of teaching. In so doing, they create their own new understandings of teaching, which are expanded and revised as they tackle new problems and deepen their experiential and knowledge base of teaching.

Many of the issues highlighted in this section will reappear throughout this collection of papers. In many of the papers, the writers describe approaches to teaching which are informed by educational theory and practice and exemplify many of the issues Brown touches on in his paper, as well as one or another of the conceptions of teaching described by Richards. At the same time, many of the papers illustrate the personal and unique solutions to problems and issues that individual teachers or groups of teachers often find in their teaching, demonstrating that for many teachers the day-to-day process of teaching is a kind of ongoing research and experimentation.

Discussion Questions

Before Reading

1. What experience do you have of learning a second or foreign language? How would you characterize the teacher's teaching method? How effective did you find it?
2. What do you understand by a teaching "method" and what is the source of different methods? How do methods often differ from one another?
3. Is your teaching based on a particular method of teaching? If so, how did you learn to teach in this way?
4. Do you agree that the notion of "method" presents a restrictive view of the nature of teaching? When might it be useful to teach according to a specific method?
5. How do you understand the differences between an "approach" and a "method"? Is this a useful distinction?
6. Why do you think many teachers are attracted to the idea of "a best method"?
7. What are the three most important principles that you think a teacher has to be aware of in teaching an ESL class? Where do these (and other principles) come from?
8. Some learners appear to be more effective language learners than others because they use more effective learning strategies. What do you understand by a "learning strategy"? Can you give examples of strategies that successful learners might use?
9. How important do you think risk taking is in language learning?
10. What role do you think motivation plays in learning a language? How can learner motivation be developed?
11. Which of these words do you think can be used to describe teaching? What view of teaching do these terms suggest to you: *a science, a profession, an art, a craft, a technology, an industry?*
12. What role does theory play in shaping teaching practice? Is good practice dependent on theory?

After Reading

1. Examine the twelve principles proposed by Brown. Do some of them seem more important than others? Are there any you would wish to add or delete?
2. How can teachers gather and make use of the kind of information Brown discusses under "diagnosis"?
3. Examine the suggestions Brown gives for developing "strategic investment." Can you suggest other activities that address each of the ten principles Brown discusses?
4. Select a group of learners you are familiar with. What do you think are their primary motivations for learning English? In what ways can learner motivations be explored and addressed in a language program?
5. Reflect on your own experiences as a language learner. To what extent were you taught strategies for language learning? Did you develop independently an awareness of the importance of strategies? What examples can you give?
6. What do you think is the role of research in improving our understanding of teaching?
7. How do you think teachers develop their ideas about teaching? What sources do you think shape their beliefs and practice?

8. What do you think are the most essential skills of a good language teacher? What is the source of your ideas about the nature of teaching skills?
9. Describe your personal philosophy of teaching and some of the key beliefs about teachers, learners, and teaching that influence your approach to teaching. How would this philosophy be evident to someone observing you teaching a class?
10. How do you think teachers change their approach to teaching over time? What do you think are some of the differences between a novice teacher and an expert teacher? How can teachers with different levels of experience learn from each other?

CHAPTER 1

English Language Teaching in the "Post-Method" Era: Toward Better Diagnosis, Treatment, and Assessment

H. Douglas Brown

INTRODUCTION

In the century spanning the mid-1880s to the mid-1980s, the language teaching profession was involved in what many pedagogical experts would call a search. That search was for a single, ideal method, generalizable across widely varying audiences, that would successfully teach students a foreign language in the classroom. Historical accounts of the profession tend, therefore, to describe a succession of methods, each of which is more or less discarded in due course as a new method takes its place. I will comment on "the changing winds and shifting sands" (Marckwardt, 1972, p. 5) of that history momentarily; but first, we should try to understand what we mean by *method.*

What is a method? More than three decades ago, Edward Anthony (1963) gave us a definition that has quite admirably withstood the test of time. His concept of method was the second of three hierarchical elements, namely, *approach*, *method*, and *technique*. An approach, according to Anthony, was a set of assumptions dealing with the nature of language, learning, and teaching. Method was defined as an overall plan for systematic presentation of language based on a selected approach. It followed that techniques were specific classroom activities consistent with a method, and therefore in harmony with an approach as well.

Some disagreement over Anthony's definition can occasionally be found in the literature. For Richards and Rodgers (1986), method was an umbrella term to capture redefined approaches, designs, and procedures. Similarly, Prabhu (1990) thought of method as both classroom activities and the theory that informs them. Despite these and a handful of other attempted redefinitions (see Pennycook, 1989), we still commonly refer to methods in terms of Anthony's earlier understanding. For most researchers and practicing teachers, a method is a set of theoretically unified classroom techniques thought to be generalizable across a wide variety of contexts and audiences. Thus, for example, we speak of the

Audiolingual Method, the Direct Method, and of the Silent Way or Suggestopedia, all as methods.

Methods: A Century-Old Obsession

Ironically, the whole concept of separate methods is no longer a central issue in language teaching practice (see Kumaravadivelu, 1994, among others). In fact, in the mid-1980s, H. H. Stern (1985, p. 251) lamented our "century-old obsession," our "prolonged preoccupation [with methods] that has been increasingly unproductive and misguided," as we vainly searched for the ultimate method that would serve as the final answer.

That search might be said to have begun around 1880 with François Gouin's publication of *The Art of Teaching and Learning Foreign Languages* (1880), in which his Series Method was advocated. This was followed at the turn of the century by the Direct Method of Charles Berlitz. The Audiolingual Method of the late 1940s and the so-called Cognitive-Code Learning Method of the early 1960s followed. Then, in a burst of innovation, the "spirited seventies," as I like to refer to them, brought us what David Nunan (1989) termed the "designer" methods: Community Language Learning, the Silent Way, Suggestopedia, Total Physical Response, and others. This latter flurry was not unlike an earlier period in the field of psychotherapy which burgeoned with a plethora of "methods" of therapy; some of the "designer" terms of that era were *T group*, *encounter group*, *analytical*, *Gestalt*, *marathon group*, *conjoint family*, *shock*, *client-centered*, and *narcosis therapy*, *electro-narcosis*, *biochemotherapy*, and *analytic psychobiology*!

Why are methods no longer the milestones of our language teaching journey through time? Our requiem for methods might list four possible causes of demise:

1. Methods are too prescriptive, assuming too much about a context before the context has even been identified. They are therefore overgeneralized in their potential application to practical situations.
2. Generally, methods are quite distinctive at the early, beginning stages of a language course and rather indistinguishable from each other at later stages. In the first few days of a Community Language Learning class, for example, the students witness a unique set of experiences in their small circles of translated language whispered in their ears. But, within a matter of weeks, such classrooms can look like any other learner-centered curriculum.
3. It was once thought that methods could be empirically tested by scientific quantification to determine which one is "best." We have now discovered that something as artful and intuitive as language pedagogy cannot ever be so clearly verified by empirical validation.
4. Methods are laden with what Pennycook (1989) referred to as "interested knowledge" – the quasi-political or mercenary agendas of their proponents. Recent work in the power and politics of English language teaching (see, especially, Pennycook, 1994; Tollefson, 1995; and Holliday, 1994) has demonstrated that methods, often the creations of the powerful "center," become vehicles of a "linguistic imperialism" (Phillipson, 1992) targeting the disempowered periphery.

David Nunan (1991, p. 228) summed it up nicely:

> It has been realised that there never was and probably never will be a method for all, and the focus in recent years has been on the development of

classroom tasks and activities which are consonant with what we know about second language acquisition, and which are also in keeping with the dynamics of the classroom itself.

A Principled Approach

And so, as we lay to rest the methods that have become so familiar to us in recent decades, what assurance do we have today of the viability of our language teaching profession?

Through the 1970s and into the early 1980s, there was a good deal of hoopla about the "designer" methods. Even though they were not widely adopted standards of practice, they were nevertheless symbolic of a profession at least partially caught up in a mad scramble to invent a new method when the very concept of method was eroding under our feet. We did not need a new method. We needed, instead, to get on with the business of unifying our *approach*[1] to language teaching and of designing effective tasks and techniques informed by that approach.

By the end of the 1980s, such an approach was clearly becoming evident in teaching practices worldwide. We had learned some profound lessons from our past wanderings. We had learned to make enlightened choices of teaching practices that were solidly grounded in the best of what we knew about second language learning and teaching. We had amassed enough research on learning and teaching in a multiplicity of contexts that we were indeed formulating an integrated approach to language pedagogy. Of course, we had not attained a theoretical mountaintop by any means; much remained – and still remains – to be questioned and investigated.

It should be clear from the foregoing that, as "enlightened" teachers, we can think in terms of a number of possible methodological – or, shall we say, pedagogical – options at our disposal for tailoring classes to particular contexts. Our approach – or theory of language and language learning – therefore takes on great importance. One's approach to language teaching is the theoretical rationale that underlies everything that happens in the classroom. It is the cumulative body of knowledge and principles that enables teachers, as "technicians" in the classroom, to diagnose the needs of students, to treat students with successful pedagogical techniques, and to assess the outcome of those treatments.

An approach to language pedagogy is not just a set of static principles "set in stone." It is, in fact, a dynamic composite of energies within a teacher that changes (or should change, if one is a growing teacher) with continued experience in learning and teaching. There is far too much that we do not know collectively about this process, and there are far too many new research findings pouring in, to assume that a teacher can confidently assert that he or she knows everything that needs to be known about language and language learning.

One teacher's approach may, of course, differ on various issues from that of a colleague, or even of "experts" in the field, who differ among themselves. There are two reasons for variation at the approach level: (1) an approach is by definition dynamic and therefore subject to some "tinkering" as a result of one's observation and experience; and (2) research in second language acquisition and pedagogy almost always yields findings that are subject to interpretation rather than giving conclusive evidence.

The interaction between one's approach and classroom practice is the key to dynamic teaching. The best teachers are able to take calculated risks in the classroom: as new student needs are perceived, innovative pedagogical techniques are attempted, and the follow-up assessment yields an observed judgment on their effectiveness. Initial inspiration for such innovation comes from the approach level, but the feedback that teachers gather from actual implementation then reshapes and modifies their overall understanding of what learning and teaching are – which, in turn, may give rise to a new insight and more innovative possibilities, and the cycle continues.

Twelve Principles

I would like to suggest that viable current approaches to language teaching are "principled," in that there is perhaps a finite number of general research-based principles on which classroom practice is grounded. The twelve principles that I list and define in this section (see Brown, 1994a, for a complete discussion with definitions and examples) are an inexhaustive number of what I would assert to be relatively widely accepted thoretical assumptions about second language acquisition. There is sometimes disagreement in their interpretation and their application in the classroom, but they nevertheless comprise a body of constructs which few would dispute as central to most language acquisition contexts. They are briefly summarized here.

1. Automaticity

Efficient second language learning involves a timely movement of the control of a few language forms into the automatic processing of a relatively unlimited number of language forms. Overanalyzing language, thinking too much about its forms, and consciously lingering on rules of language all tend to impede this graduation to automaticity.

2. Meaningful Learning

Meaningful learning will lead toward better long-term retention than rote learning. One among many examples of meaningful learning is found in content-centered approaches to language teaching.

3. The Anticipation of Reward

Human beings are universally driven to act, or "behave," by the anticipation of some sort of reward – tangible or intangible, short-term or long-term – that will ensue as a result of the behavior. Although long-term success in language learning requires a more intrinsic motive (see 4 below), the power of immediate rewards in a language class is undeniable. One of the tasks of the teacher is to create opportunities for those moment-by-moment rewards that can keep classrooms interesting, if not exciting.

4. Intrinsic Motivation

Sometimes, reward-driven behavior is dependent on extrinsic (externally administered by someone else) motivation. But a more powerful category of reward is one which is intrinsically driven within the learner. When behavior stems from needs, wants, or desires within oneself, the behavior itself has the potential to be self-rewarding. In such a context, externally administered rewards are unnecessary; learners are likely to maintain the behavior beyond the immediate presence of teachers, parents, and other tutors.

5. Strategic Investment

Successful mastery of the second language will be, to a large extent, the result of a learner's own personal "investment" of time, effort, and attention to the second language in the form of an individualized battery of strategies for comprehending and producing the language.

6. Language Ego

As human beings learn to use a second language, they develop a new mode of thinking, feeling, and acting – a second identity. The new "language ego," intertwined with the second language, can easily create within the learner a sense of fragility, defensiveness, and a raising of inhibitions.

7. SELF-CONFIDENCE

The eventual success that learners attain in a task is partially a factor of their belief that they indeed are fully capable of accomplishing the task. Self-esteem, at least global self-esteem, lies at the roots of eventual attainment.

8. RISK TAKING

Successful language learners, in their realistic appraisal of themselves as vulnerable beings yet capable of accomplishing tasks, must be willing to become "gamblers" in the game of language, to attempt to produce and to interpret language that is a bit beyond their absolute certainty.

9. THE LANGUAGE–CULTURE CONNECTION

Whenever you teach a language, you also teach a complex system of cultural customs, values, and ways of thinking, feeling, and acting.

10. THE NATIVE LANGUAGE EFFECT

The native language of learners will be a highly significant system on which learners will rely to predict the target-language system. Although that native system will exercise both facilitating and interfering (positive and negative transfer) effects on the production and comprehension of the new language, the interfering effects are likely to be the most salient.

11. INTERLANGUAGE

Second language learners tend to go through a systematic or quasi-systematic developmental process as they progress to full competence in the target language. Successful interlanguage development is partially a factor of utilizing feedback from others. Teachers in language classrooms can provide such feedback, but more important, can help learners to generate their own feedback outside of the language classroom.

12. COMMUNICATIVE COMPETENCE

Given that communicative competence is the goal of a language classroom, instruction needs to point toward all of its components: organizational, pragmatic, strategic, and psychomotoric. Communicative goals are best achieved by giving due attention to language use and not just usage, to fluency and not just accuracy, to authentic language and contexts, and to students' eventual need to apply classroom learning to heretofore unrehearsed contexts in the real world.

DIAGNOSIS, TREATMENT, AND ASSESSMENT

A principled approach to language teaching encourages the language teacher to engage in a carefully crafted process of diagnosis, treatment, and assessment. It enables us initially to account for communicative and situational needs anticipated among designated learners, and to diagnose appropriate curricular treatment for those specific learners in their distinctive context and for their particular goals. It helps us then to devise effective pedagogical objectives which have taken into account all the contextual variables in a classroom. A sound, comprehensive approach underlies the creation of a set of learning experiences that are appropriate, given specific contexts and purposes, for realizing established objectives. It enables teachers to assess what went right and what went wrong in a lesson, that is, to systematically evaluate the accomplishment of curricular objectives. And it assists them in revising activities, lessons, materials, and curricula.

DIAGNOSIS

The first phase of the diagnostic stage of language pedagogy begins with curricular plans and continues as an ongoing monitoring process in the classroom. Language curricula call for an initial study of what Richards (1990) calls "situational" needs, or the context of the teaching. Situational needs include consideration of the country of the institution, the socioeconomic and educational background of the students, the specific purposes the students have in learning a language, and institutional constraints that are imposed on a curriculum. Some of the twelve principles cited earlier come into play in isolating situational needs:

- Is language proficiency perceived by students as intrinsically motivating?
- To what extent will the language in question involve students in wrestling with a "new identity" and therefore imply a language ego issue?
- What is the relationship between the target language and the native culture of the students?

A host of other educational, sociological, and administrative principles come to bear in specifying situational needs; these are but a few.

The second phase of curricular development is typified by the specification of linguistic – sometimes called "communicative" – needs: the specific language forms and functions that should be programmed into a course of study. Here again, certain principles of learning and teaching inform our choices:

- To what extent are native-language and target-language contrasts important to consider?
- How should interlanguage systematicity and variation affect curriculum designs?
- What do studies of contrastive analysis, interlanguage, and communicative competence tell us about the sequencing of linguistic forms and functions in a curriculum?
- How can the curriculum realize the principle of authenticity?

Of equal importance in the planning stages of language courses is the specific diagnostic assessment of each student upon entering a program. Once courses have been carefully planned, with pedagogical options intricately woven in, how can teachers and/or administrators become diagnostic scientists and artists, carefully eliciting language production and comprehension on the part of every student? How should those elicitations be measured and assessed in such a way that the language course can be either slightly or greatly modified to meet the needs of the particular students who happen to be in one's class at this moment?

None of these complex questions can be answered with the language teaching profession's recently interred methods! The crucial import of the diagnostic phase of language courses precludes any consideration of methods that are prepackaged for delivery to all learners. One of the principal fields of inquiry in the profession today is this very stage of diagnosis, that of more adequately pinpointing learners' linguistic needs as they enter a program of study.

TREATMENT

One may be tempted to think of "treatment" as the appropriate stage for the application of methods. One can still find people arguing, for example, that if a diagnostic phase discovered learners who need a great deal of physical activity, little metalinguistic explanation, and a strongly directive teacher, then surely Total Physical Response (TPR) is the treatment that should be offered. The problem with this conclusion is that it is over-generalized and much too restrictive. Certain learners can indeed benefit from occasional doses of "TPR-like" techniques, but certainly the complexity of the second language acquisition process warrants a multiple-treatment, multiphase approach to a language course. The principles that collectively underlie the method as we knew them provide a few valid correlates of an approach to diagnosis and treatment, but a single method covers far too narrow a band of possibilities to suffice for a whole curriculum.

Second language "treatments" may be thought of as courses of study or, better, sets of learning experiences, designed to target learner needs exposed by diagnostic assessments. For such treatments, the profession offers an extraordinarily large number of options. Consider, just as a start, the thirty-eight language teaching techniques categorized by Crookes and Chaudron (1991, pp. 52–54), ranging from controlled (drills, dialogues, reading aloud, display questions/answers, etc.) to semicontrolled (referential questions/answers, cued narratives, information gap activities, etc.) to free (role-plays, problem solving, interviews, discussions, etc.). Consider as well an abundance of whole-class, group-work, and pair-work activities at our disposal. Then, just take a look at the mountain of textbooks and other materials represented at a major language teaching conference! It is the teacher's task to carefully and deliberately choose among these many options to formulate a pedagogical sequence of techniques in the classroom. And this is where a teacher's choices must be "principled."

One way of looking at principled choices for treatment is the extent to which a technique promotes a desired goal. For example, let's suppose a teacher wishes to deliver techniques that seek to create *intrinsic motivation* in learners. The principle of intrinsic motivation implies more than a few corollaries that can act as a "test" of a technique's potential for creating or sustaining intrinsic motivation (see Brown 1994b, pp.33–46, for a full development of intrinsic motivation in the classroom). Consider the following checklist, each item of which represents a facet of the principle of intrinsic motivation:

1. Does the technique appeal to the genuine interests of your students? Is it relevant to their lives?
2. Is the technique presented in a positive, enthusiastic manner?
3. Are students clearly aware of the purpose of the technique?
4. Do students have some choice in: (*a*) choosing some aspect of the technique? and/or (*b*) determining how they go about fulfilling the goals of the technique?
5. Does the technique encourage students to discover for themselves certain principles or rules (rather than simply being "told")?
6. Does it encourage students in some way to develop or use effective strategies of learning and communication?
7. Does it contribute – at least to some extent – to students' ultimate autonomy and independence (from you)?
8. Does it foster cooperative negotiation with other students in the class? Is it a truly interactive technique?
9. Does the technique present a "reasonable challenge"?
10. Do students receive sufficient feedback on their performance (from each other or from you)?

By the careful delivery of techniques that incorporate many of these criteria, teachers can be more assured of offering treatments that are specifically designed to accomplish the goal of fostering intrinsic motivation. This is a far more sophisticated and effective option than grabbing at a particular method and programming it into a course of study regardless of diagnosed student needs.

Another way of looking at the relationship between approach and treatment is illustrated in the following list of suggestions for building a sense of *strategic investment* in the classroom. Each of the ten considerations is a principle of language learning/teaching which is reasonably well accepted (see Brown 1994b, pp.189–215). They are "good language learner" characteristics that we would all be wise to foster among students in second language classrooms. Each principle implies certain activities that may be appropriate.

1. LOWER INHIBITIONS

Play guessing and communication games; do role-plays and skits; sing songs; use group work; laugh with your students; have them share fears in small groups.

2. ENCOURAGE RISK TAKING

Praise students for making sincere efforts to try out language; use fluency exercises where errors are not corrected at that time; give outside-of-class assignments to speak or write or otherwise try out the language.

3. BUILD STUDENTS' SELF-CONFIDENCE

Tell students explicitly (verbally and nonverbally) that you do indeed believe in them; have them make lists of their strengths, of what they know or have accomplished so far in the course.

4. HELP STUDENTS DEVELOP INTRINSIC MOTIVATION

Remind students explicitly about the rewards for learning English; describe (or have students look up) jobs that require English; play down the final examination in favor of helping students to see rewards for themselves beyond the final exam.

5. PROMOTE COOPERATIVE LEARNING

Direct students to share their knowledge; play down competition among students; get your class to think of themselves as a team; do a considerable amount of small-group work.

6. ENCOURAGE STUDENTS TO USE RIGHT-BRAIN PROCESSING

Use movies and tapes in class; have students read passages rapidly; do skimming exercises; do rapid "free writes"; do oral fluency exercises where the object is to get students to talk (or write) a lot without being corrected.

7. PROMOTE AMBIGUITY TOLERANCE

Encourage students to ask you, and each other, questions when they do not understand something; keep your theoretical explanations very simple and brief; deal with just a few rules at a time; occasionally you can resort to translation into a native language to clarify a word or meaning.

8. HELP STUDENTS USE THEIR INTUITION

Praise students for good guesses; do not always give explanations of errors – let a correction suffice; correct only selected errors, preferably just those that interfere with learning.

9. GET STUDENTS TO MAKE THEIR MISTAKES WORK FOR THEM

Tape-record students' oral production and get them to identify errors; let students catch and correct each other's errors; do not always give them the correct form; encourage students to make lists of their common errors and to work on them on their own.

10. GET STUDENTS TO SET THEIR OWN GOALS

Explicitly encourage or direct students to go beyond the classroom goals; have them make lists of what they will accomplish on their own in a particular week; get students to make specific time commitments at home to study the language; give "extra credit" work.

Here again, we see a practical example of the way a principled approach to language teaching consistently and directly leads to practical classroom techniques. Ten principled maxims or "rules" for good language learning can focus teachers on sound classroom practices.

ASSESSMENT

Finally, our requiem for methods has propelled us into a new and fruitful domain of language pedagogy, namely, improved approaches and techniques for assessing students' accomplishment of curricular objectives. The methods of old offered nothing in the way of assessment techniques; at the very best they may have implied a continuing process of assessment as the method is being practiced. Today, the language-testing field has mushroomed into a highly developed and sophisticated field with numerous facets.

One of these facets is the increased emphasis on ongoing assessment of students' performance as a course progresses, or, what has commonly been called *formative evaluation.* With the advent of techniques for performance-based assessment, portfolio development, oral production inventories, cooperative student-student techniques, and other authentic testing rubrics, we are quickly developing the capacity to provide an ongoing program of assessment throughout a student's course of study. With formative processes of assessment in place, teachers can make appropriate midcourse pedagogical changes to more effectively reach goals.

The notion that evaluation must be confined to summative, end-of-term or end-of-unit tests alone is vanishing. However, it is important to note that summative evaluation is also an important component of a language program. The difference between current summative testing philosophy and the presupposition behind methods – that "one size fits all" – can be seen in a wide variety of assessment batteries that cover both production and comprehension skills, a range of assessment tasks, individualized (including computer-adaptive) tests, and increased attention to the communicative properties of tests.

CONCLUSION

"Methods," as we historically understand the term in the profession, are not a relevant issue in the sophisticated process of diagnosing, treating, and assessing learners of foreign languages. We have emerged well beyond the dark ages of language teaching when a handful of prepackaged elixirs filled up a small shelf of options. Although traces of the principal ingredients of the old methods still effectively find their way into our array of pedagogical options for treatment, our profession has emerged into an era of understanding a vast number of language teaching contexts and purposes, and an even larger number of student needs, learning styles, and affective traits. As teachers and teacher trainees develop and carry out classroom techniques, they can benefit by grounding everything they do in well-established principles of language learning and teaching. In so doing, they will be less likely to bring a prepackaged – and possibly ineffective – method to bear, and more likely to be directly responsive to their students' purposes and goals.

References

Anthony, E. M. (1963). Approach, method, and technique. *English Language Teaching, 17*(2), 63–67.

Brown, H. D. (1994a). *Principles of language learning and teaching.* 3rd ed. Englewood Cliffs, NJ: Prentice Hall Regents.

Brown, H. D. (1994b). *Teaching by principles: An interactive approach to language pedagogy.* Englewood Cliffs, NJ: Prentice Hall Regents.

Crookes, G., & Chaudron, C. (1991). Guidelines for classroom language teaching. In M. Celce-Murcia (Ed.), *Teaching English as a second or foreign language,* 2nd ed. Boston, MA: Heinle & Heinle.

Gouin, F. (1880). *L'art d'enseigner et d'étudier les langues.* Paris: Librairie Fischbacher.

Holliday, A. (1994). *Appropriate methodology and social context.* Cambridge: Cambridge University Press.

Kumaravadivelu, B. (1994). The postemethod condition: (E)merging strategies for second/foreign language teaching. *TESOL Quarterly, 28*, 27–48.

Marckwardt, A. (1972). Changing winds and shifting sands. *MST English Quarterly, 21*, 3–11.

Nunan, D. (1989). *Understanding language classrooms: A guide for teacher-initiated action.* Englewood Cliffs, NJ: Prentice-Hall.

Nunan, D. (1991). *Language teaching methodology: A textbook for teachers.* New York: Prentice-Hall.

Pennycook, A. (1989). The concept of method, interested knowledge, and the politics of language teaching. *TESOL Quarterly, 23*, 589–618.

Pennycook, A. (1994). *The cultural politics of English as an international language.* London: Longman.

Phillipson, R. (1992). *Linguistic imperialism.* Oxford: Oxford University Press.

Prabhu, N. S. (1990). There is no best method–why? *TESOL Quarterly, 24*, 161–176.

Richards, J. (1990). *The language teaching matrix.* New York: Cambridge University Press.

Richards, J., & Rodgers, T. S. (2001). *Approaches and methods in language teaching,* 2nd ed. New York: Cambridge University Press.

Stern, H. H. (1985). Review of methods that work: A smorgasbord of ideas for language teachers. *Studies in Second Language Acquisition, 7*, 249–251.

Tollefson, J. W. (Ed.). (1995). *Power and inequality in language education.* Cambridge: Cambridge University Press.

Endnote

[1] I use the term *approach* here in much the same way that Anthony (1963) used it: our collective wisdom on the nature of language, learning, and teaching. However, I part company with Anthony in assuming that method is in any way the next logical layer in a theory of language pedagogy.

CHAPTER 2

Theories of Teaching in Language Teaching

Jack C. Richards

INTRODUCTION

The field of TESOL is shaped in substantial ways by how the nature of language teaching is conceptualized. As with teaching in general, language teaching can be conceived in many different ways – for example, as a science, a technology, a craft, or an art. Different views of language teaching lead to different views as to what the essential skills of teaching are, and to different approaches to the preparation of teachers. The purpose of this paper is to examine conceptualizations of teaching which are found in TESOL and to consider the implications of different views of teaching for second language teacher education.

In an important paper on the relationship between theories of teaching and teaching skills, Zahorik (1986) classifies conceptions of teaching into three main categories: science-research conceptions, theory-philosophy conceptions, and art-craft conceptions. I will take this classification as my starting point, illustrating it with examples from the field of language teaching. I will then examine how each conception of teaching leads to differences in our understanding of what the essential skills of teaching are.

SCIENCE-RESEARCH CONCEPTIONS

Science-research conceptions of language teaching are derived from research and are supported by experimention and empirical investigation. Zahorik includes operationalizing learning principles, following a tested model, and doing what effective teachers do, as examples of science-research conceptions.

OPERATIONALIZING LEARNING PRINCIPLES

This approach involves developing teaching principles from research on memory, transfer, motivation, and other factors believed to be important in learning. Mastery learning and programmed learning are examples of science-research conceptions of teaching in general education. In TESOL, Audiolingualism, Task-Based Language Teaching, and Learner Training represent applications of learning research to language teaching.

Audiolingualism was derived from research on learning associated with behavioral psychology. Laboratory studies had shown that learning could be successfully manipulated if three elements were identified: a stimulus, which serves to elicit behavior; a response, triggered by a stimulus; and reinforcement, which serves to mark the response as being appropriate (or inappropriate) and encourages the repetition (or suppression) of the response in the future. Translated into a teaching method this led to the Audiolingual Method, in which language learning was seen as a process of habit formation and in which target-language patterns were presented for memorization and learning through dialogs and drills.

A more recent example of attempts to develop a teaching methodology from learning research is referred to as Task-Based Language Teaching. Proponents of Task-Based Language Teaching point out that second language acquisition research shows that successful language learning involves learners in negotiation of meaning. In the process of negotiating with a speaker of the target language, the learner receives the kind of input needed to facilitate learning. It is proposed that classroom tasks which involve negotiation of meaning should form the basis of the language teaching curriculum, and that tasks can be used to facilitate practice of both of language forms and communicative functions. Research is intended to enable designers to know what kinds of tasks can best facilitate acquisition of specific target-language structures and functions. Prahbu (1983) initiated a large-scale application of this approach in schools in India, developing a syllabus and associated teaching materials around three major types of tasks: information-gap tasks, opinion-gap tasks, and reasoning-gap tasks.

Learner Training is an approach which draws on research on the cognitive styles and learning strategies used by learners in carrying out different classroom learning tasks. This research may involve observing learners, asking them to introspect about their learning strategies, or probing learners in other ways. Once successful learning strategies are identified, these can be taught to other learners. This is referred to as Learner Training.

FOLLOWING A TESTED MODEL OF TEACHING

This approach involves applying the results of empirical or experimental research to teaching. In this approach, "a view of good teaching is developed through logical reasoning and previous research; good teaching is defined in terms of specific acts" (Zahorik, 1986, p. 21). An example of research of this kind which has been used to develop theories of good teaching across both regular and ESL classrooms is research on teachers' question patterns and wait time. Long (1984) argued that research had established the contribution of these to the quality of classroom interaction in second language classrooms. In applying this research to teacher preparation, a simple training model was developed in which teachers were taught the differences between display questions (those for which answers are known in advance) and referential questions (those for which answers are not known) and the advantages of providing longer wait-time after questions. Teachers' question use and wait time before and after training were measured, and "it was found that the training modules affected teaching behaviors, and that the new behaviors affected student participation patterns in ways believed to be significant for these students' language acquisition" (Long, 1984, p. vi).

With approaches of this kind, if the specific teaching behaviors such as question patterns and wait time are effective in bringing about second language acquisition, a conception of good teaching will have been identified and validated.

DOING WHAT EFFECTIVE TEACHERS DO

Another approach to developing a theory of teaching is to derive teaching principles from studies of the practices of effective teachers. This involves identifying effective teachers and then studying their teaching practices. Effective teachers are typically defined as those whose students perform better on standardized achievement tests.

In a study of effective teachers in bilingual education programs in California and Hawaii, for example, Tikunoff (1985) observed teachers to find out how they organize instruction, structure teaching activities, and enhance student performance on tasks. Teachers were interviewed to determine their instructional philosophies and goals, and the demands they structured into class tasks. An analysis of the classroom data revealed that there was a clear linkage between the following:

1. teachers' ability to clearly specify the intent of instruction, and a belief that students could achieve accuracy in instructional tasks
2. the organization and delivery of instruction such that tasks and institutional demands reflected this intent, requiring intended student responses
3. the fidelity of student consequences with intended outcomes

In a summary of research of this kind (Blum, 1984, p. 3–6), twelve characteristics of effective teaching were identified:

1. Instruction is guided by a preplanned curriculum.
2. There are high expectations for student learning.
3. Students are carefully oriented to lessons.
4. Instruction is clear and focused.
5. Learning progress is monitored closely.
6. When students do not understand, they are retaught.
7. Class time is used for learning.
8. There are smooth and efficient classroom routines.
9. Instructional groups formed in the classroom fit instructional needs.
10. Standards for classroom behavior are high.
11. Personal interactions between teachers and students are positive.
12. Incentives and rewards for students are used to promote excellence.

Advocates of effective teaching use findings of this kind as guidelines to train teachers. An approach to teaching which reflects these principles has been labeled Direct Instruction or Active Teaching.

THEORY-PHILOSOPHY CONCEPTIONS

The next approach to theories of teaching Zahorik terms "theory-philosophy conceptions." "Their truth is not based on a posteriori conditions or on what works. Rather, their truth is based on what ought to work or what is morally right" (Zahorik, 1986, p. 22). Teaching conceptions which are derived from what ought to work are essentially theory-based or rationalist in approach, whereas those which are derived from beliefs about what is viewed as morally right are values-based approaches.

THEORY-BASED APPROACHES

The conceptions underlying many teaching methods or proposals can be characterized as theory-based or rationalist in approach. This suggests that the theory underlying the method is ascertained through the use of reason or rational thought. Systematic and principled thinking, rather than empirical investigation, is used to support the method. These conceptions of teaching tend not to draw support from classroom results as such (e.g., by showing pre- and post-test gains resulting from the use of a method), but defend themselves through logical argumentation.

Examples of theory-based or rationalist approaches in TESOL are Communicative Language Teaching and the Silent Way. Each of these is based on a set of carefully elaborated assumptions.

Communicative Language Teaching, for example, arose as a reaction to grammar-based approaches to teaching realized in teaching materials, syllabuses, and teaching methods in the 1960s. The proponents of Communicative Language Teaching established it through convincing critiques of the inadequacy of the linguistic and pedagogical theory underlying grammar-based approaches. It was often described as a "principled approach." Communicative Language Teaching was an attempt to operationalize the concept of communicative competence and to apply it across all levels of language program design, from theory, to syllabus design, to teaching techniques. Its proponents, however, never felt compelled to produce any evidence to demonstrate that learning was more successful if "communicative" teaching methods and materials were adopted; the theory itself was considered sufficient to justify the approach.

A method such as the Silent Way, on the other hand, is derived not so much from a linguistic theory as from a learning theory. It is based on a set of claims and beliefs as to how learning takes place in adults. The classroom procedures which are distinctive to the method attempt to draw on the learning principles espoused by Gattegno (1982, p. 203), who attests:

> there are no really difficult forms which cannot be illustrated through the proper situation involving rods and actions on them about which one makes statements by introducing specific words whose associated meaning is obvious. What teachers must do is to arrange for practice so that students' minds are triggered to use these new words spontaneously.

Gattegno takes the theory underlying the Silent Way as self-evident; neither the theory nor the method has been subject to any form of empirical verification.

VALUES-BASED APPROACHES

A different approach to a theory of teaching is to develop a teaching model from the values one holds about teachers, learners, classrooms, and the role of education in society. Certain ways of going about teaching and learning are then seen to be educationally justifiable and should therefore form the basis of teaching practice. In some situations, this leads to certain approaches to teaching being viewed as politically justifiable (and therefore good) and others seen as not morally, ethically, or politically supportable (and therefore bad).

Values-based approaches in education are not hard to identify. For example, advocates of "literature in the language curriculum," "school-based curriculum development," or "the teacher as action researcher" essentially appeal to educational or social value systems in justifying their proposals.

Other examples of values-based approaches in language teaching include "team teaching," "humanistic approaches," the "learner-centered curriculum" movement, and "reflective teaching." Team teaching is based on a view that teachers work best when they work in collaboration with a peer, and that the interaction with a colleague in all phases of teaching is beneficial to both teachers and learners.

Humanistic approaches in language teaching refer to approaches which emphasize the development of human values, growth in self-awarenes and in the understanding of others, sensitivity to human feelings and emotions, and active student involvement in learning and in the way human learning takes place. Community Language Learning is sometimes cited as an example of a humanistic approach, as is the work of Stevick and Moskowitz.

The "learner-centered curriculum" is one of a number of terms used to refer to approaches to language teaching which are based on the belief that learners are self-directed, responsible decision makers. Learners are seen to learn in different ways and to have different needs and interests. Language programs and the teachers who work in them should therefore set out to provide learners with efficient learning strategies, to assist learners in identifying their own preferred ways of learning, to develop skills needed to negotiate the curriculum, to encourage learners to set their own objectives, to encourage learners to adopt realistic goals and time frames, and to develop learners' skills in self-evaluation.

Reflective teaching is an approach to teaching which is based on a belief that teachers can improve their understanding of teaching and the quality of their own teaching by reflecting critically on their teaching experiences. In teacher education, activities which seek to develop a reflective approach to teaching aim to develop the skills of considering the teaching process thoughtfully, analytically, and objectively as a way of improving classroom practices. This is brought about through using procedures which require teachers to collect data on their own teaching practices (e.g., through audio or video recordings), to reflect on their own decision making (e.g., through journal writing), and to examine their own values and assumptions about teaching (e.g., through peer or group discussion or observation of videos).

Art-Craft Conceptions

Another way of conceptualizing teaching is to view it as an art or craft, and as something which depends on the teacher's individual skill and personality. Zahorik (1986, p. 22) characterizes this approach to teaching in these terms: "The essence of this view of good teaching is invention and personalization. A good teacher is a person who assesses the needs and possibilities of a situation and creates and uses practices that have promise for that situation."

Art-craft approaches to teaching seek to develop teaching as a unique set of personal skills which teachers apply in different ways according to the demands of specific situations. There are no general methods of teaching; rather, teachers should develop an approach to teaching which allows them to be themselves and do what they feel is best. Teacher decision-making is an essential competency in this approach, because a good teacher is seen as one who analyses a situation, realizes that a range of options is available based on the particular class circumstances, and then selects an alternative which is likely to be most effective for the circumstances. This does not deny the value of knowing about different methods of teaching and how to use them, but it suggests that commitment to a single method of teaching may impede the teacher's full potential as a teacher.

The Essential Skills of Teaching

A central issue in a theory or conception of teaching is what the essential skills of teaching are assumed to be. Science-research conceptions, theory-philosophy conceptions, and art-craft conceptions represent different points of view about what teaching is. Science-research conceptions use learning theory or learning research to validate selection of instructional tasks and tend to support the use of specific teaching strategies and techniques. Teachers are expected to select and monitor learners' performance on tasks to ensure that the tasks are generating the appropriate use of language or choice of learning strategy. The effective teaching model of teaching is similarly a top-down philosophy of teaching, in the sense that once the characteristics of effective teaching are identified, teachers must aim to implement such practices in their own classes.

Theory-philosophy conceptions require teachers first to understand the theory underlying the methodology and then to teach in such a way that the theory is realized in classroom practice. With Communicative Language Teaching, for example, lessons, syllabi, materials, and teaching techniques can be judged as more or less "communicative." Specifications as to what constitutes "communicative teaching" have been proposed, and a teacher's performance can be assessed according to the degree of "communicativeness" found in his or her lessons. Likewise, Gattegno's views on teaching, which form the basis of the Silent Way, lead to prescriptions as to what teachers should and should not do in the classroom. The essential skills the teacher needs to acquire are those that reflect the theory and spirit of the Silent Way approach. There is little room for personal interpretations of the method.

Philosophical or values-based approaches are prescriptive in a different kind of way, since the choice of instructional means in this case is not based on educational criteria (e.g., on effectiveness or learning criteria) but on a wider set of values which are not subject to accountability (e.g., religious, political, social, or personal beliefs). Art-craft conceptions, on the other hand, are more "bottom-up" than top-down. Teachers should not set out to look for a general method of teaching or to master a particular set of teaching skills, but should constantly try to discover things that work, discarding old practices and taking on board new ones.

The different principles underlying the three conceptions of teaching can thus be summarized in terms of the following statements of what teachers should do according to each conception of teaching.

SCIENCE-RESEARCH CONCEPTIONS

These see the essential skills in teaching as the following:

- Understand the learning principles.
- Develop tasks and activities based on the learning principles.
- Monitor students' performance on tasks to see that desired performance is being achieved.

THEORY-PHILOSOPHY CONCEPTIONS

These see the essential skills in teaching as:

- Understand the theory and the principles.
- Select syllabi, materials, and tasks based on the theory.
- Monitor your teaching to see that it conforms to the theory.

VALUES-BASED CONCEPTIONS

In the case of values-based approaches, the essential skills in teaching are:

- Understand the values behind the approach.
- Select only those educational means which conform to these values.
- Monitor the implementation process to ensure that the value system is being maintained.

ART-CRAFT CONCEPTIONS

The essential skills of teaching in this approach are:

- Treat each teaching situation as unique.
- Identify the particular characteristics of each situation.
- Try out different teaching strategies.
- Develop personal approaches to teaching.

Since these three conceptions of teaching offer quite different perspectives on what the essential skills of teaching are, it is not the case that they can simply be regarded as alternatives, that can be exchanged according to the whims of the moment. Eclecticism is not an option here, since the different conceptions of teaching represent fundamentally different representations of what teaching is and how teachers should approach their work.

However, it is possible to view these three conceptions as forming a continuum. Teachers entering the teaching profession need technical competence in teaching, and the confidence to teach according to proven principles. Science-research conceptions of teaching might well provide a good starting point for inexperienced teachers. As they gain experience, they can then modify and adapt these initial theories of teaching, moving toward the more interpretive views of teaching implicit in theory-philosophy conceptions. Eventually, as they develop their own personal theories of teaching, they can teach more from an art-craft approach, creating teaching approaches according to the particular constraints and dynamics of the situations in which they work. In this way, teacher development can be seen as a process of ongoing self-discovery and self-renewal, as top-down approaches to teaching become replaced by more bottom-up approaches, or approaches which blend the two. This moves the teacher's work beyond the routine, creating both the challenges and rewards of teaching.

References

Blum, R. E. (1984). *Effective schooling practices: A research synthesis*. Portland, OR: Northwest Regional Educational Laboratory.

Gattegno, C. (1982). *Teaching foreign languages in schools*. New York: Educational Solutions.

Long, M. H. (1984). *The effect of teachers' questioning patterns and wait-times.* Department of ESL, University of Hawaii.

Prahbu, N. S. (1983). Procedural syllabuses. Paper presented at the RELC Seminar, Singapore.

Tikunoff, W. S. (1985). *Developing student functional proficiency for LEP students.* Portland, OR: Northwest Regional Educational Laboratory.

Zahorik, J. A. (1986). Acquiring teaching skills. *Journal of Teacher Education* (March–April), 21–25.

SECTION 2

LESSON PLANNING AND CLASSROOM MANAGEMENT

INTRODUCTION

The two articles in this section focus on two aspects of a language lesson: planning the lesson and managing learner behavior during a lesson. Planning is often viewed as a key aspect of teaching a successful lesson. During the planning phase, the teacher makes decisions about goals, activities, resources, timing, grouping, and other aspects of the lesson. Harmer (1991) includes the following elements in a lesson plan:

a. Description of the class
b. Recent work
c. Objectives
d. Contents (context, activity and class organization, aids, language, possible problems)
e. Additional possibilities

Even though a lesson may have already been planned (by the textbook writer), a teacher will still need to make decisions that relate to the needs of his or her specific class, adapting the lesson from the book in different ways to make it better suit the class. This process of planning and adaptation is a crucial dimension of teaching because during this process the teacher makes many decisions that are essential for a successful lesson. Planning can be regarded as a process of transformation during which the teacher creates ideas for a lesson based on understanding of learners' needs, problems, and interests, and on the content of the lesson itself. This does not necessarily result in a detailed, written lesson plan. Many teachers teach successful lessons based on mental plans or on brief lesson notes. What is important is not the extent and detail of the teacher's plan but the extent to which the teacher has developed ideas for turning a potential lesson (such as a textbook lesson) into the basis for an engaging and effective lesson.

Lesson planning involves decisions about the pedagogical dimensions of the lesson. But another important aspect of a lesson concerns the management of learners during the lesson. This includes eliciting students' attention, maintaining their engagement in the lesson, and organizing them into pairs or groups. If these aspects of a lesson are not well handled by a teacher, much of the time available for teaching can be lost in nonproductive activity. Classroom management refers to the ways in which teachers manage a class in order to make it maximally productive for language learning.

Farrell discusses the processes involved in the planning, implementation, and evaluation of a lesson. At the planning stage, teachers need to think about questions such as what the objective(s) of the lesson will be, what materials and activities will be used, what type of interaction will be encouraged, and how the learning will be monitored. At the implementation stage, the teacher's job is not simply to carry out the lesson as previously planned. During the lesson, interactive and evaluative decisions will often have to be made in response to the dynamics of the class. It may be necessary for teachers to adjust or even change the original plan when the lesson is not going well. Having implemented the lesson, the teacher must evaluate the success or failure of the lesson. This phase is important as it provides an opportunity for the teacher to reflect on what has gone on in the lesson vis-à-vis the objectives of the lesson. Important questions to ask at this phase include what the pupils learned in the lesson, which tasks were successful, whether the material was appropriate, whether the pace of the lesson was right, and what changes need to be made in future lessons. Farrell concludes by saying that carefully thought-out lesson plans are likely to result in more efficient use of instructional time and more fruitful teaching and learning opportunities.

Lewis describes how classroom learning can be more effectively managed to produce the desired outcomes of language learning, that is, for learners to use the new language for a variety of communicative purposes and contexts. Three aspects of classroom management are the focus of her chapter: (1) motivation, (2) constraints, and (3) the teacher's role. Lewis offers numerous practical ideas of how to deal with low learner motivation, which often results in off-task behavior, how to overcome classroom constraints such as large classes and limited resources, and how to help teachers better understand their new roles in the communicative language classrooms. Effective management of these three aspects, Lewis points out, can lead to a classroom atmosphere that helps pupils "make the most of the opportunities for learning and practicing language."

Discussion Questions

Before Reading

1. How important do you think a lesson plan is to a successful lesson? What features do you think a lesson plan should include?
2. Do you think it is a good idea to strictly follow a lesson plan? Why?
3. Some people think that lesson plans severely restrict teachers' creativity. Do you agree? Explain your answer.
4. Do you think teachers should review the lessons they have just taught? Why?
5. What are the goals of classroom management? What do you think are the most important principles of classroom management?
6. What techniques do teachers normally use to get students on task in class?
7. What do teachers do to limit learners' use of L1 in their class?

After Reading

1. If possible, arrange to observe a teacher's class. Ask the teacher to provide a copy of his or her lesson plan. In what ways does the lesson follow the lesson plan? What aspects of the lesson are not anticipated by the plan?
2. What classroom management problems have you observed (or experienced) in language classes? How did the teacher deal with them?
3. Observe a lesson and identify points in the lesson during which the teacher dealt with off-task behavior. How did he or she handle this? Was he or she successful?
4. Plan a lesson for a class you are familiar with. Describe how you incorporate group work in your lesson and how you will deal with students who refuse to work in groups.
5. Devise a form that could be used as the basis for evaluating a lesson. Then try it out. What kind of information did you collect?
6. Review Lewis's article. Do you think motivation is a serious problem in a second or foreign language class? How useful is the article in helping you understand the issue of low motivation among your students? Can you suggest other ways of dealing with reluctant learners?
7. According to Lewis, what roles do teachers have to adopt in the communicative language classroom? Do you agree with her? What other roles do you think teachers should play?
8. Review Farrell's article. Describe Tyler's (1969) rational-linear model of lesson planning. Do you agree that the model is too limiting? In what ways is Yinger's (1980) framework an improvement of Tyler's model?
9. According to Farrell, how important is lesson planning for the success of a lesson? What happens if a lesson is not going according to what has been planned before? How easy or difficult is it to adjust or change a lesson plan at the implementation phase?

Further Reading

Harmer, J. (1991). *The practice of English language teaching.* Harlow, UK: Longman.

CHAPTER 3

Lesson Planning

Thomas S. C. Farrell

"Would you tell me, please, which way I ought to go from here?" asked Alice.
"That depends a good deal on where you want to get to," said the Cheshire Cat.

Lewis Carroll (1963). *Alice's Adventures in Wonderland* (p. 59). New York: Macmillan.

INTRODUCTION

Teachers may wonder "which way they ought to go" before they enter a classroom. This usually means that teachers need to plan what they want to do in their classrooms. Most teachers engage in yearly, term, unit, weekly, and daily lesson planning (Yinger, 1980). Yearly and term planning usually involve listing the objectives for a particular program. A unit plan is a series of related lessons around a specific theme such as "The Family." Planning daily lessons is the end result of a complex planning process that includes the yearly, term, and unit plans. A daily lesson plan is a written description of how students will move toward attaining specific objectives. It describes the teaching behavior that will result in student learning.

This chapter addresses the daily planning decisions that English language teachers make before they enter the classroom. Included in this discussion are the interactive and evaluative decisions teachers make during and after the lesson. Richards (1998) stresses the importance of lesson planning for English language teachers: "The success with which a teacher conducts a lesson is often thought to depend on the effectiveness with which the lesson was planned" (p. 103). For the purposes of this chapter, lesson planning is defined as the daily decisions a teacher makes for the successful outcome of a lesson. This chapter discusses the following issues associated with lesson planning:

- Why plan?
- Models of lesson planning.
- How to plan a lesson.

WHY PLAN?

Language teachers may ask themselves why should they bother writing plans for every lesson. Some teachers write down elaborate daily plans; others do the planning inside their heads. Preservice teachers say they write daily lesson plans only because a supervisor, cooperating teacher, or school administrator requires them to do so. After they graduate, many teachers give up writing lesson plans. However, not many teachers enter a classroom without some kind of plan. Lesson plans are systematic records of a teacher's thoughts about what will be covered during a lesson. Richards (1998) suggests that lesson plans help the teacher think about the lesson in advance to "resolve problems and difficulties, to provide a structure for a lesson, to provide a 'map' for the teacher to follow, and to provide a record of what has been taught" (p. 103).

There are also internal and external reasons for planning lessons (McCutcheon, 1980). Teachers plan for internal reasons in order to feel more confident, to learn the subject matter better, to enable lessons to run more smoothly, and to anticipate problems before they happen. Teachers plan for external reasons in order to satisfy the expectations of the principal or supervisor and to guide a substitute teacher in case the class needs one. Lesson planning is especially important for preservice teachers because they may feel more of a need to be in control before the lesson begins.

Daily lesson planning can benefit English teachers in the following ways:

- A plan can help the teacher think about content, materials, sequencing, timing, and activities.
- A plan provides security (in the form of a map) in the sometimes unpredictable atmosphere of a classroom.
- A plan is a log of what has been taught.
- A plan can help a substitute to smoothly take over a class when the teacher cannot teach. (Purgason, 1991)

Daily planning of lessons also benefits students because it takes into account the different backgrounds, interests, learning styles, and abilities of the students in one class.

MODELS OF LESSON PLANNING

There are a number of approaches to lesson planning. The dominant model of lesson planning is Tyler's (1949) rational-linear framework. Tyler's model has four steps that run sequentially: (1) specify objectives; (2) select learning activities; (3) organize learning activities; and (4) specify methods of evaluation. Tyler's model is still used widely in spite of evidence that suggests that teachers rarely follow the sequential, linear process outlined in the steps (Borko & Niles, 1987). For example, Taylor (1970) studied what teachers actually did when they planned their lessons and found that they focused mostly on the interests and needs of their students. More important, he found that teachers were not well prepared in teacher-education programs for lesson planning.

In response to these findings, Yinger (1980) developed an alternative model in which planning takes place in stages. The first stage consists of "problem conception" in which planning starts with a discovery cycle of the integration of the teacher's goals, knowledge, and experience. The second stage sees the problem formulated and a solution achieved. The third stage involves implementing the plan along with its evaluation. Yinger sees this process as becoming routine, whereby each planning event is influenced by what went on before and what may happen in the future. He also sees a place for considering each teacher's experiences as influencing this ongoing process of planning.

Research on what English language teachers actually do when planning lessons has shown that many teachers, when they do write lesson plans (Richards & Lockhart, 1994), tend to deviate from the original plan. Also, when English language teachers do write daily lesson plans, they do not state them in terms of behavioral objectives, even though they are taught this method in preservice teacher education courses (Richards & Lockhart, 1994; Freeman, 1996; Bailey, 1996). Instead, English language teachers, especially more experienced teachers, are more likely to plan their lessons as sequences of activities (Freeman, 1996), teaching routines, or to focus on the need of particular students (Richards & Lockhart, 1994).

Bailey's (1996, p. 38) study of six experienced English language teachers came up with the following interesting reasons (stated as principles) why teachers deviate from the original lesson plan: (1) "Serve the common good." Here teachers are willing to deviate from the original lesson plan because one student raised an issue that the teacher perceives to be relevant for the other students. (2) "Teach to the moment." Sometimes, teachers may completely abandon the lesson plan to discuss some unplanned event because the teacher thinks it is timely for the class. (3) "Further the lesson." Teachers make a procedural change during the lesson as a means of promoting the progress of the lesson. (4) "Accommodate students' learning styles." Teachers may sometimes depart from their lesson plans in order to accommodate their students' learning styles if the original plan has not accounted for them. (5) "Promote students' involvement." Teachers sometimes eliminate some steps in their lesson plans in order to have more student involvement, especially if the students are not responding. (6) "Distribute the wealth." This last principle has teachers changing lesson plans to encourage quiet students to participate more and to keep the more active students from dominating the class time. These findings show that teacher decision making is a dynamic process involving teachers making choices before, during, and after each lesson.

The question that arises out of these studies is, What kinds of lesson plans should English language teachers write? The next section discusses how to develop, implement, and evaluate a lesson plan.

How to Plan a Lesson

DEVELOPING THE PLAN

An effective lesson plan starts with appropriate and clearly written objectives. An objective is a description of a learning outcome. Objectives describe the destination (not the journey) we want our students to reach. Clear, well-written objectives are the first step in daily lesson planning. These objectives help state precisely what we want our students to learn, help guide the selection of appropriate activities, and help provide overall lesson focus and direction. They also give teachers a way to evaluate what their students have learned at the end of the lesson. Clearly written objectives can also be used to focus the students (they know what is expected from them).

For English language lessons, Shrum and Glisan (1994) point out that effective objectives "describe what students will be able to do in terms of observable behavior and when using the foreign language" (p. 48). Hence, the language a teacher uses for stating objectives is important. I suggest action verbs be used to identify desired student behavior; these can include action verbs similar to those used in Bloom's *Taxonomy of Thinking Processes* (see Appendix B). Vague verbs such as *understand*, *appreciate*, *enjoy* (although these can still be used for certain types of lessons, e.g., English poetry or reading novels), or *learn* should be avoided because they are difficult to quantify. Action verbs such as *identify*, *present*,

Lesson Phase	Role of Teacher	Role of Students
I. *Perspective* (opening)	Asks what students have learned in previous lesson	Tell what they've learned previously
	Previews new lesson	Respond to preview
II. *Stimulation*	Prepares students for new activity	Relate activity to their lives
	Presents attention grabber	Respond to attention grabber
III. *Instruction/Participation*	Presents activity	Do activity
	Checks for understanding	Show understanding
	Encourages involvement	Interact with others
IV. *Closure*	Asks what students have learned	Tell what they have learned
	Previews future lessons	Give input on future lessons
V. *Follow-up*	Presents other activities to reinforce same concepts	Do new activities
	Presents opportunities for interaction	Interact with others

Adapted from Shrum & Glisan (1994)

Figure 1 Generic Components of a Lesson Plan.

describe, *explain*, *demonstrate*, *list*, *contrast*, and *debate* are clearer and easier for teachers to design a lesson around. Use of these action verbs also makes it easier for the students to understand what will be expected from them in each lesson.

After writing the lesson objectives, teachers must decide the activities and procedures they will use to ensure the successful attainment of these objectives. Planning at this stage means thinking through the purposes and structures of the activities. This step involves planning the shape of the lesson. To highlight some generic components of a language lesson plan, I use Shrum and Glisan's (1994) adaptation of the Hunter and Russell (1977) model (Figure 1). They have built in a place for greater student involvement in the lesson.

The generic lesson plan as shown in Figure 1 has five phases:

I. *Perspective or opening.* The teacher asks the students (or himself or herself) the following questions: What was the previous activity (what was previously learned)? What concepts have they learned? The teacher then gives a preview of the new lesson.

II. *Stimulation.* The teacher (*a*) poses a question to get the students thinking about the coming activity; (*b*) helps the students to relate the activity to their lives; (*c*) begins with an attention grabber: an anecdote, a little scene acted out by peer teachers or lay assistants, a picture, or a song; and (*d*) uses it (the response to the attention grabber) as a lead into the activity.

III. *Instruction/participation.* The teacher presents the activity, checks for student understanding, and encourages active student involvement. Teachers can get students to interact by the use of pair work and/or group work.

IV. *Closure.* For this phase the teacher checks what the students have learned by asking questions such as "What did you learn?" and "How did you feel about these activities?" The teacher then gives a preview about the possibilities for future lessons.

V. *Follow-up.* The last phase of the lesson has the teacher using other activities to reinforce some concepts and even to introduce some new ones. The teacher gives the students opportunities to do independent work and can set certain activities or tasks taken from the lesson as homework.

Of course, teachers can have variations on this generic model. Shrum and Glisan (1994) point out that as time passes in language lessons and as students gain competence, the students "can gradually take on a larger role in choosing the content and even in the structure of the lessons themselves" (pp. 187–188). English language teachers should also realize that language lessons may be different from other content lessons because the same concepts may need to be reinforced time and again using different methods. The following questions may be useful for language teachers to answer before planning their lessons:

- What do you want the students to learn and why?
- Are all the tasks necessary – worth doing and at the right level?
- What materials, aids, and so on, will you use and why?
- What type of interaction will you encourage – pair work or group work – and why?
- What instructions will you have to give and how will you give them (written, oral, etc.)? What questions will you ask?
- How will you monitor student understanding during the different stages of the lesson?

An example of an authentic lesson plan for an English reading class is given in Appendix A. The lesson plan should not be seen as a prescription or "how to," because each teaching context will be different. After writing the plan, the next step is to implement it by teaching the class.

IMPLEMENTING THE PLAN

Implementing the lesson plan is the most important (and difficult) phase of the daily lesson planning cycle. In this phase, the lesson plan itself will retreat into the background as the reality of the class takes over. As many experienced teachers know, it is easy to get sidetracked by unplanned events. However, teachers should remember that the original plan was designed with specific intentions in mind and the plan was based on the teacher's diagnosis of the learning competence of the students. Nonetheless, teachers may need to make certain adjustments to the lesson at the implementation phase. I would suggest two broad reasons for teachers to deviate from their original lesson plan: first, when the lesson is obviously going badly and the plan is not helping to produce the desired outcome; second, when something happens during an early part of the lesson that necessitates improvisation.

When the lesson is not succeeding, teachers should make immediate adjustments to the original plan. This is difficult for beginning teachers because they may not have the necessary experience to recognize that things are going badly. They may also lack sufficient knowledge to develop contingency plans to substitute in such cases. No teacher's guide can anticipate what problems might occur during a lesson (e.g., out-of-class problems such as interruptions from a visitor); however, they must be dealt with quickly. Teachers can build up this professional knowledge with experience.

When implementing their lesson plan, teachers might try to monitor two important issues, namely, lesson variety and lesson pacing. Variety in lesson delivery and choice of activity will keep the class lively and interested. To vary a lesson, teachers should frequently change the tempo of activities from fast-moving to slow. They can also change the class organization by giving individual tasks, pair work, group work, or full class interaction.

Activities should also vary in level of difficulty, some easy and others more demanding. The activities should also be of interest to the students, not just to the teacher. Ur (1996, p. 216), however, cautions that varied activities should not be "flung together in random order." The result of this would be restlessness and disorder. Consequently, Ur (1996) suggests that the harder activities and tasks be placed earlier in the lesson and the quieter activities before lively ones. Teachers may want to try variations of this to see what works best in their particular class.

Pace is linked to the speed at which a lesson progresses, as well as to lesson timing. In order for teachers to develop a sense of pace, Brown (1994) suggests the following guidelines: (1) activities should not be too long or too short; (2) various techniques for delivering the activities should "flow" together; (3) there should be clear transitions between each activity. If teachers remember to work for the benefit of their students rather than their own, then they can avoid falling into the trap of racing through different activities just because they have been written on the lesson plan.

EVALUATING THE PLAN

The final part of daily lesson planning happens after the lesson has ended (although Brown [1994] reminds us that evaluation can take place during the lesson too), when the teacher must evaluate the success (or failure) of the lesson. Ur (1996) says it is important to think after teaching a lesson and ask "whether it was a good one or not, and why" (p. 219). This form of reflection, she says, is for self-development. Of course, both "success" and "failure" are relative terms and their definitions will vary according to each individual teacher's and student's perspective. Nevertheless, Brown (1994) says that without an evaluative component in the lesson, the teacher has no way of assessing the success of the students or what adjustments to make for the next lesson.

Brown (1994) defines evaluation in lesson planning as an assessment that is "formal or informal, that you make after students have sufficient opportunities for learning" (p. 398). Ur (1996) says that when evaluating a lesson, the first and most important criterion is student learning because that is why we have a lesson in the first place. Even though it may be difficult to judge how much has been learned in a lesson, Ur says that we can still make a good guess. This guess can be based "on our knowledge of the class, the type of activity they were engaged in, and some informal test activities that give feedback on learning" (p. 220). Ur offers the following criteria for evaluating lesson effectiveness and orders them as follows: (1) the class seemed to be learning the material well; (2) the learners were engaging with the foreign language throughout; (3) the learners were attentive all the time; (4) the learners enjoyed the lesson and were motivated; (5) the learners were active all the time; (6) the lesson went according to plan; (7) the language was used communicatively throughout (p. 220). Readers might wish to reflect on these criteria and reorder them in their own list of priority.

The following questions may also be useful for teachers to reflect on after conducting a lesson (answers can be used as a basis for future lesson planning):

- What do you think the students actually learned?
- What tasks were most successful? Least successful? Why?
- Did you finish the lesson on time?
- What changes (if any) will you make in your teaching and why (or why not)?

Additionally, for further clarification of the success of a lesson, teachers can ask their students the following four questions at the end of each class; the answers can assist teachers with future lesson planning (I avoid overly judgmental questions such as "Did you enjoy the lesson?" as these types of questions are highly subjective):

- What do you think today's lesson was about?
- What part was easy?
- What part was difficult?
- What changes would you suggest the teacher make?

Conclusion

I have focused on the day-to-day lesson planning decisions that face language teachers (both preservice and in-service). Because we all have different styles of teaching, and therefore planning, the suggestions in this chapter are not meant to be prescriptive. Teachers must allow themselves flexibility to plan in their own way, always keeping in mind the yearly, term, and unit plans. As Bailey (1996) points out, a lesson plan is like a road map "which describes where the teacher hopes to go in a lesson, *presumably taking the students along*" (p. 18; emphasis added). It is the latter part of this quote that is important for teachers to remember, because they may need to make "in-flight" changes in response to the actuality of the classroom. As Bailey (1996) correctly points out, "In realizing lesson plans, part of a skilled teacher's logic in use involves managing such departures [from the original lesson plan] to maximize teaching and learning opportunities" (p. 38). Clearly thought-out lesson plans will more likely maintain the attention of students and increase the likelihood that they will be interested. A clear plan will also maximize time and minimize confusion of what is expected of the students, thus making classroom management easier.

Appendix A: Lesson Plan

Time: 12:00 P.M. to 12:35 P.M. **Subject:** English language **Class:** Secondary 2 English (mixed-ability level)
Language Focus: Reading **Topic:** Sport

Objectives:
To teach the students how to skim for main idea of the passage – identify key words.

Prior Knowledge:
Students have learned how to locate information by reading and finding the main sentence of each paragraph.

Materials:
1. Reading materials – article from book on Sport
2. Overhead projector/OHTs
3. Whiteboard

Step	Time	Tasks (Teacher)	Tasks (Pupils)	Interaction	Purpose
1	5–10 mins	**Opening:** Introduction to the topic sport. T activates schema for sport.	Listen	T ⟷ Ss (T = teacher; Ss = students)	Arouse interest. Activate schema for sport.
		T asks Ss to help him or her write down as many different kinds of sport on the whiteboard within 3 minutes.	Ss call out the answer to the question as the T writes the answers on the board.		
		T asks Ss to rank their favorite sports in order of importance.	T writes the answers.		

Step	Time	Tasks (Teacher)	Tasks (Pupils)	Interaction	Purpose
2	5–7 mins	T distributes handout on sports schedule from the newspaper.	Ss read the handout and answer the questions.	T ⟷ Ss	Focus attention of Ss on the concept of skimming for general gist with authentic materials.
		T asks Ss to read it quickly and answer the true/false questions that follow it within 3 minutes.	Ss call out their answers to the T.	Ss ⟷ T	
		T goes over the answers and shows Ss how he or she found the answers based on key words in the article.	Ss check their answers.		
3	15 mins	T tells Ss that they just practiced skimming to get the general meaning or gist of a passage.	Ss read the handout and answer the questions.	T ⟷ Ss	Getting Ss to read passage quickly to get the overall meaning.
		T gives another handout on sports from the textbook (*New Clue*). T asks Ss to read and answer the true/false questions written on the paper within 5 to 7 minutes. T asks Ss for answers and writes them on the board. T explains how key words can give the answers.	Ss call out their answers to the T.	Ss ⟷ T (S ⟷ S possible also)	
			Ss check their answers.	T ⟷ Ss	
4	5 mins	T summarizes the importance of reading a passage quickly first in order to get the gist.	Ss listen.	T ⟷ Ss	To remind Ss what they have just done and why – to develop pupil metacognitive awareness.
		T gives homework of reading the next day's newspaper's front-page story and writing down the gist of the story in 4 sentences.			
		Follow-up: Next lesson: To teach the students to find the main idea of the passage by scanning.			

Key: Interaction: T ⟷ Ss means teacher interacts with the whole class.

Appendix B: Bloom's Taxonomy of Thinking Processes

BLOOM'S TAXONOMY OF THINKING PROCESSES (ADAPTATION)

Level of Taxonomy	Definition	Student Roles	Action Verbs
Knowledge	Recall of specific information	responds absorbs remembers recognizes	tell; list; define; name; identify; state; remember; repeat
Comprehension (understanding)	Understanding of communicated information	explains translates demonstrates interprets	transform; change; restate; describe; explain; review; paraphrase; relate; generalize; infer
Application (using)	Use of rules, concepts, principles, and theories in new situations	solves problems demonstrates uses knowledge constructs	apply; practice; employ; use; demonstrate; illustrate; show; report
Analysis (taking part)	Breaking down information into parts	discusses uncovers lists dissects	analyze; dissect; distinguish; examine; compare; contrast; survey; investigate; separate; categorize; classify; organize
Synthesis (creating new)	Putting together of ideas into a new or unique plan	discusses generalizes relates contrasts	create; invent compose; construct; design; modify; imagine; produce; propose; what if…
Evaluation (judging)	Judging the value of materials or ideas on the basis of set standards or criteria	judges disputes forms opinions debates	judge; decide; select; justify; evaluate; critique; debate; verify; recommend; assess

Adapted from Shrum & Glisan (1994)

References

Bailey, K. M. (1986). The best-laid plans: Teachers' in-class decisions to depart from their lesson plans. In K. M. Bailey & D. Nunan (Eds.), *Voices from the language classroom: qualitative research in second language classrooms* (pp. 15–40). New York: Cambridge University Press.

Borko, H., & Niles, J. (1987). Descriptions of teacher planning: Ideas for teachers and researchers. In V. Richardson-Koehler (Ed.), *Educators' handbook: A research perspective* (pp. 167–187). New York: Longman.

Brown. H. D. (1994). *Teaching by principles: An interactive approach to language pedagogy*. Englewood Cliffs, NJ: Prentice Hall Regents.

Freeman, D. (1996). Redefining the relationship between research and what teachers know. In K. M. Bailey & D. Nunan (Eds.), *Voices from the language classroom: Qualitative research in second language classrooms* (pp. 88–115). New York: Cambridge University Press.

Hunter, M., & Russell, D. (1977). How can I plan more effective lessons? *Instructor, 87*, 74–75.

McCutcheon, G. (1980). How do elementary school teachers plan? The nature of planning and influences on it. *Elementary School Journal, 81*(1), 4–23.

Purgason, K. B. (1991). Planning lessons and units. In M. Celce-Murcia (Ed.), *Teaching English as a second or foreign language* (2nd ed., pp. 419–431). Boston, MA: Heinle & Heinle.

Richards, J. C. (1990). *The language teaching matrix*. Cambridge: Cambridge University Press.

Richards, J. C. (1998). What's the use of lesson plans? In J. C. Richards (Ed.), *Beyond training* (pp. 103–121). New York: Cambridge University Press.

Richards, J. C., & Lockhart, C. (1994). *Reflective teaching in second language classrooms*. Cambridge: Cambridge University Press.

Shrum J. L., & Glisan, E. (1994). *Teacher's handbook: Contextualized language instruction*. Boston, MA: Heinle & Heinle.

Taylor, C. (1970). The expectations of Pygmalion's creators. *Educational Leadership*, *28*, 161–164.

Tyler, R. (1949). *Basic principles of curriculum and instruction*. Chicago: University of Chicago Press.

Ur, P. (1996). *A course in language teaching: Practice and theory*. Cambridge: Cambridge University Press.

Yinger, R. (1980). A study of teacher planning. *Elementary School Journal, 80* (3), 107–127.

CHAPTER 4

Classroom Management

Marilyn Lewis

Teachers' Concerns

Language teachers are familiar with the intended outcomes of Communicative Language Teaching, namely, for students to use the new language in speech and in writing for a variety of purposes and in a range of contexts. Teachers also have access to many textbooks setting out activities for doing this. What they often struggle with in their own classes is how to manage classroom learning to achieve these ends. The following comments are grouped into three broad categories: motivation, constraints, and the teacher's role.

Some teachers are concerned about *students' motivation:*

> Students in our school are learning English because they have to. It makes motivation really difficult for the teacher.
>
> Students don't want to use English in class when they can say the same thing faster in their own language. What do other teachers do if one or two students refuse to speak?

For others, *constraints* are things that teachers believe are stopping them from managing an ideal learning atmosphere:

> How can we organize group work when the desks are all fixed to the floor in rows?
>
> Our classes are huge. Whenever I organize tasks, things get messy, such as some students finishing ahead of the others and wasting their time.

> How do experienced teachers manage when all the students are at different levels?
>
> We have to achieve examination results. Anything that doesn't lead there is not valued by the school or the parents.
>
> It's hard to access authentic materials for my teaching.

Finally, some comments relate to *new roles for teachers* in language classrooms.

> In this school, the tradition is for the teacher to be at the front by the board all the time, but in our teacher-training course they mentioned walking around the room. How could I keep control if I did that?
>
> I was trained to teach in a traditional way and now the government has decided to introduce Communicative Language Teaching. My English isn't good enough to answer students' questions.

Elsewhere in this volume, writers address general principles and approaches to language teaching. This chapter deals with the "how" of classroom management. The concerns just cited are discussed in three sections: motivating students, managing constraints, and managing the teacher's role. The situation will be presented first, followed by some solutions.

MOTIVATING STUDENTS

THE SITUATION

The statement about learning in general, that it "never takes place in a vacuum" (Williams & Burden, 1997, p. 188), is even more true in the language class. When it comes to creating a classroom climate for language learning, Williams and Burden point to three levels of influence: national and cultural influences on the language being learned, the education system where the language is being learned, and the immediate classroom environment. Influences on the language being learned are already determined, as is the education system. School policy, the textbook, and a national curriculum all influence the way students feel about language learning in general and about learning English in particular. However, teachers do influence the classroom environment by motivating unmotivated students. There are many ways in which students can be "off-task": They fail to take part by sitting in silence, they distract other students by talking off the topic, and they provide "nonlanguage" entertainment. All of these call for teachers' management skills. Even taking into account differences from country to country and class to class, teachers of a range of learners and subjects believe that they can make a difference, as the examples that follow show.

TEACHERS' RESPONSES

In language learning, motivation is more specific than in a content-based subject. The history teacher can motivate students to take an interest in the subject, but the language teacher is looking for more than interest. Language is a skill, and a skill needs to be applied, not just stored in the head or admired at a distance.

Teachers encourage language use through both intrinsic and extrinsic motivation. Some students have strong intrinsic motivation; they know the benefits of learning a particular language. Others need to be reminded of where success could lead. For example, in societies where studying literature is an important part of the education system, teachers emphasize the benefits of being able to read English poetry, short stories, and novels in the original. In other contexts, teachers build on the career and commercial benefits to students: Fluent speakers of English are employed as interpreters, they travel abroad on business, and they work in tourism. Reminding students about the jobs waiting for fluent language speakers can be an important part of motivation.

Extrinsic motivation can come through rewards. Teachers supply interesting additional reading materials, they show a video to follow a difficult language task, or they invite guest speakers so that students can use the new language in an authentic way. Occasionally, though, rewards can take over and destroy enjoyment, as van Lier (1996) reports from one of his classes. He had organized a grammar game involving two teams as a means of motivating students, but unfortunately the teams became so competitive that they argued over every point and were quickly diverted from the grammar point.

In monolingual classes teachers report particular difficulty in persuading students to speak English. The following ideas have worked in small and large classes in different countries:

Role-play, with one student taking the role of a foreigner

Native-speaking visitors answer questions on specific topics

Pen friends, by mail or E-mail

Group presentations of topics students have researched

Interclass debates

Speech competitions

Concerts with plays and singing

Although the ultimate goal is to speak English, in classes where students speak different first languages, it can help motivation to allow limited use of the first language in class for specific purposes. For example, the L1 helps in clarifying a difficult point or planning the organizational part of projects, particularly when the teacher does not speak the languages of all the students.

An ongoing aspect of motivation is dealing with the behavior of particular students. Experienced teachers usually have a scale of responses to off-task behavior, which helps them decide whether to ignore or attend to the problem. Here are three examples of how a teacher might move through stages in managing a particular type of behavior.

CASE 1: THE BACK-ROW DISTRACTOR

The same student always sits at the back and distracts others.

Use eye contact while continuing to speak.

Stop mid-sentence and stare until the student stops.

Talk with the student after class to investigate the cause.

CASE 2: THE NONPARTICIPANTS

Several students are not taking part in the assigned activity.

Ignore them if they are not distracting others.

Walk past their desks and ask if there is a problem.

Ask colleagues how the same students participate in other classes.

CASE 3: THE OVEREXUBERANT STUDENT

In a language class, teachers want students to speak. Sometimes, though, the pleasure of hearing the language in use sours when one outgoing student dominates question time, comment time, and all the rest of the talking time. This calls for tact, because the person is often a good language model for others.

Interrupt with "Thanks for that" and call on someone else to continue.

Remind the student that there will be more talking time soon in groups.

Talk to the student individually later.

In summary, making quick decisions on what to do about a problem depends on answers to questions like the following:

Does the behavior hinder other students' learning?

Is this just a single occurrence not worth wasting time on?

Is it a whole-class problem or specific to one or two people?

Teachers also know that if large numbers of students are failing to attend to the lesson, there could be a problem with the lesson itself. The task may be too difficult, or it may have continued for too long, or the content may be boring. On the other hand, the problem may not be within the class at all. A forthcoming sports match or even unusual weather can change the mood of a class and signal to the teacher the need for a change of activity.

The suggestions in the rest of this chapter are intended to prevent off-task behavior before it starts.

MANAGING CONSTRAINTS

THE SITUATION

There are very few contexts in which students learn English only for the purposes of listening and reading, without any need to interact with others in speech or writing. When it comes to giving students opportunities to talk, constraints such as large, multilevel classes with fixed furniture, traditions of learning ("Games are for children. This is an adult class"), an examination-oriented curriculum ("We have to pass exams. Exams are not about group work"), and difficulty in accessing resources all seem to stand in the way of organizing talk. Resources frequently head the list of constraints. Some teachers have no photocopiers or no funds to make copies for the whole class, no tape recorders or video recorders, and their students have no source of interesting reading material, even in a library. The teacher may have a single copy of a useful article, colored photographs relevant to the topic but too small to be seen at the back of a large class, or half a dozen copies of commercial readers at the right level for a class of forty students. Managing with scarce resources is a challenge, but rather than abandoning these great resources, teachers often find ways around the problems.

TEACHERS' RESPONSES

Reading the many accounts of how other teachers have overcome constraints is one practical way of picking up ideas. For example, the encouraging news about group work despite large numbers and fixed furniture is that it happens in many parts of the world. The journal *English Teaching Forum* is a good source of articles, many of them written about classroom contexts where conditions seem less than ideal. Teachers have described how they organize group work in large classes with benches fixed to the floor by asking students to turn around and form groups of four with the students sitting in the row behind. Sometimes the group leader scrambles over desks to reach the teacher to discuss progress.

If traditions of learning make students reluctant to join in group work, then the first step is to overcome their preconceptions and "sell" the idea of groups.

- Explain that groups are a chance to speak without the teacher noticing mistakes.
- When students complain about having to listen to all the other students' bad English when they get into groups, point out that communication involves listening to everyone and making sense whether people speak slowly or fast, formally or informally.
- Make the activities age-appropriate. Avoid the word *games* with older learners.
- Make the purpose of each activity clear beforehand.
- Call for student feedback on group activities. What went well? What could be changed?
- Start with self-selected groupings, so that students are working with people they know or like.
- Show connections between group activities and the rest of the program to overcome the belief that group work is an extra.

In some cultures, students are very anxious about making mistakes in front of others. Oxford (1999) suggests a number of ways of reducing anxiety, including talking about the problem and minimizing conditions that might increase it. In particular, she recommends laughter and music as antidotes to anxiety.

To overcome photocopying constraints, a single article can be photocopied just once and cut up so that each student has one sentence. This becomes the basis of a "divided information" communicative activity. Colored photographs and a limited number of readers can be supplemented by self-access worksheets so that students work through the tasks and materials individually or in pairs on different days. Another resource is the blackboard sketch. Observation in many classrooms in different countries suggests that teachers underestimate their own artwork, whereas students enjoy it. Quick drawing while talking can enliven a dialogue, illustrate word meaning, or prompt student talk.

If the barrier to group work is managing large numbers, the teacher could experiment with different types of group work which call for different management skills: free discussion, projects, and the particular type of group work described as "tasks." In free-discussion groups, the teacher can use the multilevel nature of the class to advantage by appointing specific roles to avoid problems such as having one student dominating the group and others sitting passively. A chairperson invites people to speak and holds back those who have talked long enough; a timekeeper watches that the group moves on to the various stages of the activity; a reporter takes notes ready for reporting back.

Another type of group work is the project. Projects involve collating material from a number of sources – inanimate and human. The teacher needs to check out availability beforehand with librarians and specialist informants. The informants could be students from other language classes, in which case time-tabling needs to be checked, or other teachers whom students interview between classes. E-mail informants also appreciate hearing from the class teacher before spending time answering questions from students.

The most specific type of small-group activity in the language class is the task. Tasks are described in detail elsewhere in this volume, but the concern here is how to manage them in large classes. A task requires input data, procedures, goals, and specific roles for teachers and learners, all of which need to be explained to the class. If photocopying facilities are limited, an alternative is to use the board or an overhead transparency. For example, a collection of words which students have to categorize and label can be written up in just a couple of minutes. Some teachers play music as the task input. Procedures can also be listed on the board, or, if they are short enough, the teacher can dictate them.

Whether the group activity is a discussion, a project, or a more specific task, it can have a variety of goals, which students select depending on their level and their interest. In a multilevel class, goals can be graded for different members of the group, according to their language competence, by modifying:

- the topic (more abstract or more applied)
- the language difficulty (two versions of the same text)
- the amount of input
- the graphic support (more or fewer pictures)
- the time taken to finish
- the level of language students are expected to use for the same purpose
- the length of the final "product"
- the amount of support from the teacher and from other students

Because some groups finish before others, teachers often organize an individual activity to follow, and return to a discussion of outcomes when everyone has finished. May (1996, p. 8), in his book *Exam Classes*, suggests:

- different word limits for different groups of students, since it takes the same amount of homework time for individual students to complete different amounts of material.
- providing more able students with different extra tasks rather than just more of the same.

An alternative is not to treat the discussion of goals as a whole-class activity, but to discuss with students group-by-group how their goals have been reached.

As with any other form of organization, group work can be overdone. The teacher's challenge is to decide which class activities can best be done individually, which work well in pairs or groups, and which call for whole-class work. Creative thinking will show teachers on a particular day with a particular class which form of organization to choose for activities such as the following:

- marking homework
- solving a word puzzle
- practicing new language
- answering students' questions
- listening to tapes
- writing a letter

Managing the Teacher's Role

THE SITUATION

The final aspect of classroom management is the role of the teacher. Teachers sometimes fear losing their central classroom role as practiced in the traditional classroom, where students asked questions that teachers could answer. In communicative language classrooms, on the other hand, they may ask how to say something that the teacher or textbook has not yet introduced or even that the teacher cannot answer.

The teacher's role includes relationships with colleagues. A typical situation is that one teacher is encouraging everyone to talk in pairs, and the talk is so successful that the teacher next door complains. Often it is not a question of actual noise level. Anyone who has taught next to a room where fifty students are chorusing drills loudly will know what noise is. It is more a question of the type of noise that people are accustomed to. When a whole department operates by the same approach, there are fewer misunderstandings.

TEACHERS' RESPONSES

One way of considering a teacher's role is in terms of metaphors. The teacher of a traditional grammar-based class could be described as a tap pouring water into an empty vessel. The teacher has all the knowledge about the new language and the empty vessels have to be filled with the grammar rules and the meaning of words. Then, in situationally based classrooms, where there was an emphasis on memorizing fixed dialogues, the teachers' roles changed. They became conductors of orchestras, bringing in the different players in turn and stopping the orchestra from time to time when someone hit the wrong note. In communicative language classes, there is far more scope for imagination in finding a metaphor: for example, the teacher is a gardener, supplying materials for growth (resources, encouragement) and rearranging the environment (the furniture) for this to happen. Stevick (1996, p. 180) uses the metaphor of a chessboard on which the teacher is "the most powerful single piece." According to this metaphor, the teacher is the most powerful player in classroom dynamics and determines the class structure.

Whatever the metaphor, the teacher has to manage a number of situations, predictable as well as unpredictable. Let's consider two aspects of classroom management: one being the way time is managed, and the other the managing of students' questions. These two are selected because the former is an example of something which can be planned, whereas the latter involves more spontaneous management skills.

One way of managing the large, multilevel class is to plan for the teacher to work with different groups of students at different times during the lesson. An example of this has been reported elsewhere (Lewis, 1998). In summary, four time slots can be used as follows:

Organization	Activity	Purposes
whole class	theme-based building on individual interests	social, language input, fluency
class in two halves, one with self-access materials, the other with the teacher	1. independent tasks 2. direct teaching	language practice, self-assessment preparation for independent work
as above, reversed	1. communicative tasks 2. independent work	focus on meaning follow-up to direct teaching
individual, pairs, or small groups	choice of tasks	one-to-one interaction with teacher and other students

In this model, the teacher has different roles at different times. For example:

- answering or asking questions
- up-front roles or supporting individuals
- language informant or eliciting language
- congratulating or encouraging individuals
- designer of tasks or materials

In detail, the lesson could flow like this: When the class arrives students work together on something that builds group dynamics. For example, the teacher might show graphics (on the overhead projector, for example) of a theme of common interest. Because of the graphics, the topic is accessible to everyone. The language input is oral and comes from both teacher and students. At the second, divided phase, each group builds on the theme that has been introduced. The more advanced group works independently on extra reading, on a traditional exercise, or in the computer laboratory. Meanwhile, the more elementary group is with the teacher, receiving further input on the theme.

At the third phase, this elementary group is ready to work independently, either individually or in pairs, practicing the language that has been introduced, while the advanced group has direct teaching from the teacher. Students in both groups could start by reviewing whatever they were doing at Phase 2 or they could move on to new work. Finally, everyone in the class is working at materials and tasks at their own level. This gives the teacher freedom to move around the room, responding to questions and identifying needs.

A second, and unplanned, aspect of classroom management is dealing with students' spontaneous questions. Teachers have to make quick decisions about whether to answer, postpone, or dismiss a question. As usual in classroom-management decisions, there are many possible responses. Being honest about why a question is not being answered can give students information about the learning process. Saying "Let me look that up so I can check all the details" is a reminder that everyone, teachers as well as students, should make use of reference material. Postponing the question is something teachers do whether or not they need to look it up. They might say, "That's an important question, but if I answer it now I think it will muddle you about the grammar point we are looking at today. Let me come back to that next week." Making a scribbled note of the question as the students watch lets them see that the teacher is taking the question seriously. If a student asks a question about a point the teacher has just explained, the first step is to gauge whether others too need further explanation ("Please put your hands up if you would like to hear the answer to that"). A huge show of hands suggests that more explanation is needed. If only a few hands go up, the teacher can ask those students to listen later when most of the class has started an exercise.

Conclusion

Many themes run through current interpretations of Communicative Language Teaching: cooperative learning, authenticity, and task-based syllabuses, to name just three. Underpinning them all is the ability of a teacher to manage students and the environment to make the most of the opportunities for learning and practicing language.

The final word in this chapter goes to Stevick (1996, p. 250), who brings a lifetime of teaching to his six-point summary of what he hopes for in a classroom. He has three hopes for students and three for teachers. He wants students to be involved, to feel comfortable while involved in intellectual activity, and to be listening to one another as well as to the teacher.

He wants teachers to be in general control, to allow and encourage originality in students, and to look "relaxed and matter-of-fact ... giving information about ... appropriateness or correctness ..., rather than criticising or praising."

References

Lewis, M. (1998). Diverse levels and diverse goals in a community class. In J. C. Richards (Ed.), *Case studies from second language classrooms*. Alexandria, VA: TESOL.

May, P. (1996). *Exam classes*. Oxford: Oxford University Press.

Oxford, R. (1999). Anxiety and the language learner. In J. Arnold (Ed.), *Affect in language learning*. Cambridge: Cambridge University Press.

Stevick, E. W. (1996). *Memory, meaning and method*. Boston, MA: Heinle & Heinle.

van Lier, L. (1996). *Interaction in the language curriculum: Awareness, autonomy and authenticity*. London: Longman.

Williams, M., & Burden, R. (1997). *Psychology for language teachers*. Cambridge: Cambridge University Press.

SECTION 3

CLASSROOM DYNAMICS

INTRODUCTION

Most teachers would hope for a small class size in which students are more or less homogeneous in terms of proficiency. Except for a lucky few, however, most teachers find themselves working with a class of fifty students or more, and, to make matters worse, these students often exhibit a wide variety of abilities. This less than ideal situation often leads to the use of teaching methodology which does not promote optimal learning. For example, teacher-centered methodology, which largely ignores individual differences and the contribution of the learners in the learning process is, unfortunately, still ubiquitous in many ESL classrooms. Walk into a typical ESL classroom and you will observe a familiar situation where interaction in the classroom is dominated by the teacher, with the students mainly responding to the teacher's initiatives. Another familiar characteristic is one in which every student in class is doing more or less "the same thing, at the same time, and in the same way" (Ur, 1996, p. 233). The two papers in this section explore ways of making students become more active contributors in the learning process and examine principles for the design of learning activities and materials which allow for some degree of individualization in the classroom.

The first paper, by Jacobs and Hall, looks at the techniques and principles for implementing cooperative learning. When carefully planned and executed, cooperative learning can lead to a more dynamic classroom interaction that promotes more learning. Benefits of cooperative learning include

- less teacher talk
- increased student talk
- more varied student talk

- more negotiation of meaning
- a greater amount of comprehensible input
- a more relaxed classroom atmosphere
- greater motivation for learning

These are factors which second language researchers believe contribute significantly to language acquisition. Although many other things can be done to create a conducive learning environment, cooperative learning techniques are definitely among those which have received considerable empirical support, and should be used more frequently in second language classrooms. For those interested in the successful implementation of cooperative learning in the classroom, Jacobs and Hall offer some practical tips on how to form groups, how to deal with students who refuse to work cooperatively, how to deal with the noise level of the class, how to determine group size, and so on.

The second paper, by Bowler and Parminter, offers practical help in dealing with the mixed-ability classroom. They view mixed-ability classes from a positive perspective and suggest a number of teaching approaches. They discuss how listening and reading tasks can be adapted to meet the varied needs of the students. They provide examples showing how students working on the same text could be assigned easier or harder tasks based on their ability level. One of the greatest advantages of designing multilevel tasks is that no student feels left out as each one of them is suitably challenged.

Discussion Questions

Before Reading

1. Do you enjoy working in groups? Share your experience of working in groups.
2. Do you use a lot of group work in your teaching? How do your students respond to it?
3. What are some of the problems associated with teaching a class of, say, fifty or sixty students? How do you deal with these problems?
4. Do you think Communicative Language Teaching principles can be applied to large class size? Why or why not?
5. In your experience, what is the optimal number of students in a group? Explain your answer.
6. List the advantages and disadvantages of teaching (1) a homogeneous class and (2) a mixed-level class. Which one do you prefer to teach? Why?

After Reading

1. What is cooperative learning? How is it different from group work?
2. What are some of the most important benefits of cooperative learning? What is the theory behind cooperative learning?
3. Develop a 1-hour reading lesson for a group of students you are familiar with, incorporating the "Numbered Heads Together" technique discussed in the Jacobs and Hall paper.
4. How can the principles of cooperative learning be applied to teaching of writing? Do you think students will produce a better piece of written work if they work cooperatively in groups?

5. How can cooperative learning techniques be applied to the teaching of
   - vocabulary
   - reading
   - listening
   - speaking

   Give a concrete example for each.
6. Review the paper by Bowler and Parminter. What do they mean by tiered tasks and bias tasks? How would you apply the concepts of tiered tasks and bias tasks in your own classroom? What are some of the limitations of this approach?
7. Select a short reading passage. Design a three-tiered task that can accommodate the needs of the high-, mid-, and low-level students in your class.

Further Reading

Ur, P. (1996). *A course in language teaching: Practice and theory.* Cambridge: Cambridge University Press.

CHAPTER 5

Implementing Cooperative Learning

George M. Jacobs and Stephen Hall

Introduction

In the last decade there has been a growing interest among ESL/EFL teachers in using cooperative learning activities. With cooperative learning, students work together in groups whose usual size is two to four members. However, cooperative learning is more than just putting students in groups and giving them something to do. Cooperative learning principles and techniques are tools which teachers use to encourage mutual helpfulness in the groups and the active participation of all members.

These principles can be seen in the cooperative learning technique Numbered Heads Together (Kagan, 1992) that can be used, for example, in an ESL/EFL reading class. There are four steps in doing Numbered Heads Together:

1. Each student in a group of four gets a number: 1, 2, 3, or 4.
2. The teacher or a student asks a question based on the text the class is reading.
3. Students in each group put their heads together to come up with an answer or answers. They should also be ready to supply support for their answer(s) from the text and/or from other knowledge.
4. The teacher calls a number from 1 to 4. The person with that number gives and explains their group's answer.

Numbered Heads Together encourages successful group functioning because all members need to know and be ready to explain their group's answer(s) and because,

This is a slightly revised version of the article that appeared in *English Teaching Forum, 32* (4) (October 1994), 2–13.

when students help their groupmates, they help themselves and their whole group, because the response given belongs to the whole group, not just to the group member giving it.

A good deal of research exists in other areas of education suggesting that cooperative learning is associated with benefits in such key areas as learning, self-esteem, liking for school, and interethnic relations (Johnson, Johnson, & Holubec, 1993; Slavin, 1995). In second and foreign language learning, theorists propose several advantages for cooperative learning: increased student talk, more varied talk, a more relaxed atmosphere, greater motivation, more negotiation of meaning, and increased amounts of comprehensible input (Liang, Mohan, & Early, 1998; Olsen & Kagan, 1992).

However, implementing cooperative learning is not like waving a magic wand: Just say a few magic words, and *whoosh!* everything is working great. In fact, in planning and executing cooperative learning, teachers have many decisions to make.

In the planning stage of cooperative learning, there are many philosophical questions to think about, such as whether to stress intrinsic or extrinsic motivation (Graves, 1990), how much choice to give students in such matters as how, about what, and with whom they will collaborate, and how tightly to structure activities to help encourage effective cooperation (Sapon-Shevin & Schniedewind, 1991). These questions demand the attention of all teachers interested in cooperative learning. However, the focus of this article is the more mechanical aspects of actually executing cooperative learning in the classroom.

From our experience doing workshops and courses for teachers about cooperative learning, we have chosen ten of the most commonly asked nuts-and-bolts questions. The suggestions listed come from our own ESL and EFL classes, ideas from colleagues and from the teacher participants in our cooperative learning workshops and courses, and books and articles in the field.

This article presents a wide range of options. Readers will want to choose those options which match their own teaching styles and their learners' backgrounds and needs. You may well come up with ideas not mentioned here. (If so, please send them to us. We will add them to our list.) If cooperative learning is new to you and your students, remember that you all may need time to adjust. We suggest that you explain to students why you are using cooperative learning; start slowly, be patient, and be persistent.

How Big Should Groups Be?

1. Even two people are a group.
2. Generally speaking, the smaller the group, the more each member talks and the less chance there is that someone will be left out. If time is short, smaller groups can usually do an activity more quickly. Smaller groups also require fewer group-management skills. Thus, when starting with cooperative learning, groups of two or three may be best.
3. Larger groups are good because they provide more people for doing big tasks, increase the variety of people in terms of skills, personalities, backgrounds, and so on, and reduce the number of groups for the teacher to monitor.
4. Many books on cooperative learning recommend groups of four. For example, Kagan (1992) suggests foursomes and uses many cooperative learning techniques in which students first work in pairs, and then the two pairs of the foursome interact with one another.

How Should Groups Be Formed?

1. Most experts on cooperative learning suggest that teacher-selected groups work best, at least until students become proficient at collaboration. Teacher-selected groups usually aim to achieve a heterogeneous mix. Such a mix promotes peer tutoring, helps to break down barriers among different types of students, and encourages on-task behavior.
2. In creating teacher-assigned teams, factors to consider include language proficiency, first language, sex, race, and diligence.
3. An effective way to set up mixed-proficiency groups is to band the learners' names into, say, four proficiency clusters from high to low and then select randomly from within each band so that groups will involve learners with a range of proficiencies. Other criteria, such as sex, race, and diligence, can be considered when deciding whom to choose from which band.
4. Random grouping is quick and easy and conveys the idea that one can work with anyone.
5. Many ways exist for randomizing groups. The most common is counting off. Take the number of students in your class, divide by the number of students you want per group, and the result will be the number students should count to. For example, if there are 56 students in the class and you want groups of 4, divide 56 by 4, which is 14; so, students should count to 14.
6. Other ways to set up random groups include using playing cards, giving out numbered pieces of paper, and distributing cards with different categories on them and letting students group themselves according to the category. An example of the latter procedure would be to have some cards with names of animals, others with names of plants, others with names of countries, and so on. All the animals would find each other and form a group, all the plants would look for the other plants, and so forth.
7. The number of students in the class may not fit evenly with the number of students per group. For example, if there are forty-seven students in the class, and you want groups of four, three students will be left over. It might be best to from eleven groups of four and one group of three.
8. When students become good at cooperative group work, they can group themselves – for example, by interests – for self-directed projects (Sharan & Sharan, 1992).

When Students Are Working in Their Groups, How Can the Teacher Get the Class's Attention?

1. A signal can be used to tell students that groups should quickly bring their discussions to a temporary halt and face the teacher. One popular signal is the teacher raising a hand. When students see this, they are to raise their hands also, bring their discussion to a close, alert other students who have not seen the teacher's raised hand, and face the teacher. One way to remember this is RSPA (Raise hand, Stop talking, Pass the signal to those who have not seen it, Attention to teacher).
2. Other possible signals include ringing a bell, playing a musical instrument, blowing a whistle, snapping one's fingers, and flicking the lights on and off. One teacher we know starts to sing! Another puts two signs on the board, one to stop working and face the teacher, and the other to continue but more quietly. She knocks on the board to get students' attention and then points to the appropriate sign.

3. Some teachers play music in the background as groups study together. In this case, turning off the music can be the attention signal (Saeki, 1994).
4. When students lead class activities, they can use the same signal.
5. One student in each group can take the role of group checker with the responsibility of watching out for the teacher's signal and being sure the group responds to the signal quickly. Many other types of roles can be used to facilitate group functioning (Ilola, Power, & Jacobs, 1989).
6. If some groups are not responding quickly to the attention signal, rewards, such as praise, can be given to encourage this component of smooth-functioning group activities.

What Can Be Done if the Noise Level Becomes Too High?

1. One student per group can be the noise monitor or quiet captain whose function is to urge the group to collaborate actively, yet quietly.
2. The closer together students sit, the more quietly they can talk. Having students sit close together not only helps reduce the noise level, but also helps foster cooperation and minimizes the chance of someone being left out.
3. Along with sitting close together, students can use special quiet voices, for example, "6-inch" voices or "30-centimeter" voices.
4. A signal similar to the one used to get the class's attention (see the preceding section) can be used as a sign to continue working but a bit more quietly. For example, for "Stop working," the signal might be hand raised straight up, and for "work more quietly," the signal could be hand raised with arm bent at elbow.
5. Kagan (1992) suggests stoplight cards. A green card goes on the desk of groups if they are working together quietly. A yellow card indicates they need to quiet down a bit. When a red card is put on their desk, the group should become completely silent, and all should silently count to ten before starting work again.

What if a Student Does Not Want to Work in a Group?

1. Discussing the advantages that students can derive from learning in groups may help overcome resistance to group activities. These potential advantages include learning more, having more fun, and preparing for tasks away from school in which collaboration is necessary.
2. Students may look more favorably on cooperative learning if they understand that talking with others is a language learning strategy that they can apply outside of class as well (Oxford, 1990).
3. Students should realize that studying in groups is only one of several ways of learning that will go on in the class.
4. Group games may encourage students to look forward to other group-learning activities. Many enjoyable games also teach academic and social skills.
5. Start with pairs and tasks that require exchange of information (Nation, 1990). Provide language support in terms of useful vocabulary and structures, so that

students are more likely to succeed (Richards, 1995). Success here will build confidence in the ability to work in groups.

6. Students who do not want to study in groups can be allowed to work on their own. In our experience, after a while, they will want to take part in the group interaction and will ask to join a group.

What if Some Groups Finish Earlier Than Others?

1. Check to see if the groups have done the assignment properly.
2. Have groups that finish early compare what they have done with other groups that also finished early.
3. Have groups discuss how they worked together. Then, because sometimes smooth-functioning groups can provide good models for others, you might want to have exemplary groups explain their group process. This might help all groups work together more efficiently.
4. Develop one or two "sponge activities." Sponge activities are short activities, related to the main task, that soak up the extra time between when the first and last groups finish.
5. Set time limits to discourage groups from dawdling. These time limits are flexible. If groups are working well, but need more time, the limit can be extended.
6. Ask students to help other groups that have not yet finished.
7. Groups that finish early can work on homework or other assignments.

What if a Few Students Are Frequently Absent?

1. Assign these students as extra members of groups. For example, if students are working in groups of four, add such students as the fifth member of groups.
2. Assign tasks that can be accomplished in one class period.
3. Being a member of a group may give such students a feeling of belonging and a reason to come to school that they did not have before. Groups may also help them to be more successful in school, and thus to enjoy being at school more.
4. Coach students in how to use appropriate peer pressure to encourage frequently absent members to come to school and to complete their portion of group tasks. (In some cases, of course, absent students may have family obligations or other nonschool reasons for missing class.)
5. If a group is working cooperative Jigsaw activities (Kagan, 1992), give the missing piece to the whole group.
6. Make sure that groups have contingency plans in case members are missing. Learning to make such plans is an important group skill, because absences are also a common problem in groups outside of school.
7. In an ongoing activity, ask groups to update absent members when they return to school. This encourages students to develop peer-tutoring skills.
8. Let groups be responsible for contacting absent members to inform them of what they missed and to make sure that they know what the assignments are.
9. Be prepared to adjust grading if such students leave their groups in a lurch, giving absent student a lower mark.

How Long Should Groups Stay Together?

1. Keeping groups together for fairly long periods, 4 to 8 weeks, gives them a chance to become comfortable with one another, allows them to form a group identity and bond, and gives them the opportunity to learn how to overcome difficulties they have working together. This is where spending time during or after cooperative activities to have groups process their interaction comes in handy (Dishon & O'Leary, 1993).
2. Groups that stay together for at least a few weeks facilitate long-term projects, such as those using the cooperative learning method Group Investigation (Sharan & Sharan, 1992).
3. Try to resist the temptation to disband groups that are not working well. Stress to students that we need to learn to be able to work with all sorts of people, including those whom we, at least initially, do not like. Use team-building activities and instruction in collaborative skills to help create a spirit of togetherness in groups (Kagan, 1992).
4. Forming heterogeneous groups according to such criteria as proficiency, sex, first language, and personality is a lot of work for teachers. Therefore, one would not want to do that too often.
5. Even while students are in long-term groups, short one-shot activities can be done with different grouping configurations. This may add a bit of variety.
6. Avoid keeping groups together if they begin to become cliquish (Dishon & O'Leary, 1993).

How Should Groups Be Ended?

1. All groups can end with statements by learners and the teacher not only about the content learned, but also about the learning process.
2. When long-standing groups are disbanded, there should be some kind of closure activity for members to thank each other for their help and to sum up what has been learned about working in groups. This can be in oral or written form.
3. Groupmates can write "letters of reference" to be given to members of the person's new group.
4. Group pictures can be taken.
5. Group products can be posted or published. This aids a sense of achievement and gives credibility to the group's work. Also, group products can serve as vehicles for assessment by individuals, groups, and teachers.

What Percentage of the Time Should Cooperative Learning Be Used?

1. No one suggests that the class be organized in cooperative groups all the time.
2. Many cooperative learning activities combine a group component with components in which the teacher lectures or demonstrates, and others in which students work alone (e.g., Slavin, 1995).
3. When students and/or teachers are unfamiliar with cooperative learning, it is best to start slowly. Use one cooperative learning technique, such as Three-Step Interview or

Numbered Heads Together (Kagan, 1992), several times to allow students to become accustomed to collaboration.

4. Discuss with students the whys and hows of learning together.
5. Making cooperation a content theme helps students tune in to working together. For example, once we asked students to write individually about a successful group experience in which they had participated. Then, groups were used to provide feedback.
6. Interact with colleagues for support and ideas.
7. Find the right balance of teaching modes according to your philosophy of education, your reading of the research (including your own research), students' preferences, and what seems to be working best. Students need to know how to cooperate, compete, and work alone.

References

Dishon, D., & O'Leary, P. W. (1993). *A guidebook for cooperative learning: A technique for creating more effective schools* (rev. ed.). Holmes Beach, FL: Learning Publications.

Graves, T. (1990). Are external rewards appropriate or desirable in a cooperative classroom? *Cooperative Learning, 11*, 15–17.

Ilola, L. M., Power, K. M., & Jacobs, G. M. (1989). Structuring student interaction to promote learning. *English Teaching Forum, 27*, 12–16.

Johnson, D. W., Johnson, R. T., & Holubec, E. J. (1993). *Circles of learning*. 4th ed. Edina, MN: Interaction Book Company.

Kagan, S. (1992). *Cooperative learning*. San Clemente, CA: Kagan Cooperative Learning.

Liang, X., Mohan, B. A., & Early, M. (1998). Issues of cooperative learning in ESL classes: A literature review. *TESL Canada Journal, 15*(2), 13–23.

Nation, I. S. P. (1990). *Language teaching techniques*. Wellington: English Language Institute, Victoria University.

Olsen, R. E. W-B., & Kagan, S: (1992). About cooperative learning. In C. Kessler (Ed.), *Cooperative language learning: A teacher's resource book* (pp. 1–30). Englewood Cliffs, NJ: Prentice Hall.

Oxford, R. L. (1990). *Language learning strategies: What every teacher should know*. New York: Newbury House.

Richards, J. C. (1995). Easier said than done. In A. C. Hidalgo, D. Hall, & G. M. Jacobs (Eds.), *Getting started: Materials writers on materials writing* (pp. 95–135). Singapore: SEAMEO Regional Language Center.

Saeki, K. (1994). Stimulating classes with background music. *English Teaching Forum, 32*, 30–31.

Sapon-Shevin, M., & Schniedewind, N. (1991). Cooperative learning as empowering pedagogy. In C. E. Sleeter (Ed.), *Empowerment through multicultural education* (pp. 159–178). Albany, NY: State University of New York Press.

Sharan, Y., & Sharan, S. (1992). *Expanding cooperative learning through group investigation*. Colchester, VT: Teachers College Press.

Slavin, R. E. (1995). *Cooperative learning: Theory, research, and practice*. 2nd ed. Boston, MA: Allyn & Bacon.

CHAPTER 6

Mixed-Level Teaching: Tiered Tasks and Bias Tasks

Bill Bowler and Sue Parminter

No one wants to use three different course books with one class: one for strong students, one for weak students, and one for midlevel students. But when faced with mixed-level classes and an unhelpful course book, what do you do? How exactly can you adapt reading and listening activities to suit stronger and weaker students?

This article aims to provide clear guidelines for teachers who, from time to time, want to make their course book reading and listening materials more flexible.

Communicative Teaching Principles

Two communicative teaching principles underline the multilevel techniques we are going to outline:

1. We do not believe that it is necessary for students to understand or translate every word of a reading or a listening text. If students complete the task we set – answering a certain number of questions, marking a given number of sentences true or false – we feel that they have read or listened successfully.
2. We believe that students' ability to read or listen successfully is governed by a simple equation: text level of challenge + task level of support = student success.

With a long, complex text, a simple task makes the reading or listening achievable for weaker students. With a shorter, simpler text, the task can be more demanding. Bearing these principles in mind, we have isolated two ways of adapting reading or listening activities for mixed-level classes. We call them tiered tasks and bias tasks.

Imagine a wedding cake, on the one hand, and a pie sliced unequally in two, on the other. The top tier of the wedding cake gives the most support (the most layers of supporting pillars) and the least freedom for error (the smallest area of cake to move around on). This is a good task for weaker students. The bottom tier gives the least support (no pillars) and the most freedom to experiment (the largest area of cake to move around on). This is a good task for stronger students. Tiered tasks produce the same or similar results for all students.

The bigger slice of the pie is for those with bigger appetites (stronger students). The smaller slice is for those with smaller appetites (weaker students). Bias tasks produce complementary results.[1]

Tiered Tasks

Now let us look at examples of these two task types, starting with tiered tasks. The following three task sheets all accompany a reading about *The Spirit of London* exhibit at Madame Tussaud's wax museum in London.

EXAMPLE 1

Top Tier

Task A: For Weaker Students

1. How much of London's history does *The Spirit of London* show?
2. How do you go around it?
3. What special effects does it have?
4. What can you see in the modern-day section?

Answers

a. lights, sound, music, and smells
b. police, punks, and tourists
c. more than 400 years
d. in a taxi

Middle Tier

Task B: For Midlevel Students

1. How much of London's history does *The Spirit of London* show?
   a. 400 years
   b. more than 400 years
   c. 399 years
2. How do you go around it?
   a. in a taxi
   b. in a train
   c. on foot

3. What special effects does it have?
   a. lights
   b. sound and music
   c. smells
4. What can you see in the modern-day section?
   a. police
   b. punks
   c. tourists

BOTTOM TIER

Task C: For Stronger Students

1. How much of London's history does *The Spirit of London* show?
2. How do you go around it?
3. What special effects does it have?
4. What can you see in the modern-day section?

- Task A gives all the answers on the page for support. They are jumbled for challenge. Weaker students manipulate the given material, and can use logic to help match the task items, together with the information in the reading text.
- Task B gives multiple-choice answers to help the average students. This is slightly different from the conventional "one answer only is correct" multiple choice, since in questions 3 and 4 there is more than one correct answer.
- Task C gives open questions – with no extra support – to challenge the strongest students in the group.

A useful feature of a tiered task activity is that, whichever level of task students get, the result is the same or similar for all. Oral feedback can therefore take place with the whole class.

We ourselves can assign task sheets to individual students, based on our knowledge of students' abilities. (Sometimes the teacher knows best, especially after conducting a diagnostic test, or after working with a class for a long period of time!)

Alternatively, we can let students choose the lettered tasks, unseen, according to whether they want a lot of help, some help, or no help with the reading activity. Initially, students may overestimate their abilities and choose the most difficult task, or they may play safe and take the easy task. However, when we have offered students a choice of tasks in the classroom a number of times – perhaps with some advice – they will begin to select a realistic task for their level: one that is achievable, yet challenging and not boring.

EXAMPLE 2

Another very simple form of tiered task which works on two levels is a dual-choice gapfill. It is good to vary things by dividing the class into two groups from time to time instead of three. As with all level grouping, where exactly we draw the line is a subjective decision. What follows is the first part of a dual-choice gapfill that accompanies a rap.

The Dead Sad Animal Rap

Listen to the rap. What are the missing words?

		MISSING WORDS
Humans ...	a) ... the dear old dodo,	killed / shot
It was ...	b) ... It couldn't fly	easy / simple
Humans ...	c) ... all the passenger pigeons	hunted / shot
From the ...	d) ... American sky.	South / North

As they listen, weaker students circle one of the words in the box to fill each gap. Stronger students get the same task sheet, but with the missing words box cut off. The task is therefore more challenging for them.

Bias Tasks

Now let us look at bias tasks. The following two task sheets accompany a Penpal Ad Page reading text.

EXAMPLE 1

Task A: For Weaker Students

1. How many of the young people are 13 years old? (Three . . .)
2. How many boys are there?
3. Who doesn't eat meat?
4. Who likes football?
5. Who lives in the country?

Task B: For Stronger Students

Write questions for these answers, based on the Penpal Page.

1. How many of them are 13? *Three of them are.*
2. . . . . ? *There are four.*
3. . . . . ? *Eloise doesn't.*
4. . . . . ? *James does.*
5. . . . . ? *Chris does.*

With Task A, weaker students answer questions about the text. With Task B, stronger students write questions for given answers related to the text.

Because the answers to these two tasks are complementary, it would not be an efficient use of class time for the teacher to conduct postactivity feedback with the whole class. Instead, student–student feedback would be a good idea, with the students in AB pairs. The teacher should naturally be available as an arbiter if there are any questions. These may come from stronger students – who might come up with alternative questions of their own.

If these are grammatically correct, and fit the given answers, the teacher should confirm them as also correct.

This type of feedback, in weak/strong pairs, is very motivating for the weaker students. They have got the difficult questions that the strong students have struggled to reconstruct. For weak students, already knowing key information is a pleasant change from traditional whole-class oral feedback, which often turns into a dialogue between the teacher and the brightest and most forthcoming students, while the weaker students feel left out.

EXAMPLE 2

Another very simple form of bias task activity is a jigsawed gapfill. To prepare a jigsawed gapfill of a song, photocopy the lyrics twice. Label one photocopy "A" and the other "B". On photocopy A, blank out with correction fluid nine words. On photocopy B, blank out eleven words, making sure that the gaps on photocopy A are in different places from the gaps on photocopy B. In this example, photocopy B is the high-level task (with more gaps to fill), and photocopy A is the the low-level task (with fewer gaps). The simplicity or complexity of the words you gap can also make the task easier or more difficult.

A positive feature of this kind of bias activity is that, because the jigsawed gaps are in different places, students are not necessarily aware of who has more gaps and who has fewer. We could easily add a third task sheet (C) for the weakest students, with six gaps in different places from the gaps on photocopies A and B. This would mean conducting feedback in groups of three.

Reduce Your Preparation

Many course books now provide support for mixed-level teaching. This is good news. If your course book includes multilevel task sheets, for example, this means less preparation for you.

Even if your course book is a more traditional one, we hope that our guidelines will help you to adapt the listenings and readings it contains for use with mixed-level classes. Cooperation with colleagues who are using the same book can naturally reduce your preparation time. Divide up the work and exchange the reading and listening task sheets you prepare individually. And if you are teaching the same course book next year, you can recycle your multilevel task sheets with a new mixed-level class.

Once you have the principles of tiered tasks and bias tasks clearly in mind, you should be able to generate many of your own variations on our example task sheets.

Endnote

[1] To take the wedding cake image further: Imagine the reflection of the wedding cake in a polished tabletop. Now the stronger students are at the top of the picture and the weaker students are at the bottom. This is perhaps a more traditional view of a mixed-level class. In this reversed image, the pillars below the "top" tier represent a high level of challenge (challenge and support being complementary factors that frame all mixed-level activities).

SECTION 4

SYLLABUS DESIGN AND INSTRUCTIONAL MATERIALS

INTRODUCTION

The processes of curriculum development and syllabus design in language teaching usually involve assessing the needs of learners in a language program, developing goals and objectives, planning a syllabus, selecting teaching approaches and materials, and deciding on assessment procedures and criteria. The papers in this section focus on issues relating to syllabus design and materials development. Since a syllabus reflects a view of language and of language learning, it is not surprising that the nature of language syllabuses has received a great deal of attention in the recent history of language teaching. As communicative approaches to teaching became dominant in the 1980s, attempts have been made to replace grammatical syllabuses with ones that reflect a communicative understanding of language. The move away from grammatically based syllabuses in the 1960s led to a variety of syllabus proposals, including notional-functional, situational, lexical, task-based, and procedural, all of which claim to be examples of a communicative syllabus. Finney examines three major curriculum design models and their origins in underlying educational traditions. She then proposes an integrated, mixed-focus model for curriculum design, within which there is the flexibility to respond to the changing needs of learners and recognition of learners as active participants in the language learning process. The teacher, in this model, is responsible not only for teaching language for communication and language as knowledge, but also for encouraging learners to take responsibility for their own learning so that they develop skills and strategies for continuing to learn outside of the classroom.

The other paper in this section examines the role of teaching materials. Teaching materials are a key component in most language programs. Whether the teacher uses a textbook, institutionally prepared materials, or makes use of his or her own materials, instructional materials generally serve as the basis for much of the language input learners receive and the language practice that occurs in the classroom. These may take the form of *(a)* printed materials such as books, workbooks, worksheets, or readers, *(b)* nonprint materials such as cassette or audio materials, videos, or computer-based materials, and *(c)* materials that comprise both print and nonprint sources such as self-access materials and materials on the Internet. In addition, materials not designed for instructional use, such as magazines, newspapers, and TV materials, may also play a role in the curriculum.

Some teachers use instructional materials as their primary teaching resource. The materials provide the basis for the content of lessons, the balance of skills taught, and the kinds of language practice students take part in. In other situations, materials serve primarily to supplement the teacher's instruction. For learners, materials may provide the major source of contact they have with the language apart from the teacher. Hence, the role and uses of materials in a language program is a significant aspect of language curriculum development.

Crawford discusses the advantages and disadvantages of the use of commercial textbooks in teaching. Among the principal advantages are the following:

a. They provide structure and a syllabus for a program: Without textbooks, a program may have no central core and learners may not receive a syllabus that has been systematically planned and developed.
b. They help standardize instruction: The use of a textbook in a program can ensure that the students in different classes receive similar content and therefore can be tested in the same way.
c. They maintain quality: If a well-developed textbook is used, students are exposed to materials that have been tried and tested, that are based on sound learning principles, and that are paced appropriately.
d. They provide a variety of learning resources: Textbooks are often accompanied by workbooks, CDs and cassettes, videos, CD-ROM, and comprehensive teaching guides, providing a rich and varied resource for teachers and learners.
e. They are efficient: They save teachers' time, enabling teachers to devote time to teaching rather than materials production.
f. They can provide effective language models and input: Textbooks can provide support for teachers whose first language is not English and who may not be able to generate accurate language input on their own.
g. They can train teachers: If teachers have limited teaching experience, a textbook, together with the teacher's manual, can serve as a medium of initial teacher training.
h. They are visually appealing: Commercial textbooks usually have high standards of design and production and hence are appealing to learners and teachers.

However, there are also potential negative effects of commercial textbooks, such as the following:

a. They may contain inauthentic language: Textbooks sometimes present inauthentic language since texts, dialogues, and other aspects of content tend to be specially written to incorporate teaching points and are often not representative of real language use.
b. They may distort content: Textbooks often present an idealized view of the world or fail to represent real issues. In order to make textbooks acceptable in many different contexts, controversial topics are avoided and, instead, an idealized, white, middle-class view of the world is portrayed as the norm.
c. They may not reflect students' needs: Since textbooks are often written for global markets, they often do not reflect the interests and needs of students and hence may require adaptation.

d. They can deskill teachers: If teachers use textbooks as the primary source of their teaching, allowing the textbook and teacher's manual to make the major instructional decisions for them, the teacher's role can become reduced to that of a technician whose primary function is to present materials prepared by others.
e. They are expensive: Commercial textbooks represent a financial burden for students in many parts of the world.

In making decisions about the role of commercial textbooks in a program, the impact of textbooks on the program, on teachers, and on learners has to be carefully assessed. Crawford proposes a number of principles for the design of effective teaching materials:

- Language is functional and must be contextualized.
- Language development requires learner engagement in purposeful use of language.
- The language use should be realistic and authentic.
- Classroom materials will usually seek to include an audiovisual component.
- Learners need to develop the ability to deal with written as well as spoken genres.
- Effective teaching materials foster learner autonomy.
- Materials need to be flexible enough to allow for individual and contextual differences.
- Learning needs to engage learners both affectively and cognitively.

Discussion Questions

Before Reading

1. What different types of language syllabuses are you familiar with?
2. What use do you make of syllabuses in your teaching?
3. Is a syllabus different from a curriculum? In what ways are these terms similar or different?
4. What steps are involved in developing a language curriculum?
5. What is meant by a communicative curriculum?
6. What are some of the advantages and limitations of using a commercial textbook as the basis for a language program?
7. What qualities do you look for when selecting a textbook?
8. What do you think are the essential qualities of good teaching materials?

After Reading

1. Review the article by Finney. How do Classical Humanism, Reconstructionism, and Progressivism differ in their assumptions about a curriculum?
2. What other philosophies can be used to provide the underlying rationale for a curriculum?
3. Give an example of an objective as part of a language course. What are the advantages and disadvantages of using objectives in syllabus planning?
4. In what ways has a focus on learners influenced views of the curriculum?
5. What does Finney mean by an "integrated approach" to curriculum development?
6. In what ways do teachers normally have to adapt textbooks? Examine a unit from a textbook and suggest how you would adapt it for a specific group of learners.

7. Examine a set of commercial materials (e.g., a textbook series) and consider its appropriateness for a specific group of learners. What criteria would you use to evaluate the materials?
8. What do you think is the role of authentic materials in a language program? What advantages do such materials have over other kinds of materials? What disadvantages?
9. If possible, observe a teacher using a textbook or other forms of materials in a lesson. How did the materials influence the way the teacher taught the class? How much use of the materials did the teacher make?
10. Examine the principles outlined by Crawford for materials design. Develop your own set of principles that could guide materials writers in a materials development project.

CHAPTER 7

The ELT Curriculum: A Flexible Model for a Changing World

Denise Finney

INTRODUCTION

It is clear that it is no longer enough to teach merely the structures and rules of a language – the myriad approaches to curriculum design which have sprung up in the last four decades under the umbrella of 'the communicative approach' have illustrated the shortcomings and lack of relevance of the grammar-systems model of language teaching. Language is communication, and as teachers we must develop in our learners the ability to communicate effectively in a wide range of professional and social contexts. But is it possible to *teach* a language within the four walls of a classroom? I think not – and so we also need to help our learners to learn how to learn and to keep on learning. I would like to quote the famous educator Carl Rogers, who makes a strong plea for learner- and learning-centred learning as the only possible model for education in a world that is changing faster than ever before:

> We are, in my view, faced with an entirely new situation in education where the goal of education, if we are to survive, is the *facilitation of change and learning*. The only man who is educated is the man who has learned how to learn; the man who has learned how to adapt and change; the man who has realized that no knowledge is secure, that only the process of *seeking* knowledge gives a basis for security. Changingness, a reliance on *process* rather than upon static knowledge, is the only thing that makes any sense as a goal for education in the modern world. (Rogers, 1983, p. 120)

In this paper, I will briefly survey three dominant models of curriculum design which are rooted in educational traditions and see how they relate to the field of English language teaching (ELT). I will then propose a model for curriculum design which provides the teacher with the security of a coherent framework within which there is the flexibility to respond to the changing needs of learners and which recognises learners as active participants in the language learning process. This integrated, mixed-focus model is concerned both with the *products* of learning in which teachers *equip* the learners with the "knowledge, skill or pattern of behaviour envisaged as educational ends" (Prabhu, 1987, p. 190) and with the *processes* of learning, which Prabhu refers to as the "enabling procedure . . . a process of developing the learner's capacity to extend and adapt what is learnt in the face of varied and emerging demands" (ibid.).

CURRICULUM: A DEFINITION

The term *curriculum* is open to a variety of definitions; in its narrowest sense it is synonymous with the term *syllabus*, as in specification of the content and the ordering of *what* is to be taught; in the wider sense it refers to all aspects of the planning, implementation and evaluation of an educational program, the *why, how* and *how well* together with the *what* of the teaching-learning process. A.V. Kelly, in his survey of curriculum theory and practice, makes a strong case for understanding *curriculum* as 'the overall rationale for the educational programme of an institution' and argues that any definition must include the following:

> the intentions of the planners, the procedures adopted for the implementation of those intentions, the actual experiences of the pupils resulting from the teachers' direct attempts to carry out their or the planner's intentions, and the 'hidden learning' that occurs as a by-product of the organization of the curriculum, and, indeed, of the school. (Kelly, 1989, p. 14)

From the field of applied linguistics, a similar definition of curriculum is proposed by Richards, Platt and Platt in the Longman *Dictionary of Applied Linguistics* (1992, p. 94): An educational programme which states:

a. the educational purposes of the programme (the ends)
b. the content, teaching procedures and learning experiences which will be necessary to achieve this purpose (the means)
c. some means for assessing whether or not the educational ends have been achieved

These definitions also imply the *who*, the participants within the curriculum design process: the planners, the administrators, the teachers and the learners.

Although there has been a long history of research and development of curriculum theory and practice within the field of education in general, the field of Teaching English as a Second or Foreign Language (ESL or EFL) has largely ignored or been isolated from mainstream developments, informed rather by research in linguistics and applied linguistics. In recent years, there has been an increasing awareness by ESL/EFL practitioners and theorists that indeed there are parallels (Stern, 1983; Richards, 1984; Nunan, 1988; Johnson, 1989), and that curriculum theory has much to offer.

> Changes in thought on language and language learning and changes in educational policy constantly impinge on language pedagogy, and curriculum change frequently occurs. Unfortunately, language pedagogy has not yet much use of the available collective wisdom in curriculum theory to cope with curriculum decisions in an economical and effective way.
>
> Educational theory provides a broad framework and essential concepts for language pedagogy (Stern, 1983, pp. 442, 446).

Models of Curriculum Planning

Both Clark (1987) and White (1988) refer to the framework developed by Skilbeck (1982) to explore the 'value systems' underlying educational traditions, and relate it to language teaching. The three traditions are identified as Classical Humanism, Reconstructionism and Progressivism, which they relate to the structural grammar/systems approach, the notional-functional syllabus, and the process-procedural approach, respectively.

THE CONTENT MODEL: CLASSICAL HUMANISM

The central focus of the curriculum in this model is the content of what is to be learned by, or transmitted to, the learner. In the Classical Humanist tradition, the content is a valued cultural heritage, the understanding of which contributes to the overall intellectual development of the learner; and, from the point of view of epistemological objectivism, the content is knowledge which has been identified and agreed to be universal, unchanging and absolute. This model has been the dominant philosophy underlying the history of the Western educational system for centuries, derived from theories of knowledge going back to Aristotle and Plato. Its attraction lies in the fact that most people, when challenged, would have fairly definite ideas of what they consider as essential to a 'good' education, for example, literature, ethics/religion, the physical sciences, the biological sciences, history, a second language, with a resultant ability in the learner "to think effectively, to communicate thought, to make relevant judgements, to discriminate among values" (Hirst, 1965, p. 2). Undoubtedly, this owes much to the power this model holds over us as products of a largely content-based curriculum.

However, as Kelly (1989, pp. 45–46) points out, the model is inadequate as the basis for curriculum design because it is unable to cope with a discussion of the wider purposes of education, and does not take into account the abilities or problems of the individual learner or the complexities of the learning proces itself. In the era of globalisation and the growth of multicultural societies, it cannot justify the transmission of one particular culture; within the ethos of 'education for all' it is unable to take account of the widely differing needs of a massive student population, where the 'educated' are no longer an elite trained to rule the next generation of workers; as the basic premises of science no longer rest on objective, logical, value-free theories but are shaken by the discoveries and uncertainties of quantum physics, the foundations of universal knowledge are no longer secure and an educational philosophy based on these foundations is no longer acceptable.

That is not to say that 'content' has no role whatsoever in curriculum design, only that as a model it is too simplistic, and too much a product of an earlier, very different society, to be the central planning factor for curricula today.

In the field of English language teaching, this model underpins the grammar-based curriculum, where the syllabus is concerned with the grammar and vocabulary of the language. If we return to Richards's definition of curriculum, then the *purposes* of the programme are to transmit knowledge of the language system to the learners and to ensure that they master the grammar rules and vocabulary of the language; the *content*, or the syllabus, is a selection and sequencing of individual grammar points and lexis; the *teaching procedures* and *learning experiences* will include drilling of grammatically correct sentences, explanations of theory and memorization of lists of vocabulary; and *assessment* is based on the learner's ability to produce grammatically accurate language. The starting point for the grammar-based curriculum, then, is the target language as a relatively fixed concept and it largely ignores factors such as context, appropriacy of use, modes of discourse or individual learner needs; as such, it reflects an essentialist (or objectivist) approach to meaning.

With the advent of the communicative approach to language learning in the late 1960s and 1970s, this approach to language curriculum design has increasingly fallen out of favour. Although it still has a place in content for syllabus design, as a basis for planning a curriculum, the grammar-based approach is not the primary factor.

THE OBJECTIVES MODEL: RECONSTRUCTIONISM

The starting point for this model of curriculum planning is no longer the content, but the *objectives* of the teaching-learning program; as such, it relates to the second educational tradition identified by Skilbeck (1982), Reconstructionism, where the main purpose of education is to bring about some kind of social change. Its origins lie in the movement for the scientific management of education and the work of behavioural psychologists in the first half of the twentieth century, who defined learning as a process of observable changes in behaviour which could be measured. It was the influential curriculum designer R. W. Tyler who promoted the use of behavioural objectives as the basis for curriculum design in the 1930s, long before the movement really took off in the 1960s, when Mager (1962) published *Preparing Instructional Objectives*, and gave the clearest definition available of behavioural objectives, as having three essential characteristics:

1. They must unambiguously describe the behaviour to be performed.
2. They must describe the conditions under which the performance will be expected to occur.
3. They must state a standard of acceptable performance (the criterion).

Today, there is a welter of terms used to describe intended learning outcomes: performance indicators, learning objectives, performance objectives, expected outputs which are particularly relevant to the business ethos and the emphasis on public or client accountability which form some of the constraints within which educational development takes place.

The attraction of the model is that it provides:

1. *Clarity of goals*: The objectives of a learning programme are clear to both the teacher and the learners, which facilitates the selection of learning materials and activities.
2. *Ease of evaluation*: Where there are clearly specified objectives, the success of the learners, and of the programme, can easily and accurately be evaluated to the extent that the objectives have been fulfilled.
3. *Accountability*: In both formal and business sectors, the model provides clear methods for needs identification, establishing learning purpose and providing measurable 'products' of the educational programme.

Some severe criticisms of the approach have been summarised by Kelly (1989), and he points out that the most fundamental criticism is that philosophically it reduces people to the level of automatons who can be trained to behave in particular ways and precludes such concepts as autonomy, self-fulfilment and personal development. As such, it is too unsophisticated, and attempts to impose a linear process on something that is spiralling and cyclical. Kelly does acknowledge, however, that the objectives model can be appropriate in the area of vocational training and in subjects which require the transmission of particular skills.

Reviewing the role of behavioural objectives in foreign language learning, Tumposky (1984, p. 302) claims that "There has been a mixed, but largely negative, reaction to behavioral objectives from teachers of foreign languages, including teachers of ESL/EFL". She explores some of the same contra arguments as Kelly, emphasising the limits such objectives place on creativity and the cognitive and affective aspects of learning, in their reduction of education to an instrument for behavioural change. Her perspective is very much that of the teacher and an interpretation of the objectives model in its narrowest sense. The objectives model, however, was the basis of the Council of Europe Threshold Level project in the 1970s, one of the most important movements in the transition from a grammar-based approach to a communicative approach to language teaching, which resulted in the notional-functional syllabus and an emphasis on needs analysis and the eventual ends of language learning rather than a narrow linguistic focus.

THE PROCESS MODEL: PROGRESSIVISM

Kelly sums up the objections to the contents and objectives models as "the fact that neither offers any real help with that decision which must precede all others, namely the choice of content and/or aims and objectives," and proposes the process model as an approach to curriculum planning which attempts to deal with this "value issue as the prime concern in educational planning" (1989, p. 84). The purpose of education from the point of view of the process model is to enable the individual to progress towards self-fulfilment. It is concerned with the development of understanding, not just the passive reception of 'knowledge' or the acquisition of specific skills. The goals of education are not defined in terms of particular ends or products, but in terms of the processes and procedures by which the individual develops understanding and awareness and creates possibilities for future learning. Content, then, is based on principles derived from research into learning development and the overall purposes of the educational process, which allows the formulation of objectives related to the procedural principles.

The model rests on concepts of learner needs, interests and development processes and is thus open to the criticism of subjectivity in the definition of these concepts, but, as the body of research in the field of developmental psychology expands, there is an increasing acceptance of its underlying philosophy. In practice, however, as a basis for national curriculum development projects, it is less attractive than the objectives model for large-scale curriculum development and planning related to government trends in the West towards vocational training to meet employment needs.

In the language teaching world, there has been a move towards the 'learner-centred curriculum' (Nunan, 1985, 1988; Candlin, 1984), and even towards a definition of a 'learning-centred curriculum' (Dickinson, 1987). Although these ideas inform much of the work done in curriculum research and development, as the central principle for curriculum design they are, as yet, peripheral rather than mainstream.

The analyses by Clark and White show that language teaching has not been entirely isolated from the educational mainstream, but has been influenced by philosophical trends and *broad* educational developments. Their view is echoed by Johnson in his introduction to *The Second Language Curriculum* (1989, p. xi), where he suggests that language teaching, after the "communicative revolution" and a period of "piecemeal reconstruction", is now characterised by "a growing interest in the curriculum process as a whole, attempts to put language teaching back in touch with educational theory in general and curriculum studies in particular".

Although Skilbeck's scheme neatly summarises the ideologies underlying curriculum models, the actuality of developments in ELT over the last three decades has not been so neat or coherent. Johnson refers to the communicative 'revolution', and a revolution cannot be achieved without a certain degree of chaos before reconstruction (Johnson refers to this period as "epitomised by the flowering of a thousand methods" (1989, p. ix) – and then consolidation. The move away from the structural grammar-systems approach began in the late 1960s, and the 1970s saw the proliferation of many different approaches under the umbrella of the communicative syllabus and a growing interest in curriculum design rather than teaching methodology. The concept of 'communicative competence' was much debated and analysed, and finer distinctions were created. For a time, a communicative approach was equated with the notional-functional syllabus, but as other approaches were developed and presented as equally – or more – communicative, the concept began to be defined more by negation of what was clearly *noncommunicative*, that is, the structural approach. Henry Widdowson, a leading member of what is known as 'the London school' of applied linguists and author of a book titled *Teaching Language as Communication*, even went so far as to state: "there is no such thing as a communicative syllabus: there can only be a methodology that stimulates communicative learning" (Widdowson, 1984, p. 26).

For the ELT curriculum designer in the 1990s, informed by research in first and second language acquisition, theories of discourse and genre analysis, and developments in socio- and psycholinguistics, constrained by funding and public or client accountability, there is a need for a framework of curriculum design which allows flexibility but gives a clear direction in which to move.

The 'New Pragmatism': A Mixed-Focus Curriculum

In practice today, too often the claim to be using a *communicative* syllabus or curriculum approach is heard, without any real agreement of what the term *communicative* means in this context and without clarification of the principles and processes of curriculum design. In the opinion of Dubin and Olshtain (1986, p. 68), three areas are central to the concept of a communicative curriculum: "a view of the nature of language as seen by the field of . . . sociolinguistics; a cognitively based view of language learning; and a humanistic approach in education". Their book on course design is one of several which contribute to the long overdue discussion of curriculum issues in language teaching. Through all the publications (Richards, 1984; Dubin & Olshtain, 1986; Nunan, 1988; Yalden, 1987; Johnson, 1989) runs an awareness of what previous models have contributed to current approaches; concepts which remain central include needs analysis, an emphasis on process as well as product, a focus on the learner and learning, evaluation at every stage, and, most important, the need for interaction between and integration of the different aspects of the design and implementation process.

In this section, I will examine some of the issues raised, and suggest that the framework most applicable to ELT today is an *integrated* approach which is essentially learner-centred and is an attempted "synthesis of the product-oriented ends-means model and the process-oriented approach" (Nunan, 1988, p. 20). This mixed-focus model is not without its difficulties, and a good deal of research will need to take place to establish an adequate theoretical base. It does, however, suggest the direction in which language curriculum development could move in the future. The following subsections broadly follow the framework proposed by Johnson (1989, p. xii):

> The framework I propose has three dimensions: that of policy, the aims of the curriculum, or what it seems desirable to achieve; pragmatics, the constraints on what it is possible to achieve; and finally the participants in the decision-making process, whose task it is to reconcile policy and pragmatics. Four stages of decision-making are identified: curriculum planning, ends/means specification, programme implementation, and implementation in the classroom . . . 'evaluation' is not seen as a stage in itself, but as a necessary and integral part of each and all of the stages already mentioned.

CURRICULUM POLICY

The role of the policy maker who establishes the broad principles and purposes of the curriculum and expresses them in a curriculum design document is that of a juggler, keeping aloft the 'balls' representing the needs of the learners, the needs of the institution or planning committee, the needs, possibly, of society, or at least specific interest groups within society, and also the needs of the teachers and administrators, the implementers of the curriculum. These diverse needs encapsulate both opportunities and constraints which must be analysed and balanced in the expression of the controlling principles and educational goals of the program. In the integrated curriculum, the policy guides all other decisions but is itself open to modification; I return to the concept of curriculum *renewal*, which recognises that most planning does not begin from zero but from an evaluation of what already is in place.

NEEDS ANALYSIS

Needs analysis is now seen as the logical starting point for the development of a language program which is responsive to the learner and learning needs, but there has been some disagreement as to what is entailed. Brindley (1989, p. 64) suggests that two orientations are now generally recognised:

1. a narrow, product-oriented view of needs which focuses on the language necessary for particular future purposes and is carried out by the 'experts'
2. a broad, process-oriented view of needs which takes into account factors such as learner motivation and learning styles as well as learner-defined target language behaviour

He further suggests (p. 64) that both types of need analysis are necessary: 'one aimed at collecting factual information for the purposes of setting broad goals related to language content, the other aimed at gathering information about learners which can be used to guide the learning process once it is underway'.

The results of the needs analysis are applied in the development of programme objectives and in the choice of appropriate teaching methodology. The participants in the needs analysis ideally should include as many of the programme participants as possible, and ideally the learners themselves – where they are involved in the specification of course content, there is a greater likelihood that they will perceive it as relevant to their needs and can take an active role in course evaluation. In the integrated approach, needs analysis takes place not only at the pre-course planning stage, but also during the course, contributing to the development of teacher–learner negotiated learning objectives.

SYLLABUS DESIGN

Course content and procedures will usually be expressed in the form of goals or learning objectives; within language teaching there are a number of different ways of expressing objectives, and indeed considerable debate on the role and nature of objectives. Earlier in the paper, I discussed the drawbacks of *performance objectives*, but many would argue that there is a place for them in a language teaching syllabus, particularly where they are negotiated by the teacher and the learners and provide a means of ongoing feedback and a move towards self-direction and self-evaluation on the part of the learner. An alternative – or addition – to performance objectives is the formulation of *process-related objectives*, for example, from an English for academic purposes (EAP) course: 'the student will be able to select and apply reading strategies appropriate to his or her needs'. Another form is *instructional objectives*, which are more related to methodology (e.g., 'To develop the learner's confidence in speaking'). The debate will – and should – continue: for both the teacher and the learner, objectives provide a guide and framework for what goes on in the classroom.

Course content is usually presented in the form of a syllabus, which I will take to mean 'a public document, a record, a contract, an instrument which represents negotiation among all the parties involved' (Yalden, 1984, p. 13). So far in this paper, several syllabus frameworks have been outlined within the discussion of different models of curriculum planning: the structural syllabus, the notional-functional syllabus, and the process syllabus in particular have been highlighted and have been treated as separate, mutually exclusive entities. However, one of the most widely used syllabus models is one that integrates aspects of all three, a *variable focus* (Allen, 1984) or *proportional* (Yalden, 1987) syllabus. The three principles which can inform language syllabus design, according to Yalden, are (1) a view of how language is *learned*, which would result in a structure-based syllabus; (2) a view of how language is *acquired*, which would result in a process-based syllabus; and (3) a view of how language is *used*, which would result in a function-based syllabus. By integrating all three, Yalden proposes a proportional syllabus, with a semantic-grammatical organisational base, a linguistic component based on language functions and themes based on learners' interests. In the early stages of language learning, one might place more emphasis on structure, before moving on to functions and then using tasks or topics to apply and creatively use the language. Allen's formulation of the variable focus syllabus is similar to this. He defines three components: structural, functional and experiential. The syllabus includes all levels all the time, but the emphasis changes at different stages of learning.

Structure/Function	**Function/Skills**	**Task/Theme**
Greater emphasis on structure and functions	Targeting specific functions	Remedial structural work
Introduction of learning strategies & techniques	Application through task-based and problem-solving activities	Task-based syllabus, focus on learning processes and strategies to encourage creative language use
Elementary levels	Pre-Intermediate levels	Intermediate and above

The advantages of this mixed-focus model are summed up by Yalden (1987, p. 120) when she states that it 'would seem to allow the syllabus designer the most freedom to respond to changing or newly perceived needs in the learners, and at the same time provides a framework for the teacher who may not be able or willing to 'go fully communicative'.' I would add that it provides the experienced teacher with a framework that allows for choice in how to implement the syllabus, and with further development can create space for learner–teacher negotiation in 'real-life' communication in the classroom.

METHODOLOGY

The syllabus provides the framework, but learning ultimately depends on the interaction between the teacher and the learners in the classroom, and on the teaching approaches, activities, materials and procedures employed by the teacher. From the perspective of communicative language teaching, learners' needs and wants inform the teaching–learning process, and the emphasis is on using the language in stimulating communicative activities.

The main point to be made in the context of an integrated approach to curriculum development is that teacher training and development is a necessary and ongoing process, involving the exploration of a range of materials, methods and approaches to learner training and evaluation. Teachers must be reflective, analytic and creative, open to new methods and ideas; the aim of teacher-training courses must be to develop teachers who are researchers, not just technicians and deliverers of the syllabus. In this way, teaching methodology can reflect curriculum goals, and teachers' experiences in turn contribute to the process of curriculum renewal.

EVALUATION

Evaluation must take place at all stages of curriculum planning and implementation, and involve all participants. The primary purpose of evaluation is to determine whether or not the curriculum goals have been met, which, in the case of a language programme, will be based on an assessment of the participants in the programme. Another purpose is to determine the effectiveness of the curriculum and to evaluate the language programme itself, which will focus on the teachers, the methodology, the materials and so on. The information gathered forms the basis of accountability to the client and also the basis for decisions regarding curriculum renewal. Brown (1989, p. 222) identifies it as 'the systematic collection and analysis of all relevant information necessary to promote the improvement of a curriculum, and assess its effectiveness and efficiency, as well as the participants' attitudes within the context of the particular institution involved'.

In the integrated approach, both formative evaluation during the planning and implementation of the curriculum, and summative evaluation at the end of the program, are important and complementary.

CONCLUSION

In drawing parallels between curriculum processes in the educational mainstream and the world of English language teaching, this paper has tended to present 'ideal' versions of the applications of major types of curriculum models: content, objectives and process; the reality is likely to be a blend of all three. I would suggest that this is the most realistic approach, given the constraints operating on any educational enterprise: external expectations and client accountability, teacher preconceptions and experiences, learner preferences, and, not least, financial and administrative constraints. Certainly, it is the mixed-focus *product* and *process* model which best fits my own experience of the curriculum.

What has emerged from this brief survey of curriculum development in ELT is that there is a need for flexibility and openness to change and influences from the broader perspective of general educational theory, and for much more discussion and research before it can be said that there is a coherent model for ELT curriculum planning and development. It is clear, however, that there is growing support for Richards's (1984, p. 25) exhortation:

> The language teaching profession has yet to embrace curriculum development as an overall approach to the planning of teaching and learning. Our profession has evolved a considerable body of educational techniques, but little in the way of an integrated and systematic approach to language curriculum processes. Such an approach may be crucial, however, if we are to develop a more rigorous basis for our educational practices.

There is also a move in ELT toward consolidation and integration, informed by educational theory.

References

Allen, J. P. B. (1984). General-purpose language teaching: A variable focus approach. In C. J. Brumfit (Ed.), *ELT Documents* 118 (pp. 61–74). Oxford: Pergamon Press.

Brindley, G. P. (1989). The role of needs analysis in adult ESL programme design. In R. K. Johnson (Ed.), *The second language curriculum* (pp. 63–78). Cambridge: Cambridge University press.

Brown, J. D. (1989). Language program evaluation: A synthesis of existing possibilities. In R. K. Johnson (Ed.), *The second language curriculum* (pp. 222–241). Cambridge: Cambridge University Press.

Brumfit, C. J. (1984). General English syllabus design: Curriculum and syllabus design for the general English classroom. *ELT Documents* 118. Oxford: Pergamon Press.

Brumfit, C. J., & Johnson, K. (Eds.). (1979). *The communicative approach to language teaching*. Oxford: Oxford University Press.

Candlin, C. N. (1984). Syllabus design as a critical process. In C. J. Brumfit (Ed.), *ELT Documents* 118 (pp. 29–46). Oxford: Pergamon Press.

Clark, J. L. (1987). *Curriculum renewal in foreign language learning*. Oxford: Oxford University Press.

Dickinson, L. (1987). *Self-instruction in language learning*. Cambridge: Cambridge University Press.

Dubin, F., & Olshtain, E. (1986). *Course design: Developing programs and materials for language learning*. Cambridge: Cambridge University Press.

Hirst, P. H. (1965). Liberal education and the nature of knowledge. In R. D. Archambault (Ed.), *Philosophical analysis and education* (pp. 113–138). London: Routledge & Kegan.

Johnson, R. K. (Ed.). (1989). *The second language curriculum*. Cambridge: Cambridge University Press.

Kelly, A. V. (1989). *The curriculum: Theory and practice*. London: Paul Chapman Publishing.

Mager, R. F. (1962). *Preparing instructional objectives*. California: Fearon Press.

Nunan, D. (1985). *Language teaching course design: Trends and issues*. Adelaide: National Curriculum Recource Centre.

Nunan, D. (1988). *The learner-centred curriculum*. New York: Cambridge University Press.

Prabhu, N. S. (1987). Language education: Equipping or enabling? In B. K. Das (Ed.), *Language education in human resource development* (pp. 190–201). Singapore: SEAMEO RELC.

Richards, J. C. (1984). Language curriculum development. *RELC Journal, 15*(1), 1–29.

Richards, J. C., Platt, J., & Platt, H. (1992). *Dictionary of applied linguistics*. 2nd ed. Harlow, UK: Longman.

Rogers, C. (1983). *Freedom to learn*. New York: Macmillan.

Skilbeck, M. (1982). Three educational ideologies. In T. Horton & P. Raggatt (Eds.), *Challenge and change in the curriculum.* London: Hodder & Stoughton.

Stern, H. H. (1983). *Fundamental concepts of language teaching*. Oxford: Oxford University Press.

Tumposky, N. (1984). Behavioral objectives, the cult of efficiency, and foreign language learning: Are they compatible? *TESOL Quarterly, 18*(2), 295–310.

Tyler, R. W. (1949). *Basic principles of curriculum and instruction*. Chicago: University of Chicago Press.

White, R. (1988). *The ELT curriculum: Design, innovation and management*. Oxford: Blackwell.

Widdowson, H. G. (1984). Educational and pedagogic factors in syllabus design. In C. J. Brumfit (Ed.), *ELT Documents* 118 (pp. 23–27). Oxford: Pergamon Press.

Yalden, J. (1984). Syllabus design in general education: Options for ELT. In C. J. Brumfit (Ed.), *ELT Documents* 118 (pp. 11–21). Oxford: Pergamon Press.

Yalden, J. (1987). *Principles of course design for language teaching*. Cambridge: Cambridge University Press.

CHAPTER 8

The Role of Materials in the Language Classroom: Finding the Balance

Jane Crawford

INTRODUCTION

What about meeting learner needs? How can a course book meet the needs of a specific group of students?

These questions, posed by a teacher looking for the first time at *Words Will Travel* (Clemens & Crawford, 1994), a set of integrated resources colleagues and I had just spent 3 years developing, set me thinking about the role of preplanned materials and why I have always been interested in resource production. It also recalled my concern, both as a teacher and as a teacher educator, about the incoherence of many language programs when teachers create their own materials or, as seems more frequently the case, pick and choose from a range of authentic and published materials and worksheets, often originally prepared for other classes.

This discussion is divided into two sections. The first looks at attitudes to teaching materials, including textbooks, and explores two opposing points of view. For some, commercial materials deskill teachers and rob them of their capacity to think professionally and respond to their students. They are also misleading in that the contrived language they contain has little to do with reality. For others, the role of teaching materials is potentially more positive. They can, for example, be a useful form of professional development for teachers, and foster autonomous learning strategies in students. Such arguments and the proliferation of teaching materials suggest that the issue is not so much whether teachers should use commercially prepared materials, but rather what form these should take so that the outcomes are positive for teachers and learners rather than restrictive. The second part of the discussion explores eight key assumptions which the author believes should underpin materials if they are to enhance the learning environment of the classroom.

Preplanned Teaching Materials – Helpful Scaffold or Debilitating Crutch?

Concern whether pre-prepared materials can meet individual learner needs is part of the dilemma teachers face in trying to implement learner-centred language programs in a group setting. This is not a new issue. Two decades ago, O'Neill (1982) queried the assumption that each group is so unique that its needs cannot be met by materials designed for another group. Such a view not only presupposes that it is possible to predict the language needs of students beyond the classroom, but also ignores the common linguistic and learning needs of many learners.

Textbooks nevertheless remain a contentious issue for many teachers and researchers. Littlejohn (in Hutchinson & Torres, 1994, p. 316), for example, claims that textbooks 'reduce the teacher's role to one of managing or overseeing preplanned events'. A similar negative view emerged during a recent discussion of the role of textbooks on the Internet (TESL-L [Teachers of English as a Second Language List], City University of New York). One participant, for example, claimed that textbooks are for poor teachers, those without imagination. In the same discussion, a Canadian colleague suggested that there are cultural differences in attitudes to textbooks and referred specifically to 'the Australian prejudice' against them. One reason for this prejudice may well be that so many of the ESL books available are British or American and so culturally removed from learners in Australia. Certainly when asked what they saw as the major strengths of a recent set of materials (Clemens & Crawford, 1994), more than one in three of the participants at introductory workshops explicitly mentioned the Australian characters, content and contexts (see Table 1 in the Appendix). The discussion on TESL-L, however, confirmed that attitudes to textbooks are complex (see Table 2 in the Appendix) and represent a mix of pedagogical and pragmatic factors and the different weightings given to these in different contexts.

It is, of course, relatively easy to criticise published materials. Their very visibility makes them more publicly accountable than those produced by teachers. The grounds for criticism are wide-ranging. Not only do published materials make decisions which could be made by the teacher and/or students (Allwright, 1981), but they often exhibit other shortcomings. Some materials, for example, fail to present appropriate and realistic language models (Porter & Roberts, 1981; Nunan, 1989). Others propose subordinate learner roles (Auerbach & Burgess, 1985) and fail to contextualise language activities (Walz, 1989). They may also foster inadequate cultural understanding (Kramsch, 1987). Further weaknesses include failure to address discourse competence (Kaplan & Knutson, 1993) or teach idioms (Mola, 1993), and lack of equity in gender representation (Graci, 1989). The fact that the textbook market flourishes despite such criticisms – Sheldon (1988), for example, reports that, in the United States alone, twenty-eight publishers offer more than 1,600 ESL textbooks – reflects perhaps teachers' understanding that these same shortcomings also occur in teacher-produced materials; indeed, they may do so more frequently because of the time constraints under which these materials are prepared.

There appears to be very little research, however, on the exact role of textbooks in the language classroom. Allwright (1981) suggests that there are two key positions. The first – the *deficiency view* – sees the role of textbooks or published materials as being to compensate for teachers' deficiencies and ensure that the syllabus is covered using well thought out exercises. Underlying this view is the assumption that 'good' teachers always know what materials to use with a given class and have access to, or can create, them. They thus neither want, nor need, published materials. The *difference view*, on the other hand, sees materials as carriers of decisions best made by someone other than the teacher because of differences in expertise. This view was mentioned by several of the teachers participating in the TESL-L debate (see Table 2 in the Appendix), who argued for the use of published materials on the grounds that these are better – and cheaper in terms of cost and effort (McDonough & Shaw, 1993) – than what teachers can produce consistently in the time available to them.

For many, however, both the deficiency and difference views challenge teachers' professionalism and reduce them to classroom managers, technicians or implementers of others' ideas. This attitude is not limited to language teachers. Loewenberg-Ball and Feiman-Nemser (1988), for example, found that preservice primary school teachers in two American universities were taught explicitly that textbooks should be used only as a resource, and that following a textbook is an undesirable way to teach.

Such views seem problematic. Obviously, teaching materials are not neutral and so will have a role to play in deciding what is learnt (Apple, 1992). For this reason, it is essential that materials writers be familiar with the learning and teaching styles and contexts of those likely to use their materials, and be able to exemplify a variety of good practice. In other words, teachers and their experience have a crucial role to play in materials production as well as in their critical classroom use, and the best writers are probably practising teachers. The difference (or is it a deficiency?) is thus not in terms of expertise, but in access to time and technology. We live in a multimedia age, and educational materials need to be of an adequate level of sophistication if the language class and learner are not to be devalued. Desktop publishing facilitates the production of convincing print materials, but many teachers still have neither the time nor access to adequate technology to create 'authentic' audiovisual materials (i.e., videos, cassettes and computer programs which reflect the real-world products the learners encounter outside the classroom). Without such authenticity, however, it is difficult to provide culturally rich input, or to develop coping strategies that will enable students to take advantage of the extracurricular input to which they have access.

The assumption seems to be that teachers will slavishly follow the textbook, let it control the classroom and what occurs therein, and fail to respond to learner feedback or to challenge received ideas contained in the materials. Is such a view justified, and, if teachers do behave in this way, is it realistic to expect them to prepare their own materials? In any case, as Allwright (1981) points out, materials may contribute to both goals and content but they cannot determine either. What is learnt, and indeed, learnable, is a product of the interaction between learners, teachers and the materials at their disposal. Furthermore, teachers do not necessarily teach what materials writers write just as learners do not necessarily learn what teachers teach (Luxon, 1994), perhaps because of differences in perceptions of proposed tasks (Block, 1994). In one of the few studies which has actually looked at teacher use of textbooks, Stodolsky (1989) found considerable variation which suggests that mistrust of textbooks may be misplaced. She concluded: 'teachers are very autonomous in their textbook use and . . . it is likely that only a minority of teachers really follow the text in the page-by-page manner suggested in the literature' (p. 176).

There is a need for more research into the dynamics of textbook use. Appropriate textbooks, for example, may actually assist inexperienced teachers to come to terms with content and ways of tackling this with different learners:

> Teachers' guides may provide a helpful scaffold for learning to think pedagogically about particular content, considering the relationship between what the teachers and students are doing and what students are supposed to be learning. *This kind of thinking about ends and means is not the same as following the teacher's guide like a script.* (Loewenberg-Ball & Feiman-Nemser, 1988, p. 421; emphasis added)

Donoghue (1992, p. 35) extends this pedagogical role for textbooks from inexperienced to experienced teachers. His survey of seventy-six teachers showed that the majority reported using teachers' guides at least once or twice a week, suggesting their potential as '*an essential source of information and support*' and a medium of ongoing professional development. This, of course, will only occur if teachers' guides include adequate information about the materials provided, and clear and theoretically explicit rationales for the activities proposed.

Hutchinson and Torres (1994) also see the textbook as a possible *agent for change.* This can be achieved if a number of conditions are met. First, the textbook needs to become a vehicle for teacher and learner training. In other words, as well as an explicit and detailed teacher's guide, the student book should also include appropriate learning-how-to-learn suggestions. Second, the textbook must provide support and help with classroom management, thus freeing the teacher to cope with new content and procedures. Third, the textbook will become an agent for change if it provides the teacher with a clear picture of what the change will look like, and clear practical guidance on how to implement it in the classroom. Finally, if adopted by a school, a textbook can result in collegial support and shared responsibility for, and commitment to, the change. Again, more research is needed to see whether preplanned materials actually do change practice or are simply adapted to maintain the status quo. Stodolsky's study of the use of textbooks by social-studies teachers (1989) suggests that innovative curriculum packages may produce stricter adherence to content and procedures than standard textbooks, but that teachers frequently make instruction more teacher-centred by eliminating group projects and the use of exploratory, hands-on activities, or those focused on higher-order mental processes. In other words, the textbook writer's aims may be overridden or vitiated by the teacher's implementation skills (Jarvis, 1987) or reading of the text (Apple, 1992).

Another function for textbooks that is often overlooked is their role as *a structuring tool.* Communicative language classes are social events, and so, inherently unpredictable and potentially threatening to all participants (e.g., Reid, 1994). This is particularly so in periods of change (Luxon, 1994) such as those experienced by teachers implementing new programs or working with unfamiliar learner types. Learners are, of course, by definition, always facing enormous and possibly threatening change as their language skills develop. One strategy both teachers and students use in dealing with this uncertainty is 'social routinisation', the process by which classroom interaction becomes increasingly stereotyped to reduce the unpredictability and, thereby, the stress. Materials can play a key role in this process: 'Textbooks survive . . . and prosper primarily because they are the most convenient means of providing the structure that the teaching-learning system – particularly the system in change – requires' (Hutchinson & Torres, 1994, p. 317). A textbook, from this perspective, does not necessarily drive the teaching process, but it does provide the structure and predictability that are necessary to make the event socially tolerable to the participants. It also serves as a useful map or plan of what is intended and expected, thus allowing participants to see where a lesson fits into the wider context of the language program. Hutchinson and Torres (1994) suggest that this is important because it allows for:

1. *Negotiation*: The textbook can actually contribute by providing something to negotiate about. This can include teacher and learner roles as well as content and learning strategies.
2. *Accountability*: The textbook shows all stakeholders 'what is being done . . . in the closed and ephemeral world of the classroom' (Hutchinson and Torres, 1994).
3. *Orientation*: Teachers and learners need to know what is happening elsewhere, what standards are expected, how much work should be covered, and so on.

Again, it is a question of balance. Using a textbook does reduce some options for learners, but it can also allow for greater autonomy. They can, for example, know what to expect and better take charge of their own learning. It may well be this sense of control which explains the popularity of textbooks with many students. Consequently, a teacher's decision *not* to use a textbook may actually be a 'touch of imperialism' – in the words of a TESL-L colleague – because it retains control in the hands of the teacher rather than in the learners'.

Therefore, despite the frequently expressed reservations about published materials, these do not need to be a debilitating crutch used only by those unable to do without. Indeed, the preceding discussion suggests that use of appropriate teaching materials can advantage both teachers and learners. The issue, then, is not whether teachers should or should not use such materials – most do so at some point in their career (Cunningsworth, 1984) – but what form these materials should take if they are to contribute positively to teaching and learning.

Effective Teaching Materials

Materials obviously reflect the writers' views of language and learning, and teachers (and students) will respond according to how well these match their own beliefs and expectations. If materials are to be a helpful scaffold, these underlying principles need to be made explicit and an object of discussion for both students and teachers. The remainder of this paper looks at the assumptions about language and learning which the author believes should underpin materials used in language classrooms. Individual end-users will, of course, weigh these factors differently, and so need to adapt the materials to their own context and learners. In terms of our present understanding of second language learning, however, effective materials are likely to reflect the following statements:

LANGUAGE IS FUNCTIONAL AND MUST BE CONTEXTUALISED

Language is as it is because of the purposes we put it to. For this reason, materials must contextualise the language they present. Without a knowledge of what is going on, who the participants are and their social and psychological distance in time and space from the events referred to, it is impossible to understand the real meaning of an interaction. In other words, language, whether it is input or learner output, should emerge from the context in which it occurs. One possible way to build a shared context for learners and their teachers is to use video drama. Familiarity with the context helps make the language encountered meaningful, and also extends the content of the course beyond that other rich source of contextualised language use, the classroom itself. That is to say, the fictitious world of a video drama can provide a joint focus which is culturally broader than the classroom, and which serves as a springboard into other real-world contexts. These will need to be negotiated carefully, however, because they are not shared by all members of the group. Again, it is the teacher who must ensure that a balance is achieved between input and the reapplication of this to the unique context of a given class.

LANGUAGE DEVELOPMENT REQUIRES LEARNER ENGAGEMENT IN PURPOSEFUL USE OF LANGUAGE

The focus of input and output materials should thus be on whole texts, language in use, rather than on so-called building blocks to be used at some later date. This does not mean that there should be no focus on form, but rather that form normally comes out of whole texts which have already been processed for meaning. Study of grammar looks at how such texts use the system to express meaning and achieve certain purposes. Depending on the background and goals of their learners, teachers can decide whether to enhance or reduce this focus on form and the language used to do this. For the majority of learners, however, some explicit discussion of language at the whole-text level is presumably useful and will contribute positively to the language learning process and learner autonomy (Borg, 1994). Materials need to include such information for students so that they can be used as references beyond the classroom and independently of the teacher.

THE LANGUAGE USED SHOULD BE REALISTIC AND AUTHENTIC

An outcome of our understanding that language is a social practice has been an increased call for the use of 'authentic' materials, rather than the more contrived and artificial language often found in traditional textbooks (Grant, 1987). The problem with using authentic materials (in Nunan's sense of 'any material which has not been specifically produced for the purpose of language teaching' [1989, p. 54]) is that it is very difficult to find such materials which scaffold the learning process by remaining within manageable fields. It is also difficult for teachers legally to obtain a sufficient range of audiovisual materials of an appropriate quality and length. The quality of the materials is, nevertheless, important because of its impact on learners and their motivation:

> Hi-tech visual images are a pervasive feature of young people's lives. Textbooks, worksheets and overheads are a poor match for these other, more complex, instantaneous and sometimes spectacular forms of experience and learning. In this context, the disengagement of many students from their curriculum and their teaching is not hard to understand. Teachers are having to compete more and more with this world and its surrounding culture of the image. (Hargreaves; 1994, p. 75)

Materials, therefore, need to be authentic-like, that is, 'authentic, in the sense that the language is not artificially constrained, and is, at the same time, amenable to exploitation for language teaching purposes' (MacWilliam, 1990, p. 160). Another related aspect of authenticity concerns the classroom interaction to which the materials give rise (Crawford, 1990; Taylor, 1994). The more realistic the language, the more easily it can cater to the range of proficiency levels found in many classes. At the same time, the proposed activities must be varied and adaptable to classroom constraints of time and concentration span. Vernon (1953), for example, found that there was a steep decline in the amount of aural information retained during the course of a half-hour transmission, and that 6 to 7 minutes is probably the optimal maximum even for native-speaking viewers. A video drama which contained 5-minute episodes would not, therefore, be authentic in terms of typical TV programs, but it would be pedagogically practical and efficient in terms of language comprehension.

CLASSROOM MATERIALS WILL USUALLY SEEK TO INCLUDE AN AUDIO VISUAL COMPONENT

This statement is true not only because we live in an increasingly multimedia world in which advances in technology allow for expanding flexibility in delivery, but also because such materials can create a learning environment that is rich in linguistic and cultural information about the target language. Materials such as video and multimedia allow teachers and learners to explore the nonverbal and cultural aspects of language as well as the verbal. Intonation, gesture, mime, facial expression, body posture and so on, are all essential channels of communication which not only help learners understand the verbal language to which they are exposed, but also are an integral part of the system of meaning which they are seeking to learn. The distance created by the video and the replay/pause options allows for analysis and cross-cultural comparisons which can then be extended to members of the class and local community. Visuals also provide information about the physical context of the interaction. This crucial comprehension support occurs particularly with formats such as soap opera, where there is greater convergence between the audio and visual strands than in other video materials, such as documentaries with voice-overs (MacWilliam, 1986).

IN OUR MODERN, TECHNOLOGICALLY COMPLEX WORLD, SECOND LANGUAGE LEARNERS NEED TO DEVELOP THE ABILITY TO DEAL WITH WRITTEN AS WELL AS SPOKEN GENRES

Reading materials will normally need to cover a range of genres, possibly including computer literacy. These will emerge from the context and be accompanied by activities and exercises which explore both their meaning in that context and, if appropriate, their schematic structure and language features. The extent to which teachers focus explicitly on the latter will depend on the needs and goals of their learners, and whether this kind of analysis fits with learning preferences. For many learners, however, these reading materials will provide models which can be used to develop familiarity with the structure of such texts, and provide a scaffold to assist with the learners' subsequent attempts to write similar texts. Materials should be integrated and not require students to write genres which have not already been encountered. This means that when learners do begin their analysis, they have already had an opportunity to acquire a certain familiarity with the genre. These previous examples can then be used for additional practice in identifying the schematic structure and language features, thus providing learners with an opportunity to elaborate and revise their interlanguage (Ellis, 1989).

Writing in a second language is sometimes daunting for L2 learners, especially because, as native speakers know, we tend to be less forgiving of grammatical and other inaccuracies. Learners need to come to terms with this aspect of written language, and develop appropriate strategies for tackling written tasks. Except for informal notes, most writing involves more than one draft. Materials can incorporate learning cycles which allow learners to explore choices and options and choose the most appropriate to their purpose before they begin working on their own. Individual writing will usually occur at the end of a number of activities in which learners have (*a*) worked with examples of the genre but with the focus on meaning, not form; (*b*) analysed examples of the genre to determine its social purpose and generic structure; (*c*) built up their knowledge of the topic through discussion, reading and so on, so that they have something to write about and have covered the necessary vocabulary; and (*d*) engaged in a joint construction, either as a whole group or in smaller groups. The discussion such collaborative work provokes engages learners in purposeful interaction and gives them an opportunity to check their understanding of the requirements of the task.

EFFECTIVE TEACHING MATERIALS FOSTER LEARNER AUTONOMY

Given the context-dependent nature of language, no language course can predict all the language needs of learners and must seek, therefore, to prepare them to deal independently with the language they encounter as they move into new situations. The activities and materials proposed must be flexible, designed to develop skills and strategies which can be transferred to other texts in other contexts. The materials writer can also suggest follow-up activities to encourage this process and to provide additional practice for those who need it. This not only assists teachers in catering to a range of learning styles and levels, but also contributes to developing their teaching repertoire. Learners can likewise be asked to explore the strategies they and their fellow students use and, where appropriate, try new ones.

One of the advantages of talking about language as proposed here is that such discussion contributes to the development of skills for continued autonomous learning (Borg, 1994), and students gain confidence in their ability to analyse the data available in the language to which they have access. Making generic and cultural aspects of the language explicit and available to learners in their textbook gives them more control over their learning environment. Another important aspect of the move to greater self-direction is the ability to evaluate the performance of oneself and others. Materials, therefore, need to build in self-assessment tasks which require learners to reflect on their progress.

MATERIALS NEED TO BE FLEXIBLE ENOUGH TO CATER TO INDIVIDUAL AND CONTEXTUAL DIFFERENCES

Although language is a social practice, learning a language is largely an individual process as learners seek to integrate newly perceived information into their existing language system. It is essential for teachers to recognise the different backgrounds, experiences and learning styles that students bring to the language classroom, and the impact these experiences have on what aspects of the input are likely to become intake. In other words, it is to a large extent the learners, not the teachers, who control what is learnt since it is they who selectively organise the sensory input into meaningful wholes.

This diversity of response provides classroom teachers with a rich source of potential communication as learners and teachers share their reactions to the materials and compare cultural differences. This presupposes that the teacher is prepared to adopt an interpretive rather than a transmissive methodology (Wright, 1987) and to adapt the materials to the context in which learning is taking place. Without opportunities to interact with one another, the teacher and the language, students will not be able to confront their hypotheses about how the language system is used to convey meaning, and then check these intuitions against the understanding of their fellow students and the teacher. It is this kind of open interaction which helps make explicit the underlying cultural and linguistic assumptions and values of both teachers and learners. Such assumptions and values become negotiable when they are made overt.

LEARNING NEEDS TO ENGAGE LEARNERS BOTH AFFECTIVELY AND COGNITIVELY

The language classroom involves an encounter of identities and cultures, and it needs to be recognised that language learning (particularly in a second language context but increasingly in foreign language contexts as the world shrinks) requires the active participation of the whole learner. The integration of new knowledge into the learner's existing language system occurs with certainty only when the language is used spontaneously in a communicative (purposeful) situation to express the learner's own meaning. Such real communication, however, implies the engagement of genuine interest and will depend, in part at least, on the presence of a positive group dynamic in the classroom. The input from the materials provides linguistic and cultural preparation before, or in parallel with, the learner-generated language which is the ultimate goal of the learning process. As O'Neill (in Rossner & Bolitho, 1990, pp. 155–156) suggests:

> Textbooks can at best provide only a base or a core of materials. They are a jumping-off point for teacher and class. *They should not aim to be more than that*. A great deal of the most important work in a class may start with the textbook but end outside it, an improvisation and adaptation, in spontaneous interaction in the class, and the development of that interaction. (Emphasis added)

Conclusion

In this article, I have looked at the roles preplanned teaching materials can play, and argued that their contribution need not be debilitating to teachers and learners; they can scaffold the work of both teachers and learners and even serve as agents of change, provided they act as guides and negotiating points, rather than straitjackets. In selecting materials, of course, practitioners need to look carefully at the principles underpinning such materials to ensure that they contribute positively to the learning environment. This article outlined eight assumptions about language and learning which seem appropriate in the light of our current understanding of the learning process, and which suggest that we take advantage, not just of print, but also of different audiovisual media, to enrich the classroom learning context.

We obviously need much more information about how we and our students use such materials to facilitate learning. Wright (1987) suggests that we teach with, rather than through, materials, thus being free to improvise and adapt in response to learner feedback. Effective teaching materials, by providing cultural and linguistic input and a rich selection of integrated activities, are thus a professional tool which can actually assist teachers to be more responsive, both by leaving them time to cater to individual needs and by expanding their teaching repertoire. Learners, too, can benefit from access to the materials used in class, and the control and structure this allows them to put on their learning. Both teachers and materials writers, of course, walk a tightrope. The teachers' challenge is to maintain the balance between providing a coherent learning experience which scaffolds learner comprehension and production, and modelling effective strategies without losing responsiveness to the unique situation and needs of each learner. The textbook writer's challenge is to provide materials which support, even challenge, teachers and learners, and present ideas for tasks and the presentation of language input without becoming prescriptive and undermining the teacher's and the learner's autonomy. It is a fine balancing act.

References

Allwright, R. L. (1981). What do we want teaching materials for? *ELT Journal, 36*(1).

Apple, M. W. (1992). The text and cultural politics. *Educational Researcher, 21*(7), 4–11.

Auerbach, E. R., & Burgess, D. (1985). The hidden curriculum of survival ESL. *TESOL Quarterly, 19*, 475–496.

Block, D. (1994). A day in the life of a class: Teacher-learner perceptions of task purpose in conflict. *System, 22*(4), 473–486.

Borg, S. (1994). Language awareness as methodology: Implications for teachers and teacher training. *Language Awareness, 3*(2), 61–71.

Clemens, J., & Crawford, J. (eds). (1994). *Words will travel.* Sydney: ELS Pty.

Crawford, J. (1990). How authentic is the language in our classrooms? *Prospect, 6*(1), 47–54.

Cunningsworth, A. (1984). *Evaluating and selecting EFL teaching materials.* London: Heineman Educational Books.

Donoghue, F. (1992). Teachers' guides: A review of their function. *CLCS Occasional Papers (30).*

Ellis, R. (1989). Sources of intra-learner variability in language use and their relationship to second language acquisition. In S. Gass, C. Madden, D. Preston, & L. Selinker (Eds.),*Variation in second language acquisition: Psycholinguistic issues* (Vol. 2, pp. 22–45). Clevedon, Avon: Multilingual Matters.

Graci, J. P. (1989). Are foreign language textbooks sexist? An exploration of modes of evaluation. *Foreign Language Annals, 22*(5), 77–86.

Grant, N. (1987). *Making the most of your textbook*. London: Longman.

Hargreaves, A. (1994). *Changing teachers, changing times*. London: Cassell.

Hutchinson, T., & Torres, E. (1994). The textbook as agent of change. *ELT Journal, 48*(4), 315–328.

Jarvis, J. (1987). Integrating methods and materials: Developing trainees' reading skills. *ELT Journal, 41*(3), 179–184.

Kaplan, M. A., & Knutson, E. (1993). Where is the text? Discourse competence and foreign language textbook. *Mid-Atlantic Journal of Foreign Language Pedagogy, 1*, 167–176. ED 335802.

Kramsch, C. J. (1987). Foreign language textbooks' construction of foreign reality. *Canadian Modern Languages Review, 44*(1), 95–119.

Loewenberg-Ball, D., & Feimen-Nemser, S. (1988). Using textbooks and teachers' guides: A dilemma for beginning teachers and teacher educators. *Curriculum Inquiry, 18*(4), 401–423.

Luxon, T. (1994). The psychological risks for teachers in a time of methodological change. *Teacher Trainer, 8*(1), 6–9.

MacWilliam, I. (1986). Video and language comprehension. *ELT Journal, 40*(2). Reprinted in R. Rossner & R. Bolitho (Eds). *Currents of change in English language teaching.* (pp. 157–161). Oxford: Oxford University Press, 1990.

McDonough, J., &. Shaw, C. (1993). *Materials and Methods in ELT*. Oxford: Basil Blackwell.

Mola, A. J. (1993). *Teaching idioms in the second language classroom: A case study of college-level German*. ED 355826.

Nunan, D. (1989). *Designing tasks for the communicative classroom.* Cambridge: Cambridge University Press.

O'Neill, R. (1982). Why use textbooks? *ELT Journal,* 36(2). Reprinted in R. Rossner & R. Bolitho (Eds.), *Currents of change in English language teaching* (pp. 148–156). Oxford: Oxford University Press, 1990.

Porter, D., & Roberts, J. (1981). Authentic listening activities. *ELT Journal, 36*(1).

Reid, J. (1994). Change in the language classroom: Process and intervention. *English Teaching Forum, 32*(1).

Sheldon, L. E. (1988). Evaluating ELT textbooks and materials. *ELT Journal, 42*(4), 237–246.

Stodolsky, S. (1989). Is teaching really by the book? In P. W. Jackson & S. Haroutunian-Gordon (Eds.), *From Socrates to software: The teacher as text and the text as teacher*. Chicago: National Society for the Study of Education.

Taylor, D. S. (1994). Inauthentic authenticity or authentic inauthenticity. *TESL-EJ, 1*(2), 1–12.

Vernon, M. D. (1953). Perception and understanding of instructional television. *British Journal of Psychology, 44*, 116–126.

Walz, J. (1989). Context and contextualised language practice in foreign language teaching. *Modern Language Journal, 73*(2), 160–168.

Wright, A. (1987). *Roles of teachers and learners*. Oxford: Oxford University Press.

Appendix A

Table 1

What do you see as the major strengths of the materials you have seen today?	
Australian characters, content, context	90
Video material	75
Wide variety of activities	44
Integrated materials	43
Authentic/realistic/real life	38
Recycling of language	33
Entertaining/interesting	27
Sound methodology/communicative approach	22
Good focus on and balance on all skills	21
Good audio material	21
Relevant to students' lives/needs	13
Well structured	12
Multicultural presentation of language	11
Genres presented/well covered	11
Professional production/high-quality materials	9
Addresses competencies	8
Photocopy pages	6
Flexibility	6
Useful/suitable/appropriate pronunciation	5
Presents Australian idioms	5
Assessment tasks	5
	TOTAL: 474

N = 251

What do you see as the major weaknesses of the materials you have seen today?	
Too long/too much material	21
Hard to use just bits and pieces/continuous program	19
Level too high for stage 2	8
Not suitable for ELICOS/short courses	8
Cost	5
Difficult to use with continuous enrolments	3
Insufficient video-based activities	3
Insufficient grammar and structure	3
Stereotyped characters	3
Instructions in Student's Book too difficult	3
Poor Student's Book	2
Not very groovy, won't interest young people	2
Faked accents	2
Set in NSW	2
Speech too Australian and too fast	2
Insufficient language focuses	1
Prefer city-based context (more relevant to students)	1
Readings "a bit difficult"	1
Narrative nature makes the material a bit prescriptive	1
Insufficient speaking activities	1
Teacher's Book unnecessary	1
Not sufficiently workplace-oriented	1
Not relevant to all levels of skills in the class	1
Not sufficiently student-centred	1
Audio materials too difficult	1
Not everyone is familiar with genres	1
No functional grammar activities	1
	TOTAL: 98

TABLE 2

TESL-L responses in favour of the use of textbooks (& number of times mentioned) TESL-L responses opposed to the use of textbooks (& number of times mentioned)

(i)	Materials better than teacher can produce consistently in time	5
(ii)	Textbook can/should be supplemented or adapted	4
(iii)	A basis for teacher preparation to meet individual needs	2
(iv)	Why reinvent the wheel?	2
(v)	A source of revision/reference for students	2
(vi)	Students expect a textbook	2
(vii)	NOT using a textbook "a touch of imperialism"	1
(viii)	Textbooks a basis for negotiation	1
(ix)	Integrity and authority of books – Ss respect books more than handouts	1
(x)	Textbook provides secure base for individual development	1
(xi)	Copyright – rights of materials writers	1
(xii)	Cost of copying unjustified	1
(xiii)	Textbooks (with keys) save teachers/learners time	1
(xiv)	Texts should be available to teachers as references only	1

TESL-L responses opposed to the use of textbooks (& number of times mentioned)

(i)	Textbooks boring/difficult to understand	1
(ii)	Textbooks don't do what is wanted	1
(iii)	Cultural difference – 'the Australian prejudice'	1
(iv)	Textbooks are inadequate	1
(v)	Textbooks are inappropriate to learner-centred methodology	1
(vi)	Textbooks appropriate in one context not appropriate in another	1
(vii)	Textbooks are for poor teachers, those without imagination	1
(viii)	Textbooks reinforce teacher-driven syllabus /reduce teacher response to learner feedback	1

N = 21

Countries of origin of posters: Australia, Canada, Holland, Japan, Korea, Malaysia, South America, Switzerland, Thailand, USA

SECTION 5

TASK AND PROJECT WORK

INTRODUCTION

Few would question the need to make language classrooms a place where genuine and meaningful communication takes place and not simply one where students "practice" language for its own sake. This emphasis on making meaning the priority in syllabus design and methodology underlies many aspects of contemporary approaches to language teaching. For example:

- *Communicative Language Teaching*: The need to make communication the primary focus of teaching materials and classroom activities has long been a core assumption of communicative methodology.
- *Task-based language teaching*: The use of tasks that serve to facilitate meaningful communication and interaction lies at the heart of various proposals for "task-based instruction," which is an attempt to apply principles from second language acquisition research to language teaching.
- *Content-based instruction*: A focus on real-world content and the understanding and communication of information through language is the key to second language learning and teaching in this approach.

The articles in this section focus on task work and project work as different ways of creating opportunities for language learning through problem solving, cooperative learning, collaboration, and negotiation of meaning – processes which many believe are central to second language acquisition.

Many traditional approaches to language teaching are based on a focus on grammatical form and a cycle of activities that involves presentation of a new language item, practice of the item under controlled conditions, and a production phase in which the learners try out the form in a more communicative context. This has been referred to as the P-P-P approach and it forms the basis of such traditional methods of teaching as Audiolingualism and the Structural-Situational Approach. This approach was gradually replaced in the 1980s by teaching methods which focus on communication (rather than grammar) as the key dimension of learning and teaching. Early models of Communicative Language Teaching used functional units of organization and practice to replace grammatical ones; more recently, however, the unit of "task" has been proposed as an alternative to other units of presentation or practice.

A task is an activity which learners carry out using their available language resources and leading to a real outcome. Examples of tasks are playing a game, solving a problem, or sharing and comparing experiences. In carrying out tasks, learners are said to take part in such processes as negotiation of meaning, paraphrase, and experimentation, which are thought to lead to successful language development. In the first article in this section, Beglar and Hunt propose how tasks can be used as a basis for teaching and give a detailed account of a 12-week-long task-based learning project. The project involves students working in small groups, choosing a topic of interest, and designing a questionnaire to investigate the topic. Students then administer the questionnaire, analyze and interpret the data, and finally present their findings in class. In carrying out the task, students experience ample opportunities for meaningful language use in a realistic context.

Stoller's paper is written from the perspective of content-based instruction (CBI). CBI seeks to use content (rather than tasks) as the vehicle for developing language skills. A focus on content not only provides valuable real-world knowledge, but also provides the basis for a meaning-based pedagogy that goes beyond a focus on studying language divorced from the context of its use. Stoller gives a useful overview of the assumptions of content-based instruction and then focuses on project work as a valuable vehicle for integrating language and content learning across a variety of educational settings. Project work shares many features with task work, though it is often more extensive and linked more specifically to the demands of content subjects in the mainstream curriculum. Stoller gives a step-by-step description of how project work can be integrated into the ESL classroom, how a language focus can be incorporated into project work, and the positive benefits that can result from project-based activities.

Discussion Questions

Before Reading

1. What do you understand by a task-based approach to teaching? Do you employ tasks in your teaching? If so, what kinds, and how effective are they?
2. Have you made much use of pair work and group work in your teaching? What are some of the practical difficulties involved?
3. What do you think some of the advantages and limitations might be of organizing a course around content (e.g., environmental issues, music and the arts, world events) rather than linguistic categories? How could such a curriculum be linked to a language syllabus?
4. How could content be selected as the basis for a content-based course?
5. What might some of the advantages be of using project work in teaching? Give an example of a project and what students could learn from completing it.

After Reading

1. Do you think a language course can be planned entirely around tasks? What might the limitations be of such a course? What other types of activities might also be necessary?
2. What are the roles of teachers and learners in a task-based curriculum?
3. Choose a task and plan a sequence of activities around it based on the framework proposed by Beglar and Hunt. Discuss any problems that arise.
4. Observe learners carrying out a task. To what extent does their performance illustrate features of tasks listed by Beglar and Hunt such as the following?
   - opportunities for negotiation for meaning
   - use of communication strategies
   - contextualized linguistic input
5. Review Beglar and Hunt's article. What do they mean by code complexity, cognitive complexity, and communicative stress?
6. According to Beglar and Hunt, what should be the role of peer and self-assessment in task-based learning? Do you agree with them? What are some of the difficulties of asking students to do peer and self-assessment?
7. In what ways can grammar be incorporated into a task-based curriculum?
8. According to the two articles in this section, what are the similarities or differences between task-based instruction and project work?
9. Give examples of projects that would be relevant to *(a)* a speaking class, *(b)* a listening class, and *(c)* a writing class in an ESL program.
10. What do you think some of the difficulties might be in implementing project work in an ESL program?
11. Plan a content-based project for an ESL class, following the steps outlined by Stoller.

CHAPTER 9

Implementing Task-Based Language Teaching

David Beglar and Alan Hunt

INTRODUCTION

Language instructors and curriculum designers can choose from two broad categories of syllabuses. The first, the synthetic syllabus, segments the target language into discrete linguistic items, such as points of grammar, lexical items, and functions. Users of this type of syllabus assume that learners will be capable of resynthesizing these discrete pieces of language into a coherent whole which can then be effectively utilized in communicative situations (White, 1988). The second type, the analytic syllabus, is a noninterventionist, experiential approach which aims to immerse learners in real-life communication. It provides learners with samples of the target language which are organized in terms of the purposes for which people use language. In this case, the assumption is that the learners' analytic abilities will be equal to the task of coming to accurate conclusions about grammatical and lexical usage, since relatively little may be explicitly explained about the formal aspects of the language. Analytic syllabuses generally represent the educational value system espoused by progressivism, which stresses the growth and self-realization of the individual (White, 1988). This is a problem-posing type of education which emphasizes dialogue between learners and teachers and between the learners themselves. The purpose of the dialogue is to stimulate new ideas, opinions, and perceptions rather than simply to exchange them or regurgitate what others have said. White (1988) lists the most salient characteristics of analytic syllabuses as follows: *(a)* they are primarily concerned with *how* materials are learned (processes-oriented); *(b)* some degree of negotiation between learners and the teacher occurs; *(c)* the content is fundamentally defined as what the subject means to the learner and what the learner brings to the subject in terms of knowledge and interest; *(d)* assessment is partially decided based on the learners' own criteria of success; and *(e)* the instructional situation is far more cooperative than in more traditional, teacher-fronted classrooms. This last point has been referred to as maximizing learning opportunities (Kumaravadivelu, 1994) and is an essential aspect of what has been termed a learner-centered curriculum. Classroom discourse should be a cooperative venture in which discourse is created through the joint efforts of both the learners and the instructor.

One type of analytic syllabus is the task-based syllabus (Crookes & Long, 1992). In addition to the characteristics of analytic syllabuses just described, task-based syllabuses are largely derived from what is known about second language acquisition (SLA). For instance, SLA research supports a focus on form which uses pedagogical tasks to draw learners' attention to particular aspects of the language code which are naturally embedded in the tasks (Long & Robinson, 1998; Robinson, 1998). The inclusion of some type of instruction on the formal aspects of the target language can be found in most recent formulations of task-based language instruction (e.g., Willis, 1996; Skehan, 1998). Tasks also provide input to learners and opportunities for meaningful language use, both of which are generally considered valuable in promoting language acquisition (Swain, 1995). Opportunities for production may force students to pay close attention to form and to the relationship between form and meaning. It is assumed that this combination of contextualized, meaningful input and output will engage learners' general cognitive processing capacities through which they will process and reshape the input. In other words, tasks will likely create a rich linguistic environment capable of activating the learners' intuitive heuristics (Kumaravadivelu, 1994), which are natural cognitive processes used both consciously and unconsciously for developing the somewhat separate rules systems that underlie language comprehension and production. In addition, form–function relationships, which are a critical aspect of SLA (MacWhinney, 1997), should be more readily perceived by the learners because of the highly contextualized and communicative nature of the tasks provided by a task-based syllabus.

For these and other reasons, which we explore in the Discussion section of this paper, we believe that a task-based syllabus has the potential to play an important role in many ESL/EFL curriculums. Thus, the purpose of this paper is to describe and evaluate one implementation of task-based learning, which took the form of a unified, semester-long project.

The Project: Student-Generated Action Research

In this section we would like to briefly describe an extended task-based project which was implemented at a major private Japanese university with approximately 340 first-year students enrolled in a second-semester speaking course. The project, which we have called *student-generated action research*, required the entire 12-week semester to complete. However, as part of the same course, learners were also engaged in other activities unrelated to the project throughout the term. These activities can best be described as part of a direct approach to teaching speaking (Dörnyei & Thurrell, 1994). In this approach, learners are explicitly instructed in some of the specific microskills, strategies, and processes involved in conversation. These include phrases and strategies for turn taking, interrupting, expressing agreement or disagreement, summarizing what another person has said, and checking whether one has been understood. The knowledge of these "formulaic frameworks" (Widdowson, 1989, p. 135) forms an essential part of the communicative competence of native speakers of a language and acts as useful linguistic knowledge which the learners can make use of as they move through the project.

In brief, the project requires the learners to work in groups of two to four persons and to choose a topic they are interested in finding out more about. The groups then design a questionnaire which will be used to investigate the opinions that a specific target group holds about the chosen topic. Following this, the learners must go beyond the boundaries of the classroom and administer their questionnaire to the target group. Each group member is required to administer the questionnaire and interview a minimum of ten people. The resulting data are compiled, analyzed, and organized by the group members. Because of the extensive amount of data, the learners must select the most significant aspects of the data, summarize them, and present them to the class in a formal presentation lasting approximately 5 to 8 minutes. The general objectives of the project are to

- provide learners the opportunity to use English for authentic purposes for an extended period of time
- provide intrinsically motivating activities which take advantage of the learners' desire to improve their listening and speaking proficiency
- allow learners to take responsibility for their own English education by giving them the primary responsibility for topic selection, questionnaire creation, and deciding how they will structure and present the data they collect
- reinforce learners' ability to form grammatically and pragmatically correct questions
- enchance the learners' presentation skills
- demonstrate to students that the use of English can further enhance their own education and development
- provide opportunities for learners to work closely together with a partner or in a small group for an extended period

A more detailed look at how the project unfolds throughout the course of a semester follows.

THE 12-WEEK PLAN

WEEK 1

In class: Learners are introduced to the project, they are shown a sample questionnaire, and they view a sample presentation on videotape. Learners undertake various listening tasks while viewing the video.

Homework: All learners must form groups of two to four students before the second class meeting and brainstorm ideas for topics. They should come to the second class with at least three possible topics.

WEEK 2

In class: The teacher checks each group's ideas. With the instructor's advice, each group should tentatively settle on one topic.

Homework: Each group must write a one- to two-paragraph explanation of their topic and why they have chosen it. This must be submitted to the instructor by E-mail at least two days before the third class. The instructor will read the groups' ideas, check to make certain that the topics are suitable, and give feedback to each group by E-mail.

WEEK 3

In class: Learners discuss suitable target groups to whom they can administer their questionnaire.

Homework: Each group must write a one- to two-paragraph explanation of the people they plan to interview and why they have chosen that particular group. This must be submitted to the instructor by E-mail at least two days before the fourth class. The instructor will read the groups' ideas, check to make certain that the target groups they have chosen to interview are suitable, and give feedback to each group by E-mail.

WEEK 4

In class: Groups brainstorm the main points they wish to investigate and then brainstorm possible questions to include on their questionnaire. The instructor gives feedback to each group in class.

Homework: Each group should write ten to twelve questions for possible inclusion on their questionnaire and submit them to the instructor by E-mail at least two days before the fourth class. The instructor will read the groups' questions, check to make certain that they are appropriate, and give feedback to each group by E-mail.

WEEK 5

In class: Groups practice interviewing and using their questionnaire by asking questions to other class members. The purpose is to find out how well the questions they have formulated are eliciting the type and quantity of information they hoped for.

Homework: Learners rewrite their questionnaires as needed and send the modified questionnaires to the instructor by E-mail at least two days before the fourth class. The instructor will read the groups' questionnaires and give feedback to each group by E-mail.

WEEK 6

In class: Learners are instructed to begin gathering data by interviewing a minimum of ten people per group member (e.g., a three-member group will interview a minimum of thirty persons). All data should be gathered by week 8 of the semester.

WEEK 7

In class: Learners briefly report to other group members on their progress in gathering data and any problems they have encountered or any useful revisions to the data-gathering process that they have discovered.

WEEK 8

In class: Group members compare interview data and look for interesting trends. Groups sign up for their presentation, which will take place in either week 10 or 11.

Homework: Learners meet outside of class and continue analyzing and categorizing the questionnaire data. They should choose the information they plan to use in their presentation by the following class.

WEEK 9

In class: The instructor explains how the presentations will be evaluated, in addition to discussing presentation skills, such as eye contact, the use of gestures, and voice projection. The video shown in week 1 (or a different video) is viewed and analyzed in terms of organization, the types of visual aids utilized, the presence of concrete details and examples, and presentation skills of the presenters.

WEEK 10

In class: Half of the groups make a formal presentation of their results. The presentation is videotaped and each group member is individually responsible for viewing the video and completing a self-assessment of the presentation, which is due the following class.

WEEK 11

In class: The remaining groups make the formal presentation of their results. Once again, the presentation is videotaped and each group member must view the video and complete a self-assessment of the presentation, which is due the following class.

WEEK 12

In class: The instructor returns completed evaluations of the presentations to each student. Learners complete course evaluations, which include questions specifically related to the project. The information in these evaluations is used, along with the results of an instructor wrap-up meeting, in order to compile suggestions for possible changes to the project.

TOPIC CHOICES

A key element to the success of this project lies in the fact that the learners have primary control over the topic they investigate. Learners have been found to benefit more from the discourse which results from self- and peer-initiated topics than from topics nominated by outside sources, such as a text or their instructor. This has noticeable positive effects on their motivation and enthusiasm to carry through the project to a successful conclusion. Allowing the learners the freedom to choose the topic is in line with the fundamental principles which underlie analytic syllabuses. Moreover, through the negotiation which occurs as instructors make suggestions to the learners about preferable topics, opportunities are created for teachers and learners to engage in discussions in which an important, real-world problem is being solved. A final point is that the instructors encourage the learners to choose topics that are socially relevant. In this way, the classroom activity is embedded in the larger societal context. An idea of the variety of topics which student groups chose can be seen in the following examples:

- *The information society*: How do people get their information and news?
- *Marriage*: What do you look for in a prospective partner?
- *Marriage and the single mother*: Do all women want to get married? Why would a woman be a single mother? Can children be happy with only one parent?
- *Care for the elderly*: What do people think about caring for elderly relatives? Conversely, what do the elderly think about living with younger family members?
- *Suicide*: Have you ever thought of suicide? What are the reasons for suicide?
- *Older men dating high school girls*: Why is it popular? Who is worse: the men or the young women? Should it be considered a crime?
- *The environment*: Are elementary school children aware of environmental problems? Have they learned about the environment? If so, from whom?

DISCUSSION

In this section, we would first like to examine the aspects of the project which we believe promote language acquisition.

POSITIVE ASPECTS OF THE PROJECT

THE FUNDAMENTAL BENEFITS OF TASKS

Many individual aspects of the project clearly meet the definition of task laid out by Skehan (1998). Specifically, Skehan proposes that a task is an activity in which meaning is primary, there is a communication problem to solve, and the task is closely related to real-world activities. The project described in this paper is composed of a wide variety of tasks which fit this description. Conversely, it is also useful to look at what the project does not do. It does not give the learners other people's meanings and then require them to regurgitate those meanings. It is not concerned with the display of accurate language usage, it is not conformity-oriented, and no particular structures are embedded into any part of the project.

PRE-TASK ACTIVITIES

Pre-task activities are used at several points in the project. They are essential for providing adequate support to the learners in their attempts to deal with a series of complex, challenging tasks. In some cases, new vocabulary, grammar, or knowledge of language functions are presented in the pre-activities. This is extremely important in SLA since a great deal of evidence indicates that partial learning is the norm (see Meara, 1984, and Palmberg, 1987, for more information about the partial learning of lexical items). Thus, the initial presentation of an item will most likely result in partial, tenuous knowledge at first. Future input and production of the item as the project unfolds may then trigger a reorganization of existing structures in the learners' interlanguage system. Another benefit of pre-activities is the activation of already-existing schemata. This can ease the processing load by allowing the learners to consider ideas about the topic, retrieve relevant information, and organize their ideas before undertaking the task. Finally, pre-tasks can potentially lead learners to interpret tasks in more fluent, more complex, and more accurate ways. Increased elaboration is also more likely, and this can potentially result in the learners experimenting with new lexical and grammatical structures.

THE NEGOTIATION OF MEANING

Tasks that generate greater negotiation of meaning appear to be more beneficial for interlanguage development. Ultimately, engaging in negotiation should produce higher degrees of comprehension as it will result in more finely tuned input as a result of paraphrasing and lexical substitution. It should also promote greater flexibility in the learner's rule system by encouraging the exploration of new hypotheses about the structure of the target language (Skehan, 1998). Several conditions that have been found to have a positive effect on the negotiation of meaning are included in the project at various junctures. First, the inclusion of large amounts of pair and group interaction. It is well known that when learners work in groups, far more negotiated interaction is produced than in teacher-fronted classrooms (Kumaravadivelu, 1994). Second, two-way tasks in which both partners or group members have access to unique information result in greater negotiation of meaning (Long, 1989). Two-way tasks are utilized at numerous points in the project. A prime example is when the learners come together to discuss the results of the ten to twelve people from whom they have gathered data. Third, convergent tasks, which require participants to come to a single solution, generate more discourse between the participants (Duff, 1986). This project presents learners with numerous convergent tasks, such as deciding on a topic, creating the final form of the questionnaire, and making decisions about which information to present and how to present it. Fourth, the learners in the project overwhelmingly formed groups with their friends. This is significant because familiar pairs have been found to use more negotiation of meaning and produce more natural discourse than unfamiliar pairs (Plough & Gass, 1993). Fifth, learners undertake a task after first hearing and or seeing the task performed (Yule, Powers, & MacDonald, 1992). This was built into the project in week 1 (in which the learners were shown a sample presentation and questionnaire) and week 9 (when they were able to view the sample presentation once again).

COMMUNICATION STRATEGIES

Learners should be actively involved in using communication strategies, such as clarification, confirmation, comprehension checks, requests, repairing, reacting, and turn taking. The underlying notion is that opportunities to modify and restructure interaction until mutual comprehension is reached are what enable learners to move forward in their interlanguage development. Although the learners were not taught communication strategies as part of the project, as described earlier, they were actively taught strategies in the part of the course that focused on the direct teaching of speaking.

CONTEXTUALIZED LINGUISTIC INPUT

One of the greatest strengths of task-based teaching is the fact that much, or all, language use occurs in a natural, communicative context. As Kumaravadivelu (1994, p. 38) states, "It is . . . essential to bring to the learners' attention the integrated nature of language. . . . Introducing isolated, discrete items will result in pragmatic dissonance, depriving the learner of necessary pragmatic cues and rendering the process of meaning making harder." As a natural by-product of the high degree of contextualization of language in this project, the major language skills were closely integrated. This is the main principle of Whole Language Education (e.g., see Brown, 1994). Language is not the sum of its discrete parts and is best learned when oral language (listening and speaking) and written language (reading and writing) are integrated and mutually reinforcing.

POSSIBLE IMPROVEMENTS TO THE PROJECT

Although the learners who took part in the project benefited from it, we firmly believe that this teaching program can be improved. Indeed, curriculum and syllabus design involves a never-ending process of making adjustments aimed at enhancing the project's pedagogical usefulness to learners. This project is no different. In this section, we would like to point out some of our major concerns and areas for further improvement.

FUNDAMENTAL PROBLEMS WITH TASKS

Skehan (1998) lists several major problems which exist where task-based language teaching is concerned. First, although early empirical indications strongly support the use of task as an effective way to conceptualize language teaching, the amount of research is still insufficient. Second, and more worrisome, is the fact that no task-based program has been implemented and subjected to rigorous evaluation. Until this has been accomplished and any positive results replicated, the use of task-based courses will be open to doubts and criticisms. Moreover, assessing task difficulty and sequencing tasks is problematic. Our understanding of the many potential factors influencing task difficulty is quite limited; thus, teachers must generally fall back on their intuition about how well their learners can deal with specific tasks. Third, little is known about task "finiteness." For instance, if examined carefully, a task such as the creation of a questionnaire is composed of a large number of "microtasks" which must be successfully accomplished in order to complete the larger task. There is probably no clearer explanation of this than in the work of Anderson and his colleagues in the area of production rules (e.g., Anderson, 1993; Anderson & Lebiere, 1998). They have shown how one relatively "simple" task, such as an addition problem, can only be completed if a large number of more basic production rules are known and accurately applied. When the task is the communicative use of language, the situation is far more complex. Skehan (1998) claims that task-based language teaching may be too structured and preplanned and so slow down the rate of acquisition. However, this did not appear to be a problem with the learners in this program. Only further research on task-based teaching will provide answers to this question.

INCREASING THE FOCUS ON FORM

Skehan (1998) notes that there are two contrasting approaches to using tasks. The first, a structure-oriented approach, emphasizes form over meaning; the second, a communicatively oriented approach, focuses very little on form. Skehan argues in favor of an intermediate approach which strikes a balance between form and meaning by alternating attention between them. This project clearly falls under the umbrella of the communicatively oriented approach and, as such, one of its primary weaknesses is an overemphasis on communication. This increases the risk that learners will become overly reliant on the use of communication strategies and lexically based language, because three aspects of speaking performance – accuracy, fluency, and complexity – compete with one another. Thus, the series of tasks given to the learners in this project appear to have the greatest effect on speaking fluency and, to a lesser degree, complexity; however, because of natural limitations in attentional resources, this means that many learners will have limited cognitive capacity to attend to accuracy. This is a matter of no small concern since this situation can potentially lead to what Skehan calls *provoked fossilization* – the fossilization of incorrect lexicalized language which is acquired relatively early in the process of acquiring productive language skills. Not only should some time be reserved for a focus on form, but, ideally, this should occur more than once in the project. Skehan (1998) suggests a focus on form at the pre-task stage of task use. In addition, after learners have completed the task, form can be emphasized before undertaking the task a second time. Finally, there must be opportunities for reflection and awareness so that whatever is accomplished during the task can be more deeply processed and consolidated.

A CLOSER ANALYSIS OF THE MAJOR TASKS

Skehan (1998) proposes three dimensions for the analysis of tasks. The first dimension involves code complexity (the language required). This includes such factors as linguistic complexity and variety, vocabulary load and variety, and redundancy and information density. In the project described in this paper, there is a high degree of code complexity, which poses severe processing problems for lower-proficiency learners. This could be dealt with by encouraging learners to use various types of support, such as preparing for in-class discussions before the class, by utilizing notes during discussions, and by providing learners with details of upcoming tasks. This type of support and pre-activity would increase the chances that the level of challenge in the tasks is appropriate for the learners involved. Tasks of appropriate difficulty are likely to be more interesting and motivating to learners since they will feel that they are being asked to respond to a reasonable challenge. Moreover, given that attentional capacities are limited, learners will more likely be able to cope with the cognitive demands of tasks of appropriate difficulty. This will help to ensure that noticing new lexical items, grammatical constructions, and form–function relationships will occur and that spare attentional capacity can be devoted to such forms and will result in gains in accuracy and/or complexity.

The second dimension, cognitive complexity, involves the type of thinking required for the completion of the task. The first aspect involves the consideration of cognitive familiarity, which consists of topic familiarity, topic predictability, familiarity with the discourse genre, and familiarity with the task. The second, cognitive processing, includes the organization of the information, the amount of computation necessary, the clarity and sufficiency of the information provided, and the type of information provided. One way to reduce the cognitive complexity would be to provide learners with a brief description and outline of the major tasks in the project, how they will be sequenced, and a time line at the beginning of the course. The lower-proficiency learners would likely benefit from receiving this information in their native language.

The third dimension, communicative stress, takes the following factors into consideration: time limits and time pressure, the speed of presentation, the number of participants involved in the task, the length of texts used, the type of response expected, and the opportunities the learners have to control the interaction. In the current formulation of the project, communicative stress is largely reduced because few strict time limits are imposed on the learners and they can make use of notes and other documentation, such as handouts, when speaking and writing.

INTRODUCING MORE FLEXIBILITY INTO THE CURRICULUM

One of this language curriculum's greatest strengths is that it is coordinated. Instructors teaching the same course (e.g., first-year, second-semester speaking) are using nearly the same materials and activities in class, and there is good communication between teachers in different skill areas. Thus, a writing teacher may connect an activity in writing class with a topic which has been dealt with in reading or listening class. However, one way in which such a highly coordinated curriculum can be disadvantageous to some learners is when considerable differences in language proficiency exist between learners studying in the same skill area. The approximately 340 learners who participated in the project are placed into classes based on TOEFL scores. Although this works well in some skill areas, such as reading, which uses TOEFL reading subsection scores to place learners of similar proficiency together, it is less successful in placing students into a speaking class, since TOEFL is not designed to measure speaking proficiency. Nonetheless, there are clear differences between the eighteen different classes which participated in this project. The highest-level classes had average TOEFL scores of around 500, and the lowest-level classes had average scores of approximately 420. Therefore, consideration should be given to ways in which the project could be adjusted to a more appropriate level for the lower-proficiency learners. For example, three factors that have been found to influence task difficulty are decreasing the number of participants (Brown, Anderson, Shilcock, & Yule, 1984), the use of more familiar information (Foster & Skehan, 1996), and the use of concrete rather than abstract information (Skehan & Foster, 1997). Learners in lower-proficiency classes could be limited to working in pairs or groups of three rather than the larger groups of four which some learners formed. This would have no adverse impact on the overall effectiveness of the program. Likewise, when lower-proficiency learners initially brainstorm topics, the instructor could encourage them to choose topics which are likely to be more familiar and more concrete. This slight change would not compromise the project since the topic would still be student generated.

ENCOURAGING SELF-EVALUATION

Learners should be encouraged to consciously engage in cycles of evaluation by periodically reflecting on what they have studied. A priority in task-based approaches is to mobilize the learner's metacognitive resources to keep track of what is being learned, and what remains to be learned. Engaging in self-assessment is the first step in consciously understanding one's weaknesses. However, this must be followed by the formulation of a plan to address those weaknesses, and then that plan must be put into action, followed by another round of evaluation. This cycle is closely related to the notion of promoting greater learner autonomy, which should be a long-term goal in most programs. Although learners were required to reflect on their performance in the group presentation, they were not asked to formulate a plan designed to address the weaknesses they noticed; therefore, no concrete action could take place. In future implementations of the project, this shortcoming should be addressed.

Conclusion

The task-based project described in this paper was well received by the majority of the learners in the course. They found the experience to be rewarding, intrinsically interesting, and educationally beneficial. Many of their final presentations were impressively polished and included a considerable amount of detailed information, which was well organized and effectively supported by appropriate visual aids. Thus, the final *product* was generally of a high level. The concern of this paper, however, has been with *process* – a concern common to most analytic syllabuses. Seen from the point of view of process, the project holds great promise for helping learners in their efforts to further improve many aspects of their English-language proficiency. However, the potential of the project can only be fully manifested as more is understood about the nature of different types of tasks and as the instructors in the program gradually implement changes which they believe will result in a pedagogically sounder experience for the learners.

References

Anderson, J. R. (1993). *Rules of the mind.* Hillsdale, NJ: Lawrence Erlbaum.

Anderson, J. R., & Lebiere, C. (1998). *The atomic components of thought.* Mahwah, NJ: Lawrence Erlbaum.

Brown, H. D. (1994). *Teaching by principles: An interactive approach to language pedagogy.* Englewood Cliffs, NJ: Prentice Hall.

Brown, G., Anderson, A., Shilcock, R., & Yule, G. (1984). *Teaching talk: Strategies for production and assessment.* Cambridge: Cambridge University Press.

Crookes, G., & Long, M. (1992). Three approaches to task-based syllabus design. *TESOL Quarterly, 26*, 27–56.

Dörnyei, Z., & Thurrell, S. (1994). Teaching conversational skills intensively: Course content and rationale. *ELT Journal, 48*(1).

Duff, P. (1986). Another look at interlanguage talk: Taking task to task. In R. Day (Ed.), *Talking to learn.* Rowley, MA: Newbury House.

Foster, P., & Skehan, P. (1996). The influence of planning on performance in task-based learning. *Studies in Second Language Acquisition, 18*, 299–324.

Kumaravadivelu, B. (1994). The postmethod condition: Emerging strategies for second/foreign language teaching. *TESOL Quarterly, 28*, 27–48.

Long, M. (1989). Task, group, and task-group interaction. In L. Beebe (Ed.), *Issues in second language acquisition: Multiple perspectives.* Rowley, MA: Newbury House.

Long, M., & Robinson, P. (1998). Focus on form: Theory, research, and practice. In C. Doughty & J. Williams (Eds.), *Focus on form in second language classroom acquisition.* Cambridge: Cambridge University Press.

MacWhinney, B. (1997). Second language acquisition and the Competition Model. In A. M. B. de Groot & J. F. Kroll (Eds.), *Tutorials in Bilingualism* (pp. 113–142). Mahwah, NJ: Lawrence Erlbaum.

Meara, P. (1984). The study of lexis in interlanguage. In A. Davies, C. Criper, & A. R. P. Howatt (Eds.), *Interlanguage* (pp. 225–235). Edinburgh: Edinburgh University Press.

Palmberg, R. (1987). Patterns of vocabulary development in foreign-language learners. *Studies in Second Language Acquisition, 9*, 201–220.

Plough, I., & Gass, S. (1993). Interlocuter and task familiarity: Effect on instructional structure. In G. Crookes & S. Gass (Eds.), *Tasks in a Pedagogical Context: Integrating Theory and Practice.* Clevedon, Avon: Multilingual Matters.

Robinson, P. (1998). State of the art: SLA theory and second language syllabus design. *The Language Teacher, 22*(4), 7–13.

Skehan, P. (1998). *A cognitive approach to language learning.* Oxford: Oxford University Press.

Skehan, P., & Foster, P. (1997). The influence of planning and post-task activities on accuracy and complexity in task-based learning. *Language Teaching Research, 1*(3), 185–211.

Swain, M. (1995). Three functions of output in second language learning. In G. Cook & B. Seidlhofer (Eds.), *Principle and practice in applied linguistics* (pp. 125–144). Cambridge: Cambridge University Press.

White, R. (1988). *The ELT curriculum: Design, innovation and management.* Cambridge, MA: Basil Blackwell.

Widdowson, H. G. (1989). Knowledge of language and ability for use. *Applied Linguistics, 10*(2), 128–137.

Wills, J. (1996). A flexible framework for task-based learning. In J. Willis & D. Willis (Eds.), *Challenge and Change in Language Teaching* (pp. 52–62). Oxford: Heinemann.

Yule, G., Powers, M., & MacDonald, D. (1992). The variable effects of some task-based learning procedures on L2 communicative effectiveness. *Language Learning, 42*, 249–277.

CHAPTER 10

Project Work: A Means to Promote Language and Content

Fredricka L. Stoller

INTRODUCTION

In recent years, increasing numbers of language educators have turned to content-based instruction and project work to promote meaningful student engagement with language and content learning. Through content-based instruction, learners develop language skills while becoming more knowledgeable citizens of the world. By integrating project work into content-based classrooms, educators create vibrant learning environments that require active student involvement, stimulate higher-level thinking skills, and give students responsibility for their own learning. When incorporating project work into content-based classrooms, instructors distance themselves from teacher-dominated instruction and move toward creating a student community of inquiry involving authentic communication, cooperative learning, collaboration, and problem solving.

In this article, I shall provide a rationale for content-based instruction and demonstrate how project work can be integrated into content-based classrooms. I will then outline the primary characteristics of project work, introduce project work in its various configurations, and present practical guidelines for sequencing and developing a project. It is my hope that language teachers and teacher educators will be able to adapt the ideas presented here to enhance their classroom instruction.

A RATIONALE FOR CONTENT-BASED INSTRUCTION

Content-based instruction (CBI) has been used in a variety of language learning contexts, though its popularity and wider applicability have increased dramatically since the early 1990s. Numerous practical features of CBI make it an appealing approach to language instruction:

> In a content-based approach, the activities of the language class are specific to the subject matter being taught, and are geared to stimulate students to think and learn through the use of the target language. Such an approach lends itself quite naturally to the integrated teaching of the four traditional language skills. For example, it employs authentic reading materials which require students not only to understand information but to interpret and evaluate it as well. It provides a forum in which students can respond orally to reading and lecture materials. It recognizes that academic writing follows from listening and reading, and thus requires students to synthesize facts and ideas from multiple sources as preparation for writing. In this approach, students are exposed to study skills and learn a variety of language skills which prepare them for the range of academic tasks they will encounter. (Brinton, Snow, & Wesche, 1989, p. 2)

This quotation reflects a consistent set of descriptions by CBI practitioners who have come to appreciate the many ways that CBI offers ideal conditions for language learning. Research in second language acquisition offers additional support for CBI; yet some of the most persuasive evidence stems from research in educational and cognitive psychology, even though it is somewhat removed from language learning contexts. Four findings from research in educational and cognitive psychology that emphasize the benefits of content-based instruction are worth noting:

1. Thematically organized materials, typical of content-based classrooms, are easier to remember and learn (Singer, 1990).
2. The presentation of coherent and meaningful information, characteristic of well-organized content-based curricula, leads to deeper processing and better learning (Anderson, 1990).
3. There is a relationship between student motivation and student interest – common outcomes of content-based classes – and a student's ability to process challenging materials, recall information, and elaborate (Alexander, Kulikowich, & Jetton, 1994).
4. Expertise in a topic develops when learners reinvest their knowledge in a sequence of progressively more complex tasks (Bereiter & Scardamalia, 1993), feasible in content-based classrooms and usually absent from more traditional language classrooms because of the narrow focus on language rules or limited time on superficially developed and disparate topics (e.g., a curriculum based on a short reading passage on the skyscrapers of New York, followed by a passage on the history of bubble gum, later followed by an essay on the volcanos of the American Northwest).

These empirical research findings, when combined with the practical advantages of integrating content and language learning, provide persuasive arguments in favor of content-based instruction. Language educators who adopt a content-based orientation will find that CBI also allows for the incorporation of explicit language instruction (covering, for example, grammar, conversational gambits, functions, notions, and skills), thereby satisfying students' language and content learning needs in context (see Grabe & Stoller, 1997 for a more developed rationale for CBI).

Project Work as a Natural Extension of Content-Based Instruction

Content-based instruction allows for the natural integration of sound language-teaching practices such as alternative means of assessment, apprenticeship learning, cooperative learning, integrated-skills instruction, project work, scaffolding, strategy training, and the use of graphic organizers. Although each of these teaching practices is worthy of extended discussion, this article will focus solely on project work and its role in content-based instructional formats.

Some language professionals equate project work with in-class group work, cooperative learning, or more elaborate task-based activities. It is the purpose of this article, however, to illustrate how project work represents much more than group work per se. Project-based learning should be viewed as a versatile vehicle for fully integrated language and content learning, making it a viable option for language educators working in a variety of instructional settings, including general English, English for academic purposes (EAP), English for specific purposes (ESP), and English for occupational/vocational/professional purposes, in addition to preservice and in-service teacher training. Project work is viewed by most of its advocates "not as a replacement for other teaching methods," but rather as "an approach to learning which complements mainstream methods and which can be used with almost all levels, ages and abilities of students" (Haines, 1989, p. 1).

In classrooms where a commitment has been made to content learning as well as language learning (i.e., content-based classrooms), project work is particularly effective because it represents a natural extension of what is already taking place in class. So, for example, in an EAP class structured around environmental topics, a project which involves the development of poster displays suggesting ways in which the students' school might engage in more environmentally sound practices would be a natural outcome of the content and language learning activities taking place in class. In a vocational English course focusing on tourism, the development of a promotional brochure highlighting points of interest in the students' hometown would be a natural outgrowth of the curriculum. In a general English course focusing on cities in English-speaking countries, students could create public bulletin-board displays with pictorial and written information on targeted cities. In an ESP course on international law, a written report comparing and contrasting the American legal system and the students' home-country legal system represents a meaningful project that allows for the synthesis, analysis, and evaluation of course content. Project work is equally effective in teacher-training courses. Thus, in a course on materials development, a student-generated handbook comprising generic exercises for language-skills practice at different levels of English proficiency represents a useful and practical project that can be used later as a teacher-reference tool. The hands-on experience that the teachers-in-training have with project-based learning could, in turn, transfer to their own lesson planning in the future (J. Mohanraj, personal communication, June 5, 1997). These examples represent only some of the possibilities available to teachers and students when incorporating project work into content-based curricula.

The Primary Characteristics of Project Work

Project work has been described by a number of language educators, including Carter and Thomas (1986), Ferragatti and Carminati (1984), Fried-Booth (1982, 1986), Haines (1989), Legutke (1984, 1985), Legutke and Thiel (1983), Papandreou (1994), Sheppard and Stoller

(1995), and Ward (1988). Although each of these educators has approached project work from a different perspective, project work, in its various configurations, shares the following features:

1. Project work focuses on content learning rather than on specific language targets. Real-world subject matter and topics of interest to students can become central to projects.
2. Project work is student centered, though the teacher plays a major role in offering support and guidance throughout the process.
3. Project work is cooperative rather than competitive. Students can work on their own, in small groups, or as a class to complete a project, sharing resources, ideas, and expertise along the way.
4. Project work leads to the authentic integration of skills and processing of information from varied sources, mirroring real-life tasks.
5. Project work culminates in an end product (e.g., an oral presentation, a poster session, a bulletin-board display, a report, or a stage performance) that can be shared with others, giving the project a real purpose. The value of the project, however, lies not just in the final product but in the process of working toward the end point. Thus, project work has both a process and product orientation, and provides students with opportunities to focus on fluency and accuracy at different project-work stages.
6. Project work is potentially motivating, stimulating, empowering, and challenging. It usually results in building student confidence, self-esteem, and autonomy as well as improving students' language skills, content learning, and cognitive abilities.

Project Work and Its Various Configurations

Though similar in many ways, project work can take on diverse configurations. The most suitable format for a given context depends on a variety of factors, including curricular objectives, course expectations, students' proficiency levels, student interests, time constraints, and availability of materials. A review of different types of projects will demonstrate the scope, versatility, and adaptability of project work.

Projects differ in the degree to which the teacher and students decide on the nature and sequencing of project-related activities, as demonstrated by three types of projects proposed by Henry (1994): *Structured projects* are determined, specified, and organized by the teacher in terms of topic, materials, methodology, and presentation; *unstructured projects* are defined largely by students themselves; and *semistructured projects* are defined and organized in part by the teacher and in part by students.

Projects can be linked to real-world concerns (e.g., when Italian ESP students designed a leaflet for foreign travel agencies outside of Europe describing the advantages of the European Community's standardization of electrical systems as a step toward European unity,[1] or when general English students at an international school created a public bulletin-board display – with photos and text based on extensive interviews with EFL faculty – introducing new students to their EFL teachers).[2] Projects can also be linked to simulated real-world issues (e.g., when EAP students staged a debate on the pros and cons of censorship as part of a content-based unit on censorship).[3] Projects can also be tied to student interests, with or without real-world significance (e.g., when general English students planned an elaborate field trip to an international airport where they conducted extensive interviews and videotaping of international travelers; see Ferragatti & Carminati, 1984; Legutke, 1984, 1985; Legutke & Thiel, 1983).

Projects can also differ in data collection techniques and sources of information as demonstrated by these project types: *Research projects* necessitate the gathering of information through library research. Similarly, *text projects* involve encounters with "texts" (e.g., literature, reports, news media, video and audio material, or computer-based information) rather than people. *Correspondence projects* require communication with individuals (or businesses, governmental agencies, schools, or chambers of commerce) to solicit information by means of letters, faxes, phone calls, or electronic mail. *Survey projects* entail creating a survey instrument and then collecting and analyzing data from "informants." *Encounter projects* result in face-to-face contact with guest speakers or individuals outside the classroom. (See Haines, 1989 and Legutke & Thomas, 1991 for a more detailed description of these project types.)

Projects may also differ in the ways that information is "reported" as part of a culminating activity (see Haines, 1989). *Production projects* involve the creation of bulletin-board displays, videos, radio programs, poster sessions, written reports, photo essays, letters, handbooks, brochures, banquet menus, travel itineraries, and so forth. *Performance projects* can take shape as staged debates, oral presentations, theatrical performances, food fairs, or fashion shows. *Organizational projects* entail the planning and formation of a club, conversation table, or conversation-partner program.

Whatever the configuration, projects can be carried out intensively over a short period of time or extended over a few weeks, or a full semester; they can be completed by students individually, in small groups, or as a class; and they can take place entirely within the confines of the classroom or can extend beyond the walls of the classroom into the community or with others via different forms of correspondence.

Incorporating Project Work into the Classroom

Project work, whether it is integrated into a content-based thematic unit or introduced as a special sequence of activities in a more traditional classroom, requires multiple stages of development to succeed. Fried-Booth (1986) proposes an easy-to-follow multiple-step process that can guide teachers in developing and sequencing project work for their classrooms. Similarly, Haines (1989) presents a straightforward and useful description of project work and the steps needed for successful implementation. Both the Fried-Booth and Haines volumes include detailed descriptions of projects that can be adapted for many language-classroom settings. They also offer suggestions for introducing students to the idea of student-centered activity through bridging strategies (Fried-Booth, 1986) and lead-in activities (Haines, 1989), particularly useful if students are unfamiliar with project work and its emphasis on student initiative and autonomy.

Sheppard and Stoller (1995) proposed an 8-step sequence of activities for orchestrating project work in an ESP classroom. That model has been fine-tuned, after testing it in a variety of language classrooms and teacher-training courses. The new 10-step sequence (see Figure 1) is described here in detail. The revised model gives easy-to-manage structure to project work and guides teachers and students in developing meaningful projects that facilitate content learning and provide opportunities for explicit language instruction at critical moments in the project. These language "intervention" lessons will help students complete their projects successfully and will be appreciated by students because of their immediate applicability and relevance. The language intervention steps (4, 6, and 8) are optional in teacher-education courses, depending on the language proficiency and needs of the teachers-in-training.

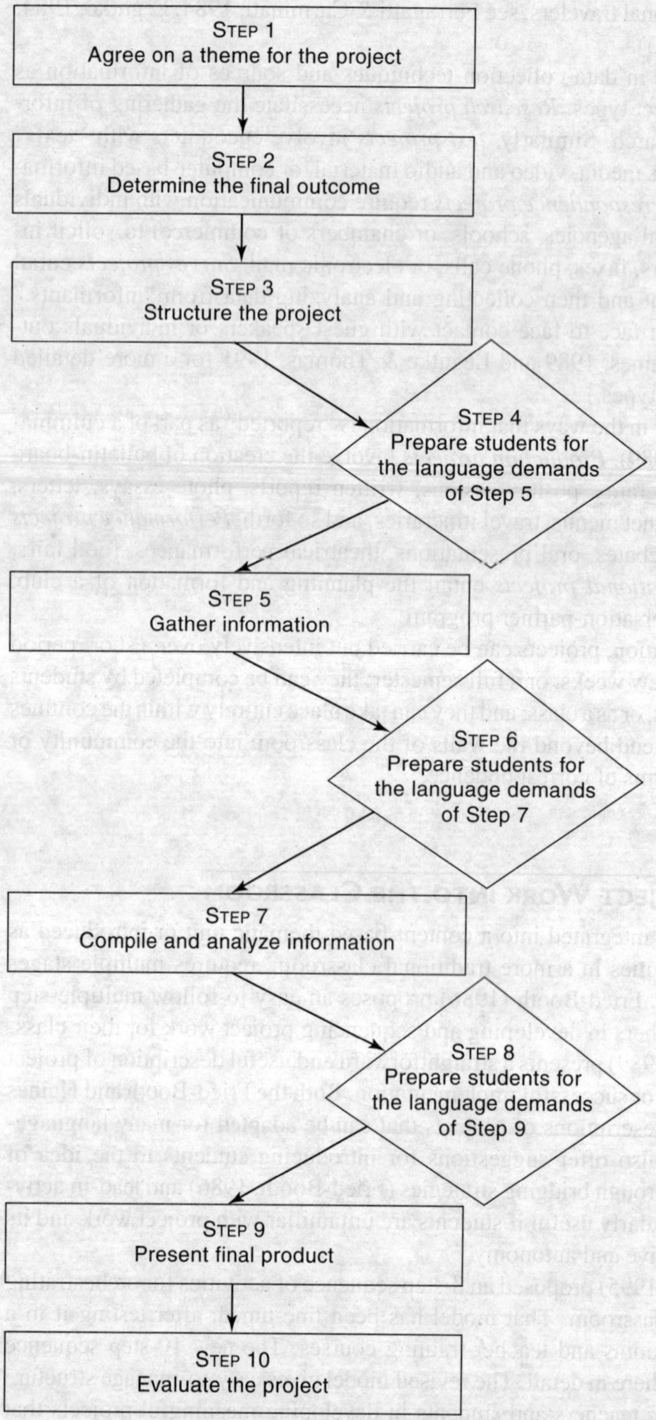

Figure 1 Developing a Project in a Language Classroom

Developing a Project in a Language Classroom

To understand the function of each proposed step, imagine a content-based EAP classroom focusing on American elections.[4] (A parallel discussion could be developed for classrooms – general English, EAP, ESP, vocational English, and so forth – focusing on American institutions, demography, energy alternatives, farming safety, fashion design, health, the ideal automobile, insects, Native Americans, pollution, rain forests, the solar system, etc.). The thematic unit is structured so that the instructor and students can explore various topics: the branches of the U.S. government, the election process, political parties with their corresponding ideologies and platforms, and voting behaviors. Information on these topics is introduced by means of readings from books, newspapers, and news magazines; graphs and charts; videos; dictocomps; teacher-generated lectures and note-taking activities; formal and informal class discussions and group work; guest speakers; and U.S. political party promotional materials. While exploring these topics and developing some level of expertise about American elections, students improve their listening and note-taking skills, reading proficiency, accuracy and fluency in speaking, writing abilities, study skills, and critical thinking skills. To frame this discussion, it should be noted that the thematic unit is embedded in an integrated-skills, content-based course with the following objectives:

1. to encourage students to use language to learn something new about topics of interest
2. to prepare students to learn subject matter through English
3. to expose students to content from a variety of informational sources to help them improve their academic language and study skills
4. to provide students with contextualized resources for understanding language and content
5. to simulate the rigors of academic courses in a sheltered environment
6. to promote students' self-reliance and engagement with learning

After being introduced to the theme unit and its most fundamental vocabulary and concepts, the instructor introduces a semistructured project that will be woven into class lessons and that will span the length of the thematic unit. The teacher has already made some decisions about the project: Students will stage a simulated political debate that addresses contemporary political and social issues. To stimulate interest and a sense of ownership in the process, the instructor will work with the students to decide on the issues to be debated, the number and types of political parties represented in the debate, the format of the debate, and a means for judging the debate. To move from the initial conception of the project to the actual debate, the instructor and students follow ten steps.

Step 1: Students and Instructor Agree on a Theme for the Project

To set the stage, the instructor gives students an opportunity to shape the project and develop some sense of shared perspective and commitment. Even if the teacher has decided to pursue a structured project, for which he or she will make most decisions, students can be encouraged to fine-tune the project theme. While shaping the project together, students often find it useful to make reference to previous readings, videos, discussions, and classroom activities.

During the initial stage of the American elections project, students brainstormed issues that might be featured in an American political debate. Through discussion and negotiation, they identified the following issues for consideration: taxes, crime, welfare, gun control, abortion, family leave, foreign policy, affirmative action, election reform, immigration, censorship, the environment, and environmental legislation. By pooling resources, information, ideas, and relevant experiences, students narrowed the scope of the debate by choosing select issues from within the larger set of brainstormed issues that were of special interest to the class and that were "researchable," meaning that resources were available or accessible for student research.

STEP 2: STUDENTS AND INSTRUCTOR DETERMINE THE FINAL OUTCOME

Whereas the first stage of project work involves establishing a starting point, the second step entails defining an end point, or the final outcome. Students and the instructor consider the nature of the project, its objectives, and the most appropriate means to culminate the project. They can choose from a variety of options, including a written report, letter, poster or bulletin-board display, debate, oral presentation, information packet, handbook, scrapbook, brochure, newspaper, or video.

In the case of the American elections project, the teacher had already decided that the final outcome would be a public debate between two fictitious political parties. In this second stage of the project, students took part in defining the nature and format of the debate and designating the intended audience. With the help of the instructor, it was decided that the class would divide itself into five topical teams, each one responsible for debating one of the issues previously identified; topical teams would generate debatable propositions on their designated issue and then divide into two subgroups so that each side of the issue could be represented in the debate. Students would also be grouped into two political parties, which they would name themselves, with one side of each issue represented in the political party; the issues and corresponding perspectives would form the party platform. The 40-minute debate was structured as follows:

Opening remarks	
Representative from first party	1 minute
Representative from second party	1 minute
Issue 1	
Party representative who supports proposition	2 minutes
Party representative who opposes proposition	2 minutes
Issue 1 rebuttals	
Another party representative who supports proposition	1 minute
Another party representative who opposes proposition	1 minute
Issues 2–5	
(Same pattern as Issue 1)	24 minutes
Questions and answers from audience to other party representatives	6 minutes
Closing remarks	
Speaker from second party	1 minute
Speaker from first party	1 minute

The class decided to invite English-speaking friends and graduate students enrolled in a TESL/TEFL program to serve as their audience and judges. It was decided that the audience would vote on which team presented the most persuasive arguments during the debate.

STEP 3: STUDENTS AND INSTRUCTOR STRUCTURE THE PROJECT

After students have determined the starting and end points of the project, they need to structure the "body" of the project. Questions that students should consider are as follows: What information is needed to complete the project? How can that information be obtained (e.g., a library search, interviews, letters, faxes, E-mail, the World Wide Web, field trips, viewing of videos)? How will the information, once gathered, be compiled and analyzed? What role does each student play in the evolution of the project (i.e., who does what?)? What time line will students follow to get from the starting point to the end point? The answers to many of these questions depend on the location of the language program and the types of information that are within easy reach (perhaps collected beforehand by the instructor) and those that must be solicited by "snail" mail, electronic mail, fax, or phone call.

In this American elections project, it was decided that topical team members would work together to gather information that could be used by supporters and opponents of their proposition before actually taking sides. In this way, topical team members would share all their resources, later using it to take a stand and plan a rebuttal. Rather than keeping information secret, as might be done in a real debate setting, the idea was to establish a cooperative and collaborative working atmosphere. Topical team members would work as a group to compile gathered information (in the form of facts, opinions, and statistics) and then analyze it to determine what was most suitable to the sides supporting and opposing their proposition. At this point, students would subdivide into groups of supporters and opponents and then work separately (and with other party members) to prepare for the debate. At that time, students would decide on different roles: the spokespersons, the "artists" who would create visuals (charts and graphs) to be used during the debate, and so forth.

STEP 4: INSTRUCTOR PREPARES STUDENTS FOR THE LANGUAGE DEMANDS OF INFORMATION GATHERING

It is at this point that the instructor determines, perhaps in consultation with the students, the language demands of the information-gathering stage (Step 5). The instructor can then plan language instruction activities to prepare students for information-gathering tasks. If, for example, students are going to collect information by means of interviews, the instructor might plan exercises on question formation, introduce conversational gambits, and set aside time for role-plays to provide feedback on pronunciation and to allow students to practice listening and note taking or audiotaping. If, on the other hand, students are going to use a library to gather materials, the instructor might review steps for finding resources and practice skimming and note taking with sample texts. The teacher may also help students devise a grid for organized data collection. If students will be writing letters to solicit information for their project, the teacher can introduce or review letter formatting conventions and audience considerations, including levels of formality and word choice. If students will be using the World Wide Web for information gathering, the instructor can review the efficient use of this technology.

STEP 5: STUDENTS GATHER INFORMATION

Having practiced the language, skills, and strategies needed to gather information, students are now ready to collect information and organize it so that others on their team can make sense of it. In the project highlighted here, students reread course readings in search of relevant materials, used the library to look for new support, wrote letters to political parties to determine their stand on the issue under consideration, looked into finding organizations supporting or opposing some aspect of their proposition (e.g., gun-control groups), and solicited information that could possibly be used in the debate. During this data-gathering stage, the instructor, knowing the issues and propositions being researched, also brought in information that was potentially relevant for student consideration, such as readings, videos, dictocomps, and teacher-generated lectures.

STEP 6: INSTRUCTOR PREPARES STUDENTS FOR THE LANGUAGE DEMANDS OF COMPILING AND ANALYZING DATA

After successfully gathering information, students are confronted with the challenges of organizing and synthesizing information that may have been collected from different sources and by different individuals. The instructor can prepare students for the demands of the compilation and analysis stage by setting up sessions in which students organize sets of materials, and then evaluate, analyze, and interpret them with an eye toward determining which are most appropriate for the supporters and opponents of a given proposition. Introducing students to graphic representations (e.g., grids and charts) that might highlight relationships among ideas is particularly useful at this point.

STEP 7: STUDENTS COMPILE AND ANALYZE INFORMATION

With the assistance of a variety of organizational techniques (including graphic organizers), students compile and analyze information to identify data that are particularly relevant to the project. Student teams weigh the value of the collected data, discarding some because of their inappropriateness for the project and keeping the rest. Students determine which information represents primary "evidence" for the supporters and opponents of their proposition. It is at this point that topical teams divide themselves into two groups and begin to work separately to build the strongest case for the debate.

STEP 8: INSTRUCTOR PREPARES STUDENTS FOR THE LANGUAGE DEMANDS OF PRESENTATION OF THE FINAL PRODUCT

At this point in the development of the project, instructors can bring in language improvement activities to help students succeed with the presentation of their final products. This might entail practicing oral presentation skills and receiving feedback on voice projection, pronunciation, organization of ideas, and eye contact. It may involve editing and revising written reports, letters, or bulletin-board display text. In the case of the American elections debate project, the instructor focused on conversational gambits to be used during the debate to indicate polite disagreement and to offer divergent perspectives (see Mach, Stoller, & Tardy, 1997). Students practiced their oral presentations and tried to hypothesize the questions they would be asked by opponents. They timed each other and gave each other feedback on content, word choice, persuasiveness, and intonation. Students also worked with the "artists" in their groups to finalize visual displays, to make sure they were grammatically correct and easily interpretable by the audience. Students also created a flyer announcing the debate (see Appendix), which served as an invitation to and reminder for audience members.

STEP 9: STUDENTS PRESENT FINAL PRODUCT

Students are now ready to present the final outcome of their projects. In the American elections project, students staged their debate in front of an audience, following the format previously agreed upon. The audience voted on the persuasiveness of each political party, and a winner was declared. In the case described here, the debate was videotaped so that students could later review their debate performances and receive feedback from the instructor and their peers.

STEP 10: STUDENTS EVALUATE THE PROJECT

Although students and instructors alike often view the presentation of the final product as the last stage in the project work process, it is worthwhile to ask students to reflect on the experience as the last and final step. Students can reflect on the language they mastered to complete the project, the content they learned about the targeted theme (in the case highlighted here, that would be American elections, party platforms, and the role of debate in the election process), the steps they followed to complete the project, and the effectiveness of their final product. Students can be asked how they might proceed differently the next time or what suggestions they have for future project work endeavors. Through these reflective activities, students realize how much they have learned and the teacher benefits from students' insights for future classroom projects.

Conclusion

Content-based instruction and project work provide two means for making English-language classrooms more vibrant environments for learning and collaboration. Project work, however, need not be limited to content-based language classes. Language teachers in more traditional classrooms can diversify instruction with an occasional project. Similarly, teacher educators can integrate projects into their courses to reinforce important pedagogical issues and provide trainees with hands-on experience, a process that may be integrated into future classrooms of their own.

Whether a project centers on American elections, demography, peace education, syllabus design, or methodology, students of varying levels and needs can benefit from the empowering experience that results from participation and collaboration in a project. Although project work may be easier to implement in second language settings because of more readily accessible content resources, teachers in foreign language settings have already proven that with adaptation and creativity, the project approach can be successful and rewarding for teachers and students alike.

References

Alexander, P., Kulikowich, J., & Jetton, T. (1994). The role of subject-matter knowledge and interest in the processing of linear and nonlinear texts. *Review of Educational Research*, *64*(2), 201–252.

Anderson, J. (1990). *Cognitive psychology and its implications*. 3rd ed. New York: W. H. Freeman.

Bereiter, C., & Scardamalia, M. (1993). *Surpassing ourselves: An inquiry into the nature and implications of expertise*. Chicago: Open Court Press.

Brinton, D., Snow, M., & Wesche, M. (1989). *Content-based second language instruction*. New York: Newbury House.

Carter, G., & Thomas, H. (1986). Dear Brown Eyes: Experiential learning in a project-orientated approach. *ELT Journal*, *40*(3), 196–204.

Ferragatti, M., & Carminati, E. (1984). Airport: An Italian version. *Modern English Teacher*, *2*(4), 15–17.

Fried-Booth, D. (1982). Project work with advanced classes. *ELT Journal*, *36*(2), 98–103.

Fried-Booth, D. (1986). *Project work*. New York: Oxford University Press.

Grabe, W., & Stoller, F. (1997). Content-based instruction: Research foundations. In M. Snow & D. Brinton (Eds.), *The content-based classroom: Perspectives on integrating language and content* (pp. 5–21). White Plains, NY: Addison-Wesley Longman.

Haines, S. (1989). *Projects for the EFL classroom: Resource material for teachers*. Walton-on-Thames Surrey, UK: Nelson.

Henry, J. (1994). *Teaching through projects*. London: Kogan Page Limited.

Legutke, M. (1984). Project Airport: Part 1. *Modern English Teacher*, *11*(4), 10–14.

Legutke, M. (1985). Project Airport: Part 2. *Modern English Teacher*, *12*(1), 28–31.

Legutke, M., & Thiel, W. (1983). *Airport: Ein project für der Englischunterricht in Klasse 6*. Hessisches Institut für Bildungsplanung und Schulentwicklung (HIBS), Abt. IE, Bodenstedstrasse 7, D 6200 Wiesbaden.

Legutke, M., & Thomas, H. (1991). *Process and experience in the language classroom*. New York: Longman.

Mach, T., Stoller, F., & Tardy, C. (1997). A gambit-driven debate. In D. Brinton & P. Master (Eds.), *New Ways in Content-Based Instruction* (pp. 64–68). Alexandria, VA: TESOL.

Papandreou, A. (1994). An application of the projects approach to EFL. *English Teaching Forum*, *32*(3), 41–42.

Sheppard, K., & Stoller, F. (1995). Guidelines for the integration of student projects in ESP classrooms. *English Teaching Forum*, *33*(2), 10–15.

Singer, M. (1990). *Psychology of language: An introduction to sentence and discourse processing*. Hillsdale, NJ: Lawrence Erlbaum.

Ward, G. (1988). *I've got a project on* … New South Wales, Australia: Primary English Teaching Association.

Endnotes

[1] This ESP project, titled "Connecting Europe with a New Plug," was designed by Italian instructors Laura Chiozzotto, Innocenza Giannasi, Laura Paperini, and Antonio Ragosa for students of electrotechnics and electronics.

[2] A project similar to this, titled "Wall Newspaper: Know Your EFL Teachers," was developed by Kris Hoover for students at the International School in Bangkok, Thailand. The project is an adaptation of Fried-Booth's (1986) "Staff Portrait Gallery" project (pp. 21–23).

[3] This debate was the culminating activity in a theme-based unit on censorship, designed by Kevin Eyraud and Gillian Giles in collaboration with their EAP students, at Northern Arizona University.

[4] The thematic unit outlined here is fashioned after a similar unit developed and implemented by Gillian Giles and Susan Koenig at Northern Arizona University.

Appendix: Student-Generated Poster Publicizing Debate

You are invited to a debate between
the Freedom Party & the International Experts Party!

Where: Liberal Arts Building, Room 110
When: November 7
Time: 11:00–11:40 A.M.

ESL students will represent two diverse political parties
and will debate each other on contemporary political issues.

You are invited to attend and then vote
on the most persuasive party.

Please come and vote! Be part of the political process!

SECTION 6

LEARNING STRATEGIES

INTRODUCTION

Interests in learning strategies began with the publication of papers collectively known as the "good language learner" studies (see Cohen & Weaver, 1998). Since then, hundreds of studies have been generated that look at different aspects of learning strategies and their roles in language learning. In an effort to make sense of the huge database and numerous research findings in this area, Oxford (1990, in Cohen & Weaver, 1998) differentiates learning strategies into the following categories:

COGNITIVE

Cognitive strategies involve the identification, retention, and retrieval of language elements. For example, students may use memory-enhancing strategies (e.g., the keyword method) to help them remember new words.

METACOGNITIVE

Strategies of this type deal with the planning, monitoring, and evaluation of language learning activities. For example, students may develop a plan for monitoring their progress by constantly comparing their current level of proficiency with the course goals outlined in the curriculum.

AFFECTIVE

Affective strategies are those that serve to regulate emotions, attitudes, and motivation. For example, students may read linguistically simplified books to develop a positive attitude toward reading materials.

SOCIAL

These strategies refer to actions learners take to interact with users of the language. For example, students may deliberately seek out opportunities to use the target language with native speakers of the language.

Language learning strategies remain an active area of research. Despite extensive research, many theoretical and practical issues still need to be addressed. In the first article in this section, Oxford surveys recent learning-strategy research with a view to identifying instructional implications that can be derived from this body of research. The implications of learning-strategy research for ESL instruction are, Oxford suggests, quite considerable, given evidence which shows that appropriate use of learning strategies can result in increased L2 proficiency. Although our knowledge of learning strategies is still not complete, the research to date suggests the following implications:

- Strategy training should form an integral part of regular classroom events.
- Strategy instruction should be embedded in meaningful communicative contexts.
- Students should be taught how to identify and analyze their preferred learning strategies by means of diaries, learning journals, interviews, and surveys.
- Teachers should provide explicit explanation and modeling of strategy use, and provide ample opportunities for practice.
- Strategy training takes time. It may take months or even years to be able to use learning strategies effectively.

Oxford concludes by saying that teachers should routinely conduct research in their own classroom to better understand the numerous factors which affect the choice and skillful use of learning strategies.

The second article, by Nunan, describes an action research project designed to find out ways to make students more active in their learning and to make them more aware of the language learning processes so that they can have a greater control over their own learning. Nunan demonstrates that tasks and activities that encourage learners to reflect on their own learning can and should be incorporated in the curriculum, as these can help learners develop skills in self-checking, monitoring, and evaluation – skills students need to become strategic and independent learners. In addition, by the end of the research project, the students were more concerned with how to learn rather than with what to learn, with the communicative dimensions of language learning rather than with the grammar of the language, and with discourse errors rather than with sentence errors. Also, as a result of the awareness of their purpose of learning English, students were more eager to seek opportunities to use English beyond the classroom.

Discussion Questions

Before Reading

1. What are learning strategies? What do you think are the roles of learning strategies in second language learning?
2. Rehearsal is a memory strategy most often employed by second language learners. How effective is this strategy?

3. Some students report using a memory-enhancing strategy known as mnemonics (e.g., the keyword method). How useful is this strategy for vocabulary learning?
4. Describe the strategies you used when learning a second or foreign language. Which strategies contributed most to your proficiency in the language?
5. In second language learning, what strategies are considered good and what strategies are considered less effective? Give some examples.
6. Can learning strategies be taught? Explain your answer.
7. What are the differences between successful and less successful learners in terms of strategy use? Do successful learners use more strategies?
8. Do younger and older learners use the same or similar strategies? Which strategies are useful for each group of learners?

After Reading

1. How do you find out about the strategies that your students use? Suggest at least three ways of identifying your students' learning strategies. Which one is the most practical for classroom teachers?
2. Review the article by Nunan. What are the key findings of the study described by Nunan?
3. Design a similar study utilizing the same procedures outlined by Nunan. In your design, include the following:
   - research questions
   - profile of your students (age, proficiency level, purpose of language study)
   - instruments (e.g., questionnaire, test)
   - research procedures
   - length of the study
4. What do you think are the strategies that good language learners use to improve their skills in reading, writing, listening, speaking, pronunciation, vocabulary, and grammar?
5. Select three good strategies each for reading, writing, listening, speaking, pronunciation, vocabulary, and grammar. Suggest ways of teaching those strategies in your lessons.
6. Learner autonomy is an important goal in many ESL programs. In what ways can strategy training help students develop autonomy?
7. Review the article by Oxford and define the following concepts:
   - cognitive strategy
   - metacognitive strategy

   Also discuss how the two types of strategies can be exploited to enhance second language learning.
8. According to Oxford, what are some of the most important implications of learning-strategy research for second language instruction? Do you agree with Oxford?

Further Reading

Cohen, A. D., & Weaver, S. J. (1998). Strategies-based instructions for second language learners. In W. A. Renandya & G. M. Jacobs (Eds.), *Learners and language learning* (pp. 1–25). Singapore: SEAMEO Regional Language Centre.

CHAPTER 11

Language Learning Strategies in a Nutshell: Update and ESL Suggestions

Rebecca L. Oxford

INTRODUCTION

In learning ESL, Trang watches TV soap operas from the United States, guessing the meaning of new expressions and predicting what will come next. Feng-ji memorizes pages of words from an English dictionary and breaks the words into their components. Amany meets with an English-speaking conversation partner for lunch three times a week. Haruko arranges to live with an American family so she can learn the culture and language in a full-time immersion situation. Masha tapes English labels to all the objects in her dorm room. Marcel practices song lyrics in English, moving freely to the music while singing. Luis regularly reads *Newsweek,* the *New York Times, Parade*, and even American comic books. Boris draws pictures of new words and creates flow charts showing how they fit together semantically. Marie-France uses a green highlighting pen to mark the main points in the notes she takes in class, and later she outlines the notes and writes a summary. Jing-Mei, who is afraid to speak English, encourages herself by using positive affirmations and self-praise. Hermann keeps a diary to evaluate his daily performance in learning English.

All these people are employing language learning strategies – specific actions, behaviors, steps, or techniques that students (often intentionally) use to improve their progress in developing L2 skills. These strategies can facilitate the internalization, storage, retrieval, or use of the new language. Strategies are tools for the self-directed involvement necessary for developing communicative ability.

An updated, brief, and practical synopsis of the latest learning-strategy research follows along with suggestions to the teacher and a summary of these instructional implications.

Learning about Learning Strategies

Frequently used techniques for assessing students' L2 strategies include informal or formal interviews, group discussions, language learning diaries, dialogue journals between student and teacher, open-ended surveys, structured three- or five-point surveys of strategy frequency, and think-aloud procedures that require students to describe their strategies aloud while using them. Observational methods are often difficult to employ because many learning strategies are internal and thus invisible to observers. Therefore, much learning-strategy research depends on learners' willingness and ability to describe their internal behaviors, both cognitive and affective (emotional) (Brown, 1989; Harlow, 1988). By conducting studies with clear instructions in nonthreatening circumstances, researchers have found that many or most L2 learners are capable of remembering their learning strategies and describing them when asked.

Results of Research on Learning Strategies

OUTSIDE THE L2 FIELD

Research on learning strategies has boomed outside the L2 field and has profoundly influenced language research. Non-L2 researchers have discovered that effective learners actively associate new information with existing information in long-term memory, building increasingly intricate and differentiated mental structures or schemata. The use of well-chosen strategies distinguishes experts from novices in many learning areas, such as physics, native language reading, and mechanical engineering.

Some might question whether studying experts' use of strategies really helps us understand how to teach novices. There may be many factors other than the use of particular strategies – factors such as maturity, comprehension of one's own learning style preferences (visual, auditory, and so on), and previous experience – that separate experts from novices. Certainly more research is needed on this topic before all the accolades go to learning strategies as the single cause of expert performance.

According to non-L2 research, successful learners often use *metacognitive* strategies such as organizing, evaluating, and planning their learning. Use of these behaviors – along with *cognitive* strategies such as analyzing, reasoning, transferring information, taking notes, and summarizing – might be considered part of any definition of truly effective learning (Brown, Bransford, Ferrara, & Campione, 1983).

Some non-L2 strategy research has concentrated on the emotional and social side of learning. Results show that a number of the best learners use *affective* and *social* strategies to control their emotions, to stay motivated, to cooperate, and to get help (Dansereau, 1985; McCombs, 1988).

IN THE L2 FIELD

EARLY LISTS

Some 15 years ago, L2 researchers made lists of strategies presumed to be essential for all "good language learners." Rubin (1975) suggested that good language learners (*a*) willingly and accurately guess, (*b*) want to communicate, (*c*) are uninhibited about mistakes, (*d*) focus on both structure and meaning, (*e*) take advantage of all practice opportunities, and (*f*) monitor their own speech and that of others. Another vintage list (Naiman, Frohlich, & Todesco, 1975) added that successful L2 learners think in the language and address the affective aspects of language learning.

EFFECTIVENESS OF STRATEGY USE

Research indicates that appropriate use of language learning strategies, which include dozens or even hundreds of possible behaviors (such as seeking out conversation partners, grouping words to be memorized, or giving oneself encouragement), results in improved L2 proficiency overall, or in specific language skill areas.

ORCHESTRATION BY EFFECTIVE LEARNERS

Research suggests that effective L2 learners are aware of the strategies they use and why they employ them, as found in both diary studies (Lavine & Oxford, forthcoming) and think-aloud procedures (O'Malley & Chamot, 1990). Skilled L2 learners select strategies that work well together and that are tailored to the requirements of the language task. For high-performing L2 learners, cognitive and metacognitive strategies often go together. Learners far less often cite social and affective strategies, perhaps because L2 researchers fail to ask about them in detail and perhaps because even skilled learners mistakenly hesitate to consider these as real strategies.

LESS SUCCESSFUL LEARNERS

Research suggests that less skilled L2 learners sometimes are not even aware of the noncommunicative or rather mundane strategies they use, such as translation, rote memorization, and repetition (Nyikos, 1987). However, more recent research indicates that many of the less effective L2 learners are indeed aware of the strategies they use, can describe them clearly, and actually use just as many strategies as effective L2 learners. However, less effective learners apply these strategies in a random, even desperate manner, without careful orchestration and without targeting the strategies to the task (Vann & Abraham, 1989). They do not construct a well-ordered L2 system, but instead retain an untidy assemblage of unrelated fragments (Galloway & Labarca, 1991; Stern, 1975).

STRATEGY TRAINING STUDIES

Studies have indicated that L2 strategy training is frequently successful, but this has not been consistently confirmed (see, for example, O'Malley & Chamot, 1990). Some strategy training has been effective in various skill areas but not in others, even within the same study. However, problems in the research methodology might have obscured some potentially important findings. Such problems include (*a*) too short a period for strategy training, (*b*) disproportionate ease or difficulty of the training task, (*c*) lack of integration of the training into normal language classwork and perceived irrelevance of the training, and (*d*) inadequate pretraining assessment of learners' initial strategy use and needs.

Unfortunately, many L2 strategy training studies have ignored powerful affective and social strategies such as positive self-talk, self-reward, and cooperative learning (Horwitz, 1990; Lavine & Oxford, 1990) in favor of a concentration on metacognitive and cognitive strategies – the more purely intellectual aspects of language learning.

However, some L2 strategy training programs have focused on a more even balance of strategies, including affective and social strategies along with a variety of others. Six very useful, naturalistic, nonquantitative case studies (Oxford, Crookall, Cohen, Lavine, Nyikos, & Sutter, 1990) show strategy training success despite very different populations.

Both L2 and non-L2 studies have shown that the most effective strategy training is explicit: Learners are told overtly that a particular behavior or strategy is likely to be helpful, and they are taught how to use it and how to transfer it to new situations. Blind training, in which students are led to use certain strategies without realizing it, is less successful, particularly in the transfer of strategies to new tasks. Strategy training succeeds best when it is woven into regular class activities on a normal basis, according to most research.

INFLUENCE ON STRATEGY USE

Research indicates that factors influencing the L2 student's choice of learning strategies include motivation, career/academic specialization, sex, cultural background, nature of task, age, and stage of language learning. More motivated L2 students typically used more strategies than less motivated students, whether in intensive classrooms, regular classrooms, or even satellite language programs (Oxford, 1989; Oxford & Nyikos, 1989; Oxford, Park-Oh, Ito, & Sumrall, 1993). Career or academic orientation was significant in strategy choice: Engineering students, for instance, chose learning strategies that were more analytic than those selected by humanities students. Females reported greater strategy use than males in several studies (summarized by Oxford, Nyikos, & Ehrman, 1988). Cultural background also correlated with strategy choice: For example, rote memorization was more prevalent among Asian ESL students than among their Hispanic counterparts. The nature of the task – conversation versus letter writing, listening for details versus listening for the main idea – helped determine the strategies used to do the activity. Students of different ages and different stages of L2 learning used different learning strategies, with more sophisticated strategies often being employed by more advanced students.

LEARNING STYLES AND STRATEGIES

Language learning style (general approach to language learning) has been identified as another key determiner of L2 strategy choice. When allowed to learn in their favorite way, unpressured by learning environment or other factors, students often use strategies that directly reflect their preferred learning. For example, students with an analytic learning style prefer strategies such as contrastive analysis, rule learning, and dissecting words and phrases, whereas students with a global style use strategies that help them find the big picture (i.e., guessing, scanning, predicting) and assist them in conversing without knowing all the words (i.e., paraphrasing, gesturing). Visually oriented students use strategies such as listing, word grouping, and so on, whereas those with an auditory preference like to work with tapes and practice aloud. Students whose style includes tolerance for ambiguity use significantly different learning strategies in some instances from those used by students who are intolerant of ambiguity.

Investigators have found a statistical link between students' L2 learning strategies and their underlying learning styles (Ehrman & Oxford, 1990; Ely, 1989). These styles are often directly related to culturally inculcated values.

Research has also shown that students can stretch beyond their learning style to use a variety of valuable L2 strategies that are initially uncomfortable. Strategy training is particularly useful in helping students use new strategies beyond their normal stylistic boundaries. Strategy training that takes learning style into account helps students avoid "style wars" with teachers and fellow students and can reveal deeply held cultural values and increase cross-cultural understanding (Scarcella & Oxford, 1992).

LIMITATIONS AND POTENTIAL OF RESEARCH

L2 researchers have spent countless hours trying to define and systematize the wide array of possible language learning strategies. These strategy systems can be categorized as follows: (*a*) systems related to behaviors of successful language learners; (*b*) systems based on psychological functions, such as cognitive, metacognitive, and affective; (*c*) linguistically based strategy systems dealing with inferencing, language monitoring, formal rule practicing, and functional (communicative) practicing; (*d*) systems based on particular language skills, such as oral production, vocabulary learning, reading comprehension, or writing; and (*e*) systems based on different types (or styles) of learners.

Although the existence of these five distinct categories representing more than two dozen strategy systems shows a great deal of ingenuity and creativity on the part of researchers, it also suggests a major problem in L2 strategy research: lack of a coherent, widely accepted system for describing strategies. Competing types of systems exist, all vying for attention in different studies. This situation makes results of investigations sometimes difficult to compare and causes direct replications of a particular study – a fundamental necessity in *any* research area – to be extremely rare.

To place strategies into a more coherent and comprehensive typology and to redress the woeful lack of research emphasis given to social and affective strategies, I developed a strategy system that contains six sets of L2 learning behaviors (Oxford, 1990). This system is based on the theory that the learner is a "whole person" who uses intellectual, social, emotional, and physical resources and is therefore not merely a cognitive/metacognitive information-processing machine. The system includes these strategy groups: (*a*) *affective*, such as anxiety reduction through laughter and meditation, self-encouragement through affirmations, and self-reward through praise and tangible reinforcement; (*b*) *social*, such as asking questions, cooperating with native speakers of the language, and becoming culturally aware; (*c*) *metacognitive*, such as paying attention, consciously searching for practice opportunities, planning for language tasks, self-evaluating progress, and monitoring errors; (*d*) *memory-related*, such as grouping, imagery, rhyming, moving physically, and structured reviewing; (*e*) *general cognitive*, such as reasoning, analyzing, summarizing, and practicing; and (*f*) *compensatory* (to make up for limited knowledge), such as guessing meanings from the context and using synonyms and gestures to convey meaning. Several hundred strategies (and/or subordinate tactics) have been identified, each fitting into one of these six groups. Although this typology is by no means perfect, its "whole person" theoretical orientation toward L2 learning behaviors has the potential to expand the traditionally limited conception of what happens when learning a new language.

More strategy training studies should be conducted in both informal and formal L2 settings, so that we can be more certain about the optimum procedures for helping students improve their strategies. It is likely that most of the principles noted earlier (e.g., explicit training interwoven into normal classroom activities, spread out over a long period of time with plenty of practice and transfer opportunities) will be validated, but different ethnic and cultural groups might need somewhat different strategy instruction techniques. For instance, students from Korea might want the teacher-as-strategy-trainer to remain a serious authority figure, whereas students from Colombia might feel comfortable with the teacher serving in a more facilitating and less directive role.

Encouraging Effective Language Learning Strategy Use: Suggestions for ESL Instructors

1. It is relatively easy to find out about your students' learning strategies. The simplest methods to use regularly are strategy diaries, structured surveys (such as the Strategy Inventory for Language Learning), and informal classrom discussions about strategies that students use.
2. Be concerned about a wide range of strategies, not just the commonly discussed cognitive and metacognitive strategies. Help your students understand the whole spectrum of strategies, including affective and social ones.
3. When time is limited or with large ESL classes, some teachers globally classify each student as an "A" student or a "C" student, or as a "quiet person" or a "talkative

person." These are not very useful descriptions because they do not give enough details. Look more closely at each of your ESL students regarding the features of "good language learners" listed earlier. Identify which of these characteristics each student has and which he or she lacks. Identify learning strategies you might teach your student to move him or her closer to the profile of a "good language learner."

4. Study the effectiveness of the particular learning strategies your ESL students use. Through strategy surveys, observations, and talking with students, figure out which language learning strategies are most closely allied to good performance in your ESL classes. Notice which strategies are most useful for which kinds of language tasks.

5. You can teach students to orchestrate their use of strategies by having them systematically combine and use strategies relevant to the ESL task at hand. For example, begin with a metacognitive strategy (such as planning for the task), then unite a cognitive with a social strategy (analyzing or practicing expressions in cooperation with other students), and finally combine a metacognitive strategy and an affective strategy (such as self-evaluating progress and self-rewarding for good performance). You can encourage students to use the affective strategy of self-talk at any time. These activities help students see that two keys to successful ESL learning are combining strategies and linking them to the specific language task.

6. Help your ESL students understand that for most language learners, the organized, reasoned use of learning strategies is more important than the sheer frequency of strategy use. Give students examples of random strategy use (e.g., simultaneously using strategies that do not support each other well, such as outlining, visualizing, scanning, guessing, and using circumlocution) and show why it does not help. Provide them with practice in tailoring and orchestrating their strategy use as discussed earlier.

7. Give explicit directions about strategy use and offer practice in transferring the strategies to new situations and tasks. Integrate strategy training with your regular instructional activities over an extended period of time (say, a semester or a year); do not separate it as a minicourse on language learning strategies.

   Base the strategy training that you give your students on their own ESL communication needs. Be sure to include affective and social strategies along with other types of strategies. Choose strategies that mesh with and support each other so that they fit the requirements of the language task and the learners' goals. Provide plenty of strategy practice with meaningful, communicative ESL materials. Ask learners to evaluate their success in using strategies. Observe any changes in language performance based on strategy use. (See Chamot & Kupper, 1989, and Oxford, 1990, for additional strategy training tips.)

8. Pay attention to the range of factors influencing strategy use among your ESL students and those you can personally affect. For instance, you can control the nature of the language tasks in the ESL classroom, and you have a great deal of influence on students' motivation level. Take advantage of the factors that you can control, and be aware of those over which you have no control (e.g., cultural background, gender, age).

9. Assess the learning styles and strategies your students use. Many different learning style surveys exist (see Oxford, Ehrman, & Lavine, 1991). Explain the nature and significance of learning styles to your students, and how their learning style preferences strongly determine their favorite learning strategies. During strategy training, explain that you are encouraging students to stretch beyond their natural style to use learning strategies that are very helpful but that may not be instantly comfortable. For instance, for certain tasks, global students sometimes need to use

analytic strategies such as reasoning deductively (from a rule to a specific case), and analytic students sometimes need to move away from the details to look at the general meaning through global strategies such as skimming and summarizing.

Summary of Implications for ESL Instruction

Although complete evidence is not yet available, and although the research improvements cited earlier are necessary, there are some potentially important implications for ESL instruction based on existing findings.

ESL teachers can help their students recognize the power of consciously using language learning strategies to make learning quicker, easier, more effective, and more fun. To help all students become more aware of their strategy choices, ESL teachers can assist students in identifying their own current learning strategies by means of diaries, surveys, or interviews.

ESL teachers can then weave learning strategy training into regular classroom events in a natural but highly explicit way, providing ample opportunity for practicing strategies and transferring them to new tasks. Strategy instruction can include information about learning styles on which the students partially base their choice of learning strategies and can highlight cultural differences in learning strategies and styles that exist in any ESL classroom. ESL teachers should tailor strategy training to the real, communicative needs of learners in the particular situation.

Strategy training can help students make effective use of multiple strategies. Metacognitive strategies help students keep themselves on track; cognitive, memory, and compensation strategies provide the necessary intellectual tools; and affective and social strategies offer continuous emotional and interpersonal support. Teachers' action research on language learning strategies or on strategy training should cover this wide array of strategies and should not be limited to just one or two types of techniques.

L2 learning strategy research is in its early stages, having only begun in earnest in the 1980s. As might be expected in any new research area, difficulty still exists in conceptualizing and defining learning strategies in a uniformly meaningful, comprehensive way. Nevertheless, recent L2 strategy research offers potentially significant implications for all ESL teachers who want to improve their instructional effectiveness. These teachers and their students can benefit greatly from what the research has already found and will gain more from future investigations.

References

Brown, A. L., Bransford, J. D., Ferrara, R. A., & Campione, J. C. (1983). Learning, remembering, and understanding. In J. H. Flavell & E. M. Markham (Eds.), *Carmichael's manual of child psychology* (Vol. 1). New York: Wiley.

Brown, H. D. (1989). *A practical guide to language learning: A fifteen-week program of strategies for success*. New York: McGraw-Hill.

Chamot, A. U., & Kupper, L. (1989). Learning strategies in foreign language instruction. *Foreign Language Annals, 22*, 13–24.

Dansereau, D. (1985). Learning strategy research. In J. W. Segal, S. F. Chipman, & R. C. Glaser (Eds.), *Thinking and learning skills: Relating learning to basic research* (pp. 209–240). Hillsdale, NJ: Erlbaum.

Ehrman, M. E., & Oxford, R. L. (1990). Adult language learning styles and strategies in an intensive training setting. *Modern Language Journal, 74*, 311–327.

Ely, C. (1989). Tolerance of ambiguity and use of second language learning strategies. *Foreign Language Annals, 22*, 437–445.

Galloway, V., & Labarca, A. (1991). From students to learners: Style, process, and strategy. In D. W. Birchnichler (Ed.), *New perspectives and new directions in foreign language education* (pp. 111–158). Lincolnwood, IL: National Textbook Company and American Council on the Teaching of Foreign Languages.

Harlow, L. (1988). The effects of the yellow highlighter – second language learner strategies and their effectiveness: A research update. *Canadian Modern Language Review, 45*, 91–102.

Horwitz, E. K. (1990). Attending to the affective domain in foreign language learning. In S. S. Magnan (Ed.), *Shifting the instructional focus to the learner* (pp. 15–33). Middlebury, VT: Northeast Conference on the Teaching of Foreign Languages.

Lavine, R. Z., & Oxford, R. L. (1990, December). Addressing affective issues in the second and foreign language classroom. Paper presented at the annual meeting of the Modern Language Association, Chicago.

Lavine, R. Z., & Oxford, R. L. (Forthcoming). *Language learning diaries: Let the learners tell us.*

McCombs, B. L. (1988). Motivational skills training: Combining metacognitive, cognitive, and affective learning strategies. In C. Weinstein, E. T. Goetz, & P. A. Alexander (Eds.), *Learning and study strategies: Issues in assessment, instruction, and evaluation* (pp. 141–169). New York: Academic Press.

Naiman, N., Frohlich, M., & Todesco, A. (1975). The good second language learner. *TESL Talk, 6*, 68–75.

Nyikos, M. (1987). The effect of color and imagery as mnemonic strategies on learning and retention of lexical items in German. Unpublished doctoral dissertation, Purdue University, West Lafayette, IN.

O'Malley, J. M., & Chamot, A. U. (1990). *Learning strategies in second language acquisition*. Cambridge: Cambridge University Press.

Oxford, R. L. (1989). Use of language learning strategies: A synthesis of studies with implications for strategy training. *System, 17*, 235–247.

Oxford, R. L. (1990). *Language learning strategies: What every teacher should know*. New York: Newbury House/Harper & Row.

Oxford, R. L., Crookall, D., Cohen, A. D., Lavine, R. Z., Nyikos, M., & Sutter, W. (1990). Strategy training for language learners: Six situational case studies and a training model. *Foreign Language Annals, 22*, 197–216.

Oxford, R. L., Ehrman, M. E., & Lavine, R. Z. (1991). Style wars: Teacher-student style conflicts in the language classroom. In S. S. Magnan (Ed.), *Challenges in the 1990s for college foreign language programs* (pp. 1–35). Boston, MA: Heinle & Heinle.

Oxford, R. L., & Nyikos, M. (1989). Variables affecting choice of language learning strategies by university students. *Modern Language Journal, 73*, 291–300.

Oxford, R. L., Nyikos, M., & Ehrman, M. E. (1988). Vive la différence: Reflections on sex differences in the use of language learning strategies. *Foreign Language Annals, 21*, 321–329.

Oxford, R. L., Park-Oh, Y., Ito, S., & Sumrall, M. (1993). Learning Japanese by satellite: What influences student achievement? *System, 21*(1).

Rubin, J. (1975). What the "good language learner" can teach us. *TESOL Quarterly, 9*, 41–51.

Scarcella, R., & Oxford, R. L. (1992). *The tapestry of language learning: The individual in the communicative classroom*. Boston, MA: Heinle & Heinle.

Stern, H. H. (1975). What can we learn from the good language learner? *Canadian Modern Language Review, 31*, 304–318.

Vann, R., & Abraham, R. (1989, April). Strategies of unsuccessful language learners. Paper presented at the annual meeting of Teachers of English to Speakers of Other Languages, San Francisco, CA.

CHAPTER 12

Learner Strategy Training in the Classroom: An Action Research Study

David Nunan

When I was in secondary school, I seldom asked questions. The reason was that the teacher always tried to explain the stuffs as detailed as possible, leaving no queries among students. Only the most curious student will ask questions. This method is well-known as the spoon-feeding education system in which we are fed with piles of notes and text books. On the other hand, students . . . only care about getting results good enough to enter a university. Students gradually become examination oriented. Eventually less and less students care about acquiring knowledge, which should be the aim of education. But in universities, things are totally different. Lecturers only give a brief talk on the topics, leave a hugh area for students to explore by themselves. This means that spoon-feed system no longer exists. Students cannot rely on the knowledge acquired in lectures.

(Sandy [pseudonym], a first-year student at the University of Hong Kong)

Introduction

It was students such as Sandy who prompted me to carry out an action research study at the University of Hong Kong. Because of my students' prior schooling experience, they expect the teacher to structure the learning situation for them, telling them what to learn and how to learn, as their high school teachers have done. Many of them have difficulty coming to terms with the very different learning environment that they encounter once they enter college. I decided, therefore, to see whether incorporating a learning strategy and self-monitoring dimension into the classroom would help my students develop the self-reflective orientation they would need to realize their potential as university students.

The Project

This small-scale action research project involved several groups of first-year undergraduate liberal arts students at the University of Hong Kong. In all, sixty students were involved in the project. The central purpose of the strategy training was to experiment with ways of making the students more active participants in their language learning. Through providing the learners with systematic opportunities to focus on the processes underlying their language learning and the patterns of their language use, I hoped to help them gradually achieve a greater sensitivity to their language acquisition and thus be in a better position to be in control of their subsequent English language development.

The action research questions that I explored were the following:

1. Would learner strategy training lead to greater sensitivity to the language learning process on the part of my students?
2. What effect would guided reflection and self-reporting have on the development of learning skills?
3. To what extent would guided reflection and self-reporting lead these learners to formulate more realistic learning goals?
4. Would strategy training encourage my students to apply their language skills beyond the classroom?

Procedure

At the beginning of the semester, I introduced students to the aim of the project and invited them to take part in it. They were told that, although the strategy training course was part of their regular program, they did not have to participate in the action research component if they did not want to. The research project, they were told, would involve having them monitor and report on their strategy use and personal goals for strategy development. In fact, almost all of the students did take part.

At the end of the first week, guided journals were filled out by those participating in the project. These journals contained the following sentence starters, which students were asked to complete.

This week I studied:

This week I learned:

This week I used my English in these places:

This week I spoke English with these people:

This week I made these mistakes:

My difficulties are:

I would like to know:

I would like help with:

My learning and practicing plans for next week are:

Over a 12-week period, all students (whether or not they were participating in the research) took part in the program designed to help them reflect on their own learning; develop their knowledge of and ability to apply learning strategies: assess their own progress; and apply their language skills beyond the classroom. The program was based on a bank of tasks that were divided into four categories. These are described and illustrated below.

Categories of Tasks

CATEGORY 1: STIMULATING A FOCUS ON THE LEARNING PROCESS

DESCRIPTION

Tasks in this section focus on general aspects of the learning process. Such tasks are designed to help learners identify how they like to learn best, to think about what works for them and what does not work, and to compare their approaches to learning with those of other students.

EXAMPLE

The three tasks (see Figure 1) were designed to encourage students to start thinking about some of the general processes underlying the learning process. They have proved useful for students who are just embarking on a new course of study. In the project described here, they were particularly appropriate, as the students were making the rather dramatic transition from high school to university.

When I tabulated the responses given by students to these tasks, the results were quite interesting. By far the most frequently reported concern was worry and embarrassment at being required to speak in front of fellow students. Another concern was a feeling of not being good as a language learner. A third general worry was that students would not be able to understand what was required. I was delighted when the students themselves came up with a proposed solution to the problem of speaking in front of others. They suggested that they be given adequate opportunities to rehearse tasks in pairs and small groups before being asked to speak publicly. I readily agreed to this. I also sought to assure them that I would make the tasks clear to them in ways that they could understand.

CATEGORY 2: FOCUSING ON THE CONTEXT AND ENVIRONMENT OF THE LEARNING PROCESS

DESCRIPTION

This second category includes tasks that encouraged learners to focus on different modes of learning. These are intended to help learners develop skills in working in a variety of different modes, including whole-class work, individualized learning, cooperative learning, pair and group work, self-access learning, and learning beyond the classroom.

EXAMPLE

Tasks in this category were designed to encourage students to think about the how and the where of the learning process. Students are involved in thinking about and discussing questions such as the following:

- What makes a good teacher?
- What are the characteristics of an effective learner?
- How can one make use of resources beyond the classroom itself for learning?

Task 1: Looking Ahead

This is a list of things that often worry students at the beginning of a new course. Read the statements and check off those that you think might apply to you. Now add three to five items of your own.

	YES	MAYBE	NO
1. I'm not sure how much work I'll have to do on this course.	.....	.....	.....
2. I'm worried that there will be too much work to do.	.....	.....	.....
3. I'm worried that I won't be able to understand the teacher.	.....	.....	.....
4. I'm worried that I won't understand what I'm required to do.	.....	.....	.....
5. I'm worried/embarrassed about speaking in front of other students.	.....	.....	.....
6. I don't think I'm very good as a language learner.	.....	.....	.....
7. I don't really feel very motivated to learn.	.....	.....	.....
8. I'm nervous about taking tests.	.....	.....	.....
9. I'm worried that others will think I'm stupid.	.....	.....	.....
10. I'm worried that the course will take up too much of my time.	.....	.....	.....

Task 2: Major Concerns

Compare your responses with those of another student, and make a note of the three most important concerns.

1. ____________________
2. ____________________
3. ____________________

Task 3: Possible Solutions

Compare your major concerns with those of another pair, and take turns brainstorming possible ways of dealing with them.

1. ____________________
2. ____________________
3. ____________________

Now help the other pair with their concerns.

Figure 1

Task 1

Study the following descriptions of small-group tasks and evaluate them according to the following key.

1. I don't like this type of task at all.
2. I don't like this type of task very much.
3. I don't mind this type of task.
4. I like this type of task very much.

A. The class is split into two groups, A and B. You listen to a discussion between three people talking about these aspects of their lifestyle: where they go on vacation. what they like to do on the weekend, their favorite hobby. The other half of the class listens to a discussion between three people talking about these aspects of their lifestyle: their favorite forms of entertainment, their favorite kinds of food, the kinds of sports they play. You then work in pairs with a student from the other group to complete the following form:

	PERSON 1	PERSON 2	PERSON 3
VACATIONS			
ENTERTAINMENT			
WEEKENDS			
FOOD			
HOBBIES			
SPORTS			

TASK RATING: _____

B. You work in pairs. You are given a job description and three job applications. You have to decide which person should get the job.

TASK RATING: _____

C. You read a short passage containing a number of grammatical errors. You have to correct the errors and say what rules have been broken.

TASK RATING: _____

D. You listen to a conversation and then practice it with another student.

TASK RATING: _____

E. You bring an English-language newspaper to class. You work with three or four other students to select an article, and prepare a set of reading comprehension questions to accompany the article. You exchange the article and questions with another group. They read your article and answer your questions. You read their article and answer their questions.

TASK RATING: _____

F. You read a passage in which every fifth word has been deleted. You have to work out which words were deleted and replace them.

TASK RATING: _____

(*continued*)

G. Working with several other students, you carry out a discussion task. You record the discussion. At the conclusion, you listen to the tape and identify your errors.

TASK RATING: ____

H. You take part in a role-play with three or four other students. One of you pretends to be someone who is being interviewed for a job. The other students pretend to be the interviewing panel.

TASK RATING: ____

Task 2

Compare responses with three or four other students and note similarities and differences. Rank the tasks from most to least popular.

Most Popular __ __ __ __ __ __ **Least Popular**

Task 3

Based on the responses you gave to Tasks 1 and 2, decide what makes a good classroom task. (List up to five characteristics.)

1. ______________________
2. ______________________
3. ______________________
4. ______________________
5. ______________________

Task 4

Compare your list with that of another group.

Figure 2

In the activity (see Figure 2), students are encouraged to think about the kinds of tasks that they enjoy, to compare their choices with several other students, and, on the basis of these comparisons, to decide what it is that makes for a good classroom task.

This activity was done twice during the semester, once at the beginning and once again at the end. At the beginning of the semester, the most popular classroom tasks nominated by students were C, D, and F. This was not really surprising, as these are the kinds of tasks that students were familiar with from their English lessons in school. However, by the end of the semester, after they had an opportunity to experiment with more communicative, experiential learning, students gave high ratings to A, B, and H. For this group of learners, at least, the opportunity of exploring new ways of learning was reflected in important attitudinal changes toward the tasks they valued in class.

Other activities that I designed for this second category included tasks for exploring self-access learning facilities, exercises for evaluating the advantages and disadvantages of small-group learning, and simulations in which students explore the various role relationships inherent in different tasks.

CATEGORY 3: DEALING WITH THE MACROSKILLS

DESCRIPTION

Tasks in the third category teach learners strategies for developing the macroskills of reading, writing, listening, and speaking.

EXAMPLE

The example (see Figure 3) gives learners an opportunity to practice selective listening. This is a key processing skill in all second and foreign language contexts, as it teaches students that they need not understand every single word for listening to be successful. It is particularly important in a context such as the University of Hong Kong, where many of the lectures are delivered in English, often by lecturers who are unused to dealing with speakers whose first language is not English.

SELECTIVE LISTENING

At the beginning of the semester, I introduced the students to the range of learning strategies underpinning the tasks in this category. The lowest rating was given to selective listening. However, once students had an opportunity to experiment with and reflect on this particular strategy, it became one of the most popular. This provides further evidence of the usefulness of incorporating a learning-strategy dimension into the curriculum.

Task 1

Selective listening is listening for the most important words and information without trying to understand everything. Working with a student, list situations in which selective listening would be a useful strategy.

Situation 1: ______________________________

Situation 2: ______________________________

Situation 3: ______________________________

Task 2

You are going to hear people talking about how they learned another language. Listen and write down the languages you hear them mention.

Byron: ______________________________

Monica: ______________________________

George: ______________________________

Task 3

Listen again. What strategies do the people use to learn languages?

Byron: ______________________________

Monica: ______________________________

George: ______________________________

Task 4

Compare your responses with those of three or four other students.

(Adapted from Nunan, 1995b)

Figure 3

Task 1

Inductive learning can be an effective way of finding out about grammar. Learning inductively means studying examples of language in use, and finding underlying patterns and rules. Working with another student, think of times when you have used inductive learning techniques. As a student, have your learning experiences been mainly inductive or deductive? (In deductive learning, you are told the rule and asked to apply it, or asked to find examples of the rule in action.) Where or when do you think that inductive learning might be useful?

Task 2

Working with another student, study the following conversation and identify examples of the simple past and present perfect tenses.

A: Tell me, why did you decide to go to Japan?

B: Well, I've always been fascinated by things Japanese, and I've read a lot about the place and its people, and I wanted to see it for myself.

A: And what did you think?

B: Well, it was the most incredible experience I've ever had.

Task 3

Working with another student, match the uses of the simple past and present perfect with the examples by writing a letter next to the appropriate use. Indicate which tense, simple past (SP) or present perfect (PP), is being referred to by writing letters in Column 2.

USE	EXAMPLE	TENSE
1. A state continuing from past to present.	___	___
2. Events in a time period leading up to the present.	___	___
3. Completed events at a definite time in the past.	___	___
4. Habits or recurring events in a period leading to the present.	___	___

EXAMPLES

a. I've been to ten parties in the past month.
b. She didn't come to the party because she was sick.
c. I have decided I'm not the party type.
d. We've been here for hours.

Figure 4

CATEGORY 4: STRATEGIES FOR DEALING WITH PRONUNCIATION, VOCABULARY, GRAMMAR, AND DISCOURSE

DESCRIPTION

The final bank of tasks introduces strategies through which students can work with the various language systems, that is, the development of pronunciation, vocabulary, grammar and discourse. Students are shown how to use context to work out the meaning of unknown words, how to monitor their pronunciation, and how to develop their grammatical knowledge through inductive and deductive learning experiences. Inductive learning is important in all kinds of learning, but is particularly important in language learning. It is particularly valuable to these students because in secondary school they were given few opportunities to figure out the English linguistic system for themselves.

EXAMPLE

The sample presented in Figure 4 is inductive learning, which involves looking for patterns and regularities. In this example, students work through a series of exercises, and then identify the rule underlying the exercises.

INDUCTIVE LEARNING

Working with these inductive activities proved to be very fruitful. Students commented on their newly awakened self-confidence and self-reliance in their language learning. The learners reported that they could see the value of putting themselves in the position of information gatherers.

Results and Discussion

What effect did opportunities for self-monitoring, self-assessing, and strategy development have on the students who took part in the program?

Twice during the course, and again at the end, students taking part in the project completed and handed in their guided journals. These were copied, commented on, and handed back to the students. They were thus part of the teaching/learning process as well as being part of the action research project. (It should be noted that the written teacher comments were in the form of reactions to the substance of the student journals, not to the form. Thus, there was no error correction here.)

If we compare the sorts of responses students provided at the beginning of the program with those they provided at the end, we can see that there are some clear differences. At the end of this section, I have presented responses made by several of the students in the study at the beginning of the course and again at the end (see Figure 5).

Here are some of the conclusions I derived from an analysis of the data provided by the students.

This week I studied: There was a gradual shift over the course of the study from a linguistic focus to a more communicative and applied focus. Students began to see language less as an object to be studied than as a tool to be used.

This week I learned: The point just made can be reiterated here. Student comments began to take on more of a process rather than a product orientation. In other words, they began to reflect on how they learned as much as on what they learned.

This week I used my English in these places: The striking point here was how the very act of posing the question led to change. Simply reflecting on the question seemed to encourage students. It not only promoted a greater sensitivity to the opportunities for communicating outside of the classroom, and, indeed, the university, but it also seemed to encourage students actively to seek out such opportunities.

This week I spoke English with these people: Again, the act of posing the question seemed to have a consciousness-raising function. It seemed to help the students become more aware of their initial limitations in this area. During the 12 weeks, students extended the communicative networks in which they used English. They also seemed to be more prepared to speak to strangers.

This week I made these mistakes: This probe revealed a shift in focus away from errors of pronunciation, grammar, and vocabulary, that is, product errors, toward process errors.

Probe	At the beginning of the course	At the end of the course
This week I studied:	The nature of verbs.	I read a journal article called "Geographic" which is published in New Zealand. I have spent an hour to discuss with my psychology classmates.
This week I learned:	Some more information about English in English linguistics lesson.	The principles of morphology. How to use the self-access centre for learning English.
This week I used my English in these places:	Tutorials. My German lessons.	In the library, Knowles building, KK Leung building. At home. Along the street near my home.
This week I spoke English with these people:	History lecturer, EAS classmates and tutor, linguistics tutor	A foreigner—he asked me where is Lok Fu MTR station. The waiter in Mario restaurant.
This week I made these mistakes:	Using incorrect words.	I spent too much time watching TV while answering questions; I created a word "gesturally."
My difficulties are:	Lack of time.	Understanding the theme of a topic or an article. Writing fluent English essays.
I would like to know:	How to improve my English.	The method that can improve both my listening and speaking skills.
I would like help with:	Dictionaries.	Ensuring I would spend some time on reading but not on other leisure activities. Communicating with foreigners. Watching foreign films. Human resources that can improve my language ability.
My learning and practicing plans for next week are:	To talk more.	To speak up in class and to use English to ask about anything I don't understand in any of my subjects. To try to understand by explaining to my schoolmates some topics of the essay before writing it.

Figure 5

Several students began to explore in their journals causes of cross-cultural communicative breakdown.

My difficulties are: In this and in other areas, students' responses gradually became more detailed, and, at the same time, more precise. All students developed a more accurate understanding of the nature of their difficulties, and some even began to identify ways in which these might be tackled.

I would like to know/I would like help with: Responses in both of these areas tended to overlap. In addition to developing greater precision in their responses, students began to take greater control of their own learning processes. Again, the shift seemed to be away from the content of learning toward the process of learning. During the course of the semester, students started to ask for strategies for getting additional practice outside of the formal language classroom.

My learning and practicing plans for next week are: The most striking finding of this final probe was the way in which students began to make connections between their English study and their other academic subjects. They began to see the value of the English courses for their other subjects and started to seek out ways of using opportunities presented by, for example, departmental tutorials and seminars, for deploying their English.

CONCLUSION

From this action research study, it seems that strategy training, plus the systematic provision of opportunities for learners to reflect on the learning process, did lead to greater sensitivity to the learning process over time. By the end of the course, the learners who took part in the action research project were much more likely to exploit opportunities that existed for language learning and use beyond the classroom than they were at the beginning. The diary entries also indicate that they also seemed to make greater connections between English and content courses. There is also evidence in the diary reports that through engaging in tasks that focus on learning processes as well as language content, learners develop skills for identifying what they want to learn and how they want to learn. Finally, opportunities to reflect on the learning process, and to develop new learning skills, helped learners to identify and articulate differences between their school experiences and those encountered at university.

In practical terms, this study supported the idea that language classrooms should have a dual focus – not only on teaching language content, but also on developing learning processes. (For more detailed information on ways in which these techniques can be incorporated into the classroom, see Ellis & Sinclair, 1989; Nunan, 1995a, 1995b; Willing, 1990.) In the project described here, this was achieved by incorporating a conscious focus on strategies into the curriculum and by encouraging learners themselves to develop skills in self-checking, monitoring, and evaluation.

References

Ellis, G., & Sinclair, B. (1989). *Learning to learn English: A course in learner training.* Cambridge: Cambridge University Press.

Nunan, D. (1995a). Closing the gap between instruction and learning. *TESOL Quarterly, 29*(1), 133–158.

Nunan, D. (1995b). *ATLAS: Learning-centered communication. Levels 1–4*. Boston, MA: Heinle & Heinle/International Thomson.

Willing, K. (1990). *Teaching how to learn.* Sydney, Australia: National Centre for English Language Teaching and Research.

SECTION 7

TEACHING GRAMMAR

Introduction

The role of grammar is perhaps one of the most controversial issues in language teaching. In the early parts of the twentieth century, grammar teaching formed an essential part of language instruction, so much so that other aspects of language learning were either ignored or downplayed. The argument was that if you knew the grammatical rules of the language, you would be able to use it for communication. This concept was strongly challenged in the early 1970s. Knowledge of the grammatical system of the language, it was argued, was but one of the many components which underlay the notion of communicative competence. To be considered a competent user of a language, one needs to know not only the rules of grammar, but also how the rules are used in real communication. During this period, grammar teaching became less prominent, and in some cases, was abandoned.

In recent years, grammar teaching has regained its rightful place in the language curriculum. People now agree that grammar is too important to be ignored, and that without a good knowledge of grammar, learners' language development will be severely constrained. There is now a general consensus that the issue is not whether or not we should teach grammar. The issue now centers on questions such as, Which grammar items do learners need most? How do we go about teaching grammar items in the most effective way? Are they best taught inductively or deductively? In this section, we consider classroom approaches to the teaching of grammar. Although there is no one best method of teaching grammar – and we have to do more research to investigate the effectiveness of the many different techniques advocated by methodologists – we do know what constitutes sound approaches to the teaching of grammar.

In the first article, Swan invites us to reflect on what grammar we teach and why we teach it. He identifies a number of reasons for grammar teaching which do not conform to sound pedagogical principles. For example, teachers often teach grammar simply because it is "easy" to teach and to test. Some attempt to teach the whole grammatical system, thinking that it is both feasible and desirable. As a consequence, we have students who may know a lot of grammar but who are unable to use their knowledge for any practical communicative purposes. Swan suggests that the teaching of grammar should be determined by the needs of the students. Thus, the selection of grammar items to be taught must depend on learners' aims in learning English. Furthermore, the teaching of grammar should be based on the principles of comprehensibility and acceptability.

The second article by Richards examines the assumptions underlying a task-based approach to teaching and identifies some of the practical difficulties that can arise. The most serious of these is the potential for students to perform a task with a poor level of grammatical accuracy, since they can often use communication strategies to bypass some of the language difficulties task performance involves. The result may be that task work develops fluency at the expense of accuracy and leads to the development of fossilized errors that may be difficult to eradicate. In order to address this issue, Richards draws on the work of Skehan and others to examine how a focus on grammatical accuracy can be built into the use of tasks. This involves adding a language-awareness dimension to tasks prior to, during, or after task performance.

The last article, by Ellis, explores the role of practice and consciousness-raising in grammar teaching. Although practice has a role to play in language learning, Ellis maintains that its value is rather limited. He argues that the available evidence seems to suggest that practice, be it controlled, contextualized, or communicative, may not be as effective as people claim it is. Consciousness-raising, on the other hand, offers an attractive alternative to traditional grammar practice. Through carefully designed consciousness-raising activities, learners will develop an explicit knowledge of the grammar of the language which facilitates their ability to communicate. Ellis admits, however, that this approach to grammar instruction has its limitations. It may not be appropriate for young learners or beginners.

Discussion Questions

Before Reading

1. How much grammar does one need in order to be able to communicate comfortably in a second or foreign language?
2. Some people claim that grammar is not very important as long as you can get your message across in the language you are studying. Do you agree with this statement?
3. What has been your experience in learning the grammar of a second language?
4. How do you go about teaching grammar? How do you decide which grammar points to present first, second, and so on?
5. Is grammar best taught in isolation or in context? Explain your answer.
6. Does one have to consciously know the rules of grammar? Why or why not?
7. How important are grammar drills in second language learning? What are the assumptions of discrete grammar practice?
8. How do you correct your students' grammar mistakes? Give at least three different techniques you usually employ in your teaching.

After Reading

1. Swan lists seven bad reasons for teaching grammar. Do you agree with him? Add a few more bad reasons to his list.

2. What does Swan mean by comprehensibility and acceptability? Design an activity that incorporates these two principles of grammar teaching.
3. Observe learners carrying out a task. To what extent does their performance illustrate the features of tasks listed by Richards?
4. Choose an example of a task and plan how it will be used in the classroom. Suggest how an accuracy component can be incorporated into the task either before, during, or after task completion, as discussed by Richards.
5. What are the goals of grammar-focused instruction according to task-based language teaching?
6. Design an activity that promotes conscious noticing of certain grammatical features.
7. What do you think is the role of grammar practice? Do you agree with Ellis that practice has a limited value in grammar learning?
8. What are some of the strengths and limitations of the approach advocated by Ellis?
9. Examine an ESL textbook series and see how grammar is dealt with. What grammar items are included? How are they presented? On what basis are they selected? What are the principles used to sequence these grammar items? To what extent do the exercises link grammar to communicative interaction?
10. Some applied linguists suggest that grammar is best learned incidentally through, for example, extensive reading. Do you agree?
11. Should grammar be taught separately or integrated into the four skills of listening, speaking, reading, and writing?

CHAPTER 13

Seven Bad Reasons for Teaching Grammar – and Two Good Ones

Michael Swan

Grammar is important, but most of the time, in most parts of the world, people probably teach too much of it. I think we can identify at least seven reasons for this.

SEVEN BAD REASONS

BECAUSE IT'S THERE

Asked why he tried to climb Everest, George Mallory famously replied, 'because it is there'. Some teachers take this attitude to the mountain of grammar in their books: It's there, so it has to be climbed. But the grammar points in the course book may not all be equally important for a particular class.

The book may have been written for students with different purposes, studying in a different environment, perhaps with different native languages and different problems. It may have been designed for learners with more time to spend on grammar than they do today. The book may simply have been written by a grammar fanatic. It is important to choose grammar points relevant to students' needs, rather than blindly going through the syllabus from left to right.

In a well-known experiment (Hughes & Lascaratou, 1982), mistakes made by Greek secondary school children were shown to Greek teachers of English, British teachers of English, and British nonteachers. Members of each group graded the mistakes on a scale from 1 (least serious) to 5. Before you read on, you might like to give your own assessment of the seriousness of the mistakes in the sentences in the box and compare your mark with the average gradings given by the Greek teachers (GT) and the British nonteachers (BN).

1. We agreed to went by car.
2. We didn't knew what happened.
3. Dizzys from the wine we decided to go home.
4. The people are too many so and the cars are too many.
5. The bus was hit in front of.
6. There are many accidents because we haven't brought (broad) roads.

Answers

(1) GT 4.6; BN 2.2 (2) GT 4.4; BN 1.8 (3) GT 4.2; BN 2.1 (4) GT 3.0; BN 4.3 (5) GT 2.6; BN 4.3 (6) GT 2.4; BN 4.1

Interestingly, the mistakes which the Greek teachers regarded as most serious were often those that troubled the native speakers least, and vice versa. The native speakers generally gave higher marks to mistakes which impeded their understanding; when discussing the reasons for their assessments, many mentioned 'intelligibility'. The nonnative teachers seemed more disturbed by infringements of common grammar rules; in discussion, they referred frequently to 'basic mistakes'. They seemed most upset by the fact that learners continued to break rules which had been taught earlier and which they 'should' therefore have mastered. Effectively, they were teaching grammar 'because it was there'.

IT'S TIDY

Vocabulary is vast and untidy. We may attempt to systematise it by teaching semantic fields, superordinates and hyponyms, notional/functional categories and the rest, but ultimately vocabulary remains a big muddle. Pronunciation is more easily analysed (especially if you leave out intonation and stress), and it can be presented as a tidy system of phonemes, allophones, syllable structure and so on. However, in Tom McArthur's immortal words, 'pronunciation is that part of a student which is the same at the end of a language course as at the beginning'. That leaves grammar. Grammar looks tidy and is relatively teachable. Although English grammar does not have the kind of inflectional apparatus which makes German or Latin look so magnificently systematic, there are still many things in English that can be arranged in rows or displayed in boxes. Grammar can be presented as a limited series of tidy things which students can learn, apply in exercises, and tick off one by one. Learning grammar is a lot simpler than learning a language.

IT'S TESTABLE

Many students like tests. It is hard to gauge your own progress in a foreign language, and a good test can tell you how you are doing, whether you have learnt what you wanted to, and what level you have reached. Tests show (or appear to show) whether students are learning and whether teachers are teaching properly; they rank learners; and (if you incorporate a pass mark) they can be used to designate successes and create failures. Unfortunately, it is time-consuming and difficult to design and administer tests which really measure overall progress and attainment. On the other hand, grammar tests are relatively simple. So grammar is often used as a testing short cut; and, because of the washback effect of testing, this adds to the pressure to teach it. So we can easily end up just teaching what can be tested (mostly grammar), and testing what we have taught (mostly grammar).

GRAMMAR AS A SECURITY BLANKET

Grammar can be reassuring and comforting. In the convoluted landscape of a foreign language, grammar rules shine out like beacons, giving students the feeling that they can understand and control what is going on. Although this feeling is partly illusory (structural competence only accounts for a portion of what is involved in the mastery of a language), anything that adds to learners' confidence is valuable. However, the 'security blanket' aspect can lead students and teachers to concentrate on grammar to the detriment of other, less codifiable but equally important, aspects of the language.

IT MADE ME WHO I AM

As a student, I worked hard to learn the rules governing capitalisation in German. In the interests of 'simplification', and without consulting me, the authorities have now changed the rules, and my investment has gone down the drain. I am not pleased. If you have struggled to learn something, you feel it must be important. Many foreign language teachers spent a good deal of time when younger learning about tense and aspect, the use of articles, relative clauses and the like; they naturally feel that these things matter a good deal and must be incorporated in their own teaching. In this way, the tendency of an earlier generation to overvalue grammar can be perpetuated.

YOU HAVE TO TEACH THE WHOLE SYSTEM

People often regard grammar as a single interconnected system, all of which has to be learnt if it is to work properly. This is an illusion. Grammar is not something like a car engine, where a fault in one component such as the ignition or fuel supply can cause a complete breakdown. It is more realistic to regard grammar as an accumulation of different elements, some more systematic than others, some linked together tightly or loosely, some completely independent and detachable. We teach – or should teach – selected subsystems, asking for each:

1. How much of this do the students know already from their native language? (A German, unlike a Japanese, knows the main facts about English article use before his or her first lesson.)
2. How much of the rest is important ?
3. How much of that have we got time for?

To try to teach the whole system is to ignore all three of these questions.

POWER

Some teachers – fortunately, a minority – enjoy the power. As a teacher, one can get a kick from knowing more than one's students, from being the authority, from always being right. In language teaching, grammar is the area where this mechanism operates most successfully. A teacher may have a worse accent than some of his or her students; there may be some irritating student in the class with a vast vocabulary of American pop idiom of which the teacher knows nothing; but there is always grammar to fall back on, with its complicated rules and arcane terminology. Even if you have a native-speaking student in your class, he or she will not be able to talk coherently and confidently about progressive infinitives or the use of articles with uncountable nouns. If you can, you win.

Societies like grammar. Grammar involves rules, and rules determine 'correct' behaviour. Education is never neutral, and the teaching methods in any society inevitably reflect attitudes to social control and power relationships. In countries where free speech is valued (up to a point), language classes are likely to let students talk, move about, and join in the decision-making (up to a point). In more authoritarian societies, students are more likely to sit in rows, listen, learn rules, do grammar exercises, make mistakes and get corrected (thus demonstrating who is in control). Examination design follows suit, showing whether the authorities want future voters who are good at expressing themselves or ones who are good at obeying rules. (Guess which !) Examination syllabi the world over also generally include a component which requires great mental agility, is of doubtful value to most people, and is regarded as a touchstone of intellectual capacity. In Western societies, math has taken over this responsibility from Latin, but the grammar of foreign languages plays a useful supporting role.

The Results

Where grammar is given too much priority the result is predictable and well known. 'Course books' become little more than grammar courses. Students do not learn English: They learn grammar, at the expense of other things that matter as much or more. They know the main rules, can pass tests, and may have the illusion that they know the language well. However, when it comes to using the language in practice, they discover that they lack vital elements, typically vocabulary and fluency: They can recite irregular verbs but cannot sustain a conversation. (As J. K. Jerome put it a century ago, few people care to listen to their own irregular verbs recited by young foreigners.) Such an approach is also psychologically counterproductive, in that it tends to make students nervous of making mistakes, undermining their confidence and destroying their motivation.

The Other Extreme

There are bad reasons for *not* teaching grammar, too. When, as sometimes happens, there is a reaction against grammar-heavy syllabi, people often fly to the other extreme and teach little or no grammar. This happened in Britain in the 1970s, when the communicative approach (in itself an excellent development) was widely taken as a justification for teaching 'functions and notions' or 'skills' *instead of* grammar. One of the results of this unfortunate trend was the appearance of a generation of British teachers and teacher trainers many of whom were seriously ignorant of the structure of the language they were professionally teaching. Doing too little grammar (whether out of misguided principle or sheer ignorance) is of course as damaging as doing too much.

Two Good Reasons

There are two good reasons for teaching carefully selected points of grammar.

COMPREHENSIBILITY

Knowing how to build and use certain structures makes it possible to communicate common types of meaning successfully. Without these structures, it is difficult to make comprehensible sentences. We must, therefore, try to identify these structures and teach them well. Precisely what they are is partly open to debate – it is difficult to measure the functional load of a given linguistic item independent of context – but the list will obviously include such things as basic verb forms, interrogative and negative structures, the use of the main tenses, and modal auxiliaries.

ACCEPTABILITY

In some social contexts, serious deviance from native-speaker norms can hinder integration and excite prejudice – a person who speaks 'badly' may not be taken seriously, or may be considered uneducated or stupid. Students may therefore want or need a higher level of grammatical correctness than is required for mere comprehensibility. Potential employers and examiners may also require a high – often unreasonably high – level of grammatical correctness, and if our students' English needs to be acceptable to these authorities, their prejudices must be taken into account.

WHAT TO TEACH

What points of grammar we choose to teach will therefore depend on our circumstances and our learners' aims. Whatever the situation, though, we must make sure that we are teaching only the points of grammar that we need to in the light of these factors, and – of course – that we are teaching them well. If we can manage to focus clearly on these principles, we have a better chance of teaching *English* instead of just teaching grammar.

Reference

Hughes, A., & Lascaratou, C. (1982). Competing criteria for error gravity. *English Language Teaching Journal, 36*(3), 175–182.

CHAPTER 14

Addressing the Grammar Gap in Task Work

Jack C. Richards

Introduction

A current interest in methodology is task-based approaches to teaching. These involve the use of tasks that engage learners in meaningful interaction and negotiation focusing on completion of a task. Learners' grammar needs are determined on the basis of task performance rather than through a predetermined grammar syllabus. However, whether learners develop acceptable levels of grammatical proficiency through such an approach is problematic. This paper reviews current views about the status of grammar learning through task work and suggests that grammar learning can be addressed at several different stages during task performance: prior to the task, during the task, and after the task. Examples are given of how this can be achieved in materials' design and in the classroom.

The status of grammar-focused teaching or, as it is currently referred to, form-focused instruction (see Doughty & Williams, 1998) has undergone a major reassessment since the 1970s. The advent of communicative language teaching ostensibly saw the demise of grammar-based instruction: Grammatical syllabuses were superseded by communicative ones based on functions or tasks; grammar-based methodologies such as the Presentation-Practice-Production (P-P-P) lesson format underlying the Situational Approach gave way to function- and skill-based teaching; and accuracy activities such as drills and grammar practice were replaced by fluency activities based on interactive small-group work. This led to the emergence of a 'fluency-first' pedagogy (Brumfit, 1979) in which students' grammar needs are determined on the basis of their performance on fluency tasks rather than predetermined by a grammatical syllabus. The present paper examines the issue of the

This chapter is reprinted from *Prospect*, 14(1), 4–19 with permission from the National Centre for English Language Teaching and Research (NCELTR), Australia.

level of language often used by learners during fluency work and reviews approaches to addressing this problem within a communicative methodology.

From Grammar-Focused to Task-Focused Instruction

The movement away from grammar-focused instruction has been supported by the findings of second language acquisition research. Skehan (1996b, p. 18) observes:

> The underlying theory for a P-P-P approach has now been discredited. The belief that a precise focus on a particular form leads to learning and automatization (that learners will learn what is taught in the order in which it is taught) no longer carries much credibility in linguistics or psychology.

A core component of fluency-based pedagogy is task work. Nunan (1989, p. 10) offers this definition:

> the communicative task [is] a piece of classroom work which involves learners in comprehending, manipulating, producing or interacting in the target language while their attention is principally focused on meaning rather than form. The task should also have a sense of completeness, being able to stand alone as a communicative act in its own right.

While carrying out communicative tasks, learners are said to receive comprehensible input and modified output, processes believed central to second language acquisition and which ultimately lead to the development of both linguistic and communicative competence (Doughty & Williams, 1998). The belief that successful language learning depends on immersing students in tasks that require them to negotiate meaning and engage in naturalistic and meaningful communication is at the heart of much current thinking about language teaching and has led to a proliferation of teaching materials built around this concept, such as discussion-based materials, communication games, simulations, role-plays and other group or pair-work activities. Skehan (1996b, p. 17) comments optimistically, 'the research strand of SLA now underpins neatly the range of classroom activities imaginatively devised by practitioners of CLT'.

The differences between traditional grammar-focused activities and communicative task work can be summarised as follows (Brumfit, 1979; Ellis, 1994; Skehan, 1996b):

Grammar-Focused Activities

- reflect typical classroom use of language
- focus on the formation of correct examples of language
- produce language for display (as evidence of learning)
- call on explicit knowledge
- elicit a careful (monitored) speech style
- reflect controlled performance
- practise language out of context
- practise small samples of language
- do not require authentic communication

Task-Focused Activities

- reflect natural language use
- call on implicit knowledge

- elicit a vernacular speech style
- reflect automatic performance
- require the use of improvising, paraphrasing, repair and reorganisation
- produce language that is not always predictable
- allow students to select the language they use
- require real communication

In advocating the use of task work in language teaching, the assumption is that learners will develop not only communicative skills but also an acceptable standard of performance through task work. Task work is not intended to promote development of a nonstandard form of English but is seen as part of the process by which linguistic and communicative competence is developed. Skehan (1996a) distinguishes between a strong and weak form of a task-based approach. A strong form sees tasks as the basic unit of teaching and as driving the acquisition process. A weak form sees tasks as a vital part of language instruction but as embedded in a more complex pedagogical context. They are necessary, but may be preceded by focused instruction, and, after use, may be followed by focused instruction which is contingent on task performance (Skehan, 1996a).

But how is an acceptable level of linguistic performance achieved during task work? The strong form of task-based teaching suggests that form will largely look after itself with incidental support from the teacher. Grammar has a mediating role, rather than serving as an end in itself (Thornbury, 1998, p. 112), something which is said to empower both teachers and learners. 'The teacher and the learner have a remarkable degree of flexibility, for they are presented with a set of general learning objectives and problem-solving tasks, and not a list of specific linguistic items' (Kumaravadivelu, 1991, p. 99). As students carry out communicative tasks, they engage in the process of negotiation of meaning, employing strategies such as comprehension checks, confirmation checks, and clarification requests. These lead to a gradual modification of their language output, which over time takes on more and more targetlike features.

Second Thoughts about Task Work

Despite the claims made for task work and the positive effects of fluency activities on classroom motivation, interest level and use of authentic language, a number of concerns remain. One relates to claims made for modification of the learner's linguistic output through the process of negotiation of meaning. In a careful reexamination of negotiation of meaning, Foster studied intermediate EFL students completing information-gap tasks in dyads and small groups. She found little evidence for negotiated interaction and modified utterances and concludes that 'contrary to much SLA theorizing, negotiating for meaning is not a strategy that language learners are predisposed to employ when they encounter gaps in their understanding' (Foster, 1998, p. 1). (See Musumeci, 1996, for similar findings.)

Another concern is the effect of extensive task-work activities on the development of linguistic competence. What is often observed in language classrooms during fluency work is communication marked by low levels of linguistic accuracy. Higgs and Clifford (1982, p. 78), for example, reporting experience with foreign language teaching programs at the Defence Language Institute, observed:

> In programs that have as curricular goals an early emphasis on unstructured communication activities – minimising, or excluding entirely, considerations of grammatical accuracy – it is possible in a fairly short time . . . to provide students with a relatively large vocabulary and a high degree of fluency. . . . These same data suggest that the premature immersion of a

> student into an unstructured or 'free' conversational setting before certain fundamental linguistic structures are more or less in place is not done without cost. There appears to be a real danger of leading students too rapidly into the creative aspects of language use, in that if successful communication is encouraged and rewarded for its own sake, the effect seems to be one of rewarding at the same time the incorrect communication strategies seized upon in attempting to deal with the communication strategies presented.

This is the issue of the grammar gap in task work referred to in the title of this paper. The grammar-gap problem has also been identified by Swain and her colleagues in Toronto, who have studied the acquisition of French by English-speaking students in French immersion classes, where it was found that,

> in spite of the input-rich communicatively oriented classrooms the students participated in, the students did not develop native-like proficiency in French. Although they are fairly well able to get their meanings across in French, even at intermediate and higher grade levels, they often do so with non-target-like morphology, syntax, and discourse patterns. (Swain, 1998, pp. 5–6)

An example of the quality of language used by students during task work is seen in the following example, observed during a role-play task in an EFL secondary school English lesson. One student is playing the role of a doctor and the other a patient, and they are discussing a health problem.

S.1: I'm thirty-four . . . thirty-five.
S.2: Thirty . . . five?
S.1: Five.
S.2: Problem?
S.1: I have . . . a pain in my throat.
S.2: [In Spanish: What do you have?]
S.1: A pain.
S.2: [In Spanish: What's that?]
S.1: [In Spanish: A pain.] A pain.
S.2: Ah, pain.
S.1: Yes, and it makes problem to me when I . . . swallow.
S.2: When do you have . . . ?
S.1: Since yesterday morning.
S.2: [In Spanish: No, I mean, where do you have the pain?] It has a pain in . . . ?
S.1: In my throat.
S.2: Ah. Let it . . . getting, er . . . worse. It can be, er . . . very serious problem and you are, you will go to New York to operate, so . . . operation, . . . the seventh, the 27th, er May. And treatment, you can't eat, er, big meal.
S.1: Big meal, I er, . . . I don't know? Fish?
S.2: Fish you have to eat, er fish, for example.

This example illustrates the point made by Higgs and Clifford (1982, p. 61) that in task work 'communicative competence is [often used as] a term for communication in spite of language, rather than communication through language'. Skehan suggests that the level of communication often observed during task work results from students relying on a lexicalised system of communication that is heavily dependent on vocabulary and memorised chunks of language as well as both verbal and nonverbal communication strategies to get meanings across. Accurate use of grammar or phonology is not necessary in such cases. In the example just cited, for instance, one student avoids asking (or does not know how to ask) 'What is your problem?' and simply says 'Problem?' Instead of saying, 'How long have you had the problem?' the student asks, 'When do you have?' Instead of negotiating for the intended question, the other student jumps straight in with the expected answer: 'Since yesterday morning'. There is no recognition of the inappropriateness of 'it makes problem to me when I . . . swallow'.

Skehan (1996b, p. 22) comments:

> This [task-based] approach places a premium on communication strategies linked to lexicalized communication. These strategies provide an effective incentive for learners to make the best use of the language they already have. But they do not encourage a focus on form. They do not provide an incentive for structural change towards an interlanguage system with greater complexity. The advantages of such an approach are greater fluency and the capacity to solve communication problems. But these advantages may be bought at too high a price if it compromises continued language growth and interlanguage development. Such learners, in other words, may rely on prefabricated chunks to solve their communication problems. But such solutions do not lead them to longer-term progress, even though they do lead to resourcefulness in solving problems.

This poses the central dilemma of communicative language teaching, namely, how can a communicative orientation to teaching be reconciled with the need to ensure that learners achieve acceptable levels of grammatical accuracy? The answer to this question depends on an understanding of the processes of second language learning.

Grammar in Relation to Second Language Acquisition Processes

Drawing on Van Patten (1993), Ellis (1994), Skehan (1996a, 1996b) and others, five stages of the learning process will be distinguished here in order to arrive at a rationale for grammar-focused instruction in teaching and teaching materials: input, intake, acquisition, access, output.

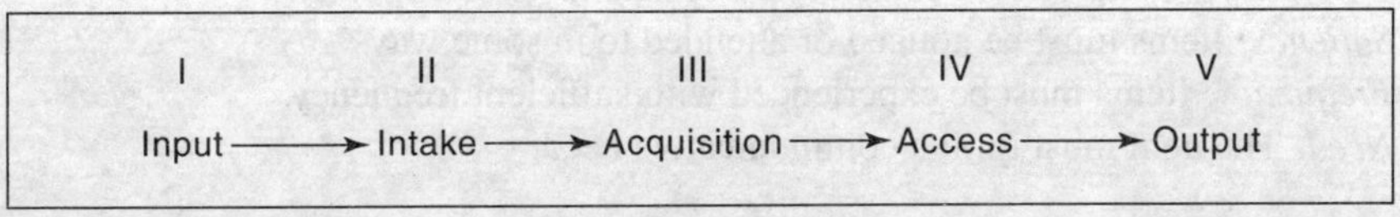

Figure 1 A Model of Second Language Learning and Use

Input

Input refers to language sources that are used to initiate the language learning process. Textbooks and commercial materials, teacher-made materials, and teacher-initiated classroom discourse all serve as input sources in language classes. Traditionally, teaching materials were planned around, or included, an explicit linguistic syllabus on the assumption that this determined the learner's acquisition of the target language. Some theorists see no need for any such syllabus, arguing that a grammar syllabus must be meaning-based and that grammar needs can be dealt with incidentally. Krashen (1985) represents this extreme position, arguing that exposure to comprehensible target-language input is in itself sufficient to trigger acquisition. Others would accept the inclusion of some form of linguistic syllabus, not on the grounds that it represents an acquisition sequence, but that it provides a way of simplifying the input. Grammatical simplification is seen as essential in providing input that is at an appropriate level of difficulty.

At the input stage in language learning, an attempt may be made to focus learners' attention on particular linguistic features of the input (sometimes known as 'input enhancement') by such means as:

- *Simplification of input:* The language corpus the learners are exposed to (via both textbooks and the teacher's discourse) may contain a restricted set of tenses and structures.
- *Frequency of exposure:* A target form may occur frequently within a source text (such as when a text is written to bring in several occurrences of the past tense or the past continuous).
- *Explicit instruction:* A target form may be presented formally together with information about how it is used, followed by practice.
- *Implicit instruction:* Students' attention may be drawn to a target form and they may have to induce the rule or system underlying its use.
- *Consciousness-raising:* Activities are provided to make learners aware of certain linguistic features in the input, without necessarily requiring them to produce them.

From a current perspective (unlike earlier perspectives where some of these processes were assumed to result in learning), none of these approaches to providing a grammatical focus at the input stage are in themselves assumed to bring about learning: They are, however, intended to facilitate the next stage in the learning process, intake.

INTAKE

Van Patten (1993) defines intake as 'that subset of the input that is comprehended and attended to in some way. It contains the linguistic "data" that are made available for acquisition.' Some portion of the input is assumed to remain in long-term memory and form the data on which the processes of language acquisition are engaged. Factors thought to affect how items pass from input to intake include:

- *Complexity:* Items should be at an appropriate level of difficulty.
- *Saliency:* Items must be noticed or attended to in some way.
- *Frequency:* Items must be experienced with sufficient frequency.
- *Need:* The item must fulfil a communicative need.

Generally speaking, we can assume frequency of occurrence in the language learning corpus (the input) to affect intake, but not always. The reason that some grammatical items such as articles, third person *-s*, and certain tense and auxiliary forms are acquired late (or never acquired) may be related to the fact that such forms have low saliency (they are not noticed) or low communicative need (they have no effect on communication), despite their high frequency of occurrence.

ACQUISITION

This refers to the processes by which the learner incorporates a new learning item into his or her developing system or interlanguage. SLA researchers have stressed the need for more powerful theories of acquisition than the simplistic 'imprinting through practice' theories of the P-P-P approach, and a number of different learning theories are currently available (Ellis, 1994). SLA research has demonstrated that learning is not a mirror image of teaching. Learners do not pass from a state of not knowing a particular target structure to a state of knowing and using it accurately. A number of processes appear to be involved:

- *Noticing:* Learners need to recognise differences between forms they are using and targetlike forms. A learner will not be motivated to try out a new linguistic structure if he or she is not aware of the differences between his or her current interlanguage system and the target-language system (Schmidt, 1990). Schmidt and Frota (1986) found that the new forms a learner incorporated into his speech were generally those that he had noticed in the speech people addressed to him. Forms that were present but not noticed were not made use of. Not all acquisition, however, is prompted by conscious awareness of linguistic features. Unconscious discovery of rules appears also to be involved.
- *Discovering rules:* According to the theory of Universal Grammar, learning also involves identification of the grammatical variables which operate in the target language and which account for the specific linguistic characteristics of that language, such as the rules underlying target-language word order, clause patterns, nominal groups, phrase structures, and so on. Currently, some researchers believe that learners have an innate understanding of grammatical variables. Universal Grammar theory (UG) suggests that 'learners are learning aspects of grammar that we are not teaching them and that they have unconscious knowledge of grammar systems which we, as teachers, are often unaware of' (Shortall, 1996, p. 38). DeKeyser adds a further clarification of this position (1998, p. 43): 'If a structure is part of UG, and UG is accessible to the second language learner, then all that is needed is sufficient input to trigger acquisition, unless L2 is a subset of L1. In the latter case, negative evidence is required. If a structure is not part of UG or cannot be acquired without negative evidence [information about what is not possible in the language] then a rather strong variant of focus on form, including rule teaching and error correction, will be required'.
- *Accommodation and restructuring:* Van Patten (1993, p. 436) describes these processes as 'those that mediate the incorporation of intake into the developing system. Since the internalization of intake is not a mere accumulation of discrete bits of data, data have to "fit in" in some way and sometimes the accommodation of a particular set of data causes changes in the rest of the system. In some cases, the data may not fit in at all and are not accommodated by the system. They simply do not make it into the long-term store'.

  As Skehan (1996b, p. 19) comments, 'The notion of learning [underlying SLA theory] is, then, a very complex one. It is certainly not a smooth progression – the elements of the target language do not simply slot into place in a predictable order'. The process which enables the learner to produce progressively more complex language is restructuring, that is, a willingness and capacity, on the part of learners, to reorganise their own underlying and developing language system, to frame and try out new hypotheses, and then to act on the feedback which is received from such experimentation.
- *Experimentation:* Much of the learner's output in the target language can be described as the result of experimentation as the learner forms hypotheses about the target language and tests them out. The learner draws on whatever

has been acquired and uses it in a tentative and uncertain way, constructing what he or she hopes will be targetlike utterances. This is seen in much of the discourse produced by the learners in the role-play task cited earlier. Researchers stress that the trying out of new language forms is essential to the acquisition process and that acquisition is most likely to occur in contexts 'where the learner needs to produce output which the current interlanguage system cannot handle . . . [and so] . . . pushes the limits of the interlanguage system to handle that output' (Tarone & Liu, 1995, pp. 120, 121, cited in Swain, 1998, p. 11).

ACCESS

Access refers to the learner's ability to draw upon his or her interlanguage system during communication. The context in which the learner is using the language as well as its purpose (in casual conversation, in a formal or public setting, to tell a story or give instructions) may affect the extent to which he or she is successful in calling up aspects of the acquired system: 'access involves making use of the developing system to create output' (Van Patten, 1993, p. 436). Skehan (1996a, p. 47) refers to this process as 'fluency', which concerns 'the learner's capacity to mobilize an interlanguage system to communicate meanings in real time'. Access may be 'totally, partially, or not at all successful, depending on task demand, previous experience (practice) and other factors' (Van Patten, 1993, p. 436). In other words, it may be much easier in some circumstances for the learners to use aspects of the acquired system than in others.

OUTPUT

Finally, output refers to the observed results of the learners' efforts. Although some theorists have proposed that output (active use of the language resulting in the production of language) is not essential to acquisition, that is, that input is sufficient (for example, Krashen, 1985), others (for example, Swain, 1985) have proposed that output is essential to acquisition but is more likely to facilitate acquisition when the learners are 'pushed', that is, required to reshape their utterances and to use the target language more coherently and accurately. This is confirmed by examples of second language users who speak a language relatively fluently but use a very restricted lexicon and syntax and show no evidence of improvement in accuracy over time (for example, taxi drivers and vendors in EFL settings), since the restricted purposes for which they use the language do not push them to expand or restructure their linguistic resources (Schmidt, 1983; Allen, Swain, Harley, & Cummins, 1990).

Addressing Grammar within Task Work

As the model of second language learning just discussed illustrates, a focus on grammar can be addressed at several different stages of the teaching/learning process – at the stages of Input, Intake, Acquisition, Access or Output. Doughty and Williams (1998, p. 3) suggest that focus on form 'entails a prerequisite engagement in meaning before attention to linguistic features can be expected to become effective'. Skehan (1996a, 1996b) proposes the following principles as the basis of a methodology that includes a focus on form as part of an overall communicative approach to teaching:

- exposure to language at an appropriate level of difficulty
- engagement in meaning-focused interaction in the language
- opportunities for learners to notice or attend to linguistic form while using the language

- opportunities to expand the language resources learners make use of (both lexical and syntactic) over time

In the remainder of this paper, I will examine how this can be attempted during the design or implementation phases of classroom tasks.

There are potentially three points at which a focus on grammar can be provided in task work – prior to the task, during the task and after the task. These will be illustrated both with general examples and with reference to the design of a typical fluency activity – a role-play task. The role-play example is from Richards and Hull (1986), which contains a set of role-play activities that are structured to provide language support at the three intervention points described here.

Addressing Accuracy prior to the Task

Pre-task activities have two goals: (1) to provide language support that can be used in completing a task; (2) to clarify the nature of the task so that students can give less attention to procedural aspects of the task and hence monitor the linguistic accuracy of their performance while carrying out a task. Skehan notes (1996a, p. 53): 'Pre-task activities can aim to teach, or mobilise, or make salient language which will be relevant to task performance'. This can be accomplished in the following ways:

1. *By pre-teaching certain linguistic forms that can be used while completing a task.* For example, prior to a role-play task which practises 'calling an apartment owner to discuss renting an apartment' (Richards & Hull, 1986), students first read advertisements for apartments and learn key vocabulary they will use in a role-play. They also listen to and practise a dialogue in which a prospective tenant calls an apartment owner for information. The dialogue serves both to display different questioning strategies and to model the kind of task the students will perform. Other pre-task activities used in the role-plays include brainstorming activities, vocabulary classification tasks and prediction tasks, all of which serve to generate language awareness as well as to develop schemata relevant to a task.
2. *By reducing the cognitive complexity of the task.* If a task is difficult to carry out, learners' attention may be diverted to the structure and management of the task, leaving little opportunity for them to monitor the language they use on the task. One way of reducing the cognitive complexity of a task is to provide students with a chance for prior rehearsal of a task. This is intended to 'ease the processing load that learners will encounter when actually doing a task' (Skehan, 1996a, p. 54). This could be achieved by watching a video or listening to a cassette of learners doing a task similar to the target task, or it could consist of a simplified version of a task similar to the one the learners will carry out. Dialogue work prior to carrying out the role-play described above serves a similar function.
3. *By giving time to plan the task.* Time allocated to planning prior to carrying out a task can likewise provide learners with schemata, vocabulary and language forms that they can call upon while completing the task. Planning activities include vocabulary-generating activities such as word classification and organisation, information-generating activities such as brainstorming, or strategy activities in which learners consider a range of strategies for solving a problem, discuss their pros and cons, and then select one which they will apply to the task. In Richards and Hull (1986), some of the planning activities include generating a set of questions that could be asked during an interview, prior to role-playing an interview. Ellis (1987) found that the

availability of planning time affects the accuracy with which the learners use some target-language forms, but only if planning time is used to focus on form (rather than, say, organisation of information).

Addressing Accuracy during the Task

A focus on form can be facilitated during the completion of a task by choosing how the task is to be carried out. The way it is implemented can determine whether it is carried out fluently and with an acceptable level of linguistic performance, or disfluently with excessive dependence on communication strategies, employment of lexical rather than grammaticalised discourse, and overuse of ellipsis and nonlinguistic resources. Task implementation factors include:

- *Participation:* whether the task is completed individually or with other learners
- *Procedures:* the number of procedures involved in completing the task
- *Resources:* the materials and other resources provided for the learners to use while completing the task
- *Order:* the sequencing of a task in relation to previous tasks
- *Product:* the outcome or outcomes students produce, such as a written product or an oral one

The effect of participation arrangement on tasks performance has been noted by Brown, Anderson, Shillcock, and Yule (1984, cited in Skehan, 1996b, p. 26): 'The greater the number of participants there are in a task the greater the pressure on those transacting a task, and the greater the likelihood that fluency will predominate as a goal over accuracy and complexity/restructuring'.

Foster found that dyads rather than groups 'coupled with the obligation to exchange information, was the "best" for language production, negotiations and modified output' (1998, p. 18).

Resources students work from can also affect task performance. The use of pictures in a storytelling task might provide an accessible framework or schema for the story, clarifying such elements as setting, characters, events, outcomes, and so on, giving the learners more opportunity to focus their planning or performance on other dimensions of the task. Or, in conducting a survey task, the design of the resources students use could have a crucial impact on the appropriateness of the language used in carrying out the task. If the survey form or questionnaire the students use provides models of the types of questions they should ask, it may result in a better level of language use during questioning and make other aspects of the task easier to manage, since less planning will need to be devoted to formulating appropriate questions. In the role-plays discussed earlier (Richards & Hull, 1986), considerable trialling was needed of the role-play cue sheets students used in carrying out their role-plays before a format was arrived at which gave partial language support and which guided but did not dominate students' improvisations during each activity.

Procedures used in completing a task can also be used to influence language output. A task that is divided into several shorter subtasks may be more manageable than one without such a structure, allowing students to deal with one section of the task at a time. For example, the procedures used in the role-play activities mentioned earlier consisted of:

1. preparatory activity designed to provide schemata, vocabulary and language
2. dialogue listening task, to model shorter version of target task

3. dialogue practice task, to provide further clarification of task
4. first practice, using role-play cues
5. follow-up listening
6. second role-play practice

The order of a task in relation to other tasks may influence use of target structures. For example, if students are to carry out a task that requires the use of sequence markers, a prior activity which explains sequence markers and models how they are used may result in more frequent use of sequence markers during the performance of the target task (see Swain, 1998).

The product focus of a task will also influence the extent to which students have an opportunity to attend to linguistic form. A task may be completed orally, it may be recorded or it may require writing. In each case, different opportunities for language awareness are involved. Swain (1998, p. 3) describes how tasks with a written product provide an opportunity for students to focus on form.

> Students, working together in pairs, are each given a different set of numbered pictures that tell a story. Together the pair of students must jointly construct the story-line. After they have worked out what the story is, they write it down. In doing so, students encounter linguistic problems they need to solve to continue with the task. These problems include how best to say what they want to say; problems of lexical choice; which morphological endings to use; the best syntactic structures to use; and problems about the language needed to sequence the story correctly. These problems arise as the students try to 'make meaning', that is, as they construct and write out the story, as they understand it. And as they encounter these linguistic problems, they focus on linguistic form – the form that is needed to express the meaning in the way they want to convey it.

Learners can also record their performance of a task and then listen to it and identify aspects of their performance that require modification.

Addressing Accuracy after the Task

Grammatical appropriateness can also be addressed after a task has been completed (see Willis & Willis, 1996). Activities of this type include the following:

- *Public performance:* After completing a task in small groups, students carry out the task in front of the class or another group. This can have the effect of prompting them to perform the task at a more complex linguistic level. Aspects of their performance which were not initially in focus during in-group performance can become conscious as there is an increased capacity for self-monitoring during a public performance of the task.
- *Repeat performance:* The same activity might be repeated with some elements modified, such as the amount of time available. Nation (1989), for example, reports improvements in fluency, control of content and, to a lesser extent, accuracy when learners repeated an oral task under time constraints and argues that this is a way of bringing about long-term improvement in both fluency and, to some extent, accuracy.

- *Other performance:* The student might hear more advanced learners (or even native speakers) completing the same task, and focus on some of the linguistic and communicative resources employed in the process (for example, Richards, 1985).

Conclusions

Although it provides an appealing alternative to grammar-based teaching, the use of communicative language tasks plus ad hoc intervention by the teacher to provide corrective feedback on errors that arise during task completion may not be sufficient to achieve acceptable levels of grammatical accuracy in second language learning. Hence there is a need to consider how a greater focus on grammatical form can be achieved during the process of designing and using tasks. Skehan (1996a, p. 51) sees this as involving 'a constant cycle of analysis and synthesis: achieved by manipulating the focus of attention of the learners and there should be a balanced development towards the three goals of restructuring, accuracy, and fluency'. In this paper, I have attempted to provide a brief overview of how this can be attempted through advocating what Skehan terms a weak form of a task-based approach. However, a number of substantive issues remain.

To begin with, we need a clear understanding of the goals of grammar-focused intervention, since, as we have seen, a number of different processes are involved in SLA as well as various stages in the learning and teaching process. DeKeyser (1998, p. 62) points out that teaching may attempt to address different stages in the learning process: 'instilling knowledge about rules, turning this knowledge into something that is qualitatively different through practice, or automatising such knowledge further in the sense that it can be done faster with fewer errors and less mental effort'. In addition, we need a better understanding of which target-language structures are most amenable to any of the forms of intervention described in this paper, and which are not. Some things can be worked out implicitly, whereas others may benefit from explicit instruction. For example, learning how to use the past tense appropriately during narrative tasks presumably involves different kinds of problems from those involving mastery of the article system. And although it has been assumed that focus on grammar should always be an integral part of a communicative task and not a discrete activity isolated from meaningful communication, this claim requires much further study, since it will depend on which stage in the acquisition process is being targeted.

Because of the importance of linguistic form in second language communication and the amount of attention currently being given to the role of form-focused instruction in language teaching, we can expect these issues to continue to be at the forefront of applied linguistic theory and research for the foreseeable future.

References

Allen, P., Swain, M., Harley, B., & Cummins, J. (1990). Aspects of classroom treatment: Towards a more comprehensive view of second language education. In B. Harley, P. Allen, J. Cummins, & M. Swain (Eds.), *The development of second language proficiency*. Cambridge: Cambridge University Press.

Brown, G., Anderson, A., Shillcock, R., & Yule, G. (1984). *Teaching talk: Strategies for production and assessment*. Cambridge: Cambridge University Press.

Brumfit, C. (1979). Communicative language teaching: An educational perspective. In C. J. Brumfit & K. Johnson (Eds.), *The communicative approach to language teaching*. Oxford: Oxford University Press.

DeKeyser, M. (1998). Beyond focus on form: Cognitive perspectives on learning and practising second language grammar. In C. Doughty & J. Williams (Eds.), *Focus on form in classroom second language acquisition*. New York: Cambridge University Press.

Doughty, C., & Williams, J. (Eds.). (1998). *Focus on form in classroom second language acquisition*. New York: Cambridge University Press.

Ellis, R. (1987). Interlanguage variability in narrative discourse: Style shifting in the use of the past tense. *Studies in Second Language Acquisition, 9*(1), 1–20.

Ellis, R. (1994). *The study of second language acquisition*. Oxford: Oxford University Press.

Foster, P. (1998). A classroom perspective on the negotiation of meaning. *Applied Linguistics, 19*(1), 1–23.

Higgs, T., & Clifford, R. (1982). The push towards communication. In T. Higgs (Ed.), *Curriculum, competence, and the foreign language teacher*. Skokie, IL: National Textbook Company.

Krashen, S. (1985). *The input hypothesis*. Harlow: Longman.

Kumaravadivelu, B. (1991). Language-learning tasks: Teacher intention and learner interpretation. *ELT Journal, 45*(2), 98–107.

Musumeci, D. (1996). Teacher-learner negotiation in content-based instruction: Communication or cross purposes? *Applied Linguistics, 17*(3), 286–325.

Nation, P. (1989). Improving speaking fluency. *System, 17*(3), 377–384.

Nunan, D. (1989). *Designing tasks for the communicative classroom*. Cambridge: Cambridge University Press.

Richards, J. C. (1985). Conversational competence through role-play activities. *RELC Journal, 16*(1): 82–100.

Richards, J. C., & Hull, J. (1986). *As I was saying*. Reading, MA: Addison-Wesley.

Schmidt, R. (1983). In N. Wolfson & E. Judd (Eds.), *Sociolinguistics and second language acquisition*. Rowley, MA: Newbury House.

Schmidt, R. (1990). The role of consciousness in second language learning. *Applied Linguistics, 11*(2), 129–158.

Schmidt, R., & Frota, S. (1986). Developing basic conversational ability in a second language. In R. Day (Ed.), *Talking to learn*. Rowley, MA: Newbury House.

Shortall, T. (1996). What learners know and what they need to learn. In J. Willis & D. Willis (Eds.), *Challenge and change in language teaching*. Oxford: Heinemann.

Skehan, P. 1996a. A framework for the implementation of task-based instruction. *Applied Linguistics, 17*(1), 38–61.

Skehan, P. 1996b. Second language acquisition research and task-based instruction. In J. Willis & D. Willis (Eds.), *Challenge and change in language teaching*. Oxford: Heinemann.

Swain, M. (1985). Communicative competence: Some roles of comprehensible input and comprehensible output in its development. In S. Gass & C. Madden (Eds.), *Input in second language acquisition*. Rowley, MA: Newbury House.

Swain. M. (1999, April). Integrating language and content teaching through collaborative tasks. In C. Ward & W. Renandya (Eds.), *Language teaching*: *New insights for the language teacher* (pp. 125–147). Anthology Series 40. Singapore: SEAMEO-RELC.

Tarone, E., & Liu, G. (1995). Situational context, variation, and second-language aquisition theory. In G. Cook & B. Seidlhofer (Eds.), *Principle and practice in applied linguistics*. Oxford: Oxford University Press.

Thornbury, S. (1998). Comments on direct approaches in L2 instruction. *TESOL Quarterly, 32*(1), 109–116.

Van Patten, W. (1993). Grammar-teaching for the acquisition-rich classroom. *Foreign Language Annals, 26*(4), 435–450.

Willis, J., & Willis, D. (Eds.). (1996). *Challenge and change in language teaching*. Oxford: Heinemann.

CHAPTER 15

Grammar Teaching – Practice or Consciousness-Raising?

Rod Ellis

Introduction

Two major questions need to be considered with regard to grammar teaching in second language (L2) pedagogy:

1. Should we teach grammar at all?
2. If we should teach grammar, how should we teach it?

The first question has been answered in the negative by some applied linguists. Krashen (1982), for instance, has argued that formal instruction in grammar will not contribute to the development of 'acquired' knowledge – the knowledge needed to participate in authentic communication. Prabhu (1987) has tried to show, with some success, that classroom learners can acquire an L2 grammar naturalistically by participating in meaning-focused tasks. Others, however, including myself, have argued that grammar teaching does aid L2 acquisition, although not necessarily in the way teachers often think it does. My principal contention is that formal grammar teaching has a delayed rather than instant effect.

The focus of this article is the second question. I am going to assume that we should teach grammar (see Ellis, 1990, for the reasons why) and turn my attention to how we should set about doing so. Specifically, I want to consider two approaches, which I shall refer to as 'practice' and 'consciousness-raising'. I shall begin by defining these. I will then briefly consider the case for practice and argue that the available evidence suggests that it may not be as effective as is generally believed. I will then present a number of arguments in support of consciousness-raising and conclude with an example of a 'CR-task'.

Defining Practice and Consciousness-Raising

For most teachers, the main idea of grammar teaching is to help learners internalise the structures taught in such a way that they can be used in everyday communication. To this end, the learners are provided with opportunities to *practise* the structures, first under controlled conditions, and then under more normal communicative conditions. Ur (1988, p. 7) describes the practice stage of a grammar lesson in these terms: 'The practice stage consists of a series of exercises . . . whose aim is to cause the learners to *absorb* the structure thoroughly; or to put it another way, to *transfer what they know from short-term to long-term memory*'.

It is common to distinguish a number of different types of practice activities – mechanical practice, contextualised practice, and communicative practice. Mechanical practice consists of various types of rigidly controlled activities, such as substitution exercises. Contextualised practice is still controlled, but involves an attempt to encourage learners to relate form to meaning by showing how structures are used in real-life situations. Communicative practice entails various kinds of 'gap' activities which require the learners to engage in authentic communication while at the same time 'keeping an eye, as it were, on the structures that are being manipulated in the process' (Ur, 1988, p. 9).

Irrespective of whether the practice is controlled, contextualised, or communicative, it will have the following characteristics:

1. There is some attempt to *isolate* a specific grammatical feature for focused attention.
2. The learners are required to *produce* sentences containing the targeted feature.
3. The learners will be provided with opportunities for *repetition* of the targeted feature.
4. There is an expectancy that the learners will perform the grammatical feature *correctly*. In general, therefore, practice activities are 'success oriented' (Ur, 1988, p. 13).
5. The learners receive *feedback* on whether their performance of the grammatical structure is correct or not. This feedback may be immediate or delayed.

These five characteristics provide a definition of what most methodologists mean by *practice*. It should be noticed that each characteristic constitutes an assumption about how grammar is learnt. By and large, though, these assumptions go unchallenged and have become part of the mythology of language teaching.

Consciousness-raising, as I use the term, involves an attempt to equip the learner with an understanding of a specific grammatical feature – to develop declarative rather than procedural knowledge of it. The main characteristics of consciousness-raising activities are the following:

1. There is an attempt to *isolate* a specific linguistic feature for focused attention.
2. The learners are provided with *data* which illustrate the targeted feature and they may also be supplied with an *explicit rule* describing or explaining the feature.
3. The learners are expected to utilise *intellectual effort* to understand the targeted feature.
4. Misunderstanding or incomplete understanding of the grammatical structure by the learners leads to *clarification* in the form of further data and description or explanation.
5. Learners may be required (although this is not obligatory) to articulate the rule describing the grammatical structure.

It should be clear from this list that the main purpose of consciousness-raising is to develop *explicit knowledge* of grammar. I want to emphasise, however, that this is not the same as *metalingual knowledge*. It is perfectly possible to develop an explicit understanding of how a grammatical structure works without learning much in the way of grammatical terminology. Grammar can be explained, and, therefore, understood in everyday language. It may be, however, that access to some metalanguage will facilitate the development of explicit knowledge.

A comparison of the characteristics of consciousness-raising with those listed for practice shows that the main difference is that consciousness-raising does not involve the learner in *repeated production*. This is because the aim of this kind of grammar teaching is not to enable the learner to perform a structure correctly but simply to help her to 'know about it'. Here is how Rutherford and Sharwood-Smith (1985) put it: 'CR is considered as a potential facilitator for the acquisition of linguistic competence and has nothing directly to do with the use of that competence for the achievement of specific communicative objectives, or with the achievement of fluency'.

Whereas practice is primarily behavioural, consciousness-raising is essentially concept-forming in orientation.

The two types of grammar work are not mutually exclusive, however. Thus, grammar teaching can involve a combination of practice and consciousness-raising and, indeed, traditionally does so. Thus, many methodologists recommend that practice work be preceded by a presentation stage, to ensure that the learners have a clear idea about what the targeted structure consists of. This presentation stage may involve an inductive or deductive treatment of the structure. Also, practice work can be rounded off with a formal explanation of the structure. Even strict audiolingualists such as Brooks (1960) recognised the value of formal explanations of patterns as 'summaries' once the practice activities had been completed. Indeed, it is arguable that no grammar teaching can take place without some consciousness-raising occurring. Even if the practice work is directed at the implicit learning of the structure and no formal explanation is provided, learners (particularly, adults) are likely to try to construct some kind of explicit representation of the rule.

Nevertheless, the distinction is a real and important one. Whereas practice work cannot take place without some degree of consciousness-raising (even if this is incidental), the obverse is not the case; consciousness-raising can occur without practice. Thus, it is perfectly possible to teach grammar in the sense of helping learners to understand and explain grammatical phenomena without having them engage in activities that require repeated production of the structures concerned. One way this occurs is by presenting learners with rules for memorisation – teaching about grammar. This is what occurred in the grammar-translation method. Such an approach has been discredited on a number of grounds, and it is not my intention to advocate its reintroduction. There are other ways of raising consciousness that are compatible with contemporary educational principles, however. Before considering them, I want to consider the extent to which the faith methodologists have in practice is justified.

Does Practice Work?

A number of empirical studies have investigated whether practice contributes to L2 acquisition (cf. Ellis, 1988, for a review). These studies are of two kinds: those that seek to relate the *amount* of practice achieved by individual learners with general increases in *proficiency* (e.g., Seliger, 1977; Day, 1984) and those that have examined whether practising a specific linguistic structure results in its acquisition (e.g., Ellis, 1984).

The results of both types of research are not encouraging for supporters of practice. Correlational studies (i.e., the first kind just referred to) have produced mixed results. Some studies have found a relationship between amount of practice and gains in proficiency, but others have failed to do so. Even when a study does show a strong relationship, it does not warrant claiming that practice *causes* learning. In order to say something about cause and effect, we have to interpret a correlational relationship. It is perfectly possible to argue that it is the learners' proficiency that influences practice, rather than vice versa. Teachers may direct more practice opportunities at those learners who they think are able to supply correct answers – thus, the more proficient receive more practice. Indeed, one of the requirements of practice – that it be success-oriented – would lead us to predict that this will happen. The detailed analysis of classroom interactions that result from practice activities supports such an interpretation.

Studies which have investigated whether practising a specific structure results in its acquisition provide evidence to suggest that practice does not result in the autonomous ability to use the structure. In other words, practising a grammatical structure under controlled conditions does not seem to enable the learner to use the structure freely. I carried out a study (Ellis, 1984) to see whether practising 'when' questions enabled learners to acquire this structure. It did not. Ellis and Rathbone (1987) investigated whether practising a difficult word-order rule with learners of L2 German resulted in its acquisition. Again, it did not. There are also doubts that learners are able to transfer knowledge from controlled to communicative practice. Once learners move into a meaning-focused activity, they seem to fall back on their own resources and ignore the linguistic material they have practised previously in form-focused activity.

There are, of course, problems with such studies as these, and it would be unwise to claim that they conclusively demonstrate that practice does not work. It may be that the practice was of the wrong kind, that it was poorly executed, or that there was not enough of it. It may be that practice only works with some kinds of learners. Nevertheless, the studies cast doubts on the claims methodologists make about practice.

There are also strong theoretical grounds for questioning the effectiveness of practice. Pienemann (1985) has proposed that some structures are *developmental* in the sense that they are acquired in a defined sequence. It is impossible for the learner to acquire a developmental structure until the psycholinguistic processing operations associated with easier structures in the acquisitional sequence have been acquired.

According to Pienemann's *teachability hypothesis*, a structure cannot be successfully taught (in the sense that it will be used correctly and spontaneously in communication) unless the learner is developmentally ready to acquire it. In other words, the teaching syllabus has to match the learner's developmental syllabus. For practice to work, then, the teacher will have to find out what stage of development the learners have reached. Although it is technically possible for the teacher to do this, it is impractical in most teaching situations.

Of course, it does not follow from these arguments that practice is without any value at all. Practice probably does help where pronunciation is concerned – it gives learners opportunities to get their tongues around new words and phrases. Also, practice may be quite effective in helping learners to remember new lexical material, including formulaic chunks such as 'How do you do?', 'Can I have a . . . ?', and 'I don't understand'. Some learners – extroverts who enjoy speaking in the classroom, for example – may respond positively to practice activities. For these reasons, practice will always have a place in the classroom. It needs to be recognised, however, that practice will often not lead to immediate procedural knowledge of grammatical rules, irrespective of its quantity and quality.

To sum up, there are strong grounds – empirical and theoretical – which lead us to doubt the efficacy of practice. 'Practice' is essentially a *pedagogical* construct. It assumes that the acquisition of grammatical structures involves a gradual automatisation of production, from controlled to automatic, and it ignores the very real constraints that exist on the ability of the teacher to influence what goes on inside the learner's head. Practice may have limited *psycholinguistic* validity.

The Case for Consciousness-Raising

We have seen that the goal of practice activities is to develop the kind of automatic control of grammatical structures that will enable learners to use them productively and spontaneously. We have also seen that there are reasons to believe that this may not be achievable. The problem lies in assuming that we can teach grammar for use in communication. If we lower our sights and instead aim to develop the learner's awareness of what is correct but without any expectancy that we can bring the learner to the point where she can use this knowledge in normal communication, then the main theoretical objections raised against practice disappear. Consciousness-raising is predicated on this lesser goal.

Practice is directed at the acquisition of *implicit* knowledge of a grammatical structure – the kind of tacit knowledge needed to use the structure effortlessly for communication. Consciousness-raising is directed at the formation of *explicit* knowledge – the kind of intellectual knowledge which we are able to gather about any subject, if we so choose. Of course, the construction of explicit representations of grammatical structures is of limited use in itself. It may help the learner to perform successfully in certain kinds of discrete-item language tests. It may also help to improve her performance in planning her discourse, as when we monitor our output in order to improve it for public perusal. But, crucially, it will not be of much use in the normal, everyday uses of language. Explicit knowledge is not much use when it comes to communicating. For this, we need implicit knowledge.

We need to ask, therefore, whether the more limited goal of consciousness-raising – to teach explicit knowledge – has any value. Ultimately, consciousness-raising can only be justified if it can be shown that it contributes to the learner's ability to communicate. I want to argue that, although consciousness-raising does not contribute directly to the acquisition of implicit knowledge, it does so indirectly. In other words, consciousness-raising *facilitates* the acquisition of the grammatical knowledge needed for communication.

The acquisition of implicit knowledge involves three processes:

1. noticing (the learner becomes conscious of the presence of a linguistic feature in the input, whereas previously she had ignored it)
2. comparing (the learner compares the linguistic feature noticed in the input with her own mental grammar, registering to what extent there is a 'gap' between the input and her grammar)
3. integrating (the learner integrates a representation of the new linguistic feature into her mental grammar)

The first two processes involve conscious attention to language; the third process takes place at a very 'deep' level, of which the learner is generally not aware. Noticing and comparing can take place at any time; they are not developmentally regulated. But integration of new linguistic material into the store of implicit knowledge is subject to the kinds of psycholinguistic constraints discussed earlier.

How, then, does consciousness-raising contribute to the acquisition of implicit knowledge? I would like to suggest that it does so in two major ways:

1. It contributes to the processes of noticing and comparing and, therefore, prepares the grounds for the integration of new linguistic material. However, it will not bring about

integration. This process is controlled by the learner and will take place only when the learner is developmentally ready.

2. It results in explicit knowledge. Thus, even if the learner is unable to integrate the new feature as implicit knowledge, she can construct an alternative explicit representation which can be stored separately and subsequently accessed when the learner is developmentally primed to handle it. Furthermore, explicit knowledge serves to help the learner to continue to notice the feature in the input, thereby facilitating its subsequent acquisition.

Consciousness-raising, then, is unlikely to result in immediate acquisition. More likely, it will have a *delayed* effect.

There are also educational reasons that can be advanced for grammar teaching as consciousness-raising. The inclusion of foreign languages in the school curriculum is not motivated entirely by the desire to foster communication between speakers of different languages, although this has become the most prominent aim in recent years. This inclusion has, and always has had, a more general goal – that of fostering intellectual development. 'Grammar' embodies a corpus of knowledge the study of which can be expected to contribute to students' cognitive skills. It constitutes a serious content and, as such, contrasts with the trivial content of many modern textbooks.

It is not my intention, however, to advocate a return to 'teaching about grammar', or, at least, not in the form that this was carried out in the past. The arguments that I have presented in favour of consciousness-raising do not justify giving lectures on grammar. Such a transmission-oriented approach runs contrary to progressive educational principles. What I have in mind is a task-based approach that emphasises discovery learning by asking learners to solve problems about grammar. The following is an example of this approach.

An Example of a Consciousness-Raising Task

Consciousness-raising tasks can be *inductive* or *deductive*. In the case of the former, the learner is provided with data and asked to construct an explicit rule to describe the grammatical feature which the data illustrate. In the case of the latter, the learner is supplied with a rule which is then used to carry out some task. We do not know, as yet, which type results in the more efficient learning of explicit knowledge – probably both will prove useful.

Table 1 provides a simple example of an inductive task designed to raise learners' awareness about the grammatical differences between 'for' and 'since'. This problem has been designed with a number of points in mind. First, the intention is to focus on a known source of difficulty; learners frequently fail to distinguish 'for' and 'since'. Second, the data provided must be adequate to enable the learners to discover the rule that governs the usage of these prepositions in time expressions. In the case of this task, the data include both grammatical and ungrammatical sentences. Third, the task requires minimal production on the part of the learners; instead, emphasis is placed on developing an 'idea' of when the two forms are used. Fourth, there is an opportunity to apply the rule in the construction of personalised statements. This is not intended to 'practise' the rule but to promote its storage as explicit knowledge; production, therefore, is restricted to two sentences and there is no insistence on automatic processing. Such tasks as these can be designed with varying formats. They can make use of situational information, diagram, charts, tables, and so on. They can also be used in both lockstep teaching (i.e., when the teacher works through a problem with the whole class) or small-group work.

TABLE 1. AN EXAMPLE OF A CR PROBLEM-SOLVING TASK

1. Here is some information about when three people joined the company they now work for and how long they have been working there.

Name	Date Joined	Length of Time
Ms Regan	1945	45 yrs
Mr Bush	1970	20 yrs
Ms Thatcher	1989	9 mths
Mr Baker	1990 (Feb)	10 days

2. Study these sentences about these people. When is 'for' used and when is 'since' used?
   a. Ms Regan has been working for her company *for* most of her life.
   b. Mr Bush has been working for his company *since* 1970.
   c. Ms Thatcher has been working for her company *for* 9 months.
   d. Mr Baker has been working for his company *since* February.
3. Which of the following sentences are ungrammatical? Why?
   a. Ms Regan has been working for her company for 1945.
   b. Mr Bush has been working for his company for 20 years.
   c. Ms Thatcher has been working for her company since 1989.
   d. Mr Baker has been working for his company since 10 days.
4. Try and make up a rule to explain when 'for' and 'since' are used.
5. Make up one sentence about when you started to learn English and one sentence about how long you have been studying English. Use 'for' and 'since'.

CONCLUSION

In this paper I have argued the case for grammar teaching as consciousness-raising. In one respect, this does not constitute a radical departure from what teachers have always done. Many teachers have felt the need to provide formal explanations of grammatical points. But in another respect, it does represent a real alternative in that it removes from grammar teaching the need to provide learners with repeated opportunities to produce the target structure. So much effort has gone into devising ingenious ways of eliciting and shaping learners' responses, more often to little or no avail as learners do not acquire the structures they have practised. Consciousness-raising constitutes an approach to grammar teaching which is compatible with current thinking about how learners acquire L2 grammar. It also constitutes an approach that accords with progressive views about education as a process of discovery through problem-solving tasks.

There are, of course, limitations to consciousness-raising. It may not be appropriate for young learners. Some learners (e.g., those who like to learn by 'doing' rather than 'studying') may dislike it. It can only be used with beginners if the learners' first language is used as the medium for solving the tasks. However, the alternative in such situations is not practice. Rather, it is to provide opportunities for meaning-focused language use, for communicating in the L2, initially perhaps in the form of listening tasks. All learners, even those who are suited to a consciousness-raising approach, will need plenty of such opportunities. Consciousness-raising is not an alternative to communication activities, but a supplement.

References

Brooks, N. (1960). *Language and language learning*. New York: Harcourt, Brace & World.

Day, R. R. (1984). Student participation in the ESL classroom. *Language Learning, 34*, 69–89.

Ellis, R. (1984). The role of instruction in second language acquisition. In D. Singleton & D. Little (Eds.), *Language learning in formal and informal contexts*. IRAAL.

Ellis, R. (1988). The role of practice in classroom language learning. *Teanga 8*, 1–25.

Ellis, R. (1990). *Instructed second language acquisition*. Oxford: Basil Blackwell.

Ellis, R., & Rathbone, M. (1987). *The acquisition of German in a classroom context*. London: Ealing College of Higher Education.

Krashen, S. (1982). *Principles and practice in second language acquisition*. Oxford: Pergamon.

Pienemann, M. (1985). Learnability and syllabus construction. In K. Hyltenstam & M. Pienemann (Eds.), *Modelling and assessing second language acquisition*. Clevedon, Avon: Multilingual Matters.

Prabhu, N. (1987). *Second language pedagogy*. Oxford: Oxford University Press.

Rutherford, W., & Sharwood-Smith, M. (1985). Consciousness-raising and universal grammar. *Applied Linguistics, 6*, 274–281.

Seliger, H. (1977). Does practice make perfect? A study of interaction patterns and L2 competence. *Language Learning, 27*, 263–275.

Ur, P. (1988). *Grammar practice activities*. Cambridge: Cambridge University Press.

SECTION 8

TEACHING PRONUNCIATION

INTRODUCTION

The papers in this section deal with an aspect of learning which could either be the focus of a lesson or form a component of any lesson – pronunciation. Pronunciation (also known as phonology) includes the role of individual sounds and sound segments, that is, features at the segmental level, as well as suprasegmental features such as stress, rhythm, and intonation. The fact that few second language learners are able to speak a second language without showing evidence of the transfer of pronunciation features of their native language is evidence of the difficulty of acquiring a nativelike pronunciation, but also of the goals learners set for themselves. Many learners are quite comfortable to show evidence of their native language on their second language phonology, since it is sometimes viewed as a core part of their cultural identity.

Approaches to the teaching of pronunciation have changed significantly throughout the recent history of language teaching, moving beyond an emphasis on the accurate production of individual speech sounds to concentrating more on the broader, communicative aspects of connected speech. Many teachers, however, are unsure as to the status of pronunciation and whether or how it should receive systematic attention in a language course. Commonly asked questions are: Is pronunciation something that is worth teaching? How effective are any of the various approaches to teaching pronunciation found in course books and teaching materials? Is a direct or an indirect approach more effective? Is there any value in using drills on specific sounds and sound patterns? What should one do about persistent and intrusive pronunciation errors from learners? And can one "teach" the more subtle dimensions of pronunciation, such as rhythm and intonation, or are they simply picked up through exposure? In many textbooks devoted to pronunciation, the focus may reflect more recent ideas of the nature of pronunciation, but the teaching techniques and task types continue to be based on behaviorist notions of second language learning, largely relying on imitation and discrimination drills, reading aloud, and contrastive analysis of L1 and L2 sound systems.

Within the field of language teaching, ideas on the value of teaching pronunciation are often at variance: Some believe that teachers can do little to influence the natural course of L2 phonological development with its often less than satisfactory results; others believe that teaching can play an important role, not only in helping learners develop ways of improving their pronunciation, but also in shaping their attitudes toward the nature and importance of pronunciation.

In his paper in this section, Jones briefly reviews recent research into the acquisition of second language phonology and examines if and how these research findings are reflected in currently used pronunciation teaching materials. Suggestions are made for developing materials that incorporate activities more fully, addressing the communicative, psychological, and sociological dimensions of pronunciation. In her paper, Hebert argues that teachers often neglect pronunciation or focus on problems of single sounds at the expense of more significant global features. In addition to teaching learners how to produce specific sounds, teaching must also address the prosodic features of language, such as stress and rhythm, intonation, pitch variation, and volume. Hebert demonstrates how teachers can construct a diagnostic profile of their learners' pronunciation difficulties as a basis for providing feedback and for planning instruction. She provides an approach with some detailed examples of how to teach these global features.

Discussion Questions

Before Reading

1. Why do you think it is difficult for adults to acquire a nativelike pronunciation in a second or foreign language even if other aspects of their speech are nativelike?
2. What do you think is a suitable target in the learning of pronunciation – a nativelike accent or a fluent but accented style of speaking?
3. What factors do learners need to attend to or become conscious of in learning new sounds or correcting fossilized pronunciation habits?
4. What is the role of imitation-based activities in teaching pronunciation?
5. Do you think young learners have less difficulty with pronunciation than older learners? If so, why might this be the case?
6. Have you learned to speak a foreign language? What difficulties did you have with pronunciation? How did you address these difficulties?
7. Do you think some people have a better "ear" for accents and pronunciation in a new language than others?
8. Do you think explaining to learners how to produce difficult sounds has a role in the teaching of pronunciation?
9. Why do you think much pronunciation teaching appears to be ineffective?
10. What personality factors do you think might play a role in learning pronunciation?
11. To what extent do you think intelligibility is a sufficient goal in the learning of pronunciation?

After Reading

1. Examine a textbook for teaching pronunciation. What aspects of pronunciation does it teach? What exercise types does it employ? To what extent do the exercises link pronunciation to communicative interaction?
2. Jones suggests that older learners "might benefit from a more descriptive or analytic approach" to the teaching of pronunciation than younger learners. What might the implications of this be for program design and teaching strategies?
3. Design an activity that teaches pronunciation within a communicative task.
4. Do you agree that teachers and classrooms seem to have very little to do with how well students pronounce English?
5. What is the role of the teacher in a pronunciation class? What is the role of the learners?
6. What are the arguments for and against the use of pronunciation drills?
7. What is the role of focused listening in the teaching of pronunciation? Give examples of activities of this kind.
8. What is the role of monitoring in the learning of pronunciation? Suggest activities that can develop this capacity.
9. How can learners be included "in the decision-making process concerning the areas in which they would like to improve their speaking," according to Hebert?
10. Listen to some samples of low-level second language learners speaking, and use the diagnostic profile proposed by Hebert to identify their pronunciation problems.
11. Choose a topic for a speaking lesson and plan a lesson that builds in a pronunciation focus, following the approach illustrated by Hebert.

CHAPTER 16

Beyond 'Listen and Repeat': Pronunciation Teaching Materials and Theories of Second Language Acquisition

Rodney H. Jones

INTRODUCTION

Over the past half century, the fortunes of pronunciation teaching have waxed and waned. Irrelevant in the grammar translation approach, pronunciation grew in prominence with the rise of the Direct Method and Audiolingualism, only to be pushed again to the sidelines with the ascendency of Communicative Language Teaching (CLT) and the Natural Approach (Krashen, 1982). Today, pronunciation teaching is experiencing a new resurgence, fuelled largely by the increasing awareness of the communicative function of suprasegmental features in spoken discourse (Brazil, Coulthard, & Johns, 1980; Brown & Yule, 1983). In the late 1980s, researchers called for a more 'top-down' approach to pronunciation teaching (Pennington & Richards, 1986; Pennington, 1989), emphasizing the broader, more meaningful aspects of phonology in connected speech rather than practice with isolated sounds, thus ushering pronunciation back into the communicative fold. Materials writers responded with a wealth of courses and recipe books focusing on suprasegmental pronunciation (Bradford, 1988; Gilbert, 1984; Rogerson & Gilbert, 1990). A closer look at such materials, however, reveals that, with notable exceptions (Bowen & Marks, 1992; Bowler & Cunningham, 1991), most commercially produced course books on pronunciation today present activities remarkably similar to the audiolingual texts of the 1950s, relying heavily on mechanical drilling of decontextualized words and sentences. Although they profess to teach the more communicative aspects of pronunciation, many such texts go about it in a decidedly uncommunicative way. The more pronunciation teaching materials have changed, it seems, the more they have stayed the same.

Meanwhile, research into second language phonology has suggested a wide range of factors affecting the acquisition of pronunciation beyond the behaviourist notion of habit formation, including those relating to cognitive development, linguistic universals and psychological and sociological conditions. This paper examines the extent to which the results of such research have made their way into commercially produced pronunciation materials and suggests ways in which materials can be brought more in line with research findings.

PRONUNCIATION TEACHING AND THEORIES

CAN PRONUNCIATION BE TAUGHT?

Arguments against the explicit teaching of pronunciation rely on two basic assumptions about the acquisition of second language phonology: the first, based on the *critical period hypothesis*, claims that it is virtually impossible for adults to acquire nativelike pronunciation in a foreign language (for review, see Burrill, 1985); the second, arising primarily from the work of Krashen (1982), insists that pronunciation is an acquired skill and that focused instruction is at best useless and at worst detrimental.

A number of studies have supported the popular notion that children enjoy an advantage over adults in learning the pronunciation of a second language (Asher & Garcia, 1969; Scovel, 1969; Siegler, Krashen, & Ladefoged, 1975). Such studies, however, fail to prove that it is impossible for adults to acquire nativelike pronunciation, and several researchers have presented strong evidence to the contrary (Neufeld, 1980; Tarone, 1978). A widely cited study by Snow and Hoefnagel-Hohle (1977) found that adults were actually superior to children in the areas of pronunciation and sound discrimination, at least in the first stages of learning, and, although children excelled in later stages, the only subject in the study identified as acquiring nativelike pronunciation was the teenager. Flege (1987), in a review of the literature, notes that the results of many empirical studies are 'inconsistent with the expectations generated by *the critical period hypothesis*' (p. 174) and points out that the hypothesis itself is difficult to test, as it is hard to isolate speech learning from other factors associated with age. Others have suggested that age-related differences might be the result of wider sociocultural and general maturational variables (Leather & James, 1991), or of differences in learning strategies among different age groups. The social pressures for phonological conformity and the ways these are manifested, for instance, might be different for children than for older learners (Tarone, 1978). It has further been pointed out that adults and adolescents have skills such as 'ability to compare and contrast and recognise patterns in speech' not available to children (Pennington, 1995, p. 102). The implication of such research on the development of pronunciation teaching materials is not that adults should be denied pronunciation training, but that learners of different ages may respond differently, both emotionally and cognitively, to different kinds of teaching approaches and task types: whereas imitation activities might be more successful with younger learners, older learners might benefit from a more descriptive or analytic approach (Brown, 1992).

The second argument against pronunciation teaching claims that the factors affecting second language pronunciation are chiefly acquisition variables, which cannot be affected by focused practice and the teaching of formal rules (Krashen, 1982). The enormous influence of this argument is evidenced by the virtual disappearance of pronunciation work in 'communicative' course books of the 1970s. Proponents of this idea often point to a study by Purcell and Suter (1980), which concludes that the factors which most affect the acquisition of L2 phonology (native language, aptitude for oral mimicry, interaction with native speakers and motivation) 'seem to be those which teachers have the least influence on' (p. 285). 'Teachers and classrooms', Purcell and Suter claim, 'seem to have very little to do with how well our students pronounced English' (p. 285). The problem with Purcell and Suter and other studies that support this claim is that, for the most part, they have focused on acquisition in a second language environment, and that they tend to underestimate the effect teachers and classrooms can have in the areas of motivation and exposure. Again, the implication for materials is not that pronunciation should be ignored, but that pronunciation teaching methods should more fully address the issues of motivation and exposure by creating an awareness of the importance of pronunciation and providing more exposure to input from native speakers.

LISTEN AND REPEAT: PHONOLOGY AND BEHAVIOURISM

Perhaps the oldest method of teaching pronunciation involves exercises in elocution: imitation drills and reading aloud. The popular image of students chanting 'the rain in Spain falls mainly on the plain' is still the reality of many language classrooms. With the development of recording technology and the rise of Audiolingualism, such methods became the stock-in-trade of language teaching, and, although now widely discredited in the areas of grammar and vocabulary teaching, the 'listen and repeat' approach has persisted in the teaching of pronunciation. Even materials which claim to be communicative often offer only a variation on this approach in which simple dialogue reading or practice with minimal pairs is passed off as 'communicative' (see, for example, Gilbert, 1984, 1993). Part of the reason for the focus on habit formation in acquiring L2 phonology is the special characteristics of pronunciation, which, unlike other language skills, involves both cognitive and motor functions: few would deny that repeated practice of motor functions results in increased dexterity. Recent research, however, has revealed the limitations of this approach, finding that, as with grammar, students who exhibit accuracy in controlled practice may fail to transfer such gains to actual communicative language use (Cohen, Larson-Freeman, & Tarone, 1991), and that accuracy of pronunciation varies according to the type of task learners are engaged in (Dickerson, 1975). Others have pointed out that the benefits of imitation drills may depend on learners' aptitude for oral mimicry. For learners without 'good ears', drills may cause production to stabilize before reaching the target (Kenworthy, 1987).

Central to this debate is the question of which half of the 'listen and repeat' equation results in increased accuracy – perception or production. Some teaching materials emphasise the importance of sound discrimination, insisting that students who cannot hear a particular English contrast have no chance of reproducing it (O'Connor & Fletcher, 1989). Several studies, however, suggest that this is not the case. Goto (1971), in his examination of Japanese learners' ability to produce and perceive the *r/l* contrast, found that some subjects with poor discrimination could still pronounce the sounds correctly, suggesting that perception may not precede production and that kinaesthetic sensation may be at least as important as auditory feedback. Similarly, Leather and James (1991) found that 'training in one modality tended to be sufficient to enable a learner to perform in another' (p. 320). Listening and repeating seem to be a two-way street: Focused listening can improve oral production and practice in oral production can improve auditory perception (Pennington, 1996).

It appears that although both imitation and discrimination drills have an important place in the teaching of pronunciation as a means to help articulation become more automatic and routinised, they are best seen as a step toward more meaningful, communicative practice (Pennington, 1996). To be truly effective, drills have to move beyond the simple identification and mimicking of decontextualised sound contrasts to the perception of more meaningful, communicative characteristics of input (Wong, 1987) and the ability to move beyond accurate production of discrete sounds to integrating those sounds into effective communication. Drills can also be made more lively and memorable by concentrating not just on oral and aural modalities, but also including visual representations and training in the awareness of kinaesthetic sensation (Acton, 1984; Pennington, 1996).

Many materials have sought to integrate perception and production as equal components in pronunciation training. Gilbert (1984, 1993) and Rogerson and Gilbert (1990) promote their books as both pronunciation and listening comprehension courses. Other materials writers have begun to recognise the importance of other modalities (visual and kinaesthetic) in pronunciation training, combining pictures, gestures and physical activities (such as the stretching of rubber bands) with drills, along the lines of Total Physical Response (Acton, 1984; Gilbert, 1993; Pennington, 1996).

INTERLANGUAGE PHONOLOGY

It is a widely held belief that interference from learners' first language affects the acquisition of the second language sound system more than other systems (such as grammar) (Kranke & Christison, 1983). This belief is reflected in the large number of pronunciation teaching materials which include sections on contrastive analysis (Baker, 1977; Bowler & Cunningham, 1991; Kenworthy, 1987; O'Connor & Fletcher, 1989). These sections, however, usually alerting teachers to 'special problems' likely to be encountered by particular L1 speakers, are often simplistic and misleading, treating the production of specific sounds and sound contrasts divorced from the natural stream of speech and usually ignoring suprasegmental features of nonnative accents.

The extent to which interlanguage phonology is affected by L1 transfer, and the relative value of providing L1-specific pronunciation practice, are very much in debate. Tarone (1978) suggests that there is a universal tendency in language acquisition to reduce complex forms, and that 'transfer is only a part – and often a small part – of the influence on interlanguage phonology' (p. 15), with other factors such as overgeneralization, approximation and avoidance being much more significant. It may be that the influence of learners' native language on their pronunciation is not really stronger than on other areas of language use, but simply more noticeable to the casual observer.

Recently, contrastive analysis has given way to the more sophisticated theories of equivalence classification, whereby learners approach a new sound system by mapping it onto their L1 sound system, using existing categories where similarities exist and creating new categories for unfamiliar features (Flege, 1987), and 'markedness' (Eckman, 1977), which posits that certain features are inherently more difficult than others, regardless of the learners' language backgrounds. Several researchers claim that universal constraints of human speech production and perception and nonphonological developmental characteristics might be much more important than L1 interference. Maken and Ferguson (1987) point out, for example, that phonological processes such as substitution, assimilation, deletion and reduplication, evident in L1 acquisition, are also present in L2 acquisition, suggesting that acquisition of a second language sound system may involve continued operation or reactivation of universal phonological processes. Furthermore, episodes of overgeneralization and experimentation in interlanguage phonology indicate that the process of building a phonological system 'is not an automatic one, but rather an active one' (Maken & Ferguson, 1987, p. 17).

In light of these findings, materials writers should approach predicting pronunciation problems based on learners' native language with caution. On the one hand, activities and methods that encourage inappropriate equivalence classification, such as overemphasis on orthography or use of simplified systems of phonetic transcription based on the L1, should be avoided (Pennington, 1996). On the other hand, L1 transfer should not be seen automatically as something negative, but rather as a natural stage and valuable strategy in the process of the acquisition of the L2 sound system (Kenworthy, 1987; Tarone, 1978). Consciousness-raising activities which sensitise learners to the differences between L1 and L2 systems and the L2 system and their own interlanguage might be more beneficial than error correction.

PHONOLOGY AND THE MONITOR

Since the publication of Morley's classic *Improving Spoken English* (1979), there has been increased attention in pronunciation materials to training students to monitor their production through the teaching of formal rules, feedback and reflective activities (Acton, 1984; Bradford, 1988; Crawford, 1987; Firth, 1987; Pennington, 1996; Wong, 1987). This trend is based on the assumption that 'pronunciation improves through gradual monitoring of the acquired system based on conscious knowledge of the facts learned about the language' (Crawford, 1987, p. 109). Krashen and his colleagues, of course, would argue against training that strengthens the monitor as useless for improving spoken language, which normally does not involve enough time for the monitor to operate. In fact, such training, they might add, could actually encourage 'monitor overuse' resulting in a decrease in fluency. Other theories incorporating the monitor model, however (such as that suggested by Bialystok), posit a more porous boundary between learned and acquired systems through which 'information stored in explicit linguistic knowledge may become automatic and transferred to implicit linguistic knowledge after continued use via the monitor' (Crawford, 1987, p. 113). Dickerson (1987), in a study involving Chinese, Japanese and Korean learners, found that formal rules do result in improvement when used for monitoring speech, and, although they can interfere with production when used for initiating speech, subjects gained in both fluency and accuracy after a period of 'covert rehearsal'. He hypothesised that formal rules may help acquisition by 'generate input for the acquisition device' in the form of learners 'talking to themselves' (p. 134), and calls for a 'better balance in our instructional activities between supplying ideal input and equipping learners to supply their own ideal input' (p. 137). Similarly, Jones, Rusman, and Evans (1994) found that students with prior exposure to phonological rules and principles, although they do not always produce more accurate pronunciation, seem to be better equipped to assess their own speech and more aware of their particular pronunciation problems. Acton (1984) suggests '*post hoc* monitoring', where learners reflect on the accuracy of their productions after the fact, and 'kinaesthetic monitoring', where learners attempt to monitor their output based on correct 'feel' rather than auditory feedback.

Although rule teaching that is too complicated or elaborate, such as all the varied rules governing intonation in discourse, might overwhelm the monitor and thus be detrimental (Kenworthy, 1987), there seems to be no justification for denying learners linguistic information which may empower them to improve on their own. The explicit presentations of rules has been a standard feature of pronunciation textbooks for more than two decades, ranging from detailed explanations of phonological concepts (O'Connor, 1980) to simple, graphic representations of articulatory processes (as in Baker, 1977). Most of these materials, however, fail to take Morley's (1979) lead and go beyond abstract presentation to the application of rules in follow-up activities such as self- or peer monitoring. Furthermore, most rule teaching focuses on single narrow models (such as Received Pronunciation) to the exclusion of local varieties, and is laid out in a deductive, prescriptive fashion. A particularly intriguing direction taken by some materials writers is to present rules more inductively through 'discovery activities' in which students listen and attempt to articulate the rules governing what they have heard with the help of cues, or collaborate with their classmates to find patterns in written or spoken text. This technique has many advantages: It can make rules more memorable to learners in that they are formulated by themselves; it can increase awareness of the communicative aspects of pronunciation; and it can provide an opportunity for communicative practice as learners interact with their peers (for examples, see Bowler & Cunningham, 1991; Bradford, 1988).

COMMUNICATION AND CONTEXTUALISATION

Perhaps the most criticized aspect of pronunciation teaching materials is their widespread reliance on decontextualized language and lack of grounding in the realities of actual communication. It is one of Krashen's (1982) chief tenets that language is best taught when it is being used to transmit messages, and this sentiment has been echoed in relation to pronunciation teaching by such researchers as Pennington and Richards (1986), who point out that it is 'artificial to divorce pronunciation from communication and other aspects of language use' (p. 208). 'In order to become a competent speaker and listener', writes Pennington (1996), 'a language learner needs to attend to not only the strictly mechanical, articulatory aspects of pronunciation, but also to the meaningful correlates of those articulatory features in the immediate linguistic context, as well as the larger context of human communication'. Pica (1984) goes so far as to attribute the widespread ineffectiveness of pronunciation training for adults to the failure of teachers and materials writers to approach the skill communicatively.

Some, though not many, materials writers have attempted to incorporate a more communicative dimension in their design of tasks and activities. Bradford (1988), for example, organises her course according to discourse functions (highlighting, telling and referring, etc.) rather than the traditional phonological categories. Other writers have included interactive activities where there is a phonological 'information gap' such that only proper pronunciation and perception can lead to the correct outcome in the task (see, for example, Gilbert, 1993). There has also been an attempt to make repetitive practice of rhythm and sound more natural and meaningful through the use of poetry and song (Gilbert, 1993; Maley, 1987). Finally, several materials writers have attempted to integrate pronunciation practice into broader communicative activities by either finding lexical/grammatical contexts with naturally occurring instances of target sounds or features (Celce-Murcia, 1987) or simply altering the language in texts used in such activities (such as the names of dishes on a menu or the names of streets on a map) to include target sounds. A large number of materials, however, offer activities which, though at first glance seeming more communicative, are actually just more elaborate forms of drilling, such as dialogue reading and highly structured pair practice such as questionnaire completion, which learners are able to engage in without attending to meaning or communication at all. In Gilbert's (1993) widely used *Clear Speech*, for example, more than a quarter of the activities are discrimination or repetition drills using decontextualised words, phrases or sentences; another 25% of the activities are reading tasks in which students read aloud printed words, sentences, dialogues, poems or paragraphs; and only about 2% of the activities in the book actually involve meaningful interaction and the transfer of information beyond one or two sentences.

Absent from most materials is the opportunity for freer practice that allows students to participate in discourse situations that exemplify a variety of suprasegmental features, such as the free conversation and 'fluency workshop' activities advocated by Wong (1987).

It is obvious that creating a stronger link between pronunciation and communication can help increase learners' motivation by bringing pronunciation beyond the lowest common denominator of 'intelligibility' and encouraging students' awareness of its potential as a tool for making their language not only easier to understand but more effective.

PSYCHOLOGICAL AND SOCIOLOGICAL FACTORS

Two aspects of pronunciation teaching that have been virtually ignored in teaching materials are the psychological and sociological dimensions. The way one speaks has a great deal to do with the impression he or she wants to create in a particular context. It has been claimed that the more learners identify with native speakers of a second language, the more likely they are to sound like native speakers. Conversely, learners who wish to retain identification with their own culture or social category may consciously or unconsciously retain a foreign accent as a marker of in-group affiliation. Such L2 social marking can occur even in the very early stages of second language acquisition (Dowd, Zuengler, & Berkowitz, 1990). Consequently, a number of researchers have claimed that work on pronunciation 'needs to be tied in with work on the individual's value set, attitudes and socio-cultural schemata' (Pennington, 1995, p. 104), and that targets for pronunciation teaching should be appropriate for the particular sociological context in which the teaching takes place (Brown, 1989).

Similarly, the way an individual pronounces has much to do with his or her personality and psychological or emotional state at any given time. Acton (1984) sees preparing students psychologically as a necessary correlate to improving their pronunciation. Phonology, he says, has both 'inside-out' and 'outside-in' dimensions which function in a kind of loop: 'Not only does personality or emotional state show in pronunciation . . . but the converse is also true: speakers can control their nerves or inner states by speaking properly. This is the basic tenet of successful programs in voice training and public speaking' (p. 75). Others (such as Guiora & Schonberger, 1990) point to the importance of empathy and the development of a 'second language ego'.

Finally, learners' reasons for learning a second language and the uses they plan to put the language to can have an effect on how nativelike they may want or need to sound. Learners who expect to have a large amount of interaction with native speakers in business or professional contexts, for example, will have different needs and expectations from learners who plan to use the language primarily for communication with other nonnative speakers.

Of course, it is difficult for teaching materials prepared for an international market to cater to learners with different needs, personalities, learning styles and cultural backgrounds. Some writers, however, have attempted to include opportunities for personalisation and student-centred learning in their activities (Bowen & Marks, 1992; Kenworthy, 1987; Morley, 1979). Such opportunities can be realized through questionnaires asking learners to reflect on their attitudes toward nonnative-like pronunciation of their own language, their pronunciation needs in their future careers, and their perceptions of their ability to change their pronunciation, as well as activities in which learners are asked to comment on their impressions of recordings of speakers with different varieties and degrees of foreign accent.

CONCLUSION: PRONUNCIATION TEACHING MATERIALS IN THE FUTURE

Contemporary materials for the teaching of pronunciation, though still retaining many of the characteristics of traditional audiolingual texts, have begun to incorporate more meaningful and communicative practice, an increased emphasis on suprasegmentals, and other features such as consciousness-raising and self-monitoring which reflect current research into the acquisition of second language phonology. Much, however, remains to be done to bring materials in line with SLA research findings.

Writers of pronunciation teaching materials in the coming years will likely pay more attention to learners' sociolinguistic situations and the political implications of attitudes toward nonnative accents. They will also increasingly find ways of dealing with the psychological aspects of pronunciation training, integrating confidence building and reflective activities into their courses. More attention will also be given to the order in which phonological principles are presented, with increased focus on the broader, more communicative aspects of pronunciation such as 'voice quality' (Jones & Evans, 1995). Like other aspects of language teaching, pronunciation materials must adapt to changes within ESL, addressing, for example, the more specialized needs of ESL, and the changing role of the learners in Self-Access Language Learning (Rogerson-Revell & Miller, 1994). Listening will continue to play a large part in pronunciation training, with perhaps more authentic listening tasks with a variety of accents. The explicit teaching of rules will remain, but will be tempered with more and more opportunities for free practice, and training at the monitor will continue to be emphasised with exercises in self-assessment. Finally, pronunciation will, whenever possible, be taught in concert with other skills, not as a separate entity, but as another string in the communicative bow.

References

Acton, W. (1984). Changing fossilized pronunciation. *TESOL Quarterly*, *18*(1), 69–83.

Asher, J., & Garcia, R. (1969). The optimal age to learn a foreign language. *Modern Language Journal*, *53*, 334–341.

Baker, A. (1977). *Ship or sheep*. Cambridge: Cambridge University Press.

Bowen, T., & Marks, J. (1992). *The pronunciation book*. London: Longman.

Bowler, B., & Cunningham, S. (1991). *Headway: Upper-intermediate pronunciation*. Oxford: Oxford University Press.

Bradford, B., (1988). *Intonation in context*. Cambridge: Cambridge University Press.

Brazil, D., Coulthard, M., & Johns, C. (1980). *Discourse intonation and language teaching*. London: Longman.

Brown, A. (1989). Models, standards, targets/goals and norms in pronunciation teaching. *World Englishes*, *8*(2), 193–200.

Brown, A. (1992). Twenty questions. In A. Brown (Ed.), *Approaches to pronunciation teaching*. London: Macmillan.

Brown, G., & Yule, G. (1983). *Teaching the spoken language*. Cambridge: Cambridge University Press.

Burrill, C. (1985). The sensitive period hypothesis: A review of literature regarding acquisition of a native-like pronunciation in a second language. Paper presented at a meeting of the TRI-TESOL Conference. Bellevue, WA, 15 November.

Celce-Murcia, M. (1987). Teaching pronunciation as communication. In J. Morley (Ed.), *Current perspectives on pronunciation* (pp. 1–12). Washington, DC: TESOL.

Cohen, A. D., Larson-Freeman, D., & Tarone, E. (1991). The contribution of SLA theories and research to teaching language. Paper presented at the Regional Language Centre Seminar on Language Acquisition and the Second/Foreign Language Classroom. Singapore, 22–26 April.

Crawford, W. W. (1987). The pronunciation monitor: L2 acquisition considerations and pedagogical priorities. In J. Morley (Ed.), *Current perspectives on pronunciation* (pp. 103–121). Washington, DC: TESOL.

Dickerson, L. (1975). The learner's interlanguage as a set of variable rules. *TESOL Quarterly*, *9*(4), 401–408.

Dickerson, W. B. (1987). Explicit rules and the developing interlanguage phonology. In A. James & J. Leather (Eds.), *Sound patterns in second language acquisition* (pp. 121–140). Dordrecht, Holland: Foris.

Dowd, J., Zuengler, J., & Berkowitz, D. (1990). L2 social marking: Research issues. *Applied Linguistics*, *11*(1), 16–29.

Eckman, F. R. (1977). Markedness and the contrastive analysis hypothesis. *Language Learning*, *27*, 315–330.

Firth, S. (1987). Developing self-correcting and self-monitoring strategies. *TESL Talk*, *17*(1), 148–152.

Flege, J. (1987). A critical period for learning to pronounce second languages? *Applied Linguistics*, *8*, 162–177.

Gilbert, J. B. (1984). *Clear speech: Pronunciation and listening comprehension in American English* (1st ed.) New York: Cambridge University Press.

Gilbert, J. B. (1993). *Clear speech: Pronunciation and listening comprehension in North American English*. New York: Cambridge University Press.

Goto, H. (1971). Auditory perception by normal Japanese adults of the sounds "l" and "r". *Neuropsychologia*, 317–323.

Guiora, A., & Schonberger, R. (1990). Native pronunciation of bilinguals. In J. Leather & A. James (Eds.), *NEW SOUNDS 90: Proceedings of the 1990 Amsterdam Symposium on the Acquisition of Second-Language Speech* (pp. 26–36). Amsterdam: University of Amsterdam.

Jones, R. H., & Evans, S. (1995). Teaching pronunciation through voice quality. *English Language Teaching Journal*, *49*(3), 244–251.

Jones, R. H., Rusmin, R., & Evans, S. (1994). Self-assessment of pronunciation by Chinese tertiary students. In D. Nunan, R. Berry, & V. Berry (Eds.), *Language awareness in language education: Proceedings of the International Language in Education Conference 1994* (pp. 169–180). Hong Kong: University of Hong Kong, Department of Curriculum Studies.

Kenworthy, J. (1987). *Teaching English pronunciation*. London: Longman.

Kranke, K., & Christison, M. A. (1983). Recent language research and some language teaching principles. *TESOL Quarterly*, *17*(4), 635–650.

Krashen, S. D. (1982). *Principles and practice in second language acquisition*. Fairview Park: Pergamon.

Leather, J., & James, A. (1991). The acquisition of second language speech. *Studies in Second Language Acquisition*, *13*, 305–331.

Maken, M. A., & Ferguson, C. A. (1987). Phonological universals in language acquisition. In G. Ioup & S. H. Weinberger (Eds.), *Interlanguage phonology* (pp. 3–22). Cambridge: Newbury House.

Maley, A. (1987). Poetry and song as effective language learning activities. In W. M. Rivers (Ed.), *Interactive language teaching* (pp. 93–109). Oxford: Oxford University Press.

Morely, J. (1979). *Improving spoken English*. Ann Arbor: University of Michigan Press.

Neufeld, G. G. (1980). On the adult's ability to acquire phonology. *TESOL Quarterly*, *14*, 285–298.

O'Connor, J. D. (1980). *Better English pronunciation* (2nd ed.). Cambridge: Cambridge University Press.

O'Connor, J. D., & Fletcher, C. (1989). *Sounds English*. Harlow, UK: Longman.

Pennington, M. C. (1989). Teaching pronunciation from the top down. *RELC Journal*, *20*(1), 20–38 .

Pennington, M. C. (1995). Recent research in second language phonology: Implications for practice. In J. Morley (Ed.), *Pronunciation, pedogogy and theory: New views, new directions* (pp. 94–108). Alexandria, VA: TOESL.

Pennington, M. C. (1996). *Phonology in English language teaching: An international approach*. London: Longman.

Pennington, M. C., & Richards, J. C. (1986). Pronunciation revisited. *TESOL Quarterly*, *20*(2), 207–225.

Pica, T. (1984). Pronunciation activities with an accent on communication. *English Teaching Forum*, *22*(3), 2–6.

Purcell, E., & Suter, R. (1980). Predictors of pronunciation accuracy: A reexamination. *Language Learning*, *30*(2), 271–287.

Rogerson, P., & Gilbert, J. B. (1990). *Speaking clearly*. Cambridge: Cambridge University Press.

Rogerson-Revell, P., & Miller, L. (1994). Developing pronunciation skills through self-access learning. In D. Gardner & L. Miller (Eds.), *Directions in self-access language learning*. Hong Kong: Hong Kong University Press.

Scovel, T. (1969). Foreign accents, language acquisition and cerebral dominance. *Language Learning*, *19*(3), 245–253.

Siegler, H. W., Krashen, S. H., & Ladefoged, P. (1975). Maturational constraints in the acquisition of second language accent. *Language Sciences*, *36*, 20–22.

Snow, C. E., & Hoefnagel-Hohle, M. (1977). Age differences in the pronunciation of foreign sounds. *Language and Speech, 20*, 357–365.

Tarone, E. (1978). The phonology of interlanguage. In J. C. Richards (Ed.), *Understanding second and foreign language learning* (pp. 15–33). Rowley, MA: Newbury House.

Wong, R. (1987). Learner variables and prepronunciation considerations in teaching pronunciation. In J. Morley (Ed.), *Current perspectives on pronunciation* (pp. 13–28). Washington, DC: TESOL.

CHAPTER 17

PracTESOL: It's Not What You Say, but How You Say It!

Julie Hebert

INTRODUCTION

To communicate effectively, language learners need to become proficient in using the semantic, syntactic, lexical, morphological and phonological elements of the language being learnt. They also need to understand its pragmatic use. The focus in ESL literature has tended to be on grammatical, thematic and functional approaches to ESL syllabus design. As the title of this paper suggests, intelligibility entails more than simply using appropriate lexical items and correct word order: Words stressed incorrectly or with inappropriate pitch or intonation will impede the learner in getting the intended message across. Phonology, then, should be an integral part of any ESL lesson/syllabus. What follows is an outline of one way to approach incorporating a phonological component into ESL lessons. It is based on the following assumptions about oral communication:

1. Speaking usually involves two or more people who use language for interactional or transactional purposes. It is not the oral expression of written language. This should be reflected in the types of activities used in ESL classrooms.
2. Spoken language imparts referential and affective meaning. When we speak, we reveal our interest and attitudes toward the topic being discussed and toward the people we are speaking with. These messages are largely conveyed through the prosodic features of language: stress and rhythm, intonation, pitch variation and volume. For these reasons, it would seem essential that phonology be learned in context and not treated incidentally and/or separately. In addition to making decisions about content, grammatical structures, lexical items, functions, skills, methodology and materials, we need to identify phonological elements as well.
3. Nativelike speech, especially for adult learners, takes time. For low-level learners, it is probably better to focus on the global aspects of oral production than on accuracy

(except in cases where inadvertent mispronunciations will cause embarrassment). A learner's intelligibility will not be affected if she substitutes one phoneme for another. For example, /dis iz di kæt/ instead of /ð is iz ð ə kæt/. However, if she says the former with a rising intonation contour when her intent is to impart information, the listener will encounter some difficulty in understanding her meaning. All ESL learners want to be understood by others, but not all will want to sound like native speakers; psychosocial and individual factors will influence their attitudes and motivation to modify their accent.

4. Not all 'problems' will be at the level of production; some will be associated with perception. The techniques used need to mirror the types of 'problems' the learners are encountering. A diagnosis of learners' spoken English will provide information as to the types of activities and techniques that will be required.
5. Learners need to have some understanding of the role phonology plays in language learning. Learning will be enhanced if learners are included in the decision-making process concerning the areas in which they would like to improve their speaking.

Where to Begin

As just indicated, I believe that learners benefit from having some understanding of the pedagogical basis of classroom activities. Most learners understand the need for a focus on grammatical structures, lexis and particular content areas. The role phonology plays in ESL is not so obvious and needs to be explained. By introducing learners to some of the prosodic features of English, learners can understand the reasons for activities used in the classroom. This knowledge also allows them to evaluate their own progress and provides them with strategies to use in communicative exchanges outside the classroom. With higher levels, this presents few problems since learners have enough language to understand the concepts involved and to ask questions where doubts arise. With lower levels, a different approach is required, which includes simplified terminology and graphic and gestural representations. I will outline how this can be done with low-level and more advanced learners.

Example 1: Class: ASLPR $0^{+}/1^{-}$*

Step 1: Setting the Context

You are teaching a unit of work on personal identification. You have introduced the relevant lexical items and grammatical structures using your preferred methodology. You want to introduce some prosodic features. Word stress can be introduced in the following way: List the nationalities represented in the class on the chalkboard; make sure that they are grouped according to similar stress patterns (e.g., *Chin'ese, Vietnam'ese, Japan'ese*). Ask learners which part of the word sounds 'stronger, louder and longer'. Indicate what you mean by these terms; clench your fist for strong, raise your voice for louder and draw out an utterance for longer by exaggerating the *-ese* (e.g., *Chin'E-S-E*). Mark the stressed syllable. Make sure the learners understand that the symbol used is to mark the stress. Shift the stress onto another syllable to show how it alters the sound of the word. Use the grammatical structures associated with personal identification to illustrate some of the functions of intonation in English. Introduce students to the intonation patterns of *wh-* questions and yes/no questions at the same time; otherwise they may draw the conclusion that all questions in English are uttered with rising intonation. Make a list of both on the chalkboard.

*Australian Second Language Proficiency Rating Level $0^{+}/1^{-}$

Where do you come from?

What's your nationality?

Do you come from Afghanistan?

Are you from Afghanistan?

Ask learners to listen to both types of questions and whether the voice goes up or down at the end of the question. Mark with appropriate contour. Demonstrate with arm movement; make sure your arm moves from right to left. Now show how the intonation changes in question-answer routines:

What's your nationality?	*Are you Chinese?*
I'm Chinese	*Yes, I am.*

Use the same question-answer routines to show how pitch variation indicates the speaker's attitude, status or mood. Utter the routines in a sad, happy, friendly, superior, surprised, angry and tired way. Ask learners to indicate how you feel about what you're saying (*Am I happy?* etc.). Through these activities the learners have some idea of the role phonology plays in spoken English. Tell them that they'll be doing activities to help them improve their speaking throughout the course.

STEP 2: DIAGNOSING LEARNERS' SPOKEN ENGLISH

The phonological features you focus on need to be related to the 'problems' the learners are encountering. By collecting data of the learners' general speaking habits, you can identify individual learner 'problems' and those common to the group. Collect samples of learners' speech, on cassette or video. For the first analysis, it is probably least traumatic for the learners if you collect a monologue of learners speaking about themselves for 1 minute. At a later date you can collect spontaneous samples of dialogues between learners. Devise a one-page diagnostic learner profile with the following headings: clarity, speed, loudness, breathing, fluency, voice, gestural expressions, eye gaze, intonation, stress rhythm, consonants and vowels. Diagnose learners' speech according to these categories. I have found Firth's (1987) diagnostic profile particularly useful for determining those elements which reflect the needs of the majority of learners in the class.

DIAGNOSTIC PROFILE

Suprasegmental level

General speaking habits

1. *Clarity.* Is the learner's speech clear?
   Are there instances where there is a breakdown in communication?
   What are the major factors?
2. *Speed.* Does the learner speak too quickly?
   Is her speech unintelligible because she speaks too quickly?
3. *Loudness.* Does the learner speak too softly?
   Does the lack of volume affect intelligibility?
4. *Breathing.* Does the learner speak with appropriate pauses, breaking each utterance into thought groups?
5. *Fluency.* Does the learner speak with either long silences between words *or* too many 'filled pauses' (e.g., 'ah . . . ummm')?

6. *Voice.* Is there enough variation in pitch?
7. *Eye gaze.* Does the learner use eye-gaze behaviour appropriate to the context (e.g., facing a conversational partner or looking at the audience if delivering an oral presentation)?
8. *Expressive behaviour.* Does the learner overuse gestures? Does the facial expression match the utterance?

Intonation

1. Is the learner using appropriate intonation patterns in utterances? Can the learner use intonation contours to signal whether utterances are statements, lists, *wh-* questions or yes/no questions?
2. Is the learner changing pitch at the major stressed words?

Stress and rhythm

1. *Word-level stress*. Does the learner produce the schwa in unstressed syllables?
   Does the learner use loudness and length to differentiate between stressed and unstressed syllables?
2. *Sentence-level stress*. Does the learner stress each syllable equally?
   Is she able to produce appropriate strong and weak stresses?
   Are lexical words stressed and ungrammatical words unstressed?
   Does the learner place the tonic stress on the appropriate words?
3. *Linking*. Is the learner linking words appropriately? Are identical consonants linked (e.g., top position)?
   Are vowels linked (e.g., *pay up*)? Are consonants linked to vowels (e.g., *top of*)?

Segmental level

Consonants

1. *Substitution.* Is the learner substituting one phoneme for another?
2. *Omission.* Is the learner omitting consonants?
3. *Articulation.* Is the consonant being articulated properly (e.g., is /p/ aspirated word-initially)?
4. *Clusters.* Are consonant clusters articulated properly?
5. *Linking.* Are consonants linked to each other?

Vowels

1. *Substitution.* Is one vowel being substituted for another?
2. *Articulation.* Is the learner articulating vowels correctly (e.g., lip rounding)?
3. *Length.* Do vowels have their appropriate length?
4. *Reduction.* Are vowels reduced in unstressed syllables?
5. *Linking.* Are vowels properly linked to other vowels across word boundaries?

After you have analysed the data, you can identify the problems common to the majority of learners and you can provide feedback to individual learners. You now have to make some decisions concerning what you can achieve in the time you have available, the areas that should be given priority, the source of the problems (e.g., perception or production) and the types of activities that will help learners improve their oral production. How you determine teaching priorities will largely depend on where you perceive the problems to be. For example, some teachers might feel that accuracy is important and therefore might focus more on the segmental level; others might feel that the learner's overall intelligibility is more important than the correct articulation of particular phonemes. Personally, I think that with lower levels the focus should be on improving the learner's intelligibility; that is to say, to focus primarily on the suprasegmental level. If a learner's intelligibility is affected because her volume is too low, then it doesn't really matter how she articulates a particular phoneme. The listener will eventually tire of the strain of trying to hear what she is saying and the communicative exchange will suffer. Where the articulation of particular phonemes is causing the learner 'problems', these should be dealt with in context. For example, the way in which /p/ is articulated depends on its occurrence with other phonemes. Consider, for example, /p/ in *pin*, *spit*, *upper*, *captain* and *topmost*.

Activities that help the learner to perceive and produce utterances should be given equal weight. Activities that deal with perception of the input enable learners to process the information they are hearing. Between perceiving aural input and the production of output, learners need time to filter, assimilate, recognise, fix, store and structure information. In order to process the information, learners need to hear the auditory input many times.

On the basis of your decisions provide feedback to the students. Again this needs to be done in a simplified manner. Tell students that different languages have different 'music'. Ask representatives of the different language groups in the class to say something. Students listen to the different music. You will show them how to learn the music of English. Outline some of the areas common to all learners.

STEP 3: SELECTING THE CONTENT

Learning is enhanced when learners are involved in the decision making process and the content of courses is directly related to their immediate needs and context. For these reasons, I believe that it is prudent to not only diagnose the learners' phonological problems, but also the communicative contexts in which they use English outside the classroom. With lower levels this can be done in the following way: Introduce learners to the notion of neighbourhood. On the chalkboard, draw pictures of where you talk to people in a typical week (e.g., school, bank, library, post office, tram, home, swimming pool.) Rub out. Ask learners to draw a picture of where they use English in their neighbourhood. Give them 3 minutes. Draw a happy, sad and neutral face on the chalkboard. Ask learners to draw in the face that matches their feelings in each situation. In pairs, ask learners to 'discuss' similarities and differences in their drawings and why they feel this way. Move around and talk with each student; note down students' comments. Collect drawings and note those contexts where the learners indicate they are unhappy. Provide feedback: For example, ten people were unhappy using the telephone, nine at the bank, eight at the post office, six at the DSS, seven using public transport, one at the bottle shop, one at the cinema, and so on. Ask learners to vote on those areas they would like to be covered and in what order. Tell them that in the next few weeks you will cover these topics and ask them to do activities that will help them to understand and produce utterances in these contexts.

At this stage, you have introduced learners to some of the phonological features of English, diagnosed their spoken English and ascertained those contexts in the community where they wish to improve their language. How does this all relate to the lessons you plan?

STEP 4: INCORPORATING PHONOLOGY INTO ESL LESSONS

You've established that the majority of learners have problems with stress and rhythm and intonation patterns. They've indicated that banking is a topic they are interested in. You select relevant material for the level you're teaching. I will outline how a lesson (series of lessons or session, whatever applies) might proceed using Unit 28, 'An Interesting Discussion', from Corbel, *Using the System* (1985). The conversation in this unit is about a woman called Judy who withdraws money and then asks to see the manager about a loan. The function involved is making polite requests; the notion is banking systems; the grammatical structures include question forms, *will* used as future marker and *would* used as a request; the lexical focus is on numerals. Given your diagnosis, you decide that the phonological objective for this unit will be how to make polite requests, using the appropriate stress patterns and intonation contours.

PROCEDURE

Review stage:

Let's assume you've completed the initial steps of the lesson, communicative activities such as matching the title with the picture, predicting what the conversation will be about, listing names of banks,and so on.

Perception stage

Learners have picture of Judy and the teller in the bank.

1. Learners look at the picture again. *Which bank is Judy in?* *What's she doing?* *What time is it?* *What day is it?* Think about it silently for one minute. Group discussion. In pairs, look at the picture while the tape is playing. One person points to Judy when she speaks, the other to the teller when she speaks. Provide model for activity. Learners to change roles.	Structuring pause. Shows you that learners have associated the correct voice with the appropriate intonation contour. Different cultures attribute different characteristics to pitch and tonal variations. If learners miscue first time, they can self-correct the second time around.
2. Listen again to tape; this time half the class raises their hand when Judy speaks, the other when the teller speaks. Each half changes roles. *Think about the people speaking. How old are they? What do they look like?* etc. *Who speaks first, Judy or the teller?*	Teacher can *see* if students have recognised the appropriate voice and character. Structuring pause.
3. Give out sheet as outlined below. **Teller:** **Judy:** **Teller:** **Judy:** **Teller:** **Judy:**	Develops knowledge of utterances length. Provides visual representation of the auditory input. Useful for developing appropriate breathing patterns.

(Continued)

Perception stage

Learners have picture of Judy and the teller in the bank.

Students are to listen and draw a continuous line to match the length of the utterances they hear. Provide model of what is required (e.g., *How do you want the money?*). *Ah, a fifty, two twenties and a ten.* Play the tape again to allow learners to check their work.	Develops awareness of function of intonation curves. Falling intonation for statements. Rising intonation for yes/no questions and rise/fall patterns for *wh-* questions. Focus here is on pauses in utterances. Develops awareness of organisation of thought groups.
Listen again, this time for the intonation contours each time the person speaking takes a breath. Provide a model. e.g., Judy: ______ ______. Listen again, this time mark in where the speakers pause. Teacher provides model. e.g., ______ ______. Listen again, mark where stressed words occur in the utterance. e.g., ______ ______. Learners compare their work with a partner.	Here the focus is on stress patterns. Learners identify the words that are stressed and which word has the most stress (tonic) in the utterance. Move around groups and check learners' work to gain an idea of where difficulties are occurring. This will give you an idea of where further work is needed and highlight where difficulties will occur at the proudction stage.
4. *How do you think the teller feels?* *How do you think Judy feels?* *How do you know?* *What sorts of gestures would both use?* *Show me for the teller.* *Now show me for Judy.*	Relates the way in which people are speaking to the way they feel. Develops knowledge and use of appropriate body language. Helps learners to synchronise language with actions.
5. *Take 5 minutes with a partner or in small groups to talk about banks in your country.* *What do they look like?* *Who works in them?* *What are the hours?* *How do you say these numbers in your language?* Write 10, 20, 30, 50, 70, 90 and 100 on the chalkboard. After learners have said these numbers in their own language, ask where the stress occurs in English.	Structuring pause. Allows learners to have a break from concentrating. A freer type of activity allows them to be creative and active in a different way. All learners can succeed in this activity.

Production

6. Listen to tape and mouth utterances for each speaker. Change roles.	Chance for learners to mouth utterance without interference of vowel/consonant combinations.
7. Hand out text. Allow learners to read silently. When learners have read text, play tape so that they can read the text while listening to it.	Time for silent and individual work. Use tape and text together to minimise graphic interference.

(Continued)

Production	
Leaners shadow the tape, that is, speak with the tape while it plays. Change roles. Learners listen to text and add appropriate gestures as they apply to utterances (e.g., hand movements when teller counts out money).	
8. Isolate requests and questions. *How would you like the hundred?* *I'd like to see the manager.* *What was it about?* *Would you like to wait or come back?* *How long will he be?*	Useful to place stress markers, pause and intonation curves on text on an overhead transparency. Focus on the intonation patterns. Shows that a request need not always be in question form.
Provide half the class with a prompt (e.g., *hundred*); they ask the other half (*How would you like the hundred?*) as if they were: a. sad b. happy c. angry d. tired e. superior	Shows that there are a variety of responses to the same request. Allows learners to be creative.
The other half responds accordingly. Indicate the role volume, pitch variation, breathing, and speed play in showing attitude and status of the speaker. Demonstrate how gestures are also related to attitude and status of the speaker/listener.	Different emotions/attitudes are signalled by changes in pitch and volume levels. Breathing patterns also change, as do the gestures and facial expressions.
Hand out strips with prompts on them (e.g., *hundred* for *How would you like the hundred?*; *fifties* for *Two fifties please*). Learners walk around saying their utterance until they find their respective partners. When all learners have found their pairs, they stand in circle and repeat the request-answer couplets. Class comments on whether pairs are grouped correctly or not. Change pairs if and where necessary.	Allows you to check learning and it's fun.
9. Teacher and learners discuss what happens in the text. *First*, ... *Then*, ... Learners work in groups. Discuss any problems they encountered with grammar, phonology, or cultural aspects associated with the text. Teacher moves round the group.	Structuring activity. Allows for learners to reflect on lesson content and to check any doubts they many have. Another way to check that learners have understood basic ideas in text.
10. Discuss whether Judy will get the loan. How much? Follow-up activities could include a word find for lexical items, a comprehension exercise, a reading activity, a fill the gap exercise, or a role-play.	Focus for next unit.

Numerous other techniques could be used. These were just a few to illustrate how some prosodic features can be incorporated into lessons. They derive from the Structuro-Global Audio Visual (SGAV) approach to language learning. For further discussion, see *All's Well 1* and *All's Well 2* teacher's manuals (Dickinson, Levegue, & Sagot, 1976, 1977).

I will now outline how the same approach can be used with a higher level.

Example 2: ASLPR 2, Course Length 5 Months

The same procedure is used, only it can be more complex as the learners have greater knowledge of the language.

STEP 1: SET THE CONTEXT

1. Show a video of a short communication exchange. After viewing, ask students what the participants were talking about and how they felt. Then ask them how they deduced these facts. Introduce the notion that it is not so much 'what you say, but the way and why you say it'. Using the utterances from the exchange on the video, introduce the terminology of prosodic features of English. Include stress, rhythm, intonation, pitch and loudness. To introduce the terms, ask the following questions:

   Which words or syllables were spoken with more effort by the speakers?

   What do you notice about the words that are not spoken with effort?

   Did the speaker's voice go up or down at the end of the utterance?

   If there was a pause during the utterance, what happened to the speaker's voice?

   Was there any variation in the speaker's voice during the exchange? If so, where did it occur and why?

   Students' answers can be graphically represented on the chalkboard using utterances from the video. Stress can be represented by using a dash over the stressed syllable. Stressed syllables are louder and longer and produced at a higher pitch than unstressed syllables. Show this as outlined in the section on low-level learners. Introduce notation for marking unstressed syllables. Pitch variation can be introduced by using a musical metaphor. Explain that just as music goes up and down the scale, so too does our speaking. Draw three lines; call them keys. There are three keys: high, middle and low. We usually use the middle key for normal speaking – when we are speaking with friends or with others we consider as equals. However, if we want to convey other attitudes about the topic or person we are speaking to, we change the key to reflect those emotions. Think about what happens when you are angry. What happens to your voice? Depending on how angry you are, it can go up a key and the speed at which you speak increases dramatically. Conversely, it can go down a key and become almost a whisper and the rate will slow down considerably. Changing keys in conversations also signals status. Imagine the prime minister trying to convince one of his Cabinet ministers to change her mind about a policy. Because the prime minister is the dominant partner in the exchange, he will signal this by using the high key throughout the exchange. Watch televised Parliament for some examples of this feature. Conclude with the comment that languages vary in their use of these features.

2. Ask learners to say *Yes, I like learning English* in their own languages. As each language group does this, ask the other learners to comment on how similar and/or

different each of the utterances sounded. The purpose of this activity is to attune students to the differences between their language and English. It also highlights the fact that they will not all encounter the same sorts of problems, which might explain why some learners might appear to be 'better' speakers than others.

3. Give each language group a handout on phonological differences (both suprasegmental and segmental) between their language and English; they are to read and discuss it amongst themselves. Having set the context, outline how phonological elements can be incorporated into the syllabus, and ask students for their opinions.

STEP 2: PROPOSE AN APPROACH

1. Diagnose individual learner oral production. Give learners an example of the phonological diagnostic profile outlined earlier and discuss each category. Suggest that learners speak about themselves, or any topic of their choosing, on video for a minimum of 1 minute. Comment on learners' spoken English on the basis of handout and highlight two areas that need attention (i.e., where the strategies the learner is using make him/or her unintelligible).
2. Discuss your analysis of learners' oral production on both an individual and a group basis.
3. Learners write the teacher a personal letter outlining how they feel about their spoken English and where they would like to improve. The teacher selects topics and the medium to be used on the basis of learners' comments.

Here are some of the comments learners made in their personal letters:

> When I first came to Australia, 8 months ago, I had a few problems understanding the Australian accent. But the big problem was when I wanted to speak. I was so embarrassed and so scared that even though I knew what to say I couldn't open my mouth, or if I said, I was making mistakes.... There is something else I have to get used to with now, and that is speaking on the phone. I can talk to anybody I have never spoken to before. I can fix appointments or interviews throw [through] the phone, as long as I am by myself in the room: When someone else is in the room and I have never spoken on the phone with that person, I can't do it, my voice is trembling, I have problems breathing and I sound very stupid.
>
> I have come across too many difficulties which regards to my volume and speed as I think my English volume is too low and my speed is too fast. But during the last 3 months I got some Australian born friends and the amazing thing is that I don't have a problem while I'm around with my friends. But when I go some public places – for instance – shopping I find some discommunictate problems so how can I overcome these misunderstandings?
>
> I am so happy that you are going to help us with our pronunciation. Here I would like to tell you something about my English speaking. I had come across of my problem in speaking with people at public and my friend and also at the shopping centre or other shop. When I was talking to them I also have to do some actions to show them what I want. Like what I want to buy something, where I can get it or I want to cook something.

Learners were given their profiles and these were discussed individually and as a group.

STEP 3: PLAN A SERIES OF LESSONS BASED ON LEARNER DATA

Content was chosen on the basis of learners' expressed needs. These initially included telephone and interview skills, casual conversations and expressing opinions in a polite, mildly impolite and aggressive manner. As indicated in the lesson outlined earlier, the type of phonological elements focused on in each lesson depended on their appropriateness to the topic or activity. For example, rise-fall intonation patterns for tag questions were dealt with when the function involved was initiating a conversation with a stranger (as in *It's a beautiful day, isn't it?*). The fall-rise and the rise-fall intonation pattern's in tag questions were contrasted when the listening activity involved speakers expressing agreement and/or doubt. Each lesson highlighted a particular aspect, but those dealt with in previous lessons were continually reinforced, as was the case with grammatical structures, functions and lexical items.

Midway through the course the learners were shown the video recording made at the beginning of the course. They were asked to indicate those areas where they thought their oral production had improved. Learners were asked to comment on each other's progress. They were able to be quite explicit about their own progress as well as their peers'. *X's speaking is much better now, she stresses the right words. Before Y use to speak too quickly, now we can understand what he is saying.*

By the end of the course, learners had a good working knowledge of syllable stress patterns, schwa, sentence stress and rhythm, tonic stress, weak forms, linking. the function of rise-fall, fall-rise intonation patterns and how these patterns combined in utterances. They felt confident that they could use the strategies learned and apply them to situations where misunderstandings might occur in the wider community. As a consequence they were more confident speakers. Rather than describing a lesson in detail I will outline how learners prepared for a Stage 3 competency: delivering an oral presentation.

PROCEDURE

1. In the lead-up lesson, learners were asked to research a topic of interest. Library visits were organised so that they could locate information on their topic. They were asked to write assignments. I will not outline how this was done as the focus in this paper is on oral production.
2. The learners were shown the performance criteria for delivering an oral presentation and these were discussed with them.
3. Learners were to make notes from their written assignments. Their talk was to have an introduction, main body and conclusion. They were asked to weight the talk in the following way: 15% to the introduction, 60% to developing the topic and 25% to the conclusion. They were then given a handout showing the difference between Spoken Academic English and Broad Australian English in which the authors were speaking about the same topic. How did the speakers weigh their talks? In groups, learners discussed other differences between the two extracts. These included choice of appropriate lexical items (*Australians* versus *Aussies*), use of attention-getting devices (*Look, it's like this* versus *It seems that* . . .), and use of contractions versus full forms.
4. To focus on phonological elements, learners were shown a short excerpt of a video of a person from a current affairs show presenting an opinion on a subject. They were asked to analyse where and why the speaker used the pitch changes, how the speaker used pitch and pause to signal the end of a thought group, what sorts of intonation patterns he used and where the tonic stresses occurred. They were then asked to consider what sorts of intonation contours they would be using for lists and for

statements; which words they would be stressing and how they would vary pitch to maintain the audience's interest; and so on. They were asked to go through their notes and handouts from all previous lessons where various phonological aspects had been covered. These aspects were revised and discussed.

5. Other features of oral presentations were also dealt with, such as maintaining eye contact with the audience, how to use props and the chalkboard, starting slowly and calmly and ways to overcome nervous body language that might appear.
6. Over a number of days, the learners gave their talks. These were recorded and transcribed.
7. Learners handed back transcriptions of their talks. Copies of the tapes were made so that learners could work in groups of four. They were given time to read the transcripts. The transcripts were marked in the following way. Unintelligible words or phrases were circled, '*?*' was used to indicate where they had paused in an utterance, *S* stood for stress, and *Gr* for grammar. Three areas where the learners' talk could be improved were specified (e.g., vary pitch, organise utterances into thought groups, focus on stress and rhythm). Using these comments as a guide, learners worked in groups and listened to one an other's talk on cassette and commented on them. When they had finished their discussions, they worked on their own transcripts. The teacher moved around each group discussing the comments on each learner's transcript. Encouraging comments preceded discussion of problematic areas.
8. At a later date, learners gave another talk. Some chose another topic; others spoke on the same topic but changed the content.

CONCLUSION

I have attempted in this paper to present a procedural approach for incorporating phonological elements into an ESL syllabus. The process can be applied to any ESL context; it is not confined to an adult ESL context. A novel study in a secondary context could incorporate phonological elements in the same manner as outlined in the discussion. Let's say one of the functions involved is expressing opinions about the novel. In addition to providing the learners with the appropriate grammatical structures to do this, one could also attune learners to appropriate phonological information. In the same way, direct speech in the text could be analysed. If a character says sarcastically, *How will I ever live without you? You're my everything!*, how would this be said? What would it sound like if the character was highly emotional and serious about what he was saying? If a video was used in conjunction with a text, then further phonological work could be done on gestures, stress, rhythm and intonation.

The focus on the suprasegmental level has been deliberate, as it is my opinion that this area causes most communication breakdowns between ESL learners and native speakers. Moreover, numerous texts are available for ideas on how to deal with problems at the segmental level.

I strongly believe that in making learners aware of phonological concepts, the learning process becomes more comprehensible and enjoyable. It's not only about putting *s* on plurals /s/, /z/ or /ɪz/, or marking past events with past-tense markers /t/ or /d/. By making learners aware of the role of phonological elements in discourse, we provide them with a means for decoding and encoding meaning in exchanges: who the people are, what their perceived status is, how they feel about what they are saying, cues for signalling a change in topic, the status of the message ('I'm imparting information, you listen', 'I'm asking you, answer me' or 'I'm not sure about what I'm saying') and boundary marking ('I'm finished', 'I'm not finished yet'). We provide learners with a key to how the culture is articulated through language and how to use language. Without this key, it is difficult to understand 'why and how' people convey their intended meanings.

References

Corbel, C. (1985). *Using the system*. Melbourne: AE Press.

Dickinson, A., Leveque, J., & Sagot, H. (1975). *All's well 1*. Paris: Didier.

Dickinson, A., Leveque, J., & Sagot, H. (1976). *All's well 2*. Paris: Didier.

Firth, S. (1987). Pronunciation syllabus design: A question of focus. *TESL Talk*, *17*(1).

SECTION 9

TEACHING SPEAKING

INTRODUCTION

A large percentage of the world's language learners study English in order to develop proficiency in speaking. The ability to speak a second or foreign language well is a very complex task if we try to understand the nature of what appears to be involved. To begin with, speaking is used for many different purposes, and each purpose involves different skills. When we use casual conversation, for example, our purposes may be to make social contact with people, to establish rapport, or to engage in the harmless chitchat that occupies much of the time we spend with friends. When we engage in discussion with someone, on the other hand, the purpose may be to seek or express opinions, to persuade someone about something, or to clarify information. In some situations, we use speaking to give instructions or to get things done. We may use speaking to describe things, to complain about people's behavior, to make polite requests, or to entertain people with jokes and anecdotes. Each of these different purposes for speaking implies knowledge of the rules that account for how spoken language reflects the context or situation in which speech occurs, the participants involved and their specific roles and relationships, and the kind of activity the speakers are involved in. In the last 20 or so years, linguists have provided a great deal of information on how speakers use language appropriately in different situations and clarified the complex nature of what is involved in developing spoken fluency in a second or foreign language. The papers in this section describe the nature of spoken interaction and suggest approaches to the teaching of different aspects of spoken English.

In the first paper, Kang discusses a number of factors that need to be considered in planning a speaking course. She refers to the influence of age, listening ability, sociocultural knowledge, and affective factors on the ability to speak a second or foreign language, and introduces the useful model developed by Canale and Swain to account for the components of speaking ability. This model describes speaking proficiency as depending on grammatical competence, discourse competence, sociolinguistic competence, and strategic competence, each of which needs to be addressed in a speaking course. Kang describes a variety of classroom activities which can be used to practice different aspects of conversational proficiency.

In the second paper, Tsang and Wong describe a study which sought to demonstrate the effectiveness of teaching university students in Hong Kong a set of conversational microskills and a working vocabulary needed to handle everyday conversations. Their study focused on the use of conversation starters, and with only 15 hours of instruction using videotaped conversation practice, they found that students did achieve considerable gains in fluency and in the use of conversation starters. There was little improvement in pronunciation or grammar, however.

In the final paper in this section Green, Christopher, and Lam examine one aspect of speaking proficiency – discussion skills – and explore how these can be developed in the classroom. They begin from the observation that teachers often experience difficulties in using discussion activities. The topics chosen may not lead to productive discussion, students pay little attention to the language they or others use during discussions, and learners receive insufficient feedback on their performance. The approach discussed in the article is learner-centered, which allows students to choose and organize their own topics, carry out peer- and self-observation and evaluation, and analyze the information they gather.

The papers in this section demonstrate that in developing a speaking course, the nature of speaking as well as the factors involved in producing fluent and appropriate speech needs to be understood. Classroom activities should be selected on the basis of problems learners experience with different aspects of speaking and the kinds of interaction the activities provide. In addition, consideration needs to be given as to how learners will receive feedback on the language they use during speaking tasks.

Discussion Questions

Before Reading

1. What needs do your learners (or a group of learners you are familiar with) have for interactional functions of language?
2. What aspects of speaking (e.g., pronunciation, intonation, grammatical accuracy, fluency) do you emphasize most in your teaching? Why?
3. Getting learners to produce the language orally at the very early stage of learning can result in fossilization. Do you agree with this statement? Why?
4. Besides grammar rules, what other rules do learners need to know? How do you teach these rules?
5. What types of speaking activities do you normally use in your classroom? Do they serve different purposes?
6. What kinds of materials do you use for teaching speaking skills? Why do you use them?
7. Beginning second language learners are often asked to memorize short dialogues. Is this useful? What do you think is the rationale behind this?

After Reading

1. Can you give examples of situations you know where second language learners have broken one of the rules of conversation? What was the rule? Were there any consequences of breaking the rule?

2. Examine an ESL textbook for teaching speaking skills. What aspects of speaking skills are taught? How adequate do you think the coverage of speaking skills is in the book?
3. Within the framework of a speaking course, discuss activities that can be used to address grammatical competence, sociolinguistic competence, discourse competence, and strategic competence.
4. Review the four kinds of activities discussed by Kang and suggest other activities that fit these categories.
5. What factors do you think account for the lack of improvement in pronunciation and accuracy in Tsang and Wong's study?
6. Examine the microskills addressed in Tsang and Wong's study. Suggest activities that could be used to teach some of these skills.
7. Discuss ways in which students can be given feedback on their performance on oral activities, and the advantages and disadvantages of different feedback strategies.
8. Suggest a lesson plan for a lesson on discussion skills.

CHAPTER 18

Factors to Consider: Developing Adult EFL Students' Speaking Abilities

Kang Shumin

INTRODUCTION

Learning to speak a foreign language requires more than knowing its grammatical and semantic rules. Learners must also acquire the knowledge of how native speakers use the language in the context of structured interpersonal exchange, in which many factors interact. Therefore, it is difficult for EFL learners, especially adults, to speak the target language fluently and appropriately. In order to provide effective guidance in developing competent speakers of English, it is necessary to examine the factors affecting adult learners' oral communication, components underlying speaking proficiency, and specific skills or strategies used in communication. This paper explores these aspects so that teachers can more effectively help adult learners develop their abilities to communicate in the target language.

Speaking a language is especially difficult for foreign language learners because effective oral communication requires the ability to use the language appropriately in social interactions. Diversity in interaction involves not only verbal communication, but also paralinguistic elements of speech such as pitch, stress, and intonation. In addition, nonlinguistic elements such as gestures and body language/posture, facial expression, and so on may accompany speech or convey messages directly without any accompanying speech. In addition, "there is tremendous variation cross-culturally and cross-linguistically in the specific interpretations of gestures and body language" (Brown, 1994, p. 241). Furthermore, different cultural assumptions about the purposes of particular interactions and expected outcomes of encounters also affect communication. Consequently, owing to minimal exposure to the target language and contact with native speakers, adult EFL learners in general are relatively poor at spoken English, especially regarding fluency, control of idiomatic expressions, and understanding of cultural pragmatics. Few can achieve nativelike proficiency in oral communication.

EFL learners need explicit instruction in speaking, which, like any language skill, generally has to be learned and practiced. However, in practice, it is too often assumed that spoken-language skills can be developed simply by assigning students general topics to discuss or by getting them to talk on certain subjects. Evidently, not enough attention is given to the factors that inhibit or facilitate the production of spoken language. Therefore, in order to provide guidance in developing competent speakers of English, instructors of EFL should keep these questions in mind: What affects adult EFL learners' oral communication? What are the components underlying speaking effectiveness? And how can adult EFL learners' speaking abilities be improved?

Factors Affecting Adult EFL Learners' Oral Communication

Age or Maturational Constraints

The interactive behavior of EFL learners is influenced by a number of factors. Age is one of the most commonly cited determinant factors of success or failure in L2 or foreign language learning. Krashen, Long, and Scarcella (1982) argue that acquirers who begin learning a second language in early childhood through natural exposure achieve higher proficiency than those beginning as adults. Oyama's study (1976) also shows that many adults fail to reach nativelike proficiency in a second language. Their progress seems to level off at a certain stage, a phenomenon which is usually called "fossilization" – the permanent cessation of second language development. This shows that the aging process itself may affect or limit adult learners' ability to pronounce the target language fluently with nativelike pronunciation (Scarcella & Oxford, 1992). Even if they can utter words and sentences with perfect pronunciation, problems with prosodic features such as intonation, stress, and other phonological nuances still cause misunderstandings or lead to communication breakdown. Adult learners do not seem to have the same innate language-specific endowment or propensity as children for acquiring fluency and naturalness in spoken language.

Aural Medium

The central role of listening comprehension in the L2 or foreign language acquisition process is now largely accepted. And there is little doubt that listening plays an extremely important role in the development of speaking abilities. Speaking feeds on listening, which precedes it. Usually, one person speaks, and the other responds through attending by means of the listening process. In fact, during interaction, every speaker plays a double role – both as a listener and as a speaker. "While listening, learners must comprehend the text by retaining information in memory, integrate it with what follows, and continually adjust their understanding of what they hear in the light of prior knowledge and of incoming information" (Mendelsohn & Rubin, 1995, p. 35). If one cannot understand what is said, one is certainly unable to respond. So, speaking is closely related to or interwoven with listening, which is the basic mechanism through which the rules of language are internalized. The fleetingness of speech, together with the features of spoken English – loosely organized syntax, incomplete forms, false starts, and the use of fillers – undoubtedly hinders EFL learners' comprehension and affects the development of their speaking abilities.

Sociocultural Factors

Many cultural characteristics of a language also affect L2 or foreign language learning. From a pragmatic perspective, language is a form of social action because linguistic communication occurs in the context of structured interpersonal exchange, and meaning is thus socially regulated (Dimitracopoulou, 1990). In other words, "shared values and beliefs create the traditions and social structures that bind a community together and are expressed in their language" (Carrasquillo, 1994, p. 55). Thus, to speak a language, one must know how the language is used in a social context. It is well known that each language has its own rules of usage as to when, how, and to what degree a speaker may impose a given verbal behavior on his or her conversational partner (Berns, 1990). Because of the influence or interference of their own cultural norms, it is hard for nonnative speakers to choose the forms appropriate to certain situations. For instance, in Chinese culture, paying a compliment to someone obligates that person to give a negative answer (such as "No. It is not so good.") in order to show "modesty," whereas in North American culture such a response might be both inappropriate and embarrassing.

In addition, oral communication, as mentioned, involves a very powerful nonverbal communication system, which sometimes contradicts the messages provided through the verbal listening channel. Because of a lack of familiarity with the nonverbal communication system of the target language, EFL learners usually do not know how to pick up nonverbal cues. As a result, ignorance of the nonverbal message often leads to misunderstanding. The following example is a case in point. One day, when a Chinese student heard "Let's get together for lunch sometime," he immediately responded by proposing to fix a specific date without noticing the native speaker's indifferent facial expression. Undoubtedly, he was puzzled when his interlocutor left without giving him an expected answer. It is evident that the student had not understood the nonverbal message, which illustrates that the sociocultural factor is another aspect that greatly affects oral communication.

AFFECTIVE FACTORS

"The affective side of the learner is probably one of the most important influences on language learning success or failure" (Oxford, 1990, p. 140). The affective factors related to L2 or foreign language learning are emotions, self-esteem, empathy, anxiety, attitude, and motivation. L2 or foreign language learning is a complex task that is susceptible to human anxiety (Brown, 1994), which is associated with feelings of uneasiness, frustration, self-doubt, and apprehension. Speaking a foreign language in public, especially in front of native speakers, is often anxiety-provoking. Sometimes, extreme anxiety occurs when EFL learners become tongue-tied or lost for words in an unexpected situation, which often leads to discouragement and a general sense of failure. Unlike children, adults are concerned with how they are judged by others. They are very cautious about making errors in what they say, for making errors would be a public display of ignorance, which would be an obvious occasion of "losing face" in some cultures, as in China. Clearly, the sensitivity of adult learners to making mistakes, or fear of "losing face," has been the explanation for their inability to speak English without hesitation.

Components Underlying Speaking Effectiveness

Language proficiency is not a unidimensional construct but a multifaceted modality, consisting of various levels of abilities and domains (Carrasquillo, 1994, p. 65). Hymes (1971) also assumes that L2 learners need to know not only the linguistic knowledge, but also the culturally acceptable ways of interacting with others in different situations and relationships. His theory of communicative competence consists of the interaction of grammatical, psycholinguistic, sociolinguistic, and probabilistic language components. Building on Hymes's theory, Canale and Swain (1980) propose that communicative competence includes grammatical competence, discourse competence, sociolinguistic competence, and strategic competence, which reflect the use of the linguistic system and the functional aspects of communication, respectively. In the framework of Canale and Swain (1980), we can show graphically the abilities underlying speaking proficiency.

GRAMMATICAL COMPETENCE

"Grammatical competence is an umbrella concept that includes increasing expertise in grammar (morphology, syntax), vocabulary, and mechanics. With regards to speaking, the term mechanics refers to basic sounds of letters and syllables, pronunciation of words, intonation, and stress" (Scarcella & Oxford, 1992, p. 141). In order to convey meaning, EFL learners must have the knowledge of words and sentences: That is, they must understand how words are segmented into various sounds, and how sentences are stressed in particular ways. Thus, grammatical competence enables speakers to use and understand English-language structures accurately and unhesitatingly, which contributes to their fluency.

DISCOURSE COMPETENCE

In addition to grammatical competence, EFL learners must develop discourse competence, which is concerned with intersentential relationships. In discourse, whether formal or informal, the rules of cohesion and coherence apply, which aid in holding the communication together in a meaningful way. In communication, both the production and comprehension of a language require one's ability to perceive and process stretches of discourse, and to formulate representations of meaning from referents in both previous sentences and following sentences. Therefore, effective speakers should acquire a large repertoire of structures and discourse markers to express ideas, show relationships of time, and indicate cause, contrast, and emphasis (Scarcella & Oxford, 1992). With these, learners can manage turn taking in conversation (see Figure 1).

SOCIOLINGUISTIC COMPETENCE

Knowledge of language alone does not adequately prepare learners for effective and appropriate use of the target language. Learners must have competence which involves knowing what is expected socially and culturally by users of the target language; that is, learners must acquire the rules and norms governing the appropriate timing and realization of speech acts. Understanding the sociolinguistic side of language helps learners know what comments are appropriate, how to ask questions during interaction, and how to respond nonverbally according to the purpose of the talk. Therefore, "adult second language learners must acquire stylistic adaptability in order to be able to encode and decode the discourse around them correctly" (Brown, 1994, p. 238).

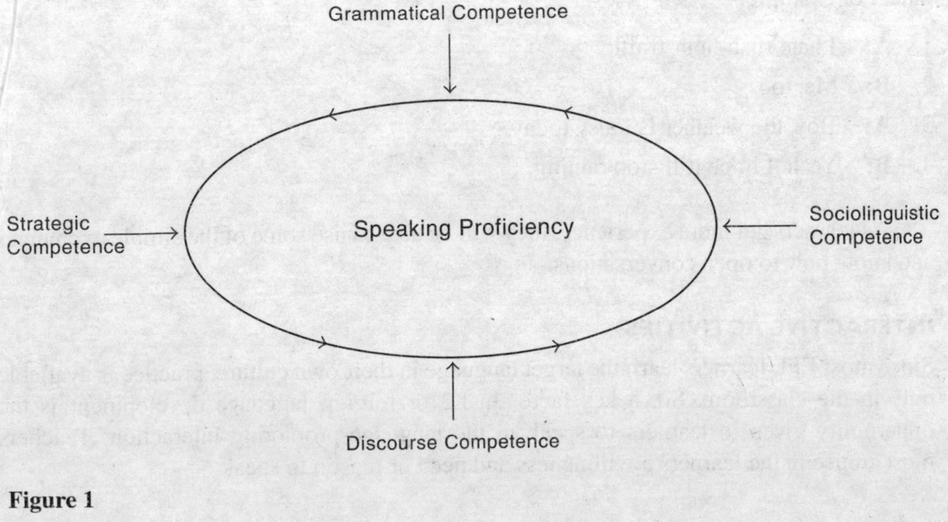

Figure 1

STRATEGIC COMPETENCE

Strategic competence, which is "the way learners manipulate language in order to meet communicative goals" (Brown, 1994, p. 228), is perhaps the most important of all the communicative competence elements. Simply put, it is the ability to compensate for imperfect knowledge of linguistic, sociolinguistic, and discourse rules (Berns, 1990). With reference to speaking, strategic competence refers to the ability to know when and how to take the floor, how to keep a conversation going, how to terminate the conversation, and how to clear up communication breakdown as well as comprehension problems.

Interaction as the Key to Improving EFL Learners' Speaking Abilities

The functions of spoken language are interactional and transactional. The primary intention of the former is to maintain social relationships, whereas that of the latter is to convey information and ideas. In fact, much of our daily communication remains interactional. Being able to interact in a language is essential. Therefore, language instructors should provide learners with opportunities for meaningful communicative behavior about relevant topics by using learner-learner interaction as the key to teaching language for communication because "communication derives essentially from interaction" (Rivers, 1987, p. xiii).

Communication in the classroom is embedded in meaning-focused activity. This requires teachers to tailor their instruction carefully to the needs of learners and teach them how to listen to others, how to talk with others, and how to negotiate meaning in a shared context. Out of interaction, learners will learn how to communicate verbally and nonverbally as their language store and language skills develop. Consequently, the give-and-take exchanges of messages will enable them to create discourse that conveys their intentions in real-life communication.

SMALL TALK

The ability to get along with people in society may correlate somewhat with how well a person can engage in brief, casual conversation with others or in an exchange of pleasantries. Talk of weather, rush-hour traffic, vocations, sports events, and so on may seem "meaningless," but such talk functions to create a sense of social communion among peers or other people. So, at the initial stage, adult EFL learners should develop skills in short, interactional exchanges in which they are required to make only one or two utterances at a time. For example:

1. **A:** I hate rush-hour traffic.
2. **B:** Me, too.
3. **A:** Boy, the weather is lousy today.
4. **B:** Yeah. I hope it'll stop raining.

As learners get more experience, they will be able to use some of the simple exchanges and know how to open conversations.

INTERACTIVE ACTIVITIES

Since most EFL learners learn the target language in their own culture, practice is available only in the classroom. So, a key factor in L2 or foreign language development is the opportunity given to learners to speak in the language-promoting interaction. Teachers must arouse in the learners a willingness and need or reason to speak.

A possible way of stimulating learners to talk might be to provide them with extensive exposure to authentic language through audiovisual stimuli and with opportunities to use the language. Likewise, teachers should integrate strategy instruction into interactive activities, providing a wealth of information about communicative strategies to raise learners' awareness about their own learning styles so that they can tailor their strategies to the requirements of learning tasks.

In designing activities, teachers should consider all the skills conjointly as they interact with each other in natural behavior, for in real life as in the classroom, most tasks of any complexity involve more than one macroskill (Nunan, 1989). Effective interactive activities should be manipulative, meaningful, and communicative, involving learners in using English for a variety of communicative purposes. Specifically, they should (1) be based on authentic or naturalistic source materials; (2) enable learners to manipulate and practice specific features of language; (3) allow learners to rehearse, in class, communicative skills they need in the real world; and (4) activate psycholinguistic processes of learning.

Based on these criteria, the following activities appear to be particularly relevant to eliciting spoken-language production. They provide learners with opportunities to learn from auditory and visual experiences, which enable them to develop flexibility in their learning styles and also to demonstrate the optimal use of different learning strategies and behaviors for different tasks.

1. *Aural: oral activities.* With careful selection and preparation, aural materials such as news reports on the radio will be fine-tuned to a level accessible to particular groups of learners. These materials can be used in some productive activities as background or as input for interaction. In practice, students are directed to listen to taped dialogues or short passages and afterwards to act them out in different ways. One example which we have used in our microteaching practice in Northern Illinois University is jigsaw listening. A story is recorded into several segments on an audiocassette tape. Teachers either have each student listen to a different segment or divide the class into small groups and make each group responsible for one segment. After each student (or group) has listened to a segment, students are provided with a worksheet of comprehension questions based on the story. Then, students work together in groups on an information-gap activity. They negotiate the meaning of the story and answer questions, which motivates students to speak.

2. *Visual: oral activities.* Because of the lack of opportunity in foreign language settings to interact with native speakers, the need for exposure to many kinds of scenes, situations, and accents as well as voices is particularly critical. This need can be met by audiovisual materials such as appropriate films, videotapes, and soap operas. They can provide (*a*) "the motivation achieved by basing lessons on attractively informative content material; (*b*) the exposure to a varied range of authentic speech, with different registers, accents, intonation, rhythms, and stresses; and (*c*) language used in the context of real situations, which adds relevance and interest to the learning process" (Carrasquillo, 1994, p. 140). While watching, students can observe what levels of formality are appropriate or inappropriate on given occasions. Similarly, they can notice the nonverbal behavior and types of exclamations and fill-in expressions that are used. Also, they can pay attention to how people initiate and sustain a conversational exchange and how they terminate an interactive episode. Subsequent practice of dialogues, role-playing, and dramatizations will lead to deeper learning.

Visual stimuli can be utilized in several ways as starter material for interaction. Short pieces of films can be used to give "eyewitness" accounts. An anecdote from a movie can be used to elicit opinion-expressing activity.

Likewise, nonverbal videos can be played to have students describe what they have viewed. While watching, students can focus on the content and imitate the "model's" body language. In this way students will be placed in a variety of experiences with accompanying language. Gradually, they will assimilate the verbal and nonverbal messages and communicate naturally.

3. *Material-aided: oral activities*. Appropriate reading materials facilitated by the teacher and structured with comprehension questions can lead to creative production in speech. Storytelling can be prompted with cartoon strips and sequences of pictures. Oral reports or summaries can be produced from articles in newspapers or from some well-designed textbooks such as *Culturally Speaking*, by Genzel and Cummings (1994). Similar material input, such as hotel brochures, can be used for making reservations; menus can be used for making purchases in the supermarket or for ordering in a restaurant. In fact, language input for oral activities can be derived from a wide range of sources that form the basis for communicative tasks of one sort or another, which will help learners deal with real situations that they are likely to encounter in the future.

4. *Culture awareness: oral activities*. Culture plays an instrumental role in shaping speakers' communicative competence, which is related to the appropriate use of language (e.g., how native speakers make an apology and what kind of form the apology takes). Generally, appropriateness is determined by each speech community. In other words, it is defined by the shared social and cultural conventions of a particular group of speakers. Therefore, it is essential to recognize different sets of culturally determined rules in communication. Just as Brown and Yule (1983, p. 40) say, "a great number of cultural assumptions which would be normally presupposed, and not made explicit by native speakers, may need to be drawn explicitly to the attention of speakers from other cultures." Cultural learning illustrated by activities and strengthened through physical enactment will motivate students.

Teachers can present situations in which there are cultural misunderstandings that cause people to become offended, angry, and confused. Then, thought-provoking information and questions can follow each description or anecdote for in-class discussion. Students can be asked to analyze and determine what went wrong and why, which will force them to think about how people in the target culture act and perceive things, and which will inevitably provide a deeper insight into that culture. This kind of exercise can strike a healthy balance between the necessity of teaching the target culture and validating the students' native culture, which will gradually sharpen students' culture awareness.

By and large, using audiovisual stimuli brings sight, hearing, and kinesthetic participation into interplay, which gets students across the gulf of imagination into the "real experience" in the first place. Meanwhile, the task-oriented activities give students a purpose to talk. Ideally, the flexibility and adaptability of these activities are essential if the communicative needs of learners are to be met. With the limited time available in class, it is necessary to follow open language experiences with more intensive structured situations, dialogues, and role-playing activities. These will give students both the chance and the confidence actually to use the language.

Conclusion

In conclusion, speaking is one of the central elements of communication. In EFL teaching, it is an aspect that needs special attention and instruction. In order to provide effective instruction, it is necessary for teachers of EFL to carefully examine the factors, conditions, and components that underlie speaking effectiveness. Effective instruction derived from the careful analysis of this area, together with sufficient language input and speech-promotion activities, will gradually help learners speak English fluently and appropriately.

References

Berns, M. (1990). *Contexts of competence: Social and cultural considerations in communicative language teaching*. New York: Plenum Press.

Brown, G., & Yule, G. (1983). *Teaching the spoken language: An approach based on the analysis of conversational English*. New York: Cambridge University Press.

Brown, H. D. (1994). *Principles of language learning and teaching*. Englewood Cliffs, NJ: Prentice Hall.

Canale, M., & Swain, M. (1980). Theoretical bases of communicative approaches to second language teaching and testing. *Applied Linguistics, 1*, 1–47 .

Carrasquillo, A. L. (1994). *Teaching English as a second language: A resource guide*. New York: Garland Publishing.

Dimitracopoulou, I. (1990). *Conversational competence and social development*. Cambridge: Cambridge University Press.

Genzel, R. B., & Cummings, M. G. (1994). *Culturally speaking*. Boston, MA: Heinle & Heinle.

Hymes, D. (1971). *On communicative competence*. Philadelphia: University of Pennsylvania Press.

Krashen, S. D., Long, M., & Scarcella, R. (1982). Age, rate, and eventual attainment in second language acquisition. In S. D. Krashen, R. Scarcella, & M. Long (Eds.), *Child-adult differences in second language acquisition* (pp. 175–201). Rowley, MA: Newbury House.

Mendelsohn, D. J., & Rubin, J. (1995). *A guide for the teaching of second language listening*. San Diego: Dominie Press.

Nunan, D. C. (1989). *Designing tasks for the communicative classroom*. Cambridge: Cambridge University Press.

Oxford, R. L. (1990). *Language learning strategies: What every teacher should know*. New York: Newbury House.

Oyama, S. (1976). A sensitive period for the acquisition of a nonnative phonological system. *Journal of Psycholinguistic Research, 5*, 3.

Rivers, W. M. (1987). *Interactive language teaching*. Cambridge: Cambridge University Press.

Scarcella, R. C., & Oxford, R. L. (1992). *The tapestry of language learning: The individual in the communicative classroom*. Boston, MA: Heinle & Heinle.

CHAPTER 19

Conversational English: An Interactive, Collaborative, and Reflective Approach

Wai King Tsang and Matilda Wong

Introduction

Conversations are listener- or person-oriented (Brown & Yule, 1983; Slade, 1986). As in other speaking tasks, a conversation requires the speaker to 'face temporal constraints and the social pressures of face-to-face interaction' (Chafe, 1986, p. 16). A conversation is a truly communicative event which is 'a dynamic exchange in which linguistic competence must adapt itself to the total informational input, both linguistic and paralinguistic' (Savignon, 1971, cited in Higgs & Clifford, 1982, p. 58).

Conversations 'begin with greetings and progress through various ordered moves: the speaker's and hearer's roles are ascertained, topics are introduced, rights to talk are assumed, new topics are raised, and at the appropriate time, the conversation is terminated in a suitable manner' (Richards, 1983, p. 118). Put briefly, the speaker and the hearer have to take the initiative, ask questions, or express disagreement in the conversation, all of which require a command of particular language features and which 'can be learnt' (Underhill, 1987, p. 45). The conversation class reported here is based on this assumption of learnability.

In the researchers' opinion, traditional conversation classes in Hong Kong are characterised by the following features:

1. *Input*: There is a focus on formal aspects of language and a lack of attention to the processes of conversational interaction, including the collaborative aspects of conversational interaction, and the negotiation of conversational meanings and messages (Richards, 1985). Class input is typically provided by the teacher.

This chapter is reprinted from *Prospect* 10, 1 with permission from the National Centre for English Language Teaching and Research (NCELTR), Australia. © Macquarie University.

2. *Error treatment and feedback*: Errors are corrected by the teacher and the teacher alone during the practice, or forgotten entirely after it, with little attention to paralinguistics.
3. *Role of teacher*: The teacher is the sole source of input and feedback and often a dominating participant in the practice, exemplifying a typical pattern of teacher stimulus followed by student response, further followed by teacher evaluation of student response (Long, 1975).

To avoid the counterproductive aspects of a traditional conversation class, the present program incorporated the following features:

- brainstorming vocabulary with the learners as a source of input (addressing features 1 and 3 above)
- using conversation starters, which are statements expressing an opinion, making a suggestion, or describing a fact, to trigger realistic communication (addressing feature 1)
- videotaping students' conversational practices in the teacher's absence from the conversation to minimise threat, and to maximise learner participation (addressing features 2 and 3)
- reviewing tapes for intensive self- and peer feedback, involving the learner actively in the learning process (addressing features 2 and 3)

The present program is *interactive*, as it allows for free conversations with the aid of starters and a working vocabulary. It is *collaborative* between the teacher and the learners in developing sources of input, and between the individual learners in providing feedback to each other. It also encourages *reflective* learning through having the students fill out worksheets for self- and peer feedback.

METHOD

OBJECTIVE

The purpose of this investigation was to evaluate the effectiveness of the program with particular reference to the use of starters, brainstorming techniques, taped practices in the teacher's absence and self- and peer feedback.

Through presentation, practice and review, the students in the conversational English program aimed to:

1. operationalise conversational dynamics (volume, amount of participation, pauses, overlap and communication breakdown, backtracking and body language)
2. build up conversational vocabulary through brainstorming and teacher prompts
3. use the appropriate microskills[1] (forms and functions) and vocabulary to initiate, maintain and terminate a conversation

SUBJECTS

The seven subjects were all Hong Kong Cantonese speakers who are learners of English as an auxiliary language. They were students from the Faculty of Humanities and Social Sciences, the Faculty of Business, and the Faculty of Science and Technology recommended to the English Foundation Program of the City Polytechnic of Hong Kong in Year 1.

PROCEDURE

ABOUT THE PROGRAM

The conversational English program reported in this paper was of 15 hours' duration, spread out over 8 weeks. In the first hour of the program, a needs analysis in two parts was conducted. It included a questionnaire on conversational competence, and a 20-minute writing task on needs and expectations. In the second hour of the program, the students moved into two groups freely and had two taped conversations using Starters 1a and 1b (Appendix A) as a pretest.

In the 10 hours following the needs analysis, the students were introduced to various conversational microskills through demonstration, audiovisual input, elicitation of interaction routines from the students, matching forms and functions of conversational expressions, and role-plays. They were also introduced to a working vocabulary for conversational English through brainstorming. In every lesson, the students formed two groups, and were given two conversation starters (see Starters 2–5 in Appendix A) for free practice. At the same time, their performance was videotaped in the absence of the teacher, who withdrew to the control room in the video laboratory after the conversation started. The students knew at the very beginning that their performance would be taped for review. Afterwards, they reviewed the tapes and filled out a worksheet to keep track of the frequency of appropriate use of conversational microskills and to make any general remarks on the speakers. The teacher also gave feedback on their performance at the end of the review.

In the thirteenth hour, the students had two taped conversations using Starters 1a and 1b again as a post-test. They did not know beforehand that these two starters would be used again in this week. In the fourteenth hour, the students evaluated what they had done in this conversational English program by completing the first two parts of the evaluation, a questionnaire survey on the effectiveness of the program, and a 20-minute writing task on their thoughts and feelings about the program.

In the final hour, the students were asked to fill out an action plan form, which was the third part of the evaluation, to set themselves specific and realistic goals from which to proceed in the program for the improvement of their conversational competence in the future.

EVALUATING THE PROGRAM

To evaluate the program, the following procedures were built into the investigation:

1. A pretest and a post-test were administered to compare the gain.
2. Practices were taped and evaluated for a course-work grade.
3. An individual profile, consisting of the pretest, course work and post-test grades for each student concerned was compiled.
4. A matching of the students' perceptions of needs and expectations before the conversational English class with their perceptions after taking the class as expressed in two questionnaires and two writing tasks was conducted.
5. An action plan for future development of their English was drawn up by each student at the end of the program.

ANALYSIS

CONTINUAL ASSESSMENT OF TAPED PRACTICES

At the end of each lesson, the two researchers graded the students' performance using Conversational English Proficiency Ratings[2] (as cited in Higgs & Clifford, 1982) (see Appendix B). In Table 1 the ratings of each student are averaged and reported

TABLE 1. COURSE-WORK GRADES

Student	Starter 2	Level	Starter 3	Level	Starter 4	Level	Starter 5	Level	Average	Level
A	44.0	2	42.0	1+	46.0	2	46.0	2	44.5	2
B	44.0	2	56.5	2+	53.5	2+	50.0	2	51.0	2
C	47.0	2	42.0	1+	42.0	1+	42.0	1+	43.3	2
D	46.0	2	38.0	1+	58.5	2+	44.0	2	46.6	2
E	55.5	2+	48.0	2	48.0	2	61.0	2+	53.1	2+
F	41.5	1+	43.5	2	42.5	1+	44.0	2	42.9	1+
G	40.5	1+	41.5	1+	42.0	1+	45.5	2	42.4	1+

as his or her coursework grade (for discussion, see section titled 'Individual Profile' below).

ANALYTICAL SCORING ON THE PRETEST AND POST-TEST

The pretest and post-test tapes were randomly ordered for blind rating. They were analytically scored by two independent raters (not the authors) using the Conversational English Proficiency Ratings for accent, grammar, vocabulary, fluency, and comprehension (Appendix B). All of the subjects except D and E showed no gain in proficiency levels (for a discussion on D and E, see below).

INDIVIDUAL PROFILE

To gain an overview of individual progress, the researchers combined both formative and summative assessments by compiling the pretest, course work and post-test scores into individual profiles, which are presented in Table 2.

Interrater reliability was demonstrated both in the scores of the course work assigned by the researchers and the scores of the pretest and post-test assigned by the two independent raters. In both cases, the scores of the two raters were close to the extent that they did not exceed a difference of one intermediate level of proficiency (e.g., between 1 and 1+, or 1+ and 2).

TABLE 2. INDIVIDUAL PROFILE

Student	Pretest Score	Pretest Level	Course work Score	Course work Level	Post-test Score	Post-test Level
A	52.3	2	44.5	2	47.5	2
B	47.5	2	51.0	2	52.8	2
C	31.3	1	43.3	2	31.5	1
D	19.3	0+	46.6	2	45.3	2
E	52.5	2	53.1	2+	69.5	3
F	52.8	2	42.9	1+	49.0	2
G	50.3	2	42.4	1+	48.3	2

Two conversational areas were looked into: topic switches[3] during the tests and taped practices, and turns during the pretest and post-test. The researchers reviewed all the tapes on the tests and practices, and recorded the flow of topics. For instance, in the pretest using Starter 1a, the students switched topics a few times once they began their conversation with the given starter. This occurred as follows:

> admit being lazy – sleeping hours – biological clock in the body – when to go to bed – television programmes and channels – TV advertisement – Mass Transit Railway commercial – the dog in the advertisement

The students were not evaluated on whether they changed topics or not, or on the number of topics they covered in their conversation; rather, they were evaluated on their ability to maintain a conversation by using any flexible and appropriate strategies, of which topic switching is a major one.

As far as the second focus is concerned, the pretest and post-test were transcribed as the researchers heard them, using conventions further adapted from Jefferson (1978; first adapted in van Lier, 1988), The turns, taken as an indicator of individual effort in participating in a conversation, were then tallied.

Discussion

THE SEVEN STUDENTS

Qualitatively, all the subjects made improvements in this program. They were able to build up a working vocabulary to handle everyday conversation, make appropriate use of conversational microskills to initiate, maintain and terminate a conversation, and gain confidence in speaking. However, their improvement, except in the case of students C, D and E, was not so great as to upgrade their conversational proficiency levels.

Given the reliability described earlier, the difference of one or more than one full level of proficiency, progressing from the pretest, through the course work, to the post-test, as found in the profiles of three individual students, C, D and E, is important and worth discussing (see Table 2). The following sections focus on these three students.

STUDENT C

Throughout the program, C showed steady progress. Her level of proficiency rose from Level 1 to Level 2 in her course work, although it remained at Level 1 in the post-test (see Table 2). In her course-work performance, she built up more confidence in speaking and was more willing to express herself. As indicated in the researchers' comments on her course work, C was able in later practices to ask questions and express opinions.

In the pretest, C's performance improved from scoring 17.5 points with Starter 1a to scoring 45.0 points with Starter 1b. The low score obtained in Starter 1a might have been owing to her initial shyness; but after some warm-up, she performed better in Starter 1b. Indeed, her interest in the given starter might also be a reason for the higher score with Starter 1b. In the post-test, C's total scores dropped from Starter 1a to 1b by 27 points, which led to a drop in proficiency by two levels. Her participation in terms of the number of turns dropped by about 2%, which is not substantial.

However, the length and nature of turns demonstrated an obvious change from short turns with 1a (e.g., 'yes. most of the people did not have the chance to study because there are only one or two university at that time'.) to very short turns with 1b (e.g., 'I quite agree with you'.), and from a combination of eliciting and giving suggestions and opinions with 1a to only brief responses to elicitation with 1b, without any effort to initiate a topic, or elicit responses from her colleagues in the latter case. For example, in Conversation 1a, C took up the turn, assisting A by giving suggestions:

> **A:** . . .[4] they commit suicide . usually because they do not I mean . because they are . what can I put it.
>
> **C:** maybe the . the . pressure from . from . from their parents may be one of the factors

In Conversation 1b, C responded briefly to E's question:

> **E:** just only one example . any chemical reaction that you have experience in your in your life
>
> **B:** I can't think of any chemical reaction yet . at this moment
>
> **E:** how about you. C?
>
> **C:** no I don't think so.

This change can be traced to the last 3 minutes of the post-test conversation for Starter 1a, when E, the latecomer, first joined the group on that day. Before E arrived, C was able to give and take turns. For example:

> **B:** this will in turn . create a . a . a . a . a not very positive effect on them . what do you think C?
>
> **C:** I agree with you because we have seen that most of the students they commit suicide because of the pressure come from school. they have a lot of work to do . and did not have . any time to . relax . and what's your opinion (turn to A)

After E's arrival, C responded either with interjections 'oh!', 'yeah', or one-sentence answers to questions. These changes may have been triggered by E's arrival. For example:

> **E:** but now what are you talking about?
>
> **C:** we talk our study

The presence of E might have been a factor in other participants' performance. E, a very active participant, not only competed with C, a less active participant, but also with A, B and D. With Starter 1a in the post-test, once E started her first turn ('what are you talking about?'), the utterances of all the other participants were responses to E's questions (with the exception of one turn taken by B: 'I want to know why are you so late?'). Moving from post-test 1a to 1b, A and D, like C, participated less as measured by the number of turns. In 1a, A tended to be the natural leader, starting the conversation, eliciting as well as responding to her colleagues. Although A took more turns than the others, the turns were not substantially longer than her colleagues'. Moreover, the whole conversation evolved naturally, with speakers eliciting and responding back and forth.

However, with Starter 1b in the post-test, the conversation seemed to be dominated by E's questions, with communication in the pattern of E's question and another participant's response, followed by E's question and a third participant's response.

These changes might also have been owing to C's personality. Unless her colleagues were encouraging and unthreatening, C would be passive and quiet. In one instance, one of her colleagues, D, actually asked her to 'try to participate more in the conversation. Don't be shy!' when D gave her peer feedback on her performance in the conversation practice. In fact, even the researchers in their after-class review described her as a 'passive listener (never takes initiative) . . . has to be urged . . . to give more suggestions'.

As Underhill (1987, p. 45) points out, conversational microskills 'can be learnt, like any other language feature. But they also require the kind of personality willing to do such things'. In the presence of more extrovert and talkative learners (such as E), C had to be constantly encouraged to overcome her shyness.

STUDENT D

Student D showed steady improvement throughout the program. In fact, her conversational proficiency rose from Level 0+ in the pretest to Level 2 in her course work, as well as in the post-test (see Table 2). This indicated a distinct gain in her proficiency level. In her evaluation, she wrote, 'can express my ideas more easily (maybe result from practices). My English is more fluent than before'.

Throughout the program, D's proficiency level stayed at 2 or 2+, except for the conversation practice with Starter 3. In fact, D's improvement impressed not only the researchers, but also her own colleagues. Peer feedback indicated that D did not participate enough in the early part of the program, but, as the program continued, she received very positive feedback from her colleague, C, on her practice with Starter 4b: 'You have done your best to make use of the expressions and also take an active role', 'loud enough – clear', and 'Well done!'

As far as the researchers' comments are concerned, in the first two taped practices with Starters 2a and 3b, D was described as 'rather quiet', and 'mainly as a listener'. In the researchers' opinion, D's performance in Starter 4b was 'well done', and Starter 5a revealed D as taking 'equal participation' with the others in the conversation group.

As these records show, all except one of the practices involving D were carried out without E. In the only taped practice (using Starter 3b) at which E was present, D's proficiency scores dropped to 38.0, which constituted Level 1+ (Table 1). As mentioned earlier, E was a very active participant. The possibility that E's presence pressurised the group cannot be discounted. It is indeed interesting to note that the other participants in that conversation group, A and C, received their lowest scores in this practice.

Even E herself admitted in her evaluation that 'I did not do well in giving turn to other students because I was too keen to give my own opinion'. In her action plan, E wrote that she spoke too much in the program, and, as a result, 'some people didn't have [a] chance to speak'. In the Action column, E actually wrote 'Self-control'. This is a good indicator of E's dominance over the whole conversation in some practices, which deprived other colleagues of an equal chance of participation.

On the whole, D's improvement was evident and consistent throughout the program, except when she faced E in the conversation practice. In fact, other participants in the same group were also affected by E's dominance, and became quieter and more passive.

STUDENT E

Although E herself admitted in her reflection that she was domineering in the conversation practices, her performance throughout the program showed considerable improvement. Her proficiency rose by one full level, from Level 2 to Level 3. In fact, the rise in her individual profile was smooth, from Level 2, through Level 2+, to Level 3.

THE PROGRAM AS A WHOLE

From the students' rating of eight on a ten-point scale in the program evaluation, it is noted that their needs and expectations were generally met. Their comments on the different aspects of the program can be categorised as follows:

1. *Use of starters and brainstorming techniques*: The students were positive toward using a starter for each conversation practice and having a session on brainstorming for vocabulary before the practice. As commented by B, 'Although there is a starter, we are supposed to practice [*sic*] English, you can talk anything you like'.
2. *Taped practice*: The students found the taped practice useful. This is evident in the students' written evaluation of the program. A student wrote: 'It helps me a lot, not only in the conversation, but also the gesture and 'small motion'. These comments justified the use of videotaping in the programme and confirmed Rodriguez and White's (1983, p. 251) opinion of using videotaping 'as a basis for discussion in class, for error analysis and correction, and for the amusement and motivation of the students'.
3. *Teacher's absence from practice*: The students appreciated the absence of the teacher while they were having their conversation practices. In her own journal, the teacher recorded one student's reaction to the teacher's absence: the student felt he could be 'fully in charge of the conversation; because . . . [it] gives us more chance like the real situation'.
4. *Self- and peer feedback*: The students were able to observe their own or their peers' major strengths (in the appropriate use of conversational microskills) and weaknesses (as demonstrated by low or soft voice, and little participation). As Murphy (1986, p. 146) points out, 'correction does not have to come from the teacher alone, . . . it will come just as appropriately (if not more so) from fellow learners'.

CONCLUSIONS

Overall, the students made several achievements in this program. As seen on the tapes and as commented upon in students' own evaluations, they were able to build up a working vocabulary to handle everyday conversation; make appropriate use of conversational microskills to initiate, maintain and terminate a conversation; and gain confidence in speaking. The starters used in the conversation practices provided enough basis to develop free conversation which approximated reality. Taping in the teacher's absence was effective. In addition, self- and peer feedback was effective. Indeed, teacher feedback confirmed self- and peer feedback, and complemented it.

Apart from these achievements, other possible directions for future programs of this kind include the following:

1. further strengthen pronunciation and vocabulary, as indicated in the students' action plans
2. deal more with grammatical accuracy, an area where the present programme failed to effect major improvement

References

Brown, G., & Yule, G. (1983). *Teaching the spoken language*. Cambridge: Cambridge University Press.

Chafe, W. (1986). Writing in the perspective of speaking. In C. R. Cooper & S. Greenbaum (Eds.), *Studying writing: Linguistic approaches*. London: Sage Publications.

Higgs, T. V., & Clifford, R. (1982). The push toward communication. In T. V. Higgs (Ed.), *Curriculum, competence, and the foreign language teacher*. Skokie, IL: National Textbook Company.

Jefferson, G. (1978). Sequential aspects of storytelling in conversation. In J. Schenkein (Ed.), *Studies in the organisation of conversational interaction*. New York: Academic Press.

Keitges, D. J. (1982). Language proficiency interview testing: An overview. *JALT Journal, 4*, 17–45.

Long, M. H. (1975). Group work and communicative competence in the ESOL classroom. *On TESOL '75: New Directions'*. Washington, DC: TESOL.

Murphy, D. F. (1986). Communication and correction in the classroom. *ELT Journal, 40*(2), 146–151.

Richards, J. C. (1983). Communicative needs in foreign language learning. *ELT Journal, 37*(2), 111–120.

Richards, J. C. (1985). Conversational competence through role play activities. *RELC Journal, 16*(1), 82–100.

Rodriguez, R. J., & White, R. H. (1983). From role play to the real world. In J. W. Oller Jr. & P. A. Richard-Amato (Eds.), *Methods that work*. Newbury House.

Slade, D. (1986). Teaching casual conversation to adult ESL learners. *Prospect, 2*(1), 68–87.

Underhill, N. (1987). *Testing spoken language*. Cambridge: Cambridge University Press.

van Lier, L. (1988). *The classroom and the language learner*. London: Longman.

Endnotes

We are indebted to Miss Chan Pui Wah and Miss Mo Kit Ling, who rendered their expertise in the independent rating of videotaped conversation samples.

[1] The conversational microskills taught included asking for repetition; checking and showing understanding; confirming what is heard and asking for clarification; eliciting opinions and suggestions; giving opinions and suggestions; agreeing and disagreeing; giving and taking turns; filling gaps.

[2] In operationalising FSI Ratings, the researchers balanced traditional criteria of accent, grammar, vocabulary, fluency and comprehension with communication criteria specified by Keitges (1982) as: quality and amount of communication, effort to communicate and communicative effectiveness. Three assumptions are made in adapting the FSI Rating scale and procedures:

a. Without a reasonable mastery of conversational microskills, the learner will not be able to participate enough for a fair assessment.
b. Although paralinguistic features in face-to-face interaction play a part in communication, they are not so important as to constitute an independent factor in an oral proficiency scale.
c. All participants in one conversation should be reviewed simultaneously but possibly assigned different grades; otherwise, the rater will be losing the perspective of individual performance in a truly interactive environment (nevertheless, the rater should avoid comparing the individuals against each other while grading).

[3] The topic switches were coded by the researchers. As van Lier (1988, p. 131) believes, the coding has to rely on 'intuitive judgements' as to what constitutes something new and what does not.

[4] Three periods approximate one second in all tapescripts. Periods are separated from the preceding word by a space.

Appendix A

Conversation Starters

1. a. Hong Kong students should be forced to work harder.
   b. We are just lazy. In fact we do not need more than 4 hours' sleep a day.
2. a. I didn't sleep well last night.
   b. The test was too difficult.
3. a. The Earth is affected by the greenhouse effect.
   b. A computer virus can be damaging.
4. a. I am planning to go to Europe this summer.
   b. Let's have a surprise party to celebrate Peter's birthday.
5. a. Students are too young for romantic love.
   b. Vegetarians are healthier than people who eat meat.

Note: Each pair of starters ('a' and 'b') was used on the same date.

Appendix B

Part I: Conversational English Proficiency Ratings

Five Levels

Adapted from the FSI Proficiency Ratings (as cited in Higgs & Clifford, 1982).

Level 1: Able to satisfy minimum courtesy requirements. Can ask and answer questions on very familiar topics; within the scope of his or her very limited language experience, can understand simple questions and statements, allowing for slowed speech, repetition or paraphrase; speaking vocabulary inadequate to express anything but the most elementary needs; errors in pronunciation and grammar are frequent, but can be understood by a native speaker used to dealing with foreigners attempting to speak his or her language.

Level 2: Able to deal with routine social exchanges. Can handle with confidence but not with facility the simplest type of conversation, including introductions and chat about autobiographical information; can get the gist of most conversations on nontechnical subjects (i.e., topics that require no specialised knowledge) and has a speaking vocabulary sufficient to express himself or herself simply with some circumlocutions; accent, though often quite faulty, is intelligible; can usually handle elementary constructions quite accurately and appropriately but does not have thorough or confident control of the grammar.

Level 3: Able to speak with sufficient structural accuracy and appropriateness and vocabulary to participate effectively in most informal conversations on practical and social topics. Can discuss particular interests and special fields of competence with reasonable ease; comprehension is quite complete for a normal rate of speech; vocabulary is broad enough that he or she rarely has to grope for a word; accent may be obviously foreign; control of grammar is good; errors never interfere with understanding and rarely disturb the native speaker.

Level 4: Able to use the language fluently, accurately and appropriately on all levels normally pertinent to conversational needs. Can understand and participate in any conversation within the range of his or her experience with a high degree of fluency and precision of vocabulary; would rarely be taken for a native speaker, but can respond appropriately even to unfamiliar topics; errors of pronunciation and grammar quite rare; can handle informal interpreting from and into the language.

Level 5: Conversational proficiency equivalent to that of an educated native speaker. Has complete fluency in the language such that his or her speech on all levels is fully accepted by educated native speakers in all of its features, including breadth of vocabulary and idiom, colloquialisms and pertinent cultural references.

PART 2: CHECKLIST OF CONVERSATION PERFORMANCE

FACTORS AND DESCRIPTORS

Adapted from the FSI Proficiency Ratings (as cited in Higgs & Clifford, 1982).

Accent

1. Pronunciation frequently unintelligible.
2. Frequent gross errors and a very heavy accent make understanding difficult, require frequent repetition.
3. 'Foreign accent' requires concentrated listening and mispronunciations lead to occasional misunderstanding and apparent errors in grammar or vocabulary.
4. Marked 'foreign accent' and occasional mispronunciations that do not interfere with understanding.
5. No conspicuous mispronunciations, but would not be taken for a native speaker.
6. Native pronunciation, with no trace of 'foreign accent'.

Grammar

1. Grammar almost entirely inappropriate or inaccurate, except in stock phrases.
2. Constant errors showing control of very few conversational microskills or major patterns, and frequently preventing communication.
3. Frequent errors showing inappropriate use of some conversational microskills or some major patterns uncontrolled, and causing occasional irritation and misunderstanding.
4. Occasional errors showing imperfect control of some conversation microskills or some patterns, but no weakness that causes misunderstanding.
5. Few errors, with no patterns of failure.
6. No more than two errors during the conversation.

Vocabulary

1. Vocabulary limited to minimum courtesy requirements.
2. Vocabulary limited to basic personal areas and very familiar topics (autobiographic information, personal experiences, etc.).
3. Choice of words sometimes inaccurate, limitations of vocabulary prevent discussion of some common familiar topics.
4. Vocabulary adequate to discuss special interests and any nontechnical subject with some circumlocutions.
5. Vocabulary broad, precise and adequate to cope with complex practical problems and varied topics of general interest (current events, as well as work, family, time, food, transportation).

6. Vocabulary apparently as accurate and extensive as that of an educated native speaker.

Fluency

1. Speech is so halting and fragmentary that conversation is virtually impossible.
2. Speech is very slow and uneven, except for short or routine sentences; frequently punctuated by silence or long pauses.
3. Speech is frequently hesitant and jerky; sentences may be left uncompleted.
4. Speech is occasionally hesitant, with some unevenness caused by rephrasing and groping for words.
5. Speech is effortless and smooth, but perceptibly nonnative in speed and evenness.
6. Speech on all general topics as effortless and smooth as a native speaker's.

Comprehension

1. Understands too little to respond to conversation initiations or topic nominations.
2. Understands only slow, very simple speech on topics of general interest; requires constant repetition and rephrasing.
3. Understands careful, somewhat simplified speech directed to him or her, with considerable repetition and rephrasing.
4. Understands quite well normal educated speech directed to him or her, but requires occasional repetition or rephrasing.
5. Understands everything in normal educated conversation, except for very colloquial or low-frequency items or exceptionally rapid or slurred speech.
6. Understands everything in informal and colloquial speech to be expected of an educated native speaker.

PART 3: CONVERSATIONAL ENGLISH PROFICIENCY RATINGS

RATING SHEET

Student: (ID)_____ (Name)_____ Rater:_____ Date:_____

Conversational English Proficiency Weighting Table

Proficiency Description	->	1	2	3	4	5	6	Total
Accent		0	1	2	2	3	4	
Grammar		6	12	18	24	30	36	
Vocabulary		4	8	12	16	20	24	
Fluency		2	4	6	8	10	12	
Comprehension		4	8	12	15	19	23	
Total								

Comments: ____

Conversational English Proficiency Conversion Table

Total Score	Level
16–25	0+
26–32	1
33–42	1+
43–52	2
53–62	2+
63–72	3
73–82	3+
83–92	4
93–99	4+

CHAPTER 20

Developing Discussion Skills in the ESL Classroom

Christopher F. Green, Elsie R. Christopher, and Jacqueline Lam

Introduction

Discussion skills are often undeveloped in the EFL/ESL classroom. A combination of potent inhibitors are responsible for this situation: large class size, students' level of proficiency and time constraints. As a result, many teachers never attempt discussions or, as a result of negative experiences, simply stop holding them. A solution adopted by many teachers involves the use of structured or guided discussions. These typically provide a framework within which learners are constrained to operate. Learners receive content input just before the discussion itself; they are then given roles to play, and follow predetermined steps through to the end of the discussion. Language prompts or appropriate wordings are usually provided. Finally, the teacher provides feedback on the whole performance. Examples of this approach, including some exceptionally good ones, are to be found in Alexander (1968), Wallace (1980), Hargreaves and Fletcher (1981), Heyworth (1984) and Ur (1981).

Although the guided approach provides some security for learners, and may help prevent communication breakdown, there is little direct learner involvement in the discussion process. Learners do not choose the topic, or decide on specific lines of enquiry to pursue; nor are they engaged in observing and evaluating their peers or themselves. The learner's perception may be that there is no real reason to participate actively in the discussion. As a result, learner cognitive engagement with the task, and motivation to develop the topic to any significant degree, are likely to be poor. Since the topic for discussion is imposed, defined and structured, we might call this approach *objective* and *non-heuristic*. The critical factors of personal involvement and unpredictability are mostly absent in this approach. It provides oral practice of a more or less controlled nature, based on role-play, but largely ignores the experiences, values and existing knowledge that individual learners might bring to bear on a discussion topic. The approach is overly concerned with linguistic factors, and downplays the cognitive and interpersonal factors which must be present in any meaningful discussion (Green, 1993).

Developing Learner Autonomy

Underpinning the rationale for a learner-centred approach to the development of discussion skills is the need to encourage students to become increasingly independent and self-directed in their learning. Haswell (1993, p. 90) describes how self-evaluation, in particular, helps students to 'learn in their own voice'. In fact, both peer and self-evaluation raise students' awareness of the links between learning objectives, processes and outcomes, by requiring them to reflect directly on their own and others' performances rather than relying on formal prestructured modes of formal evaluation. This active engagement between students and their learning allows them to integrate mentally the various stages in the learning process in a holistic way. As a result, learners develop a metacognitive awareness of the recursive nature of the learning process, which, in turn, is likely to help them to evolve into effective lifelong learners.

Selection of Topics for Discussion

It is worth noting that there is an almost total lack of research data on the effects of second language learners controlling the selection of topics for discussion. However, Ellis (1990) offers some evidence to support the notion that acquisition is enhanced when teachers allow students relatively free choice of topic. Further supporting evidence is offered in a small-scale action learning project carried out by Slimani (1992). Free choice of topic may well be of particular importance in monolingual classrooms, in which the common cultural background of the learners might limit the range of topics of potential interest; it may also determine the degree of convergence students adopt to target-language phonological and lexico-grammatical norms. In such situations, learners choosing their own topics and expressing their views in a nonstandard or localized form of the target language – at least initially – may help to bolster the cultural solidarity of the class, and lower the affective barriers (often so firmly in place) against the use of the target language in peer interaction in the classroom.

A Heuristic Approach

We would argue that discussion skills work should be subjective in orientation, and that it should provide learners with a very substantial element of evaluation and feedback, so that they are aware of the degree of cognitive-linguistic success being achieved. Discussion activities are often deemed appropriate for advanced classes only, on the grounds that relatively high levels of linguistic competence have to be reached before discussions may be attempted. However, our experience is that a learner-centred approach, with carefully chosen groupings, may be used effectively with most levels of learners, and for any type of course. We offer now an overview of the approach we advocate, and which we have trialled extensively in our university, where English is the medium of academic communication.

Implementing a Classroom Discussion

In our approach there are three stages in the implementation of a classroom discussion:

Pre-discussion. Viable discussion and associated partner groups are formed. We have found groups of four to be the most appropriate number of participants for fluent interaction. Each group draws up a list of possible discussion topics, deriving principally from their current professional, academic or developmental concerns. Next, a topic for discussion is selected and divided into manageable areas of enquiry for the time available. Responsibility may then be apportioned among individuals for researching and exploring particular aspects of the topics. If preferred, the whole topic may be researched and thought about by each participant.

Discussion. The groups discuss the topic while partner groups of observer-evaluators monitor the process, using a variety of instruments to record data. This procedure is described in detail later.

Post-discussion. First, there should be peer feedback from the observer-evaluators. The teacher may then give feedback on content, intragroup dynamics and linguistic appropriateness to groups and individuals. Finally, the groups decide on ways to enrich and extend the topic or, alternatively, to choose a new topic.

PRE-DISCUSSION

FORMING THE GROUPS

Discussions depend for success primarily on the willingness of all the participants to make substantial and coherent contributions to the process. Individual contributions depend on a knowledge or experience of the topic under discussion, willingness to express oneself in the target language and personality type. Krashen (1981) has taken account of the basic personality types in his model of second language acquisition, claiming that extroverts are more likely to communicate effectively than introverts, at least in the early stages of the second language learning programme.

Problems caused by the silent participant are better known than those created by socially skilled and overly assertive group members. If heterogeneous groups are formed, introverted personalities may well feel crushed by the more expressive participants, and lose the little confidence they possess, while the confident ones might feel that no satisfactory progress is being made, and so become bored and discouraged. Discussions carried out in relatively homogeneous groups might well lead the more introverted student away from his or her concern with rule obedience and correctness to a more unselfconscious and fluent expression of personal knowledge and views. Groups, then, should be as homogeneous as possible in terms of both linguistic ability and personality type.

The next step is the formation of partner groups of observer-evaluators. The reason for having these groups is to ensure that students have reasonably frequent opportunities not just to participate in discussions, but also to observe, describe and evaluate the process. In this way, the discussion and post-discussion stages, as well as the pre-discussion stage, become substantially learner-centred. This allows the teacher to focus feedback far more effectively, by targeting points not picked up by the learners, and providing opportunities to repair and develop relevant language points.

IDENTIFYING AND ORGANIZING THE TOPIC

Some learners find it difficult to generate and organize discussion topics in their first language; the extra pressure of trying to think and communicate in a second language adds considerably to the problems in the early stages of the discussion programme. Instead of reverting to the use of L1 or L2 prompts to complete this stage, we believe that it is far more desirable for the teacher to pre-teach brainstorming and mind-mapping techniques (Buzan, 1974, 1988, 1989); this helps to increase confidence and fluency in the use of the second language, and provides a means of mapping out possible content areas, as well as a framework for the investigation of each topic area.

The topic areas chosen by groups are often so broad as to require breaking down into manageable areas of enquiry to suit the time constraints of particular programmes. Learners can help to solve this problem by identifying and listing subtopics, and setting objectives for their coverage. In this way, the initial framework the groups derived from the brainstorming stage begins to take the form of a more substantial framework for use in guiding the discussion along relevant lines of enquiry. Part of the teacher's role will be to check that the framework is sound, and to offer advice, if necessary, for its modification.

Discussion

PEER OBSERVATION AND EVALUATION

We decided to examine possible means of observing and evaluating the discussion. Peer evaluation may be carried out in one, two, or all of three main ways (the observer ring, shadowing and the reviewing of video- and audiotape recordings of discussions). The role of the teacher in the discussion stage is to pass unobtrusively from group to group, forestalling possible breakdowns in communication caused by students having insufficient language to realize intended meanings. Systematic repair and enrichment of language should take place at the post-discussion stage.

Observer ring. While a group conducts its discussion, the observer-evaluators sit with the discussion group and monitor the proceedings. Their findings are reported back in the post-discussion stage.

Although this exercise is of receptive value for the observers, and of feedback value for the participants, it leaves no permanent record for subsequent reference. For the collection of storable data, observers need to complete observation and evaluation sheets (see Figure1).

A less structured way of carrying out this exercise would be for observers simply to draw a horizontal line across the middle of a piece of paper. Those participants making a large number of contributions would have their names recorded above the line, and those making fewer contributions below it. This exercise could be carried out regularly and when, say, five assessments have been carried out, the results could be analysed to find out who is predominantly above the line, who is usually below and who has changed position. Provided the findings are not interpreted in a judgemental way, this kind of exercise can be a great

	Number of Contributions					
Behaviour	**Student A**	**Student B**	**Student C**	**Student D**	**Student E**	**Student F**
1 Total number of contributions made						
2 Responding supportively						
3 Responding aggressively						
4 Introducing a new (relevant) point						
5 Digressing from the topic						

Figure 1

Functions	Language used	Pronunciation	Gestures
1 To prevent interruption and finish speaking	*Please . . . I must finish . . .*	Voice gets louder and faster	Holds up one page
2 Helping somebody to begin speaking	*I wonder if Amy has an opinion about this . . . ?*	Stress *Amy*; voice rises towards end of question	Smiling; eyes wide open
3 Interrupting to disagree	*Sorry, but I can't agree . . .*	Stress the negative	Eye contact made with speaker
4 Interrupting to obtain more information	*What do you mean by . . . ?*	Stress on uncertain term; voice falls at end of question	Leans forward
5 Supporting the previous speaker	*I think Peter made a good point about . . .*	Stress *good*	Looks at Peter
6 Not supporting the previous speaker	*Unlike Peggy, I think that . . .*	Stress *Peggy*	Looks around the group for support

Figure 2

motivator. The data collected might also provide evidence of a poorly constituted grouping in need of reorganisation.

Shadowing. Whereas the observer ring involves all observer-evaluators in recording data on all the discussion participants, shadowing provides for intensive one-to-one peer evaluation, and the possible development of long-term, reciprocal, 'buddy' pairings. A specified member of the partner group sits next to, or better, just behind, a discussion group participant. This technique may also be used for empathy building. At a prearranged point in the discussion, the shadow may substitute for the participant and adopt his or her line of argument. We have found that some practice in contributing and responding empathetically can be very useful in getting learners to understand how others think and express themselves.

An example of an observation exercise best carried out by one-on-one shadowing is given in Figure 2. The functions are given for guidance, and to raise observer awareness of what to focus on while observing intragroup dynamics. Any details missed during the discussion may be added in the post-discussion stage.

Using video and audio recorders. This means of collecting data is perhaps the most obvious, yet not always the easiest to exploit in practice. The presence of cameras and recorders can be very distracting, and the poor sound quality often obtained sometimes mocks the effort put into setting up the recording. However, excellent results can be obtained if the camera is fixed on a tripod, and there are sufficient remote microphones in position. If possible, the recording of each group should be made away from the classroom, in a quiet space.

Video gives the best possible feedback because it provides a simultaneous display of contributions, sociolinguistic strategies, group dynamics, language use and accuracy. Replaying early videos of a group discussion, and comparing these to later recordings of the same group, should help students to perceive that progress has been made. This in turn may strengthen their resolution to progress still further.

KEEPING REFLECTIVE JOURNALS

Another advantage of recording discussion sessions is that the video may be reviewed by individual students as a post-discussion activity. This is of particular benefit to students who feel uncomfortable about giving and receiving peer-evaluation feedback in front of the whole class. Data gleaned from video review were frequently in evidence in the reflective journals students were expected to keep, where they entered a paragraph of commentary on each discussion session. The journal was used to create a written dialogue between individual students and the teacher, as in the following sample entry from a first-year student:

> I think my performance in the discussion is better than the last time. I am active on this topic and express my own opinion confidently. I can speak more fluently. But there are also some aspects I can improve in the future, like that I can use more appropriate body language.

ASSESSMENT

The teacher will be particularly busy recording data during the discussion stage. He or she might like to consider assessing students at a later date, using assessment criteria. The great advantage of this procedure is that it can deliver a far more complete profile of discussion performance than any other technique. We have used a four-band scale, which we find works quite effectively (see Appendix).

POST-DISCUSSION

The main concern during this phase will be for learners to review and discuss the strengths and weaknesses of the discussion with peers and the teacher, to make recommendations for future modifications and improvements. This is also the time for the teacher to give one-to-one feedback, making reference to the assessment criteria or any other collected or recorded data.

Most repair and enrichment of grammar and vocabulary will also take place during this phase. Both the learners and the teacher will have recorded linguistic data, which can be used as a point of departure for systematic practice and future application. This is also the most appropriate time to practise and raise awareness of the prosodic and paralinguistic phenomena recorded during the discussion stage. In addition, writing tasks may be carried out. Summaries of the main points of the discussion, and compositions which extend and elaborate the topic discussed, are particularly valuable.

Another worthwhile post-discussion activity is to practise elements of group dynamics within the parameters of a moves frame. This technique helps more reserved participants to develop confidence in making contributions, and encourages the smooth flow of the discussion. A short section from a moves frame follows, by way of illustration:

A: Starts practice discussion by giving opinion.
B: Responds to A, agreeing or disagreeing.
C: Responds to both A and B. Not giving a new idea, but expressing either agreement or disagreement with A and B.

D: Introduces new idea.
E: Responds to D.
F: Asks E a question to clarify his or her opinion.
E: Answers F.
D: Relates his opinion to either A or B.
B: Responds to D, agreeing or disagreeing.
A: Responds to D, agreeing or disagreeing, etc.

Of equal importance is the need for learners to establish lines of enquiry for future discussions. This is essential to lend a sense of progression and coherence to a series or programme of discussions. It is not desirable for a single discussion to be seen as a completed and closed task; rather, it should link in coherently with preceding and subsequent discussions. A major aim in developing discussion skills should be the creation of a recursive flow between the various phases. In fact, the paramount aim should be to merge the phases into a seamless whole.

Conclusion

We have attempted to provide a rationale to support an experiential and process-oriented approach to the development of discussion skills in a second language. Although we have used English as the language of exemplification, this approach could be used to develop discussion skills in any second language. It could also be used on ESP, EAP, and general English courses, and at all post-elementary linguistic levels.

If the role of the teacher appears to have been understated in our description of the discussion process, this is simply a consequence of the approach advocated here, since we view the teacher's role as being crucial, providing as it does a source of information, animation and feedback for the discussion participants. However, the teacher does have to restrain his or her involvement, particularly during the pre-discussion and discussion stages. A heuristic approach to discussions also demands that learners take more responsibility for organizing and carrying out their own learning. Clearly, if participants fail to reflect on and research their particular areas of enquiry, they will not be able to contribute effectively to the discussion and, as a consequence, intragroup dynamics are likely to suffer. For the teacher, this will not necessarily mean a complete breakdown of the process of discussion, since extra peer pressure will be brought to bear on recalcitrant participants to prepare more effectively. This approach to discussion skills work can contribute to an important educational initiative, that is, the development of the efficient, independent, self-directed learner competent in organizing his or her own learning long after programmes of formal instruction have ceased.

References

Alexander, L. G. (1968). *For and against*. London: Longman.

Buzan, T. (1974). *Use your head*. London: BBC.

Buzan, T. (1988). *Make the most of your mind*. London: Pan.

Buzan, T. (1989). *Use your memory*. London: BBC.

Ellis, R. (1990). *Instructed second language acquisition*. Oxford: Blackwell.

Green, C. F. (1993). Learner drives in second language acquisition. *English Teaching Forum 31*(1), 2–5, 11.

Hargreaves, R., & Fletcher, M. (1981). *Arguing and discussing*. London: Evans.

Haswell, R. (1993). Student self-evaluations and developmental change. In J. Macgregor (Ed.), *Student self-evaluation: Fostering reflective learning*. San Francisco: Jossey-Bass.

Heyworth, F. (1984). *Discussions: Advanced role play for EFL*. London: Hodder and Stoughton.

Krashen, S. D. (1981). *Second language acquisition and second language learning*. Oxford: Pergamon.

Slimani, Y. (1992). Evaluating classroom interaction. In J. C. Alderson & A. Beretta (Eds.), *Evaluating second language education*. Cambridge: Cambridge University Press.

Ur, P. (1981). *Discussions that work: Task-centered fluency practice*. Cambridge: Cambridge University Press.

Wallace, M. J. (1980). *Study skills in English*. Cambridge: Cambridge University Press.

Appendix

BAND D

- A standard of speech problems which makes comprehension markedly difficult
- Use of mostly fragmented language items and phrases
- Little understanding of what others say
- Little evidence of preparing and reflecting on the topic
- Low level of ability to respond to new ideas
- General reluctance to contribute, either by initiating or by helping to maintain the discussion dynamic

BAND C

- A standard of speech production that does not consistently hinder comprehension
- Control of language more or less adequate for discussion
- Evidence of general understanding of the issues raised in the discussion
- Sharing of ideas and experiences that are basically relevant to the issues
- Ability to respond more or less appropriately to new ideas raised in discussion

BAND B

- Ability to express ideas clearly and accurately to other participants in the discussion
- Readiness and ability to participate confidently in discussion
- Appropriate turn taking and sensitivity to other people and ideas
- Evidence of considerable reflection on issues under discussion
- Ability to take in the ideas of fellow participants and build on them
- Ability to formulate fundamentally logical and coherent arguments
- Ability to sum up conclusions reached

BAND A

- Control of language that allows finer shades of meaning to be expressed, and complex issues debated
- Ability to question assumptions and existing beliefs, and turn a discussion in useful directions
- Ability to stimulate others' ideas and lead discussions
- Ability to counter arguments logically and persuasively

SECTION 10

TEACHING LISTENING

INTRODUCTION

For many years, listening skills did not receive priority in language teaching. Teaching methods emphasized productive skills, and the relationship between receptive and productive skills was poorly understood. Until recently, the nature of listening in a second language was ignored by applied linguists, and it was often assumed that listening skills could be acquired through exposure but not really taught. This position has been replaced by an active interest in the role of listening comprehension in second language acquisition, by the development of powerful theories of the nature of language comprehension, and by the inclusion of carefully developed listening courses in many ESL programs. Some applied linguists go so far as to argue that listening comprehension is at the core of second language acquisition and therefore demands a much greater prominence in language teaching. The papers in this section explore the nature of second language listening and principles for the design of teaching activities and classroom materials.

In the first paper, Nunan points out that in order to develop appropriate approaches to teaching listening skills, it is first necessary to understand the nature of listening. Two models of listening can be identified: the bottom-up and the top-down processing models. The bottom-up processing holds that listening is a linear, data-driven process. Comprehension occurs to the extent that the listener is successful in decoding the spoken text. The top-down model of listening, by contrast, involves the listener in actively constructing meaning based on expectations, inferences, intentions, and other relevant prior knowledge. The language data serve as cues to activate this top-down process. In teaching listening, Nunan suggests that we design activities that teach both bottom-up and top-down processing skills as they both play important, but different, roles in listening. It is also important to teach learners specific strategies that can help them understand the processes underlying listening, so that gradually they can assume greater control of their own learning. Among the key strategies that can be taught are predicting, selective listening, listening for different purposes, inferencing, and personalizing.

The second paper, by Field, examines a commonly used format for the teaching of listening, one which involves three stages in a listening activity: pre-listening, listening, and post-listening. He points out the limitations of some activities often used at these different points in a lesson: Materials and teaching often tend to test listening rather than teach it and do not practice the kind of listening that takes place in real life. Field advocates the use of preset questions, the use of task-based listening activities, a focus on strategies, and a greater use of authentic materials and shows how these recommendations affect the typical three-part listening lesson. He also shows how the teacher's role is crucial in the teaching of listening. The teacher is not there simply to check answers, but rather to actively guide learners through the processes of listening, monitoring their listening difficulties, and reshaping classroom tasks to provide maximum opportunities for learner involvement and to develop a better awareness of how to listen.

Finally, Lam points out that many ESL listening materials fail to provide examples of genuine spoken language since devices typically used by speakers, such as filler, fragments, and compensation devices, are often omitted. She illustrates ways in which learners can develop awareness of the syntax and organization of spoken discourse in order to facilitate their ability to process spoken texts. These activities integrate both listening and speaking and seek to prepare learners to handle the demands of real-world communication.

Discussion Questions

Before Reading

1. What listening needs do your learners (or a group of learners you are familiar with) have? What do you do to meet those needs?
2. What do you think are second language learners' greatest difficulties with listening? If possible, interview the learners to confirm your impressions.
3. To what extent do you think listening can be taught? What do you think the role of the teacher is in a listening class?
4. Discuss some of the differences between spoken and written texts in terms of vocabulary, syntax, and discourse structure.
5. Describe listening activities that you think are effective in enhancing students' listening skills.
6. What are the similarities and differences between listening and reading comprehension processes?
7. How effective is the language lab in promoting listening skills?

After Reading

1. How do schemata influence the way we listen? Discuss with reference to the following situations:
   - listening to someone recount a traffic accident
   - listening to someone describe his or her apartment
   - listening to casual conversation at a social gathering
2. Design a pre-listening activity that you can use to activate students' schemata.

3. Record an example of authentic speech (e.g., a casual conversation) and then examine it carefully. What examples do you find of differences between spoken language and written language?
4. Examine a unit from an ESL/EFL listening text. What types of pre-listening, listening, and post-listening activities does it make use of? Are the criticisms Field makes of standard exercise types for this lesson format true of the text?
5. Choose a listening extract (e.g., an authentic sample from radio or TV or an interview or discussion that you record) and suggest how it could be used to teach listening skills. Prepare a lesson plan following the suggestions given by Fields.
6. Prepare an activity, similar to those discussed by Lam, for developing students' awareness of the features of authentic spoken discourse.
7. Select some listening strategies and discuss how you can teach them to a group of students with the following proficiency levels: elementary; intermediate; advanced.
8. Review the paper by Nunan. What are the differences between the bottom-up and top-down views of listening? Which of the two processes is more useful for listening comprehension?
9. According to Nunan, what are the differences between reciprocal and nonreciprocal listening tasks? Which one will you stress more in your listening class?

CHAPTER 21

Listening in Language Learning

David Nunan

Introduction

Listening is the Cinderella skill in second language learning. All too often, it has been overlooked by its elder sister – speaking. For most people, being able to claim knowledge of a second language means being able to speak and write in that language. Listening and reading are therefore secondary skills – means to other ends, rather than ends in themselves.

Every so often, however, listening comes into fashion. In the 1960s, the emphasis on oral language skills gave it a boost. It became fashionable again in the 1980s, when Krashen's (1982) ideas about comprehensible input gained prominence. A short time later, it was reinforced by James Asher's (1988) Total Physical Response, a methodology drawing sustenance from Krashen's work, and based on the belief that a second language is learned most effectively in the early stages if the pressure for production is taken off the learners. During the 1980s, proponents of listening in a second language were also encouraged by work in the first language field. Here, people such as Gillian Brown (see, for example, Brown, 1990) were able to demonstrate the importance of developing oracy (the ability to listen and speak) as well as literacy, in school. Prior to this, it was taken for granted that first language speakers needed instruction in how to read and write, but not in how to listen and speak, because these skills were automatically bequeathed to them as native speakers.

The Nature of the Listening Process

Listening is assuming greater and greater importance in foreign language classrooms. There are several reasons for this growth in popularity. By emphasising the role of comprehensible input, second language acquisition research has given a major boost to listening. As Rost

(1994, pp. 141–142) points out, listening is vital in the language classroom because it provides input for the learner. Without understanding input at the right level, any learning simply cannot begin. Listening is thus fundamental to speaking.

Two views of listening have dominated language pedagogy since the early 1980s. These are the bottom-up processing view and the top-down interpretation view. The bottom-up processing model assumes that listening is a process of decoding the sounds that one hears in a linear fashion, from the smallest meaningful units (phonemes) to complete texts. According to this view, phonemic units are decoded and linked together to form words, words are linked together to form phrases, phrases are linked together to form utterances, and utterances are linked together to form complete, meaningful texts. In other words, the process is a linear one, in which meaning itself is derived as the last step in the process. In their introduction to listening, Anderson and Lynch (1988) call this the 'listener as tape recorder view' of listening because it assumes that the listener takes in and stores messages sequentially, in much the same way as a tape recorder – one sound, one word, one phrase, and one utterance at a time.

The alternative, top-down view suggests that the listener actively constructs (or, more accurately, reconstructs) the original meaning of the speaker using incoming sounds as clues. In this reconstruction process, the listener uses prior knowledge of the context and situation within which the listening takes place to make sense of what he or she hears. Context and situation include such things as knowledge of the topic at hand, the speaker or speakers, and their relationship to the situation, as well as to each other and prior events.

These days, it is generally recognised that both bottom-up and top-down strategies are necessary. In developing courses, materials, and lessons, it is important to teach not only bottom-up processing skills, such as the ability to discriminate between minimal pairs, but also to help learners use what they already know to understand what they hear. If teachers suspect that there are gaps in their learners' knowledge, the listening itself can be preceded by schema-building activities to prepare learners for the listening task to come.

There are many different types of listening, which can be classified according to a number of variables, including purpose for listening, the role of the listener, and the type of text being listened to. These variables are mixed in many different configurations, each of which will require a particular strategy on the part of the listener.

Listening purpose is an important variable. Listening to a news broadcast to get a general idea of the news of the day involves different processes and strategies from listening to the same broadcast for specific information, such as the results of an important sporting event. Listening to a sequence of instructions for operating a new piece of computer software requires different listening skills and strategies from listening to a poem or a short story. In designing listening tasks, it is important to teach learners to adopt a flexible range of listening strategies. This can be done by holding the listening text constant (working, say, with a radio news broadcast reporting a series of international events) and getting learners to listen to the text several times – however, following different instructions each time. They might, in the first instance, be required to listen for gist, simply identifying the countries where the events have taken place. The second time they listen, they might be required to match the places with a list of events. Finally, they might be required to listen for detail, discriminating between specific aspects of the event, or perhaps comparing the radio broadcast with newspaper accounts of the same events and noting discrepancies or differences of emphasis.

Another way of characterising listening is in terms of whether the listener is also required to take part in the interaction. This is known as reciprocal listening. When listening to a monologue, either live or through the media, the listening is, by definition, nonreciprocal. The listener (often to his or her frustration) has no opportunity of answering back, clarifying understanding, or checking that he or she has comprehended correctly. In the real world, it is rare for the listener to be cast in the role of nonreciprocal "eavesdropper" on a conversation. However, in the listening classroom, this is the normal role.

Listening in Practice

A challenge for the teacher in the listening classroom is to give learners some degree of control over the content of the lesson, and to personalise content so learners are able to bring something of themselves to the task. There are numerous ways in which listening can be personalised. For example, it is possible to increase learner involvement by providing extension tasks which take the listening material as a point of departure, but which lead learners into providing part of the content themselves. For example, students might listen to someone describing his or her work, and then create a set of questions for interviewing the person.

A learner-centred dimension can be lent to the listening class in one of two ways. First, tasks can be devised in which the classroom action is centered on the learner, not the teacher. In tasks exploiting this idea, students are actively involved in structuring and restructuring their understanding of the language and in building their skills in using the language. Second, teaching materials, like any other types of materials, can be given a learner-centred dimension by getting learners involved in the processes underlying their learning and in making active contributions to the learning. This can be achieved in the following ways:

- making instructional goals explicit to the learner
- giving learners a degree of choice
- giving learners opportunities to bring their own background knowledge and experience into the classroom
- encouraging learners to develop a reflective attitude to learning and to develop skills in self-monitoring and self-assessment

I try to simulate the interactive nature of listening and to involve learners personally in the content of the language lesson through activities in which they listen to one side of a conversation, and react with written responses. Obviously, this is not the same thing as taking part in an actual conversation, but I find that it does generate a level of involvement on the part of learners that goes beyond the usual sort of nonparticipatory listening task. Because learners are providing personalised responses, there is variation between learners, and this creates the potential for follow-up speaking tasks, in which learners compare and share their responses with other learners.

Nonreciprocal listening tasks can draw on a rich variety of authentic data, not just lectures and one-sided anecdotes. In my own listening classes, I have used the following data: answering-machine messages, store announcements, announcements on public transportation, minilectures, and narrative recounts. The increasing use of computerised messages on the telephone by companies and public utilities can also provide a rich source of authentic data for nonreciprocal listening tasks.

A recurring theme in recent books and papers on language teaching methodology is the need to develop learners' awareness of the processes underlying their own learning so that, eventually, they will be able to take greater and greater responsibility for that learning. This can be done through the adoption of a learner-centred strategy at the level of classroom action, and through equipping students with a wide range of effective learning strategies. Through these, students will not only become better listeners, they will also become more effective language learners because they will be given opportunities to focus on, and reflect upon, the processes underlying their own learning. This is important because if learners are aware of what they are doing, if they are conscious of the processes underlying the learning they are involved in, learning will be more effective. Key strategies that can be taught in the listening classroom include selective listening, listening for different purposes, predicting, progressive structuring, inferencing, and personalising. These strategies should not be separated from the content teaching, but woven into the ongoing fabric of the lesson, so that learners can see the applications of the strategies to the development of effective learning.

Conclusion

In this paper, I have set out some of the theoretical, empirical, and practical aspects of listening comprehension. I have suggested that listening classrooms need to develop both bottom-up and top-down listening skills in learners. I have also stressed the importance of a strategies-based approach to the teaching of listening. Such an approach is particularly important in classrooms where students are exposed to substantial amounts of authentic data, because they will not (and should not expect to) understand every word.

In summary, an effective listening course will be characterized by the following features (see also the design features set out in Mendelsohn, 1994):

- The materials should be based on a wide range of authentic texts, including both monologues and dialogues.
- Schema-building tasks should precede the listening.
- Strategies for effective listening should be incorporated into the materials.
- Learners should be given opportunities to progressively structure their listening by listening to a text several times and by working through increasingly challenging listening tasks.
- Learners should know what they are listening for and why.
- The task should include opportunities for learners to play an active role in their own learning.
- Content should be personalised.

References

Anderson, A., & Lynch, T. (1988). *Listening*. Oxford: Oxford University Press.

Asher, J. (1988). *Learning another language through actions: The complete teacher's guidebook.* 3rd ed. Los Gatos, CA: Sky Oaks Productions.

Brown, G. (1990). *Listening to spoken English.* 2nd ed. London: Longman.

Krashen, S. (1982). *Principles and practice in second language acquisition.* Oxford: Pergamon.

Mendelsohn, D. (1994). *Learning to listen.* San Diego: Domine Press.

Rost, M. (1994). *Introducing listening*. London: Penguin.

CHAPTER 22

The Changing Face of Listening

John Field

INTRODUCTION

There was a time when listening in language classes was perceived chiefly as a means of presenting new grammar. Dialogues on tape provided examples of structures to be learned, and this was the only type of listening practice most learners received. Ironically, much effort was spent on training learners to express themselves orally. Sight was lost of the fact that one is (to say the least) rather handicapped in conversation unless one can follow what is being said, as well as speak.

From the late 1960s, practitioners recognised the importance of listening and began to set aside time for practising the skill. A relatively standard format for the listening lesson developed at this time:

- **Pre-listening**

  Pre-teaching of all important new vocabulary in the passage

- **Listening**

  Extensive listening (followed by general questions establishing context)
  Intensive listening (followed by detailed comprehension questions)

- **Post-listening**

  Analysis of the language in the text (*Why did the speaker use the present perfect?*)
  Listen and repeat: teacher pauses the tape, learners repeat words

This is a slightly revised version of an article that appeared in *English Teaching Professional*, Issue 6, 12–14, January 1998.

Over the past several decades, teachers have modified this procedure considerably. It is worthwhile reminding ourselves of the reasons for these changes. In doing so, we may come to question the thinking behind them and/or conclude that the changes do not go far enough.

Pre-listening

Critical words

Pre-teaching of vocabulary has now largely been discontinued. In real life, learners cannot expect unknown words to be explained in advance; instead, they have to learn to cope with situations where part of what is heard will not be familiar. Granted, it may be necessary for the teacher to present three or four critical words at the beginning of the listening lesson – but 'critical' implies absolutely indispensable key words without which any understanding of the text would be impossible.

Pre-listening activities

Some kind of pre-listening activity is now usual, involving brainstorming vocabulary, reviewing areas of grammar, or discussing the topic of the listening text. This phase of the lesson usually lasts longer than it should. A long pre-listening session shortens the time available for listening. It can also be counterproductive. Extended discussion of the topic can result in much of the content of the listening passage being anticipated. Revising language points in advance encourages learners to focus on examples of these particular items when listening – sometimes at the expense of global meaning.

One should set two simple aims for the pre-listening period:

1. to provide sufficient context to match what would be available in real life
2. to create motivation (perhaps by asking learners to speculate on what they will hear)

These can be achieved in as little as 5 minutes.

Listening

The intensive/extensive distinction

Most practitioners have retained the extensive/intensive distinction. On a similar principle, international examinations usually specify that the recording is to be played twice. Some theorists argue that this is unnatural because in real life one gets only one hearing. But the whole situation of listening to a cassette in a language classroom is, after all, artificial. Furthermore, listening to a strange voice, especially one speaking in a foreign language, demands a process of *normalisation* – of adjusting to the pitch, speed, and quality of the voice. An initial period of extensive listening allows for this.

Preset questions

There have been changes in the way that comprehension is checked. We recognise that learners listen in an unfocused way if questions are not set until after the passage has been heard. Unsure of what they will be asked, they cannot judge the level of detail that will be required of them. By presetting comprehension questions, we can ensure that learners listen with a clear purpose, and that their answers are not dependent on memory.

LISTENING TASKS

More effective than traditional comprehension questions is the current practice of providing a task where learners *do* something with the information they have extracted from the text. Tasks can involve labelling (e.g., buildings on a map), selecting (e.g., choosing a film from three trailers), drawing (e.g., symbols on a weather map), form filling (e.g., a hotel registration form), and completing a grid.

Activities of this kind model the type of response that might be given to a listening experience in real life. They also provide a more reliable way of checking understanding. A major difficulty with listening work is that it is difficult to establish how much a learner has understood without involving other skills. For example, if learners give a wrong answer to a written comprehension question, it may be because they have not understood the question (reading) or because they cannot formulate an answer (writing) rather than because their listening is at fault. The advantage of listening tasks is that they can keep extraneous reading or writing to a minimum.

A third benefit is that tasks demand individual responses. Filling in forms, labelling diagrams, or making choices obliges every learner to try to make something of what he or she hears. This is especially effective if the class is asked to work in pairs.

AUTHENTIC MATERIALS

Another development has been the increased use of authentic materials. Recordings of spontaneous speech expose learners to the rhythms of natural everyday English in a way that scripted materials cannot, however good the actors. Furthermore, authentic passages where the language has not been graded to reflect the learners' level of English afford a listening experience much closer to a real-life one. It is vital that students of a language be given practice in dealing with texts where they understand only part of what is said.

For these two reasons (naturalness of language and real-life listening experience), it is advisable to introduce authentic materials early on in a language course. In general, students are not daunted or discouraged by authentic materials – provided they are told in advance not to expect to understand everything. Indeed, they find it motivating to discover that they can extract information from an ungraded passage. The essence of the approach is as follows: *Instead of simplifying the language of the text, simplify the task that is demanded of the student*. With a text above the language level of the class, one demands only shallow comprehension. One might play a recording of a real-life stall holder in a market and simply ask the class, to write down all the vegetables that are mentioned.

Students may have difficulty in adjusting to authentic conversational materials after hearing scripted ones. It is worthwhile introducing your learners systematically to those features of conversational speech which they may find unfamiliar – hesitations, stuttering, false starts, and long, loosely structured sentences. Choose a few examples of a single feature from a piece of authentic speech, play them to the class, and ask them to try to transcribe them.

STRATEGIC LISTENING

The type of foreign language listening that occurs in a real-life encounter or in response to authentic material is very different from the type that occurs with a scripted passage whose language has been graded to fit the learner's level. In real life, listening to a foreign language is a *strategic activity*. Nonnative listeners recognise only part of what they hear (my research suggests a much smaller percentage than we imagine) and have to make guesses which link these fragmented pieces of text. This is a process in which our learners need practice and guidance. Cautious students need to be encouraged to take risks and to make inferences based on the words they have managed to identify. Natural risk takers need to be encouraged to check their guesses against new evidence as it comes in from the speaker. And all learners need to be shown that making guesses is not a sign of failure.

Post-listening

We no longer spend time examining the grammar of the listening text; that reflected a typically structuralist view of listening as a means of reinforcing recently learned material. However, it remains worthwhile to pick out any functional language and draw learners' attention to it. ('Susan threatened John. Do you remember the words she used?'). Listening texts often provide excellent examples of functions such as apologising, inviting, refusing, suggesting, and so on.

The 'listen-and-repeat' phase has been dropped as well – on the argument that it is tantamount to parroting. This is not entirely fair: In fact, it tested the ability of learners to achieve lexical segmentation – to identify individual words within the stream of sound. But one can understand that it does not accord well with current communicative thinking.

As part of post-listening, one can ask learners to infer the meaning of new words from the contexts in which they appear – just as they do in reading. The procedure is to write the target words on the board, replay the sentences containing them, and ask learners to work out their meanings. Some teachers are deterred from employing this vocabulary-inferring exercise by the difficulty of finding the right places on the cassette. A simple solution is to copy the sentences to be used onto a second cassette.

To summarise, the format of a good listening lesson today differs considerably from that of four decades ago:

Pre-listening

Set context. Create motivation.

Listening

Extensive listening (followed by questions on context, attitude)
Preset task/Preset questions
Intensive listening
Checking answers

Post-listening

Examining functional language
Inferring vocabulary meaning

Where Do We Go from Here?

Listening methodology has changed a great deal, but some would argue that many of the changes have been cosmetic, and that what is really needed is a rethinking of the aims and structure of the listening lesson. The following are some of the limitations of our present approach.

WE STILL TEND TO TEST LISTENING RATHER THAN TEACH IT

The truth is that we have little option but to use some kind of checking procedure to assess the extent of understanding that has been achieved. What is wrong is not what we do, but *how we use the results*. We tend to judge successful listening simplistically in terms of correct answers to comprehension questions and tasks. We overlook the fact that there may be many ways of achieving a correct answer. One learner may have identified two words and made an intelligent guess; another may have constructed a meaning on the basis of 100% recognition of what was said.

We focus on the product of listening when we should be interested in the *process* – what is going on in the heads of our learners. Wrong answers are more informative than right ones; it makes sense to spend time finding out where and how understanding broke down. On this view, the main aim of a listening lesson is diagnostic: identifying listening problems and putting them right. Armed with evidence of why a misunderstanding occurred, teachers can design remedial microlistening exercises which tackle the cause of the problem. Here, dictation is a particularly useful tool. Suppose that learners find it difficult to recognise weak forms (/wəz/ for 'was', /tə/ for 'to', /ʊ/ for 'who'). A series of sentences can be dictated containing examples of the weak forms, to ensure that students interpret them correctly the next time they encounter them.

Remedial exercises should not be restricted to low-level skills such as word recognition; they can also be used to develop higher-level ones (distinguishing important pieces of information, anticipating, noticing topic markers, and so on).

A diagnostic aim for the listening lesson implies a change in lesson shape. Instead of the kind of long pre-listening period which some teachers employ, it is much more fruitful to allow time for an extended post-listening period in which learners' problems can be identified and tackled.

WE DO NOT PRACTISE THE KIND OF LISTENING THAT TAKES PLACE IN REAL LIFE

If we are to use authentic texts, it is pointless to operate on the assumption that learners will identify most of the words they hear. We need a new type of lesson, which models much more closely the kind of process that takes place in a real-life situation where understanding of what is said is less than perfect. The process adopted by nonnative listeners seems to be:

- Identify the words in a few fragmented sections of the text. Feel relatively certain about some, less certain about others.
- Make inferences linking the parts of the text about which you feel most confident.
- Check those inferences against what comes next.

This kind of strategy is not confined to low-level learners; my evidence suggests that it is used up to the highest levels. One of the most dangerous mistakes we make is to assume that because students have a good knowledge of vocabulary or grammar, they can necessarily *recognise* the words and structures they know when they encounter them in a natural spoken context.

We need to reshape some (not all) of our listening lessons to reflect this reality. Let us encourage learners to listen and write down the words they understand; to form and discuss inferences; to listen again and revise their inferences; then to check them against what the speaker says next. In doing this, we not only give them practice in the kind of listening they are likely to do in real life, we also make them realise that guessing is not a sign of failure, but something that most people resort to when listening to a foreign language.

LISTENING WORK IS OFTEN LIMITED IN SCOPE AND ISOLATING IN EFFECT

Our current methodology reinforces the natural instinct of the teacher to provide answers. We need to design a listening lesson where the teacher has a much less interventionist role, encouraging learners to listen and relisten and to do as much of the work as possible for themselves. On the other hand, we should also recognise the extent to which listening can prove an isolating activity, in which the liveliest and most vocal class can quickly become a group of separate individuals, each locked up in their own auditory efforts.

The solution is to play a short passage, then get learners to compare their understanding of it in pairs. Encourage them to disagree with each other – thus increasing motivation for a second listening. Play the passage again, and let the pairs revise their views, then share their interpretations with the class. *Resist the temptation to tell them who is right and who is wrong*. When the whole class has argued about the accuracy of different versions, play the text again and ask them to make up their minds, each student providing evidence to support his or her point of view. In this way, listening becomes a much more interactive activity, with learners listening because they have a vested interest in justifying their own explanation of the text. By listening and relistening, they improve the accuracy with which they listen and, by discussing possible interpretations, they improve their ability to construct representations of meaning from what they hear.

The methodology of the listening lesson has come a long way, but let us not be complacent. Unless we address the three problem areas just outlined, our teaching will remain hidebound and we will miss our true aim – which is not simply to provide practice, but to produce better and more confident listeners.

CHAPTER 23

Raising Students' Awareness of the Features of Real-World Listening Input

Wendy Y. K. Lam

INTRODUCTION

Many learners of English encounter more difficulties in listening and speaking than in reading and writing. One of the contributing factors is that much emphasis is laid on the written text in the teaching syllabus. The effect is that young learners start learning the written form of the language with little regard to its aural-oral aspect. When listening to natural, unscripted speech, students are exposed to loose, flowing texts. On the other hand, when reading, they are exposed to dense, structured texts. Many teachers fail to highlight this difference to the students and subsequently the teaching and learning of listening and speaking skills can only achieve minimal results.

Even when the aural-oral aspect is dealt with, the symbiotic relationship between listening and speaking practices is often overlooked. In many real-life situations, listening is reciprocal. The listener has the opportunity to indicate understanding or nonunderstanding, and to intervene when clarification is needed during communication (Anderson & Lynch, 1988). As listening and speaking are part and parcel of the spoken language, I would therefore argue that any effective listening course should help learners recognize the unique characteristics of spoken language (Allison & Martyn, 1993).

In this article, I focus on the description of these characteristics and the ways to alert learners to these characteristics in order that they can cope with real-world listening input and real-life communication more effectively.

FEATURES OF REAL-WORLD LISTENING INPUT

THE USE OF TIME-CREATING DEVICES

To ease the production of speech, the speaker normally uses time-creating devices. These are "used to gain time for the speaker so that he can formulate what to say next in spontaneous speech" (Wu, 1993). One typical example of these devices is the use of pause fillers. These belong to one of the five types of speech markers identified by Olynak (1990), necessary even in fluent speech. Olynak (1990) argue that the occurrence of speech markers such as pause fillers at the end of a completed speech unit or a transitionally relevant place (e.g., at a grammatical juncture) is very frequent. Despite the lack of syntactic or lexical functions that pause fillers such as "um," "urh," or "eh" serve, they do have a primary aim – to help the speaker to solicit more time to plan and in turn to furnish the listener with more processing time.

THE USE OF FACILITATION DEVICES

The pressure of time in real-life communication also renders it necessary for the speaker to use facilitation devices to ease speech production (Bygate, 1987). Effective listeners need to identify and be familiar with these devices in free speech. The use of less complex structures is one of these devices. In spoken language, learners have to know that it is not uncommon to find fragments of utterances which are reductions of complete "underlying" or "understood" constructions. Many constructions are less than complete clauses. Ellipses are very common because they help the speaker to cut short any unnecessary elements. Common examples are "Yes, I did," "Me too," "So am I," and so on. If learners are not prepared for these in listening and fail to recover the full meaning of these constructions, they will encounter problems in real-life communication. This problem is particularly prevalent among Hong Kong students.

The use of fixed and conventional phrases is another device to facilitate speech production. The use of speech formulas is a good example. Fluency in speech is related to formulaic language use, which includes two main kinds: memorized sequences and lexicalized sentence stems (Pawley & Syder, 1983). Stock phrases such as "I see what you mean," "I'm sure you're right but . . . " "you know," "I mean," "kind of," and so on, are just some of the memorized chunks of discourse. The use of these ready-made phrases simplifies the speaker's task, thereby increasing speed and fluency. Memorized and routine utterances are building blocks of fluent spoken discourse. In fact, such phrases as "you know," "I mean," and "well" may serve as pause fillers as well. These phrases will normally give the impression of fluency; they serve the function of filling unwanted pauses. As effective listeners, students need to understand their function.

THE USE OF COMPENSATION DEVICES

Unlike the written text, spoken discourse cannot be retrieved during normal interaction. The speed of natural speech and the fact that one cannot ask the speaker to repeat more than once means that listening input has to be processed very quickly. Fortunately, redundancy in natural speech does allow the listener some processing time.

The three typical ways to build in redundancy and help relieve memory load are repetition, reformulation, and rephrasing. Speakers always find themselves correcting or improving what they have already said. They may repeat part of the speech at the request of the listener or express their ideas in a different way. This kind of redundancy is necessary to help understanding on the part of the listener. Effective listeners therefore identify these elements of redundancy and are able to guess meanings from the help of compensation devices.

PEDAGOGICAL IMPLICATIONS

If time-creating, facilitation, and compensation devices are necessary "evils," the EFL learner has to recognize their locations and functions in running speech. The learner needs to understand that these devices are there to facilitate the speaker's production and the listener's processing of speech, and not to distract the listener's attention or to impede understanding. ESL students who are so used to reading the written form of the language need to be alerted to this so that they will not expect to hear uninterrupted, perfect flow of speech. Knowing what to expect is necessary if they are to be effective listeners.

To sum up, spoken language is not written language spoken aloud. Learners need to be aware of the use of these time-creating, facilitation, and compensation devices, which are virtually nonexistent in any text to which students are so conventionally accustomed. In fact, many of the listening materials available in the market for foreign learners of English are so heavily edited that many of the features of real speech are missing. No wonder learners find it hard to understand unedited speech or real-life interactions. Therefore, I would reiterate that students should be given opportunities to be exposed to real-life listening input.

Classroom Implementation

AWARENESS-RAISING EXERCISES

I shall now describe how the implications of these features of real speech can be put into classroom practice. The first step toward developing learners' listening skills is to raise their awareness of the difference between written and spoken language. Take the following as an example:

Spoken Text

"Somebody told me you once did some busking. Is that right?"

"Oh, yeah. Um, yes, I mean, it is I did. I went busking what? Just after university, or was it while I was at university? But anyway in the summer once in Hong Kong."

Written text

"I went busking once in Hong Kong during the summer holidays. However, I am not sure whether it was while I was still at university or after I had just left."

By comparing these short extracts of written and spoken texts that convey the same message, the teacher can highlight pause fillers such as "oh, yeah," "um, yes," the stock phrase "I mean," and less complex structures such as "it is I did," "Just after university, or was it while I was at university?" Let the learners listen to the spoken text on the tape. The teacher would then discuss with the learners the functions of these devices.

Alternatively, the teacher can focus on the grammar and lexis of the listening input, which bear elemental differences from the written text. The written text, which is a far more stable system than the spoken text, can be shown to the students to illustrate differences between written and spoken texts. Students would then read the scripts and discuss the differences:

Spoken Text

"You really/you realize/you know how hard it must've been/for them to come into a country/uh/where they've came from/you know I worked for one lady/and um/four times she'd missed being gassed."

Written Text

"You realize how hard it was for them to come to a new country. I worked for a lady once who avoided the gas chambers four times."

SKILLS ENABLING EXERCISES

After the consciousness-raising exercises, the teacher can provide learners with opportunities to identify time-saving, facilitation, and compensation devices in running speech. Listening materials produced for students are often "artificial" in order to suit the level of the students. Typically, such materials do not have hesitations, repetitions, very loose organization, and incomplete sentences. To make sure that the listening input is authentic and comprehensible and pitched at the right level of students, the teacher can help students produce their own listening materials. Not only would this help students comprehend the listening input, but it would also integrate both listening and speaking skills practices.

Helping students write semi-scripted simulated authentic speeches is one of the simple ways to produce appropriate listening input (Geddes & White, 1978). To reflect real-world listening input, the students do not need to write out everything that has to be said. Instead, a semi-script, rather than a full script in complete sentences, just gives the main ideas to the student who will speak into the tape. In this way, the speakers have to choose their language while they are speaking and their speech is more natural and rich in features of real speech.

There are two basic ways to guide learners to write semiscripts. First, the teacher can use brief notes or flow charts. The gist of the exchanges or the moves that students should take can be given to students to follow (Appendixes 1 and 2). Second, the teacher can think of a role-play situation in which different students have different roles to play (e.g., a radio interview with a social worker, a nonsmoker, an information officer, and a businessman to talk about cigarette advertisements). The teacher writes down information about each role on a role card and has different students take on different roles (Appendix 3).

Another suggestion is to have students produce their own authentic speech (Wu, 1993). The teacher can prepare a number of topics which are of general interest and within the scope of students' experiences (friends, stars and fans, part-time jobs, computer games, etc.). Then students can work in pairs. In each pair, one student chooses a topic and gives an unprepared talk on the topic for about three minutes. The student should not mention the actual topic and his or her partner has to guess what the topic is.

Using the aforementioned suggestions, extracts of student talk can be played to the whole class. The teacher should pause the tape whenever necessary for discussion. The teacher asks the students to identify pause fillers (e.g., "actually," "well," "um"). Similarly, students can do the same with the use of formulaic expressions, repetitions, simplified structures, and so on (e.g., "you know, I um er kind of urh like Al Pacino. Don't know why. But er – actually he's attractive. Really first class. I mean really good. See what I mean?"). In short, these skill enabling exercises aim to highlight the features of listening input and to integrate the listening and speaking practices.

CONCLUSION

In this article, I have emphasized the importance of addressing the differences between spoken and written texts in the teaching of listening skills. It is only when learners are aware of the unique characteristics of authentic listening input that can they be equipped with skills to handle real-life communication. Awareness-raising and skills-enabling exercises that provide students with opportunities to monitor the difficulty level of listening input and integrate listening and speaking skills have also been discussed.

References

Allison, D., & Martyn, E. (1993). The teaching of spoken English. In *Teaching grammar and spoken English: A handbook for Hong Kong schools*. Hong Kong: Education Department, Hong Kong Government Printer.

Anderson, A., & Lynch, T. (1988). *Listening*. Oxford: Oxford University Press.

Bygate, M. (1987). *Speaking*. Oxford: Oxford University Press.

Geddes, M., & White, R. (1978). The use of semi-scripted simulated authentic speech and listening comprehension. *Audio Visual Language Journal 16*(3).

Olynak, M., (1990). A quantitative and qualitative analysis of speech markers in the native and second language speech of bilinguals. In R. C. Scarcella, E. S. Anderson, & D. Karshen (Eds.), *Developing communicative competence in a second language: Series on issues in second language research*. New York: Newbury House.

Pawley, A., & Syder, F. (1983). Two puzzles for linguistic theory: Nativelike selection and nativelike frequency. In J. Richards & R. Schmidt (Eds.), *Language and communication*. New York: Longman.

Wu, K. Y. (1993). Teaching time-creating devices in spontaneous speech: A focused-learning approach. *English Teaching Forum*,

Appendix 1

Writing *notes* to help learners to speak and listen.

Hobbies A

You can answer your partner's questions either by using the following notes or by talking about your own hobbies.

photography, swimming, playing video games, taking photos on holiday, playing chess with a friend once a week, swimming in summer, brother likes computer games, got camera as birthday present, swimming is fun, can play chess anywhere, film is expensive, many beaches in Hong Kong

Hobbies B

Ask your partner about his or her hobbies. Use the following notes to help you. You can ask other questions as well.

What hobby?
Others?
How much time?
How started?
Why these?
Bad points?

Appendix 2

Writing *moves* to help learners to speak and listen.

Keeping Fit A

Talk with your partner about keeping fit.

Start like this:

1. Ask what he or she does about keeping fit.
2. Ask if he or she wants to do more or less.
3. Ask the same question. Carry on in this way.

Keeping Fit B

Talk with your partner about keeping fit.

Answer his or her question, then go on.

1. Also ask what he or she does about keeping fit.
2. Ask about his or her opinion of the importance of health and fitness.
3. Carry on in this way.

Appendix 3

Writing information about each *role* on a role card.

SU WING FOOK

You are compère of the radio talk show *Your View*, and tonight's topic is "All cigarette advertisements should be banned from TV commercials." Introduce the topic and the guests, keep the discussion moving, then sum up after 10 minutes.

SATWANT SINGH

You are a businessman. You do not feel that people smoke simply because of the influence of commercials. After all, the target audience of these advertisements are smokers who smoke anyway. You also believe that this is a free world. Consumers should be given informed choices and, hence, advertisements are just a fact of life.

WONG MEILING

You are a nonsmoker and love watching TV. You find that many TV commercials, including cigarette advertisements, depict a glamorous lifestyle, and you enjoy watching them. You strongly believe that people should be educated enough not to be easily influenced by what they see on the screen.

MARIA PAVLOVA

You are a social worker working in three different schools. You have handled quite a number of cases in which students have been caught smoking in school. Your experience in counseling these students has convinced you that TV commercials have insidious and powerful effects on young people.

TANG KIN HONG

You are an information officer in a government department. You have been invited to attend the radio interview. Your main role is to support the government's decision to have the warning sign "Smoking is hazardous to health" appear in all cigarette advertisements. But at the same time you do not want to offend the businessman. So you need to be tactful in defending the government's policy.

SECTION II

TEACHING VOCABULARY

INTRODUCTION

In the past, vocabulary teaching and learning were often given little priority in second language programs, but recently there has been a renewed interest in the nature of vocabulary and its role in learning and teaching. Traditionally, vocabulary learning was often left to look after itself and received only incidental attention in many textbooks and language programs. Thus, although the course curriculum was often quite specific about aspects of teaching such as grammar, reading, or speaking, little specification was given to the role of vocabulary. The status of vocabulary now seems to be changing. For one thing, the notion of a word has been "broadened" to include lexical phrases and routines, and it has been suggested that in the initial stages of learning these play a primary role in communication and acquisition. In addition, access to lexical corpora has made it possible for applied linguists to access huge samples of language in order to find out how words are used, both by native speakers and by second language learners. Such research has enabled applied linguists to identify common patterns of collocation, word formation, metaphor, and lexical phrases that are part of a speaker's lexical competence. The papers in this section discuss the role of vocabulary in teaching and learning.

Vocabulary is a core component of language proficiency and provides much of the basis for how well learners speak, listen, read, and write. Without an extensive vocabulary and strategies for acquiring new vocabulary, learners often achieve less than their potential and may be discouraged from making use of language learning opportunities around them such as listening to the radio, listening to native speakers, using the language in different contexts, reading, or watching television. Research on vocabulary in recent years has done a great deal to clarify the levels of vocabulary learning learners need to achieve in order to read both simplified and unsimplified materials and to process different kinds of oral and written texts, as well as the kinds of strategies learners use in understanding, using, and remembering words.

Hunt and Beglar discuss three approaches to vocabulary teaching and learning: incidental learning (i.e., learning vocabulary as a by-product of doing other things such as reading or listening), explicit instruction, and independent strategy development. A major source of incidental learning is extensive reading, which Hunt and Beglar recommend as a regular out-of-class activity. Explicit instruction depends on identifying specific vocabulary-acquisition targets for learners. Information is now available on what such targets should be for learners at different proficiency levels. For example, a target of 4,500 words is identified in the *Cambridge English Lexicon* (Hindmarsh, 1980), a core vocabulary for secondary school learners in EFL contexts. An additional 3,000 to 5,000 words is suggested for learners continuing to tertiary education studies. These words may have to be taught directly. Hunt and Beglar discuss techniques that can be employed for this purpose. In addition, learners need to be taught strategies for inferring words from context as well as those which can help learners retain the meanings of words they have encountered. Hunt and Beglar recommend a combination of all three approaches – indirect, direct, and strategy training – as the basis for a vocabulary program.

Nation argues for a systematic rather than an incidental approach to the teaching of vocabulary and argues that such a focus is an essential part of a language course. He points out the limitations of incidental learning and the fact that L2 learners are often unable to benefit from incidental vocabulary acquisition through reading because of limitations in their vocabulary knowledge. Nation illustrates a number of strategies for building in a focus on vocabulary as a part of the design of communicative tasks and argues that vocabulary instruction should be integrated into the listening, speaking, reading, and writing components of a language program.

Discussion Questions

Before Reading

1. Do you think learners acquire vocabulary more effectively through incidental learning or through explicit instruction?
2. What opportunities do learners have to acquire vocabulary through incidental learning?
3. What do you think are some of the strategies employed by a learner who is a "good vocabulary learner"?
4. Do you think textbooks provide sufficient support for vocabulary learning? How could further support be provided?
5. In what ways can learners accelerate the rate at which they learn vocabulary?
6. Why do you think learners forget many of the words they encounter or study in their course materials? How can the rate of retention of vocabulary be increased?
7. For languages you have learned, what strategies have you found helpful in learning new vocabulary?
8. What role do you think dictionaries can play in assisting vocabulary development? How do you use dictionaries in your teaching?

After Reading

1. Suggest ways in which learners can consolidate vocabulary they encounter through extensive reading.

2. Examine an ESL textbook series to see how vocabulary is dealt with. What vocabulary targets does the series teach? On what basis is vocabulary chosen? Is vocabulary dealt with incidentally or explicitly throughout the series?
3. How useful do you think bilingual word lists are in learning new vocabulary? What other strategies can learners use to help learn important words?
4. Develop vocabulary exercises for teaching the following:
   - a set of prefixes or suffixes
   - members of a lexical set (e.g., adjectives to describe appearances)
   - a set of words and their synonymns

   Review the exercises you developed. What learning principles are they based on?
5. Develop a list of vocabulary learning strategies that you would recommend to a specific group of intermediate-level learners.
6. Suggest ways in which dictionary use can be incorporated into ESL teaching.
7. What factors influence the learning of vocabulary through reading, according to Nation?
8. Why is the spoken production of vocabulary during a task likely to benefit the learning of vocabulary?
9. How might language-focused instruction assist vocabulary learning? Give an example of tasks that involve explicit language focus and suggest how this might facilitate vocabulary development.

Further Reading

Hindmarsh, R. (1980). *Cambridge English lexicon.* Cambridge: Cambridge University Press.

CHAPTER 24

Current Research and Practice in Teaching Vocabulary

Alan Hunt and David Beglar

INTRODUCTION

The purpose of this article is to present a systematic framework for vocabulary development by combining three approaches to vocabulary instruction and learning (modified from Coady, 1997a; Hulstijn, Hollander, & Greidanus, 1996). These three approaches – incidental learning, explicit instruction, and independent strategy development – are presented in this article as seven teaching principles. The incidental learning of vocabulary requires that teachers provide opportunities for extensive reading and listening. Explicit instruction involves diagnosing the words learners need to know, presenting words for the first time, elaborating word knowledge, and developing fluency with known words. Finally, independent strategy development involves practicing guessing from context and training learners to use dictionaries.

Although all of these approaches and principles have a role to play in vocabulary instruction, the learners' proficiency level and learning situation should be considered when deciding the relative emphasis to be placed on each approach. In general, emphasizing explicit instruction is probably best for beginning and intermediate students who have limited vocabularies. On the other hand, extensive reading and listening might receive more attention for more proficient intermediate and advanced students. Also, because of its immediate benefits, dictionary training should begin early in the curriculum.

Before proceeding, it is necessary to clarify the definition of a word. In this article, *a word* (also called a base word or a word family) is defined as including the base form (e.g., *make*) and its inflections and derivatives (e.g., *makes*, *made*, *making*, *maker*, and *makers*). Since the meanings of these different forms of the word are closely related, it is assumed that little extra effort is needed to learn them (Read, 1988). While this may be true, a study of Japanese students showed that they did not know many inflections and derivative suffixes for English verbs (Schmitt & Meara, 1977). Thus, these forms should be taught.

Although this definition of *a word* is convenient and commonly used in vocabulary research, it should be remembered that vocabulary learning is more than the study of individual words. Nattinger and DeCarrico (1992) have observed that a significant amount of the English language is made up of lexical phrases, which range from phrasal verbs (two or three words) to longer institutionalized expressions (Lewis, 1993, 1997). Because lexical phrases can often be learned as single units, the authors believe that the following principles apply to them as well as to individual words.

INCIDENTAL LEARNING

PRINCIPLE 1: PROVIDE OPPORTUNITIES FOR THE INCIDENTAL LEARNING OF VOCABULARY

In the long run, most words in both first and second languages are probably learned incidentally, through extensive reading and listening (Nagy, Herman, & Anderson, 1985). Several studies have confirmed that incidental L2 vocabulary learning through reading does occur (Chun & Plass, 1996; Day, Omura, & Hiramatsu, 1991; Hulstijn, Hollander, & Greidanus, 1996; Knight, 1994; Zimmerman, 1997). Although most research concentrates on reading, extensive listening can also increase vocabulary learning (Elley, 1989). Nagy, Herman, and Anderson (1985) concluded that (for native speakers of English) learning vocabulary from context is a gradual process, estimating that, given a single exposure to an unfamiliar word, there was about a 10% chance of learning its meaning from context. Likewise, L2 learners can be expected to require many exposures to a word in context before understanding its meaning.

The incidental learning of vocabulary through extensive reading can benefit language curricula and learners at all levels (Woodinsky & Nation, 1988). According to Coady (1997b), the role of graded (i.e., simplified) readers is to build up the students' vocabulary and structures until they can graduate to more authentic materials. Low-proficiency learners can benefit from graded readers because they will be repeatedly exposed to high-frequency vocabulary. Many students may never have done extensive reading for pleasure, so it may be initially useful to devote some class time to Sustained Silent Reading (SSR) (Pilgreen & Krashen, 1993). Once students develop the ability to read in a sustained fashion, then most of the reading should be done outside of class.

EXPLICIT INSTRUCTION

PRINCIPLE 2: DIAGNOSE WHICH OF THE 3,000 MOST COMMON WORDS LEARNERS NEED TO STUDY

Knowing approximately 3,000 high-frequency and general academic words is significant because this amount covers a high percentage of the words on an average page. The 2,000 high-frequency words in West's (1953) *General Service List* (GSL) cover 87% of an average nonacademic text (Nation, 1990) and 80% of an average academic text (P. Nation, personal communication, September 18, 1997). The 800 general academic words from Xue and Nation's (1984) "*University Word List*" account for about 8% of an academic text. For second language learners entering university, Laufer (1992) found that knowing a minimum of about 3,000 words was required for effective reading at the university level, whereas knowing 5,000 words indicated likely academic success. One way to estimate vocabulary size is to use Nation's (1990) Vocabulary Levels Test or a checklist test which requires learners to mark the words on a list that they believe they know (for more information on checklist tests, see Read, 1988; Meara, 1992, 1996).

PRINCIPLE 3: PROVIDE OPPORTUNITIES FOR THE INTENTIONAL LEARNING OF VOCABULARY

The incidental learning of vocabulary may eventually account for a majority of a advanced learners' vocabulary; however, intentional learning through instruction also significantly contributes to vocabulary development (Nation, 1990; Paribakht & Wesche, 1996; Zimmerman, 1997). Explicit instruction is essential for beginning students whose lack of vocabulary limits their reading ability. Coady (1997b) calls this the beginner's paradox. He wonders how beginners can "learn enough words to learn vocabulary through extensive reading when they do not know enough words to read well" (p. 229). His solution is to have students supplement their extensive reading with study of the 3,000 most frequent words until the words' form and meaning become automatically recognized (i.e., "sight vocabulary"). The first stage in teaching these 3,000 words commonly begins with word pairs in which an L2 word is matched with an L1 translation.

Translation has a necessary and useful role in L2 learning, but it can hinder learners' progress if it is used to the exclusion of L2-based techniques. Prince (1996) found that both "advanced" and "weaker" learners could recall more newly learned words using L1 translations than using L2 context. However, "weaker" learners were less able to transfer knowledge learned from translation into an L2 context. Prince claims that weaker learners require more time when using an L2 context as they have less developed L2 networks and are slower to use syntactic information. To discourage the learners from overrelying on translation, he advises that teachers talk with them about their expectations of language learning and "the pitfalls of low-effort strategies like translation" (p. 489). Furthermore, translation needs to be followed up with other L2-based exercises and learning strategies (see Principles 4 through 7).

Vocabulary lists can be an effective way to quickly learn word-pair translations (Nation, 1990). However, it is more effective to use vocabulary cards because learners can control the order in which they study the words (Atkinson, 1972). Also, additional information can easily be added to the cards. When teaching unfamiliar vocabulary, teachers need to consider the following:

1. Learners need to do more than just see the form (Channell, 1988). They need to hear the pronunciation and practice saying the word aloud as well (Ellis & Beaton, 1993; Fay & Cutler, 1977; Siebert, 1927). The syllable structure and stress pattern of the word are important because they are two ways in which words are stored in memory (Fay & Cutler, 1977).
2. Start by learning semantically unrelated words. Also avoid learning words with similar forms (Nation, 1990) and closely related meanings (Higa, 1963; Tinkham, 1993) at the same time. For example, because *affect* and *effect* have similar forms, simultaneously studying them is likely to cause confusion. Also, bilingual vocabulary books often simply list words in alphabetical order, increasing the chances of confusing words that start with the same syllable. Likewise, words with similar, opposite, or closely associated (e.g., types of fruit, family members) meanings may interfere with one another if they are studied at the same time.
3. It is more effective to study words regularly over several short sessions than to study them for one or two longer sessions. As most forgetting occurs immediately after

initial exposure to the word (Pimsleur, 1967), repetition and review should take place almost immediately after studying a word for the first time.

4. Study five to seven words at a time, dividing larger numbers of words into smaller groups. As learners review these five to seven cards, they will more quickly get repeated exposure to the words than when larger groups (twenty to thirty) are studied.
5. Use activities such as the keyword technique to promote deeper mental processing and better retention (Craik & Lockhart, 1972). Associating a visual image with a word helps learners remember the word.
6. A wide variety of L2 information can be added to the cards for further elaboration. Newly met words can be consciously associated with other L2 words that the learner already knows (Prince, 1996), and this word can be added to the card. Sentence examples, parts of speech, definitions, and keyword images can also be added (see Schmitt & Schmitt, 1995).

PRINCIPLE 4: PROVIDE OPPORTUNITIES FOR ELABORATING WORD KNOWLEDGE

Prince (1996) states that simply knowing translations for L2 words does not "guarantee that they will be successfully accessed for use in an L2 context" (p. 488), because knowing a word means knowing more than just its translated meaning or its L2 synonyms. Drawing upon Richards's (1976) list, Nation (1994) identifies various aspects of word knowledge such as knowing related grammatical patterns, affixes, common lexical sets, typical associations, how to use the word receptively and productively, and so on. Receptive knowledge means being able to recognize one of the aspects of knowledge through reading and listening, and productive knowledge means being able to use it in speaking and writing. Teachers should be selective when deciding which words deserve deeper receptive and/or productive practice, as well as which types of knowledge will be most useful for their students. Many of the two thousand high-frequency words from the GSL or other lists would be good candidates for exercises that elaborate upon both receptive and productive knowledge.

Elaboration involves expanding the connections between what the learners already know and new information. One way to do this is to choose L2 words from the surrounding context and to explain their connections to the recently learned word (Prince, 1996). In addition to presenting this new information, teachers should create opportunities to meet these useful, recently learned words in new contexts that provide new collocations and associations (Nation, 1994). Exercises that can deepen students' knowledge of words include the following: sorting lists of words and deciding on the categories; making semantic maps with lists either provided by the teacher or generated by the learners; generating derivatives, inflections, synonyms, and antonyms of a word; making trees that show the relationships between superordinates, coordinates, and specific examples; identifying or generating associated words; combining phrases from several columns; matching parts of collocations using two columns; completing collocations as a cloze activity; and playing collocation crossword puzzles or bingo (see Lewis, 1993; McCarthy & O'Dell, 1994; Nation, 1994; Redman & Ellis, 1990).

PRINCIPLE 5: PROVIDE OPPORTUNITIES FOR DEVELOPING FLUENCY WITH KNOWN VOCABULARY

Fluency-building activities recycle already known words in familiar grammatical and organizational patterns so that students can focus on recognizing or using words without hesitation. As Nation (1994) points out, developing fluency "overlaps most of all with developing the skills of listening, speaking, reading, and writing" (p. 208), so giving learners many opportunities to practice these skills is essential.

Fluency partly depends on developing sight vocabulary through extensive reading and studying high-frequency vocabulary. Fluency exercises include timed and paced readings. In timed readings, learners may try to increase their speed by sliding a 3 × 5 card or a piece of paper down the page to increase their speed while attempting to comprehend about 80% of a passage. Also, learners need to be given practice in looking at groups of words rather than each individual word when reading. Teachers can ask learners to practice timed reading on passages that have already been read. In paced readings, the teacher determines the time and pushes the learners to read faster. One type of paced reading is the "reading sprint" in which learners read their pleasure-reading book for 5 minutes and count the number of pages they have read. Then they try to read the same number of pages while the time they have to read decreases from 5 minutes to 4 to 3 to 2 minutes for each sprint. Finally, they read for five minutes again at a relaxed pace and count the number of pages they have finished (Mikulecky & Jeffries, 1996).

Independent Strategy Development

PRINCIPLE 6: EXPERIMENT WITH GUESSING FROM CONTEXT

Guessing from context is a complex and often difficult strategy to carry out successfully. To guess successfully from context, learners need to know about 19 out of every 20 words (95%) of a text, which requires knowing the 3,000 most common words (Liu & Nation, 1985; Nation, 1990). Even if one knows these words, however, Kelly (1990) concludes that "unless the context is very constrained, which is a relatively rare occurrence, or unless there is a relationship with a known word identifiable on the basis of form and supported by context, there is little chance of guessing the correct meaning" (p. 203). He also asserts that, because guessing from context fails to direct attention to word form and meaning, relatively little learning occurs.

Although this strategy often may not result in gaining a full understanding of word meaning and form, guessing from context may still contribute to vocabulary learning. Just what is and is not learned will partly depend on text difficulty as well as the learners' level. More proficient learners using texts that are not overly difficult can be expected to use this strategy more effectively than low proficiency learners. It should be remembered that learning vocabulary also includes learning about collocations, associations, and related grammatical patterns as well as meaning. Therefore, if regularly practiced, this strategy may contribute to deeper word knowledge for advanced learners as long as they pay attention to the word and its context.

However, given the continuing debate about the effectiveness of guessing from context, teachers and learners should experiment with this strategy and compare it to dictionary training. Guessing from context is initially time-consuming and is more likely to work for more proficient learners. A procedure for guessing from context begins with deciding whether the word is important enough (e.g., is part of an important idea and/or is repeated often) to warrant going through the subsequent steps. This decision is itself a skill that requires practice and experience. Teachers can assist learners by marking words which learners should try to infer before using other sources, as well as by providing glosses (Hulstijn, Hollander, & Greidanus, 1996). Once learners decide that a word is worth guessing, they might follow a five-step procedure such as that of Nation and Coady (1988, pp. 104–150):

1. Determine the part of speech of the unknown word.
2. Look at the immediate context and simplify it if necessary.

3. Look at the wider context. This entails examining the clause with the unknown word and its relationship to the surrounding clauses and sentences.
4. Guess the meaning of the unknown word.
5. Check that the guess is correct.

In Step 5, the guess needs to be the same part of speech as the unknown word. Moreover, the learner should try to see if the unknown word can be analyzed into parts (*unlock* becomes *un* + *lock*) and to check if the meaning of the parts matches the meaning of the unknown word. Finally, the guess should be tried out in the context to see whether it makes sense, and a dictionary may be consulted to confirm the guess. In the case of a wrong or partially correct guess, it is important for learners to reanalyze how the "correct" answer is more appropriate in the context. Finally, Liu and Nation (1985) suggest practicing this strategy as a class rather than as individual work, and Williams (1986) advises that it be demonstrated on an overhead transparency or a chalkboard by circling the unknown word and drawing arrows from other words that give clues to its meaning.

PRINCIPLE 7: EXAMINE DIFFERENT TYPES OF DICTIONARIES AND TEACH STUDENTS HOW TO USE THEM

Bilingual dictionaries have been found to result in vocabulary learning (Knight, 1994; Luppescu & Day, 1993). Hulstijn, Hollander, and Greidanus (1996) showed that, compared to incidental learning, repeated exposure to words combined with marginal glosses or bilingual dictionary use leads to increased learning for advanced learners. Luppescu and Day's (1993) study on Japanese students reports that bilingual dictionaries did result in vocabulary learning, unless the unfamiliar word had numerous entries, in which case the dictionaries may have confused learners. Finally, a bilingual dictionary may be much more likely to help lower-proficiency learners in reading comprehension because their lack of vocabulary can be a significant factor in their inability to read (Knight, 1994).

Bilingualized dictionaries may have some advantages over traditional bilingual or monolingual dictionaries. Bilingualized dictionaries essentially do the job of both a bilingual and a monolingual dictionary. Whereas bilingual dictionaries usually provide just an L1 synonym, bilingualized dictionaries include L2 definitions, L2 sentence examples, as well as L1 synonyms. Bilingualized dictionaries were found to result in better comprehension of new words than either bilingual or monolingual dictionaries (Laufer & Hader, 1997). A further advantage is that they can be used by all levels of learners: Advanced students can concentrate on the English part of the entry, and beginners can use the translation. For beginners, teachers may want to examine the bilingualized *Longman-Mitsumura English-Japanese Dictionary for Young Learners* (1993), which includes Japanese translations, definitions, and examples. Currently, neither Collins COBUILD, Longman, nor Oxford (all publishers with access to large, updated computerized English language databases) has bilingualized dictionaries for intermediate and advanced learners.

Electronic dictionaries with multimedia annotations offer a further option for teachers and learners. Chun and Plass's (1996) study of American university students learning German found that unfamiliar words were most efficiently learned when both pictures and text were available for students. This was more effective than text alone or combining text and video, possibly because learners can control the length of time spent viewing the pictures. Hulstijn, Hollander, and Greidanus (1996) suggest that, because computerized entries are easier to use than traditional dictionaries, students will be more likely to use them. Teachers may want to investigate the CD-ROM dictionaries published by Collins COBUILD, Longman, and Oxford. However, unlike the dictionary in the Chun and Plass study, these CD-ROM dictionaries do not link most of their entries to a visual image. The one exception is *The New Oxford Picture Dictionary CD-ROM* (1997), which includes 2,400 illustrated words (mainly concrete nouns) and is available in a bilingual version.

Finally, training in the use of dictionaries is essential. Unfortunately, in most classrooms, very little time is provided for training in dictionary use (Graves, 1987; Summers, 1988). In addition to learning the symbols and what information a dictionary can and cannot offer, learners may need extra practice for words with many entries. Furthermore, learners need to be taught to use all the information in an entry before making conclusions about the meaning of a word (Laufer & Hader, 1997). The learners' attention should also be directed toward the value of good sentence examples which provide collocational, grammatical, and pragmatic information about words. Finally, teachers should emphasize the importance of checking a word's original context carefully and comparing this to the entry chosen, because context determines which sense of a word is being used.

Conclusion

Learning vocabulary through incidental, intentional, and independent approaches requires teachers to plan a wide variety of activities and exercises. The amount of emphasis that teachers and programs decide to place on any given activity will depend on the learners' level and the educational goals of the teacher and the program. In general, it makes most sense to emphasize the direct teaching of vocabulary for learners who still need to learn the first 3,000 most common words. As learners' vocabulary expands in size and depth, extensive reading and independent strategies may be increasingly emphasized. Extensive reading and listening, translation, elaboration, fluency activities, guessing from context, and using dictionaries all have a role to play in systematically developing the learners' vocabulary knowledge.

References

Atkinson, R. C. (1972). Optimizing the learning of a second language vocabulary. *Journal of Experimental Psychology, 96*, 124–129.

Channell, J. (1988). Psycholinguistic considerations in the study of L2 vocabulary acquisition. In R. Carter & M. McCarthy (Eds.), *Vocabulary and language teaching.* London: Longman.

Chun, D., & Plass, J. (1996). Effects of multimedia annotations on vocabulary acquisition. *Modern Language Journal, 80*, 183–198.

Coady, J. (1997a). L2 vocabulary acquisition: A synthesis of the research. In J. Coady & T. Huckin (Eds.), *Second language vocabulary acquisition* (pp. 273–290). Cambridge: Cambridge University Press.

Coady, J. (1997b). L2 vocabulary acquisition through extensive reading. In J. Coady & T. Huckin (Eds.), *Second language vocabulary acquisition* (pp. 225–237). Cambridge: Cambridge University Press.

Craik, F. I. M., & Lockhart, R. S. (1972). Depth of processing and the retention of words in episodic memory. *Journal of Experimental Psychology, 104*, 268–284.

Day, R., Omura, C., & Hiramatsu, M. (1991). Incidental EFL vocabulary learning and reading. *Reading in a Foreign Language, 7*, 541–549.

Elley, W. (1989). Vocabulary acquisition from listening to stories. *Reading Research Quarterly, 24*, 174–187.

Ellis, N., & Beaton, A. (1993). Psychological determinants of foreign language vocabulary learning. *Language Learning, 43*(4), 559–617.

Fay, D., & Cutler, A. (1977). Malapropisms and the structure of the mental lexicon. *Linguist Inquiry, 8*(3), 505–520.

Graves, M. (1987). The roles of instruction in fostering vocabulary development. In M. G. McKeown & M. E. Curns (Eds.), *The nature of vocabulary acquisition* (pp. 167–184). Hillsdale, NJ: Lawrence Erlbaum.

Higa, M. (1963). Interference effects of intralist word relationships in verbal learning. *Journal of Verbal Learning and Verbal Behavior, 2*, 170–175.

Hulstijn, J., Hollander, M., & Greidanus, T. (1996). Incidental vocabulary learning by advanced foreign language students: The influence of marginal glosses, dictionary use, and reoccurrence of unknown words. *Modern Language Journal, 80*, 327–339.

Kelly, P. (1990). Guessing: No substitute for systematic learning of lexis. *System, 18*, 199–207.

Knight, S. (1994). Dictionary use while reading: The effects on comprehension and vocabulary acquisition for students of different verbal abilities. *Modern Language Journal, 78*, 285–299.

Laufer, B. (1992). How much lexis is necessary for reading comprehension? In H. Bejoint & P. Arnaud (Eds.), *Vocabulary and applied linguistics* (pp. 126–132). London: MacMillan.

Laufer, B.,& Hadar, L. (1997). Assessing the effectiveness of monolingual, bilingual, and "bilingualized" dictionaries in the comprehension and production of new words. *Modern Language Journal, 81*, 189–196.

Lewis, M. (1993). *The lexical approach*. Hove, UK: Language Teaching Publications.

Lewis, M. (1997). L2 vocabulary acquisition through extensive reading. In J. Coady & T. Huckin (Eds.), *Second language vocabulary acquisition* (pp. 255–270). Cambridge: Cambridge University Press.

Liu, N., & Nation, I. S. P. (1985). Factors affecting guessing vocabulary in context. *RELC Journal, 16*(1), 33–42.

Longman-Mitsumura English-Japanese Dictionary for Young Learners. (1993). Harlow, UK: Longman and Mitsura Book Publishing Company.

Luppescu, S., & Day, R. (1993). Reading, dictionaries, and vocabulary learning. *Language Learning, 43*, 263–287.

McCarthy, M., & O'Dell, F. (1994). *English vocabulary in use*. Cambridge: Cambridge University Press.

Meara, P. (1992). *EFL vocabulary tests*. Centre for Applied Language Studies University College Swansea. (ERIC Document Reproduction Service No. ED 362 046).

Meara, P. (1996). The dimensions of lexical competence. In G. Brown, K. Malmkjaer, & J. Williams (Eds.), *Performance and competence in second language acquisition* (pp. 35–53). Cambridge: Cambridge University Press.

Mikulecky, B. S., & Jeffries, L. (1996). *More reading power.* Reading, MA: Addison-Wesley.

Nagy, W. E., Herman, P., & Anderson, R. C. (1985). Learning words from context. *Reading Research Quarterly, 20*, 233–253.

Nation, I. S. P. (1990). *Teaching and learning vocabulary*. New York: Newbury House.

Nation, I. S. P. (Ed.). (1994). *New ways in teaching vocabulary*. Alexandria, VA: TESOL.

Nation, I. S. P., & Coady, J. (1988). Vocabulary and reading. In R. Carter & M. McCarthy (Eds.), *Vocabulary and language teaching.* London: Longman.

Nattinger, J., & DeCarrico, J. (1992). *Lexical phrases and language teaching*. Oxford: Oxford University Press.

The New Oxford Picture Dictionary CD-ROM. (1997). Oxford: Oxford University Press.

Paribakht, T., & Wesche, M. (1996). Enhancing vocabulary acquisition through reading: A hierarchy of text-related exercise types. *Canadian Modern Language Review, 52*, 155–178.

Pilgreen, J., & Krashen, S. (1993). Sustained silent reading with English as a second language high school students: Impact on reading comprehension, reading frequency, and reading enjoyment. *School Library Media Quarterly, 22*, 21–23.

Pimsleur, P. (1967). A memory schedule. *Modern Language Journal, 51*, 73–75.

Prince, P. (1996). Second language vocabulary learning: The role of context versus translations as a function of proficiency. *Modern Language Journal, 80*, 478–493.

Read, J. (1988). Measuring the vocabulary knowledge of second language learners. *RELC Journal, 19*(2), 12–25.

Redman, S., & Ellis, R. (1990). *A way with words book 2.* Cambridge: Cambridge University Press.

Richards, J. C. (1976). The role of vocabulary teaching. *TESOL Quarterly, 10*(1), 77–89.

Schmitt, N., & Meara, P. (1997). Researching vocabulary through a word knowledge framework. *Studies in Second Language Acquisition, 19*, 17–36.

Schmitt, N., & Schmitt, D. (1995). Vocabulary notebooks: Theoretical underpinnings and practical suggestions. *ELT Journal, 49*(2), 133–143.

Seibert, L. C. (1927). An experiment in learning French vocabulary. *Journal of Educational Psychology, 18*, 294–309.

Summers, D. (1988). The role of dictionaries in language learning. In R. Carter & M. McCarthy (Eds.), *Vocabulary and language teaching* (pp. 111–125). London: Longman.

Tinkham, T. (1993). The effect of semantic clustering on the learning of second language vocabulary. *System, 21*(3), 371–380.

West, M. (1953). *A general service list of English words*. London: Longman.

Williams, R. (1986). Teaching vocabulary recognition strategies in ESP reading. *ESP Journal, 4*, 121–131.

Woodinsky, M., & Nation, P. (1988). Learning from graded readers. *Reading in a Foreign Language, 5*(1), 155–161.

Xue, G., & Nation, I. S. P. (1984). A university word list. *Language Learning and Communication, 3*(2), 215–229.

Zimmerman, C. B. (1997). Do reading and interactive vocabulary instruction make a difference?: An empirical study. *TESOL Quarterly, 31*, 121–140.

CHAPTER 25

Best Practice in Vocabulary Teaching and Learning

Paul Nation

INTRODUCTION

Research on second language acquisition can be interpreted to show that a well-balanced language course should contain four major strands: meaning-focused input, meaning-focused output, fluency development and language-focused instruction. The inclusion of a language-focused instruction strand is not a reaction to communicative approaches but is the result of research findings that courses that contain such a strand are likely to achieve better results than courses that do not contain such a strand (Long, 1988; Ellis, 1990). For most second language learners, language-focused vocabulary instruction is an *essential* part of a language course.

The aim of this article is to show how the vocabulary component of a language course fits into these four strands. The assumption is that vocabulary growth is such an important part of language acquisition that it deserves to be planned for, deliberately controlled and monitored. There is a growing body of theory and research findings that can guide us in doing this.

VOCABULARY AND MEANING-FOCUSED INPUT

Reading has long been seen as a major source of vocabulary growth. Research indicates that, for several reasons, there is a fragility to this kind of learning. First, research with native speakers of English shows that the amount of vocabulary learning that occurs during the reading of a text is rather small (Nagy, Herman, & Anderson, 1985). It is necessary to use sensitive tests of vocabulary knowledge to show any learning at all. However, it is likely to be cumulative if there are repeated opportunities to meet the partially learned vocabulary again. This suggests that there will be a close relationship between vocabulary growth and the amount and variety of meaning-focused input.

Frequency counts show us that there is a very rapid drop-off in frequency of occurrence of vocabulary after the most frequent 2,000 to 3,000 high-frequency words of the language. For example, in a diverse 1,000,000 running word corpus, words outside the most frequent 6,000 occur less than eight times. This drop-off is even more noted in texts belonging to the same genre (Sutarsyah, Nation, & Kennedy, 1994). One million running words is about 3,000 pages of text or the equivalent number of pages of ten to fifteen novels. Clearly, beyond the most frequent words of the language, considerable meaning-focused input is needed for vocabulary growth to continue at a reasonable pace.

The second reason why vocabulary learning through meaning-focused input is fragile is that it depends heavily on the quality of the learners' control of the reading skill. Chall (1987) argues that for native speakers there is little vocabulary growth through reading while learners gain control of the skill of reading. For native speakers of English, this takes several years. Once this skill is developed, reading can then become a major means of vocabulary growth. Nonnative speakers are in a different situation, but with similar results. Adult learners of another language may already be fluent readers of their first language. One of the major barriers to reading in the second language is vocabulary size.

For this reason, Michael West and others saw the importance of providing series of graded readers with careful vocabulary control. These allow second language learners to draw on the reading skill developed in their first language to expand their vocabulary in the second language. These are an important resource for learners and a vital part of a language course. Their effective use for vocabulary growth, however, depends on learners' reading skill.

The third reason why vocabulary learning through meaning-focused input is fragile is that the type of reading that is done will strongly influence vocabulary learning. If learners read in familiar areas where they bring a lot of relevant background knowledge to their reading, they will easily cope with unknown words in context, but they will probably not learn them. If they read in unfamiliar areas, there is greater chance of learning new vocabulary because they have to pay close attention to the language of the text to get the meaning.

Research in another area of meaning-focused input supports the value of giving attention to the language as a system and not just as messages. Elley's (1989) studies of vocabulary learning through listening to stories show that if the teacher briefly interrupts the story to comment on the meaning of a word, or to put it on the chalkboard, the learning of those items increases significantly. This shows that deliberately drawing attention to language items as a part of the language system (language-focused instruction) makes learning more certain. Relying on meaning-focused input alone is leaving too much to chance.

This examination of the fragility of vocabulary learning through meaning-focused input is not intended to show that such learning is not worthwhile. Vocabulary learning through reading and listening is an essential strand of a language course. Best practice in vocabulary teaching and learning should aim to reduce this fragility by providing large quantities of suitably graded input, by providing it across a range of genres and topics, and by providing language-focused activities to support it. This will ensure that the learning condition of noticing will occur.

Vocabulary and Meaning-Focused Output

It may seem a little strange to see meaning-focused speaking and writing as ways of expanding learners' vocabulary, but the most exciting findings of recent research on vocabulary learning have revealed how spoken production of vocabulary items helps learning and how teachers and course designers can influence this spoken production. The research is reported in Newton (1995), Joe (1995) and Joe, Nation, and Newton (1996). The main findings of this research into spoken communicative activities are as follows:

- The written input to a communicative task has a major effect on what vocabulary is used and negotiated during the task. Newton (1995) found that all of the vocabulary negotiated in the ranking and problem-solving tasks he investigated was in the written task sheet handed out to the learners. Joe (1995) found that in a retelling task, vocabulary from the written text was produced during the retelling even when the written text could not be consulted and some of the vocabulary items were previously unknown.
- Negotiation of the meaning of unknown vocabulary meant that words had a greater chance of being learned. However, because much more previously unknown vocabulary was used and not negotiated, quantitatively more vocabulary was learned through being used productively or receptively.
- The quality of learning depends on the quality of use of the previously unknown vocabulary during the communicative task (Joe, 1995). The more the vocabulary is observed or used in contexts which differ from its occurrence in the written input, the better it is learned.
- Learners are able to provide useful information to each other on most of the vocabulary in a typical communicative task; that is, if someone in a group does not know a particular word, there is likely to be someone else in the group who knows something useful about it and who can communicate this information effectively.
- Learners who actively negotiate the meaning of unknown words do not seem to learn more than learners who observe the negotiation.
- Only a small amount of the negotiation in a communicative task (about 6% in Newton's study) is negotiation of word meaning. The other kinds of negotiation include negotiation of procedure, negotiation of comprehension, negotiation of mishearing, and so on.
- Research on learning from negotiation needs to be careful about distinguishing what is negotiated.

The significance of these findings for vocabulary learning is that by carefully designing and monitoring the use of the handout sheets for spoken tasks, teachers can have a major influence on determining what vocabulary could be learned from such tasks, and how well it is learned.

There is no research on how tasks involving written production can result in vocabulary learning. It is not difficult to imagine that writing requiring the synthesis of information from several related sources could provide very favorable conditions for learning from input and strengthening this learning through generative use in written output.

Developing Fluency with Vocabulary

Here, "fluency" means making the best use of what you already know, and fluency development tasks have the characteristics of involving no new language items, dealing with largely familiar content and discourse types, including some kinds of preparation or repetition so that speed and smoothness of delivery can improve, and involving some kind of encouragement to perform at a faster than normal level of use. Fluency tasks are typically meaning-focused tasks.

Surprisingly, given its effect on vocabulary knowledge, fluency development is still largely an unexplored area.

There are some vocabulary items that need to be learned to a very high degree of fluency as quickly as possible. These include numbers, polite formulas, items for controlling language use (for example, to ask someone to repeat, speak more slowly and so on), times, and periods of time and quantities. In addition to this, it is important that all high-frequency vocabulary be learned to a reasonable degree of fluency so that it can be readily accessed when it is needed.

The following learning conditions favor the development of fluency:

- The demands of the task are largely within the experience of the learners; that is, the learners are working with known language items, familiar ideas, and familiar tasks. Fluency activities should not involve unfamiliar vocabulary.
- The learners' focus is on the message.
- The learners are encouraged to reach a higher than usual level of performance, through the use of repetition, time pressure, and planning and preparation.

Repetition and focus on the message may work against each other – the more something is repeated, the less likely it will continue to be seen as a message-focused activity. The teaching methodology solution to this is to balance the ease provided by the repetition against a challenge provided by new but similar material, reducing time, a new audience, and increasing complexity. Initially, activities such as number dictation, prepared talks, interviews, and questionnaires would be most suitable. Later activities could include retelling tasks.

Vocabulary and Language-Focused Instruction

Language–focused instruction occurs when learners direct their attention to language items not for producing or comprehending a particular message, but for gaining knowledge about the item as a part of the language system. Language-focused instruction thus includes focusing on the pronunciation and spelling of words; deliberately learning the meanings of a word; memorizing collocations, phrases and sentences containing a word; and being corrected for incorrect use of a word.

Negotiation of vocabulary is also a kind of language-focused instruction if it involves discussing the word's spelling or pronunciation, or giving an explanation of its meaning.

Language-focused instruction can affect implicit knowledge of a language in several ways. If knowing the word is not dependent on a developmental sequence of knowledge, then language-focused instruction on each word can add directly to both implicit knowledge and explicit knowledge. Some concepts – for example, family relationships – are probably acquired developmentally, and language-focused instruction may have no effect if the learners are not at an appropriate stage of conceptual development. It is not known what other learning conditions apply for language-focused instruction on vocabulary to directly affect implicit knowledge, but it seems likely that only some learning of vocabulary items that are not affected by a developmental sequence directly enters implicit knowledge.

A second effect of language-focused instruction is that it can raise learners' consciousness or awareness of particular items so that they are then more readily noticed when they occur in meaning-focused input. The causal chain is (1) language-focused instruction, (2) explicit knowledge about a word, (3) increased awareness of the word, (4) noticing of the word in meaning-focused input, and (5) implicit knowledge of the word. The quality

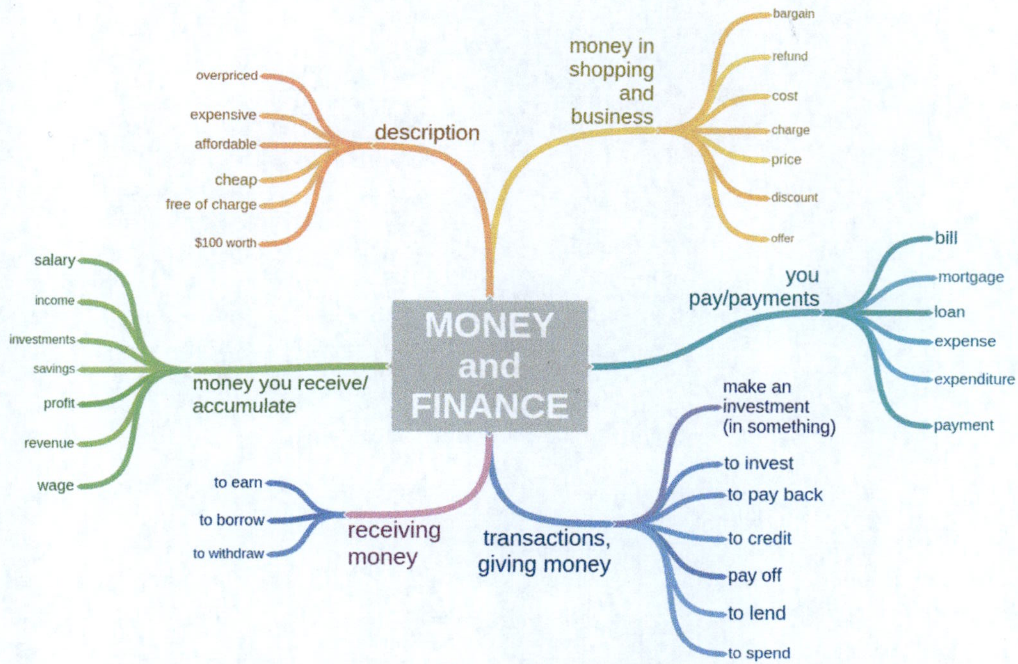
MONEY and FINANCE
description
overpriced
expensive
affordable
cheap
free of charge
$100 worth
money in shopping and business
bargain
refund
cost
charge
price
discount
offer
you pay/payments
bill
mortgage
loan
expense
expenditure
payment
money you receive/ accumulate
salary
income
investments
savings
profit
revenue
wage
receiving money
to earn
to borrow
to withdraw
transactions, giving money
make an investment (in something)
to invest
to pay back
to credit
pay off
to lend
to spend

of the language-focused instruction will determine how readily a word is noticed and what aspects of the word are noticed.

A third effect of language-focused instruction is similarly indirect: (1) language-focused instruction, (2) explicit knowledge, (3) output constructed from the explicit knowledge (that is, the word is used in a consciously constructed sentence), (4) the output acting as meaning-focused input to the same learner, and (5) implicit knowledge of the word.

What kinds of language-focused vocabulary instruction are likely to be of benefit? The following list is ranked in order of importance. Each suggestion is matched with its likely effect on implicit knowledge.

GUESSING UNKNOWN WORDS FROM CONTEXT

Although this may seem to be a meaning-focused activity, at least in the early stages of the development of the guessing skill, it involves learners consciously focusing on unknown words, interrupting their normal reading, and systematically drawing on the available clues to work out the unknown word's meaning.

Guessing from context focuses on the particular reference of a word as determined by the context rather than on its underlying meaning. It is likely that this knowledge will directly enter implicit memory as it will be less complicated than the concept of the word. Guessing may also serve to raise consciousness of the word.

There are various effects of guessing procedures. Their main effect should be to raise learners' confidence in guessing from context, to make them sensitive to the range of clues available, and to help them avoid strategies – such as focusing too quickly on the form of the word – that will reduce their chances of guessing accurately.

LEARNING THE MEANINGS OF UNKNOWN WORDS

There is an assumption in much that is written about vocabulary learning that all vocabulary learning should be in context. This assumption is not supported by research and by what successful learners do. Considerable research shows that

- Explicit, decontextualized study of vocabulary is an effective way of rapidly increasing learners' vocabulary size.
- The learning achieved in this way can last for a very long time.
- This knowledge can be made available for meaning-focused use of the language.
- There are ways that considerably increase the efficiency of language-focused learning and learners benefit from being able to make use of these. They include the use of mnemonic techniques, using vocabulary cards which encourage retrieval, the spacing and organizing of learning, and the deliberate avoidance of interference among items.

The deliberate learning of vocabulary may contribute directly to implicit knowledge if the words learned are not complicated and if the learning is meaningful. At the very least, the results of deliberate learning will be available for language-focused use, which may then indirectly contribute to implicit knowledge through production or through making meaning-focused input meaningful. There is a lack of research on the effect of deliberate vocabulary learning on meaning-focused use.

STUDY OF WORD PARTS AND MNEMONIC DEVICES

The majority of words in English come from French, Latin, or Greek and the majority of these have word parts, particularly prefixes and suffixes, which occur in many words. Knowledge of these word parts can be used to improve the learning of many words through relating unknown word forms and meanings to known word parts. This is similar to the effect of mnemonic devices on vocabulary learning, the best researched of which is the keyword technique.

The effect of such learning is probably to add to explicit knowledge. This will contribute to implicit knowledge receptively because it is a very strong form of consciousness-raising, and productively through the deliberate production of meaning-focused output.

A well thought-out vocabulary component of a course would be largely indistinguishable from the listening, speaking, reading, and writing parts of the language program. The main differences would lie in the language-focused learning and in the deliberate planning and manipulation of the written input to listening, speaking, reading, and writing activities to provide optimal conditions for vocabulary growth.

References

Beebe, L. M. (Ed.). (1988). *Issues in second language acquisition.* New York: Newbury House.

Chall, J. S. (1987). Two vocabularies for reading: Recognition and meaning. In M. G. McKeown & M. E. Curtis, *The nature of vocabulary acquisition* (pp. 7–17). Hillsdale, NJ; Lawrence Erlbaum.

Elley, W. R. (1989). Vocabulary acquisition from listening to stories. *Reading Research Quarterly, 24*(2), 174–187.

Ellis, R. (1990). *Instructed second language acquisition.* London: Blackwell.

Joe, A. (1995). Text-based tasks and incidental vocabulary learning. *Second Language Research, 11*(2), 149–158.

Joe, A., Nation, P., & Newton, J. (1996). Speaking activities and vocabulary learning. *English Teaching Forum, 34*(1), 2–7.

Long, M. (1988). Instructed interlanguage development. In L. M. Beebe (Ed.), *Issues in second language development.* New York: Newbury House.

McKeown, M. G., & Curtis, M. E. (Eds.) (1987). *The nature of vocabulary acquisition.* Hillsdale, NJ: Lawrence Erlbaum.

Nagy, W. E., Herman, P., & Anderson, R. C. (1985). Learning words from context. *Reading Research Quarterly, 20*, 233–253.

Newton, J. (1995). Text-based interaction and incidental vocabulary learning: A case study. *Second Language Research, 11*(2), 159–177.

Sutarsyah, C., Nation, P., & Kennedy, G. (1994). How useful is EAP vocabulary for ESP? A corpus-based study. *RELC Journal, 25*(2), 34–50.

SECTION 12

TEACHING READING

INTRODUCTION

In many second or foreign language teaching situations, reading receives a special focus. There are a number of reasons for this. First, many foreign language students often have reading as one of their most important goals. They want to be able to read for information and pleasure, for their career, and for study purposes. In fact, in most EFL situations, the ability to read in a foreign language is all that students ever want to acquire. Second, written texts serve various pedagogical purposes. Extensive exposure to linguistically comprehensible written texts can enhance the process of language acquisition. Good reading texts also provide good models for writing, and provide opportunities to introduce new topics, to stimulate discussion, and to study language (e.g., vocabulary, grammar, and idioms). Reading, then, is a skill which is highly valued by students and teachers alike. But, what is reading instruction like in the classroom? How do we teach reading? Do teachers teach according to principles derived from research findings? The three articles in this section, to varying degrees, seek to throw light on the principles and practice of teaching reading.

In the first paper, Grabe critically examines the relationship between research and practice in both L1 and L2 reading. He points out that the relationship between research and instruction in the L1 reading contexts is quite straightforward. L1 reading instruction has to a large extent been influenced by research findings. For example, L1 reading teachers are now aware of

- the importance of developing letter–sound correspondence for early reading
- the need for a large vocabulary for fluent reading
- the need for students to become effective strategy users
- the value of extensive reading
- the usefulness of Content-Based Instruction

- the benefits of developing reasonable reading rates
- the importance of explicit teacher modeling in reading instruction

But such is not the case with the L2 reading contexts, as Grabe makes clear. Despite advances that have been made in research on second language reading (and the findings are not dissimilar to those for L1 reading), a lot of problems remain to be addressed before research findings can be applied in the classroom. The most crucial problem, Grabe maintains, lies in the fact that research in L2 reading tends to be short-term and less programmatic. As a result, we do not have enough converging evidence to enable us to say with confidence what works best in which L2 contexts. If L2 reading research is to have any significant impact on instruction, it is imperative that we encourage more systematic and programmatic research studies that examine aspects of reading instruction under a variety of contexts and over a longer period of time. Results of longitudinal studies of this nature are likely to reduce the gap between theory and practice.

Janzen attempts to shed light on the practical issues of translating findings in reading strategy research into the classroom. She is concerned with two questions: (1) How do we go about teaching reading strategies? (2) How do we incorporate reading strategies in an ongoing classroom reading program? Drawing on relevant research findings, Janzen suggests that a sound approach to strategy instruction should have the following characteristics:

- The teaching of strategies is contextualized.
- Strategies are taught explicitly through direct explanation, modeling, and feedback.
- There is a constant recycling of strategies over new texts and tasks.
- Strategies are taught over a long period of time.

She then describes how this approach to strategy instruction can be successfully implemented in one ESL classroom. Throughout the whole semester of her reading program, she organizes her activities in such a way as to enable her students not only to understand the *whats* and *hows*, but also the *whys* of reading strategies. She claims that without a solid understanding of the values of reading strategies, students will not get the most benefits of strategy instruction.

Renandya and Jacobs argue strongly for including extensive reading in the second language curriculum. There is now a compelling evidence that extensive reading can have a significant impact on learners' second language development. Not only can extensive reading improve reading ability, it can also enhance learners' overall language proficiency (e.g., spelling, grammar, vocabulary, and writing). In addition, extensive reading, with its emphasis on encouraging learners to read self-selected, large amounts of meaningful language, is in line with current principles for good second and foreign language pedagogy. Experts now agree that some of the most important principles include providing a rich linguistic environment, respecting and capitalizing on learners' contribution to the learning process, and giving more emphasis to fluency than to accuracy. Renandya and Jacobs describe what extensive reading is, how it is different from intensive reading, what its learning benefits are for students, and what theories underlie extensive reading. They also discuss some of the reasons why many teachers are still not implementing extensive reading.

Discussion Questions

Before Reading

1. What roles does reading play in first and second language development?
2. What are some of the differences between good readers and poor readers? What can you do to help the latter improve their reading ability?

3. To what extent do research findings in reading inform classroom practice?
4. What is your approach to teaching reading? Where does this approach come from?
5. What are the arguments for incorporating reading strategies? Can strategies be taught?
6. What do you understand is meant by a "reading strategy"? As a reader, what reading strategies do you use? Are they equally effective?
7. What is the role of prior knowledge in reading? What types of prior knowledge do you know?
8. What are some of the key factors that affect fluent reading? Why are they important?
9. What role does vocabulary play in fluent reading? How much vocabulary is needed for fluent reading?
10. What is the place of simplified readers in a second language reading program? Is the language used in those texts authentic?

After Reading

1. Review "Dilemma 1" in the article by Grabe. What does "replication" mean? What is the rationale for this?
2. Select a recent research article on reading and then develop a research plan to replicate the study.
3. According to Grabe, what does " explicit teacher modeling" mean? Give one or two examples of how you would do this when teaching a reading strategy.
4. Examine the principles of teaching reading strategies outlined by Janzen. In what ways have you used these principles in your own teaching?
5. Select one or two reading strategies. Then develop a plan for teaching the strategy using the principles outlined by Janzen.
6. Review the article by Renandya and Jacobs. What is an intensive reading approach to teaching reading? How is it different from an extensive reading approach? Which approach do you think plays a more important role in developing learners' reading ability?
7. What are the characteristics of a good extensive reading program? What are some of the most important benefits of extensive reading?
8. Renandya and Jacobs discuss some reasons why teachers are not including extensive reading in their reading lessons. Can you suggest other reasons?
9. Examine the benefits of extensive reading discussed by Renandya and Jacobs. Are there any others you would like to add?
10. As a classroom teacher, what can you do to bridge the gap between research and practice?
11. To what extent does your approach to teaching reading reflect findings from L2 research?
12. Do you use a lot of authentic materials in your reading instruction? What do you think is the role of authentic materials in developing learners' reading skills?

CHAPTER 26

Dilemmas for the Development of Second Language Reading Abilities

William Grabe

Introduction

Since the 1980s, a number of advances have been made in research on reading, both in first and second language contexts. Although the advances in first language contexts have led to a number of improvements in reading instruction, the corresponding research in second language contexts has not made as much headway. The reasons for these differences will be discussed in the form of dilemmas for second language reading instruction. By way of introduction to these dilemmas, research findings that have influenced L1 reading instruction are briefly reviewed, and the corresponding advances in second language research are noted. The larger discussion will then focus on the dilemmas that second language contexts impose on reading instruction and the possible responses to these dilemmas.

First Language Reading Research and Instruction

In first language settings, research has demonstrated at least ten major findings for reading instruction. These highlight the

- importance of developing letter–sound correspondences for beginning reading
- importance of word recognition and the relatively complete processing of words in a text
- necessity for a large recognition vocabulary for fluent reading
- need for reasonable reading rates for processing
- usefulness of graphic representations for comprehension instruction
- value of extensive reading
- importance of dialogue and teacher modelling in comprehension instruction

This chapter is reprinted from *Prospect,* 10(2), 38–51 with permission from the National Centre for English Language Teaching and Research (NCELTR), Australia.

- facilitating role of Content-Based Instruction
- need for students to become strategic readers
- influence of varying social contexts on the development of reading abilities

Although documenting these general developments would require a separate paper, essential sources for these developments include Stanovich (1986, 1992), Adams (1989), Rayner and Pollatsek (1989), Barr, Kamil, Mosenthal, and Pearson (1991), Heath (1991), Palincsar and David (1991), Rieben and Perfetti (1991), Samuels and Farstrup (1992), Guzzetti, Snyder, Glass, and Gamas (1993), and Pressley et al. (1994).

These research results impact strongly on reading instruction in various L1 settings. In early reading instruction, no one now denies the need for students to develop letter–sound correspondences; rather, the issue centres on the best means for achieving these abilities. The finding that readers process texts relatively completely – that is, read most words on a page – means that students should have many opportunities to encounter words, to read predictable texts, and to reread texts to develop word-recognition skills. The need to build a large vocabulary is developed by reading to students, by having students read extensively, and by focusing attention on key vocabulary. Fluency in reading rate is established by having students reading extensively and by practice with a combination of timed readings, paced reading, rapid recognition exercises, and rereading techniques.

Reading for comprehension is the primary purpose for reading (though this is sometimes overlooked when students are asked to read overly difficult texts); raising student awareness of main ideas in a text and exploring the organisation of a text are essential for good comprehension. As a consequence, the use of graphic representations to highlight text organisation and to indicate the ordering of the content information is an important resource for comprehension instruction. Similarly, teachers who model reading skills and strategies overtly, facilitate student performances of these abilities in comprehending texts, and provide students with many opportunities for practice are encouraged in a number of comprehension-enhancing approaches – the best known of which are reciprocal teaching, cooperative learning, and reading recovery. These approaches often provide the context for specific strategy instruction and for transforming the student into a strategic reader (see also Gaskins, 1994; Pressley et al. 1994). Finally, the translation of research findings into realistic classroom settings has led to greater emphasis on Content-Based Instruction as the most effective means for learning from texts and for using text information to carry out other academic activities.

Second Language Reading Research and Instruction

Research on second language reading has also provided a number of insights for reading development and instruction. The many different L2 contexts, however, do not lead to exactly the same set of findings as those noted earlier for L1 contexts. Research insights for L2 reading development have informed at least the following eight issues:

- the importance of discourse structure and graphic representations
- the importance of vocabulary in language learning
- the need for language awareness and attending to language and genre form
- the existence of a second language proficiency threshold in reading
- the importance of metacognitive awareness and strategy learning
- the need for extensive reading
- the benefits of integrating reading and writing
- the importance of Content-Based Instruction

These L2 research findings have been persuasively argued (Mohan, 1990; Bernhardt, 1991; Carrell, 1991; 1992; Hulstijn, 1991; Tang, 1992; Zamel, 1992; Crandall, 1993; Devine, 1993; Huckin, Haynes, & Coady, 1993; Krashen, 1993; Koda, 1994). Despite these research developments, little progress has been made in translating these L2 findings into practice. There are many reasons for this gap between research and practice (as well as between L1 and L2 research). The remainder of this article will examine nine major dilemmas for L2 reading research and instructional practices and, in a few cases, suggest possible ways in which the gap can be bridged. There are certainly additional dilemmas (issues to be discussed, explored, and resolved) to consider; however, the nine noted here represent fundamental issues for L2 reading and they should provide a useful starting point for dialogue.

Dilemmas for Second Language Reading Instruction

Dilemma 1

A most obvious dilemma for L2 instruction is the many different contexts for L2 reading instruction. This dilemma also represents an underlying cause for many other dilemmas facing L2 reading instruction. Second language students can be classified into dozens of instructional contexts, but the following is a general set of distinctions which point out the first dilemma: How can any reading approach be relevant to *all* different L2 reading acquisition contexts? How can reading instruction adjust in line with the rapidly changing proficiencies of L2 reading students? And how can research be carried out with sufficiently large groups of students over a long enough period of time that the results instil confidence in terms of reliability and validity? In a related vein, how can we know what to apply to instruction from L2 reading research when research publications do not promote replications, near replications, and research variations? This last L2 situation is quite different from L1 reading research contexts: L1 publications encourage many overlapping studies in such areas as phonological awareness, orthographic knowledge, word recognition, sentence processing, exposure to reading, morphological knowledge, and so on.

It is certainly true that L2 contexts for reading instruction are more complex; they include all the contexts for L1 instruction and add the L2 learning dimension to all of the others. The L2 contexts also include far greater diversity in terms of ethnic and cultural variation. This situation is not about to change, so the complexity in L2 contexts must lead L2 researchers to be cautious with their results and with possible suggestions from L1 reading contexts. Careful attention must be paid to the similarities and/or differences that research and controlled training contexts have with practical instructional contexts. One resolution to this dilemma is to ask researchers and relevant journals to promote replications, near replications (but in distinct contexts), and overlapping research studies. Converging evidence would then allow for stronger connections to diverse instructional situations. A telling discussion in this regard is Stanovich's (1992) review of phonemic awareness as a critical predictor of subsequent L1 reading development. He notes that 10 years of continual research and numerous related studies made this finding one of the breakthroughs in reading research. A similar sense of multiple studies and converging evidence is needed for many issues in L2 reading development and instruction.

Dilemma 2

A second dilemma for L2 reading instruction derives from the (U.S.-based) generative linguistic foundation of most research in second language acquisition (SLA) and the subsequent irrelevance of much of SLA for L2 reading research. This Chomskyan foundation explains why most L2 reading researchers do not see their work as part of SLA. A much more fruitful foundation for L2 reading research can be found in a functional linguistics approach (such as Halliday, 1985) combined with learning theories from cognitive psychology and educational psychology. These latter resources should include both qualitative and quantitative methods and should carry out training studies that attend to ecological validity (reflecting natural classroom contexts as much as possible). Learning theories, whether sociohistorical (e.g., Vygotsky, 1978) or cognitive (e.g., Anderson, 1990, or Gardner, 1991), should also be given careful attention, as should affective and motivation theories.

SLA, in contrast, follows a number of assumptions of generative linguistics which make it irrelevant for most L2 reading issues. For example, SLA accepts the primacy of oral language as a major underlying assumption, it accepts second language learning as a natural process reflecting oral-first language learning processes (language is acquired rather than learned), and it accepts the Chomskyan assumption that 'creative' algorithmic rule learning is central to second language learning. Given these assumptions, it is not clear to what extent L2 reading research and SLA research perspectives are reconcilable.

DILEMMA 3

Formal aspects of language and genre structure contribute to readers' developing comprehension and inferencing abilities. Awareness of text structure is a critical aspect of reading comprehension and learners who are aware of text structure have better comprehension abilities. Yet few reading instruction curricula focus on text structure awareness as a consistent component. Nor is the ability to discuss and teach awareness of text structure well developed in a variety of L2 teaching contexts (see Christie, 1992; Christie, 1990; Mohan, 1990; Tang, 1992; Martin, 1993). In many educational contexts (particularly in North America), social constructionist views, reader-response theories and language learning assumptions obscure the contribution of the textual component, even though much L1 reading research has demonstrated the importance of discourse structure knowledge for reading comprehension (e.g., Beck, McKeown, Sinatra, & Loxterman, 1991; Pearson & Fielding, 1991).

Recent work on social construction theory, as well as literary criticism research (e.g., Foucault, Derrida, Eco, Fish, Rosenblatt), argues that the coherence of a text resides within the reader. To some extent, this claim is undeniable. However, a number of lines of research in cognitive psychology and educational psychology argue that a significant portion of textual coherence resides in the text and the intended reading is made apparent through various discourse structuring mechanisms. This poses a dilemma for reading research and instruction because these discourse structuring mechanisms are often overlooked in a radical reader interpretive framework – even though a number of research studies argue persuasively that student awareness of such structures while reading significantly enhances comprehension abilities.

Controlling the formal aspects of language use in reading and writing is a way out from subordinate and marginalised uses of language – a means for empowerment (Martin, 1989, 1993; Christie, 1992). Leaving language instruction at an intuitive and 'mystical' level of 'natural language acquisition' may be easy for the teacher and may make some students feel good, but it leads to disempowerment. At the same time, however, those teachers who believe that recognition and effective use of formal aspects of language are important, need to know what is to be taught and how it is to be taught. How are structures and genres brought to students' attention in ways that will be useful for them, and will be seen as useful by them?

DILEMMA 4

A large vocabulary is critical, not only for reading, but for all L2 language skills, for academic abilities, and for background knowledge. The dilemma arises with the recognition that students in English L1 academic contexts learn an average of 40,000 words by the end of secondary school, and learn approximately 3,000 new words each year in school. How will an L2 student develop such a large vocabulary and compete with average L1 academic students? (see Nagy & Herman, 1987; Nagy, 1988; Beck & McKeown, 1991). First language research has also demonstrated that most academic vocabulary is learned incidentally through reading and discussion about reading material. This further complicates the L2 reading task since there are fewer opportunities for incidental contexts, and it is unlikely that so many words can be directly taught to L2 students. In L2 reading contexts, it is now recognised that the best way to develop such a large vocabulary is to read extensively, but this knowledge has not translated over to many L2 instruction contexts. In few L2 teaching contexts is silent, free reading in class seen as important, nor is extensive reading at home treated as a high priority.

First language reading research stresses the importance of extensive reading (both in school and at home), direct instruction in key vocabulary, and strategies for accessing word meanings independently when necessary. In L2 reading instruction, vocabulary is gaining in importance, although both the notion of nuclear vocabulary and the related notion of teaching the 2,000 most frequent core words for reading tend to simplify issues centring on vocabulary development.

Reading fluency requires that a reader know 95% or more of the words encountered in a text for *minimal* comprehension (Laufer, 1989); and these words need to be recognised automatically with minimal conscious effort. But that sort of vocabulary knowledge requires knowledge of 12,000–20,000 different words (see Laufer, 1989; Nation, 1990). Students will only develop such a large automatically recognised vocabulary from consistent, extensive reading. Fluency, then, is closely tied to a large reading vocabulary and extensive reading.

DILEMMA 5

A further complication for students, in both L1 and L2 reading instruction situations, is that the social context of the student's home environment strongly influences reading development; in particular, social class differences do appear to have an indirect effect on reading development. Typical middle-class families provide children with an estimated 1,000 hours of 'tutoring' before the children arrive at school (Adams, 1990, p. 45). For the 'untutored' learners, how can schools be expected to make up this amount of literacy exposure at the same time that the better prepared students are moving ahead from the moment they arrive in school? This is especially problematic when literacy studies today typically promote natural discovery learning, multiple literacies, and the rights of students to their own literacy practices; yet students will still be evaluated, promoted, and encouraged based on their performances with the genres most associated with middle-class home support. One response is to provide an intensive tutoring program such as reading recovery (Pinnell, DeFord, & Lyons, 1988; DeFord, Lyons, & Pinnell, 1991; cf. Wasik & Slavin, 1993), though for many schools such an option is not financially feasible. The most basic response to this dilemma is to encourage students to read extensively, but this advice itself poses another dilemma.

DILEMMA 6

We learn to read by reading a lot, yet reading a lot is not the emphasis of most reading curricula. There is now considerable evidence that the best way to learn to read (as opposed to translating, or studying) is by extensive reading. Many additional language learning benefits are created by reading extensively as well (Elley, 1991; Krashen, 1993; West, Stanovich, & Mitchell, 1993). Yet extensive reading is not the central component of reading instruction in most L2 contexts. The dilemma is not a simple one to respond to. School administrators do not typically support daily silent reading in class; teachers do not feel that they are 'teaching' when students are reading something enjoyable; and students often are not motivated to read, because they have not yet experienced the pleasure of reading material that they want to read. How do we motivate students to read and see reading as both useful and enjoyable? Most students do not read much, or enjoy reading in their first language either. This lack of motivation is also reflected in teaching contexts in which reading for pleasure is not given priority, but rather is treated as unimportant, or even irrelevant. Both teachers and students come to feel that there are 'more important things to do' in EFL contexts; and in many ESL contexts, students are uninterested (as are some teachers).

The more immediate solution to this dilemma rests partly with educating administrators and teachers about the importance of extensive pleasure reading. Classrooms and libraries must be supplied with reading resources that can excite students to read. Specific time in the school curriculum should be devoted to pleasure reading, during which teachers read to, and with, students on a regular basis. Additionally, time must be devoted to developing students' motivation and to turning them into independent readers.

A long-term solution will require a model of L2 reading development which can influence future instruction and teacher-training practices. Both the need to compensate for certain home contexts and certain teacher orientations (dilemmas 5 and 6) also point out the need to integrate socialisation issues into a more comprehensive interpretive theory of L2 reading development. Such a comprehensive theory may provide the best foundation for more relevant research, more appropriate instructional practices, and more effective teacher training. (In fact, issues of social contexts for reading instruction influence all of the dilemmas noted here.)

DILEMMA 7

Although it is important that L2 students increase reading fluency, develop a large recognition vocabulary and engage in extensive reading, these issues in themselves are not sufficient for reading comprehension. A critical component for comprehension is the ability to use appropriate reading strategies and to know when to use them and in what combinations, depending on different reading purposes and tasks. However, the teaching of reading strategies is not without its own dilemmas.

Teaching students to use reading strategies is now recognised as important, but helping students to develop a large set of independently operating, efficient reading strategies that are relevant to varying needs and contexts has proven to be extremely difficult. How do students learn strategies? How do they learn to use them appropriately? How do students know when and where to use them (or not use them) and in what combinations to use strategies, depending on the situation and their needs? In L2 contexts, we seem only to have created taxonomies of reading skills and to have carried out a few treatment studies. The dilemma is that we have to make students into strategic readers rather than teach them reading strategies. How to do this is a major educational dilemma for L2 contexts, and how to do the relevant research also poses an interesting set of dilemmas.

Work along these lines has been a major focus of recent L1 reading research. In particular, long-term studies of training strategic teachers have been one of the more eye-opening and informative areas of research, and an area which should have a profound influence on L2 teacher training and reading instruction as well. This research focuses on commitments by entire schools and programmes to becoming strategic schools: while teaching various content material or thematic cycles, teachers learn to raise student awareness of strategies, demonstrate strategies overtly for students, assist students to use these strategies where relevant, and have students gradually take on more responsibilities for using the appropriate strategies independently (Pressley, Gaskin, Wile, Cunicelli, & Sheridan, 1991; Pressley et al., 1994; Duffy, 1993; Gaskins, 1994).

DILEMMA 8

The uncritical acceptance of schema theory represents a major dilemma for higher comprehension processes. The common assumption is that schema theory supports comprehension by calling up stable background knowledge representations that support and interpret the text knowledge. The dilemma is that schema theory is hardly a theory, and there is very little research which actually explores what a schema is or how it would work for reading comprehension. Rather, it is a useful simplifying metaphor for the more general notion of prior knowledge. As Spiro, Vispoel, Schmitz, Samarapungavan, and Boerger (1987, p. 177) note:

> A fundamental tenet of all recent theories of comprehension, problem solving and decision making is that success in such cognitive arenas depends on the activation and appropriate application of relevant pre-existing knowledge. Despite the substantial agreement on this general claim, we know very little about the organization of background knowledge and the method of its application to the understanding of new situations.

There are a number of problems associated with the 'schema' dilemma. First, teachers are taught that previewing a text and discussing an idea generally related to a reading will help students activate relevant schemata. However, with reading texts that are instructional, students are just as likely to activate the wrong information, or only partially useful information (Gardner, 1991). Second, there is a lack of appropriate scepticism with respect to schemata because of the 'theory' label. Teachers and teacher trainers both tend to assume that there is strong theoretical evidence for the 'theory'. However, much research is questioning the concept of schema theory as a theoretical orientation to a person's prior knowledge and memory retrieval (Spiro et al., 1987; Alexander, Schallert, & Hare, 1991; Sadoski, Paivio, & Goetz, 1991; Carver, 1992). Third, there are viable alternative interpretations of prior knowledge which need to be explored, and their implications considered for instruction (Alexander, Schallert, & Hare, 1991; Kintsch, 1988; Margolin, 1987; Paivio, 1990).

Exploring this critique of schema theory in detail would require its own paper. However, it is an important issue for second language reading because the concept is so readily accepted by teachers and teacher trainers alike, and schema theory has become a rationale for many teaching suggestions. It is hoped that the concept of schema theory, seen as a dilemma, will initiate further discussion and contribute to a more flexible understanding of the role of background knowledge for second language reading.

DILEMMA 9

At some point in all students' academic careers, they must learn to make the transition from learning to read to reading to learn other information. However, there is little discussion in most discussions of second language reading development on how this transition to academic learning-from-reading is to be made. What is the relationship between reading instruction and Content-Based Instruction (CBI)? What role should CBI play in reading instruction? A strong case can be made that CBI is very useful for language skills development in many L2 contexts (Mohan, 1990; Crandall, 1993). CBI has the potential to motivate students strongly, to develop strategic readers, to provide contexts for reading extensively, and to promote larger and more useful vocabularies. Moreover, CBI can be readily integrated with various learning theories (e.g., reciprocal teaching, Vygotsky activity theory, research on expertise), all of which can be used to argue the importance of CBI for reading instruction. Finally, CBI provides a natural framework for incorporating text-structure awareness and formal knowledge of language structure, demonstrating how language serves useful functions for communicating and achieving goals. So why is it not at the centre of curriculum discussion in reading instruction? And how is it to be made applicable in a wide range of L2 contexts? These questions suggest a future line of research which should inform reading instruction for L2 students in many school contexts.

Conclusions

The dilemmas presented in this article are intended to provoke discussion and, in some cases, lead to reconsideration of L2 instructional practices. They can also be seen as important research agendas. The nine dilemmas do not represent the full set of dilemmas that could be posed; indeed, a careful reading of this article will, in all likelihood, suggest additional dilemmas to inform research and instruction.

The dilemmas have a number of possible resolutions and some have been noted, although the most interesting research to date is generally not directed to various L2 reading contexts. The dilemmas also point out a number of implied political and social issues related to L2 reading instruction which need to be addressed, although, for reasons of space, such a discussion is not possible in this article. I hope that the dilemmas posed will open up some debates on the sorts of L2 reading research that is needed, as well as open new possibilities for L2 reading instruction. Finally, I hope that this article will suggest additional dilemmas which can contribute to our reflections and actions as teachers of second language reading abilities.

References

Adams, M. (1989). *Beginning to read: Thinking and learning about print.* Cambridge, MA: MIT Press.

Adams, M. (1990). *Beginning to read: Thinking and learning about print. A summary* (S. Stahl, J. Osborn, & F. Lehr, eds.). Urbana, IL: Center for the Study of Reading.

Alexander, P., Schallert, D., & Hare, V. (1991). Coming to terms: How researchers in learning and literacy talk about knowledge. *Review of Educational Research, 61*, 315–343.

Anderson, J. R. (1990). *Cognitive psychology and its implications.* 3rd ed. New York: W. H. Freeman.

Barr, R., Kamil, M., Mosenthal, P., & Pearson, P. D. (Eds.). (1991). *Handbook of reading research.* Vol. 2. New York: Longman.

Beck, I., & Mckeown, M. (1991). Conditions of vocabulary acquisition. In R. Barr, M. Kamil, P. Mosenthal, & P. D. Pearson (Eds.), *Handbook of reading research* (Vol. 2). New York: Longman.

Beck, I., McKeown, M., Sinatra, G., & Loxterman, J. (1991). Revising social studies text from a text-processing perspective: Evidence of improved comprehensibility. *Reading Research Quarterly, 26*(3), 251–276.

Bernhardt, E. (1991). *Reading development in a second language.* Norwood, NJ: Ablex.

Carrell, P. (1991). Strategic reading. In J. E. Alatis (Ed.), *Linguistics and language pedagogy: The state of the art.* Georgetown University Round Table on Languages and Linguistics 1991. Washington, DC: Georgetown University Press.

Carrell, P. (1992). Awareness of text structure: Effects on recall. *Language Learning, 42*(1), 1–20.

Carver, R. (1992). Effect of prediction activities, prior knowledge, and text type upon the amount of comprehension: Using rauding theory to critique schema theory research. *Reading Research Quarterly, 27*(2), 164–174.

Christie, F. (1990). *Exploring reports.* Sydney: Harcourt Brace Jovanovich.

Christie, F. (1992). Literacy in Australia. In W. Grabe (Ed.), *Annual Review of Applied Linguistics, 12*: Literacy. New York: Cambridge University Press.

Crandall, J. (1993). Content-centered learning in the US. In W. Grabe (Ed.), *Annual Review of Applied Linguistics, 13*: Issues in second language teaching and learning. New York: Cambridge University Press.

DeFord, D., Lyons, C., & Pinnell, G. (Eds.). (1991). *Bridges to literacy: Learning from reading recovery*. Portsmouth, NH: Heinemann.

Devine, J. (1993). The role of metacognition in second language reading and writing. In J. Carson & I. Leki (Eds.), *Reading in the composition classroom.* New York: Heinle & Heinle.

Duffy, G. (1993). Teachers' progress toward becoming expert strategy teachers. *Elementary School Journal, 94*(2), 109–120.

Elley, W. (1991). Acquiring literacy in a second language: The effect of book-based programs. *Language Learning, 41*(3), 375–411.

Gardner, H. (1991). *The unschooled mind.* New York: Basic Books.

Gaskins, I. (1994). Classroom applications of cognitive science: Teaching poor readers how to learn, think, and problem solve. In K. McGilly (Ed.), *Classroom lesson: Integrating cognitive theory.* Cambridge, MA: MIT Press.

Guzzetti, B., Snyder, T., Glass, G., & Gamas, W. (1993). Promoting conceptual change in science: A comparative meta-analysis of instructional interventions from reading education and science education. *Reading Research Quarterly, 28*(2), 116–159.

Halliday, M. A. K. (1985). *Introduction to functional grammar*. London: Edward Arnold.

Heath, S. B. (1991). The sense of being literate: Historical and cross-cultural features. In R. Barr, M. Kamil, P. Mosenthal, & P. D. Pearson (Eds.), *Handbook of reading research* (Vol. 2). New York: Longman.

Huckin, T., Haynes, M., & Coady, J. (Eds.). (1993). *Second language reading and vocabulary learning.* Norwood, NJ: Ablex.

Hulstijn, J. (Ed.). (1991). *Reading in two languages*. Amsterdam: Free University Press.

Kintsch, W. (1988). The role of knowledge in discourse comprehension: A construction-integration model. *Psychological Review, 95*, 163–182.

Koda, K. (1994). Second language reading research: Problems and possibilities. *Applied Psycholinguistics, 15*(1), 1–28.

Krashen, S. (1993). *The power of reading*. Englewood, CO: Libraries Unlimited.

Laufer, B. (1989). What percentage of text-lexis is essential for comprehension? In C. Lauren & M. Nordmann (Eds.), *Special language: From humans thinking to thinking machines* (pp. 316–323). Clevedon, Avon: Multilingual Matters.

Margolin, H. (1987). *Patterns, thinking, and cognition.* Chicago: University of Chicago Press.

Martin, J. R. (1989). *Factual writing*. New York: Oxford University Press.

Martin, J. R. (1993). Genre and literacy – modeling context in educational linguistics. In W. Grabe (Ed.), *Annual Review of Applied Linguistics, 13: Issues in second language teaching and learning* (pp. 141–172). New York: Cambridge University Press.

Mohan, B. (1990). LEP students and the integration of language and content: Knowledge structures and tasks. In C. Simich-Dudgeon (Ed.), *Proceedings of the first research symposium on limited English proficient students' issues* (pp. 113–160). Washington, DC: Office of Bilingual Education and Minority Language Affairs.

Nagy, W. (1988). *Teaching vocabulary to improve reading comprehension.* Urbana, IL: National Council of Teachers of English.

Nagy, W., & Herman, P. (1987). Breadth and depth of vocabulary knowledge: Implications for acquisition and instruction. In M. McKeown & M. Curtis (Eds.), *The nature of vocabulary acquisition* (pp. 19–35). Hillsdale, NJ: Lawrence Erlbaum.

Nation, I. S. P. (1990). *Teaching and learning vocabulary.* New York: Newbury House.

Paivio, A. (1990). *Mental representations: A dual coding approach.* New York: Oxford University Press.

Palincsar, A., & David, Y. (1991). Promoting literacy through classroom discourse. In E. Hiebert (Ed.), *Literacy for a diverse society* (pp. 122–140). New York: Teachers College Press.

Pearson, P. D., & Fielding, L. (1991). Comprehension instruction. In R. Barr, M. L. Kamil, P. Mosenthal, & P. D. Pearson (Eds.), *Handbook of reading research* (Vol. 2; pp. 815–860). New York: Longman.

Pinnell, G., DeFord, D., & Lyons, C. (Eds.). (1988). *Reading recovery: Early intervention for at-risk first graders.* Arlington, VA: Educational Research Service.

Pressley, M., Alsami, J., Shuder, T., Bergman, J., Hite, S., El-Dinary, P., & Brown, R., (1994). Transactional instruction of comprehension strategies: The Montgomery County, Maryland, SAIL Program. *Reading and Writing Quarterly, 10*(1), 5–19.

Pressley, M., Gaskin, I., Wile, D., Cunicelli, E., & Sheridan, J. (1991). Teaching literacy strategies across the curriculum: A case study at Benchmark school. In J. Zutell & S. McCormick (Eds.), *Learner factors/teacher factors: Issues in literacy research and instruction* (pp. 219–228). Chicago: National Reading Conference.

Rayner, K., & Pollatsek, A. (1989). *The psychology of reading.* Englewood Cliffs, NJ: Prentice Hall.

Rieben, L., & Perfetti, C. (Eds.). (1991). *Learning to read: Basic research and its implications.* Hillsdale, NJ: Lawrence Erlbaum.

Sadoski, M., Paivio, A., & Goetz, E. (1991). Commentary: A critique of schema theory in reading and a dual coding alternative. *Reading Research Quarterly, 26*(4), 463–484.

Samuels, S., & Farstrup, A. (Eds.). (1992). *What research has to say about reading instruction.* 2nd ed. Newark, DE: International Reading Association.

Spiro, R., Vispoel, W., Schmitz, J., Samarapungavan, A., & Boerger, A. (1987). Knowledge acquisition for application: Cognitive flexibility and transfer in complex cognitive domains. In B. Britton & S. Glynn (Eds.), *Executive control processes in reading* (pp. 177–199). Hillsdale, NJ: Lawrence Erlbaum.

Stanovich, K. (1986). Matthew effects in reading: Some consequences of individual differences in the acquisition of literacy. *Reading Research Quarterly, 21*(4), 360–407.

Stanovich, K. (1992). The psychology of reading: Evolutionary and revolutionary developments. In W. Grabe (Ed.), *Annual Review of Applied Linguistics, 12*: Literacy (pp. 3–30). New York: Cambridge University Press.

Tang, G. (1992). The effects of graphic representation of knowledge structures on ESL reading comprehension. *Studies in Second Language Acquisition, 14*(2), 177–195.

Vygotsky, L. S. (1978). *Mind in society: The development of higher psychological processes.* Cambridge: Cambridge University Press.

Wasik, B., & Slavin, R. (1993). Preventing early reading failure with one-to-one tutoring: A review of five programs. *Reading Research Quarterly, 28*(2), 178–200.

West, R., Stanovich, K., & Mitchell, H. (1993). Reading in the real world and its correlates. *Reading Research Quarterly, 28*(1), 34–50.

Zamel, V. (1992). Writing one's way into reading. *TESOL Quarterly, 26*(3), 463–485.

CHAPTER 27

Teaching Strategic Reading

Joy Janzen

Mircea is a conscientious student. When he is told he will be tested on the contents of Chapter 2 in the textbook, he looks up every unknown word in the dictionary in an effort to fix the information in his memory. Despite his extended preparations, he doesn't do very well on the test, though he says he spent hours preparing. Lia, on the other hand, excels on the exam, but she has approached the text in a very different way. Before she reads the chapter, she skims through it, looking at subheadings and graphics so as to give herself a general idea of what the text will be about. As she reads, she connects the material in the chapter to what she already knows. She frequently asks herself questions about the text, looking back or ahead to link one part of the text to another. When she is puzzled by the content, she searches for clues in the context, tries to paraphrase, or considers what she knows about text structure. In short, Lia is reading like an expert, while Mircea is relying on just one technique. The difference between the two is in their use of reading strategies.

Implications of Reading Strategy Research for Teachers

Reading strategies can be defined as "plans for solving problems encountered in constructing meaning" (Duffy, 1993, p. 232). They range from bottom-up vocabulary strategies, such as looking up an unknown word in the dictionary, to more comprehensive actions, such as connecting what is being read to the reader's background knowledge. Research in the L1 and L2 fields has demonstrated that strategy use is different in more proficient and less proficient readers. More proficient readers use different types of strategies, and they use them in different ways (Block, 1986, 1992; Jimenez, Garcia, & Pearson, 1995; Pressley, Beard El-Dinary, & Brown, 1992). Moreover, reading strategies can be taught to students, and when taught, strategies help improve student performance on tests of comprehension and recall (Carrell, 1985; Carrell, Pharis, & Liberto, 1989; Pearson & Fielding, 1991).

But what do these research results really mean for the classroom teacher? Given that strategies can be taught, and that one goal of teaching reading is to help students develop as strategic readers, how should this teaching be carried out? Strategy instruction has been discussed in general (see, e.g., Chamot & O'Malley, 1994), but in TESOL little has been published that relates to teaching reading strategies in an ongoing classroom reading program. This is not the case, however, in the L1 field, and one answer to the pedagogical dilemma is to adapt methods that have been found successful in L1 teaching to an ESL situation. In the teaching approach of Brown and Palincsar (1989), for example, students are taught four reading strategies: summarizing, predicting, clarifying, and asking questions. Versions of this have been tried with L2 students and have been found helpful (Cotterall, 1990; Hewitt, 1995). In the L1 field today, however, state-of-the-art reading strategy instruction has moved to a more comprehensive approach.

Teaching Reading: A Comprehensive Approach

What is sometimes termed the *transactional* teaching approach to strategy instruction has several characteristics that deserve attention.

1. It is embedded in a content area so that students are learning strategies while they are engaged in their regular reading for a variety of purposes.
2. Strategies are taught through direct explanation, teacher modeling, and feedback. Students are never in doubt as to what the strategies are, where and when they can be used, and how they are used. The teacher models expert behavior by reading and thinking aloud. The students also read and think aloud in class, and their strategy use is supported by teacher feedback.
3. Strategies are constantly recycled over new texts and tasks. The students encounter individual strategies and groups of strategies time and time again. In this way, students better understand the usefulness of strategies, and there is transfer of training from one type of text or task to another.
4. Strategy use develops over the long term. It is estimated that it takes several years for L2 students to develop as strategic readers (Beard El-Dinary, Pressley, & Schuder, 1992). Certainly, the decontextualized teaching of individual strategies for a short period is not likely to have long-term impact on students or to effectively help them develop as strategic readers (Gaskins, 1994; Pressley, Beard El-Dinary, & Brown, 1992).

The purpose of this article is to describe how a version of this global approach to teaching strategic reading is working successfully in one ESL classroom.

One ESL Classroom: How We Approach Group Reading Activities

I teach a reading lab class in an intensive university-level English program. The intensive program is designed to prepare students for mainstream study at either the graduate or the undergraduate level. The reading lab is one of a number of skills courses that supplement a content-based curriculum. In the reading class, we offer several activities: group reading, word-recognition exercises, and individualized reading, as well as work with vocabulary. I will focus on the group reading activities in this article.

Because this reading class is oriented toward instruction in one skill, it was not possible to embed strategy teaching entirely in content instruction, where all four skills would be addressed. The next-best alternative was to focus on one text for the course of a semester so that some of the benefits of content instruction could be present (e.g., heightened knowledge of a given topic and recurring vocabulary, both of which aid in reading comprehension). The text I selected was *Special Effects in the Movies* (Powers, 1989), a book written for high school students who are native speakers of English. While using this approach to teaching reading strategies in an earlier semester, I found *Special Effects* to be on an appropriate level for a similar group of students. The topic has also proved to be a fruitful one because all of the students in the class have seen many movies and can make immediate and extended connections between their own background knowledge and the text content.

CLASSROOM PROCESSES

Effective instruction in strategic reading entails a number of classroom processes or moves. I see five (which overlap to a certain extent) as primary. These are:

1. general strategy discussion
2. teacher modeling
3. student reading
4. analysis of strategies used by the teacher or by students when thinking aloud
5. explanation/discussion of individual strategies on a regular basis.

I organized my class activities to reflect these processes.

GENERAL STRATEGY DISCUSSION

In general strategy discussion, reading strategies and strategic reading are defined. The teacher explains and the class discusses why learning and practicing strategies are important. The following three points are examples of what I try to elicit from students: (1) Strategies help to improve reading comprehension as well as efficiency in reading; (2) By using strategies, students will be reading in the way that expert readers do; (3) Strategies help readers to process the text actively, to monitor their comprehension, and to connect what they are reading to their own knowledge and to other parts of the text.

I use this type of discussion not just in initial class periods as a part of explaining the method I am using to approach reading, but also on a recurring basis to ensure that students are aware of the value of what they are doing, and to ensure that they are connecting their progress in reading to the use of strategies. Another goal of our general discussions about the value of strategies is to encourage transfer of training to other reading tasks. Although initially the teacher may need to explain the value of using strategies, the students are soon able to relate their own views on strategies and strategy use. Through discussion, students gain a deeper understanding of their reading behavior, and they come to realize that they use strategies in reading in their L1.

TEACHER MODELING

A second important feature of strategy instruction is regular teacher modeling of expert behavior. In doing this, I read aloud a short portion of the text, and, as I do so, I think aloud. Here is a short excerpt from a transcript early in the semester. (Words in italics represent the actual text.)

> Okay, um, the chapter, the title of the chapter is *Dreams and Screams* – um, well, what does that mean? Um. I know the book is about special effects, but what, why is the chapter called *Dreams and Screams*? I don't know. *Movies have always had the power to make people believe that what they are seeing on screen is really happening*. Okay, so is this what the author means by special effects? I don't know. Um, okay. *Special effects add to that power*. Oh, so the author means that movies without special effects make people believe they're seeing what's on the screen, but special effects make those movies more surprising, more amazing. (Someone says "um-hum".) *By using special effects, filmmakers make "impossible" scenes seem real.* Okay, so movies seem real when we watch them, and special effects can make impossible things seem real. So may be the author will say next what impossible things can seem real. . . . *Through special effects, filmmakers have shown actors parting the waters of the Red Sea, flying to distant planets, and chopping off heads on Friday the 13th.* Okay, so I was right. The author is giving examples of special effects, impossible things that can seem real.

Here I can be observed using several strategies, which include asking questions, making predictions, checking those predictions, and summarizing or paraphrasing.

STUDENT READING

I also encourage students to read and think aloud from the very beginning, though I expect that familiarity with this process will take time. Reading and thinking aloud presents a very high cognitive load for L2 readers, yet not an impossible one. Here is an example of one student reading, also taken from early in the semester. (Words in italics represent the actual text.)

> The title of the next is "*Simple mattes* " . . . And, so I think it would be, explain something more about, uh, this kind of special effect. *In its, in its simplest form, a matte is a black card held in front of the camera lens. This matte card can have many different shapes*. I think he, he's going to explain some more about the, um, maybe technical, some infor- some technical information. *It can be used to cover a large part of the image or just a small part, like a window or doorway. When a camera operator photographs a scene, the area hidden behind the matte, the matte card does not show up on the filmed image*. I was almost right, he's, uh, he was explaining the, the use, how do they use, how they use this kind of effect. I think that the next we can, maybe we can find some example.

In this excerpt, the reader can be heard predicting and checking the correctness of her predictions.

ANALYSIS OF STRATEGY USE

After the students or I have read a portion of the text, we immediately analyze the strategy use of the reader through full class discussion: What did the reader do, and when did he or she do it? What strategies did the reader use? Analyzing the teacher's reading is a step toward ensuring that the students get the full benefit from the teacher's modeling behavior. By discussing what the teacher did, they will be better able to incorporate effective strategy use into their own reading. When a student's reading is under discussion, the

TABLE 1. SAMPLE STRATEGIES TAKEN FROM STUDENTS' OWN WORK

What	When	Why
Connecting • What I already know (to) what I'm reading • Previous part (to) what I'm reading	While reading After reading	To clarify ideas To help paraphrase To evaluate content
Evaluating	While reading After Reading	To judge the author's idea To make own opinion To develop knowledge
Asking questions	While reading Before reading	To evaluate To check To have more interest
Checking for answers to questions	While reading	To pay attention to what I'm reading
Translating	While reading	To get exact meaning

identification and analysis of strategy use is intermixed with teacher feedback on the reader's behavior. This feedback can include prompting to use specific strategies or eliciting suggestions from other students as to what strategies might be helpful in solving comprehension problems.

STRATEGY EXPLANATION AND DISCUSSION

The process of strategy identification and feedback entails the naming of strategies and repeated explanations on the teacher's or students' parts as to how to use the strategies. The explanation process can be facilitated by use of graphic organizers such as the one in Table 1. From the first session, I ask the students to write down the strategies I or other readers use, as well as when they were used, as soon as each section of reading is completed. After they have written down this information individually, we name the strategies as a class and discuss their value, that is, why they should be used. After a few weeks of this type of discussion, I ask the class to work in small groups and to fill in charts such as the one in Table 1, with three columns headed: What, When, and Why. The examples are taken from charts made by the students themselves.

In subsequent sessions, we add to the charts, and at intervals during the semester we revamp them completely. In this way, the students can remember the array of strategies we have covered, and we can also discuss how the strategies interconnect. The charts are always mounted on the chalkboard during class and serve as reference lists for strategies that have been used, or could be used, while reading.

HOMEWORK

Strategy use is reinforced outside the classroom through two types of homework. In the first type, students finish reading the material that we have begun in class and respond to various written prompts. Before finishing the chapter, they may preview the rest of the assigned text and predict what it will be about. While reading, they note questions they have and describe what other strategies they are using or could be using while they read. After reading, they can summarize the chapter and predict what future chapters will be about. At the same time that they use these strategies, they also explain why using them is helpful or worthwhile. In this way, strategy homework does not become simply rote skill learning but requires thought and concentration. In the second type of homework, students keep track of the reading they do outside of class for pleasure or for other courses. They note down what they have read, how much they have read, what strategies they have used in reading, and their evaluation of the text. This type of homework is meant to reinforce strategic behavior and to encourage transfer of strategy training to other tasks. In completing these assignments in recent semesters, students listed a wide variety of strategies, as can be seen in the list in Table 2. Their evaluations of the texts also indicated that they were reading in an attentive, thoughtful manner. Occasionally, the students would note that they had not used any strategies to read a given text. This point makes it probable that the strategies the students did list were ones they had genuinely employed and that they did not simply put them down after the fact to finish off a homework assignment.

TABLE 2. STUDENT-GENERATED STRATEGY LIST

Title	How Much to Read	Evaluation	Strategies Used
Us and Them: A History of Intolerance in America	20 pages	Interesting issues of different kinds of intolerance Lack of background but very interesting stories, written with simple style	Skim – look at pictures and heading Predict Check predictions Ask questions of the author and of the teacher in class Underline Use dictionary Guess Take notes Translate
Harriet Tubman: Freedom Girl	All the book	The issue was interesting and the book was written in an easy style Very complete about the personal story, but not about historical events	Predict Check predictions Underline Take notes Ask questions Paraphrase
"Flex Time – Meet the Ultimate Body Builder"	Whole article	It was more difficult than the text which we used in class, a lot of metaphors, different text structure, a lot of new vocabulary	Reread Think about (text) structure Ask questions Use the dictionary

CONCLUSION

I have used this approach with high-intermediate level university students, but it has potential for students at any level of instruction. It should be emphasized that transactional teaching, the basis for the method I am describing, was originally designed for elementary school classrooms. In adapting instruction in strategic reading from an L1 situation to an L2 environment, a very important issue to consider is how fast the teacher should introduce new strategies. The rate depends mostly on whether the students appear to be identifying strategies easily and articulating strategy use as they read. Another factor to consider is how much information about strategic reading should be explained, rather than elicited. When students are already proficient in reading in their L1, they are often immediately able to relate what we are doing with strategies in English to their reading behavior in their L1. This would not be the case with younger students, who may need more direct explanation about the meaning and value of strategies. The results of using this method to date have been very positive. In class, all the students are able to read and think aloud, articulating strategy use as they go. They can identify strategies that other readers have used, as well as come up with convincing reasons why these strategies are important. When students fill out charts describing the reading they do outside of class, they identify strategies they have used. In class, students have said that strategy training helps them to understand their reading process better, in both their L1 and their L2.

Acknowledgment

I would like to thank Angela Barker, Bill Grabe, and Sarah Rilling for reading this article and providing helpful comments.

References

Beard El-Dinary, P., Pressley, M., & Schuder, T. (1992). Teachers learning transactional strategies instruction. In C. Kinzer & D. Leu (Eds.), *Literary research, theory, and practice: Views from many perspectives: Forty-first yearbook of the National Reading Conference* (pp. 453–462). Chicago: National Reading Conference.

Block, E. (1986). The comprehension strategies of second language readers. *TESOL Quarterly, 20*, 46392.

Block, E. (1992). See how they read: Comprehension monitoring of L1 and L2 readers. *TESOL Quarterly, 26*, 319–342.

Brown, A., & Palincsar, A. (1989). Guided, cooperative learning and individual knowledge acquisition. In L. B. Resnick (Ed.), *Knowledge, learning and instruction: Essays in honor of Robert Glaser* (pp. 393–451). Hillsdale, NJ: Lawrence Erlbaum.

Carrell, P. (1985). Facilitating ESL reading by teaching text structure. *TESOL Quarterly, 19*, 727–752.

Carrell, P., Pharis, B. G., & Liberto, J. C. (1989). Metacognitive strategy training for ESL reading. *TESOL Quarterly, 23*, 647–678.

Chamot, A. U., & O'Malley, M. (1994). *The CALLA handbook*. Reading, MA: Addison-Wesley.

Cotterall, S. (1990). Developing reading strategies through small-group interaction. *RELC Journal, 21*, 55–69.

Duffy, G. (1993). Rethinking strategy instruction: Four teachers' development and their low achievers' understandings. *Elementary School Journal, 93*, 231–247.

Gaskins, I. (1994). Classroom applications of cognitive science: Teaching poor readers how to learn, think, and problem solve. In K. McGilly (Ed.), *Classroom lessons: Integrating cognitive theory and classroom practice* (pp. 129–154). Cambridge, MA: MIT Press.

Hewitt, G. (1995). Toward student autonomy in reading: Reciprocal teaching. *English Teaching Forum, 33*, 29–30.

Jimenez, R., Garcia, G., & Pearson, P. (1995). Three children, two languages, and strategic reading: Case studies in bilingual/monolingual reading. *American Educational Research Journal, 32*, 67–97.

Pearson, P. D., & Fielding, L. (1991). Comprehension instruction. In R. Barr, M. Kamil, P. Mosenthal, & P. Pearson (Eds.), *Handbook of reading research* (Vol. 11; pp. 815–860). White Plains, NY: Longman.

Powers, T. (1989). *Special effects in the movies*. San Diego: Lucent Books.

Pressley, M., Beard El-Dinary, P., & Brown, R. (1992). Skilled and not-so-skilled reading: Good information processing and not-so-good information processing. In M. Pressley, K. Harris, & J. Guthrie (Eds.), *Promoting academic competence and literacy in schools* (pp. 91–127). San Diego: Academic Press.

CHAPTER 28

Extensive Reading: Why Aren't We All Doing It?

Willy A. Renandya and George M. Jacobs

Introduction

Applied linguists have in recent years begun to move away from a preoccupation with the best methods of language teaching to a view that seeks to better understand the nature of language learning and teaching. Rather than introducing new methods of teaching, they are now more concerned with describing language pedagogy that is based on a principled understanding of second language learning. Brown (Chapter 1 of this volume) and Kumaravadivelu (1994), for example, have proposed a set of teaching/learning principles to which any good language pedagogy should conform. Examples of these principles include providing a rich linguistic environment, respecting and capitalizing on learners' contribution to the learning process, and emphasizing fluency over, but not at the expense of, accuracy (see Richards, Chapter 14 of this volume).

Extensive reading (ER), with its emphasis on encouraging learners to read self-selected, large amounts of meaningful language, fits well with current principles for good second and foreign language pedagogy (Grabe, Chapter 26 of this volume; Day & Bamford, 1998). In this paper, we briefly describe what ER is, how it is different from intensive reading, what its learning benefits can be for students, and what theories underpin ER. The paper also discusses some of the reasons why many teachers are still not implementing ER.

What Is Extensive Reading?

According to Carrell and Carson (1997, pp. 49–50), "extensive reading . . . generally involves rapid reading of large quantities of material or longer readings (e.g., whole books) for general understanding, with the focus generally on the meaning of what is being read than on the language." Although this definition provides an overview of ER, Davis (1995, p. 329) offers one description of ER from an ELT classroom implementation perspective:

> An extensive reading programme is a supplementary class library scheme, attached to an English course, in which pupils are given the time, encouragement, and materials to read pleasurably, at their own level, as many books as they can, without the pressures of testing or marks. Thus, pupils are competing only against themselves, and it is up to the teacher to provide the motivation and monitoring to ensure that the maximum number of books is being read in the time available. The watchwords are quantity and variety, rather than quality, so that books are selected for their attractiveness and relevance to the pupils' lives, rather than for literary merit.

Although ER programs come under different names, including Uninterrupted Sustained Silent Reading (USSR), Drop Everything and Read (DEAR), Silent Uninterrupted Reading for Fun (SURF), and the Book Flood Approach (Elley & Mangubhai, 1983), they all share a common purpose: that learners read large quantities of books and other materials in an environment that nurtures a lifelong reading habit. In addition, these programs share a common belief that the ability to read fluently is best achieved through an instructional program that emphasizes reading extensively in the language.

ER differs from intensive reading. In intensive reading, students normally work with short texts with close guidance from the teacher. The aim of intensive reading is to help students obtain detailed meaning from the text, to develop reading skills – such as identifying main ideas and recognizing text connectors – and to enhance vocabulary and grammar knowledge. It is important to note that these two approaches to teaching reading – intensive and extensive reading – should not be seen as being in opposition, as both serve different but complementary purposes (Carrell & Carson, 1997; Nuttall, 1996).

What are the characteristics of successful ER programs?[1] The following characteristics are generally thought to be among the most important (Bamford & Day, 1997; Davis, 1995; Hill, 1997; Hsui, 1994; Jacobs, Davis, & Renandya, 1997; Waring, 1997; Yu, 1993).

STUDENTS READ LARGE AMOUNTS OF MATERIAL

This is one of the key features that distinguishes extensive from intensive reading programs. In ER, teachers attempt to build a reading culture in which students read in quantity. The program will not obtain optimal benefits unless students are "hooked" on reading. In a study we recently completed, quantity of reading was the single most important predictor of students' gain scores (Renandya, Rajan, & Jacobs, 1999).

STUDENTS USUALLY CHOOSE WHAT THEY WANT TO READ

With highly motivated students, this feature is easy to achieve. With less motivated learners, however, the availability of materials that they do like to read can make a lot of difference. These learners usually do not read much. To get them hooked on reading, they need access to a good collection of books and other materials that they want to read. Unfortunately, the kind of material that these students are more likely to pick up (e.g., ghost stories, comics, and the like) may be hard to find, or even nonexistent, in schools (Richards, Thatcher, Shreeves, Timmons, & Barker, 1999; Worthy, Moorman, & Turner, 1999). Although we are stating that student choice of reading materials should be the norm, a place does exist for ER in which the entire class reads the same book.

READING MATERIALS VARY IN TERMS OF TOPIC AND GENRE

Students should be exposed to different types of materials so that they become familiar with different kinds of genre and accustomed to reading for different purposes and in different ways. Although younger learners may prefer fiction, they should gradually be introduced to nonfiction. Although a good selection of fiction often can be found, there is a relative scarcity of nonfiction materials for less proficient readers. Even scarcer are materials for adult learners who want to read simplified materials on such topics as law, business, technology, and medicine.

THE MATERIAL STUDENTS READ IS WITHIN THEIR LEVEL OF COMPREHENSION

Unlike in intensive reading, where the material is typically above students' linguistic level, in ER the material should be near or even below their current level. To use Second Language Acquisition (SLA) jargon, students should be reading texts at an $i + 1$, i, or $i - 1$ level, with "i" being their current proficiency level. The rule of thumb here is that to get students started in the program, it is better that they read easier texts than more challenging ones. For students who have had minimal exposure to contextualized language and who lack confidence in their reading, even $i - 2$ material may be appropriate, at least at the initial stage of the ER program.

STUDENTS USUALLY TAKE PART IN POSTREADING ACTIVITIES

The most commonly reported postreading task that teachers employ is, unfortunately, that of summary writing or book review. This task is not without value, but because writing a summary is time-consuming and often dreaded by students, it should be used less often. Other less laborious and potentially more inviting postreading tasks can be fruitfully used. These include asking students to

- design a bookmark to suit the book
- role-play the story
- design a poster to advertise the book
- read interesting/exciting/well-written parts aloud
- copy interesting words and useful expressions into a notebook
- write a letter to the author
- share their views about the book with a small group of classmates

TEACHERS READ WITH THEIR STUDENTS, THUS MODELING ENTHUSIASM FOR READING

We are less likely to be successful in encouraging our students to read if we ourselves do not read. This advice is particularly important when first beginning an ER program. We can show students the books or other materials we have just read or are reading, let them see us read silently, and read aloud to them from our favorite materials. This sends a strong message that we value reading and that our students should do the same (Campbell, 1989).

TEACHERS AND STUDENTS KEEP TRACK OF STUDENT PROGRESS

Ideally, students read on their own without the need for teachers to monitor their reading. However, regular monitoring is recommended, especially when working with reluctant readers. A simple book record can be designed to check students' progress. In addition to using book records, a monthly student–teacher conference can be scheduled to find out if students are having any problems with their reading. This conference can be as brief as

5 minutes or less. Monitoring should be seen as a way of displaying student progress and motivating students, rather than as a way for the teacher to *assess* them.

Finding the materials to suit the students' reading tastes as well as having a wide range of books at different levels can be difficult, especially where funding is insufficient. Lituañas (1997) describes how she collects materials from a wide variety of sources, including fellow teachers, past students, and community groups. Toh and Raja (1997) explain ways that teachers themselves can write ER materials suited to their students' cultural contexts and proficiency levels. Ways that students can be involved in creating reading materials for themselves and peers are explored in Davidson, Ogle, Ross, Tuhaka, and Ng (1997) and Dupuy and McQuillan (1997).

It is worth noting that not all writers on ER agree that postreading tasks should be included in the ER programs. The main objection is that postreading tasks take time away from reading and may spoil students' reading enjoyment, and that in ER, reading should be seen as its own reward. However, we feel that postreading tasks, if carefully designed, can serve useful purposes (see Yu, 1993, for a similar view). Postreading activities can be used to (1) reinforce what students have learned from their reading; (2) give students a sense of progress; and (3) help students share information about materials to read or avoid. The output hypothesis (Swain, 1993) provides additional support for the use of postreading tasks. This hypothesis states that although comprehensible input supplies an essential basis for second language acquisition, it must be supplemented by the production of comprehensible output if learners are to reach a high level of proficiency in the target language. Swain argues that production tasks push learners to notice features of the target language and to form and test hypotheses about the language.

Some educators use student groups to support ER. Group activities support reading interest and proficiency and can take place before, during, and after ER. For instance, Cockburn, Isbister, and Sim-Goh (1997) and Rodgers (1997) depict programs in which more proficient, often older readers, support less proficient, often younger students, in various literacy activities. McQuillan and Tse (1997) and Renandya, Rajan, and Jacobs (1999) describe group activities that provide readers with opportunities to discuss what they have been reading.

The Benefits of Extensive Reading

ER is seen as offering many advantages (Day & Bamford, 1998; Krashen, 1993; Nation, 1997), some of which are as follows:

1. enhanced language learning in such areas as spelling, vocabulary, grammar, and text structure
2. increased knowledge of the world
3. improved reading and writing skills
4. greater enjoyment of reading
5. more positive attitude toward reading
6. higher possibility of developing a reading habit

Rationales for these proposed advantages of ER range from the commonsense – we learn to x (in this case, read) by doing x (in this case, reading) – to the currently more esoteric, for example, chaos theory (Larsen-Freeman, 1997), which postulates that dynamic, complex, nonlinear systems such as human language are self-organizing, given sufficient input and feedback, and that reading provides one source of such input and feedback. A more common scholarly explanation of the benefits of ER argues that the human brain contains innate potential for language learning of both L1 and L2s. This potential is known as language acquisition device or universal grammar (Chomsky, 1968). The large quantities of meaningful and comprehensible input provided by ER activate that potential, thereby fostering language acquisition, as learners induce the rules of grammar and other language elements, such as spelling, from the data they receive in their environment (Krashen, 1993). In first language acquisition, this innate ability enables young children to gain mastery of most of their first language's rules and a good deal of its vocabulary regardless of their socioeconomic status and intelligence.

We generally agree with this nativist view, and feel that the same processes come into play for the learning of second languages, but we also see the possible benefit of what interactionist theorists (Larsen-Freeman & Long, 1991; Swain, 1999) have proposed, namely, that although comprehensible input is an absolutely crucial condition for second language acquisition, it may by itself not be sufficient. The effectiveness of ER may be further enhanced by such means as students engaging in activities in which they talk and write about what they have read and will read (Renandya, Rajan, & Jacobs, 1999). This talking and writing can help make the reading more comprehensible and may provide a means for students to "infect" each other with the joy of reading. Talking and writing also push students to move from the receptive language competence needed for reading to the more demanding productive competence required for speaking and writing.

From a cognitive point of view (see Day & Bamford, 1998, Chapter 2, for an excellent summary), ER is particularly crucial in aiding the development of three of the most important components of fluent reading: a large sight vocabulary, a sizable general vocabulary, and knowledge of the target language and of the world. Sight vocabulary refers to words that readers can recognize quickly and effortlessly. This rapid and automatic process of word recognition is extremely crucial for reading. If this ability is lacking, subsequent reading processes are likely to be seriously impeded, which in turn makes comprehension difficult, if not impossible. Similarly, without possessing a large stock of vocabulary, reading becomes a frustrating dictionary-thumbing exercise that disrupts smooth processing of textual information. Although these two components are necessary, they do not by themselves make comprehension happen. This is where the third component comes into the picture, as comprehension depends to a large extent on the reader's prior knowledge of syntax, text structures, and the subject of the reading. The repeated exposure to massive amounts of written language afforded by ER is believed to help readers develop these three aspects of fluent reading.

Why Aren't We All Doing Extensive Reading?

ER is not new, yet although many of us would readily acknowledge the educational benefits of ER, how many of us are actually implementing it in our second language program? If ER is good for second language development, why isn't everybody doing it? According to Day and Bamford (1998), one of the most important reasons is that many teachers believe that intensive reading alone will produce good, fluent readers. As was mentioned earlier, in intensive reading students spend lots of time analyzing and dissecting short, difficult texts under the close supervision of the teacher. The aim of intensive reading is to help students construct detailed meaning from the text, develop reading skills, and enhance vocabulary and grammar knowledge. This overemphasis on the explicit teaching of reading and language skills leaves little room for implementing other approaches. The intensive reading approach by itself, Day and Bamford further argue, may produce *skilled* readers but not skilled *readers*.

A related reason why ER is not done goes back to the whole paradigm issue of the role of the teachers: sages on the stage or guides on the side. Many teachers are perhaps still uncomfortable with the idea of playing a "less" central role in the classroom. In intensive reading, instruction is more teacher-centered in that teachers are more center stage in what is happening in the classroom. They do lots of talking and decide what skills or strategies to teach, how these are taught, and what passages to use. In contrast, with ER, roles shift as teachers not only pass on knowledge, but also "guide students and participate with them as members of a reading community" (Day & Bamford, 1998, p. 47).

Other reasons for the relative absence of ER in second language instruction are more practical in nature. In our in-service courses, we often hear teachers saying that they do not have enough time to get students to read extensively because they feel pressured by the administration to cover the predetermined materials specified in the syllabus. Some others report that since ER is not directly assessed, they feel that curriculum time would be better spent on other subjects that students are tested on. Even in places where ER has been incorporated into the second language curriculum (e.g., Singapore), full implementation of the ER programs is hampered by these practical considerations. Careful examination of these implementation variables should receive more attention in future research.

Conclusion

We hope this article has motivated those of you who do not yet use ER or use it only a little to give ER a try or expand its use. We also hope that those of you who already are "extensively" using extensive reading have gained new ideas. We are confident that a growing number of applied linguists hold the view expressed by Eskey (1986, p. 21): "Reading . . . must be developed, and can only be developed, by means of extensive and continual practice. People learn to read, and to read better, by reading." The benefits of ER, however, extend beyond the acquisition of reading fluency. After reviewing hundreds of research studies in both first and second language learning contexts, Krashen (1993, p. 23) boldly states that through extensive reading we "develop a good writing style, an adequate vocabulary, advanced grammar, and . . . become good spellers."

Beyond powerful gains in language proficiency, reading offers more. It offers a richer understanding of the world and a place in the ongoing, worldwide dialogue on a universe of topics open only to those who are literate and who exercise their literacy. Thus, ER represents much more than a teaching device. It represents a lifelong habit, a habit that brings with it the power and wealth that language offers in such large quantities. By encouraging our students to read extensively and showing them how to do so, we help them strengthen their grip on the efficacious tool of reading.

Acknowledgment

We wish to thank Lim Wai Lee, Patrick Gallo, and Jack Richards for their insightful comments on the earlier draft of this paper.

References

Bamford, J., & Day, R. R. (1997). Extensive reading: What is it? Why bother? *Language Teacher, 21*, 6–8, 12.

Campbell, R. (1989). The teacher as a role model during Sustained Silent Reading (SSR). *Reading, 23*(3), 179–183.

Carrell, P. L., & Carson, J. G. (1997). Extensive and intensive reading in an EAP setting. *English for Specific Purposes, 16*, 47–60.

Chomsky, N. (1968). *Language and mind*. New York: Harcourt, Brace & World.

Cockburn, L., Isbister, S., & Sim-Goh, M. L. (1997). Buddy reading. In G. M. Jacobs, C. Davis, & W. A. Renandya (Eds.), *Successful strategies for extensive reading* (pp. 65–80). Singapore: SEAMEO Regional Language Centre.

Davidson, C., Ogle, D., Ross, D., Tuhaka, J., & Ng, S. M. (1997). Student-created reading materials for ER. In G. M. Jacobs, C. Davis, & W. A. Renandya (Eds.), *Successful strategies for extensive reading* (pp. 144–160). Singapore: SEAMEO Regional Language Centre.

Davis, C. (1995). ER: An expensive extravagance? *ELT Journal, 49*(4), 329–336.

Day, R., & Bamford, J. (1998). *Extensive reading in the second language classroom.* Cambridge: Cambridge University Press.

Dupuy, B., & McQuillan, J. (1997). Handcrafted books: Two for the price of one. In G. M. Jacobs, C. Davis, & W. A. Renandya (Eds.), *Successful strategies for extensive reading* (pp. 171–180). Singapore: SEAMEO Regional Language Centre.

Elley, W., & Mangubhai, F. (1983). The impact of reading on second language learning. *Reading Research Quarterly, 19*, 53–67.

Eskey, D. (1986). Theoretical foundation. In F. Dubin, D. E. Eskey, & W. Grabe (Eds.), *Teaching second language reading for academic purposes* (pp. 3–23). Reading, MA: Addison-Wesley.

Hill, D. R. (1997). Setting up an ER programme: Practical tips. *Language Teacher, 21*(5), 17–20.

Hsui, V. Y. (1994). A modified sustained silent reading programme for secondary classrooms. In S. E. A. Lim, M. Sripathy, & V. Saravanan (Eds.), *Literacy: Understanding the learner's needs* (pp. 165–174). Singapore: Society for Reading and Literacy.

Jacobs, G. M., Davis, C., & Renandya, W. A. (1997). *Successful strategies for extensive reading*. Singapore: SEAMEO Regional Language Centre.

Jacobs, G. M., Renandya, W. A., & Bamford, D. (1999). *Annotated bibliography of works on extensive reading in a second language.* http://www.kyoto-su.ac.jp/information/er/

Krashen, S. (1993). *The power of reading: Insights from the research.* Englewood, CO: Libraries Unlimited.

Kumaravadivelu, B. (1994). The postmethod condition: (E)merging strategies for second/foreign language teaching. *TESOL Quarterly, 28*, 27–48.

Larsen-Freeman, D. (1997). Chaos/complexity science and second language acquisition. *Applied Linguistics, 18*(2), 141–165.

Larsen-Freeman, D., & Long, M. H. (1991). *An introduction to second language acquisition research*. London: Longman.

Lituañas, P. M. (1997). Collecting materials for extensive reading. In G. M. Jacobs, C. Davis, & W. A. Renandya (Eds.), *Successful strategies for extensive reading* (pp. 25–29). Singapore: SEAMEO Regional Language Centre.

McQuillan, J., & Tse, L. (1997). Let's talk about books: Using literature circles in second language classrooms. In G. M. Jacobs, C. Davis, & W. A. Renandya (Eds.), *Successful strategies for extensive reading* (pp. 81–89). Singapore: SEAMEO Regional Language Centre.

Nation, P. (1997). The language learning benefits of extensive reading. *Language Teacher, 21*, 13–16.

Nuttal, C. (1996). *Teaching reading skills in a foreign language.* 2nd ed. Oxford: Heinemann.

Renandya, W. A., Rajan, B. R. S., & Jacobs, G. M. (1999). Extensive reading with adult learners of English as a second language. *RELC Journal, 30*(1), 39–61.

Richards, P. O., Thatcher, D. H., Shreeves, M., Timmons, P., & Barker, S. (1999). Don't let a good scare frighten you: Choosing and using quality chillers to promote reading. *Reading Teacher, 52*, 830–840.

Rodgers, T. S. (1997). Partnership in reading and writing. In G. M. Jacobs, C. Davis, & W. A. Renandya (Eds.), *Successful strategies for extensive reading* (pp. 120–127). Singapore: SEAMEO Regional Language Centre.

Swain, M. (1993). The output hypothesis: Just speaking and writing aren't enough. *Canadian Modern Language Review, 50*, 158–164.

Swain, M. (1999). Integrating language and content teaching through collaborative tasks. In C. S. Ward & W. A. Renandya (Eds.), *Language teaching: New insights for the language teacher* (pp. 125–147). Singapore: SEAMEO Regional Language Centre.

Toh, G., & Raja, M. (1997). ELT materials: Some perceptions on the question of cultural relevance. *Guidelines, 19*, 45–72.

Waring, R. (1997). Graded and extensive reading – Questions and answers. *Language Teacher, 21*(5), 9–12.

Worthy, J., Moorman, M., & Turner, M. (1999). What Johnny likes to read is hard to find in school. *Reading Research Quarterly, 34*, 12–27.

Yu, V. (1993). ER programs: How can they best benefit the teaching and learning of English? *TESL Reporter, 26*, 1–9.

Endnote

[1] A Web site exclusively dedicated to understanding and exploring ER in second language learning was established in 1999 (http://www.kyoto-su.ac.jp/information/er/). It houses a large annotated bibliography of works on ER and many other resources for developing successful ER programs, including information on setting up a program.

SECTION 13

TEACHING WRITING

Introduction

There is no doubt that writing is the most difficult skill for L2 learners to master. The difficulty lies not only in generating and organizing ideas, but also in translating these ideas into readable text. The skills involved in writing are highly complex. L2 writers have to pay attention to higher level skills of planning and organizing as well as lower level skills of spelling, punctuation, word choice, and so on. The difficulty becomes even more pronounced if their language proficiency is weak.

With so many conflicting theories around and so many implementation factors to consider, planning and teaching a course in writing can be a daunting task. Which theoretical strands are we going to adopt? Are we going to use the process approach or the genre-based approach? Or an eclectic approach? What will be the focus of our course? What activities are likely to help students develop their writing skills? How do we treat learner errors? Do we correct all error types? How do we get students to self-edit? These are some of the issues that the four articles in this section seek to address.

Drawing on her extensive experience in research and teaching writing, Raimes outlines a set of guidelines which can make the planning of a writing course a less intimidating task. These guidelines are based on what we have long known to be the key principles of course design, which include considerations of course goals, theories, content, focus, syllabus, materials, methodology, activities, and course evaluation. Although these are of paramount importance in the design of a writing course, one should not lose sight of the fact that these are but principles. Eventually, it is the teacher who is responsible for translating these principles into practice. And for this practice to produce optimal learning benefits, teachers should constantly and systematically record, ponder, and analyze what they have done in the classroom, and use their reflective experience as a basis for improving their instructional practices.

Seow describes the process approach to teaching writing, which comprises four basic stages – planning, drafting, revising, and editing. Three other stages could be inserted after the drafting stage; these are responding, evaluating, and post-writing. For each stage, suggestions are provided as to the kinds of classroom activities that support the learning of specific writing skills. For example, at the planning stage, teachers can help students generate ideas through such activities as brainstorming, clustering, and rapid free writing. Seow concludes by offering some implementation tips for teachers.

Reppen discusses the genre-based approach, which in recent years has received a lot of attention from researchers as well as practitioners. A genre-based approach provides students with ample opportunities to become aware of the different purposes of written communication and the different ways information is organized in written texts. Unless students are exposed to these different text types and are given sufficient practice in these types of writing, their written products will leave much to be desired. In his paper, Reppen describes an action research study in which he teaches fifth-grade students using a methodology that combines the principles which underlie the genre-based and the process approaches to teaching writing. The results of his study show that his students react positively to this instructional procedure, with most of them becoming more aware of the different conventions used in different genres.

Ferris begins with an observation that although process skills are important, we have to be aware of the fact that grammatical inaccuracies can have negative effects on the overall quality of students' writing. Because of this, writing teachers need to help students develop their editing as well as their composing skills. Editing refers to the process of detecting and correcting grammatical, lexical, and other mechanical errors before publishing a final written product. Ferris then describes a three-stage approach to teaching editing skills that can help students become independent editors of their own written work. She suggests that the focus of the editing activities should be on students' most frequent errors, especially those that affect the global meaning of their written texts.

Discussion Questions

Before Reading

1. Writing is usually thought to be the most difficult skill to acquire and should only be taught after students have learned the other skills. Do you agree? Explain.
2. Writing is a matter of putting together strings of grammatically correct sentences. Do you agree with this statement?
3. Reflect on your experience as a second/foreign language learner. Did you have problems in expressing your ideas in writing? What were those problems? How did you deal with those problems?
4. Do you write a lot in your native language? Is it difficult to write in your own language? What kinds of problems do you have when you write? Do these problems have to do with vocabulary, syntax, or organization?
5. How important are the following processes in writing: planning, drafting, editing, and rewriting?
6. What approach do you use in teaching writing skills? How successful have you been in teaching writing?
7. Describe the textbook you use for teaching writing skills. Does it follow any particular approach of teaching? What kinds of activities are commonly used?

8. How do you evaluate students' writing? What criteria do you use?
9. What are the features of a good writing program?

After Reading

1. What is process writing? Is the process approach sufficient to produce competent writers? Is the approach appropriate for beginners as well as more advanced learners? Will it work with ESL as well as EFL students?
2. One of the criticisms against process writing is that it takes up a lot of classroom time to teach process skills. As a result, students do not get much writing done. Do you agree with this?
3. What is meant by a genre approach to teaching writing? In what ways does knowledge of different text types contribute to learners' growing competence in writing?
4. Review the article by Reppen. Develop a lesson plan that teaches the expository genre using the guidelines suggested in the article.
5. Reflect on how you dealt with your students' errors in writing. Did you always correct their errors? What types of errors did you correct? How did you correct them?
6. Review the article by Ferris. Develop an instructional plan that incorporates Ferris's three-stage approach to teaching editing skills.
7. If possible, arrange to observe a teacher teaching writing. Does she or he use the process approach, the genre-based approach, or a combination of the two?
8. Review Step 1 in the article by Raimes. What is the significance of this step in your own teaching situation?
9. Review Step 2 in article by Raimes. What theoretical principles do you adhere to?
10. Review the rest of the steps in Raimes's paper. Are they applicable to your teaching situation? Which points do you find most useful in your teaching situation?

CHAPTER 29

Ten Steps in Planning a Writing Course and Training Teachers of Writing

Ann Raimes

Introduction

A few years ago, I gave papers called "The Neurosis of Lesson Planning" and "Anguish as a Second Language" in which I explored the fact that both learning and teaching a language promote anxiety. There is even more anxiety when writing is involved, especially when many teachers themselves do not feel entirely comfortable with writing in English, even if it is their native language. Today, with a burgeoning of conflicting theories, planning a writing course is like walking a minefield. It involves so many choices about where to go next, what is the best step to take, and what is the best route to the goal. Taking a wrong step in this context might not be as dire as stepping on a mine, but it can undermine our confidence and detonate our students' resistance. So I have come up with ten steps that I hope can lead us to safer ground both in planning writing courses and in helping teachers to plan writing courses.

Step 1: Ascertaining Goals and Institutional Constraints

When I began writing this paper, I listed only "ascertaining goals." Then, as I worked on the paper, I found myself discussing under every heading the constraints imposed upon teachers by their institutions or, further afield, by ministries of education, examining and accreditation agencies, funding sources, and the like. Such constraints include assigned curricula, approved textbooks, and designated proficiency examinations; they lead to questions such as these about goals: Do your students have to pass an exam that values writing to a formula and rewards above all accuracy of grammar, spelling, and punctuation? Do they even have to compose at all, or just write sentences, judge grammaticality, or pick from multiple-choice responses? Do you want your students to write to demonstrate mastery of form, or to experiment with language, record experiences and reactions, and generate and communicate ideas? Or do you want simply to increase their confidence in themselves as writers? Answering questions like these is a necessary first step in designing a course. And different answers will lead in different directions.

Students in a recent ESL class of mine wrote about the times when they wrote or spoke in English. They felt worried, embarrassed, hampered by barriers, restrictions, and fears. They felt their voice was monotonous: "I'm not the real me," said one. "I feel like I'm choking on a word that won't come out," said another. And one capped it all by saying, "Inside of me I feel stupid and dumb." This was owing mainly, it seems, not to the difficulty of writing itself but to the difficulty of doing it in a new language. When students wrote in their native language they felt, they said, "comfortable, free, self-assured, open, loud, and positive"; "I feel more like me"; "I can write with feelings and anger"; "Words just come out from my brain on paper." We can see that taking direction from these students and addressing comfort, confidence, and fluency as a goal would lead to a very different course from one that sees as its goal the production of an academic essay with an introduction, three points, and a conclusion, and effective use of transition words. And what if an imposed curriculum or textbook stresses only rhetorical form and grammatical accuracy? What is the teacher to do?

If institutional constraints limit our ability to pursue our goals and what we see as the students' goals, a few courses of action are open to us:

- We can work politically to change the constraints. We can join and form committees, we can make proposals, and we can run pilot projects. Pilot projects are a good way to test out alternate methods, since administrations do not view them as too threatening.
- We can make only a part of our course address the test or the assigned curriculum.
- We can avoid seeing ends as means. If a student has to learn how to write an essay in 30 minutes on a prescribed topic, that does not mean that the whole course should consist of 30-minute writing tasks. The ends dictate only the destination, not how we get there. We need to find ways to ensure that we vary our means of working toward the prescribed ends.

Step 2: Deciding on Theoretical Principles

Articles by Santos (1992), McKay (1993), Severino (1993), and Benesch (1993) have discussed the role of ideology in teaching writing. Terry Santos tells us that ESL composition "see[s] itself pragmatically" and so "avoid[s] ideology" (1992, p. 80). And some teachers insist that their teaching is not associated with ideology in any way. Those in my graduate course have said emphatically, "In my classroom I teach English and there's no ideology in that." But Sarah Benesch points out that "all forms of ESL instruction are ideological, whether or not educators are conscious of the political implications of their instructional choices" (1993, p. 705). She illustrates this with an analysis of English for academic purposes (EAP). She points out that in its attempts "to adapt students to the status quo" (p. 714) by presenting the demands of literacy as "positive artifacts of a normative academic culture" (p. 710), EAP turns toward "an accommodationist ideology" (p. 714), which prepares students to be assimilated into systems that instructors never question and that their students never examine critically. She claims, then, that all writing is ideological.

So teachers first need to confront their ideological position and recognize their perceptions of the relationship between the type of writing they teach and the roles they are preparing students for in academia and the wider world of work. The question of ideology and who determines what is taught is a question of power and reflects local conditions. In the United States, teaching writing to immigrants and refugees raises issues of assimilation and accommodation which are obviously different from issues raised by teaching EFL writing in other parts of the world. Suresh Canagarajah discusses this in relation to Sri Lanka in a *TESOL Quarterly* article (1993). It is important for all of us to ask ourselves what English and what types of writing we teach, what content our students are exposed to, and what we expect our students to do with what they learn. What roles in society does our instruction prepare them for? How specific are the specific purposes of ESP (English for specific purposes), socioeconomically and politically?

Then, closely allied to ideology comes theory and our views of language, the nature of language learning, writing, and the nature of the learning of composition. Even if we never articulate our theories to ourselves, they become apparent to others in our syllabus and choice of materials and activities. Let's look at two examples of writing-class decisions: the use of text models and the choice of focus on content or form.

What are text models used for? Are they to be imitated or examined critically, analyzed, and compared? Fan Shen (1989) from the People's Republic of China has written about his experience learning English composition in the United States. He says that in Chinese, writers try to "reach a topic gradually and systematically." To him, the concept of a topic sentence stating the main idea of a paragraph right there up front is "symbolic of the values of a busy people in an industrialized society" (p. 462). As teachers, we have the choice of presenting a text structure as a given, as some kind of "standard," as a form to be learned and imitated, or going beyond that and exploring in our classes the notion that what writers do reflects an entire system of values and beliefs, with strong connections between the writing process and the beliefs of a culture. Sandra McKay claims that we need to examine the "social practices that surround academic discourse" (1993, p. 74), and we can do that by discussing openly in our classes the differences in approaches to writing and reading and critically examining the text forms that appear in our textbooks and curricular guides.

Another example of a writing-class decision that has clear links to theory is the choice of focus on content or form. A commitment to content, fluency, personal voice, and revising is often called *process writing*. But since all writing involves a process, whether teachers focus on it or not, I prefer to call this a *process approach to teaching writing* and to emphasize that when we pay attention to how a piece of writing is constructed, this is not necessarily at the expense of attention to the product. In addition, a process approach is not the same as an expressionist approach, focusing only on personal writing. A process approach to teaching writing can be used with personal and with academic content, with literature and with nonfiction. And in a process approach, of course the product and accuracy and grammar are important – they are just not the first and only thing that is important. A principled process approach always pays serious attention to the product – but at an appropriate stage in the process.

So what we decide to emphasize in the classroom is not just a practical matter of choosing an activity to fill the next day's lesson plan. Principled teaching will always reveal principled theoretical underpinnings. To detect these, I always ask the teachers in my teacher-training courses to ask themselves the following questions: Why am I doing this activity in my class? How does it fit into what I know about language and language learning? What will my students learn from it? What is it worth learning for?

Step 3: Planning Content

There's a healthy controversy about what the content of writing classes should be, and teachers use any or all of the following: personal experience, social issues, cultural issues, literature, or the content of other subject areas. There is no one right answer to the question of content, but I will go so far as to say that there is one wrong answer. That wrong answer is that the content of a writing course takes a back seat to practice in prescribed models of paragraph or essay form; that is, that it does not matter what you write about as long as it conforms to an accepted rhetorical model. Why is that wrong? Because it misses the point about using writing as a unique tool for language learning. It returns to an early view of writing as one (and the least important) of the four language skills to be used to test that other skills have been mastered. It neglects the real value of writing: that it is a valuable tool for learning not only about subject matter, whatever the choice, but also about language. Writing is for discovery of learning, not just demonstration of learning. For writing, unlike speaking, provides us with a way not only to generate ideas before presenting them to an audience, but also to scrutinize the ideas and language we produce; this re-vision, this seeing again, lets us receive feedback from ourselves and others and, learning as we go, make changes and corrections. If we simply ask students to analyze, manipulate, and imitate given texts, we are not allowing them to grapple for that fit between content and form that all writers need to grapple with.

However, the question of content involves more than selecting content that is not based on rhetorical models of form. It involves also the question of what content will actively encourage students to use writing as a tool for learning and for communication and to become engaged enough with their writing to have an investment in examining it, improving it, and eventually revising it for readers. So when the pursuit of so-called objective academic content in a content-based approach leads to borrowing content from such areas as history and social sciences, this serves to shoulder out personal responses to the authentic academic issue of examining culture, identity, and language. Then a lot of the advantages of writing as a language learning tool bite the dust too. Although graduate courses might address specific genres as the focus of instruction, in large numbers of ESL and EFL writing courses, language learning rather than forms of written discourse is a major consideration. So students need topics that allow them to generate ideas, find the forms to fit the ideas, and invite risk taking.

Step 4: Weighing the Elements

Writing consists of many constituent parts and we need to consider which ones will be the most important for a course: content, organization, originality, style, fluency, accuracy, or using appropriate rhetorical forms of discourse. Obviously, unless a course lasts for years, we will not be able to do all these justice. So we have to form priorities and weight the elements according to students' needs and our own philosophy.

When I first began teaching ESL in the early 1960s, a writing course existed primarily as grammar practice. I would have students write dozens of sentences about John and Mary (and the tedious, boring lives they led) and eventually, with the advent of controlled and guided compositions, moved daringly into having them write paragraphs, but they were still working with content that was already provided for them on the page. Then came the idea that writing is generative of ideas, that it is a messy and chaotic process. Contrastive rhetoricians frequently graphically present a piece of writing in English as a straight line, but that is a depiction of the product, not the process. There are, unfortunately, no neat formulas for getting to an exquisite final product, one step at a time. Giving instruction in writing is not like giving instructions for assembling a toy or a mail-order computer. It is not simply a question of getting the right tools and following directions. If it were, more people would be good writers, and more teachers and textbook writers would be very rich. We must accept the chaotic and messy nature of writing – but teachers do not like chaos, so they have sought to impose order on it by focusing on grammar, rhetorical modes, and models of academic discourse, to provide themselves with neat systems to teach.

It is helpful to do a needs analysis on the first day, balancing institutional goals with what students say they need to learn and what they need to use writing for; then we can weight the elements so that the chaos of composing is somewhat reduced for the students, since they can focus on one or two things at a time. My ESL courses usually address a theme – culture and identity, or education, for example – and within that theme and within each task, students focus on critical reading, generating ideas and expressing them with clarity, organization, style, and accuracy. My students know that I see learning to write a lab report as a priority in a physics class, not in an ESL class.

Step 5: Drawing Up a Syllabus

The next question we ask after deciding on content and weighting the elements is how we will organize that content and the learning experiences in the classroom. In *The Language Teaching Matrix*, Richards (1990) lists the kinds of syllabi commonly found in speaking and listening courses in ESL. I will adapt his list to the types of syllabus organization for writing courses, from the traditional to the more current and innovative, with a lot of overlap:

1. *Structural.* Writing courses, particularly at beginning levels, can be organized around grammar and sentence patterns. A present tense paragraph one day, then a past tense paragraph, and so on. This was common in the 1960s, but is less so now. Structural courses nowadays are often organized by patterns of writing forms or genres: paragraphs with topic sentences, descriptions, analyses, and so on.
2. *Functional.* Writing courses can be organized around rhetorical activities: describing, telling a story, writing autobiography, comparing and contrasting, classifying, defining, explaining, arguing, persuading, or supporting a thesis with examples, illustrations, and other evidence.
3. *Topical.* A writing course can be organized around themes, such as housing, health, education, or abstractions such as *success* or *courage*. In the United States, ESL writing courses in college are often linked with a content course. At Hunter College in New York, students in an intermediate-level ESL course are also enrolled in "The Greek and Latin Roots of English" and many of the readings in that course are examined in more linguistic detail in the ESL course.
4. *Situational.* Writing courses can be organized around situational transactions, such as applying for a job, complaining to a landlord, writing letters to the newspaper, writing a business memo, or writing essays to pass a course.
5. *Skills and processes.* Writing courses can be organized around skills and processes such as generating ideas, organizing ideas, revising, writing fluently, writing effective beginnings and endings, and developing an argument to convince a reader.
6. *Tasks.* Writing courses can be organized around problem-solving activities, such as producing a class magazine of accounts of student trips; comparing the structure of texts written for different audiences and purposes; writing, editing, and producing a play; and examining the differences between ESL textbook situations and the expectations of the students' culture.

Such a spread of choices is like going to a big food center. There is so much there that we do not know where to begin. I do not want to stick with Chinese noodles. I want satay and curry and those wonderful big prawns. With syllabus types, too, in practice, as Richards points out, a "combination of approaches is often used" (1990, pp. 9–10); what they are, and in what proportion they are used, depends on our students, goals, theoretical principles, and institutional constraints. And we have to make a principled selection every time we plan a lesson or a course.

Learners do not have to be excluded from the process of syllabus design, though the traditional view, expressed by Reid (1993), is that a curriculum and syllabus "should be in place and ready to use before the ESL writing class meets for the first time" (p. 73). But if a needs assessment of the students who are actually in the classroom rather than a typical body of students is preferred, then syllabus planning can become more of a collaborative than a teacher-directed process.

The easy way out of syllabus design is, of course, to simply choose a book, and build a day-by-day syllabus around it. But then we give all our power of choice to a textbook writer who does not know our students. If the book we choose fits our theoretical philosophy, we will not feel too bound by the syllabus it imposes. If a book is assigned to a class, or a syllabus is prescribed, then we all learn to drop, add, cut, paste, and select. Creative adaptation and critical analysis become the order of the day. Canagarajah reports on textbooks assigned in Sri Lanka in which the situations "assume an urbanized, technological Western culture that is alien to the students" (1993, p. 609). But even with texts such as these, students do not have to just repeat and perform the assigned dialogues and exercises. The texts can also be used as material for critical analysis and comparison with local cultural and rhetorical norms.

STEP 6: SELECTING MATERIALS

Increasingly, teachers of writing are beginning to view the main texts of a writing class as what the students write and what the teachers write in response. Certainly, students and teachers generate a lot of words on the page for analysis, discussion, and revision. But to open up the classroom to shared experiences – to topics to stimulate writing – teachers turn to other materials, such as videos, software, and books. Then the materials have to fit as far as possible with the goals, principles, content, and weighting that we have already decided on. It just won't work, for example, to decide that a process approach to writing will help our students with fluency and discovery of ideas and language, and then to use a book full of sentence-level grammar exercises with a few controlled compositions thrown in.

Before selecting a book, either as an individual or as a committee, it is advisable to take a section or a task or two and work through it to see what is asked for and what assumptions the author makes, because sometimes authors make claims on which they do not follow through. If you decide to use an ESL writing textbook and not books and articles written for authentic purposes, I would suggest looking for the following seven features:

1. *Topics.* Will they engage the students' interests? What are they based on – experience, materials in the book such as readings and pictures, activities and inquiries beyond the classroom, or out-of-the-blue random topics? Are the topics culturally appropriate for your students? Is the content relevant and engaging?
2. *Types of writing.* Are the students writing essays, letters, or paragraphs? Is that what they need to be writing?
3. *Opportunities for and instruction in methods of generating ideas.* Which of the following are included: brainstorming, free writing, listing, mapping, outlining? Which are appropriate for your students?
4. *Instruction on principles of rhetorical organization.* What information is provided to help students organize various types of writing – letters, description, narration,

exposition, and argument, for example – and which types do your students need to practice?

5. *Opportunities for collaboration.* Is group work a part of the activities? If so, how are collaborative activities viewed in your culture?
6. *Opportunities for revision.* Are students encouraged and directed to write drafts? Does the book provide instruction on what to do at various stages? Does your curriculum allow for revision of essays?
7. *Instruction in editing and proofreading.* What can students learn from the book about how to edit their own work? What instruction is provided in finding and editing grammatical errors?

Once you have chosen a book, the task is not over. No time to relax. You still have to decide how to use it in the classroom.

Step 7: Preparing Activities and Roles

In planning a lesson or a course, the tendency is for teachers to think about what they will be doing: presenting a lesson on paragraph organization, leading a class discussion on editing a student paper, and so on. One of my graduate students wrote in her journal: "I'm always scared that I'll finish early and I won't know what to do next." What if we turn that around and ask what the students will be doing next? If we are presenting, the students are listening. If we have the right answers to the questions we ask, students become passive pawns in a guessing game.

There is a lot of theoretical talk about student-centered classrooms, and teachers can find out what that means when they analyze their own classes and their own experience as students. That is why it is important for teachers to be students, too – in their own classrooms, by writing reflective teaching journals, and, wherever possible, in another teacher's classroom. When I took a course in elementary Japanese, the thing that frustrated me more than anything was the various systems for counting: different words for counting people, or cylindrical objects, or flat ones, or books, and so on. This was a result of the instructor's adopting what Paulo Freire (1988) calls the "banking" concept of education: depositing knowledge in the learners' heads. But this head was not ready for it, and in fact actively rejected it. I could not understand why I was not learning the one most useful system that would help me more than any other. Once resistance sets in, it is all over. We have to make sure that we do not try to bank too much in our students' brains all at once. It helps if we think about what students will be doing and learning in the classroom rather than the comprehensiveness of the information we will be imparting.

Step 8: Choosing Types and Methods of Feedback

Here each teacher has a lot of decisions to make: Will anyone respond, and if so, who? What will be the method and type of response – and what do I have time for? What is the purpose of my response?

First, in the case of large classes, not every piece of writing has to be corrected or even seen by the teacher. Students can do journal writing, response logs to reading, or free writing in which the aim is to generate ideas, and so increase fluency rather than accuracy. This writing can be for the student's eyes only, or students can read each other's work, with clear guidelines from the teacher about what to look for – not for accuracy, but for a response as a reader. If the teacher is to read the writing, the possible roles can be specified and distinguished: general reader, helper, copy editor, or examiner. Then the teacher will not have to look for and comment on everything all at once, in one draft.

Second, whoever responds has a variety of physical methods of responding: a comment to or a conversation with the writer; an interlinear response with computer software, using such features as the "Comment" capability and redlining; an audiotaped response; or a written response. If you choose a written response, you can write a note to the student on a separate sheet of paper or on adhesive "Post-it notes"; you can write comments on the page; you can use an analytical checklist, or guidelines. But students have to understand what you are doing and why, and what you are *not* doing and why – and also what you will do on a later draft.

Third, you have to select the type of response you prefer to give, with time and class size being important factors in the decision. Some teachers do the following:

- They evaluate by giving a grade.
- They locate, indicate the nature of, and/or correct the student's errors.
- They make suggestions for changes: "I think you need to rewrite the sentence about your boss so that we understand his point of view more clearly."
- They reflect – and subtly correct as they do so: "I'm not surprised that your grandmother felt upset." (The student had actually written: "My grandmother *feeling* upset.")
- They rewrite passages: "I am easy to change a fuse." → "Changing a fuse is easy."
- They comment on strategies: "It might be useful to define the term *success*."
- They ask questions: "Where was your grandmother born?"
- They emote: "What a terrible experience!" "I feel this way, too."
- They criticize: "The conclusion is weak. It introduces new points."
- They describe: "You start out by mentioning four ways in which language learning is beneficial. Then you provide two specific examples."
- (less frequently) They praise: "The paragraph about your aunt's language learning experience makes its point very strongly through the story you tell."
  I used to type up student sentences with errors in them for the whole class to edit. Now, to emphasize the positive, I type up those that work well and we discuss these "winners."

Fourth, you and your students need to agree on the purpose of the response. The key question here is: What are the students supposed to do next? Does the feedback help them do that? If we fail to make our expectations clear, we have only ourselves to blame if the students cast a mere cursory glance at all our hard work and file it in the circular file.

Step 9: Evaluating the Course

Teachers use sentence tests and essay tests to evaluate students' progress. They use the results of these tests in addition to questionnaires and their own reflective logs to evaluate their own success as teachers. One form of evaluation that is becoming increasingly popular in writing courses actually helps to combine student evaluation and course evalution: the use of portfolios. All semester students work on multiple drafts of their writing, which are guided by their instructor but not graded. At the end, they select three or four specified types of writing to include in the portfolio, both in-class writing and revised work. They write a cover letter assessing their work and their progress and what they have learned in the course. The portfolio is then evaluated by another instructor in the program, who assigns a grade. So the original instructor is coach, not evaluator. These portfolios lead students to want to revise, to present their best work. They also provide a valuable ongoing teacher-training tool, since teachers continually discuss appropriate assignments and the qualities of acceptable and good writing. They also see what colleagues assign and how they respond to student writing – a salutary lesson.

Probably, enough problematic considerations about planning a writing course have been presented to give you food for thought for a while. But let's round off our steps with one last, vital step.

Step 10: Reflecting the Teacher's Experience

Goals, theories, content, focus, syllabus, materials, activities, feedback, and course evaluation are substantive matters that we have to address whenever we design a writing course, but they pale into insignificance beside one thing: ourselves and our experience. In fact, we should begin – not end – with that. Teachers do not always consider themselves researchers. But any teacher who ponders why one class or activity works and another does not, any teacher who tests out a new approach and notes its effects, is a researcher, theorist, and practitioner – a busy person. We need to have confidence in what is called variously "the wisdom of practice" (Shulman, 1987, p. 11) or "a teacher's sense of plausibility about teaching" (Prabhu, 1990, p. 172). The best way for a teacher to record this sense of plausibility and analyze it is, of course, through writing. A key component of any teacher-training course should therefore be a massive amount of writing: reflective teaching logs, reports, essays, research papers, and responses to other teachers' and students' writing, with the hope that teachers in writing courses will then write along with their students and present their own writing for discussion. That way, we will keep in the forefront what we and our students learn and experience as we work together, and we will let that set the framework for the other nine steps in planning a writing course.

References

Benesch, S. (1993). ESL, ideology, and the politics of pragmatism. *TESOL Quarterly, 27*, 705–717.

Canagarajah, A. S. (1993). Critical ethnography of a Sri Lankan classroom: Ambiguities in student opposition to reproduction through *ESOL. TESOL Quarterly, 27*(4) 601–626.

Freire, P. (1988). *Pedagogy of the oppressed*. Trans. M. B. Ramos. New York: Continuum.

McKay, S. L. (1993). Examining L2 composition ideology: A look at literacy education. *Journal of Second Language Writing, 3*, 65–81.

Prabhu, N. S. (1990). There is no best method – why? *TESOL Quarterly, 24*, 161–176.

Reid, J. M. (1993). *Teaching ESL writing*. Englewood Cliffs, NJ: Regents/Prentice Hall.

Richards, J. C. (1990). *The language teaching matrix*. Cambridge: Cambridge University Press.

Santos, T. (1992). Ideology in composition: L1 and ESL. *Journal of Second Language Writing, 1*, 1–15.

Severino, C. (1993). The sociopolitical implications of response to second language and second dialect Writing. *Journal of Second Language Writing, 2*, 181–201.

Shen, F. (1989). The classroom and the wider culture: Identity as a key to learning English composition. *College Composition and Communication, 40*, 459–465.

Shulman, L. S. (1987). Knowledge and teaching: Foundations of the new reform. *Harvard Educational Review, 57*, 1–22.

CHAPTER 30

The Writing Process and Process Writing

Anthony Seow

Introduction

The writing process as a private activity may be broadly seen as comprising four main stages: planning, drafting, revising and editing. As depicted in Figure 1, the stages are neither sequential nor orderly. In fact, as research has suggested, 'many good writers employ a recursive, non-linear approach – writing of a draft may be interrupted by more planning, and revision may lead to reformulation, with a great deal of recycling to earlier stages' (Krashen, 1984, p. 17).

Process Writing

The term *process writing* has been bandied about for quite a while in ESL classrooms. It is no more than a *writing process approach* to teaching writing. The idea behind it is not really to dissociate writing entirely from the written product and to merely lead students

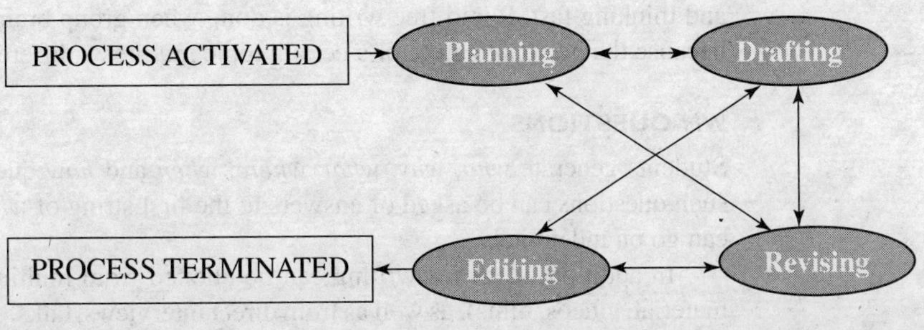

Figure 1 The Writing Process

through the various stages of the writing process but 'to construct process-oriented writing instruction that will affect performance' (Freedman, Dyson, Flower, & Chafe, 1987, p. 13). To have an effective performance-oriented teaching programme would mean that we need to systematically teach students problem-solving skills connected with the writing process that will enable them to realise specific goals at each stage of the composing process. Thus, process writing in the classroom may be construed as a programme of instruction which provides students with a series of planned learning experiences to help them understand the nature of writing at every point.

Process writing as a classroom activity incorporates the four basic writing stages – planning, drafting (writing), revising (redrafting) and editing – and three other stages externally imposed on students by the teacher, namely, responding (sharing), evaluating and post-writing. Process writing in the classroom is highly structured as it necessitates the *orderly* teaching of process skills, and thus it may not, at least initially, give way to a free variation of writing stages cited earlier. Teachers often plan appropriate classroom activities that support the learning of specific writing skills at every stage. The planned learning experiences for students may be described as follows.

Planning (Pre-writing)

Pre-writing is any activity in the classroom that encourages students to write. It stimulates thoughts for getting started. In fact, it moves students away from having to face a blank page toward generating tentative ideas and gathering information for writing. The following activities provide the learning experiences for students at this stage:

GROUP BRAINSTORMING

Group members spew out ideas about the topic. Spontaneity is important here. There are no right or wrong answers. Students may cover familiar ground first and then move off to more abstract or wild territories.

CLUSTERING

Students form words related to a stimulus supplied by the teacher. The words are circled and then linked by lines to show discernible clusters. Clustering is a simple yet powerful strategy: "Its visual character seems to stimulate the flow of association . . . and is particularly good for students who know what they want to say but just can't say it" (Proett & Gill, 1986, p. 6).

RAPID FREE WRITING

Within a limited time of 1 or 2 minutes, individual students freely and quickly write down single words and phrases about a topic. The time limit keeps the writers' minds ticking and thinking fast. Rapid free writing is done when group brainstorming is not possible or because the personal nature of a certain topic requires a different strategy.

WH-QUESTIONS

Students generate *who*, *why*, *what*, *where*, *when* and *how* questions about a topic. More such questions can be asked of answers to the first string of *wh*-questions, and so on. This can go on indefinitely.

In addition, ideas for writing can be elicited from multimedia sources (e.g., printed material, videos, films), as well as from direct interviews, talks, surveys, and questionnaires.

Students will be more motivated to write when given a variety of means for gathering information during pre-writing.

DRAFTING

Once sufficient ideas are gathered at the planning stage, the first attempt at writing – that is, drafting – may proceed quickly. At the drafting stage, the writers are focused on the fluency of writing and are not preoccupied with grammatical accuracy or the neatness of the draft. One dimension of good writing is the writer's ability to visualise an audience. Although writing in the classroom is almost always for the teacher, the students may also be encouraged to write for different audiences, among whom are peers, other classmates, pen-friends and family members. A conscious sense of audience can dictate a certain style to be used. Students should also have in mind a central idea that they want to communicate to the audience in order to give direction to their writing.

Depending on the genre of writing (narrative, expository or argumentative), an introduction to the subject of writing may be a *startling statement* to arrest the reader's attention, a *short summary* of the rest of the writing, an *apt quotation*, a *provocative question*, a *general statement*, an *analogy*, a *statement of purpose*, and so on. Such a strategy may provide the lead at the drafting stage. Once a start is made, the writing task is simplified 'as the writers let go and disappear into the act of writing' (D'Aoust, 1986, p. 7).

RESPONDING

Responding to student writing by the teacher (or by peers) has a central role to play in the successful implementation of process writing. Responding intervenes between drafting and revising. It is the teacher's *quick initial reaction* to students' drafts. Response can be oral or in writing, after the students have produced the first draft and just before they proceed to revise. The failure of many writing programmes in schools today may be ascribed to the fact that responding is done in the final stage when the teacher simultaneously *responds* and *evaluates*, and even *edits* students' finished texts, thus giving students the impression that nothing more needs to be done.

Text-specific responses in the form of helpful suggestions and questions rather than 'rubber-stamped' comments (such as 'organisation is OK', 'ideas are too vague' etc.) by the teacher will help students rediscover meanings and facilitate the revision of initial drafts. Such responses may be provided in the margin, between sentence lines or at the end of students' texts. Peer responding can be effectively carried out by having students respond to each other's texts in small groups or in pairs, with the aid of the checklist in Table 1 (adapted from Reinking & Hart, 1991).

REVISING

When students revise, they review their texts on the basis of the feedback given in the responding stage. They reexamine what was written to see how effectively they have communicated their meanings to the reader. Revising is not merely checking for language errors (i.e., editing). It is done to improve global content and the organisation of ideas so that the writer's intent is made clearer to the reader.

TABLE 1. PEER RESPONDING CHECKLIST

When responding to your peer's draft, ask yourself these questions:
What is the greatest strength of this composition?
What is its greatest weakness?
What is the central idea of this composition?
Which are the ideas which need more elaboration?
Where should more details or examples be added? Why?
What are some of the questions that the writer has not answered?
At which point does this composition fail to hold the reader's interest? Why?
Where is the organisation confusing?
Where is the writing unclear or vague?

To ensure that rewriting does not mean recopying, Beck (1986, p. 149) suggests that the teacher collect and keep the students' drafts and ask them for rewrites. 'When the students are forced to act without their original drafts, they become more familiar with their purposes and their unique messages. ... The writers move more ably within their topics, and their writing develops tones of confidence and authority'.

Another activity for revising may have the students working in pairs to read aloud each other's drafts before they revise. As students listen intently to their own writing, they are brought to a more conscious level of rethinking and reseeing what they have written. Meanings which are vague become more apparent when the writers actually hear their own texts read out to them. Revision often becomes more voluntary and motivating. An alternative to this would be to have individual students read their own texts into a tape recorder and take a dictation of their own writing later. Students can replay the tape as often as necessary and activate the pause button at points where they need to make productive revision of their texts.

Editing

At this stage, students are engaged in tidying up their texts as they prepare the final draft for evaluation by the teacher. They edit their own or their peer's work for grammar, spelling, punctuation, diction, sentence structure and accuracy of supportive textual material such as quotations, examples and the like. Formal editing is deferred till this phase in order that its application not disrupt the free flow of ideas during the drafting and revising stages.

A simple checklist might be issued to students to alert them to some of the common surface errors found in students' writing. For instance:

- Have you used your verbs in the correct tense?
- Are the verb forms correct?
- Have you checked for subject–verb agreement?
- Have you used the correct prepositions?
- Have you left out the articles where they are required?
- Have you used all your pronouns correctly?

- Is your choice of adjectives and adverbs appropriate?
- Have you written in complete sentences?

The students are, however, not always expected to know where and how to correct every error, but editing to the best of their ability should be done as a matter of course, prior to submitting their work for evaluation each time. Editing within process writing is meaningful because students can see the connection between such an exercise and their own writing in that correction is not done for its own sake but as part of the process of making communication as clear and unambiguous as possible to an audience.

Evaluating

Very often, teachers pleading lack of time have compressed responding, editing and evaluating all into one. This would, in effect, deprive students of that vital link between drafting and revision – that is, responding – which often makes a big difference to the kind of writing that will eventually be produced.

In evaluating student writing, the scoring may be analytical (i.e., based on specific aspects of writing ability) or holistic (i.e., based on a global interpretation of the effectiveness of that piece of writing). In order to be effective, the criteria for evaluation should be made known to students in advance. They should include overall interpretation of the task, sense of audience, relevance, development and organisation of ideas, format or layout, grammar and structure, spelling and punctuation, range and appropriateness of vocabulary, and clarity of communication. Depending on the purpose of evaluation, a numerical score or grade may be assigned.

Students may be encouraged to evaluate their own and each other's texts once they have been properly taught how to do it. In this way, they are made to be more responsible for their own writing.

Post-writing

Post-writing constitutes any classroom activity that the teacher and students can do with the completed pieces of writing. This includes publishing, sharing, reading aloud, transforming texts for stage performances, or merely displaying texts on notice-boards. The post-writing stage is a platform for recognising students' work as important and worthwhile. It may be used as a motivation for writing as well as to hedge against students finding excuses for not writing. Students must be made to feel that they are writing for a very real purpose.

Implementing Process Writing

Here are some pointers which teachers may like to take note of when implementing process writing:

Teacher Modelling

Teachers should model the writing process at every stage and teach specific writing strategies to students through meaningful classroom activities.

RELATING PROCESS TO PRODUCT

A first draft looks quite unlike another draft that has gone through several revisions. It is vital that as students go through the various stages of writing, they understand what kind of product is expected at each stage. Thus students need to be guided to set and achieve specific writing goals at every stage.

WORKING WITHIN INSTITUTIONAL CONSTRAINTS

It is possible to teach some process skills appropriate to a writing stage, be it planning, drafting, responding, revising or editing within a regular two-period composition lesson. The teaching of the same process skill could be repeated in subsequent composition lessons. Process skills can be systematically taught each time until the entire series of such skills is developed over a period of time.

CATERING TO DIVERSE STUDENT NEEDS

The teacher should implement a flexible programme to cater to different student needs. The teacher will need to know what the individual student knows and work from there. The teacher may also decide to have students enter into different writing groups as planners, drafters, responders, revisers or editors during a writing session. A student may be with the planners for one writing task, but move to be with the editors later for the same or another task, according to his or her need or developmental stage in writing.

EXPLOITING THE USE OF COMPUTERS IN PROCESS WRITING

Many word-processing programmes are user-friendly enough for students to handle. Their direct application to process writing, especially for the purposes of drafting, revising and editing, is rewarding for both the teacher and the students. The teacher can teach responding or editing skills via the computer hooked on to an overhead projector. The students can freely make any number of changes to their texts by deleting words or moving them around without having to retype large chunks of text all over again. Any work done can be saved on the computer for revision later.

References

Beck, T. (1986). Two activities that encourage real revision. In *Practical ideas for teaching writing as a process*. Sacramento: California State Department of Education.

D'Aoust, C. (1986). Teaching writing as a process. In *Practical ideas for teaching writing as a process*. Sacramento: California State Department of Education.

Freedman, Dyson, Flower, & Chafe, (1987). *Research in writing: Past, present and future*. Berkeley: University of California Press.

Krashen, S. D. (1984). *Writing: Research, theory and applications*. Oxford: Pergamon Institute of English.

Proett, J., & Gill, K. (1986). *The writing process in action: A handbook for teachers*. Urbana, IL: National Council of Teachers of English.

Reinking, J. A., & Hart, A. W. (1991). *Strategies for successful writing*. 2nd ed. Englewood Cliffs, NJ: Prentice Hall.

CHAPTER 31

A Genre-Based Approach to Content Writing Instruction

Randi Reppen

INTRODUCTION

Just as students learn to control different oral registers, they must also be able to write in different ways for different purposes. Writing research has shown that students need to be exposed to and have practice with various genres in addition to narrative writing (e.g., Bereiter & Scardamalia, 1987; Langer, 1986; Martin, 1989; Perera, 1984). This is important for English L1 students and crucial for English L2 learners. Simply allowing students to write a lot will not necessarily provide sufficient practice in the types of writing valued for academic learning.

Since the 1980s, researchers have been looking at the use of written language in elementary school classrooms. This research goes beyond merely describing the situations and features to proposing strategies that may enhance student performance in various situations. Other researchers (Christie, 1992; Martin, 1989) have argued for the importance of language form and structure as an integral part of meaningful language use, a view that is being seen as increasingly more important for academic L2 contexts. Poynton (1986), for example, explored the types of writing elementary grade students do and highlights the importance of helping students to realize the different purposes of writing. This metalinguistic awareness empowers students and gives them tools to manipulate information and accomplish different purposes through writing.

This focus has been a response to the occasional excesses of a process approach to writing instruction. An emphasis on a process approach often disregards the importance of written form and, in effect, takes power away from learners, particularly those from different language or culture backgrounds. For the L2 student, many writing conventions will remain a mystery unless teachers are able to bring these forms and patterns of language use to conscious awareness. Emphasizing the process to the exclusion of the product neglects direct instruction in certain text features, yet students are still evaluated by their control of these features (e.g., text organization, sentence structure). By providing students with the language to talk about texts, they can better understand how to make a piece of writing more effective and appropriate to the communicative purpose. This helps students increase their writing skills and become more effective during peer editing and revision.

In response to these concerns, I developed an ESL instructional unit that cycles content material through different writing tasks, combining writing process approaches, and integrating language arts skills activities with specific content material and direct instruction on different genre forms. This unit combines a functional approach to language with the current emphasis on content-centered instruction.

I wanted to see if it was possible to increase content knowledge while giving students practice with school-valued ways of writing. The lessons are based on two concepts. The first involves scaffolding or apprenticeship. The teacher occupies a central role in the scaffolding process and must be familiar with the learning situation, the material that is being presented, and the specific features associated with the writing students are going to produce, and must be able to guide students to help them accomplish the goal. Students practice with models to accomplish a task. As the students gain greater control, the teacher's role diminishes. Students are expected to progress from the role of active observers to autonomous learners.

The second concept focuses on increasing student awareness of how different ways of organizing information in writing interact with the purpose of the text. This is an important step in helping students become more successful writers. By discussing features of different text types, students learn the language needed to talk about texts, begin to understand how and why texts are organized in certain ways, and are able to evaluate their own writing and participate in peer editing sessions more effectively.

The Study

The Setting and the Students

I piloted the unit in a fifth-grade public school classroom in a small city in Arizona. The average socioeconomic level at this school is low, with more than 85% of the students participating in the federally funded free lunch program.

In this school, minority students are the majority. The student population consists of Native Americans, Hispanics, and European Americans fairly evenly mixed in each class throughout the school. There are also many students who speak English as a second language. Of the twenty students participating in the study, six were limited English speakers who participated in a half-day ESL pullout program and at least half of the remaining students were from homes where English is a second language.

The Unit

I selected a regular social studies unit on explorers as the content material for this pilot unit. The time period for the pilot was the same as would normally have been spent covering the unit – 5 weeks with three to four 45-minute periods of instruction per week.

During this unit, six explorers were highlighted and viewed from different genre perspectives. The content information was organized so that there would be a progression of genre forms during the 5-week period.

Each section of the unit followed a similar pattern of instruction. In this way, students became familiar, with the format and could focus their attention on the information presented. Class sessions began with a brief review of content and genre information covered in previous lessons. New information was introduced by relating it to previous material or concrete examples familiar to the students. I first modeled new patterns of writing for students to practice as a class and in small groups before working independently.

The progression of the genre forms in writing instruction during the 5-week period was narrative descriptive, persuasive, and expository (see Table 1). The rationale behind this order was twofold: to progress from the genre that students appeared to be most familiar with to the least familiar, and to follow a content-driven framework for introducing material. I presented the instructional sequence of content material to students as follows: After the explorers returned, they would have told these stories (narrative). Second, they would have given detailed descriptions of the places and people that they had seen (descriptive). Explorers would have had to persuade crew members to accompany them, and royalty or other affluent people to fund their expeditions (persuasive). Finally, explorers would have had to provide reports about their explorations (expository). Because students are sometimes expected to present reports at the end of a content unit, this seemed the appropriate genre with which to end the explorer unit.

Throughout the unit, I introduced each genre through the content material by posing questions that highlighted different aspects of various explorers. We discussed particular attributes of each genre and compared and contrasted genre characteristics. For example, students compared the verbs used in narrative, descriptive, and persuasive texts and realized that the action verbs used in narratives (e.g., *sailed*, *conquered*, *explored*) are not found in descriptions, in which *be* and *have* are common, and that the persuasive texts had a lot of emotion verbs (e.g., *think*, *feel*, *know*). Students also recognized that stories usually have an exciting part that descriptions lack.

Students began to realize the importance of framing the beginning of a text rather than just jumping in and so became increasingly aware of the reader's needs. Students also learned that for both descriptive and persuasive texts, it was necessary to view the task from a perspective other than their own. In the descriptive task, students had to consider and recognize features that would help someone visualize an object without seeing it. In the persuasive task, students realized the need to anticipate an argument and generalize reasons that would support their stand. The pre- and post-assessment writing measures reflected the students' heightened awareness of arguments and reasons used in persuasive essays.

In addition to language knowledge, map skills are an important part of social studies knowledge, so map work was a regular part of the unit. Students were constantly referring to their copy of a world map to locate various countries. This was an important part of the unit because maps gave students a sense of the distances traveled by various explorers, and students became familiar with the location of countries and regions of the world. There were discussions about various ways that countries could be categorized into groups (e.g., politically, geographically). At the beginning of this unit, no student could label a country outside the North American continent; most could identify only the United States. By the end of the unit, students were easily able to label the eleven countries featured in the unit (e.g., Italy, Iceland, China). This type of contextualized map work was a natural setting in which to introduce the need for and use of map scales and keys, and also provided practice with locating features through the use of longitude and latitude lines.

Results and Discussion

I used several types of pre- and post-assessment measures to determine changes in student writing, content knowledge, and attitudes. All reflected a positive change. Through a focus on language use and the genre demands of different ways to organize information, students also mastered content material while gaining greater skill with various school-valued ways of writing.

Through personal observation, comments from the regular classroom teacher, and journal entries, I noted that students were enthusiastic about this approach. Social studies was

TABLE 1. UNIT OUTLINE

The outline that follows presents an overview of the four genres that were highlighted in the 5-week unit on explorers through a variety of talks, reading, and other media.

I. Genre: Narrative (1 week)
   A. Explorers
      1. Ponce de León
      2. Christopher Columbus
      3. Vikings
         a. Eric the Red
         b. Leif Ericson
         c. Bjarni Herjolfsson
   B. Activities
      1. Students read a one-page story about Ponce de León. After reading the text, students are asked to
         a. underline the first time the main character appears
         b. put a box around the location of the story
         c. underline what the explorers were in search of
         d. put a line in the margin by the exciting portion of the story
      2. Students discuss the location and purpose of these narrative features in story text.
      3. Students write a story and locate Features a–d listed above in Number 1 in their stories. Then students compare the location of these various features in the text that they wrote with the text that they read.
   C. Map work: Locating countries of explorers and exploration

II. Genre: Descriptive ($1\frac{1}{2}$ weeks)
   A. Explorers
      1. Vikings
      2. Hernán Cortés
      3. Marco Polo
      4. John Wesley Powell
   B. Activities
      1. Joint text construction on the overhead projector of a description of a cactus. Teacher and students brainstorm features prior to writing the text. The need for a general topic sentence is discussed.
      2. The cactus text is compared and contrasted to the Ponce de León text. Verb types are discussed. Students become aware of the action verbs associated with the narrative in contrast to the static verbs (e.g., *be*, *have*) of the descriptive text. Students also become aware that both texts – narrative and descriptive – need an introduction or some type of initial framing to orient the reader.
      3. Students construct group texts at four poster centers depicting sights from four areas explored by the featured explorers, The posters show scenes from China, Mexico (Aztec), the Grand Canyon, and Greenland and Iceland. In addition to scenes from the area, each poster has a map of the world with that region highlighted. Students work in groups to construct a descriptive text at

TABLE 1. (Continued)

each of the four poster centers. For each poster, students also complete a sheet that identifies the country of exploration, the explorer, and the explorer's countery of origin.

4. Students then select one center that they develop into an individual descriptive text.

C. Map work: Locating countries of explorers and exploration

III. Genre: Persuasive ($1\frac{1}{2}$ weeks)

A. Explorers
1. Marco Polo
2. John Wesley Powell
3. Christopher Columbus

B. Activities
1. Oral discussion of persuasive strategies. Different types of reasons used in persuasion are discussed and related to the influence of the audience on the reasons selected. Students become aware of the need to see things from someone else's perspective in order to construct a strong argument.
2. Group work: Working in pairs, students assume the role of an explorer and try to persuade their partner of their point of view (e.g., go on an expedition, found an expedition, explore an area).
3. Joint text construction: On an overhead projector, students write a persuasive text representing an explorer's attempt to persuade royalty to fund an expedition.
4. Individual text construction: Students choose either to persuade a crew member to join them on an expedition or to persuade someone to fund their expedition.

IV. Genre: Expository (1 week)

A. Explorers
1. Vikings
2. Ponce de León
3. Marco Polo
4. Hernán Cortés
5. Christopher Columbus
6. John Wesley Powell

B. Activities
1. Various ways of organizing expository texts are discussed. Information about various explorers is brainstormed and recorded on the board according to the following types of report formats:
   a compare/contrast
   b. problem/solution
   c. pros/cons
   d. cause/effect
2. Joint text construction on the overhead projector provides students with an opportunity to practice cause/effect expository writing.

C. Map work: Reviewing all countries related to explorers

one of the least favorite subjects of students in this class. However, after this instructional approach, most of the students commented that they liked social studies. Perhaps some of the appeal was because this approach challenged students and they were aware that they were learning. Students were actively involved in the learning process and used writing to help accomplish tasks. Some students even suggested that this might be a useful way to teach science.

In retrospect, joint text construction on an overhead projector was one of the most beneficial aspects of this study. Through this process, students were made aware of my thoughts as I made informal, think-aloud comments while planning texts for the overhead. This gave students valuable insights into decisions made during text construction and provided them with opportunities and tools to talk about language.

I also discovered that when writing as individuals, students had a strong desire to turn any task into a story. However, as the instructional period progressed, they struggled to overcome this tendency. Students became aware that different tasks demanded different texts. The explicit practice and guided support provided during the instructional period allowed students to be aware of the different ways to construct texts.

The results of my study indicate that this approach may offer ESL students valuable practice in various school-valued ways of writing while they learn content material and work through steps in the writing process. The role of genre in content writing instruction should emerge naturally from the material. Caution should be exercised not to turn genre instruction into a formulaic type of instruction in which students are simply instructed to manipulate certain features. Rather, students must learn to respond to the informational and organizational demands of various settings. Instruction needs to provide a scaffolding so that students can progress toward more academically valued ways of writing, learn content material, and have a better chance to experience success in school.

Acknowledgments

I would like to thank Bill Grabe for his help in shaping this paper and the two anonymous reviewers for their comments. A special thanks to the class that participated in this study.

References

Bereiter, C., & Scardamalia, M. (1987). *The psychology of written composition.* Hillsdale, NJ: Lawrence Erlbaum.

Christie, F. (1992). Literacy in Australia. *Annual Review of Applied Linguistics, 12*, 142–155.

Langer, J. (1986). *Children reading and writing: Structures and strategies*. Norwood, NJ: Ablex.

Martin, J. (1989). *Factual writing: Exploring and challenging social reality.* New York: Oxford University Press.

Perera, K. (1984). *Children writing and reading: Analysing classroom language*. London: Basil Blackwell.

Poynton, C. (1986). Writing in the primary school. In C. Painter & J. Martin (Eds.), *Writing to mean: Teaching genres across the curriculum* (pp. 136–149). Sydney: Applied Linguistics Association of Australia.

Further Reading on Writing Research

Brewer, W. (1980). Literary theory, rhetoric, and stylistics: Implications for psychology. In R. Spiro, B. Bruce, & W. Brewer (Eds.), *Theoretical issues in reading comprehension* (pp. 221–239). Hillsdale, NJ: Lawrence Erlbaum.

Brinton, D., Snow, M., & Wesche, M. (1989). *Content-based second language instruction.* New York: Newbury House.

Bruner, J. (1983). *In search of mind: Essays in autobiography*. New York: Harper.

Bruner, J. (1986). *Actual minds, possible worlds.* Cambridge, MA: Harvard University Press.

Calkins, L. (1983). *Lessons from a child: On the teaching and Learning of writing.* Exeter, NH: Heinemann.

Christie, F. (1989). Language development in education. In R. Hasan & J. Martin (Eds.), *Language development: Learning language and culture* (pp. 152–198). Norwood, NJ: Ablex.

Crowhurst, M. (1990). The development of persuasive/argumentative writing. In R. Beach & S. Hynds (Eds.), *Developing discourse practices in adolescence and adulthood* (pp. 200–223). Norwood, NJ: Ablex.

Delpit, L. (1991). The silenced dialogue: Power and pedagogy in educating other people's children. In M. Minami & B. Kennedy (Eds.), *Language issues in literacy and bilingual/multi-cultural education* (pp. 483–502). Cambridge, MA: Harvard Educational Review.

Derewianka, B. (1990). *Exploring how texts work.* Rozelle, Australia: Primary English Teachers Association (PETA).

Dyson, A. (1989). *Multiple worlds of child writers: Friends learning to write*. New York: Teachers College Press.

Edelsky C. (1986). *Writing in a bilingual program: Había una vez.* Norwood, NJ: Ablex.

Gray, B. (1987). How natural is 'natural' language teaching; Employing wholistic methodology in the classroom. *Australian Journal of Early Childhood, 12*, 3–19.

Hynd, C., & Chase, N. (1991). The relation between text type, tone, and written response. *Journal of Reading Behavior*, 23, 281–303.

Martin, J., & Hasan, R. (1989). *Language development: Learning language, learning culture*. Norwood, NJ: Ablex.

Mohan, B. (1986). *Language and content*. Reading, MA: Addison-Wesley.

Painter, C. (1986). The role of interaction in learning to speak and learning to write. In C. Painter & J. Martin (Eds.), *Occasional paper no. 9. Writing to mean: Teaching genres across the curriculum* (pp. 62–97). Sydney, Australia: Applied Linguistics Association of Australia.

Paris, S., Wasik, B., & Turner, J. (1991). The development of strategic readers. In R. Barr, M. Kamil, P. Mosenthal, & P. Pearson (Eds.), *Handbook of reading research,* (Vol. 2; pp. 609–640). New York: Longman.

Pearson, P., & Fielding, L. (1991). Comprehension instruction. In R. Barr, M. Kamil, P. Mosenthal, & P. Pearson (Eds.), *Handbook of reading research* (Vol. 2; pp. 815–860). New York: Longman.

Reyes, M. (1991a). A process approach to literacy instruction for Spanish-speaking students: In search of a best fit. In E. Hiebert (Ed.), *Literacy for a diverse society* (pp. 157–171). New York: Longman.

Reyes, M. (1991b). Bilingual student writers: A question of fair evaluation. *English Journal*, 80, 16–23.

Teale, W., & Sulzby, E. (Eds.). (1986). *Emergent literacy: Writing and reading*. Norwood, NJ: Ablex.

CHAPTER 32

Teaching Students to Self-Edit

Dana Ferris

INTRODUCTION

Over the past couple of decades, the process approach to teaching writing has greatly improved both L1 and L2 composition pedagogy. However, though students may be much better at invention, organization, and revision than they were before, too many written products are still riddled with grammatical and lexical inaccuracies. No matter how interesting or original a student's ideas are, an excess of sentence- and discourse-level errors may distract and frustrate instructors and other readers. Because this may lead to harsh evaluation of the student's overall writing abilities, ESL writing teachers, in addition to focusing on students' ideas, need to help students develop and improve their editing skills.

In the modern process approach composition classroom, editing refers to finding and correcting grammatical, lexical, and mechanical errors before submitting (or "publishing") a final written product. A number of studies claim that a lack of grammatical accuracy in ESL student writing may impede students' progress in the university at large (Janopolous, 1992; Santos, 1988; Vann, Lorenz, & Meyer, 1991; Vann, Meyer, & Lorenz, 1984). As a university-level ESL writing teacher, I know the high standard of accuracy in student writing that the academic discourse community demands. My students will not succeed outside of the sheltered world of the ESL class unless they can learn to reduce their errors. Because I will not always be there to help my students, it is important that they learn to edit their own work.

As shown by several ESL editing textbooks (Ascher, 1993; Fox, 1992; Lane & Lange, 1993; Raimes, 1992a) and a teacher's reference on responding to ESL writing (Bates, Lane, & Lange, 1993), researchers and teachers of ESL writing have become more aware of the need to help students self-edit their writing (Lane & Lange, 1993, p. xix). In response to this need, I have developed and used a semester-long editing process approach to help advanced ESL writing students become more self-sufficient as editors. The particulars of this approach follow.

Philosophical Assumptions

I based my editing process approach on the following principles:

- Students and teachers should focus on major patterns of error rather than attempt to correct every single error (Bates, Lane, & Lange, 1993).
- Because not all students will make the same errors, it is necessary and desirable to personalize editing instruction as much as possible.
- The errors to focus on should be those that are most frequent, global (interfere with the comprehensibility of the text), and stigmatizing (would cause a negative evaluation from native speakers) (Bates, Lane, & Lange, 1993; Hendrickson, 1980).

The Editing Process

Bates, Lane, and Lange (1993) and Hendrickson (1980) advocate teaching students a discovery approach through which they will become independent self-editors. I teach my advanced ESL students through a three-stage discovery approach to become self-sufficient editors.

Stage 1: Focusing on Form

Although some teachers assume that all ESL students are obsessively concerned with grammar to the detriment of developing and presenting their ideas, I have found that many students have little interest in and pay limited attention to editing their work. They find editing tedious or unimportant or they have become overly dependent on teachers or tutors to correct their work for them. A crucial step in teaching students to become good editors is to convince them of the necessity of doing so.

To raise awareness of the importance of editing, I use in-class activities in which the students look at sentences or short student essays that contain a variety of editing problems. Rather than simply finding and correcting errors, they discuss how these errors impede their understanding of the texts, as in the following three examples:

1. My *parent* always gave me a lot of love.
2. School is the place where I *learn* things such as reading and writing.
3. I like coffee; *on the other hand*, I also like tea.

The italicized portions of these three sentences contain common ESL writing errors: respectively, an omitted plural marker, a verb tense error, and a misused transitional phrase. However, none of the sentences immediately appears ungrammatical – *parent* can be singular; the two verbs in Example 2 are both in present tense and thus appear consistent; and *on the other hand* does signal a clause expressing a different viewpoint from the one preceding it. But once the students look closely at the texts, they can see that the use of *parent* is confusing and nonidiomatic (if you really had only one parent, you would identify him or her as your father or mother), that they learned to read and write a long time ago in school, and that liking coffee is not the opposite of liking tea, as implied by the use of *on the other hand.* Even fairly minor errors can lead to problems in text processing and comprehension.

Another strategy I use to convince the students of the necessity of developing editing skills is to give them a diagnostic essay assignment and then provide them with written feedback about their ideas, detailed information about their editing problems, and an indication of what grade they would receive if still writing at this level at the end of the semester. Giving students an immediate sense of what their final grade could be is motivating, but does not seem to be intimidating if it is made clear that these initial grades are for the students' information only and will not be counted in their final course evaluation.

STAGE 2: RECOGNIZING MAJOR ERROR TYPES

Research indicates that focusing on patterns of error, rather than on individual errors, is most effective for both teachers and students, so at this stage I train students to recognize various types of errors. The categories may vary depending on the students' needs, but they should be selected from error types which are frequent, global, and stigmatizing. I sensitize students to these error patterns by going over the targeted categories, letting them practice identifying them in sample student essays, and then looking for these errors in peer-editing exercises (see Activities 1 and 2). It seems to be true that it is easier to find mistakes in others' work than in one's own. Exercises in recognizing error patterns of other writers' work help students become more aware of similar problems in their own writing. They also help lead students away from the frustrating and even counterproductive notion that they can or should attempt to correct every single error in a given essay draft.

During this stage of the editing process, I may also give brief, focused instruction on major patterns of error if there are particular errors to which most students are prone. For instance, students may be confused about when to use the simple past tense and when to use the present perfect. In-class instruction should deal directly with this difficulty, rather than attempting to give students a complete overview of the English verb tense system or even of the various uses of the present perfect. (See Activity 3, which provides an example of an overview of noun error problems: This activity takes 15–20 minutes.)

Activity 1
Editing: Major Error Categories

Type 1: Nouns

- *Noun endings*
  I need to buy some *book.*
  I gained a lot of *knowledges* in high school.
- *Articles*
  I need to buy ∧ *book.*
  A good *jobs* is hard to find.

Type 2: Verbs

- *Subject-verb agreement*
  The boys *was* hungry.
  That TV show *come* on at 8:00.
  Many students in the class *is* failing.
- *Verb tense*
  Last year I *come* to Sac State.
  I've never been to Disney World, but I *had been* to Disneyland before.
- *Verb form*
  My car *was stole.*
  My mother *is miss* her children.

Type 3: Punctuation and Sentence Structure

- *Sentence fragments*
  Wrong: *After I got home.* I washed the dishes.
  Right: After I got home, I washed the dishes.

- *Comma errors*
  When I got home ∧ I discovered my house was on fire.
  I studied hard for the test ∧ but I still got a bad grade.
  I studied hard for the test, I still got a bad grade.
- *Run-on sentences*
  I studied hard for the test I still got a bad grade.
- *Semicolon errors*
  Although I studied hard for the test; I still got a bad grade.
  I studied hard for the test ∧ I still got a bad grade.

Type 4: Word Form Errors

Examples:
My father is very *generosity.*
Intelligent is *importance* for academic success.

Type 5: Preposition Errors

Examples:
I do a lot of work *on* volunteer organizations.
For an American, I like baseball and hot dogs.

Editing Worksheet

Instructions: Read the sample essay. First, find all the nouns, and underline any noun errors. Then do the same with verbs, punctuation/sentence structure. word forms, and prepositions. Count the errors of each type and fill in the worksheet below. Turn in both your marked essay and this worksheet.

Type 1: Noun Errors

Total number of noun errors in essay: _____
Write one example from the essay. Underline the error.

Type 2: Verb Errors

Total number of verb errors in essay: _____
Write one example from the essay. Underline the error.

Type 3: Punctuation and Sentence Structure

Total number of punctuation errors in essay: _____
Write one example from the essay. Underline the error.

Type 4: Word Forms

Total number of word-form errors in essay: _____
Write one example from the essay. Underline the error.

Type 5: Prepositions

Total number of preposition errors in essay: _____
Write one example from the essay. Underline the error.

Note: The categories for this activity were taken from Fox, 1992.

An alternative to whole-class instruction is to individualize editing instruction with an editing handbook (e.g., Ascher, 1993; Fox, 1992; Lane & Lange, 1993; Raimes, 1992b). A handbook is distinct from an ESL text, which attempts to provide comprehensive coverage of grammatical concepts, as opposed to focusing on specific writing problems students may have. In addition, many ESL writing textbooks include an editing section (e.g., Raimes,

1992a; Spack, 1990). When using an editing handbook, I give students homework assignments that correspond to their particular area(s) of need as shown in their essay drafts.

Activity 2

Peer-/Self-Editing Workshop

Your Name: ______________________

Writer's Name: ______________________

Instructions: Read your partner's second essay, looking specifically for errors in grammar, spelling, and punctuation. Mark the paper using the following symbols:

- If there is a spelling error, circle it.
- If there is a grammar error, underline the word or phrase that has the problem.
- If there is a missing word, put a ∧ to show that something is missing.

After you have read and marked the essay, complete the worksheet below.

Error Types

Type 1 (Noun Errors)
Total number found in essay: ____
Example (from essay): ______________________

Type 2 (Verb Errors)
Total number found in essay: ____
Example (from essay): ______________________

Type 3 (Punctuation and Sentence Structure Errors)
Total number found in essay: ____
Example (from essay): ______________________

Type 4 (Word Form Errors)
Total number found in essay: ____
Example (from essay): ______________________

Type 5 (Preposition errors)
Total number found in essay: ____
Example (from essay): ______________________

STAGE 3: SELF-EDITING PRACTICE

In the final phase, I require students to find and correct errors in their own and other students' essay drafts (see Activity 2). Also, throughout the semester, students keep a log of their error frequencies in the different categories so they can observe their progress. As the semester progresses and the students get more and more editing practice, I gradually decrease the amount of editing feedback I provide and turn the editing task over first to peer editors and then to the writers themselves.

Activity 3

Grammar Focus: Nouns

I. Definitions: A noun is a word that names a person, place, object, idea, emotion, or quantity.

Nouns may be concrete: physical, can be touched, seen, felt, etc. (book, table, gas).

Nouns may be abstract: nonphysical (friendship, sadness, hope).

Both concrete and abstract nouns can be classified into two types:

- count nouns: may be counted (apples, students, chairs)
- noncount nouns: are not counted (money, coffee, happiness)

II. Noun trouble spots for ESL writers

A. Plural nouns must have plural markers:

1. English teachers are good spellers.
2. One of the ways to improve your spelling is to study hard.

B. Subject nouns must agree in number with their verbs.

1. *One* of the reasons I came here *is* to study English.
2. *People* who emigrate to the United States *are* usually very happy.
3. English *teachers are* good spellers.

C. *Singular count nouns must* be preceded by a determiner (*a/an*, *the*, *some*, *my*, *this*, *that*, *one*, etc.).

1. I have *a friend*.
2. My friend owns *a car*.
3. *The car* is old.
4. She bought *her car a long time ago*.
5. *Some people* think she should get *a new car*.
6. *These people* have more money than she does.

Exercises: Find and Correct the Noun Errors.

1. One of the way teacher helps her students is to talk to them outside of class.
2. Teacher in general are very hardworking.
3. This is the reason that many people don't want to become teacher.
4. Each of the students is important to a good teacher.
5. Student should come to class every day and always do homework.
6. Students should treat their teacher with respect at all time.
7. Student who come to United States have to learn English.
8. Students is very nervous.
9. A teacher who gives a lot of high grade is good teacher.
10. All of student should give presents to their teacher at the end of the semester.

Does This Editing Approach Work?

I have developed the various components of this approach over several years. In order to assess its effectiveness, I undertook two small research projects (Ferris, 1994). The first showed that nearly all students analyzed (twenty-eight to thirty) made significant progress in reducing their percentages of errors in five error categories over the course of a semester.

However, their degree of improvement varied across error types, essay topics, and writing context (in or out of class). As a result, I modified my instructional approach to editing during the following semester to allow for a more individualized treatment of student editing problems. Specifically, I gave the students individual editing assignments from a text (Fox, 1992) when each essay draft was returned, rather than providing in-class grammar-focus presentations. Research on the effects of this change is ongoing, but preliminary results indicate that student improvement was even greater than with the prior approach.

Editing is an aspect of the writing process which has been somewhat neglected by ESL writing teachers and researchers. With the introduction of new techniques and tools (such as editing handbooks) to help students edit better (and research and teacher-training books to support these efforts), working on students' sentence-level needs is likely to become a more successful and satisfying enterprise than it has been. Although we should not return to the excesses of previous generations (attempting to mark and eradicate every single error student writers make), our goal should be to have our students become skillful independent editors who can function beyond the ESL writing class.

References

Ascher. A. (1993). *Think about editing*. Boston, MA: Heinle & Heinle.

Bates, L., Lane, J., & Lange, E. (1993). *Writing clearly: Responding to ESL compositions.* Boston, MA: Heinle & Heinle.

Ferris, D. (1994). Can advanced ESL students be taught to recognize and correct their most most frequent and serious errors? Unpublished manuscript, California State University, Sacramento.

Fox, L. (1992). *Focus on editing*. London: Longman.

Hendrickson, J. (1980). Error correction in foreign language teaching: Recent theory, research, and practice. In K. Croft (Ed.), *Readings on English as a second language* (pp. 153–173). Boston, MA: Little, Brown.

Janopolous, M. (1992). University faculty tolerance of NS and NNS writing errors. *Journal of Second Language Writing, 1*, 109–122.

Lane, J., & Lange, E. (1993). *Writing clearly: An editing guide*. Boston, MA: Heinle & Heinle.

Raimes, A. (1992a). *Exploring through writing: A process approach to ESL composition.* 2nd ed. New York: St. Martin's Press.

Raimes, A. (1992b). *Grammar troublespots*. New York: St. Martin's Press.

Santos, T. (1988). Professors' reactions to the academic writing of nonnative-speaking students. *TESOL Quarterly, 22*, 69–90.

Spack, R. (1990). *Guidelines.* New York: St. Martin's Press.

Vann, R., Lorenz, F., & Meyer, D. (1991). Error gravity: Faculty response to errors in written discourse of nonnative speakers of English. In L. Hamp-Lyons (Ed.), *Assessing second language writing in academic contexts* (pp. 181–195). Norwood, NJ: Ablex.

Vann, R., Meyer, D., & Lorenz, F. (1984). Error gravity: A study of faculty opinion of ESL errors. *TESOL Quarterly, 18*, 427–440.

SECTION 14

ASSESSMENT

INTRODUCTION

In recent years, there has been a growing interest in the application of assessment procedures that are radically different from traditional forms of assessment. More authentic forms of assessment, such as portfolios, interviews, journals, project work, and self- or peer assessment have become increasingly common in the ESL classroom. These forms of assessment are more student-centered in that, in addition to being an assessment tool, they provide students with a tool to be more involved in their learning, and give them a better sense of control for their own learning. Also, authentic assessment procedures (more popularly known as alternative assessment in some quarters) provide teachers with useful information that can form the basis for improving their instructional plans and practices.

Interest in the use of nontraditional forms of assessment in the classroom reflects the changing paradigm in education in general and in second language teaching in particular. The old paradigm is slowly giving way to a new one, as exemplified below:

Old Paradigm	*New Paradigm*
1. Focus on language	1. Focus on communication
2. Teacher-centered	2. Learner-centered
3. Isolated skills	3. Integrated skills
4. Emphasis on product	4. Emphasis on process
5. One answer, one-way correctness	5. Open-ended, multiple solutions
6. Tests that test	6. Tests that also teach

The first two papers in this section examine authentic or alternative assessment procedures in terms of both theory and practice. The first paper, by Huerta-Macías, begins by asking a valid question: How can we assess our students in a way that consistently reflects their true ability in the second language? Although traditional forms of assessment can provide psychometrically valid measures of students' performance, they often fail to provide the kind of information that the typical classroom teachers are interested in, namely, what the students *can* do in their second language. Because of this, an alternative to the traditional forms of assessment has been proposed in recent years. This has come to be termed *alternative assessment*, *authentic assessment*, or *informal assessment*. This new form of assessment focuses more on measuring learners' ability to use language holistically in real-life situations and is typically carried out continuously over a period of time. In this way, a more accurate picture of students' language profile can be obtained. In her paper, Huerta-Macías describes alternative assessment procedures, addresses key issues related to validity, reliability, and objectivity, and explores the benefits of alternative assessment in teaching and learning.

Much has been written about how to teach writing, but little has been done in the area of assessment and response to student writing. In the next paper, Peñaflorida discusses a number of alternative assessment procedures that second language teachers can beneficially use in their writing classes. These include portfolio assessment, protocol analysis, learning logs, journal entries, and dialogue journals. Each of these is explored in the context of helping learners become more capable of taking charge of their own learning. Responding to students' written work forms the second part of the paper, in which she describes a variety of techniques of giving feedback on student writing, including self-response, peer feedback, and teacher response.

The third paper, while still considered traditional in nature, reflects the growing awareness among practitioners to make second language assessment more learner-friendly and shows how an oral test can be designed to obtain more accurate information about young learners' oral language ability. Hingle and Linington describe some of the problems teachers and researchers face when designing a speaking test for young second language learners of English and offer suggestions on how these problems can be dealt with.

Discussion Questions

Before Reading

1. Discuss different types of assessment you are familiar with (e.g., multiple choice, true-false). How good are these tests for measuring one's proficiency in the language?
2. How do you evaluate your students' composition? What aspects (e.g., grammar, spelling, content, organization) do you take into account when marking your students' papers?
3. What is the difference between a subjective and an objective test? Which one do you usually use? What are some of the advantages and disadvantages of these two types of test?
4. Do you agree that assessment is the sole responsibility of the teacher? Why or why not?
5. How can you involve students in assessing their learning?
6. How do you assess your students' speaking and listening skills?
7. How do you make sure that your assessment is valid and reliable?
8. Is it better to assess students' language skills separately or holistically? Why?

After Reading

1. According to Huerta-Macías, what are some of the problems associated with the traditional mode of assessment? Do you agree?

2. What is alternative assessment? How is it different from traditional assessment?
3. Have you used alternative assessment? What are the main strengths and weaknesses of alternative assessment?
4. Define the following terms and discuss how one should take them into consideration when designing a test:
   - reliability
   - validity
   - objectivity
5. What does Huerta-Macías mean by "triangulation of data"? Within the constraints of a typical ESL classroom, how can one go about doing it?
6. Review the article by Peñaflorida. How is nontraditional assessment related to the development of learner autonomy?
7. What is portfolio assessment? How is this different from the traditional form of assessing students' composition?
8. Discuss some of the differences between "dialogue journal" and "journal entries." How useful are these tools for assessing students' writing?
9. What are the rationales for including self- and peer response in your assessment?
10. According to Hingle and Linington, what are some of the key problems associated with the assessment of oral skills? Can you add some more problems of your own?
11. Discuss Hingle and Linington's proposal for assessing primary school children's oral proficiency? Do you think the same principles apply to testing older students' oral ability?

CHAPTER 33

Alternative Assessment: Responses to Commonly Asked Questions

Ana Huerta-Macías

INTRODUCTION

I was picking up my fourth-grade daughter after school one afternoon when, as she jumped into the car, she exclaimed, "Mom, I've never in my life had none of the above!" I thought for a moment and then realized what she was talking about – a multiple-choice test. Sure enough, as she continued to talk she expressed her frustration at a science test she had taken that afternoon. The teacher had decided to add the choice of "none of the above" to several of the questions, a choice my daughter had not understood. Never having seen it before on a test, she decided that it meant that she was not to circle any of the choices listed for the questions that offered "none of the above" as a response. Consequently, she failed the test.

This anecdote illustrates one of the problems found in contrived tests – including standardized tests as well as teacher-made tests such as the one my daughter took. In this case, the student knew the concept being tested, but was unfamiliar with the language and format of the test. Thus, her test-taking skills were what was lacking, not her scientific knowledge. Other problems that have been discussed in the literature with relation to traditional, standardized tests include norming on a population unlike the one being tested and cultural and language biases (García & Pearson, 1992, 1994; Wrigley & Guth, 1992). In addition, the testing situation itself often produces anxiety within the student such that she is unable to think clearly. The student may also be facing extenuating circumstances (e.g., personal problems or illness) at the time she is being tested, thus also hampering her performance on the test. The problems associated with traditional testing often mask what the student really knows, or, in the case of ESL, what the student can do in her second language. What, then, are the alternatives? How can we assess a student's acquisition of a second language in a valid and reliable way? Are there alternatives that can be adapted to all levels? In this article, I will offer responses to these questions by *(a)* describing alternative assessment procedures; *(b)* addressing issues related to validity, reliability, and objectivity that are often raised as objections to alternative assessment; and *(c)* discussing the power of alternative assessment to provide knowledge about a student.

Alternative Assessment Procedures

Alternative assessment has been described as an alternative to standardized testing and all of the problems found with such testing. There is no single definition of alternative assessment. Rather, a variety of labels has been used to distinguish it from traditional, standardized testing. García and Pearson (1994) include the following in their review of these labels: performance assessment, authentic assessment, portfolio assessment, informal assessment, situated (or contextualized) assessment, and assessment by exhibition. They also state that alternative assessment consists of all of those "efforts that do not adhere to the traditional criteria of standardization, efficiency, cost-effectiveness, objectivity, and machine scorability" (p. 355).

Alternative assessment is different from traditional testing in that it actually asks students to show what they can do. Students are evaluated on what they integrate and produce rather than on what they are able to recall and reproduce. The main goal of alternative assessment is to "gather evidence about how students are approaching, processing, and completing 'real-life' tasks in a particular domain" (García & Pearson, 1994, p. 357). Most important, alternative assessment provides alternatives to traditional testing in that it *(a)* does not intrude on regular classroom activities; *(b)* reflects the curriculum that is actually being implemented in the classroom; *(c)* provides information on the strengths and weaknesses of each individual student; *(d)* provides multiple indices that can be used to gauge student progress; and *(e)* is more multiculturally sensitive and free of norm, linguistic, and cultural biases found in traditional testing.

Alternative assessment procedures are nonintrusive to the classroom because they do not require a separate block of time to implement them, as do traditional tests. Moreover, the same day-to-day activities that a student is engaged in (e.g., writing, role-playing, group discussion) are the basis for alternative assessment. Thus, little or no change is required in classroom routines and activities to implement alternative assessment. Because alternative assessment is based on the daily classroom activities, it also reflects the curriculum, unlike traditional, standardized tests that often test skills incongruent with classroom practices. Furthermore, because the data collected are based on real-life tasks, alternative assessment provides information on the strengths as well as the weaknesses of a student. A work sample, for instance, may tell an instructor that a student's strong points are with the mechanics of English but that she needs additional work on vocabulary and organization of a written piece. Alternative assessment provides a menu of possibilities, rather than any one single method for assessment. Thus, student growth can be more reliably assessed because information from various sources is included in the process. Finally, alternative assessment procedures are multiculturally sensitive. They are particularly suited for the diverse ESL populations because they are free of those biases found in traditional testing. They are not normed instruments, and they are based on student performance in real-life tasks.

Alternative assessment includes a variety of instruments that can be adapted to varying situations. Because the literature (Anthony, Johnson, Mikelson, & Preece, 1991; Goodman, 1991; Holt, 1994; Navarrete, Wilde, Nelson, Martinez, & Hargett, 1990; Wilde, Del Vecchio, & Gustke, in press) provides ample discussion and illustrations of these procedures, I will only briefly mention them here. Although it is unlikely that any one instrument will fit the needs of a given group of students, the idea is to adopt and/or adapt existing instruments in such a way that they reflect the goals of the class and the activities being implemented in that classroom to meet those goals. Alternative assessment procedures include, for example, the use of checklists of student behaviors or products, journals, reading logs, videos of role-plays, audiotapes of discussions, self-evaluation questionnaires, work samples, and teacher observations or anecdotal records. The instructor and students can collaboratively decide which procedures are to be used for assessment in a given class. Individual students are also often given the responsibility of selecting specific products of their work (published pieces, for instance) on which they will be assessed.

Validity, Reliability, and Objectivity

Objections to alternative assessment are often voiced in terms of *validity*, *reliability*, and *objectivity* – terms that have been most often associated with standardized tests. The following questions focus on these issues (respectively):

- Does the test measure what it is supposed to measure?
- Is the test consistent in its measurement?
- Is the test unbiased? (García & Pearson, 1991)

Proponents of alternative assessment do not suggest that these criteria be overlooked, for any high-quality assessment must adhere to them. Rather, the suggestion is that we apply new words that have been borrowed from the literature on qualitative research. Concerns with validity and reliability of assessment instruments have been addressed in qualitative research through the use of the term *trustworthiness*. An instrument is deemed to be *trustworthy* if it has *credibility* (i.e., truth-value) and *auditability* (i.e., consistency). In other words, does it measure what it is supposed to measure and would the instrument give the same results if replicated (Guba & Lincoln, 1981)?

Kirk and Miller (1986) write that "In the best of worlds, a measuring instrument is so closely linked to the phenomena under observation that it is 'obviously' providing valid data" (p. 22). Alternative assessment represents the best of all worlds in that it looks at actual performance on real-life tasks, such as writing, self-editing, reading, participation in collaborative work, and doing a demonstration in front of a group. The procedures in and of themselves are, therefore, valid. Written work samples and published pieces in an ESL class, for instance, will inform a teacher as to how well the student can write in English. The pieces themselves will serve as evidence of the student's ability to express his or her ideas in writing in an organized fashion, to use appropriate mechanics, transitions, and vocabulary.

What about reliability, or consistency? It follows that if a procedure is valid, then it is reliable in that it will consistently produce the same results if audited or replicated. The probability is very high, for example, that a student's written retelling of a story will share the same, or at least highly similar, characteristics in his or her writing from one week to the next. Two instructors, or even the same instructor who is trained in the use of a holistic evaluation scale, will more than likely find that two pieces, written a week apart by a student, will exhibit similar characteristics. Thus, the rater will assign the same or a similar score on the scale because the descriptors that best fit the two pieces will most probably be the same ones.

Wilde, Del Vecchio, and Gustke (in press) further suggest the following to ensure reliability in alternative assessments:

- Design multiple tasks that lead to the same outcome.
- Use trained judges, working with clear criteria, from specific anchor papers or performance behaviors.
- Monitor periodically to ensure that raters use criteria and standards in a consistent manner.

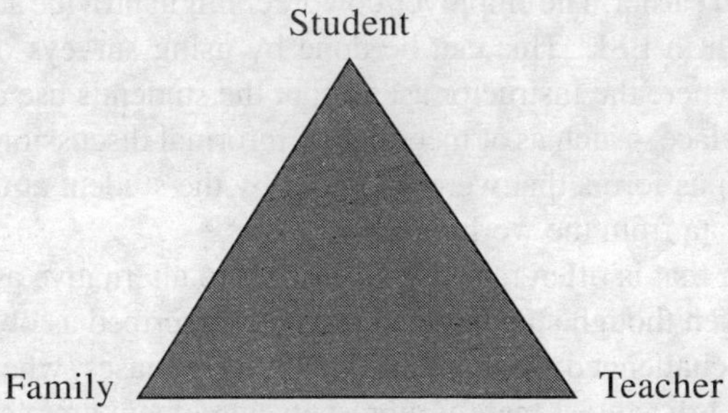

Figure 1 Triangulation of Data: Alternative Assessment for ESL Public School Class

Reliability, or consistency, in qualitative research is often ensured through yet another means, *triangulation*. In qualitative research, triangulation refers to the combination of methodologies to strengthen a study design (Patton, 1987). When applied to alternative assessment, triangulation refers to the collection of data or information from three different sources or perspectives. In the case of an ESL public school class, for instance, a teacher would want to assess students' literacy development in English. In order to do this, she or he could collect data that would paint a picture of each student's growth by describing, for example, the student's *(a)* background, *(b)* use of English (reading, writing, speaking, listening) in academic tasks within the classroom as well as in situations outside the classroom, and *(c)* ability to use literacy behaviors such as inferencing, obtaining meaning from context, and skimming through a text before reading it. In this case, the sources of data might be the parents, the students, and the teacher. Data from the parents might include information gathered through conversations, surveys, or informal interviews on the student's linguistic and cultural background, length of residence in the United States, language(s) spoken at home, language(s) spoken with friends, amount of reading in English, and the native language spoken at home, among other items. From the student, the instructor might put together a portfolio that includes data such as written work samples, audiotapes of the student engaged in conversation, a video of a role-play, a reading log, and self-evaluation sheets. The instructor would then include his or her own perspectives by adding, for instance, observations or anecdotes of events in the class that demonstrate English proficiency, teacher journals, and checklists on performance. (See Figure 1.)

Triangulation can be applied in varying contexts. Consider, for example, an adult workplace literacy class focusing on work-related English that will assist employees to more effectively carry out their duties. Triangulation in this case might be achieved by gathering data from the instructor, the student, and his or her employer or fellow coworkers (see Figure 2). Data from the instructor and the student would include the same types of

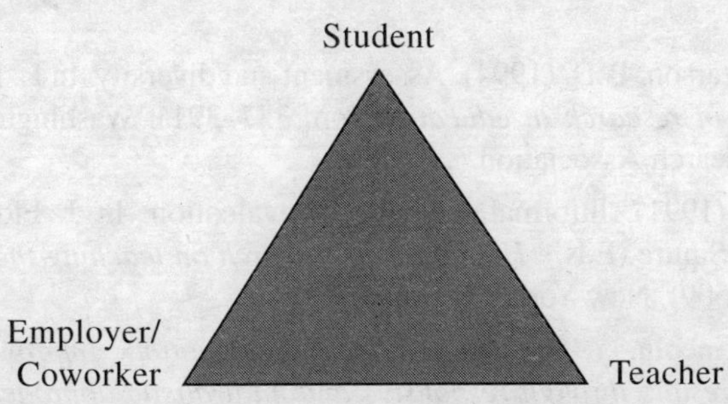

Figure 2 Triangulation of Data: Alternative Assessment for Adults in a Workplace ESL Class

information described earlier. The employer/coworker might provide additional information on a student's growth in ESL. This can be done by using surveys or informal phone or personal interviews where the instructor asks about the student's use of English in varying contexts at the workplace – such as at meetings or informal discussions. In addition, work-related samples, such as forms that were filled out by the student at the workplace, might also be included as data from the workplace.

Another concern that is often raised with respect to alternative assessment is the lack of objectivity. Yet, even though standardized tests are described as objective, the notion of objectivity has been challenged. As humans, we all have biases, whether we are aware of them or not. A standardized test merely represents agreement among a number of people on scoring procedures, format, and/or content for that specific test. In other words, these individuals are not really objective; they just collectively share the same biases. Therefore, in this sense, a standardized test is no more objective than an alternative assessment instrument. One might argue, moreover, that quantitative data – as from standardized tests – can be more subjective because the numbers or statistics can be manipulated to reflect certain biases on the part of the researcher. There is no reason, then, to consider alternative assessment as being any less objective than traditional testing.

Conclusion

I have discussed alternative assessment as consisting of valid and reliable procedures that avoid many of the problems inherent in traditional testing, including norming, linguistic, and cultural biases. There is yet another advantage to the use of alternative assessment: It has the power to tell a story. The data compiled on individual students provide a clear picture of each student's development through the various work samples and products collected. An educator who looks at this picture can determine growth, areas of weakness, and areas of strength. She can also inform herself about the student's background, interests, and goals through his or her journals, compositions, conversations, and observations. In short, the educator becomes acquainted with this person. Thus, contrary to traditional testing, which typically provides only a set of numbers, alternative assessment documents a story for every student – and what is the ultimate goal of evaluation if not to give us the knowledge to be able to reflect on, discuss, and assist a student's journey through the learning process? Alternative assessment gives us the power to do all three.

References

Anthony, R., Johnson, T., Mickelson, N., & Preece, A. (1991). *Evaluating literacy: A perspective for change*. Portsmouth, NH: Heinemann.

García, G. E., & Pearson, P. D. (1991). The role of assessment in a diverse society. In E. F. Hiebert (Ed.), *Literacy for a diverse society* (pp. 253–278). New York: Teachers College Press.

García, G. E., & Pearson, P. D. (1994). Assessment and diversity. In L. Darling-Hammond (Ed.), *Review of research in education* (pp. 337–391). Washington, DC: American Education Research Association.

Goodman, Y. M. (1991). Informal methods of evaluation. In J. Flood, J. M. Jensen, D. Lapp, & J. Squire (Eds.), *Handbook of research on teaching the English language arts* (pp. 502–509). New York: Macmillan.

Guba, E. G., & Lincoln, Y. S. (1981). *Effective evaluation: Improving the usefulness of evaluation results through responsive and naturalistic approaches*. San Francico: Jossey-Bass.

Holt, D. (1994). *Assessing success in family literacy projects: Alternative approaches to assessment and evaluation*. Washington, DC: Center for Applied Linguistics.

Kirk J., & Miller, M. L. (1986). *Realiability and validity in qualitative research*. Newbury Park, CA: Sage.

Mitchell, R. (1979). *Less than words can say.* Boston, MA: Little, Brown.

Navarrete, C., Wilde, J., Nelson, C., Martinez, R., & Hargett, G. (1990). *Informal assessment in educational evaluation: Implications for bilingual programs*. Washington, DC: National Clearinghouse for Bilingual Education.

Patton, M. Q. (1987). *Creative evaluation*. Newbury Park, CA: Sage.

Wilde, J., Del Vecchio, A., Gustke, C. (in press). Alternative assessments for Latino students. In M. González, A. Huerta-Macías, & J. Tinajero (Eds.), *The schooling of Latino students: A guide to quality practice.* Lancaster, PA: Technomic Publishing.

Wrigley, H. S., & Guth, G. A. (1992). *Bringing literacy to life: Issues and options in adult ESL literacy.* San Mateo, CA: Aguirre International.

CHAPTER 34

Nontraditional Forms of Assessment and Response to Student Writing: A Step Toward Learner Autonomy

Andrea H. Peñaflorida

Introduction

This paper will discuss new options open to the language teacher in assessing and responding to student writing, and in promoting learner autonomy in the process.

The following questions are useful to start a discussion of nontraditional forms of assessment and response to student writing:

1. What direction should nontraditional forms of assessment for writing take?
2. Should they be samples of daily work such as journal entries or portfolio assessment?
3. Or, is the notion of general assessment completely out of synchronization with the megatrends in education where assessment and response to writing have become revolutionary?

Based on this writer's experience as teacher trainer, she has observed that the teaching and subsequent assessment of writing leave much to be desired. Not much change has been undertaken in terms of approaches and classroom procedures. Might this be owing to the fact that some of the teachers teach the way they were taught, or that some of us still cling to age-old beliefs and practices in evaluating, grading and teaching, assessing and responding to student writing?

Some of the practices that many language teachers find difficult to do away with are the following:

- Teacher gives exercises and model paragraphs and essays for students to imitate. If this is all that a teacher does, then she hampers or impedes creativity on the part of the students.

- Teacher lists a number of topics on the chalkboard, then asks students to choose one and write about it. This is done without so much as a preliminary activity to the actual writing exercise.
- Teacher prescribes the exact number of words and the time limit with which to finish a piece of writing. For example, all papers have to be handed in at the end of a 40- or 60-minute period, inclusive of preliminaries such as instructions, number of words, number of paragraphs, and so on.
- Assessment, evaluation, and grading are imprecise and unsystematic. Teachers usually write marginal comments which only serve to confuse students. General comments like *improve, rephrase, vague, too broad,* or *specify* frustrate the students instead of helping them.
- Teacher gives writing assignments which take time to mark and give back to students, or worse, teacher sometimes fails to return the papers. We were students once and we know how important the teacher's feedback was. Can we blame our students today if they become indifferent to their English courses?
- Teacher corrects all errors, "bleeds" students' papers to death, figuratively and literally. Red penciling all over the paper reveals that form, rather than substance, is given more attention. By concentrating on form, students tend to turn in papers which are almost flawless in grammar but lacking in substance. Research in the teaching of writing, according to Sommer (1989), reveals that the use of red ink, marginal notes, and symbols for correction is not a sign of improvement in student writing.
- Readership is limited. Students write compositions for their teacher's eyes only. They do not get the chance to read each other's work.

These are only some of the classroom *malpractices* that confuse and disorient students. How, then, do English teachers put an end to these seemingly problematic scenarios in their writing classes?

The traditional way of evaluating papers where the teacher is the only reader for whom the students write and that the teacher's role is to assume responsibility for reading through errors and editing the paper for grammatical and mechanical mistakes is now being gradually replaced by the so-called extended readership.

Assessment and evaluation are not the sole responsibility of the teacher. Teachers need to make their students realize that their paper is their own property, thus answering the question of ownership. A paper which is excessively marked and scribbled over by the teacher is no longer the student's property. It becomes the teacher's. How, then, do we assess and respond effectively to student writing considering the negative effects of certain traditional beliefs and practices?

This paper's main objective is to present new directions in assessing and responding to student writing. Wiser and Dorsey (1991, p. 47) claim that "what we are doing now is not much; what we are going to be doing is a lot more." Some of us want assessment to play a role that is totally different from the role it now plays. Others may want to do away with traditional assessment altogether and to use alternative or nontraditional forms.

KEY TERMS

Four key terms included in the title of this paper – nontraditional, assessment, response, and learner autonomy – need clarification. The term *nontraditional* suggests the existence of other forms of assessment outside the conventional or traditional system. It gives one the impression that the so-called conventional forms of writing do not seem to be very effective; hence the need to look for other possibilities of assessing classroom-based writing.

Assessment, based on the context of the paper, involves the means of obtaining information about students' abilities, knowledge, understanding, attainments, or attitudes. An assignment in writing, for instance, will be helpful in assessing a student's ability in and understanding of the assigned activity. Sommer (1989) defines assessment as the process of finding out who the students are, what their abilities are, what they need to know, and how they perceive the learning will affect them. Assessment places the needs of the students at the center of the teacher's planning.

The third key term is *response*, which is considered an integral feature of student writing, inasmuch as it enables students to identify their own strengths and weaknesses, which, in the case of the latter, will make students know how to go about improving themselves and becoming more effective writers. In this paper, *response* and *feedback* will be used interchangeably.

Learner autonomy, the fourth key term, is a process that enables learners to recognize and assess their own needs, to choose and apply their own learning strategies or styles eventually leading to the effective management of learning.

Some Issues in Nontraditional or Alternative Forms of Assessment

There are some issues that need to be addressed if we want to move into alternative forms of assessment. We have to think about the use to which we are going to put assessment. Along with these are two other equally important issues: the issue of self-reflection through journal entries or protocol analysis and the issue of whether a teacher can do a portfolio assessment and use it to help learners develop autonomy. It is always good for writing teachers to sit down together and discuss what the issues are and their relevance to assessment and response to student writing.

Three assessment issues in the order of their importance are presented (Farr, 1991):

1. philosophical issues
2. public issues
3. implementation issues

Farr (1991, p. 80) believes that "philosophical problems of the role of assessment are fundamental and need to be considered before any assessment can gain popular support." What do teachers really want assessment to do? They differ as to the role assessment ought to play.

In the second set of issues – public issues – the public may not be ready for nontraditional assessment. For example, Farr believes that parents may not understand innovative trends in education.

Development and implementation issues are a third set of problems that Farr posits. These issues are the crucial problems and they can be ironed out with the help of research-based studies, conferences, seminars, and the like.

Nontraditional or Alternative Forms of Assessment

The answer to the question raised earlier – "How do we assess and respond effectively to student writing considering the negative effects of certain traditional beliefs and practices?" – is that teachers should explore new directions and perspectives in light of assessment and response to writing.

In terms of pedagogical concerns, this paper considers the following nontraditional or alternative forms of assessment of classroom-based writing:

- portfolio assessment
- protocol analysis
- learning logs
- journal entries
- dialogue journals

Some of these forms of assessment are familiar, but they will be discussed in terms of new trends and approaches relevant to the teaching of writing.

PORTFOLIO ASSESSMENT

Some new ideas in the teaching of English become quickly established in practice because they are *so right, so timely, so useful.* The portfolio in writing classes is a case in point. Disenchantment with the traditional modes of assessment has probably contributed to the portfolio approach to assessment of writing.

What are portfolios, and how can they be used as an alternative method of assessment? Applebee and Langer (1992, p. 30) define portfolios as a cumulative collection of the work students have done. Some of the most popular forms are the following:

1. a traditional "writing folder" in which students keep their work
2. a bound notebook with separate sections kept for work in progress and final drafts
3. a loose-leaf notebook in which students keep their drafts and revisions
4. a combination folder and big brown envelope where students' writings – exercises, tests, compositions, drafts, and so on – are kept.
5. a notebook divided into two sections: one for drafts and the other for final copies (traditionally called *original* and *rewritten* compositions back in the late 1950s and 1960s when this writer was a public school teacher in the Division of City Schools, Manila)

A typical writing portfolio contains the student's total writing output to represent his or her overall performance, but it may also contain only a selection of works which the student has chosen for the teacher to evaluate. In other words, portfolios show a student's work from the beginning of the term to the end, giving both teacher and student a chance to assess how much the latter's writing has progressed.

Here is a specific example from this writer's own experience. In April 1995, she personally handled 15 hours of a 30-hour writing class (a special writing program), which she team-taught with another teacher. The class was composed of twenty college-bound students who wanted to improve their writing skills in preparation for university studies. The writer exploited the portfolio approach, which she found effective despite the fact that the writing class was a nondegree program. Instead of taking their portfolios home, the students kept them on a writing desk which was set up in one corner of the room (they had a permanent room for the entire course). Before they left their class at noontime, the students had to put their portfolios on the desk; they got them back as soon as they arrived the following morning. The students had all the time necessary to discuss their assignments, to write, to do exercises, and to engage in other activities relevant to the subject matter. Likewise, this writer had all the time to assess their work with the assistance of the whole class. Incidentally, she also asked her students to put their journal entries in a small notebook which they kept in their portfolios. Two days before the end of classes, she required her students to prepare a table of contents for their portfolios and to write a timed reflective essay in class, which was the only timed writing they did, explaining their choice of papers for assessment and evaluation purposes. They got back their portfolios with written comments and suggestions from the teacher on the last day of classes as part of their culminating activity. This does not mean, however, that portfolio assessments should be done only once; actually, they should be done at the outset and progress along with the students' own progress in writing.

Portfolio collections may also serve as responses to student writing. Conferencing is an important component of portfolio assessment. Farr and Lowe (1991) are of the opinion that students, through conferencing and keeping a portfolio, experience making real-life decisions as well as decisions about schoolwork. In order for students to take responsibility for their learning and their lives, ownership of their own choices and actions is an all-important consideration. *This is a real step toward learner autonomy.* In the traditional approach, ownership of work and learning is looked upon more as the responsibility of the teacher than of the learner. But when students actively participate in the selection and discussion of their work, they gain a true sense of ownership, which results in personal satisfaction and feelings of self-worth.

According to Farr and Lowe (1991, p. 79), for portfolios to meet the goals of literacy assessment, they must be developed as follows:

- Teachers and students both add materials to the portfolio.
- Students are viewed as the owners of the portfolios.
- Conferencing between students and the teacher is an inherent activity in portfolio assessment.
- Conference notes and reflections of both the teacher and the student are kept in the portfolio.
- Portfolios need to reflect a wide range of student work and not only that which the teacher or student decides is the best.
- Samples of the student's reading and writing activities are collected in the portfolios, including unfinished projects.

Applebee and Langer (1992, p. 29) believe that portfolios of students' work offer one of the best vehicles for assessment of writing for two reasons: (1) They typically contain a variety of different samples of student work, and (2) they make it easy to separate evaluation from the process of instruction.

No system of assessment is as perfect as portfolio assessment, according to Gallehr (1993), because students are required to write, but within this requirement, they can choose the topic, audience, responders in the class, revision strategies, and so on. They are also free to select from their works the pieces they want to include in their portfolios. This shows that portfolios may be used as a holistic process for evaluating course work and for promoting learner autonomy. Portfolios provide a sound basis on which to document individual student progress because they incorporate a range of assessment strategies over an extended period of time.

PROTOCOL ANALYSIS

A second, though somewhat complicated, means of assessing student writing is protocol analysis. Actually, protocol analysis, as well as the other nontraditional forms of assessment, is a writing procedure that promotes the process approach to writing.

Protocol analysis is also known as the composing aloud protocol or a think aloud activity, which is the exact opposite of the fixed model used by traditional composition teachers. This type of analysis reveals the conscious processes involved in writing. In this approach, students are asked to record every thought that comes to mind during the writing process. The transcripts are analyzed and used as one of the instruments for assessing student writing. To enable the students to use protocol analysis effectively, the teacher should first serve as model. She should show the class how to proceed by making the class listen to a tape-recorded model of her own protocol analysis procedure, or by doing actual protocol analysis in the classroom with students listening and observing.

Assessment of student writing can be done using this strategy, for through protocol analysis, a teacher can tell how students write, the strategies they use to generate ideas, how often they revise and edit their work, and whether their written work has improved.

LEARNING LOGS

Learning logs help teachers see what their students are learning, particularly in the writing class, and in the language class as a whole. In a learning log, students write on the knowledge they have gained from studying in their writing classes, and from their own thinking. A teacher need not grade learning logs, but can assess how much a student has gained or benefited from the writing class.

JOURNAL ENTRIES

Journal entries may be used as an informal means of assessment by the teacher because they are personal and intimate. The teacher can write short notes in response to students' thoughts. Just as in portfolio assessment, journal entries may be a source for conferencing.

Journal keeping, being informal in nature, enables a student to get extensive writing practice. Some of its advantages are that (1) it can be enjoyable, since it gives the students free rein to write on any topic at the spur of the moment, and (2) it offers students the privacy, freedom, and safety to experiment and develop as a writer (Applebee & Langer, 1992).

Since journal keeping is a private and confidential, as well as highly individualized, process, assessing students' journal entries is also a private matter between the writer and the teacher. This writer started journal keeping at the DLSU Writing Lab in the late 1980s. She required all students to keep their journals in the Writing Lab. Because students had been keeping a journal regularly, it eventually became a habit with them. They were given a maximum of 10 minutes to write briefly on anything (e.g., family gatherings, family problems, ideas on love and courtship, travel, current events, special occasions, and other relevant issues). They wrote down their thoughts in a few sentences at the beginning, but their writing gradually improved and developed so much that at the end of the Writing Lab stint, they could already express their thoughts in longer paragraphs. Sometimes the teacher responded to journal entries through conferencing. At the beginning, for as long as students could communicate their thoughts on paper, for as long as their writings were comprehensible, evaluation of their grammatical flaws and lapses was postponed until later. What worked well at the time resulted from several factors, including the interest of the students, the patience of the lab instructors, and the collaboration between the lab instructors and the subject teachers.

This writer also suggested that the Writing Lab teachers keep journals and write their own journal entries at the same time as the students. Occasionally, some students shared their entries with their classmates. Journal entries contribute greatly to the humanistic approach to teaching and learning, an example of which is the integration of values during the sharing sessions.

DIALOGUE JOURNALS

Another nontraditional form of assessment of writing is dialogue journals. These are written conversations between teacher and student over a period of time, usually for the duration of a course, on topics that are of special interest to them. Their goal is to "communicate in writing, to exchange ideas and information free of the concern for form and correctness so often imposed on developing writers" (Jones, 1991, p. 3, in Peyton & Staton, 1991).

Dialogue journals provide guidance to the learner in expressing ideas, thoughts, feelings, and emotions. Dialogue journal interaction leads to trust between learner and teacher.

The value of a dialogue journal in assessing student writing is that it helps to make students independent and eventually able to read and respond to the teacher's entries (Peyton & Staton, 1991). This shows that reading cannot be dissociated from writing, that a link really exists between these two skills.

Jana Staton, an educational psychologist, and Leslee Reed, a sixth-grade teacher, coined the name "dialogue journal" in 1979 to describe Reed's practice of writing freely back and forth, every day, with each of her students (Peyton & Staton, 1991).

Dialogue journals have some essential ingredients that differentiate them from other forms of written communication, specifically journal entries. Some of the distinguishing characteristics between dialogue journal writing and journal keeping are as follows:

Dialogue Journal	Journal Entries
Teacher and student write to each other, taking equal turns in writing and responding.	Teacher comments on student's work, but there is no equal turn taking in responding.
Teacher and student share ideas and information.	Student is not obligated to share her writing with anybody.
Teacher and student act as equal partners in the interaction between them.	There is a hierarchical relationship between teacher and student.
Dialogue journal writing is applicable to some content area courses such as literature, social studies, or science.	Journal keeping is usually practiced in language courses only.
In dialogue journals, teacher gives students assistance beyond what they already know how to do.	In journal entries, teacher assists students on the language used or on the content of what is written.

These two forms of written communication not only have distinguishing characteristics, but also bear striking similarities. Both provide intensive writing practice, promote learner autonomy, serve as informal means of assessment, are highly private and confidential, and are interactive in varying degrees.

Response to Student Writing

In responsive teaching, the student acts and the teacher reacts. The range of reaction is extensive and diverse because an individual teacher is responding to an individual student, and the student in turn is passing through an ever-changing process of discovery through writing (Murray, 1985).

How do language teachers respond to their students' written compositions? Most teachers cannot resist the temptation to correct all errors, both global and local, in their students' compositions. Generally, in the case of global errors (errors that impede communication), teachers substitute their own words, sentences, and even ideas for their students' errors so that these students lose ownership of their writings; they can barely recognize their own work. This contributes to many students' dislike for writing. Responding to student writing, if done properly, may lead to students' improved written work and may make writing interesting, challenging, and enjoyable.

Responding or giving feedback to student writing can be both oral and written. There are a variety of response types that an English teacher can utilize in the classroom.

SELF-RESPONSE

Self-response and assessment of one's own writing or feedback is a *step toward learner autonomy.* Studies on self-assessment reveal that students are capable of analyzing and responding to their own writing given the proper training. By allowing students to react to their own work and to practice self-feedback, the teacher is encouraging them to be self-sufficient and independent. How can self-assessment be done? A few sample questions can be given as guidelines to the students. For example:

- What am I writing about?
- Is the main idea of my work clear?
- Do I have details (e.g., examples and illustrations) to support my main idea?

Many teachers are interested in having students do self-assessment and understand how they are developing as learners.

PEER RESPONSE

Peer response shows that readership does not belong exclusively to the teacher, since in this type of response, students are enjoined to share their writings with each other. Students may not like this at the beginning, but with the teacher's encouragement, they will gradually get used to the idea of communicating their ideas to each other. Elbow (1992) believes that when students write only for their teacher (which usually means for a grade), they often fall into certain bad habits, treating writing as an empty school exercise and attempting simply to just "get it right" or "give teachers what they want." When students write for their peers, they become very concerned about what they say and how they say it. Students may not be as skilled as their teachers at responding to each other's work, but they are excellent in providing the one thing that writers need most – an audience.

Kroll (1991, p. 259) says that "because ESL students lack the language competence of native speakers of English who can react instructively to their classmates' papers, peer responding in the ESL classroom must be modeled, taught, and controlled in order for it to be a valuable activity." Controlling peer response, just like self-feedback, can be done through the use of a checklist. Below are some typical questions for peer response (Kroll, 1991, p. 259):

- What is the main purpose of this paper?
- What have you found particularly effective in the paper?
- Do you think the writer has followed through on what the paper set out to do?
- Find at least three places in the essay where you can think of questions that have not been answered by the writer. Write those questions on the margin as areas for the writer to answer in the next draft.

TEACHER RESPONSE

The last to respond to a written work is the teacher. The teacher's load is lightened when students have done both individual and peer feedback. The teacher can employ peer correction gradually in the classroom so that students can get used to it.

Conferencing, which is a one-to-one conversation between teacher and student, is an effective means of teacher response to student writing. It is a form of oral teacher feedback. A short conference of 10 to 15 minutes will enable the teacher to ask the student about certain parts of the latter's writing which are problematic, but conferencing may be short or for as long as the two parties wish to talk. Only two people are involved in conferencing: the teacher and the student. Conferences make teachers better acquainted with their students.

According to Kroll (1991, p. 259), one advantage of conferencing "allows the teacher to uncover potential misunderstandings that the student might have about prior written feedback on issues in writing that have been discussed in class."

In conferencing, the teacher meets individually with students. In the context of assessment and response to student writing, one-on-one conferences round out the process of discovering the unique backing records and needs of students, especially the first conference. Sommer (1989) further suggests that the teacher should make arrangements with students to confer with him or her on a one-on-one basis after the students have finished writing their compositions.

The variations on the writing conference are almost infinite, but the basic pattern as proposed by Graves (1985, p. 148) is simple:

- The student *comments* on the draft.
- The teacher *reads* or reviews the draft.
- The teacher *responds* to the student's comments.
- The student *responds* to the teacher's response.

The purpose of this basic pattern is to help students learn to read their own drafts with increasing effectiveness. It is the responsibility of the student to write and make the first evaluation of his or her experiment in meaning. It is the responsibility of the teacher to listen to the student's response, then to listen to the text, and finally to respond to the writer's reading of the text. Then it is the responsibility of the student to respond to the teacher's response. As Murray (1985, p. 156) points out,

> As much as possible in responding orally or in writing the teacher should not praise or criticize. We need to discuss with the students how the piece is going, what is working, what needs to be done, focusing on a discussion of what is working, and what needs work.

Murray (1985, p. 156) also provides samples of some responses to avoid and to use during conferencing. Below are some responses teachers should try to avoid:

- This is no good.
- Wow! You can write.
- Didn't you learn anything about writing?
- This is great, just great.
- This is a mess, just a mess.
- I've never seen such a bad paper.
- I don't know what I can teach someone who writes like you (can be used to overpraise or overcriticize).

Aside from these, there are many other "monster responses" to drafts that writing teachers give. The problem is that they terminate discussion and the growth of the piece of writing. There is not much the writer can do with – or learn from – such comments.

The following comments may stimulate and encourage work (Murray, 1985, p. 156):

- What do you plan to work on next?
- Obviously, some of this works, but what do you plan to attack next?
- Where do you think you get off the track?

- I like the way you wove the quotes into the text. Are there other things that could be woven in in the same way?
- This looks like what happened to my draft this morning. Where do you intend to go from here? I need to find out.
- And you said you had no voice. Tell me how you made this draft so different.

Finally, Applebee and Langer (1992) have the following suggestions for teachers in providing effective response:

- Limit the amount of writing to which you, the teacher, respond.
- Respond to work in progress as a collaborator rather than as an elaborator.

CONCLUSION

New directions in teachers' assessment and response to student writing have just been presented in the hope that these new directions will become "practical alternatives, and not merely passing fads" (Farr & Lowe, 1991, p. 74). All these are possible if teachers keep a focus on their purpose for applying them in the language classroom, and possibly in other content area classrooms as well.

References

Applebee, A. N., & Langer, J. A. (1992). Integrating the language arts. In *The writer's craft* (teacher's edition). Evanston, IL: McDougal, Littel & Company.

Elbow, P. (1992). Peer sharing and peer response. In *The writer's craft* (teacher's edition). Evanston, IL: McDougal, Littel & Company.

Farr, R. (1991). Current issues in alternative assessment. In *Alternative assessment in the language arts.* IN: ERIC Clearinghouse in Reading and Communication Skills.

Farr, R., & Lowe, K. (1991). Alternative assessment in language arts. In *Alternative assessment in the language arts* (pp. –). IN: ERIC Clearinghouse in Reading and Communication Skills.

Gallehr, D. R. (1993). Portfolio assessment in the college writing classroom. In G. Kent (Ed.), *Process and portfolios in writing instruction.* Urbana, IL: National Council of Teachers of English.

Graves, D. (1985). In D. Murray, *Writer teaches writing*, 2nd ed. Boston, MA: Houghton Mifflin.

Jones, P. (1991). *What are dialogue journals?* Cited in Peyton and Staton (Eds.), *Writing our lives: Reflections on dialogue journal writing with adults learning English.* Englewood Cliffs, NJ: Prentice Hall Regents.

Kroll, B. (1991). Teaching writing in the ESL context. In C. Murcia (Ed.), *Teaching English as a second language.* New York: Newbury House.

Murray, D. (1985). *Write to learn.* 4th Ed. Orlando, FL: Harcourt Brace.

Peyton, J. K., & Staton, J. (Eds.). (1991). *Writing our lives: Reflections on dialogue journal writing with adults learning English.* Englewood Cliffs, NJ: Prentice Hall Regents.

Sommer, R. F. (1989). *Teaching writing to adults.* San Francisco: Jossey-Bass.

(1992). *The writer's craft.* (teacher's edition.) Evanston, IL: McDougal, Littell & Company.

CHAPTER 35

English Proficiency Test: The Oral Component of a Primary School

Ishbel Hingle and Viv Linington

Introduction

Many teachers feel comfortable setting pencil-and-paper tests. Years of experience marking written work have made them familiar with the level of written competence pupils need in order to succeed in a specific standard. However, teachers often feel much less secure when dealing with tests which measure speaking and listening, even though these skills are regarded as essential components of a diagnostic test which measures overall linguistic proficiency. Although the second language English pupils often come from an oral rather than a written culture, and so are likely to be more proficient in this mode of communication, at least in their own language, speaking in English may be a different matter. In English-medium schools in particular, a low level of English may impede students' acquisition of knowledge. Therefore, identifying the correct level of English of the student is all the more challenging and important.

This article outlines some of the problem areas described by researchers when designing a test of oral production for beginning-level speakers of English and suggests ways in which they may be addressed.

How does one set a test which does not intimidate children but encourages them to provide an accurate picture of their oral ability?

In replying to this question, one needs to consider briefly the findings of researchers working in the field of language testing. "The testing of speaking is widely regarded as the most challenging of all language tests to prepare, administer and score," writes Harold Madsen, an international expert on testing (Madsen, 1983, p. 147). This is especially true when examining beginning-level pupils who have just started to acquire English, such as those applying for admission to primary school. Theorists suggest three reasons why this type of test is so different from more conventional types of tests.

First, the nature of the speaking skill itself is difficult to define. Because of this, it is not easy to establish criteria to evaluate a speaking test. Is "fluency" more important than "accuracy," for example? If we agree that fluency is more important, then how will we define this concept? Are we going to use "amount of information conveyed per minute" or "quickness of response" as our definition of fluency?

A second set of problems emerges when testing beginning-level speakers of English, which involves getting them to speak in the first place, and then defining the role the tester will play while the speaking is taking place. Relevant elicitation procedures which will prompt speakers to demonstrate their optimum oral performance are unique to each group of speakers and perhaps even unique to each occasion in which they are tested. The tester will therefore need to act as a partner in the production process, while at the same time evaluating a number of things about this production.

A third set of difficulties emerges if one tries to treat an oral test like any other more conventional test. "In the latter, the test is often seen as an object with an identity and purpose of its own, and the children taking the test are often reduced to subjects whose only role is to react to the test instrument" (Madsen, 1983, p. 159). In oral tests, however, the priority is reversed. The people involved are important, not the test, and what goes on between tester and testee may have an existence independent of the test instrument and still remain a valid response.

HOW CAN ONE ACCOMMODATE THESE DIFFICULTIES AND STILL COME UP WITH A VALID TEST OF ORAL PRODUCTION?

In answering this question, especially in relation to the primary school mentioned earlier, we would like to refer to the experience we had in designing such a test for the Open Learning Systems Education Trust (OLSET) to measure the success of their English-in-Action Programme with Sub B pupils. This program is designed to teach English to pupils in the earliest grades of primary school, using the medium of the tape recorder or radio.

In devising this test, we decided to use fluency as our basic criterion, that is, "fluency" in the sense Brumfit uses it: "the maximally effective operation of the language system so far acquired by the student" (Brumfit, 1984, p. 543). To this end, we decided to record the total number of words used by each pupil on the test administration and to employ this as an overall index to rank order the testees in terms of performance.

To address the second and third set of problems just outlined, we decided to use elicitation procedures with which the children were familiar. Figures 1 and 2 would require the teacher to find a picture full of images the pupils could relate to, such as children playing. Students could participate in the following types of activities:

- an informal interview, to put the children at ease by getting them to talk about themselves, their families, and their home or school lives (see Figure 1)
- a set of guided answers to questions about a poster, to test their knowledge of the real-life objects and activities depicted on the poster, as well as their ability to predict the consequences of these activities (see Figure 2)
- narratives based on packs of story cards, to generate extended language in which the children might display such features as cohesion or a knowledge of the English tense system in an uninterrupted flow of speaking.

Instead of treating the situation as a "test," we asked testers to treat it as a "game." Both partners would be seated informally on the ground (with, in our case, a recorder placed

The Interview

The tester should capture personal details by asking the following types of questions:

What is your name?

Where do you live?

Do you have any brothers or sisters?

Does anyone else live at home with you?

Now tell me, what do you all do when you get up in the morning?

How do you all go to school and work?

Do you have any brothers or sisters in this school?

What standards are they in?

Which subject do you enjoy most? Why?

What do you do at break?

Tell me about your best friends.

What does your mother/grandmother cook for dinner?

Can you tell me how she cooks it?

Why do you all enjoy this food most?

Do you listen to the radio/watch TV in your house?

What is your favorite program?

Why do you enjoy it most?

What do you do when you are getting ready to sleep in the evening?

What time do you go to sleep. Why?

Now look at the picture and tell me what this little boy is doing. Let's give him a name.

What do you suggest?

Figure 1

unobtrusively on the floor between them because of the research nature of our test). If the occasion was unthreatening to the pupil with the tester acting in a warm, friendly way, we anticipated that the child would respond in a similar way, and thus produce a more accurate picture of his or her oral productive ability. We suggested that the tester act as a listener/speaker only while the test was being conducted, and as assessor once the test administration was over.

To maintain a more human approach to the testing situation, we decided to allow the tester a certain flexibility in choosing questions to suit each particular child, and also in the amount of time she spent on each subtest. The time allowed for testing each pupil would be limited to 8 minutes, and all three subtests would be covered during this period, but the amount of time spent on each could vary.

"Arriving at School"

Questions for guided response:

What are the children doing?

Where are they?

How many children are there?

Are there more boys than girls?

How do you know this?

What is the girl in the green dress doing?

What are the boys going to do when they finish playing marbles?

Do you think the children are happy?

Have you ever played marbles?

(If yes) How do you play marbles?

(If no) What other game do you play with your friends?

How do you play it?

Now look at the picture and tell me what this little boy is doing. Let's give him a name.

What do you suggest?

Figure 2

Question banks were provided for testers to select questions they felt were within the range of each child's experience, but there was an understanding that how and why questions were more difficult to answer than other *wh-* questions. A range of both types should therefore be used.

Story packs also provided for a range of experiences and could be used by the tester telling a story herself first, thus demonstrating what was required of the pupil. However, it was anticipated that some pupils might be sufficiently competent to use the story packs without any prompting from the teacher. Pupils could place the cards in any order they chose, as the sole purpose of this procedure was to generate language. Story packs were composed of picture stories that had been photocopied from appropriate-level books, cut up into individual pictures, and mounted on cardboard. Six pictures to a story pack were considered sufficient to prompt the anticipated length of a story that pupils could handle.

EVALUATING THE TEST

This test of oral production was administered at both rural and urban schools to children who were on the English-in-Action Programme and to those who were not. The comparative results are not relevant here, but findings about which aspects of the test worked and which did not may be of assistance to those who wish to set similar tests. In summarizing these findings, the remainder of this paper comments on the administration of the test, the success of each subtest in eliciting language, and, finally, the criteria we used for evaluating the test outcomes.

First, both testers commented that this type of test was more difficult to organize and administer than other kinds of evaluation tests they had used. This was caused by the need to find a quiet and relatively private place to administer the test and record the outcome and because the procedure could be done only on a one-to-one basis. We had anticipated this type of feedback but were also not surprised when told that subsequent administrations "were much easier and the children were more enthusiastic about participating than the previous time." The testing procedure was new to both tester and testee, but once experienced, it gave children greater freedom of expression than other kinds of tests.

Second, although the test as a whole did elicit oral language production, the amount and type of language varied from subtest to subtest. The interview produced rather less language than the other two subtests; it also elicited rather learned chunks of language, which we called "patterned responses."

The guided responses, on the other hand, produced a much greater variety of answers, couched in a fairly wide range of grammatical structures. But even these responses consisted on the whole of single words or phrases. Open-ended questions evoked longer responses from the more able students, but seemed to confound less able students. For example, the question "What can you see in the picture?" produced the answer "I can see a car and a woman going to the shop and a boy had a bicycle and the other one riding a bicycle" from a bright pupil, but only "Boy and bicycle" from a weaker pupil.

Higher-order *wh-* questions such as "What do you think is in the suitcase?" or "What will happen next?" seemed to produce only "I don't know" responses from even the most competent pupils. They seemed to lack the linguistic resources, or perhaps the cognitive resources, to predict or suggest answers.

The narrative subtest, based on the story cards, elicited the best display of linguistic ability from the testees, in terms of both amount of language produced and range of grammatical structures used.

Competent pupils were able to respond well to the tell/retell aspect and constructed sentences of seven to ten words in length, joined by a variety of coordinating devices. They also employed past-tense forms in retelling the story such as the following:

> The boys they played with the cow's what ...... what ...... a ...... bells three bells ...... then they got some apples and went to swim ...... the monkey saw them swim and putted them shirts and shorts ...... some they said hey ...... I want my shirts ...... wait I want my shirts ...... but monkey she run away

Less competent students could describe isolated images on each card without using narrative in any way to link them together.

From these results we therefore concluded that the story packs were the most successful of the three elicitation procedures we used in stimulating optimum language output.

The final issue from the findings of the OLSET test that are relevant here are the criteria used for assessing the language output. Our decision to count "number of words produced" as a measure of speaking ability was a mixed blessing. Initially, it did seem to rank order the pupils in terms of ability and gave us a base for comparison at subsequent test administrations, but nonverbal factors such as self-confidence, familiarity with the tester, and presence of the teacher may have affected even these results. In the second administration of the test, it was not at all accurate because improvement in ability to speak and respond in English was reflected more in the quality of how the testees spoke, rather than in the quantity of language they produced. Several of the more competent pupils spoke the second time in the first round but displayed knowledge and features not present in their own home languages such as prepositions and articles, used correctly subordinating and coordinating conjunctions they had been introduced to only in the course of conversation, and employed a variety of tenses in their storytelling. We therefore used these data to develop a number of assessment levels, or descriptive band scales, based on these various grammatical competencies, when evaluating the pupil's output (a band scale outlines a set of linguistic features and skills a pupil needs to display in order to be placed in that category).

In response to our discussion, some schools have begun to introduce two components in their diagnostic test. The first is a multiple-choice comprehension test and the second an oral test based on a set of story cards.

The same test will be used for pupils at all levels of the primary school, using the lead provided by a test produced by the Human Sciences Research Council for the same purpose. However, the expected proficiency levels to enter a particular grade or standard will be different.

Conclusion

In conclusion, let me summarize the advice I would give to teachers who need to design speaking tests but who are afraid to take the plunge into this area of assessment:

- Do not be afraid to set such a test in the first place.
- Draw on your own materials to set a test appropriate for your group of testees.
- Keep the factor of time constant for each test administration.
- Give the testee the opportunity to lead once he or she is at ease.
- Do not allow factors such as accent to cloud your perception of linguistic competence.
- Rely on your own instinctive judgment when assigning a value to performance on such a test.
- Try to think of this value in terms of words rather than marks.

References

Brumfit, C. (1984). *Communicative methodology in language teaching*. Cambridge: Cambridge University Press.

Madsen, H. S. (1983). *Techniques in testing*. New York: Oxford University Press.

SECTION 15

TECHNOLOGIES IN THE CLASSROOM

INTRODUCTION

The three articles in this section deal with the use of technologies in the classroom. In recent years, the use of technological aids, especially those related to computers, has increasingly become a common feature of the classroom. There is no doubt that computer-based instruction will occupy a more central role in the second language classroom in the future. However, as we eagerly explore the potential that this new technology has to offer to language learning, we should not lose sight of the fact that it is the teacher, not the technology, who determines the quality of the learning that takes place in the classroom.

In adopting a new technology, be it a tape recorder, a VCR, a CD-ROM multimedia, or other network-based communication technology, Jones and Sato (1998) suggest that we consider the following questions:

- Does the new technology facilitate the attainment of course goals?
- Is it cost-effective? Do the benefits outweigh its cost?
- Are the teachers ready to work with the new technology? Is any training required?
- Does it serve the needs of the teachers and students?
- Does it help teachers make more efficient use of class time?

There are other questions to think about, but these are some of the most important questions that need to be addressed before we decide to implement new technologies in the classroom.

Stempleski discusses the positive features of video materials and presents guidelines which can help teachers plan their video lessons effectively. With careful and systematic planning, video-based lessons can be highly stimulating, and provide a rich resource for language learning. Stempleski emphasizes the key role of the teacher in the use of video, saying that it is the teacher, not the video, who can make any video-based lesson a fruitful language learning experience. It is the teacher who chooses the video; designs tasks and activities that facilitate active learning; prepares students for the previewing, viewing, and postviewing activities; raises students' awareness of certain language points; and integrates the video with other aspects of the curriculum.

Warschauer and Whittaker examine the use of the Internet for second language teaching and present a set of guidelines for teachers who plan to integrate computer technology in the classroom. As technology is rapidly developing, the authors consider it advisable to provide a set of guidelines which are applicable across a variety of computer network-based tasks. The guidelines, which conform to sound pedagogical principles, suggest that teachers consider the following:

Goals. As in other instructional activities, the first thing for teachers to do is to clarify their goals. Once the aims are specified, appropriate tasks and activities can be designed.

Integration. For best results, computer-based activities should be integrated into the course curriculum as a whole.

Technical support. Although many students are quite knowledgeable about the computer, sufficient support should be provided to avoid problems of a technical nature.

Learner-centered teaching. As much as possible, teachers should involve learners throughout the entire instructional process. Involving the students in deciding on the class direction is likely to create the kind of classroom atmosphere that promotes optimal learning.

The authors conclude by providing an illustration of how these guidelines help a teacher deal with her new computer-based writing class.

Li and Hart look specifically at the World Wide Web and explore its potential for language learning. The Web possesses a number of features which are particularly suited for second language learners' growing proficiency in the language. These include the following:

- It provides a rich data base of authentic material.
- It offers an excellent tool for interactive learning.
- It provides an excellent context for collaborative materials development.
- Its multimedia, capabilities, which combine graphics, sounds, and movies, are particularly conducive to language learning.
- Materials stored in the Web can reach a wide audience at a relatively low cost.

Li and Hart then describe their Web magazine, which provides a forum for their ESL learners to interact and share ideas with other learners, and, at the same time, develop their writing skills. They discuss some of the problems they encountered and suggest future directions for the design and development of Web-based language learning resources.

Discussion Questions

Before Reading

1. Do you think technologies (e.g., videos, computers) should play a central or a peripheral role in second language teaching and learning? Why?
2. What are the roles of the teacher and students in a technology-based classroom?
3. Have you had any experience using the information technology in your second language classroom? What lessons can you draw from this experience?
4. Some teachers are not very comfortable using the computer in the classroom. What advice would you give to these teachers?

5. In what ways can the computer help to promote second language learning?
6. How is the language used on the Internet different from that found in traditional textbooks? What are some of the differences?
7. How can the computer be used to teach vocabulary and grammar? Give some examples.
8. How can the standard-features word-processing programs be exploited for teaching writing skills?

After Reading

1. Plan a lesson for a class you are familiar with. In what ways can you integrate the computer into the lesson so as to make it more effective?
2. Review the guidelines for using videos suggested by Stempleski. Do you think the guidelines are applicable for younger and older students, for beginners and more advanced learners?
3. Design a video-based lesson that encompasses the three-stage activities (previewing, viewing, and postviewing) suggested by Stempleski.
4. What are the criteria for selecting video and Web-based materials? How are the criteria different for choosing text-based material?
5. Log on to the Web site designed by Li and Hart (http://deil.lang.uiuc.edu/exchange/). How can you use the materials and activities in the magazine for your students? What learning benefits are your students likely to get?
6. Review the guidelines for implementing computer-based activities into the second language classroom discussed in the article by Warschauer and Whittaker. Are the guidelines sufficient? Can you add a few more points based on your own experience?
7. The World Wide Web provides a rich source of authentic material. What sort of authentic material would be suitable for the learners you are currently working with? Design an activity that would go nicely with the material.
8. How can computer-based activity make second language learning more interactive? Please give one or two concrete examples.
9. It was pointed out in the introduction to this section that before adopting the new technology in the second language classroom, we need to ask if it is cost-effective (i.e., do the benefits outweigh its cost?) and whether it can help us make more efficient use of class time. Discuss these issues in relation to your particular teaching situation.
10. Discuss the features of CD-ROM multimedia material you have used. Which features do you like most?

Further Reading

Jones, E., & Sato, J. (1998). Hardware, software, students and teachers: A look at technology in the classroom. In C. S. Ward & W. A. Renandya, *Computers and language learning* (pp. 1–20). Singapore: SEAMEO Regional Language Centre.

CHAPTER

Video in the ELT Classroom: The Role of the Teacher

Susan Stempleski

Introduction

The teacher plays a key role in the success or failure of any video used in the language classroom. It is the teacher who selects the video, relates the video to students' needs, promotes active viewing, and integrates the video with other areas of the language curriculum. Any video's chances of achieving the important goals of motivating students' interest, providing realistic listening practice, stimulating language use, and heightening students' awareness of particular language points or other aspects of communication can be improved or destroyed by the way in which the teacher introduces the video and the activities which the students carry out in conjunction with viewing.

Video is an extremely dense medium, one which incorporates a wide variety of visual elements and a great range of audio experiences in addition to spoken language. This can be baffling for many students. The teacher is there to choose appropriate sequences, prepare the students for the viewing experience, focus the students' attention on the content, play and replay the video as needed, design or select viewing tasks, and follow up with suitable postviewing activities.

Published language teaching video materials usually provide guidance for teachers. Indeed, the most sophisticated of these are usually part of a multimedia package that, in addition to the videos themselves, includes viewing guides, student textbooks, teacher manuals, and audiocassettes. ELT video series such as *The ABC News ESL Video Library* or *Family Album USA* present carefully designed or selected video material in contexts geared to students' interest and are accompanied by student workbooks featuring a variety of viewing activities. However, even if you are using a published course, you may want or need to modify the lesson materials provided, or possibly produce your own lesson plans to fit your timetable and the specific needs of your students. If you are planning to select your own authentic video material or to use language teaching video as supplementary material, you will have even more preparation to do. The aim of this brief article is to present some guidelines which will help you plan your video lessons effectively and exploit the video material to its utmost effect. Although there is no one "right way" to use video, teachers planning to use the medium for intensive language presentation and practice, especially those teachers who are less experienced in using video, might find the following suggestions helpful.

Guide Students toward Appreciating Video as a Language Learning Tool

Television and video are so closely associated with leisure and entertainment that many, if not most, students watching video in the classroom expect only to be entertained. Teachers need to lead students to an appreciation of video as a valuable tool for language learning and help them to develop viewing skills which they can apply to their video and television viewing experiences outside the classroom. When we watch television or video for entertainment, we usually do so passively. For example, we do not normally concentrate on such things as the gestures or other nonverbal signals used by the people on the screen, or listen carefully for the intonation in their voices. Elements such as these are what make video such a rich resource for language learning. It is your job as the teacher to get students to focus their eyes, ears, and minds on the video in ways that will increase both comprehension and recall and add to the satisfaction they gain from viewing. The video will still remain entertaining, but the students will also come to a recognition of how the medium can be used for learning.

Make the Video an Integral Part of the Course

Video's true potential in language learning is only achieved when it is used as an integral part of a course. If you are planning to use video as supplementary material, be sure that the sequence fits in with the overall goals of your course. One way to do this is to bring in the video to introduce or to expand on a theme or topic that is already part of the curriculum or that is dealt with in the students' textbook. For example, in my high-beginning-level ESL classes at Hunter College, I have quite successfully used the first 3 minutes of the "Koko" sequence from the National Geographic documentary *Gorilla* to introduce the unit "A Talking Gorilla" in the students' reading textbook *Explorations.* (Rice & Stempleski, 1988)

Use Short Sequences

It is difficult to specify an exact sequence length without identifying a particular video sequence, but in my own experience it is better to exploit a short (3 to 5 minutes) segment of video thoroughly and systematically rather than to play a long sequence which is likely to result in less active viewing on the part of your students.

A word of warning: When you use short, isolated sequences from authentic video documents such as situation comedies, feature films, or documentaries, you must expect your students to be interested in other parts of the video. You should be prepared to respond to this interest. For example, you might choose to eventually exploit the whole of an episode or the serial of which it forms a part, not just the sequence that you have chosen for a particular lesson. Alternatively, you might wish to make the whole video available for student viewing outside of regular class time, in a resource center, for example.

Familiarize Yourself with the Material

Most teachers would not dream of presenting a print-based lesson in class without first reviewing the materials themselves. You should follow the same practice in using video. Treat the video material as seriously as you would treat any other language teaching material. Before presenting a video in class, view the entire sequence yourself, preferably several times and with the video transcript in hand. If you are using suggested activities from a published video language course, and if time allows, try doing the activities yourself in order to anticipate difficulties or questions your students may have.

Treat the Video as Both a Visual and an Audio Text

A video sequence is a text, somewhat like a language-presentation passage in a book or a dialogue on an audiocassette. However, whereas the most important element in a written passage or on an audiocassette is usually the words, a video sequence contains not only words, but visual elements (and often sound effects and music) that provide essential evidence on behavior, character, and context, which are not usually in the script. When planning your lessons, it is important to consider not only the video script, but the video itself. Test the degree of visual support in a video sequence by viewing it first with the sound turned off to see how much you can comprehend based on the pictures alone. Does the camera focus on the person who is speaking? Does the body language suggest anything about what is being said? Are there location shots which help to establish the context by indicating where a particular scene takes place?

Scenes with a high degree of visual support are more useful for presenting language. However, if you are using video as a stimulus to elicit language from the students, some ambiguity may be desirable. For example, if you want the students to hypothesize about what is being said, you will not want the visuals to make what is being said so obvious that there is nothing left for them to hypothesize about.

Design Lessons That Provide Opportunities for Repeated Viewing

Once is not enough. Unless students are extraordinarily gifted and at near-native levels of language proficiency, they will need to see and hear a video sequence several times if they are to understand the situation, identify characters, and observe and recall the language and other facets of the video in any detail. In my own experience, students are usually happy and eager to view a well-chosen sequence again, particularly if they are provided with a variety of viewing activities that require them to focus on different aspects of the video, such as cultural differences, body language, vocabulary, or language models. Present the activities to the students *before each viewing* in order to focus their attention on the particular viewing task at hand.

Plan Activities for Three Stages

Teachers can promote active viewing and increase student comprehension and recall by planning video-related lessons for three stages of activity: previewing, viewing, and postviewing.

Previewing activities. These prepare the students to watch the video by tapping their background knowledge, stimulating interest in the topic, and lessening their fear of unfamiliar vocabulary. One way of doing this with a drama sequence is to announce the situation and ask students to predict the content. For example, students are told they will see a scene showing a man buying a plane ticket at an airport, and are asked to write down five items under each of two headings: *Sights* (things they expect to see) and *Words* (words they expect to hear).

Viewing activities. These primarily facilitate the actual viewing of the video. They involve playing and replaying the entire sequence or relevant parts and requiring students to focus on important aspects such as factual information, plot development, or the language used in a particular situation. In general, it is a good idea to provide activities that focus on the basic situation first. For example, with a drama sequence, you might ask students to watch and look for the answers to questions such as: Where are these people? Why are they there? What is their relationship? What is going on? After this more global viewing activity, you would then have students do a series of tasks that require them to concentrate on specific details, such as the sequence of events or the particular utterances used.

Postviewing activities. These require students to react to the video or to practice some particular language point. The range of postviewing activities is enormous and includes things such as discussion, role-play, debate, writing activities, and related reading.

These activities listed are merely options, and they represent just a few examples from a wide range of possibilities. You should design, select, or adapt activities that evolve naturally out of the video sequence itself and at the same time meet the needs of your students. For a more comprehensive collection of ideas, see Stempleski and Tomalin (1990).

CONCLUSION

It is worth emphasizing that the teacher, not the video, is responsible for making any video-based lesson a rewarding language learning experience. Like any teaching resource, video is best when it is used carefully and intelligently. How you, the teacher, approach the use of video in your classroom will determine how valuable it is perceived to be by your students, and how significant it will be to them, in the language learning process.

References

Rice, A., & Stempleski, S. (1988). *Explorations: An interactive approach to reading.* Boston, MA: Heinle & Heinle.

Stempleski, S., & Tomalin, B. (1990). *Video in action: Recipes for using video in language teaching.* London: Prentice Hall International.

CHAPTER 37

The Internet for English Teaching: Guidelines for Teachers

Mark Warschauer and P. Fawn Whittaker

Teachers have been using online communication in the language classroom since the 1980s. From an investigation of the experiences of dozens of teachers around the world who have used the Internet in language teaching (Warschauer, 1995a, 1995b, 1996c, 1996d), a few common guidelines emerge that can assist teachers in successfully planning and implementing network-based learning projects.

GUIDELINES

Readers will note that these guidelines are independent of the particular technological tools being used. As has been noted elsewhere, "technology is developing so rapidly that it can often be difficult or even overwhelming to harness somewhat like trying to get a drink of water from a gushing fire hydrant" (Warschauer, 1995b, p. xv). In order to make effective use of new technologies, teachers must thus take a step back and focus on some basic pedagogical requirements. The following guidelines are designed to help teachers implement computer network-based activities and technologies into the second language classroom.

CONSIDER CAREFULLY YOUR GOALS

There are several possible reasons for using the Internet in language teaching. One rationale is found in the belief that the linguistic nature of online communication is desirable for promoting language learning. It has been found, for example, that electronic discourse tends to be more lexically and syntactically complex than oral discourse (Warschauer, 1996a) and features a broad range of linguistic functions beneficial for language learning (Chun, 1994; Kern, 1995; Wang, 1993). Another possible reason for using the Internet is that it creates optimal conditions for learning to write, since it provides an authentic audience for written communication (see, for example, Janda, 1995). A third possible reason is that it can increase students' motivation (Warschauer, 1996c). A fourth possible reason is the belief that learning computer skills is essential to students' future success; this reason suggests that it is not only a matter of using the Internet to learn English, but also of learning English to be able to function well on the Internet.

None of these reasons is more or less legitimate than any of the others. However, since there are so many ways to integrate the Internet into classroom instruction, it is important for the teacher to clarify his or her goals. If, for example, one of the teacher's goals is to teach students new computer skills, the teacher may want to choose Internet applications which will be most useful outside of the classroom, with activities structured so that students steadily gain mastery of more skills. If the immediate goal is to create a certain kind of linguistic environment for students, once again, the teacher should consider what types of language experiences would be beneficial and structure computer activities accordingly. If the goal is to teach writing, Internet activities should be structured so that they steadily bring about an increase in the types of writing processes and relationships essential to becoming a better writer (see, for example, seven activities by Janda in Warschauer, 1995b).

As will be discussed later in this article, little is usually gained by just adding random online activities into a classroom. Clarifying course goals is thus an important first step toward successful use of the Internet.

THINK INTEGRATION

Most teachers who have used the Internet have started out with some kind of simple key pal (computer pen pal) exchanges. And most teachers who have used these exchanges have felt something lacking. Simply put, there is no more reason to expect a significant educational outcome from simply creating a pen pal connection than there is from simply bringing two students into a room and asking them to talk. Over time, greater involvement on the teacher's part in creating learning activities that create sufficient linguistic and cognitive demands on the student is needed to get maximum benefit from Internet exchanges. And, as a number of people have noted, this teacher intervention is most successful when it brings about activities and projects that are well integrated into the course curriculum as a whole.

Bruce Roberts, the coordinator of the Intercultural E-Mail Classroom Connections (IECC) program, explained this point well:

> There is a significant difference in educational outcome depending on whether a teacher chooses to incorporate e-mail classroom connections as (1) an ADD-ON process, [as] one would include a guest speaker, or (2) an INTEGRATED process, in the way one would include a new text-book. The e-mail classroom connection seems sufficiently complex and time consuming that if there are goals beyond merely having each student send a letter to a person at a distant school, the ADD-ON approach can lead to frustration and less-than-expected academic results – the necessary time and resources come from other things that also need to be done. On the other hand, when the e-mail classroom connection processes are truly integrated into the ongoing structure of homework and classroom interaction, then the results can be educationally transforming. (In Warschauer, 1995a, p. 95)

Of course, there are many ways that Internet activities can be integrated into the overall design and goals of a course (see Sayers, 1993, for a good overview). The teacher can work with students to create research questions which are then investigated in collaboration with foreign partners. Students and long-distance partners can work collaboratively on publications. Or students can use exchange partners as experts to supply information on vocabulary, grammar, or cultural points which emerge in the class. Again, the choice has to be made by the classroom teacher, preferably in ongoing consultation with the students. Nevertheless, as Roberts suggests, it does behoove the teacher to think about how to integrate online connections into the class rather than adding these connections on top of the rest of the classroom activities in a disconnected fashion.

DON'T UNDERESTIMATE THE COMPLEXITY

Most English teachers, even those who consider themselves computer novices, have several relative advantages when learning to use the Internet. They are in most cases skilled at English, experienced at typing or keyboarding, and have some basic computer literacy (i.e., they probably have at least used a computer for word processing). ESL students, on the other hand, at least in some cases, may lack these basic prerequisites. Although we have had students who are quite experienced with computers, we have also had students who had seldom used a computer; lacked basic knowledge such as how to operate a mouse or open a folder; and lacked the vocabulary, reading, and listening skills to follow instructions for using the computer.

Beyond these issues of learner preparation, there are a number of other complexities in introducing Internet-based activities in the ESL classroom. Activities in a single class may be dependent on scheduling the computer lab, and on students finding computers outside class time to continue their activities. Hardware and software can malfunction and computer systems can be down. Students' schedules might not permit them to return to the computer lab at a time when computers are available to complete their assignments.

Exchanges between classes are even more complex. The partner class might have absent students, or might not meet in a particular week because of holidays or other activities in that location. The partner teacher might not have the same understanding of the nature of the exchange, and working through differences can cause further delays. The students might have differences in background, language, and experience which can cause further complications.

None of these potential problems mean that Internet-based activities should not be used. But, in attempting to integrate online teaching, it is best not to be overly ambitious in the beginning. A situation which overwhelms both students and teacher in technical difficulties is not likely to bring about the desired results. It is better to start small and to create the kinds of activities which have a direct purpose and are well integrated into classroom goals. If these activities prove successful, you can build from there and attempt a more ambitious plan the following semester.

PROVIDE NECESSARY SUPPORT

Mindful of the complexities which can arise in Internet usage, teachers need to provide support sufficient to prevent students from being overwhelmed by difficulties. This kind of support can take numerous forms: creating detailed handouts that students can refer to when class is finished and the teacher's personal help is not accessible; building technology-training sessions into the class schedule, not only in the beginning but on an ongoing basis; working with the computer center to set up log-on systems and other procedures which are as simple and intuitive as possible; assigning students to work in pairs or groups, both in and out of the lab, so that they can provide assistance to each other; providing details to students about how and when they can get assistance from technology specialists or others on campus outside of class; and being available to help students at times when they are most likely to need it.

INVOLVE STUDENTS IN DECISIONS

The concept of a learner-centered curriculum (Nunan, 1988) predates, and has broader significance than, the Internet-enhanced classroom. However, this concept seems particularly important when considering network-based teaching.

First of all, network-based teaching involves a number of special complexities. It will be difficult for a teacher to be fully aware of the impact of these complexities without regular consultation with students. This might involve anonymous surveys, class discussions, or similar means of involving students in expressing their opinions about the process of implementing technologies.

Beyond that, though, the nature of computer-mediated communication is that it creates opportunities for more decentered interaction (for summaries, see Warschauer, 1996b; Warschauer, Turbee, & Roberts, 1996). To fully exploit these opportunities, the teacher must learn to become a "guide on the side" rather than a "sage on the stage." A situation which is based on communication between students, but in which the students have little say over the topics or outcomes of that communication, is not likely to lead to the kind of atmosphere optimal for language learning.

As pointed out elsewhere (Warschauer, Turbee, & Roberts, 1996), involving students in determining the class direction does not imply a passive role for teachers. Teachers' contributions in a learner-centered, network-enhanced classroom include coordinating group planning, focusing students' attention on linguistic aspects of computer-mediated texts, helping students gain metalinguistic awareness of genres and discourses, and assisting students in developing appropriate learning strategies.

AN ILLUSTRATION FROM THE CLASSROOM

An example of one network-based class will illustrate several of the points in the preceding section. A university instructor decided to organize her ESL advanced writing class largely around network-based exchanges. Class was conducted in a networked computer lab twice weekly and in a regular classroom the remaining two classes weekly. Students shared their writings in small groups within the class, both via E-mail and by exchanging rough and final drafts of their essays. They also carried out exchanges with native-English-speaking partners at other universities in the United States and Canada. The activities were carefully constructed around the teachers' goals, which were to give her students *(a)* experience in learning to write in a variety of styles to a particular audience, and *(b)* frequent opportunities for feedback on the organization and structure of their writing from peers and the teacher.

Unfortunately, the teacher somewhat underestimated the complexity of the new course design, and both the teacher and the students consequently felt overwhelmed by the many tasks. The students, a number of whom were from underdeveloped Pacific Island communities and had little experience with computers, could not keep up with their many assignments, which included lessons for learning keyboarding, grammatical lessons, frequent small-group writing activities, letters to several key pals, and formal essays. Students felt somewhat frustrated and questioned the value of many of the assignments.

Fortunately, the teacher implemented an important guideline: She listened to her students and involved them in the decision making. Based on student feedback in the middle of the semester, the teacher streamlined the course activities, focusing on the activities which most carefully integrated the use of the Internet with the goals of the course and which also gave students more say over the direction of their writing. The students' final projects included short autobiographical essays which were posted on the World Wide Web, a class video project which was directed by the students and shared with their exchange class, and an in-depth essay which incorporated research on the partner's culture compared with their own as gathered from the Web and from E-mail interviews with their key pals. At the end of the class, students expressed pride in what they had learned about writing and using computers. One student from a small Pacific village commented, "Now [that] it's the end of the class, the teacher could just give us anything and I think I can write about it now. I feel confident!"

Conclusion

A paper of this length cannot completely cover the topic of network-based language teaching. Further information on this topic is available in books (see, for example, Warschauer, 1995a, 1995b) and on the Internet itself (see, for example, NETEACH-L at http://thecity.sfsu.edu/~funweb/neteach.htm). In the end, though, each teacher will have to find her or his own way, based on the goals of the teacher and the program, the needs of the students, and the materials and technology available. It is hoped that the guidelines outlined in this paper can provide some assistance to teachers attempting to optimally combine their own goals, their students' needs, and the power of the technology-enhanced classroom.

References

Chun, D. (1994). Using computer networking to facilitate the acquisition of interactive competence. *System, 22*(1), 17–31.

Janda, T. (1995). Breaking the ice: E-mail dialogue journal introductions and responses. In M. Warschauer (Ed.), *Virtual connections: Online activities and projects for networking language learners* (pp. 57–58). Honolulu: University of Hawaii, Second Language Teaching and Curriculum Center.

Kern, R. (1995). Restructuring classroom interaction with networked computers: Effects on quantity and quality of language production. *Modern Language Journal, 79*(4), 457–476.

Nunan, D. (1988). *The learner-centered curriculum.* Cambridge: Cambridge University Press.

Sayers, D. (1993). Distance team teaching and computer learning networks. *TESOL Journal, 3*(1), 19–23.

Wang, Y. M. (1993). E-mail dialogue journaling in an ESL reading and writing classroom. Unpublished Ph.D. dissertation, University of Oregon at Eugene.

Warschauer, M. (1995a). *E-mail for English teaching.* Alexandria, VA: TESOL Publications.

Warschauer, M. (Ed.). (1995b). *Virtual connections: Online activities and projects for networking language learners.* Honolulu: University of Hawaii, Second Language Teaching and Curriculum Center.

Warschauer, M. (1996a). Comparing face-to-face and electronic communication in the second language classroom. *CALICO Journal, 13*(2), 7–26.

Warschauer, M. (1996b). *Computer-mediated collaborative learning: Theory and practice* (Research Note No. 17). Honolulu: University of Hawaii, Second Language Teaching and Curriculum Center.

Warschauer, M. (1996c). Motivational aspects of using computers for writing and communication. In M. Warschauer (Ed.), *Telecollaboration in foreign language learning:*

Proceedings of the Hawaii symposium. Honolulu: University of Hawaii, Second Language Teaching and Curriculum Center.

Warschauer, M. (1996d). *Telecollaboration in foreign language learning: Proceedings of the Hawaii symposium.* Honolulu: University of Hawaii, Second Language Teaching and Curriculum Center.

Warschauer, M., Turbee, L., & Roberts, B. (1996). Computer learning networks and student empowerment. *System, 14*(1), 1–14.

CHAPTER 38

What Can the World Wide Web Offer ESL Teachers?

Rong-Chang Li and Robert S. Hart

Introduction

The rapid growth of the Internet, which links computers all over the world into a single electronic communications network, is in the process of making widespread computer-based instruction a reality. This is owing largely to the advent of the World Wide Web, a system for accessing and viewing information on the Internet. Web browser software such as Mosaic or Netscape permits easy viewing of texts stored on machines all over the Internet and they can display graphics, transmit sounds, and even play movies in the form of digitized video.

The ease with which Web documents can be created, as well as their worldwide accessibility, multimedia capabilities, and interactive functions, make the Web an attractive environment for carrying on computer-based instruction. From the viewpoint of English language instruction, an added advantage is the fact that at present, Web documents, which cover a huge set of subject matters, are mostly written in English, with new documents continually appearing. The Web thus offers a rich database of authentic material.

We have been examining how this new medium can be utilized for ESL instruction. We have learned that the Web is not only a tremendously effective means for disseminating instructional materials, but that it can also provide a context for efficient collaborative materials development.

Design of Experimental Web Learning Material for ESL Learners

Our work has focused on creating multimedia learning environments for intermediate-level ESL learners. We targeted this group because intermediate-level learners seem to be the audience who can profit most immediately from Web-based courseware. Beginners need the carefully graded and structured material already provided by textbooks and may find it difficult to use the Web at all because their English is too limited to cope with the operating instructions of the browser programs. Nor is there a pressing need to develop special materials for advanced ESL learners because one can easily find many Web documents that are interesting and appropriate. In our multimedia work, audio rather than video has been our main focus because Web video is still too slow to be practical for anything but very short video clips. (However, this is changing rapidly.)

Before discussing our work, we want to point out how Web documents augment the capabilities of conventional text. Web browsers support hypertext, a form of cross-referencing in which a highlighted text selection is linked to another document. When a user clicks the highlighted text, the linked document, which may be anywhere within the Web, is displayed. Links not only support immediate access to cross-referenced material but also permit Web documents to be structured as elaborate menus and indices. A simple programming language called the *hypertext markup language* (usually abbreviated HTML) allows authors to annotate documents with these hypertext links and to specify text display formats. To see a particular Web document, one must provide its Internet address (called its *uniform resource locator* or *URL*), which specifies both the name of the document and the name of the computer that contains the document. Usually, an initial URL leads to a menu or index, and from that point on one can follow hypertext links.

Of course, pure display, even when equipped with links, is not sufficient for a flexible instructional environment; some way of interacting with students is also necessary. The Web supports limited interaction by means of forms, which are areas of a document (specifiable using HTML) where the user can type in a response or select a button to click. Once the user has entered some responses, they can be processed by an author-specified program in order to store them as data and send responses as E-mail, or they can be examined with a view to giving the user feedback about correctness.

*EX*CHANGE*: An ESL Web Magazine

In an initial attempt to implement language learning resources on the Web, Li and other graduate students at University of Illinois at Urbana-Champaign founded the ESL Web magazine *EX*CHANGE* (Shetzer, 1995; Zhao, Li, & Hegelheimer, 1995)[1]. Their purpose was to explore ways in which high-quality ESL learning resources could be accumulated, organized, and presented on the Web. The magazine was mainly intended to serve individual ESL learners at the intermediate level, although ESL instructors also can (and do) use it as supplementary material for their classes (see sample page that follows).

The editors of the new magazine considered two common modes of Web publishing as an accessible format for the publication. One was the bulletin board or discussion group, of which Sperling's (1995) *ESL Graffiti Wall* Web page is an example. Bulletin boards are almost always moderated, but control over what is posted is traditionally minimal, and they typically have a conversational quality. The main mode of organization is imposed by whatever conversational "threads" or topics the participants happen to evolve. The second model is traditional periodicals, in which issues appear at fixed intervals, close control is maintained over the quality and content of the materials, and overall organization is imposed by editorial decision.

Both models have their merits. The participatory, dialogue-like nature of the bulletin board was attractive, but in the end the publication model seemed more appropriate for ESL learners because the quality and grammatical accuracy of what they read would affect the quality of their learning.

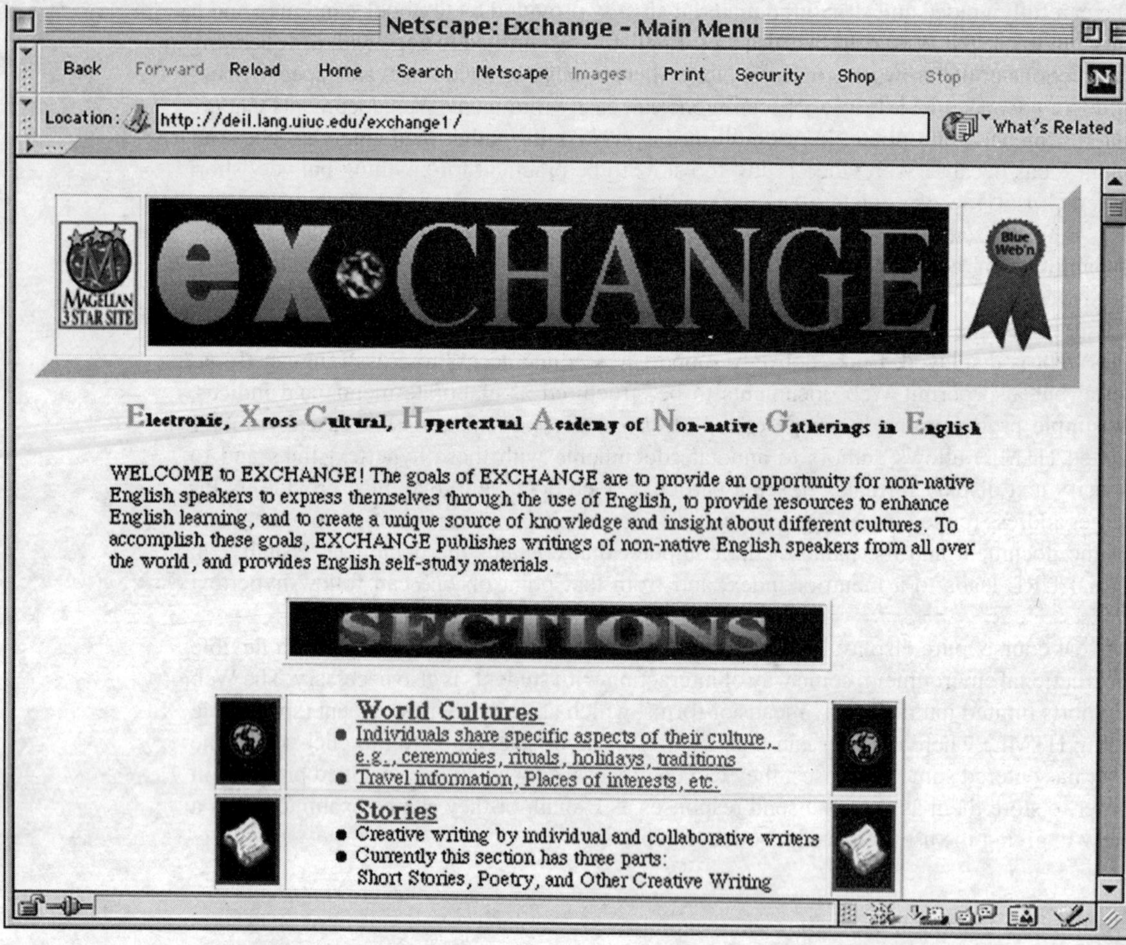

*EX*CHANGE*'s Editorial Departments

Organized to promote the dual functions of promoting communication among ESL learners and serving as a resource archive, *EX*CHANGE* arranges its content in four editorial departments, or sections: World Cultures, Current News and Events, Stories, and the Learning Resource Center. In the World Cultures section, ESL students write about aspects of their cultures such as birthdays in Germany, weddings in India, and old men in Korea. The Current News and Events section reports events that are currently happening in various countries in the world. In the Stories section, ESL students develop exciting chain stories. The topics of these sections reflect what we perceived to be important preoccupations of ESL students and were intended to encourage contributions from readers. The largest section is the Learning Resource Center, which contains reading materials with a comprehension check, discussion of writing strategies, grammar tutorials, and English conversations that help students learn oral English. There are also an English idiom bank and links to an online dictionary and some ESL newsgroups. To enable users to find what they need with a minimum of effort, *EX*CHANGE* aids its readers by offering a built-in search capability such that users can type in key words in order to locate specific materials in past issues of the magazine.

As an edited magazine, *EX*CHANGE* depends on (mainly unsolicited) submissions from its readers. Both ESL teachers and learners contribute via the forms within *EX*CHANGE* itself or by E-mail. The editors (all experienced ESL teachers) read the submissions and send them back with comments and corrections, requesting, when appropriate, that ESL student writers revise and resubmit their articles. The World Cultures, News, and Stories sections were designed to elicit participation and encourage interaction among readers. They have succeeded in doing this, but not as well as we had hoped. The intervention of an editorial apparatus slows and inhibits spontaneous interaction. Many would-be student contributors are undoubtedly intimidated by the prospect of having their errors critiqued by unknown editors and by the labor involved in revision, while instructors may feel pressure to spend time writing for professional journals for which the rewards are more tangible.

Advantages of Electronic Medium over Print

Nevertheless, *EX*CHANGE* has proved to have substantial advantages over a traditional paper magazine. As with any other electronic magazine, the time and effort needed to publish articles is reduced. Communication between editors and writers is through E-mail. All the contributions are submitted and published in electronic form, which makes it easier and faster to get the work done and possible to post new material as soon as it is available. Color pictures, audio, and even video can be presented as inexpensively as text. Archival material is easy to maintain and retrieve. Perhaps most important, it is possible to build a wide audience without extensive (and costly) promotion and advertising. As soon as *EX*CHANGE* went online, standard Web search facilities introduced it to the ESL community, and the magazine was soon linked to various other ESL sites. Readership grew almost overnight to more than one hundred readers per day from more than forty different countries.

Preferences for Audio Formats

The multimedia aspect of *EX*CHANGE* is unquestionably popular with our readers; however, we are not yet sure what kinds of audio materials readers actually want. To investigate this question, Li (1995b) created materials that incorporated text and audio in four different formats. He used short, interesting stories designed to promote the integration of reading, listening, and speaking skills.[2] The first text, *Scientists Listen in on Whales* (*Whales*), is a two hundred-word news article with point-and-click glossary help. Words likely to be difficult for ESL students are highlighted. When the student clicks on one of these words, it is pronounced aloud (using prerecorded digitized speech). Definitions of the glossed words are also given at the end of the reading material.

A second story, titled *Will the Leaning Tower Topple Over*? (*Tower*), discusses the Leaning Tower of Pisa. In this format, text is not automatically presented to the students at the beginning. Rather, they have the options of listening to the whole story without seeing the text or looking at the text, and can shift back and forth between these two modes.

A third story, *This Judge Really "Sentences" Criminals* (*Criminals*), is designed to give students oral practice with smaller text units. Students can see the text and read it. Each sentence of the text is also linked to a prerecorded audio rendition that the student can request (by clicking) to hear at any time. Students can listen to the text sentence by sentence, read after the native speaker, and imitate the pronunciation and intonation.

The last text, *Everday English*, is not a story but a collection of commonly used English expressions such as *Can you give me a ride?* A student can click an expression in order to listen to it again and again. This activity is designed for learners who want to learn to speak some limited English for a specific purpose.

The formats also vary with respect to the amount of time the user has to wait while the audio material is downloaded, that is, copied to the user's machine so that it can start playing. The audio associated with the story *Tower*, the audio of the whole story, is longest and takes the longest (up to about 1 minute depending on the speed of a local network) to download. Other audios are for individual words or sentences, which imposes a wait of only a second or so. The wait for downloading is an issue for all multimedia materials for the Web, particularly video and, to a lesser extent, still pictures.

Our intent was to see which formats our worldwide clientele of ESL students and instructors would find most acceptable. As a rough measure of acceptability, we kept track of the frequency with which each file was accessed (the Web server that we used can automatically record simple usage data in a usage log).

The frequency data indicate that, among the four formats, the first story, *Whales*, with point-and-click pronouncing glossary, has been accessed most. This may be owing in part to the fact that it occupies the first position in the menu and attracts more attention, but it may also be because it involves a shorter wait to hear the audio. We did not anticipate, however, that the third story, *Criminals*, with the format of listening to the text sentence by sentence, would be the least accessed section – only about 30% as often as the average of the other three sections. Nor did we expect that, among all the individual sound files, the longest sound file – the whole audio for the second story, *Tower* – would be accessed most, about six times more often than most other individual sound files. We thought that this sound file would be accessed infrequently because it takes so long to download. The popularity of *Tower* may indicate that ESL learners like the particular story content, or like to hear a whole story rather than listening to it sentence by sentence, or that they prefer one long wait to many short ones, or some combination of these factors. Generally, however, ESL Web learners seem to like the *Everyday English* best since the sound files in this section, which occupies the last position in the menu, have gotten much more use than the audio materials in other sections.

These statistics, of course, do not bear on the effectiveness of the different formats, only on their acceptability. They do, however, show that we cannot trust our intuition in these matters and so suggest the value of further experimental work.

Templates for Interactive Exercises

Besides the structuring of multimedia materials, attaining adequate interactivity is another problem for Web-based instruction. The greatest hurdle for HTML authors is without doubt the cumbersome process required to create interactive activities. Web forms do provide instructionally useful input formats such as scrolling and nonscrolling text areas, check-box buttons, radio buttons, and pop-up menus (see sample of Netscape Interactive Facilities on the following page). On the other hand, forms have serious drawbacks, a major one being that creating exercises generally requires tedious HTML programming.

What is needed is a way to author popular exercise types such as multiple choice, cloze, written response, free response, point-and-click glossary help and annotation, and so on, without using HTML. This can be accomplished neatly with the aid of JavaScript, a simple programming language supported by Web browsers. Hart is currently developing a set of JavaScript-based exercise templates that require instructors to provide nothing but exercise content, yet allow for response analysis, feedback, and instructional management.[3]

Other ESL Learning Resources for the Web

Our experiments are in no way unique. Web-based ESL materials are under intensive development at many locations. Most English language centers and intensive English institutes now maintain their own Web pages as a way to advertise their programs. Many ESL teachers have devoted their time and energy to developing various TESOL resources on the Web, some intended for ESL teachers, others for ESL learners. Resources for teachers include Web magazines such as the *Internet TESOL Journal* (1995), designed along the lines of a

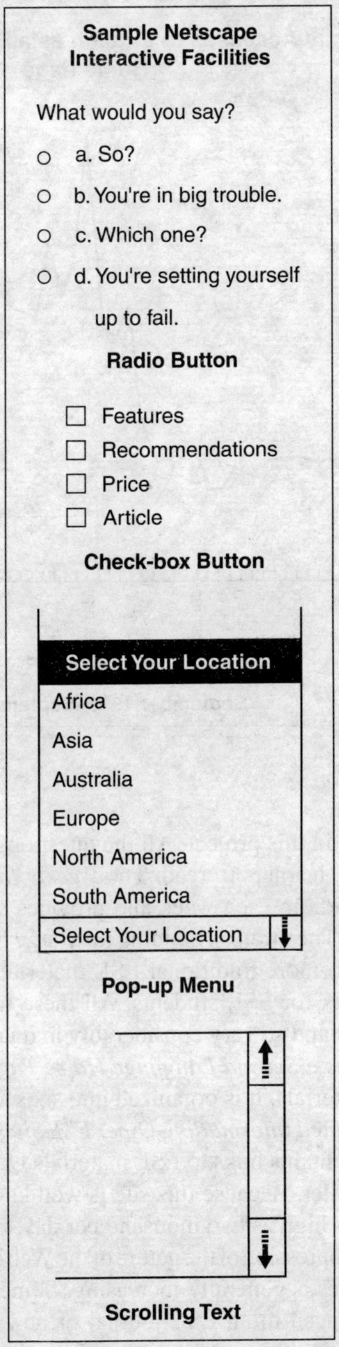

professional journal, with discussion of TESOL issues, lesson plans, and teaching ideas. Bowers (1995) put together *Resources for Teachers of English for Science and Technology*, a Web page that links many Web resources relevant for this group of teachers. Harris's (1995) *Linguistic Funland* lists resources including ESL organizations, ESL discussion lists and newsgroups, and ESL employment.

There are more Web resources for ESL learners than for ESL teachers. Sperling's (1996) *ESL Help Center on the Web* is a resource in a bulletin-like format. Any ESL learner can post a question and will get an answer from one of the ESL teachers that Sperling

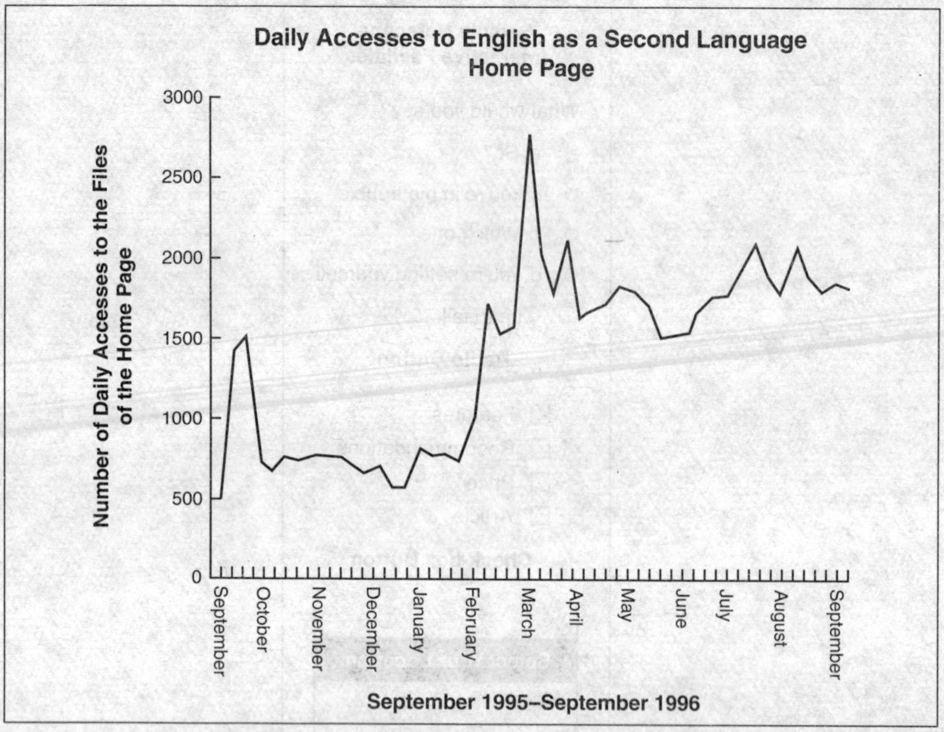

Figure 1

has recruited to participate in this project. All the questions and answers are posted on the bulletin board for any ESL learners to read. The *Weekly Idiom* Web site of the Comenius Group (1995) selects one idiom each week and provides short conversations to illustrate how the idiom can be used. The group is building up a large English-idiom learning resource on the Web. There are also more traditional ESL materials on the Web, such as English grammar and sample letters for ESL students. All these materials are subject to varying degrees of editorial control and so vary considerably in quality.

Li's (1995a) *English as a Second Language Home Page* provides general access for a large selection of these materials. It is organized into six sections: *Listening and Speaking*, *Reading*, *Writing*, *ESL-Related Information*, *Other ESL Sites on the Web*, and *ESL Learners' Web pages*. Each section contains links to ESL materials Li has found or created, including the materials discussed earlier. Because this site is well known and heavily used, with the number of files accessed as high as two thousand per day,[4] we can examine usage patterns (see Figure 1 to gain some impression of the nature of the Web ESL community and its needs).

The number of accesses is generally increasing. Sometimes a peak occurred because the home page was introduced in an ESL journal or newspaper at the time. Among the six sections of the English as a Second Language Home Page, the Listening and Speaking section is accessed most, accounting for 36% of total accesses. It is possible that the novelty of being able to receive audio over the Web has played a role in the popularity of this section, but such a high percentage also suggests that listening and speaking materials are most in demand by ESL learners on the Web.

We have tabulated the frequency of access by country of origin (see Figure 2). About 46% of the identifiable accesses come from the United States, and the rest are from more than forty other countries or regions, with Korea, Japan, Canada, Australia, Brazil, Italy, Germany, Taiwan, Hong Kong, and Israel as significant users.

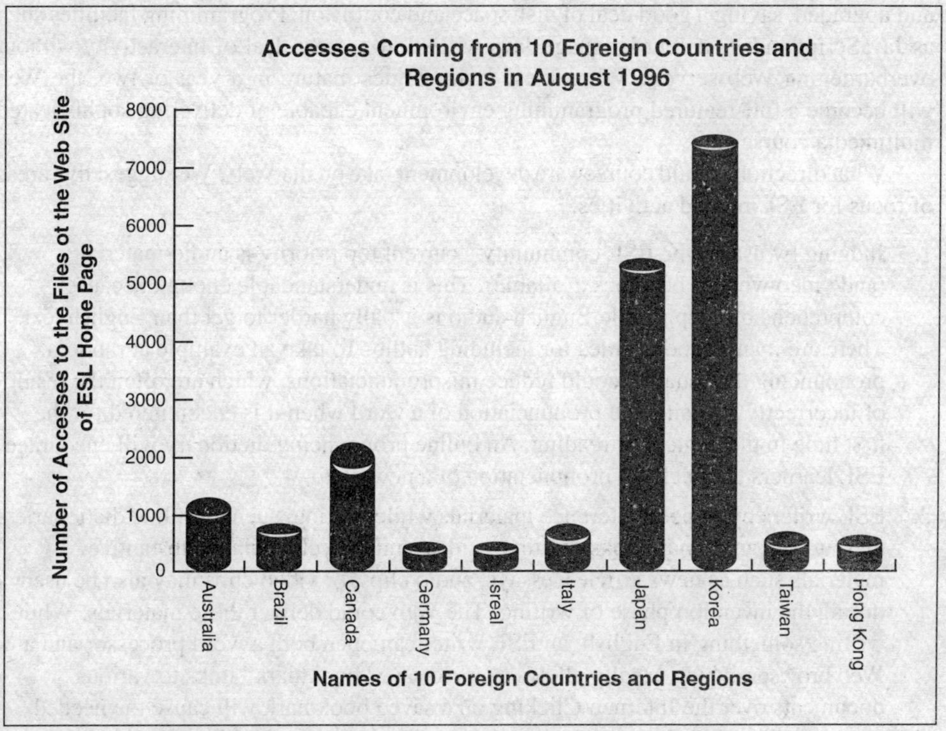

Figure 2

Most of the users are from developed countries. This is undoubtedly because a large portion of ESL learners in developing countries are still unable to access the Web owing to scarcity of suitably equipped computers or the expense of Internet communications. Because it is precisely in these countries that other authentic materials are scarce, the demand for Web-based resources will surely increase as ESL learners in these areas begin to gain Web access. A striking feature of the statistics is very high usage by Korea and Japan, each exceeding that of all European countries combined. The explanation for this phenomenon, which cannot plausibly be attributed to population totals or inferior European access, remains unclear to us.

To encourage feedback, the *ESL Home Page* allows users to type in a message and send it via E-mail. We receive messages sent by users of the page almost every day from readers in many different countries. Most of them say that the resources are very useful and ask us to make more material available. Some people asked us to help them with specific problems in using the Web. Others sent the addresses of new ESL resources they had found or created. We respond appropriately to these messages whenever possible. To date we have not received any negative comments.

Conclusions

Technology is evolving so rapidly that any TESOL courseware on the Web must be considered work in progress. We certainly consider our efforts in this light. Although predicting the future is always a risky undertaking, some short-term Web developments are clear. "Streaming" and "plug-in" technologies now under development will soon allow the delivery of good-quality audio and video to Web users in real time without a download delay. This will mean that only a single copy of multimedia materials will need to be stored, maintained, and upgraded, saving a good deal of disk space and confusion. Programming facilities such as JavaScript and its parent language Java will allow a great deal of interactivity without overburdening Web servers. When these technologies mature in a year or two, the Web will become a full-featured programming environment capable of delivering sophisticated multimedia courseware.

What direction should courseware development take on the Web? We suggest five areas of focus for ESL-related activities:

1. Judging by usage, the ESL community's current top priority is audio material (and video when it becomes available). This is understandable enough because comprehensible, replayable English audio is usually harder to get than English text. There are many opportunities for including audio. To take an example at random, pronouncing dictionaries could reduce mispronunciations, which are often the result of incorrectly guessing the pronunciation of a word when it is encountered for the first time in the context of reading. An online pronouncing dictionary will encourage ESL learners to check the pronunciation of a new word.
2. ESL writers often need reference materials while writing, such as online dictionaries, thesauruses, grammar books, writing guides, and encyclopedias. Substantive materials such as news articles, essays, audio clips, or video clips may also be used during the invention phase of writing. The Web could deliver these materials. While writing something in English, an ESL writer can open both a word processor and a Web browser, which usually allows users to save "bookmark" links to various documents over the Internet. Clicking on a saved bookmark will cause the needed corresponding document to appear on the screen instantly; in this way, the student can build up a personalized writing environment. The ESL community should encourage commercial publishers of such reference works to make their products available in a Web-accessible form.
3. The newest Web browsers allow users to post E-mail and bulletin board messages. This opens the possibility for ESL composition of a much wider use of peer editing, collaborative writing, and various peer-audience activities already popular in English composition.
4. Web forms are a convenient and efficient means for building and grading exercises, quizzes, and objective tests. The development of template systems should make this as quick and easy as putting the equivalent exercise on paper. Browsers such as Netscape support passwords and encryption to guarantee privacy and data security. However, testing activities become really useful only if there is instructional management software in place to collect and store scores, aggregate data, and produce reports for instructors. The whole issue of institutional management in the highly distributed Web environment needs careful study.
5. The Web comprises a vast and continually growing library. A library, however, is only useful if you can find the document you need. Web links and index pages can create some order by organizing documents into categories and hierarchies. Search facilities help, but sometimes fail to retrieve the desired document or else retrieve far too many. The Web can automatically collect detailed information about specialized usage, including document access. Keyword requests can be recorded and analyzed. Such tracking data can tell us how our users interact (or want to interact) with the Web, and consequently what sorts of documents, organization, and keyword coding will be most useful to them. Multiple perspectives may be required; for example, a student moving through a set of documents as part of an exploratory learning assignment may need a different organization from that of an instructor looking for materials to use in class.

Although these five areas seem particularly fruitful directions for the immediate future, there are plenty of other possibilities open to exploration. Indeed, during the next few years the evolving Web will open new possibilities for TESOL courseware; in the process, both instructors and students are sure to gain.

References

Bowers, R. (1995). *Resources for teachers of English for science and technology*. Available: http://www.wfi.fr/est/est 1.html.

Comenius Group (1995). *The weekly idiom*. Available: http://www.comenius.com./idiom/index.html.

Godwin, J. R. (1994). *Language learning and the World Wide Web*. Available: http://www.ncsa.uiuc.edu/SDG/IT94/Agenda/Papers-received.html.

Harris, K. P. (1995). *Linguistic funland*. Available: http://math.unr.edu/linguistics/linguistic.funland.html.

Internet TESOL Journal (1995). *Internet TESOL journal*. http://www.aitech.ac.jp/-iteslj/.

Li, R. C. (1995a). *English as a second language home page*. Available: http://www.lang.uiuc.edu/r-li5/esl/.

Li, R. C. (1995b). Integration of listening, reading, and speaking skills. Available: http://www.lang.uiuc.edu/r-li5/ESLproject/eslbeg.html.

Shetzer, H. (1995). *EX*CHANGE*: *El*ectronic *X*ross *C*ultural, *H*ypertextual *A*cademy of *N*on-native *G*atherings in *E*nglish. In M. Warschauer (Ed.), *Virtual connections*. Manoa, HI: University of Hawaii Press.

Sperling, D. (1995). *ESL graffiti wall*. Available: http://www.pacificnet.net/-sperling/wall.html.

Sperling, D. (1996). *ESL help center on the Web*. Available: http://www.pacificnet.net/-sperling/wwwboard2/wwwboard.html.

Zhao, Y., Li, R. C., & Hegelheimer, V (1995). *EX*CHANGE*. http://deil.lang.uiuc.edu/exchange/.

Endnotes

[1] Yong Zhao served as the first coordinator of the *EX*CHANGE* project and did much of the initial programming. Many people have helped to make *EX*CHANGE* possible, among them Volker Hegelheimer, Heidi S. Shetzer, Eric McCune, Kim Nguyen-Jahiel, Anita Pandey, Leslie K. Hammersmith, and Michael Lindeman. Professors Gary Cziko, Robert Hart, and James Levin have served as an informal *EX*CHANGE* faculty advisory committee. *EX*CHANGE*, supported in 1994–1995 by the College of Education, is now supported by Division of English as an International Language at University of Illinois at Urbana-Champaign.

[2] These texts were used with permission from the copyright holder, Scholastic, Inc.

[3] These templates, which are freely available for use, can be downloaded by link from the home page of the University of Illinois at Urbana-Champaign Language Learning Laboratory, (http://www.lang.uiuc.edu), or by FTP from (ftp://ftp.lang.uiuc.edu).

[4] Access frequencies should be interpreted conservatively. The home page contains a number of documents. The access to each document was counted as a separate file access, although graphics were filtered out in counting file accesses.

SECTION 16

PROFESSIONAL DEVELOPMENT

INTRODUCTION

The last section in this anthology deals with the central issue of teachers' professional development. Over the years we have come to realize that, to quote Hargreaves and Fullan (1992, p. ix), "the teacher is the ultimate key to educational change and school improvement." Teachers do not simply implement the curriculum. They define and refine the curriculum; they interpret and transform the curriculum in a way that makes learning more manageable for the learners. In other words, it is what teachers think and do at the classroom level that eventually determines what learners learn in the classroom. Thus, given the key role of the teachers in the classroom, it is imperative that professional growth become a top priority. Teachers should constantly develop not only their knowledge of the subject matter, but also their knowledge of pedagogy. The three articles in this section look at the different aspects of professional development.

Ur sets the scene by defining the concept of professionalism in the context of the work of the English teacher. After discussing the notion of professionalism, she asks if we English teachers can be rightly called professionals. Do we belong to a community of professionals who interact and exchange ideas for the purpose of developing our professionalism? Are we a learning community which is interested in acquiring new knowledge and experimenting with new ideas? Are we committed to achieving certain desirable standards in our profession? Are we autonomous enough to set professional standards so as to make sure that only those meeting the standards can take part in educating our students? Unfortunately, the answers to these questions are not always in the complete affirmative. Ur asserts that although we have seen a lot of progress, we have not yet reached a satisfactory level of professionalism.

Pettis begins by saying that all teachers should embark on a lifelong journey of developing professional competence. She goes on to say that it is our professional responsibility to continuously undertake a wide range of activities to improve our teaching competence. Reflecting on her personal journey to professional growth, she highlights three important areas. First, to be a true professional, teachers must constantly upgrade their knowledge and understanding of language and language learning. But this is not enough. They should also develop their skills in translating this newly acquired knowledge in their teaching. Second, teachers' professional interests and needs should change over time. As they progress in their careers, they should also seek out different professional development activities. For example, young teachers may initially be concerned with *what-to-teach* questions. But, as they gain more experience, they should be more concerned with the principles that underlie the various teaching techniques and activities that they use. Finally, professional development requires a personal and ongoing commitment. Pettis suggests that we should make the many professional development activities (in-service courses, classroom research, seminars, etc.) our *personal* plan. Our profession deserves no less than our wholehearted commitment to excellence.

Taylor discusses how teachers can develop their professionalism through conducting research in their own classroom. Knowledge gained from this type of research can be very rewarding, as teachers can develop a deeper understanding of what goes on in their classroom which in turn can become the basis for improving their instructional practices. Taylor describes the major stages of carrying out an action research study, which include generating a meaningful research question, finding out what other people have found out about the topic of our investigation, collecting, analyzing, and interpreting the data, and reporting the results. Taylor suggests that teachers should start with a small, achievable project, preferably one that deals with the most relevant classroom issues, such as how to increase student participation in class, or how to get students motivated to read extensively. After gaining experience and confidence, teachers can move on with a larger and more complicated research project.

Discussion Questions

Before Reading

1. As a teacher, what have you done to promote your professional competence?
2. Discuss in what ways the following can help you develop professionally. Which ones contribute most to your professional development?
   - teaching journal
   - materials development
   - feedback from colleagues
   - learner feedback
   - seminars and workshops
3. Some teachers seem to stop developing at some stage in their career. What do you think are the reasons?
4. How important is your work environment in promoting your professional growth?
5. In what ways has your philosophy of teaching changed over the years? Give some concrete examples.
6. What is the role of in-service, teacher-training programs in teachers' professional development?

After Reading

1. Review the article by Penny Ur. How is professionalism defined? Would you want to add anything to the definition?

2. Do you agree with Ur that despite progress that has been made in our profession, we have not reached a satisfactory level of professionalism? Suggest ways in which professionalism in our field can be further promoted.
3. Reflect on your own professional development. How has your approach to teaching changed over time? Have your needs and interests remained the same or changed over the years?
4. Pettis points out that professional development requires an ongoing and personal commitment. What else does it include?
5. What is action research? How might action research help you develop your understanding of language teaching and learning?
6. Describe an action research study that you have just completed. What were some of the difficulties that you encountered? Did you gain any useful insights from it?
7. Review the article by Taylor. What are the stages involved in doing an action research study? Think of a question of practical interest to you and develop a research plan to answer this question.

Further Reading

Hargreaves, A., & Fullan, M. G. (Eds.). (1992). *Understanding teacher development.* New York: Teachers College Press.

CHAPTER 39

The English Teacher as Professional

Penny Ur

Introduction

A 'professional' is, broadly speaking, someone whose work involves performing a certain function with some degree of expertise. But a narrower definition limits the term to apply to people such as doctors, teachers and lawyers, whose expertise involves not only skill and knowledge but also the exercise of highly sophisticated judgement, and whose accreditation necessitates extensive study, often university-based, as well as practical experience.

This notion of professionalism can be further clarified by contrasting it with others that it is often set in opposition to: concepts such as lay, amateur, technician, academic. Each contrast offers an understanding from a different perspective.

This article explores these contrasts, and relates them to the work of the English teacher.

Professional versus Lay

A 'lay' population is a population that does not belong to a specified professional group. Members of the professional group possess certain skills, knowledge, and conventions that the lay population do not have. Typically, they communicate between themselves employing vocabulary that is not readily comprehensible to a layperson (in our case, examples would be *cloze*, *L1*, *L2*, *ESP* etc.). These qualifications make them into a 'club' for the initiated to which others do not belong: a professional community.

Like many others, the professional community of English teachers has developed means of consolidating relationships between its members and created opportunities for them to benefit from each other's knowledge. It holds courses and conferences: locally or nationally and, increasingly, internationally (IATEFL, TESOL etc.). And it sets up organs through which members can exchange ideas and publish innovations (journals, newsletters, Internet sites, etc.).

PROFESSIONAL VERSUS AMATEUR

The distinction between the professional and the amateur is based on consistent differences in performance in the field, involving the quality of preparatory and ongoing learning, standards and commitment. The amateur does things for fun, for the love of it: thus someone who knows English may have a go at teaching it, as an amateur, without any particular training or commitment. He or she may do it well, or badly. But the professional cannot allow himself or herself to 'have a go' at teaching or to do it badly.

Professionalism means preparing oneself to do a competent job through learning. This learning may take the form of preservice or in-service courses, reflection on experience, reading, observation, discussion with colleagues, writing, research – the means are numerous. Such learning continues throughout the professional's working life. Similarly, the professional recognises certain standards: of knowledge (of the subject and of its methodology), of dedication and hard work, of behaviour and of relationships with clients (learners, patients) and other professionals.

Some of these standards are, in many professions, maintained through compulsory examinations and nationally or internationally recognised qualifications – this is increasingly true also of English teaching, though not universally. Finally, there is the aspect of commitment and responsibility. Just as the lawyer is committed to doing the best for the client, so professional teachers are committed to bringing about the best learning they can in their classes.

One implication of this is that we may not play around and experiment with our classes, trying out new 'fads' only because they are fashionable or fun for us: We may only try out new things if we are confident that they will benefit our students' learning; compare the situation of the doctor with new treatments.

The distinction between professional and amateur is one of general principle, and may, in individual cases, be blurred or nonexistent. As in many fields, a gifted amateur may outperform a professional. And the amateur may become a professional, provided he or she adopts the professional approach just described. Many excellent teachers in fact began as amateurs, and developed their professionalism over the course of time.

PROFESSIONAL VERSUS TECHNICIAN

The technician, craftsman, or artisan performs certain acts with skill and becomes more skillful as time goes on, through practice. The professional has not only to acquire certain skills, but also to be able to take courses of action that are based on knowledge and thought, as distinct from automatic routines. Beyond this, he or she has to understand the principles underlying both automatic and consciously designed action, and be able to articulate them, relate them to each other, and innovate.

There are, therefore, many jobs that may be done either 'technically' or 'professionally', depending on the way the worker approaches and performs them: An innovative and thoughtful carpenter may be a professional (Adam Bede, for example, in George Eliot's book of that name); a nurse who performs only routine duties as he or she is told may be more of a technician.

The native English speaker is a technician, in the sense that he or she is skilled in speaking English; the English teacher is in principle a professional: He or she cannot only speak the language, but can also explain why it works the way it does and what different bits of it mean, and knows how to 'mediate' it to learners in a form that they can grasp and learn (for a more comprehensive discussion of this point, see Shulman, 1986). The teacher also knows how to manage classrooms and relationships: Again, these are not just unthinking skills but thoughtfully evolved and flexible sets of professional behaviours. The combination of these kinds of knowledge enables the experienced teacher to make informed and appropriate real-time decisions when – as often happens – different, equally valid principles appear to conflict in a particular situation.

One important implication of this is the professional autonomy of the teacher. Because the teacher has a deep understanding of the principles of professional action, enabling him or her to innovate and to relate critically to the innovations of others, it follows that he or she may not just carry out instructions or adopt, unthinkingly, the recommendations of 'experts'. We ourselves are the experts. We should certainly listen to other people's ideas, but we should adopt them only in so far as we find them acceptable in terms of our own thinking and experience.

Professional versus Academic

An academic can be defined as a researcher, lecturer, and writer, usually based in a university. According to the contrasts defined up to now, the academic comes under the category of 'professional', and many academics would so define themselves. But there is an essential difference between the occupation of the doctor, architect, teacher on the one hand, and the research scientist on the other. The professional is, first and foremost, a bringer-about of real-world change: The doctor cures patients, the architect designs buildings, the teacher brings about or catalyses learning. Essentially, the professional prioritises real-time action, whereas the academic prioritises thought – though of course the professional also thinks about his or her actions, and the academic acts in order to develop his or her thinking. The distinction is thus one of emphasis and priorities rather than of substance.

The following list summarises the differences, as well as one important similarity.

The Academic

- is primarily occupied in thinking and researching.
- acts (researches) in order to refine thinking.
- is interested in finding out the truth or more information.
- is not an immediate agent of real-world change.
- is evaluated in the short term by his or her publications.
- is evaluated in the long term by his or her influence on the thought and action of both academics and professionals (and sometimes of the lay public).

The Professional

- is primarily occupied in real-time action.
- thinks in order to improve action.
- is interested in finding out what works.
- is an immediate agent of real-world change.
- is evaluated in the short term by the extent to which he or she brings about valuable change.
- is evaluated in the long term by his or her influence on the thought and action of both academics and professionals (and sometimes of the lay public).

The similarity is in the last item: Whatever they do during their active careers, the work of both will be judged ultimately by how they have contributed to their field in a way that can benefit future generations. Galileo would be an example of the first category, Socrates of the second.

An implication of all this is that research and thinking by the academic may not always apply or be relevant to professional practice, just as 'what works' for us may not be for them a worthwhile or generalisable scientific hypothesis. There is, obviously, much for us to learn from one another, but to impose the priorities of the one on the activity of the other is to dilute or actually mar its quality.

Thus, to claim that academic research should justify itself in terms of its usefulness or applicability to real-world professional practice is to deny academic freedom and the joy of discovery for its own sake. And it is, similarly, wrong to imply that professionals should base their professional action primarily on the results of academic research and theorising.

The English teacher is essentially a professional engaged in bringing about real-world change, who may on occasion undertake academic research. The two endeavours are different, but mutually beneficial and equally to be respected.

We English Teachers . . .

Thus, to say that we English teachers are professionals is to imply that:

- We are a community. We are an identifiable group, whose members are interested in interaction with one another for the sake of learning, and also for the enjoyment of exchanging experiences and ideas with sympathetic colleagues.
- We are committed. We are committed to reaching certain standards of performance, and we are aware of our responsibility toward our learners and their learning.
- We publish. We communicate innovatory ideas, whether theoretical or practical, to one another and to the public at large: through in-house seminars, national or international conferences, journals, or books.
- We learn. We do not just teach: We also learn, continually – about our subject matter, about teaching methods, and about many other things that make us better educated and therefore better educators. We read, we listen, we reflect, we discuss.
- We are autonomous. Nobody else can tell us what to do; we ourselves are responsible for maintaining professional standards. In principle, therefore, a professional body should set the requirements for accreditation at different levels and should act as 'gatekeeper', ensuring that teaching is not performed by ill-qualified amateurs.
- We are responsible for training new teachers. It is the professional teachers who should be organising courses and teaching the next generation of practitioners, whether through school-based, college-based, or university-based courses.

. . . Professionals?

English teaching has not yet reached the level of professionalism, as defined here, that – to me at least – seems desirable. Some of the conditions described have not yet been realised, or not to the level I would like to see. There are still too many amateurs around, who think that it is enough to know English in order to teach it, resulting in lowering of teaching standards; there are too many academics telling us how to teach, and too many 'technician' teachers. Perhaps also there are too many laypersons in positions of authority, taking or causing ill-informed decisions on the management of the learning of English in schools or on teacher training.

But things are moving. In my own working lifetime, I have seen significant progress toward professionalism. Thriving English teachers' organisations now exist in most countries, as do journals and regular seminars and conferences; professional bodies have set up courses and tests to accredit teachers; increasingly, teachers take pride in their work, invest time and effort in it, lecture and write.

References

Barrow, R. (1984). *Giving teaching back to teachers.* Brighton, Sussex: Wheatsheaf.

Shulman, L. S. (1986). Those who understand: Knowledge growth in teaching. *Educational Researcher, 15*(2), 4–14.

CHAPTER 40

Developing Our Professional Competence: Some Reflections

Joanne Pettis

INTRODUCTION

For many, the melting snows of spring and burgeoning greenery signal the advent of a new year. For others, the new year began several months earlier, in January. For me, however, the new year begins in September with the start of a new school year. It is then that my pulse quickens in anticipation of the excitement of meeting new groups of students and seeing my colleagues again after the long, lazy summer. It is also at that time that I make my professional resolutions. I promise myself that I am going to spend more time with teachers, discussing educational issues and finding out about the realities of their teaching situations, their particular concerns, solutions, innovations, and strengths. I am going to read more and reflect on the implications of my reading. I am going to find time to work with more students, trying out ideas I have been exploring, honing new techniques, and learning more, always more about adult language learners and second language acquisition.

It is the time that I become particularly aware that I am both a teacher and a learner. For just as adult ESL students realize that learning English is a possibly lifelong process, so too have I realized that the development of professional competence is equally long-term and ongoing. At the beginning of a new year, I find myself reflecting on the implications of this realization for me as an adult ESL educator.

Like many adult ESL educators, I recognize that my role is multifaceted. Some of us see ourselves as change agents, bridges to our society, and student advocates. We also no doubt recognize our fundamental and pivotal role in facilitating the development of our students' communicative competence. Although I am not working directly with adult ESL students in the classroom, I believe that my work and that of my colleagues who provide support to teachers and programs is ultimately directed to that goal. Giving a definition to the term *communicative competence*, however, has provided me with important context.

I have been influenced by a definition provided by Tedick and Walker (1994). They suggest that communicative competence is the ability to communicate and understand messages across linguistic and cultural boundaries. I like this definition because of the reciprocal nature of communication and the fundamental context of culture it portrays. The Canale and Swain paradigm of communicative competence that subsumes linguistic, discourse, strategic, and sociolinguistic competence (Richards & Rodgers, 2001) has also influenced my conception of communicative competence, particularly as it is this paradigm that has informed the development of the Canadian Language Benchmarks, which many of us are beginning to work with. The Celce-Murcia, Döornyei, and Thurrell (1995) proposal of an alternative construct with an additional actional competence and other modifications introduces an exciting new representation of communicative competence. However, whether the Canale and Swain paradigm provides my conceptual framework or the model articulated by Celce-Murcia et al., if my goal is communicative competence it behooves me to ensure that I have the requisite principles, knowledge, and skills to accomplish it.

What those principles, knowledge, and skills are will no doubt also reflect the particular conception of teaching I hold and the implications of my other roles. However, three things are clear:

1. If I am to be a professionally competent educator, I must be principled and knowledgeable in addition to skillful.
2. My professional needs and interests have changed over time and continue to evolve.
3. My commitment to professional development must be ongoing and personal.

Let me address each of these observations.

Principles, Knowledge, and Skills

Principles, knowledge, and skills are fundamentally integrated in the professionally competent teacher. If I am to be professionally effective, I believe I must ensure a balance in my expertise. To be knowledgeable and principled without the appropriate skills necessary to apply this knowledge is limiting. The knowledgeable teacher who is also skillful is a powerful educator, and the adult ESL profession has a substantial number of knowledgeable, skillful teachers. Skill, too, in the absence of knowledge is of limited value. Skillful teachers, who have amassed an effective array of activities and techniques that they can and do employ, but who have not developed a parallel level of knowledge, limit their effectiveness. Unfortunately, the application of their skill is constrained by the limitations of their cognitive framework.

The growing body of knowledge on topics such as learning styles and language learning strategies, the role of discourse in communicative language teaching, adult ESL/literacy, and the cultural dimensions of language learning and teaching beg for exploration. Even "old" standbys such as linguistics cannot be neglected, for surely knowledge about English, its vocabulary, and its grammar is a fundamental requirement of adult ESL teachers. Teachers regularly claim that the ability to speak English is insufficient preparation to teach English, yet some contradict this by saying that, because they do not overtly teach grammar, there is no need for them to acquire grammatical knowledge. I would counter that assumption: If we are not relying on a grammar syllabus, we must be particularly knowledgeable and skillful so that the necessary range of topics is addressed appropriately and sufficiently.

Some have also suggested that teachers do not need to know much linguistic information if they "just" teach beginners. I wonder how effective teachers would be in teaching reading to grade 1 students if they had no background in teaching reading, or how competent they would feel if they only read at a grade 1 level themselves. In addition, experience tells us that our students' language encounters in the real world are unlikely to follow the hierarchical organization presented in many classrooms. When a beginner student asks a teacher to explain the grammar of *Smoking is not allowed*, the teacher will no doubt want to provide a more appropriate explanation than "That's just how we say it," and needs to draw on linguistic knowledge to do so.

Even the principles that guide our decision making can change over time and deserve to be reconsidered periodically. For instance, a particular principle I have held for a number of years is the centrality of learner-centeredness in adult ESL instruction. However, I find I must reconsider this principle in light of an article by Auerbach (1993), in which she argues that learner-centeredness should not be equated with participatory education. Instead, it can be shown that learner-centeredness requires an accompanying critical analysis of the social context to be truly participatory. Without social analysis and with its focus on individualism, learner-centeredness may further marginalize learners and reinforce the status quo. Certainly food for thought and discussion.

Changing Needs

Every workshop presenter I know has at one time or another received contradictory feedback. I have received comments such as "Really practical!" versus "Not enough meat!" for the same workshop or, conversely, "Provocative ideas" versus "Too theoretical" for another. What does this tell me? Generally, I conclude that I could have done a better job of describing my workshop, and there was a mix of experienced and novice teachers in the crowd.

It is no surprise that novice teachers and experienced teachers have different needs. Research into this shows that novice teachers tend to be concerned with *What-to-teach* questions, whereas experienced teachers want to explore *How-to* and *Why* questions to a greater degree (Freeman, 1982). If this is so, then logically teachers will naturally seek out different types of professional development activities and a different content focus as their careers progress. If we find ourselves always seeking the same "practical" content or classroom activities type of workshop after 10 or 15 years of teaching experience, shouldn't we explore the reason and seek more balance in our professional development pursuits? Don't get me wrong. I love to get new activities or techniques to use in a class. However, I also love a professional development activity that challenges and changes my conceptual framework, and it is learning from these endeavors that enables me to make better decisions about those new activities and techniques.

Personal Commitment to Professional Development

Development of teaching competence is our professional responsibility, and we can undertake a wide range of activities in fulfillment of this obligation. As Crandall (1996) pointed out in her keynote address at the TESL Canada Conference, there are courses to take, journals to read, colleagues to talk with and observe, classroom research to conduct, textbooks to review, and workshops to attend. This range of professional development opportunities allows us to develop a comprehensive, yet personal professional development plan, and I am convinced it must be a personal plan. Employers and professional organizations may support our pursuit of professional development by funding us to the occasional conference or organizing a workshop, but as educators we must make a personal commitment to our own ongoing professional growth.

As I tell my son, sometimes he carries out a chore at home because he is paid for it. Then I am satisfied because the chore has been done; he is happy because he has done a good job and put some money into his wallet. However, I cannot possibly pay him for every job that needs to be done around the house, nor should I have to. He lives there; he has a stake in its maintenance and improvement. When he sees something that needs to be done and he takes it on unasked and without pay, he is demonstrating his sense of responsibility to our family's well-being in addition to his own. I think it is the same for those of us engaged in the adult ESL profession. Going to the occasional workshop because it is organized for us, or because we are funded by employers, although mutually beneficial to a degree, is not enough for our own and our profession's well-being. Each of us, I believe, must be personally committed to seeking out additional opportunities to learn and develop. If we continue to argue that adult ESL is an area of educational expertise, we must ensure that we indeed have that expertise. Knowledge and principles without skill or, conversely, skill without knowledge or principles, are professionally unacceptable states. There is no place for professional complacency in the field of adult ESL instruction. The students and our profession deserve more.

So when we begin another school year and our students return to our clean classrooms in hopeful anticipation of a dynamic and effective year, I will make my New Year's resolutions. I will promise to spend more time with teachers and students. I will promise to try out a new technique. I will promise to be more organized. And I will promise to examine my assumptions about adult ESL education regularly and make a personal commitment to the continuing development of my professional competence.

References

Auerbach, E. (1993). Putting the P back in participatory. *TESOL Quarterly, 27*, 543–545.

Celce-Murcia, M., Döornyei, Z., & Thurrell, S. (1995). Communicative competence: A pedagogically motivated model with content specifications. *Issues in Applied Linguistics, 6*, 5–35.

Crandall, J. (1996, May). The challenge of professionalism and professionalization in ESL. Keynote address presented at the national TESL Canada Conference in Winnipeg.

Freeman, D. (1982). Observing teachers: Three approaches to in-service training and development. *TESOL Quarterly, 16*, 21–28.

Richards, J. C., & Rodgers, T. S. (2001). 2nd ed. *Approaches and methods in language teaching*: *A description and analysis.* New York: Cambridge University Press.

Tedick, D. J., & Walker, C. L. (1994). Second language teacher education: The problems that plague us. *Modern Languages Journal, 78*, 300–312.

CHAPTER 41

Research in Your Own Classroom

Elizabeth Taylor

How Might I Become Interested in Investigating My Own Classroom?

Teachers want to know about their classrooms on several levels. At the most practical level, you are interested in everyday matters, such as whether the learners work better seated around tables in small groups or as a whole class led by the teacher. At a more theoretical level, you might wonder what second language acquisition research has to say about whether increasing interaction in the target language by using small groups promotes learning, or what classroom research says about patterns of interaction and roles adopted by learners in small-group settings.

How Might I Make These Links between Practice and Theory?

At the daily practical level, you might notice that some of your learners adopt 'teacher-like' roles when grouped with others, and some rarely speak at all in groups, but follow the lead of the others. Does this matter? you wonder. Some activities seem to get students talking, while others do not. What are their characteristics? If you believe mixed-language groupings produce the most amount of negotiation, does it matter what the composition of these groups is? After some time, you may want to find out whether there are any other teachers who have noticed similar patterns, successes, or problems in the way learners are grouped. At this point, you may have a casual chat about it in the staff room and ideas shared might get put into practice.

The next level might be when you generalise from your own and colleagues' experiences to the broader context of second language teaching generally and wonder what the reasons behind the apparently more successful class groupings might be. Your own learning style will probably then determine what you do next! Those of you who prefer to learn from colleagues and from talking over problems and issues might raise the topic when several teachers meet informally. If your institution has regular meetings devoted to curriculum and methodology issues, this could be an appropriate forum, although the luxury of discussing other than the most pressing needs at such a meeting could be a thing of the past in many workplaces. Research on professional development in the adult literacy and basic education field (Davison, Taylor, & Hatcher, forthcoming) shows that unless such sessions are formalised, it is largely a matter of luck as to whether teachers find themselves working with colleagues who will get involved in talking over classroom issues.

Those of you who are more print-oriented, however, might think that there is something useful written up in journals or some of the resources in a library, so you have a look through these. This reveals that there are, in fact, a few books which seem very useful (Nunan, 1989; Malamah-Thomas, 1987; Wright, 1988). On browsing through books like these you find how other people have gone about investigating the same problem you are interested in. You also find that the last section of all the books in the Oxford series, of which Malamah-Thomas and Wright form a part, has some very clearly explained ideas on how to investigate your own classroom.

Collaborate or Go It Alone?

Whether you have talked your ideas over with your colleagues or looked through some articles or books, you have decided you would like to know more. At this stage, is it best to go ahead alone or with others? As we noted, people have different ways of working and learning and you may be quite happy to go ahead on your own. If you decide you would prefer to work collaboratively, however, this could be easier for you. You may simply work informally with just one colleague or try to set up a small group where you teach (or study). If you are currently following a formal course of study in TESOL, LOTE or language and literacy, or in education generally, it will probably be quite feasible to undertake a small classroom research project as an assignment for your course. Talk it over with your lecturer.

Setting up a small group at your workplace has its practical difficulties, but you may find a couple of other interested people. Arrange a regular meeting time and read on.

What Have Other Researchers Found Out about My Area of Interest?

Although there may not be much time for reading, you feel someone may already have found out quite a lot about learner groupings in second language classrooms, and it seems a pity not to check this first so that you can either follow the same procedures they did and see if the same things happen in your classroom too, or get some ideas to try something new of your own. So what should you read?

One problem with a great deal of classroom research which has been reported in international journals such as *TESOL Quarterly* and collections of second language acquisition or classroom research (such as Allwright & Bailey, 1991; Chaudron, 1988; van Lier, 1988) is that many are carried out by a researcher from outside and therefore do not provide examples of people studying their own or a colleague's classroom. Reading about these studies will still be very useful to you, however, both in terms of what was found out and of how the researchers went about their task. You need to keep in mind, though, that these studies will be of research projects far larger than you would hope to carry out, and so it is useful and interesting to read reports of research done by other teachers as well. The main difference between the major studies and the type of study we are interested in here is that you may only look at one class, possibly only one lesson, and are not looking for the large numbers to make your research statistically viable and thus generalisable to other contexts. You are interested, at least to begin with, in a single context – your own.

Although the more 'formal' reports have the disadvantage of describing larger and more ambitious research projects, they have the advantage of being models of how to write up research clearly. The 'informal' ones have the advantage of seeming closer to reality, but have the disadvantage of being often less well explained because of teachers' inexperience of reporting back in written format. Journals publish reports of research.

How Do I Go about Investigating My Own Classroom?

A practical example: learner roles in small-group interaction compared with a teacher-directed lesson.

FOCUSING THE INVESTIGATION

The best way to see how a question can be asked and investigated is to examine the process one teacher followed with her adult ESL literacy community class, which she had been teaching for about 2 years. The teacher, Anne, had realised that her lessons seemed to be very teacher-directed. This was very largely influenced by the learning styles and experiences of her students. They expected that teaching should come from the teacher and that it was the learners' role to receive instruction. There was very little learner–learner interaction in the class even though it was very small – six to eight students. Anne was also concerned that the students were not developing learning strategies and, in particular, did not see themselves as independent readers in English. She knew from her reading that increasing learner–learner interaction was thought to be beneficial, but could not find much research done on differences between learner roles in small groups as compared with teacher-fronted groups. She therefore decided to investigate these roles in her own class.

Anne's background reading told her that in second language learning, group work is considered effective for several reasons: It increases actual participation and thus language learning opportunities; it improves the quality, or naturalness, of student talk, so that it is closer to 'genuine' interaction; it helps individualise instruction; it promotes a positive affective climate; and it increases student motivation (Long & Porter, 1985; McPherson, 1992; van Lier, 1988). Second language acquisition research also suggests that negotiation of meaning (which is better carried out in more 'natural' smaller groups) actually may lead to acquisition of the target language. As far as learner roles in small groups are concerned, Anne found that small groups encouraged learners to take on new roles which they may not have done in a teacher-fronted lesson. For instance, they may initiate more interaction instead of simply responding to the teacher.

COLLECTING INFORMATION

The next step for Anne was to collect information in her classroom so that she could examine learner roles. She decided that because one of her concerns was for the students to develop more independent reading strategies, she would use a reading-based task to focus on. They had already worked on prereading strategies for understanding the content of new texts, so she set up two activities, one teacher-fronted and one small-group, so that she could compare roles in these. In the teacher-fronted session, Anne attempted to elicit from the students the use of the four cues they had previously studied and then to apply these to the text in that lesson. These cues were:

1. looking at pictures/illustrations
2. looking at the title
3. looking at headings
4. looking for easily recognised words in the body of the text.

In the small-group session, the learners' task was to *(a)* predict what the reading would be about and *(b)* say what they did to try to work this out – in other words, to discuss their strategies. The texts Anne chose were two segments of the same government pamphlet on the environment.

The class was very small, so Anne had only two small groups and she intentionally grouped these in mixed levels, since the class had a wide range of proficiency in both oral and literacy skills and she felt the mixed groupings reflected reality in community classes.

Anne audiotaped about 15 to 20 minutes of each session. This gave her plenty of material to work with.

ANALYSING THE INFORMATION

Unfortunately, once you have a tape, you need to transcribe it! Anne ended up transcribing about eight pages of interaction for each session. This is very time-consuming, but also very revealing. You may find other aspects of the lesson you might like to follow up in the future by doing this. Anne transcribed by hand, but you may find you can get access to a transcription machine, which is a tape recorder with a headset and a foot pedal. This allows you to type with two hands and review the tape by using your foot.

The best way to analyse your transcription is to see how other people have done it. Some kind of framework and terminology are important in order to communicate to others what you have found interesting. You can, of course, invent your own framework and categories for analysis or adapt what someone else has done, and this is what many teachers investigating their classrooms for their own purposes have done.

Anne analysed the roles her learners took in the two lessons by looking at four broad categories of roles: *leader, participator, nonparticipator,* and *negative contributor*. (A *participator* was interpreted as someone who contributed to the group discussion but deferred to a leader.) Anne based this on work done by Orlich, Harder, Callahan, Kanchak, Prendergrass, and Keogh (1990). These four categories were further subdivided into three ways in which these roles may be oriented in the group. These were *task roles* (focusing on the task, e.g., initiating, asking questions); *maintenance roles* (focusing on maintaining group processes, e.g., encouraging, giving feedback, commenting on progress); and *self-serving roles* (tending to obstruct discussion by serving the learner's own interests, e.g., blocking others' contributions, off-task comments).

Anne used her transcripts to code the learners' utterances first into the functions they were performing (e.g., encouraging), then allocated these to the role they were fulfilling (e.g., maintenance). She found that there were no nonparticipators and no negative contributors, so she counted the number of times each learner filled the role of leader or participator and what aspect of the role was being carried out (e.g., task, maintenance).

MAKING SENSE OF IT

Anne had made some predictions before starting her study. One was that the learners who actively contribute in the teacher-fronted group will assume leadership roles in a small learner-centred group. This turned out to be the case.

She found that in the teacher-fronted lesson, not surprisingly, the learners adopted the role of leader only 10% of the time, but in the small groups roughly a quarter to a third of the time was spent with learners adopting the role of leader. In both the teacher-fronted session and the small-group one, the learners were strongly task-oriented rather than maintenance-oriented, although one group was a little more concerned than the other with the latter function.

This looks as if Anne was only counting utterances and describing her results in terms of percentages. Although there is no space to show the detail here, Anne, because of the small size of her class, was able to describe and discuss how each student contributed in the small-group activity, supported by quotes from her transcript. For instance, she found that one student took on a very strong 'teacher' role in the small-group discussion. This student (with an Australian Second Language Proficiency Rating reading level of 4 and with a tertiary education background) took on the role of 'instructing' the others in reading strategies. However, in teacher-fronted sessions he does not do this, and Anne speculates that *this may have been owing to his awareness of his greater ability and his desire not to dominate a class which he attends mainly for social reasons rather than learning needs.* In a small group, because of all the learners' strong task orientation, this student would not have expected to learn from the others and took on the only role he saw himself able to fulfil because of his view of what education was about, that of 'teacher':

> *First you look at the picture, then you read the heading, the title and everything and you tell me what it will be about. First the picture ... Here ... What is it?*

Both his past educational experiences and those of the other members of the group enabled him to take on this role, since they were happy to defer to him (*thank you for helping me read; you are a good teacher* are examples from their discussion). It was interesting that in the other group the student who took on the role of 'leader' did not do it by instructing, but by offering information and controlling the discussion: *Don't spend too much water. How to do?* was how she initiated discussion on the topic of saving water they had read about in the brochure.

The fact that the groups did not pay much attention to maintaining group cohesion was seen by Anne as a sign of their inexperience at working in groups, but also because they already knew each other well and had a good rapport with their fellow students.

How Can Research in My Own Classroom Help My Teaching?

How did all this help Anne in planning for and teaching the class in the future? She was able to see that even though there may be more interaction going on in small groups, a wide disparity in learner background, particularly in level of education, may result in some learners continuing to adopt 'participant' roles, responding to the 'teacher' orientation of the most highly educated and most proficient member of the group. Is this a reason to abandon group work? Probably not – learners will have more chances to participate in small groups, even if roles remain static initially. Experimentation with group composition would be interesting. Maybe Anne could try grouping the 'leaders' together and see what happens next time.

An important discovery for Anne was the effect of the nature of the task itself. She found in follow-up discussion to the task with the students (which was also recorded and transcribed) that the highly educated student was in fact the only one to grasp the 'learning-to-learn' focus of the activity. The others concentrated on understanding the reading text but not on the strategies they had studied for approaching it:

Teacher: OK! . . . What did you think it was about?
S1: the water . . . you soap, you use then the water. You have to take less time in the shower . . .
Teacher: What did this group think it was about?
S2: Shower, washing.
Teacher: Yes . . . tell me about all of it . . . not just the little bits . . . what do you think the whole thing was about?
S3: For shower . . . (*discussion continues about details of content of text*)
Teacher: Yes. You're telling me this is all about saving water – how did you know it was all about saving water?
S4 ('teacher'): We look at the picture. We look at the words to see if we know something about them?

It seems that Anne was right to decide that her learners need to be more independent in their reading strategies if they are ever to see themselves as 'readers' in English. She may now be able to recycle activities which focus on conscious awareness of reading strategies and feel it is quite all right to 'overdo' this, since continuous reinforcement is probably important for the majority of the class who have primary school backgrounds only.

How Do I Report My Findings?

If Anne wants to inform colleagues or other second language teachers about her study, how could she go about it? If, as noted earlier, you are working as a team in your institution or through other informal grouping arrangements, presenting your findings as an informal talk with time for discussion at a staff development session would be the best way to do this. You will find that you are so familiar with what you have done by now that talking about it will be easy! Simple charts or tables of findings are useful as overhead transparencies or handouts and a copy of the actual transcript will always create interest and promote discussion. This is especially important if you are trying to involve staff members who are not particularly enthusiastic about professional development. A concrete example of the students and teacher interacting works very well (accompanied by an audiotape or videotape would be even better). You will find that far more issues than the one you originally were addressing will arise.

If you are enrolled in a formal course, approach your lecturer about arranging ways for students to present their work. There may already be some kind of forum for this, but if not, new arrangements can be negotiated. It is unfortunate that in most formal courses, assignments are done after the course has finished and are then only reading material for the person marking it. If you have good feedback on your assignment, however, consider rewriting in article format and sending it to an appropriate journal.

Acknowledgements

This paper draws on the work of students enrolled in the TESOL/LOTE specialisations in the Postgraduate Diploma in Educational Studies at the University of Melbourne. I would like to thank Anne Wagner in particular, whose research in her own classroom is described in this article.

References

Allwright, D., & Bailey, K. (1991). *Focus on the language classroom – an introduction to classroom research for language teachers*. Cambridge: Cambridge University Press.

Chaudron, C. (1988). *Second language classrooms: Research on teaching and learning.* New York: Cambridge University Press.

Davison, C., Taylor, E., & Hatcher, L. (forthcoming). *Pedagogy and politics: Developing ethnic-inclusive practices in adult literacy.*

Long, M. H., & Porter, P. A. (1985). Group work, interlanguage talk and second language acquisition. *TESOL Quarterly, 19*(2).

Malamah-Thomas, A. (1987). *Classroom interaction*. Oxford: Oxford University Press.

McPherson, K. (1992). Talking behind our backs. *TESOL in Context, 2*(1), 8–12.

Nunan, D. (1989). *Understanding language classrooms.* London: Prentice Hall International.

Orlich, D., Harder, R., Callahan, R., Kanchak, D., Prendergrass, R. A., & Keogh, A. (1990). *Teaching strategies: A guide to better instruction.* Toronto: D. C. Heath.

van Lier, L. (1988). *The classroom and the language learner*. London: Longman.

Wright, T. (1988). *Roles of teachers and learners*. Oxford: Oxford University Press.

Credits

p. 9 Brown, H. Douglas. English language teaching in the "post-method" era: Toward better diagnosis, treatment, and assessment. This chapter originally appeared in *PASAA*, 27, 1–11, 1997. Reprinted by permission.

p. 52 Jacobs, George M., and Hall, Stephen. Implementing cooperative learning. This chapter originally appeared in *Forum*, 31(4), 2–5/13, 1994. Reprinted by permission.

p. 59 Bowler, Bill, and Parminter, Sue. Mixed-level teaching: tiered tasks and bias tasks. This chapter originally appeared in *English Teaching Professional*, Issue 5, 13–15, 1997. Reprinted by permission.

p. 69 Finney, Denise. The ELT curriculum: A flexible model for a changing world. This chapter originally appeared in *TEFLIN*, 8:1, 14–31, 1996. Reprinted by permission.

p. 80 Crawford, Jane. The role of materials in the language classroom: finding the balance. This chapter originally appeared in *TESOL in Context*, 5(1), 25–33. Reprinted by permission.

p. 96 Beglar, David, and Hunt, Alan. Implementing task-based language teaching. Paper presented at the 4th CULI International Conference, Bangkok, Thailand, 1–3 Dec. 1999. Reprinted by permission.

p. 107 Stoller, Fredricka L. Project work: A means to promote language and content. This chapter originally appeared in *Forum*, 35(4), 2–9/37. Reprinted by permission.

p. 124 Oxford, Rebecca L. Language learning strategies in a nutshell: update and ESL suggestions. This chapter originally appeared in *TESOL Journal*, 2(2), 18–22. Reprinted by permission.

p. 133 Nunan, David. Learner strategy training in the classroom: an action research study. This chapter originally appeared in *TESOL Journal*, 6(1), 35–41. Reprinted by permission.

p. 148 Swan, Michael. Seven bad reasons for teaching grammar – and two good ones. This chapter originally appeared in *English Teaching Professional*, Issue 7, 3–5, 1998, © Michael Swan. Reprinted by permission.

p. 153 Addressing the grammar gap in task work by Jack C. Richards, reprinted from *Prospect*, 14(1), 4–19 with permission from the National Centre for English Language Teaching and Research (NCELTR), Australia. © NCELTR 1999.

p. 167 Ellis, Rod. Grammar teaching – practice or consciousness-raising. This chapter originally appeared in *Second Language Acquisition and Language Pedagogy*, Clevedon, Avon: Multilingual Matters 79. Reprinted by permission.

p. 178 Jones, Rodney H. Beyond 'listen and repeat': pronunciation teaching materials and theories of second language acquisition. Reprinted from *SYSTEM*, 25(1), 103–112, 1997, with permission of Elsevier Science.

p. 188 Hebert, Julie. PracTESOL: it's not what you say, but how you say it. This chapter originally appeared in *TESOL in Context*, 3(1), 15–22, 1993. Reprinted by permission.

p. 204 Shumin, Kang. Factors to consider: Developing adult EFL students' speaking abilities. This chapter originally appeared in *Forum*, 35(3), 8–13/29. Reprinted by permission.

p. 212 Conversational English: An interactive, collaborative, and reflective approach by Wai King Tsang and Matilda Wong, reprinted from *Prospect* 10, 1 with permission from the National Centre for English Language Teaching and Research (NCELTR), Australia. © Macquarie University.

p. 225 Green, Christopher F., Christopher, Elsie R., and Lam, Jacqueline. Developing discussion skills in the ESL classroom. This chapter originally appeared in *The ELT Journal*, 51(2), 135–143, 1997. Reprinted by permission of Oxford University Press.

p. 238 Nunan, David. Listening in language learning. This chapter originally appeared in *The Language Teacher*, 23(9), 47–51, 1997. Reprinted by permission.

p. 242 Field, John. The changing face of listening. This chapter originally appeared in *English Teaching Professional*, Issue 6, 12–14, January 1998. Reprinted by permission.

p. 248 Lam, Wendy Y. K. Raising stduents' awareness of the features of real-world listening input. This chapter originally appeared in *Guidelines*, 19(1), 74–86, 1997. Reprinted by permission.

p. 258 Hunt, Alan, and Beglar, David. Current research and practice in teaching vocabulary. This chapter originally appeared in *The Language Teacher*, 22(1), 7–11/25, 1998. Reprinted by permission.

p. 267 Nation, Paul. Best practice in vocabulary and learning. *EA Journal*, 13(2), 7–15, 1995/96. Reprinted by permission.

p. 276 Dilemmas for the development of second language reading abilities by William Grabe, reprinted from *Prospect*, 10(2), 38–51 with permission from the National Centre for English Language Teaching and Research (NCELTR), Australia. © NCELTR 1995.

p. 287 Janzen, Joy. Teaching strategic reading. This chapter originally appeared in *TESOL Journal*, 6(1), 6–9, 1996. Reprinted by permission.

p. 306 Raimes, Ann. Ten steps in planning a writing course and training teachers of writing. This chapter originally appeared in M. L. Tickoo (ed.), *Reading and Writing: Theory into Practice*, 514–527. Singapore: SEAMEO Regional Language Centre, 1995. Reprinted by permission.

p. 315 Seow, Anthony. The writing process and process writing. This chapter originally appeared in *TELL*, 11(1), 60–63, 1995. Reprinted by permission.

p. 321 Reppen, Randi. A genre-based approach to content writing instruction. This chapter originally appeared in *TESOL Journal*, 4(2), 32–35, 1995. Reprinted by permission.

p. 328 Ferris, Dana. Teaching students to self-edit. This chapter originally appeared in *TESOL Journal*, 4(4), 18–22, 1995. Reprinted by permission.

p. 338 Huerta-Marcías, Anna. Alternative assessment: Responses to commonly asked questions. This chapter originally appeared in *TESOL Journal*, 5(1), 8–11, 1995. Reprinted by permission.

p. 344 Peñaflorida, Andrea H. Non-traditional forms of assessment and response to student writing: A step toward learner autonomy. This chapter originally appeared in W. Renandya and G. M. Jacobs (eds.), *Learners and Language Learning*, 72–88. Singapore: SEAMEO Regional Language Centre, 1998. Reprinted by permission.

p. 354 Hingle, Ishbel, and Linington, Viv. English proficiency test: The oral component of a primary school. This chapter originally appeared in *Forum*, 35(2), 26–29, 1997. Reprinted by permission.

p. 364 Stempleski, Susan. Video in the ELT classroom: the role of the teacher. This chapter originally appeared in *The Language Teacher*, 18(8), 28–29/47, 1994. Reprinted by permission.

p. 368 Warschauer, Mark and Whittaker, P. Fawn. The Internet for English teaching: guidelines for teachers. This chapter originally appeared in *TESL Reporter*, 30(1), 27–33, 1997. Reprinted by permission.

p. 374 Li, Rong-Chang and Hart, Robert S. What can the World Wide Web offer ESL teachers? This chapter originally appeared in *TESOL Journal*, 6(2), 5–10, 1996. Reprinted by permission.

p. 388 Ur, Penny. The English teacher as professional. This chapter originally appeared in *English Teaching Professional*, Issue 2, 3–5, 1997. Reprinted by permission.

p. 393 Pettis, Joanne. Developing our professional competence: some reflections. This chapter originally appeared in *TESL Canada Journal*, 14(2), 67–71, 1997. Reprinted by permission.

p. 397 Taylor, Elizabeth. Research in your own classroom. This chapter originally appeared in *TESOL in Context*, 3(2), 6–10, 1993. Reprinted by permission.

Author Index

Subject Index

Au

AutoCAD Architecture 2013 Fundamentals

Elise Moss

ISBN: 978-1-58503-745-2

SDC PUBLICATIONS

Schroff Development Corporation

www.SDCpublications.com

Schroff Development Corporation
P.O. Box 1334
Mission, KS 66222
(913) 262-2664
www.SDCpublications.com

Publisher: Stephen Schroff

Moss, Elise
Autodesk AutoCAD Architecture 2013 Fundamentals
Elise Moss
ISBN: 978-1-58503-745-2

Printed and bound in the United States of America.

Preface

No textbook can cover all the features in any software application. This textbook is meant for beginning users who want to gain a familiarity with the tools and interface of AutoCAD Architecture before they start exploring on their own. By the end of the text, users should feel comfortable enough to create a standard model, and even know how to customize the interface for their own use. Knowledge of basic AutoCAD and its commands is helpful, but not required. I do try to explain as I go, but for the sake of brevity I concentrate on the tools specific to and within AutoCAD Architecture.

The files used in this text are accessible from the Internet at www.schroff.com/resources. They are free and available to students and teachers alike.

We value customer input. Please contact us with any comments, questions, or concerns about this text.

Elise Moss
elise_moss@mossdesigns.com

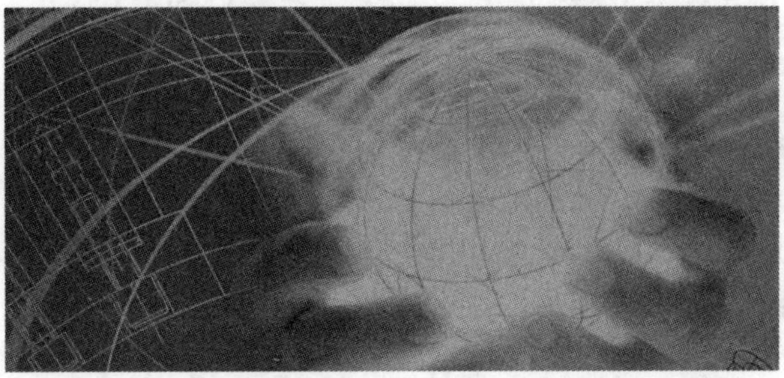

Acknowledgements from Elise Moss

This book would not have been possible without the support of some key Autodesk employees.

The effort and support of the editorial and production staff of Schroff Development Corporation is gratefully acknowledged. I especially thank Stephen Schroff for his helpful suggestions regarding the format of this text.

Finally, truly infinite thanks to Ari for his encouragement and his faith.

- Elise Moss

About the Author

Elise Moss has worked for the past thirty years as a mechanical designer in Silicon Valley, primarily creating sheet metal designs. She has written articles for Autodesk's Toplines magazine, AUGI's PaperSpace, DigitalCAD.com and Tenlinks.com. She is President of Moss Designs, creating custom applications and designs for corporate clients. She has taught CAD classes at DeAnza College, Silicon Valley College, and for Autodesk resellers. She is currently teaching CAD at SFSU, in the College for Extended Learning campus and at Laney College in Oakland. Autodesk has named her as a Faculty of Distinction for the curriculum she has developed for Autodesk products. She holds a baccalaureate degree in Mechanical Engineering from San Jose State.

She is married with three sons. Her older son, Benjamin, is an electrical engineer. Her middle son, Daniel, works with AutoCAD Architecture in the construction industry. His designs have been featured in architectural journals. Her youngest son, Isaiah, is in high school, but shows signs of being a budding engineer. Her husband, Ari, is retired from a distinguished career in software development.

Elise is a third generation engineer. Her father, Robert Moss, was a metallurgical engineer in the aerospace industry. Her grandfather, Solomon Kupperman, was a civil engineer for the City of Chicago.

She can be contacted via email at elise_moss@mossdesigns.com.

More information about the author and her work can be found on her website at www.mossdesigns.com.

Autodesk
Certified Instructor

Other books by Elise Moss

Autodesk Revit Architecture 2013 Basics

Table of Contents

Lesson 1:
Desktop Features

AutoCAD Architecture (ACA) enlists object oriented process systems (OOPS). That means that ACA uses intelligent objects to create a building. This is similar to using blocks in AutoCAD. Objects in AutoCAD Architecture are blocks on steroids. They have intelligence already embedded into them. A wall is not just a collection of lines. It represents a real wall. It can be constrained, has thickness and material properties, and is automatically included in your building schedule.

AEC is an acronym for Architectural/Electrical/Construction.
BID is an acronym for Building Industrial Design.
BIM is an acronym for Building Information Modeling.
AIA is an acronym for the American Institute of Architects.
MEP is an acronym for Mechanical/Electrical/Plumbing.

The following table describes the key features of objects in AutoCAD Architecture:

Feature Type	Description
AEC Camera	Create perspective views from various camera angles. Create avi files.
AEC Profiles	Create AEC objects using polylines to build doors, windows, etc.
Anchors and Layouts	Define a spatial relationship between objects. Create a layout of anchors on a curve or a grid to set a pattern of anchored objects, such as doors or columns.
Annotation	Set up special arrows, leaders, bar scales.
Ceiling Grids	Create reflected ceiling plans with grid layouts.
Column Grids	Define rectangular and radial building grids with columns and bubbles.
Design Center	Customize your AEC block library.
Display System	Control views for each AEC object.
Doors and Windows	Create custom door and window styles or use standard objects provided with the software.
Elevations and Sections	An elevation is basically a section view of a floor plan.
Layer Manager	Create layer standards based on AIA CAD Standards. Create groups of layers. Manage layers intelligently using Layer Filters.
Masking Blocks	Store a mask using a polyline object and attach to AEC objects to hide graphics
Model Explorer	View a model and manage the content easily. Attach names to mass elements to assist in design.
Multi-view blocks	Blocks have embedded defined views to allow you to easily change view.

Feature Type	Description
Railings	Create or apply different railing styles to a stair or along a defined path.
Roofs	Create and apply various roof styles.
Floorplate slices	Generate the perimeter geometry of a building.
Spaces and Boundaries	Spaces and boundaries can include floor thickness, room height, and wall thickness.
Stairs	Create and apply various stair types.
Tags and Schedules	Place tags on objects to generate schedules. Schedules will automatically update when tags are modified, added, or deleted.
Template Files	Use templates to save time. Create a template with standard layers, text styles, linetypes, dimension styles, etc.
Walls	Create wall styles to determine material composition. Define end caps to control opening and end conditions. Define wall interference conditions.

AutoCAD Architecture sits on top of AutoCAD. It is helpful for users to have a basic understanding of AutoCAD before moving to AutoCAD Architecture. Users should be familiar with the following:

- AutoCAD toolbars and ribbons
- Zoom and move around the screen
- Manage blocks
- *Draw* and *Modify* commands
- *Model* and *Paper space* (layout),
- Dimensioning and how to create/modify a dimension style

If you are not familiar with these topics, you can still move forward with learning AutoCAD Architecture, but you may find it helpful to have a good AutoCAD textbook as reference in case you get stuck.

TIP: The best way to use AutoCAD Architecture is start your project with massing tools (outside-in design) or space planning tools (inside-out design) and continue through to construction documentation.

The AEC Project Process Model

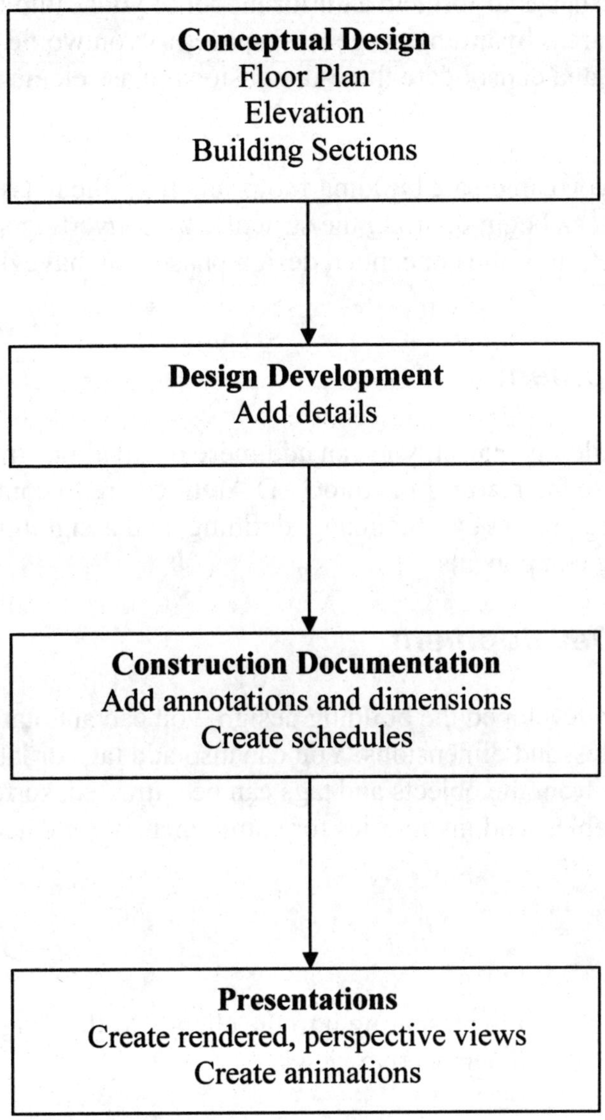

Conceptual Design

In the initial design phase, you can assemble AutoCAD Architecture mass elements as simple architectural shapes to form an exterior model of your building project. You can also lay out interior areas by arranging general spaces as you would in a bubble diagram. You can manipulate and consolidate three-dimensional mass elements into massing studies.

Later in this phase, you can create building footprints from the massing study by slicing floorplates, and you can begin defining the structure by converting space boundaries into walls. At the completion of the conceptual design phase, you have developed a workable schematic floor plan.

Design Development

As you refine the building project, you can add more detailed information to the schematic design. Use the features in AutoCAD Architecture to continue developing the design of the building project by organizing, defining, and assigning specific styles and attributes to building components.

Construction Development

After you have fully developed the building design, you can annotate your drawings with reference marks, notes, and dimensions. You can also add tags or labels associated with objects. Information from the objects and tags can be extracted, sorted, and compiled into schedules, reports, tables, and inventories for comprehensive and accurate construction documentation.

Presentations

A major part of any project is presenting it to the client. At this stage, you develop renderings, animations, and perspective views.

TIP:  If you use the **QNEW** tool, it will automatically use the template set in the Options dialog.

Express Tools

By default, Express Tools are not installed with AutoCAD Architecture.

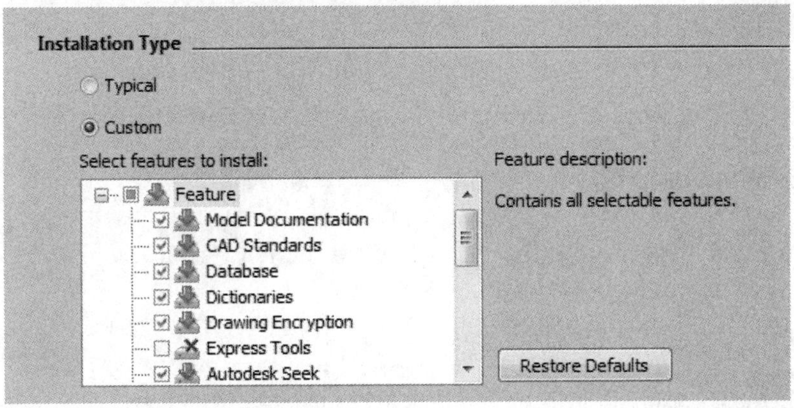

In order to install the Express Tools, you need to select the Custom Installation Type.

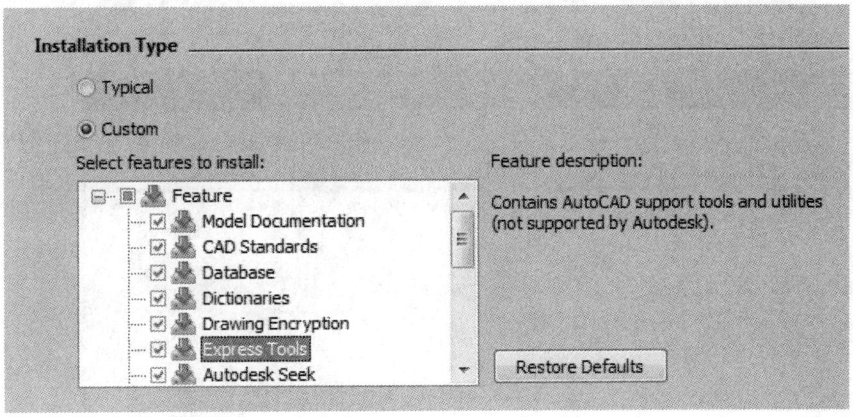

Place a check next to Express Tools to enable the installation and continue with the installation.

Express Tools can be used to create custom line types, control layers, and many other useful functions.

If you forgot to check Custom and install the Express Tools, they can be installed at any time. Refer to the next lesson for further guidance on installing the Express Tools after ACA has been installed.

Exercise 1-1:
Exploring the User Interface

Drawing Name: New
Estimated Time: 15 minutes

Note: This exercise requires the user to be connected to the internet. Some help and support features require web-browsing.

This exercise reinforces the following skills:

- Getting the user familiar with tools and the ACA environment

1. Launch ACA.

2. 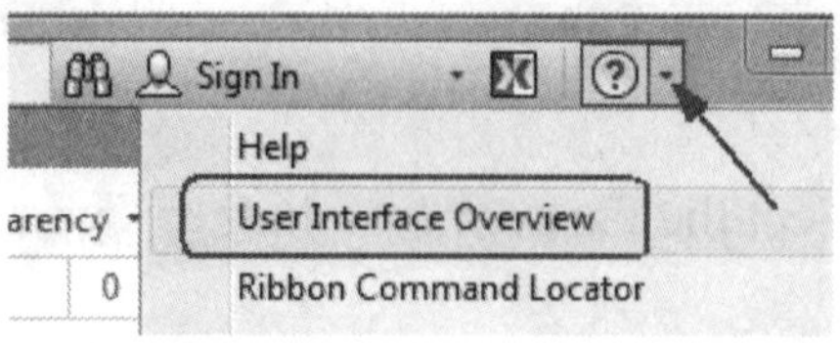

Select the down arrow next to the Help tool.

Select **User Interface Overview**.

3. Mouse over each number to identify the tools.

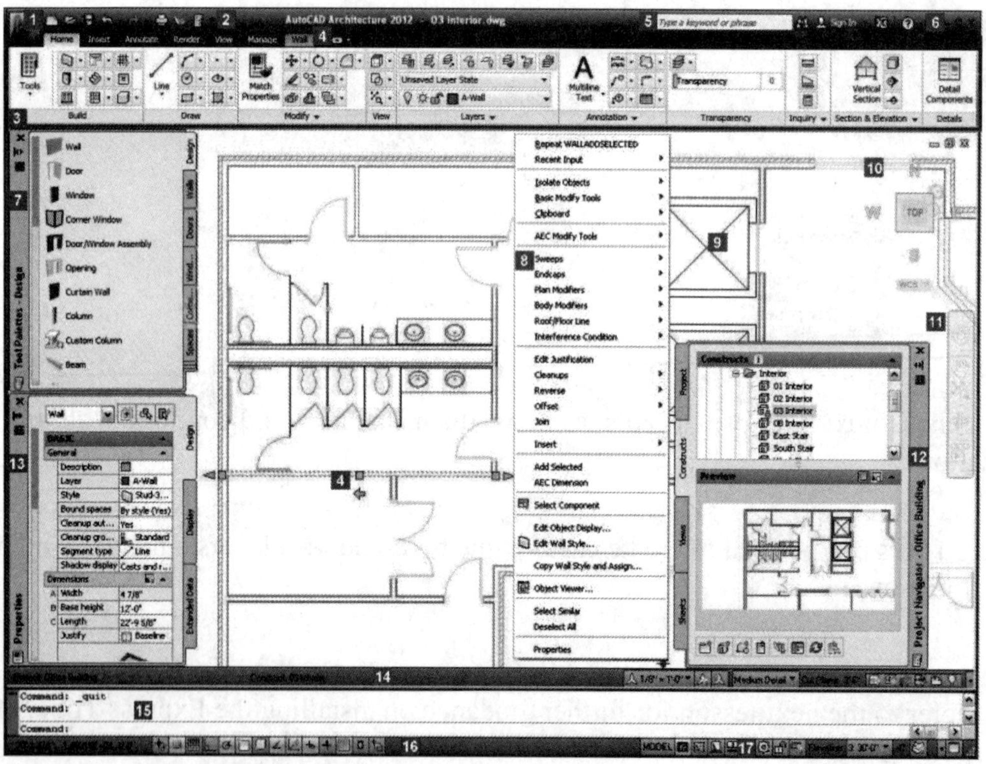

4. 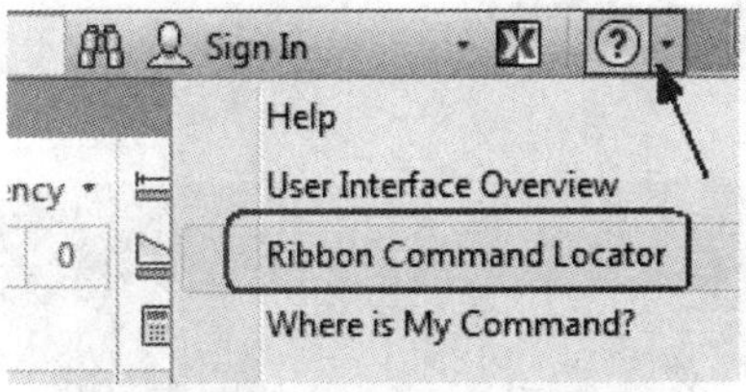

Select the down arrow next to the Help tool.

Select **Ribbon Command Locator**.

5. 

If you used older versions of AutoCAD or AutoCAD Architecture, you may wish to use this tool if you get stuck looking for a command.

Click on the link.

6. A webpage will load.

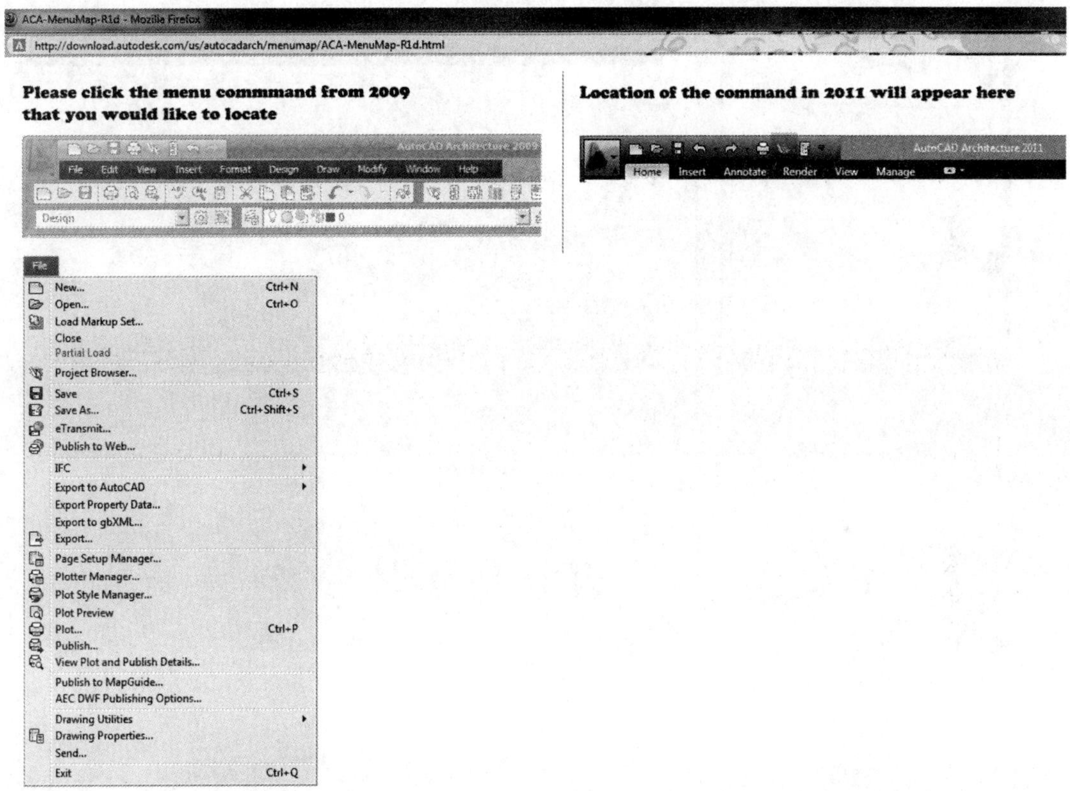

Look for a command using the old interface and the page will show you where to locate it in 2013.

7. 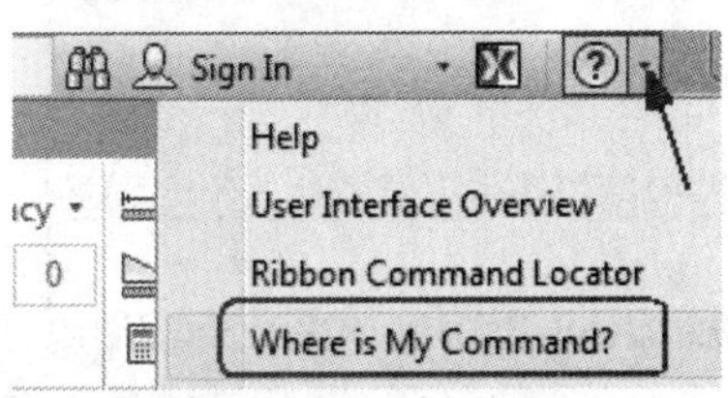

Select the down arrow next to the Help tool.

Select **Where is My Command?**

8. This help file allows you to locate where commands can be found in 2013.

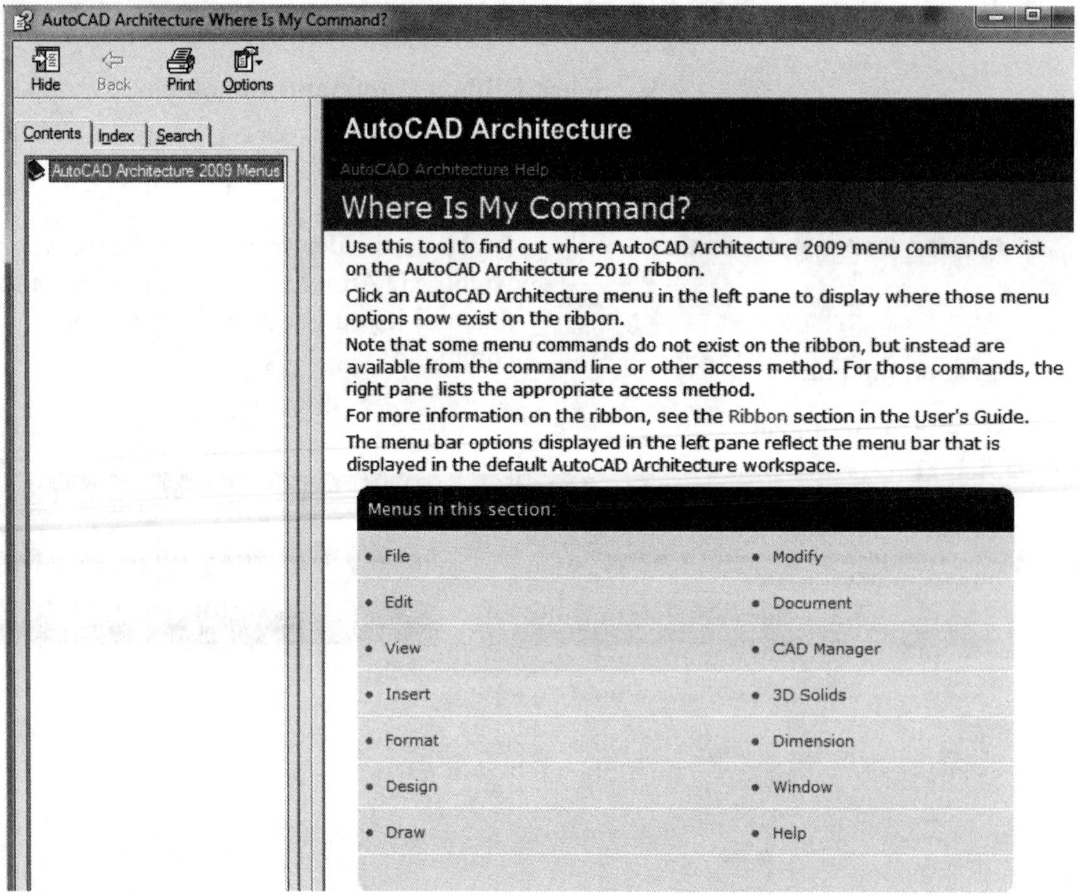
AutoCAD Architecture Where Is My Command?
Hide
Back
Print
Options
Contents
Index
Search
AutoCAD Architecture 2009 Menus
AutoCAD Architecture
AutoCAD Architecture Help
Where Is My Command?
Use this tool to find out where AutoCAD Architecture 2009 menu commands exist on the AutoCAD Architecture 2010 ribbon.
Click an AutoCAD Architecture menu in the left pane to display where those menu options now exist on the ribbon.
Note that some menu commands do not exist on the ribbon, but instead are available from the command line or other access method. For those commands, the right pane lists the appropriate access method.
For more information on the ribbon, see the Ribbon section in the User's Guide.
The menu bar options displayed in the left pane reflect the menu bar that is displayed in the default AutoCAD Architecture workspace.
Menus in this section:
File
Edit
View
Insert
Format
Design
Draw
Modify
Document
CAD Manager
3D Solids
Dimension
Window
Help

Exercise 1-2:
Setting the Template for QNEW

Drawing Name: New
Estimated Time: 15 minutes

This exercise reinforces the following skills:

- Use of templates
- Getting the user familiar with tools and the ACA environment

1. Launch ACA.

2. Place your cursor on the command line.

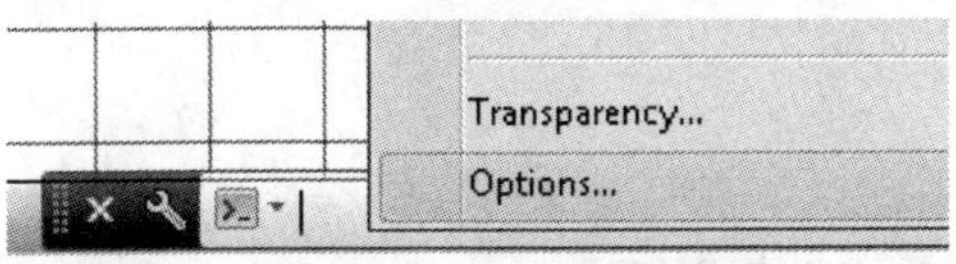

Right click the mouse.

Select **Options** from the short-cut menu.

3. Select the **Files** tab.
Locate the *Template Settings* folder.

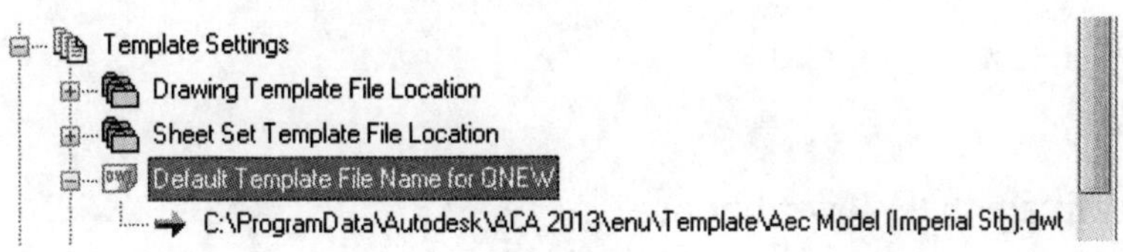

Click on the + symbol to expand.
Locate the Default Template File Name for QNEW.

4. 

Highlight the path and file name listed and select the **Browse** button.

5. Browse to the *Template* folder.

This should be listed under
Documents & Settings\[user name]\Application Data\ Autodesk\ACD-A 2013\enu
or
Program Data/Autodesk/ ACA 2013/enu

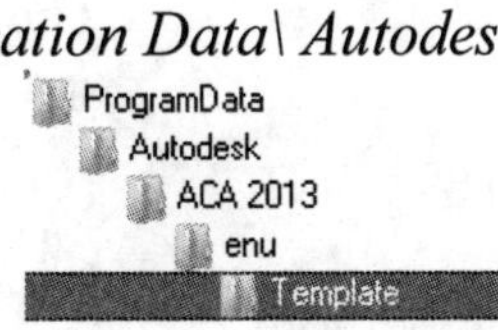

6. 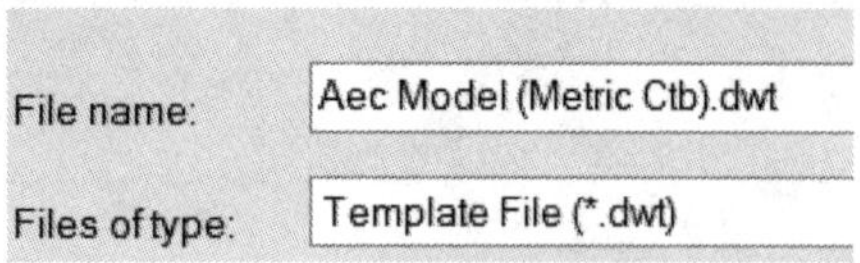

Locate the *Aec Model (Imperial Ctb).dwt [Aec Model (Metric Ctb).dwt]* file.

Press **Open**.

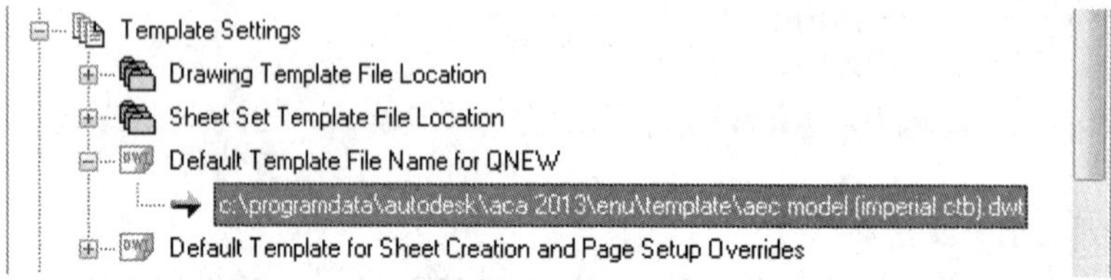

7. Note that you can also set where you can direct the user for templates. This is useful if you want to create standard templates and place them on a network server for all users to access.

   You can also use this setting to help you locate where your template files are located.

8. Press **Apply** and **OK**.

9. 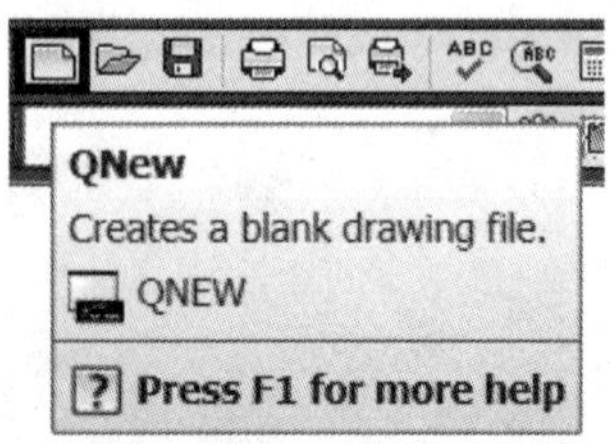

Select the **QNEW** tool button.

10. 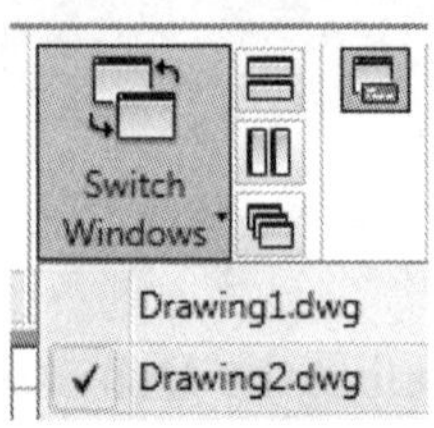

Activate the **View** ribbon.

Under **Switch Windows**, you see that you have two files open now. A check mark appears next to the active file.

11. 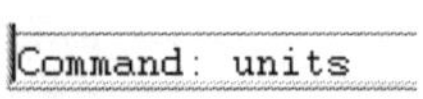

Type **units** on the *Command* line.

12. 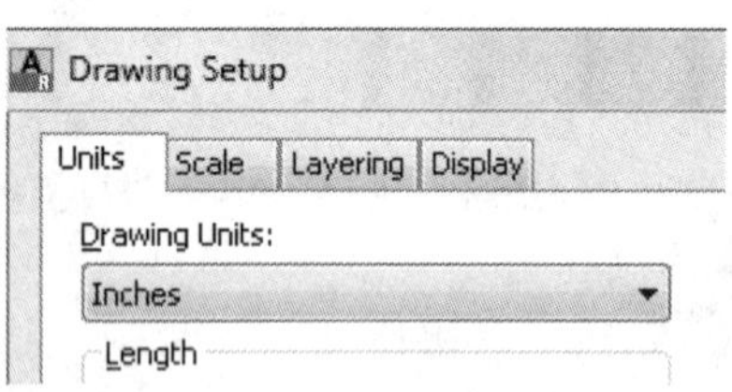

Note that the units are in inches [millimeters].

The units are determined by the template you set to start your new drawing.

13. Close the drawing without saving.

TIP: Templates can be used to preset layers, property set definitions, dimension styles, units, and layouts.

Setting AEC Drawing Options

Menu	Tools→Options
Command line	Options
Context Menu→Options	Place Mouse in the graphics area and right click
Shortcut	Place mouse in the command line and right click

Access the Options dialog box.

ACA's Options includes five additional AEC specific tabs.
They are AEC Editor, AEC Content, AEC Object Settings, AEC Dimension, and AEC Project Defaults.

AEC Editor

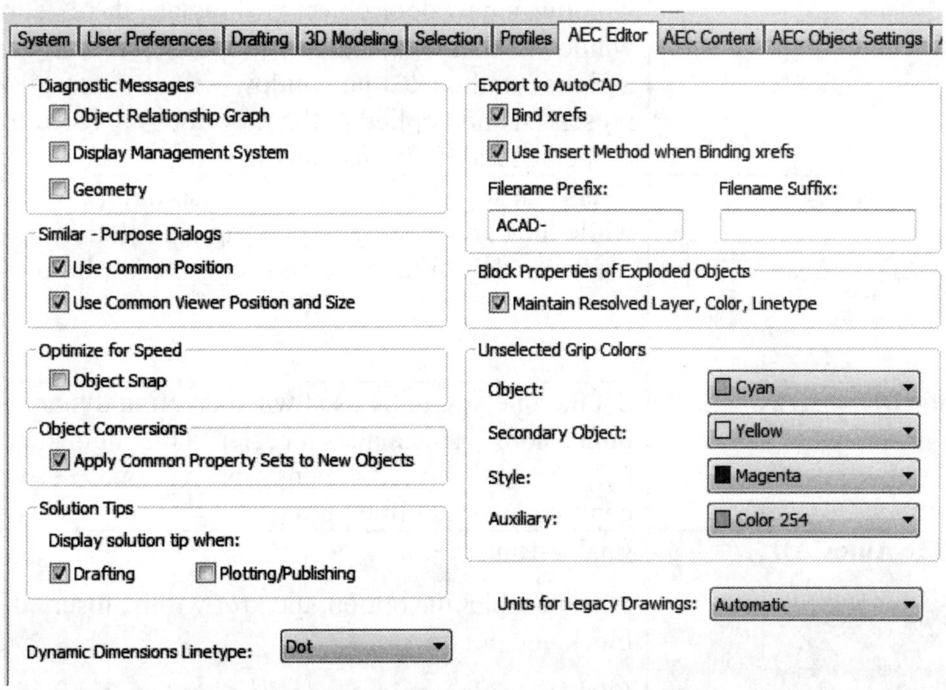

Diagnostic Messages	All diagnostic messages are turned off by default.
Similar-Purpose Dialogs	Options for the position of dialog boxes and viewers.
Use Common Position	Sets one common position on the screen for similar dialog boxes, such as door, wall, and window add or modify dialog boxes. Some dialog boxes, such as those for styles and properties, are always displayed in the center of the screen, regardless of this setting.

Use Common Viewer Position and Sizes	Sets one size and position on the screen for the similar-purpose viewers in AutoCAD Architecture. Viewer position is separately controlled for add, modify, style, and properties dialog boxes.
Optimize for Speed	Options for display representations and layer loading in the Layer Manager dialog.
Object Snap	Enable to limit certain display representations to respond only to the Node and Insert object snaps. This setting affects stair, railing, space boundary, multi-view block, masking block, slice, and clip volume result (building section) objects.
Apply Common Property Sets to New Objects	Property sets are used for the creation of schedule tables. Each AEC object has embedded property sets, such as width and height, to be used in its schedule. AEC properties are similar to attributes. Size is a common property across most AEC objects. Occasionally, you may use a tool on an existing object and the result may be that you replace the existing object with an entirely different object. For example, if you apply the tool properties of a door to an existing window, a new door object will replace the existing window. When enabled, any property sets that were assigned to the existing window will automatically be preserved and applied to the new door provided that the property set definitions make sense.
Solution Tips 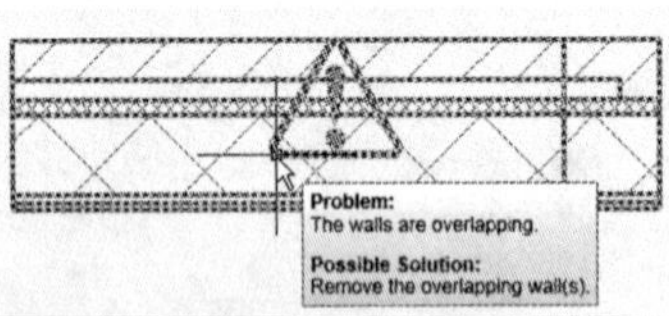	Users can set whether they wish a solution tip to appear while they are drafting or plotting. A solution tip identifies a drafting error and suggests a solution.
Dynamic Dimensions Linetype	Set the linetype to be used when creating dynamic dimensions. This makes it easier to distinguish between dynamic and applied dimensions. You may select either continuous or dot linetypes.
Export to AutoCAD 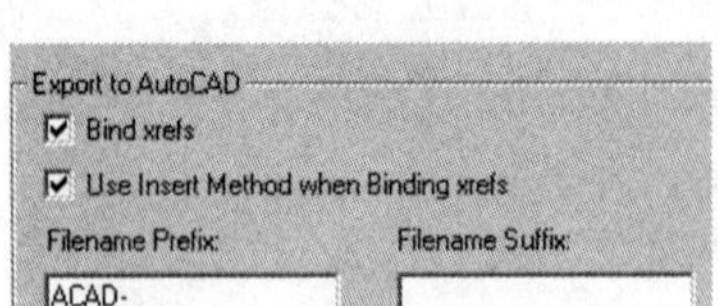	Enable Bind Xrefs If you enable this option, the xref will be inserted as a block and not an xref. Enable Use Insert Method when binding Xrefs if you want all objects from an xref drawing referenced in the

	file you export to be automatically exploded into the host drawing. If you enable this option, the drawing names of the xref drawings are discarded when the exported drawing is created. In addition, their layers and styles are incorporated into the host drawing. For example, all exploded walls, regardless of their source (host or xref) are located on the same layer. Disable Use Insert Method when binding Xrefs if you want to retain the xref identities, such as layer names, when you export a file to AutoCAD or to a DXF file. For example, the blocks that define walls in the host drawing are located on A-Wall in the exploded drawing. Walls in an attached xref drawing are located on a layer whose name is created from the drawing name and the layer name, such as Drawing1|WallA. Many architects automatically bind and explode their xrefs when sending drawings to customers to protect their intellectual property. Enter a prefix or a suffix to be added to the drawing filename when the drawing is exported to an AutoCAD drawing or a DXF file. In order for any of these options to apply, you have to use the Export to AutoCAD command. This is available under the Files menu.
Unselected Grip Colors	Assign the colors for each type of grip
Units for Legacy Drawings	Determines the units to be used when opening an AutoCAD drawing in AutoCAD Architecture. Automatic – uses the current AutoCAD Architecture units setting Imperial – uses Imperial units Metric – uses Metric units

TIP: Option Settings are applied to your current drawing and saved as the default settings for new drawings. Because AutoCAD Architecture operates in a Multiple Document Interface, each drawing stores the Options Settings used when it was created and last saved. Some users get confused because they open an existing drawing and it will not behave according to the current Options Settings.

AEC Content

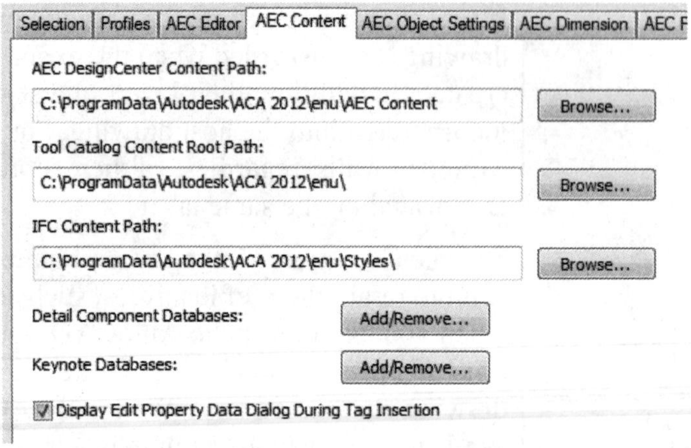

AEC DesignCenter Content Path	Type the path and location of your content files, or click Browse to search for the content files.
Tool Catalog Content Root Path	Type the path and location of your Tool Catalog files, or click Browse to search for the content files.
IFC Content Path	Type the path and location of your Tool Catalog files, or click Browse to search for the content files.
Detail Component Databases	Select the **Add/Remove** button to set the search paths for your detail component files.
Keynote Databases	Select the **Add/Remove** button to set the search paths for your keynote database files.
Display Edit Schedule Data Dialog During Tag Insertion	To attach schedule data to objects when you insert a schedule tag in the drawing, this should be ENABLED.

IFC Content is an object-based building data model that is non-proprietary. It uses open-source code developed by the IAI (International Alliance for Interoperability) to promote data exchange between CAD software. IFC Content might be created in Autodesk Revit, Inventor, or some other software for use in your projects.

Using AEC Content

AutoCAD Architecture uses several pre-defined and user-customizable content including:

- Architectural Display Configurations
- Architectural Profiles of Geometric Shapes
- Wall Styles and Endcap geometry
- Door styles
- Window styles
- Stair styles
- Space styles
- Schedule tables

Standard style content is stored in the AEC templates subdirectory. You can create additional content, import and export styles between drawings.

AEC Object Settings

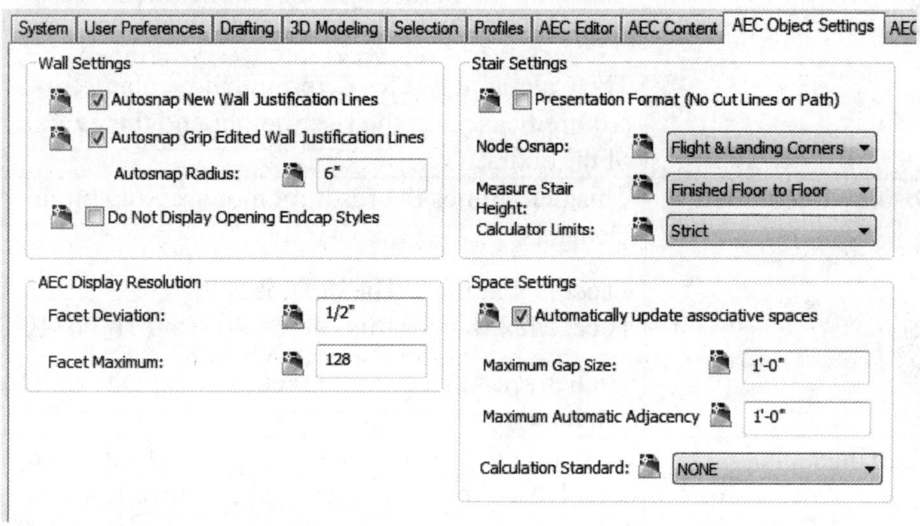

Wall Settings	
Autosnap New Wall Justification Lines	Enable to have the endpoint of a new wall that is drawn within the Autosnap Radius of the baseline of an existing wall automatically snap to that baseline. If you select this option and set your Autosnap Radius to 0, then only walls that touch, clean up with each other.
Autosnap Grip Edited Wall Justification Lines	Enable to snap the endpoint of a wall that you grip edit within the Autosnap Radius of the baseline of an existing wall. If you select this option and set your Autosnap Radius to 0, then only walls that touch clean up with each other.

Autosnap Radius	Enter a value to set the snap tolerance.
Do not display opening end cap styles	Enable Do Not Display Opening Endcap Styles to suppress the display of endcaps applied to openings in walls. Enabling this option boosts drawing performance when the drawing contains many complex endcaps.
Stair Settings	
Presentation Format (No Cut Lines or Path)	If this is enabled, a jagged line and directional arrows will not display.
Node Osnap	Determines which snap is enabled when creating stairs: Vertical Alignment Flight and Landing Corners
Measure Stair Height	Rough floor to floor – ignore offsets Finished floor to floor – include top and bottom offsets
Calculator Limits	Strict – stair will display a defect symbol when an edit results in a violation of the Calculation rules. Relaxed – no defect symbol will be displayed when the stair violates the Calculation rules. The Calculation rules determine how many treads are required based on the riser height and the overall height of the stairs.
AEC Display Resolution	This determines the resolution of arcs and circular elements. Facet Deviation – The default is ½″. Facet Maximum – this can be set from 100 to 10,000. Higher settings use more memory and may affect screen refresh rates
Space Settings 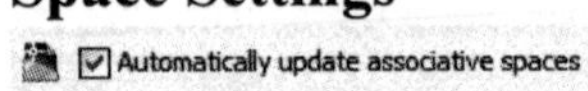 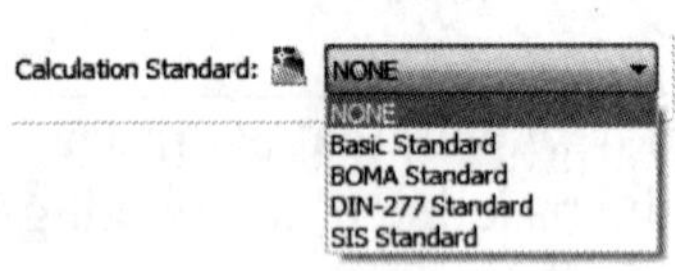	If *Automatically update associative spaces* is enabled, AutoCAD Architecture will automatically determine which spaces are adjacent to each other and update their association accordingly. The Maximum Gap Size is the allowable distance between spaces. The Maximum Automatic Adjacency sets the gap allowance between spaces for spaces to be considered adjacent. The Floor Boundary Thickness sets the value of the Floor Boundary Thickness. The Calculation Standard determines how the space values are calculated.

AEC Dimension

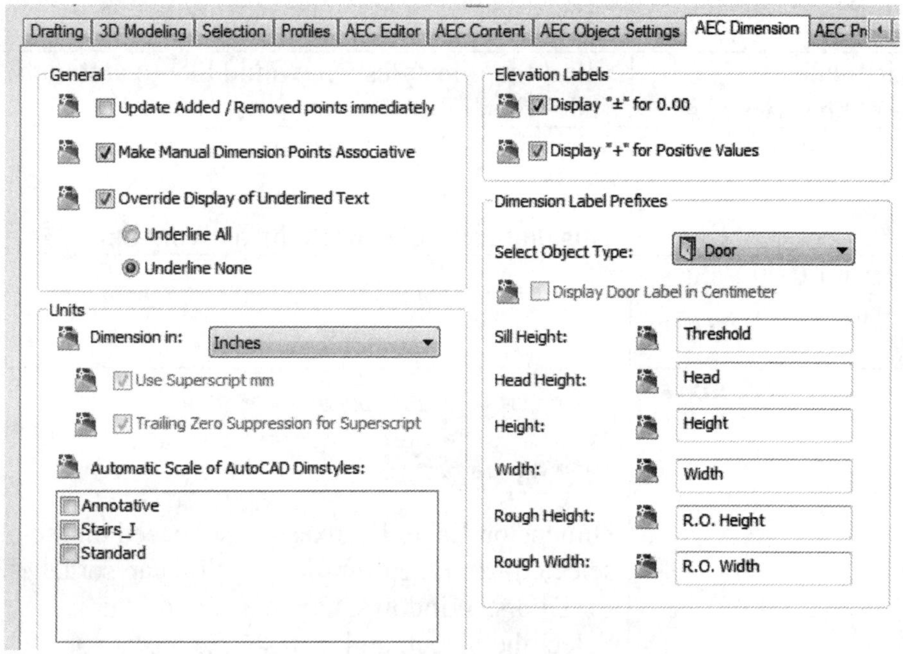

General	
Update Added/Removed points immediately	Enable to update the display every time you add or remove a point from a dimension chain.
Make Manual Dimension Points Associative	Enable if you want the dimension to update when the object is modified.
Override Display of Undefined Text	Enable to automatically underline each manually overridden dimension value.
Underline All	Enable to manually underline overridden dimension values.
Underline None	Enable to not underline any overridden dimension value.
Units	
Dimension in:	Select the desired units from the drop-down list.
Use Superscript mm	If your units are set to meters or centimeters, enable superscripted text to display the millimeters as superscript. 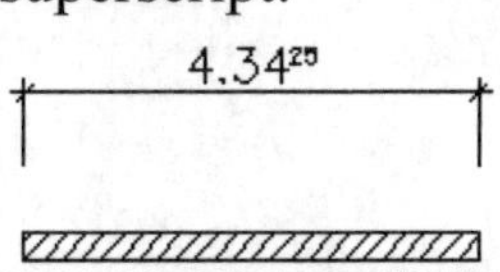
Trailing Zero Suppression for Superscript	To suppress zeros at the end of superscripted numbers, select Trailing Zeros Suppression for Superscript. You can select this option only if you have selected Use Superscript mm and your units are metric.

	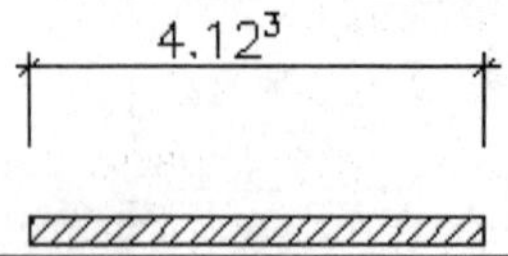
Automatic Scale of AutoCAD Dimstyles	Select the dimstyles you would like to automatically scale when units are reset.
Elevation Labels	Select the unit in which elevation labels are to be displayed. This unit can differ from the drawing unit.
Display +/- for 0.00 Values	
Display + for Positive Values	
Dimension Label Prefixes	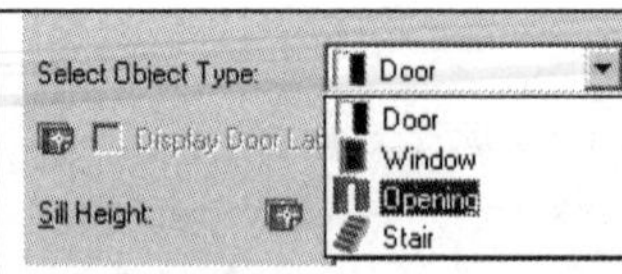 Dimension Label Prefixes are set based on the object selected from the drop-down. You can set label prefixes for Doors, Windows, Openings, and Stairs. Select the object, and then set the prefix for each designation. The designations will change based on the object selected.

AEC Project Defaults

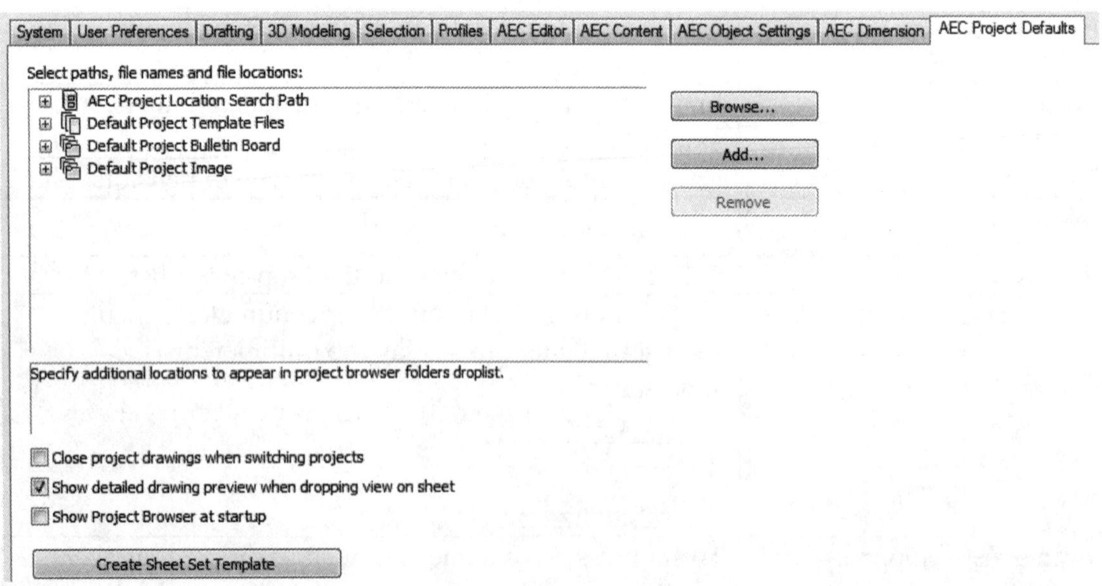

Most BID/AEC firms work in a team environment where they divide a project's tasks among several different users. The AEC Project Defaults allows the CAD Manager or team leader to select a folder on the company's server to locate files; set up template files with the project's title blocks; and even set up a webpage to post project information.

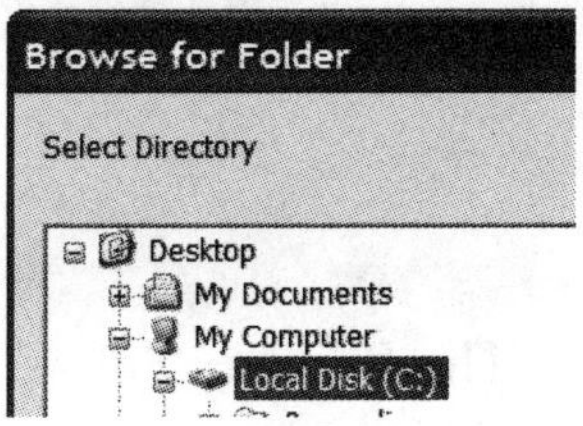

To add a path, simply expand the folder and use the Browse button to locate the desired folder.

You can add more than one path to the AEC Project Location Search Path. All the other folders only allow you to have a single location for template files, the project bulletin board, and the default project image.

TIP: I highly recommend that you store any custom content in a separate directory as far away from AutoCAD Architecture as possible. This will allow you to back up your custom work easily and prevent accidental erasure if you upgrade your software application.

You should be aware that AutoCAD Architecture currently allows the user to specify only ONE path for custom content, so drawings with custom commands will only work if they reside in the specified path.

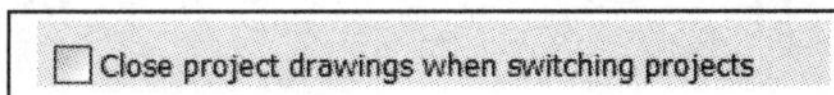	If enabled, when a user switches projects in the Project Navigator, any open drawings not related to the new project selected will be closed. This conserves memory resources.
	If enabled, then the user will see the entire view as it is being positioned on a sheet. If it is disabled, the user will just see the boundary of the view for the purposes of placing it on a sheet.
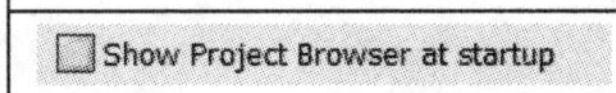	If enabled, you will automatically have access to the Project Browser whenever you start AutoCAD Architecture.

Accessing the Project Browser

Command line	AECProjectBrowser
Quick Access Toolbar	
Files Menu	Project Browser

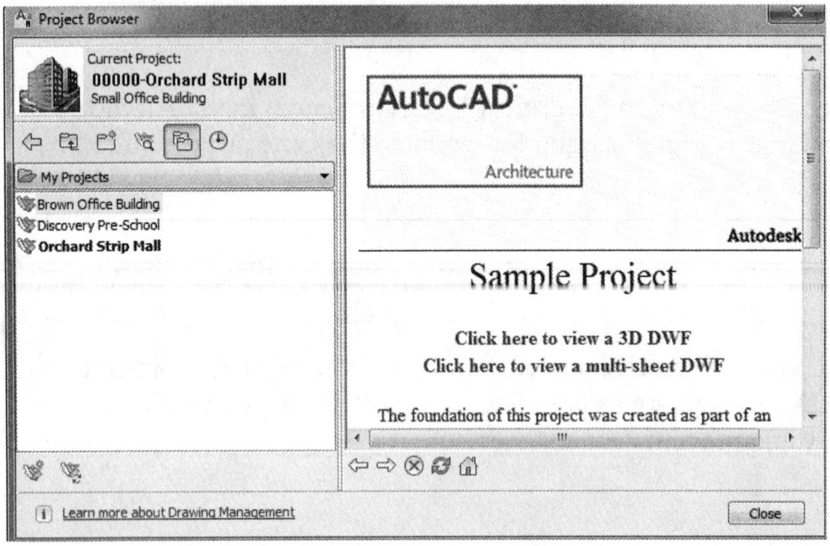

The Project Browser allows you to manage your project, similar to the old Today window in 2002, but more powerful. Projects have two parts: the building model and the reports generated from the building model.

The building model is made of two drawing types: constructs and elements. A construct is any unique portion of a building. It can be a flight of stairs, a specific room, or an entire floor. Constructs are assigned to a level (floor) and a division within a project. Elements are any AEC object or content that is used multiple times in a model. For example, furniture layouts or lavatory layouts. Elements can be converted into constructs if you decide that they will not be used repeatedly.

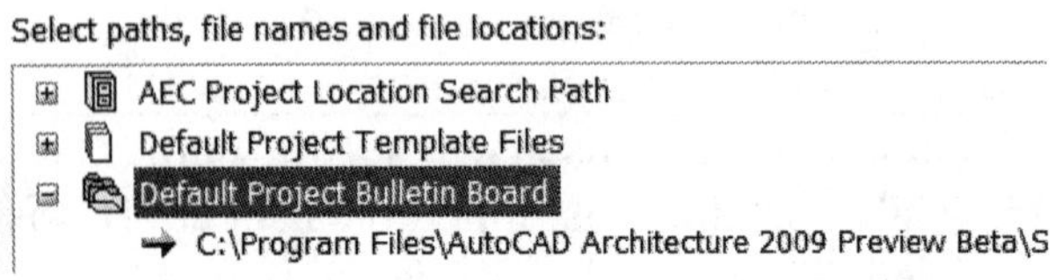

The text you see in the right window is actually an html file. The path to this file is controlled in the path for the Default Project Bulletin Board. This is set on the AEC Project Defaults tab in the Options dialog.

Architectural Profiles of Geometric Shapes

You can create mass elements to define the shape and configuration of your preliminary study, or mass model. After you create the mass elements you need, you can change their size as necessary to reflect the building design.

- **Mass element**: A single object that has behaviors based on its shape. For example, you can set the width, depth, and height of a box mass element, and the radius and height of a cylinder mass element.

Mass elements are parametric, which allows each of the shapes to have very specific behavior when it comes to the manipulation of each mass element's shape. For example, if the corner grip point of a box is selected and dragged, then the width and depth are modified. It is easy to change the shape to another form by right-clicking on the element and selecting a new shape from the list.

Through Boolean operations (addition, subtraction, intersection), mass elements can be combined into a mass group. The mass group provides a representation of your building during the concept phase of your project.

- **Mass group**: Takes the shape of the mass elements and is placed on a separate layer from the mass elements.
- **Mass model**: A virtual mass object, shaped from mass elements, which defines the basic structure and proportion of your building. A marker appears as a small box in your drawing to which you attach mass elements.

As you continue developing your mass model, you can combine mass elements into mass groups and create complex building shapes through addition, subtraction, or intersection of mass elements. You can still edit individual mass elements attached to a mass group to further refine the building model.

To study alternative design schemes, you can create a number of mass element references. When you change the original of the referenced mass element, all the instances of the mass element references are updated.

The mass model that you create with mass elements and mass groups is a refinement of your original idea that you carry forward into the next phase of the project, in which you change the mass study into floor plates and then into walls. The walls are used to start the design phase.

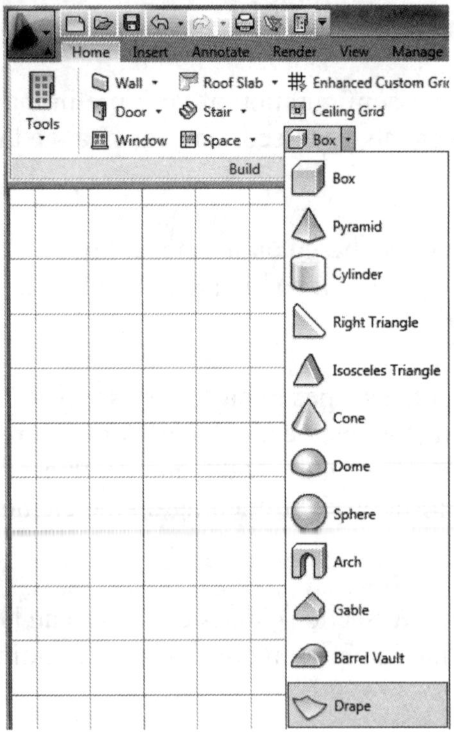

Mass Elements are accessed from the Home ribbon.

Mass Elements that can be defined include Arches, Gables, Doric Columns, etc.

The Style Manager

Menu

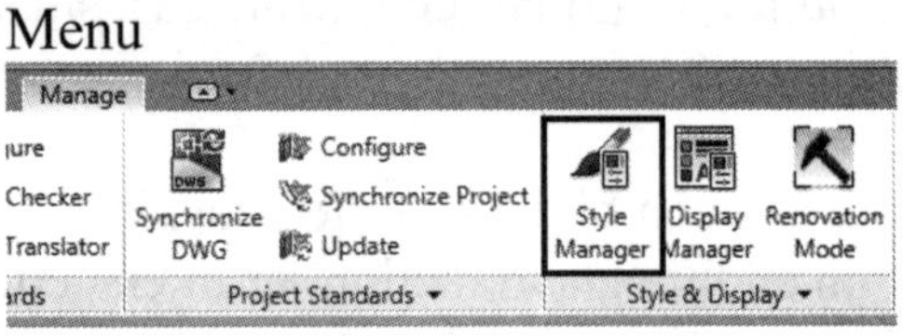

Access the Style Manager from the Manage ribbon.

The Style Manager is a Microsoft® Windows Explorer-based utility that provides you with a central location in Autodesk AutoCAD Architecture where you can view and work with styles in drawings or from Internet and intranet sites.

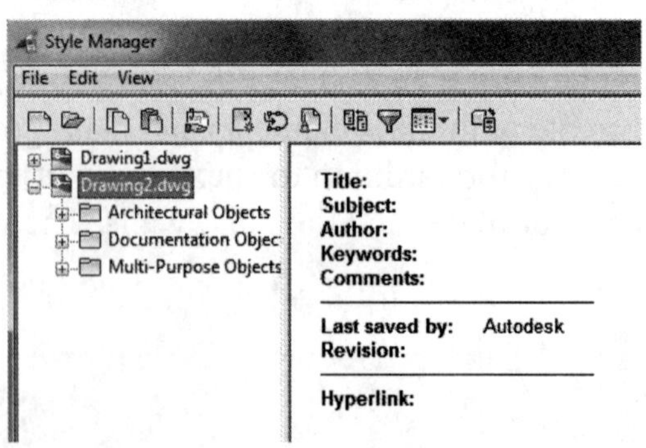

Styles are sets of parameters that you can assign to objects in Autodesk AutoCAD Architecture to determine their appearance or function. For example, a door style in Autodesk AutoCAD Architecture determines what door type, such as single or double, bi-fold or hinged, a door in a drawing represents. You can assign one style to more than one object, and you can modify the style to change the all the objects that are assigned that style.

Depending on your design projects, either you or your CAD Manager might want to customize existing styles or create new styles. The Style Manager allows you to easily create, customize, and share styles with other users. With the Style Manager, you can:

- Provide a central point for accessing styles from open drawings and Internet and intranet sites
- Quickly set up new drawings and templates by copying styles from other drawings or templates
- Sort and view the styles in your drawings and templates by drawing or by style type
- Preview an object with a selected style
- Create new styles and edit existing styles
- Delete unused styles from drawings and templates
- Send styles to other Autodesk AutoCAD Architecture users by email

Objects in Autodesk AutoCAD Architecture that use styles include 2D sections and elevations, AEC polygons, curtain walls, curtain wall units, doors, endcaps, railings, roof slab edges, roof slabs, schedule tables, slab edges, slabs, spaces, stairs, structural members, wall modifiers, walls, window assemblies, and windows.

Additionally, layer key styles, schedule data formats, and cleanup group, mask block, multi-view block, profile, and property set definitions are handled by the Style Manager.

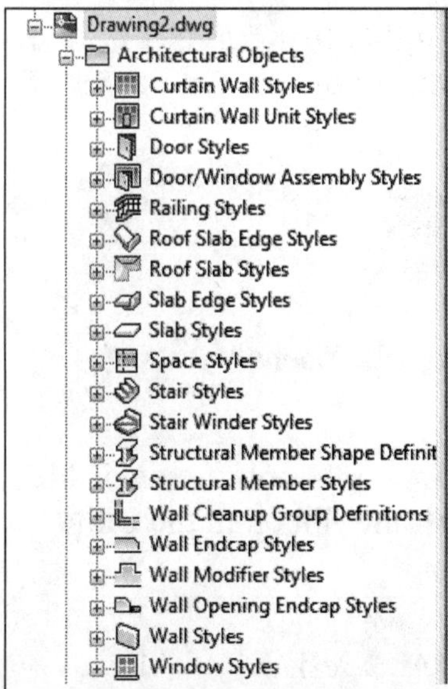

Most of the objects in Autodesk AutoCAD Architecture have a default Standard style. In addition, Autodesk AutoCAD Architecture includes a starter set of styles that you can use with your drawings. The Autodesk AutoCAD Architecture templates contain some of these styles. Any drawing that you start from one of the templates includes these styles.

You can also access the styles for doors, end caps, spaces, stairs, walls, and windows from drawings located in *Documents and Settings\All Users\ Application Data\Autodesk\... \Styles\Imperial or Metric.* Property set definitions and schedule tables are located in the *Documents and Settings\All Users\Application Data\ Autodesk...\AEC Content\ Imperial\ Documentation\Schedule Tags* folder.

> **TIP:** I do not recommend modifying AutoCAD Architecture's standard styles as this may affect drawings you bring in from outside sources. Instead, copy the existing style to a NEW style and modify it using the desired properties.

Exercise 1-3:

Creating a New Geometric Profile

Drawing Name: New
Estimated Time: 15 minutes

This exercise reinforces the following skills:

- Use of AEC Design Content
- Use of Mass Elements
- Use of Views
- Visual Styles
- Modify using Properties

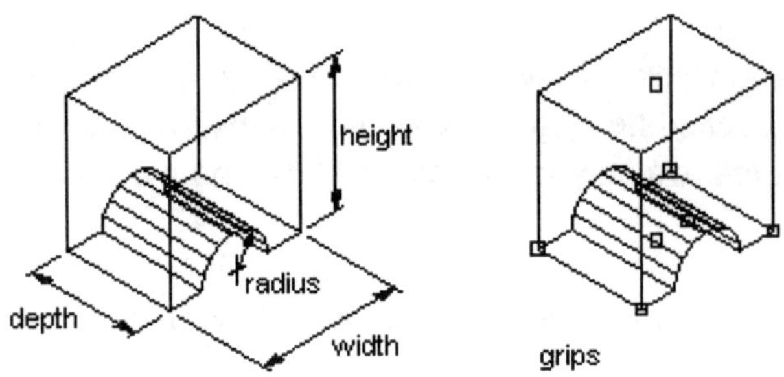

Creating an arch mass element

1. Start a New Drawing.
2.  Select the QNEW tool from the Standard toolbar.

   Because we assigned a template in Exercise 1-2, a drawing file opens without prompting us to select a template.

3. 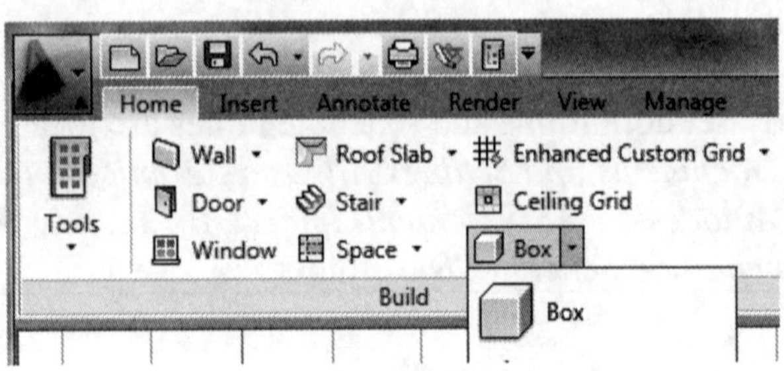

   All the massing tools are available on the **Home** ribbon in the Build section.

4. 

Select the **Arch** tool from the Massing drop down list.

5. 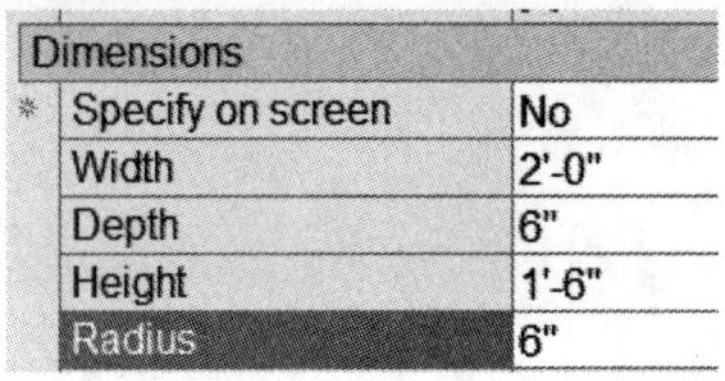

Expand the **Dimensions** section on the Properties dialog.

Set Specify on screen to **No**.
Set the Width to **2′** [**600**].
Set the Depth to **6″** [**200**].
Set the Height to **1′ 6″** [**500**].
Set the Radius to **6″** [**200**].

6. 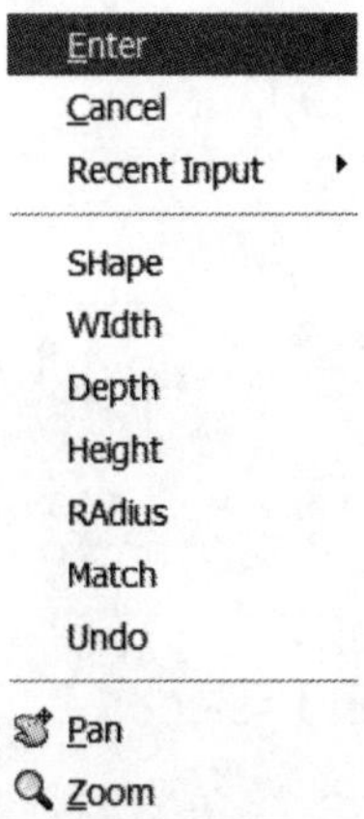

Pick a point anywhere in the drawing area.

Press ENTER to accept a Rotation Angle of 0 or right click and select **ENTER**.

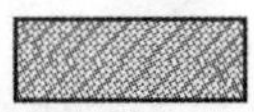

Press **ENTER** to exit the command.

7.  Switch to an isometric view.

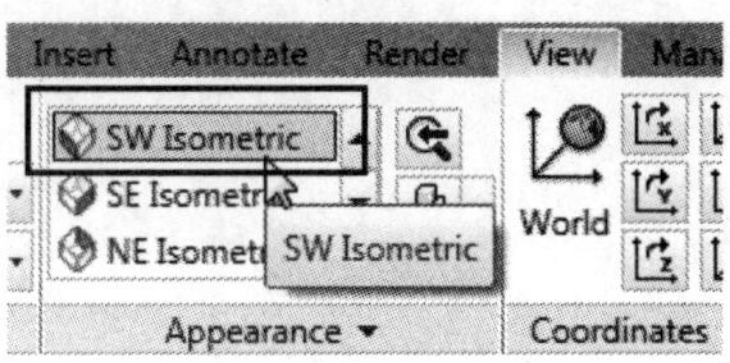

To switch to an isometric view, simply go to **View** Ribbon. Under the Views list, select **SW Isometric**.

Our model so far.

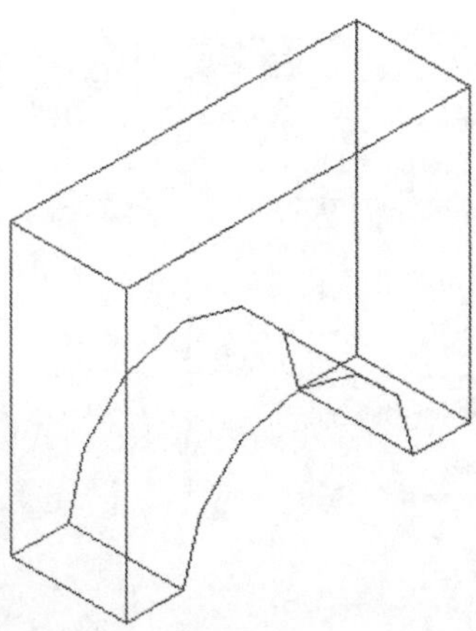

8. 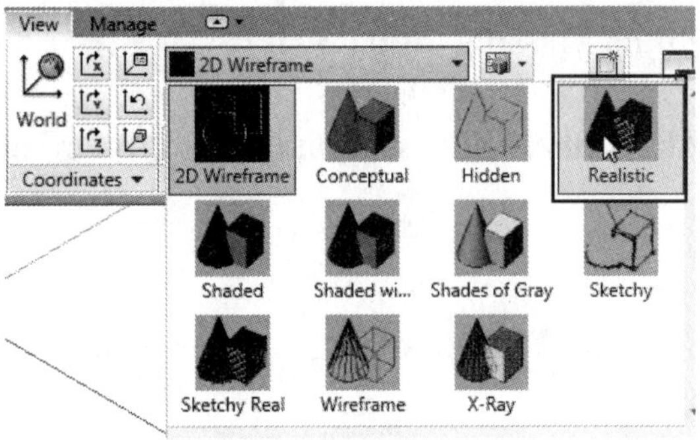

Select **Realistic** on the View ribbon under Face Effects to shade the model.

You can also type **SHA** on the command line, then **R** for Realistic.

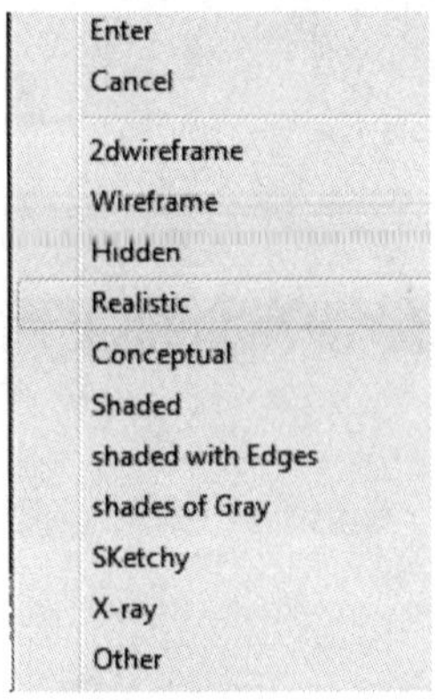

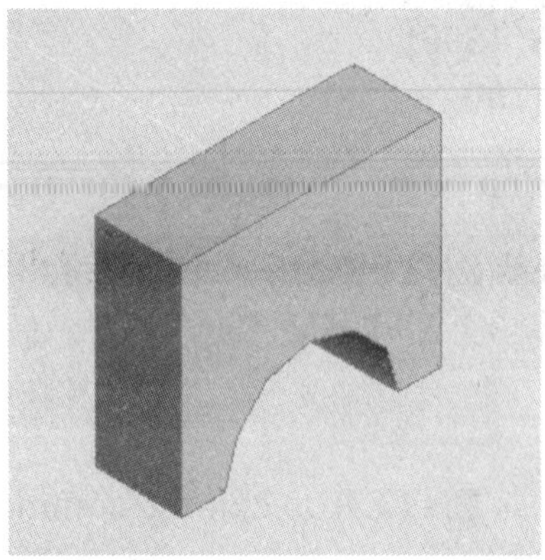

9. To change the arch properties, select the arch so that it is highlighted.
If the properties dialog doesn't pop up automatically, right click and select **Properties**.

10. 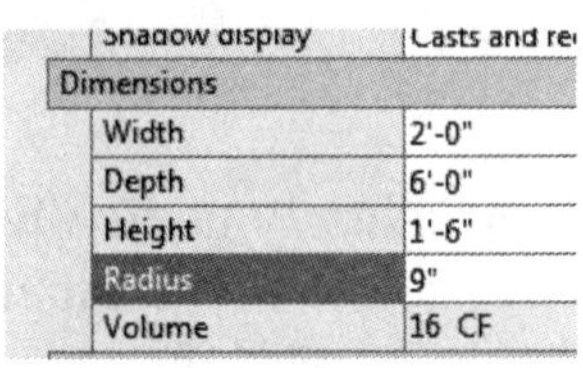

Change the Radius to **9″** [**250**].

Pick into the graphics window and the arch will update.

11. Press **ESC** to release the grips on the arc.

12. Save the drawing as *ex1-3.dwg*.

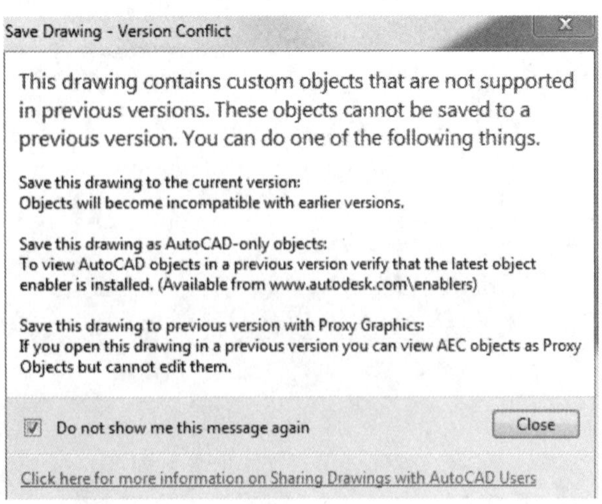

If you see this dialog, you can just ignore it and close it.

Exercise 1-4:
Creating a New Visual Style

Drawing Name: ex1-3.dwg
Estimated Time: 15 minutes

This exercise reinforces the following skills:d

- Workspaces
- Use of Visual Styles
- Controlling the Display of Objects

1. Open *ex1-3.dwg*.

2. 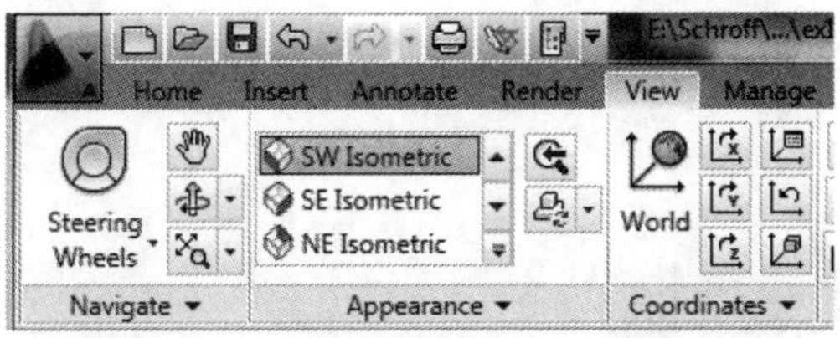

Activate the **View** ribbon.

3. 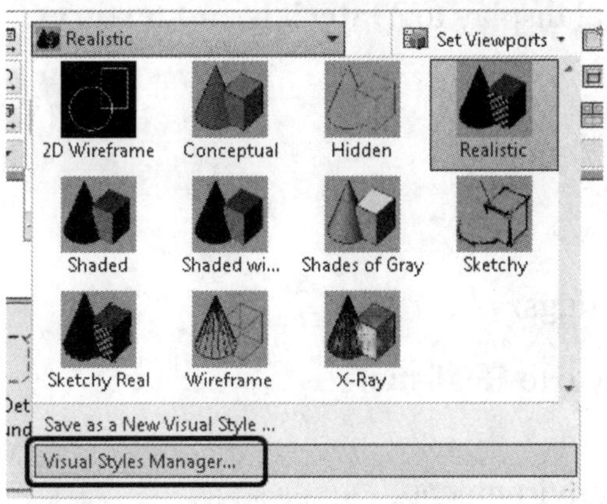

Launch the Visual Styles Manager.

To launch, select the drop-down next to the Visual Styles tool, then select **Visual Styles Manager**.

4. 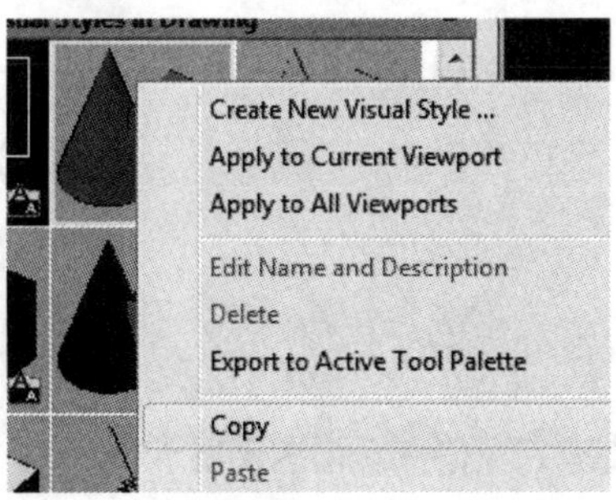

Highlight the **Conceptual** tool.

Right click and select **Copy**.

5. 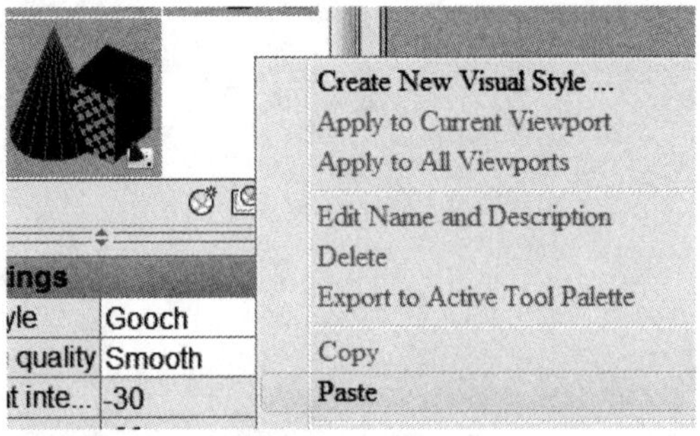

Right click and select **Paste**.

6. 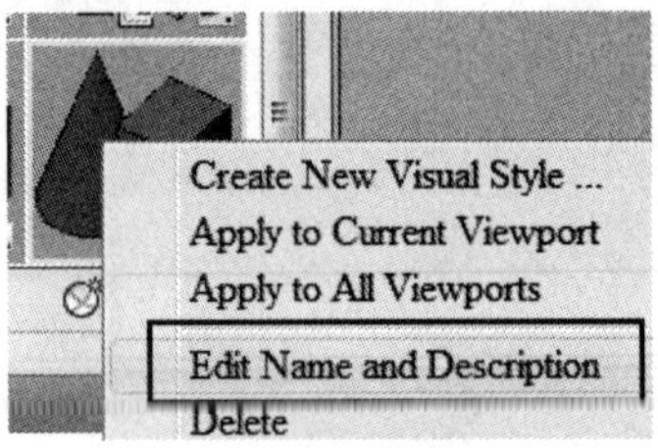

Highlight the copied tool.
Right click and select **Edit Name and Description**.

7. 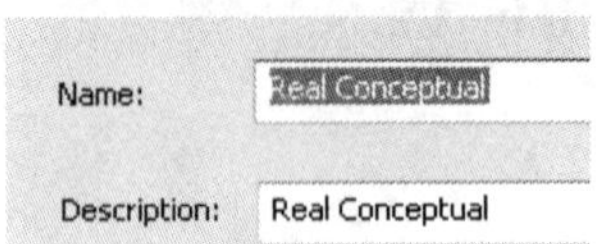

Change the name and description to **Real Conceptual**.

Press **OK**.

8. 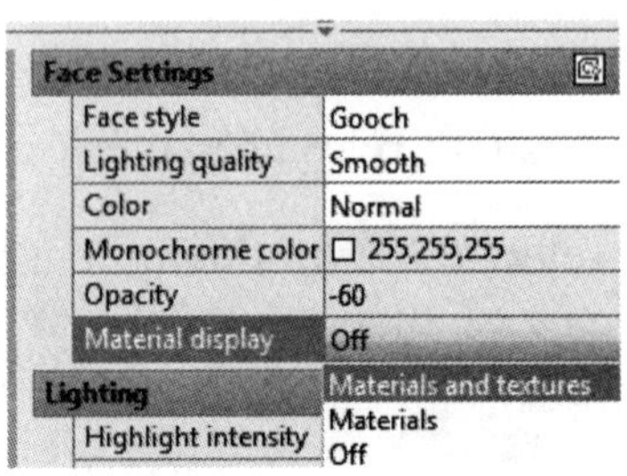

Under Face Settings:
Set Material display to **Materials and textures**.

9. 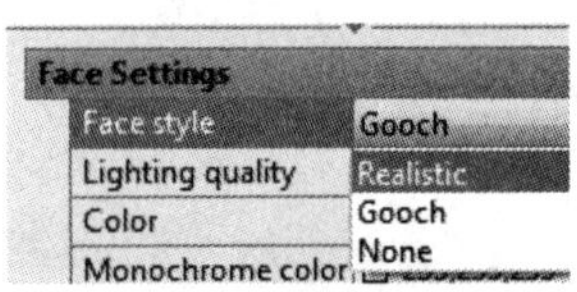

Under Face Settings:

Set the Face Style to **Realistic**.

10. 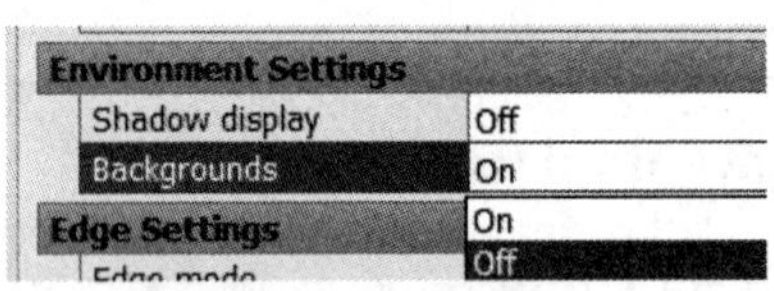

Under Environment Settings:

Set the Backgrounds to **Off**.

11. 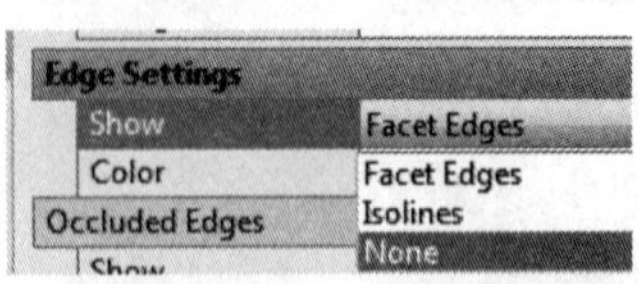

Under Edge Settings:

Set the Show to **None**.

12. 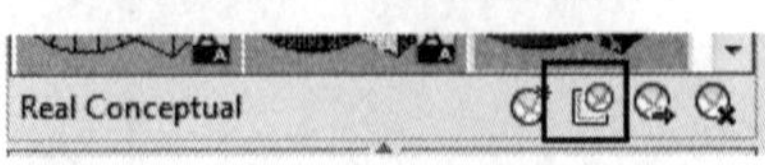

Verify that the Real Conceptual Style is highlighted/ selected.

Select the **Apply Visual Style to Current Viewport** tool.

13. Save the drawing as *ex1-4.dwg*.

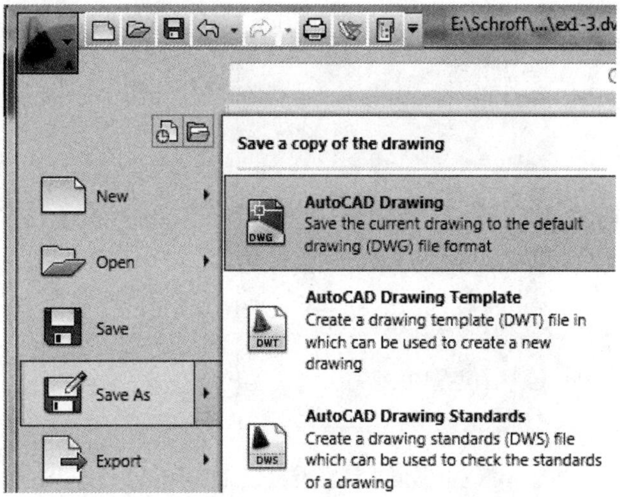

Exercise 1-5:

Creating a New Wall Style

Drawing Name: New using Imperial [Metric] (ctb).dwt
Estimated Time: 30 minutes

This exercise reinforces the following skills:

- Use of AEC Design Content
- Use of Wall Styles
- Workspaces

1.  Select the **QNEW** tool from the Standard toolbar.

2. 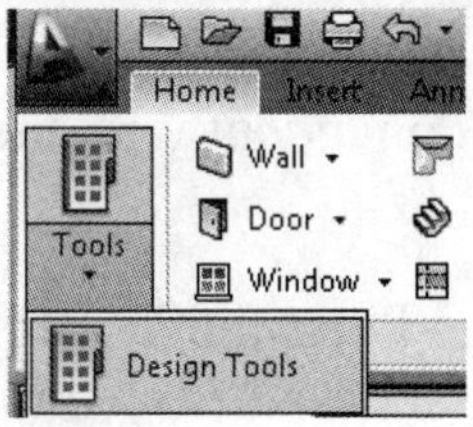

Activate the **Home** ribbon.

Select **Tools→Design Tools** from the drop down.

3. 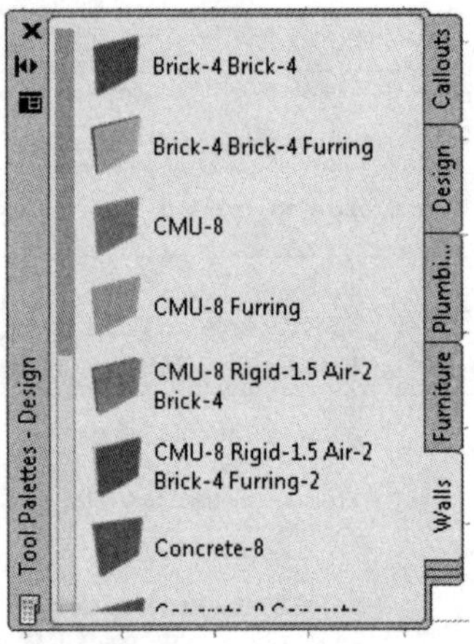

Select the **Walls** tab of the palette.

4. 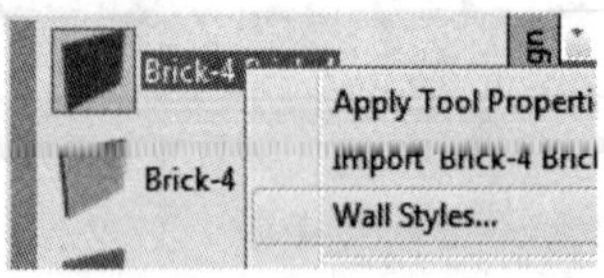

Highlight the first wall icon.
Right click and select **Wall Styles**.

5. The Style Manager is displayed, with the current drawing expanded in the tree view. The wall styles in the current drawing are displayed under the wall style type. All other style and definition types are filtered out in the tree view.

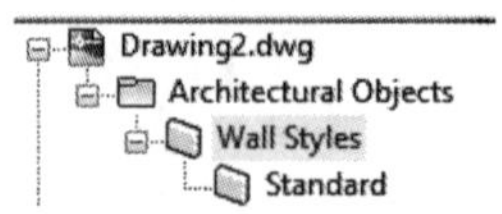

6. 

Select the **New Style** tool.

7. Change the name of the new style by typing **Brick_Block**.

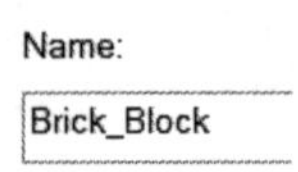

8. In the General tab, type in the description **8″ CMU and 3-1/2″ [200 mm CMU and 90 mm] Brick Wall** in the Description field as shown.

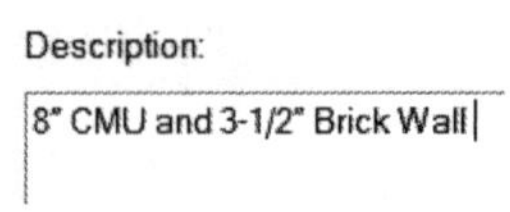

9. Select the Components tab.
Change the Name to **CMU** by typing in the Name field indicated.

Press the dropdown arrow next to the Edge Offset Button.
Set the Edge Offset to 0.

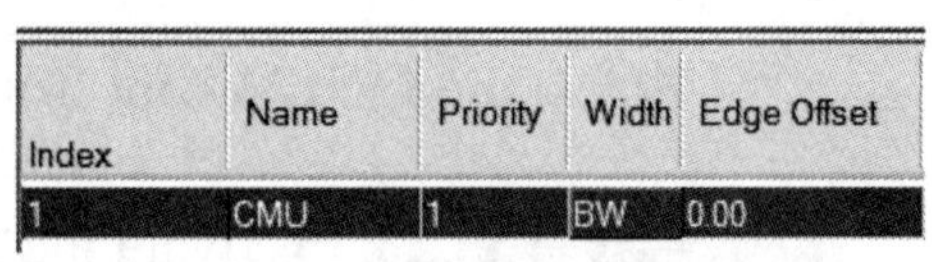

10. A 0 edge offset specifies that the outside edge of the CMU is coincident with the wall baseline.

11. 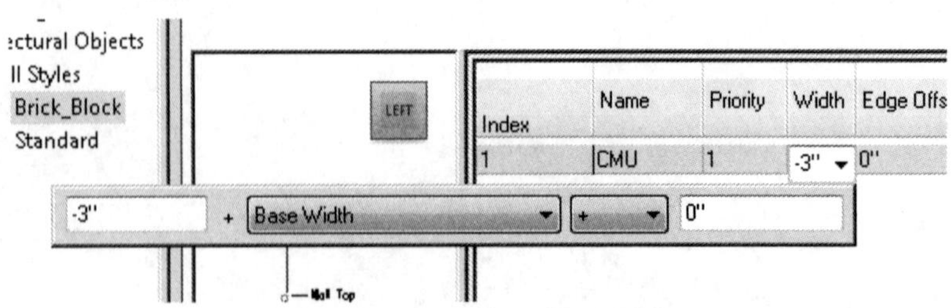

Press the **Width** down arrow button.

Set the value to **-3″ [-80]**.

This specifies that the CMU has a fixed width of 3 inches [80 mm] in the negative direction from the wall baseline (to the inside).

You now have one component defined for your wall named CMU with the properties shown.

12.  Press the **Add** Component button on the right side of the dialog box. Next, we'll add wall insulation.

13. In the Name field, type **Insulation**.

Set the Priority to 1. (The lower the priority number, the higher the priority when creating intersections.)

Set the Edge Offset with a value of **0**.

Set the Component Width as shown, with a value of **1.5″** [**38**] and the Base Width set to 0.

This specifies that the insulation has a fixed width of 1.5″ [38 mm] offset in a positive direction from the wall baseline (to the outside).

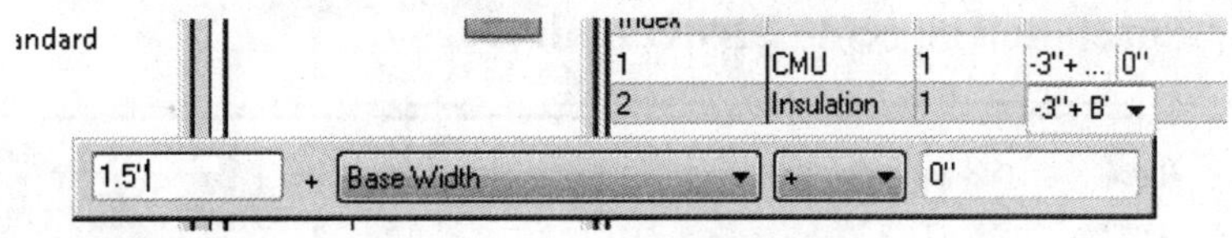

14. 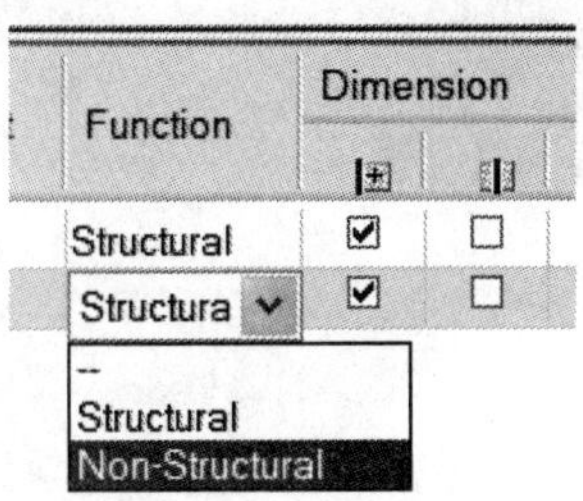

Set the Function to **Non-Structural**.

15. 

Note that the preview changes to show the insulation component.

16. Now, we add an air space component to our wall. Press the **Add Component** button.

17. Rename the new component **Air Space**. Set the Edge Offset to **0**.

    This specifies that the inside edge of the air space is coincident with the outside edge of the insulation.

Index	Name	Priority	Width	Edge Offset	Function
1	CMU	1	3"	0"	Structural
2	INSULATI...	1	1 1/2"	0"	Non-Struct...
3	AIR SPACE	1	1"	0"	Non-Struct...

    The width should be set to 1″ [25.4].

    This specifies that the air gap will have a fixed width of 1 inch [25.4 mm] offset in the positive direction from the wall baseline (to the outside).

18. Use the **Add Component** tool to add the fourth component.

    The Name should be **Brick**.
    The Priority set to **1**.
    The Edge Offset set to **2.5″** [**63.5**].
    The Width set to **3.5″** [**90**].

    The Function should be set to **Structural**.

Index	Name	Priority	Width	Edge Offset	Function	Dimension	
1	CMU	1	-3"+ BW	0"	Structural	☑	☐
2	Insulation	1	1 1/2"+ BW	0"	Non-Struct...	☑	☐
3	Air Space	1	1"+ BW	0"	Non-Struct...	☑	☐
4	Brick	1	3 1/2"+ BW	2 1/2"	Structural	☑	☐

Index	Name	Priority	Width	Edge Offset	Function
1	CMU	1	-80.0...	0.00	Structural
2	INSULATION	1	38.00...	0.00	Non-Structural
3	AIR SPACE	1	25.40...	0.00	Non-Structural
4	BRICK	1	90.00...	63.50	Structural

19. 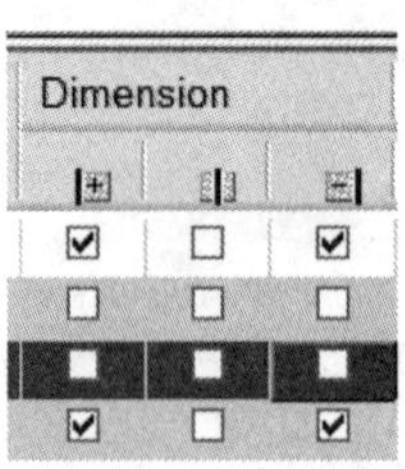

The Dimension section allows you to define where the extension lines for your dimension will be placed when measuring the wall. In this case, we are not interested in including the air space or insulation in our linear dimensions. Uncheck those boxes.

20.

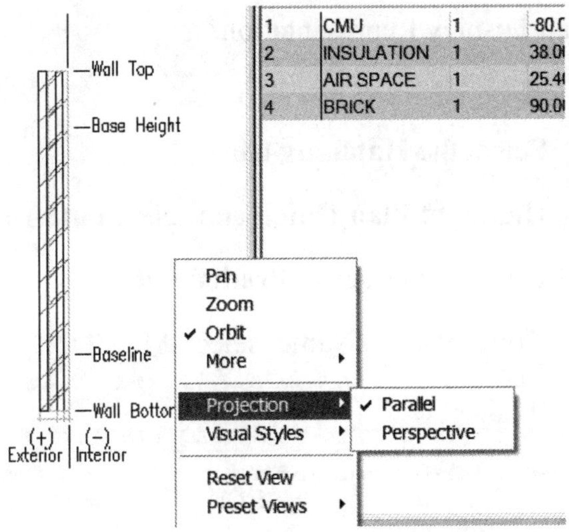

Note how your wall style previews.

If you right click in the preview pane, you can change the preview window by zooming, panning, or assigning a Preset View.

The preview pane uses a DWF-style interface.

21. Select the **Materials** tab.

Highlight the **CMU** component.

Select the **Add New Material** tool.

22.

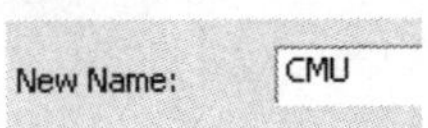

Enter **CMU** in the New Name field and press **OK**.

23. Use the **Add New Material** tool to assign new materials to each component.

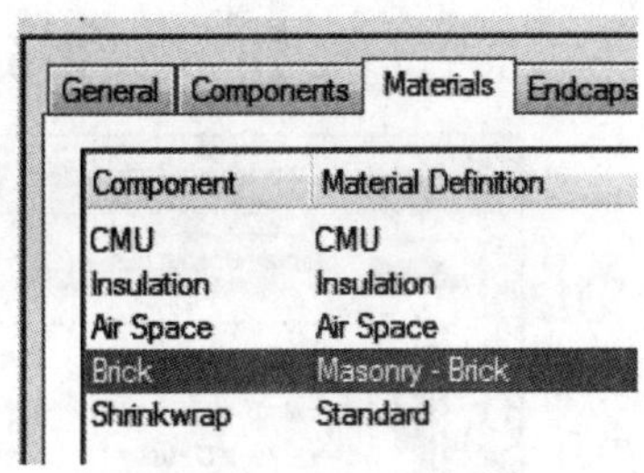

24. Highlight the **CMU** Component.

Select the **Edit Material** tool.

25. Select the **Display Properties** tab.

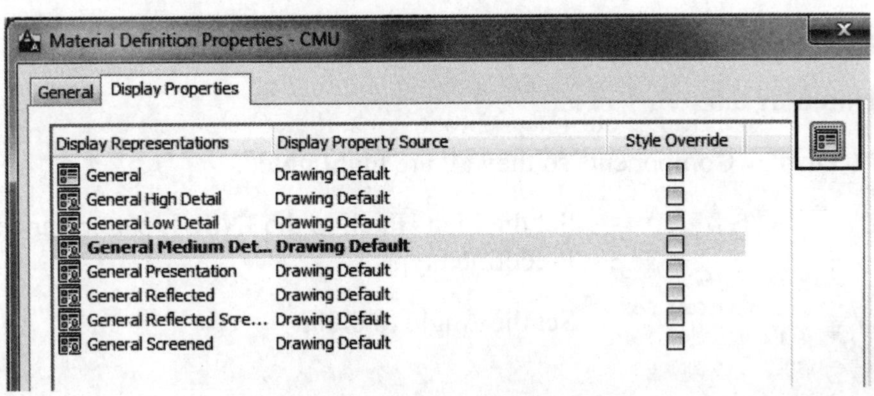

Highlight the **General Medium Detail** Display Representation.

Click on the **Style Override** button.

26. 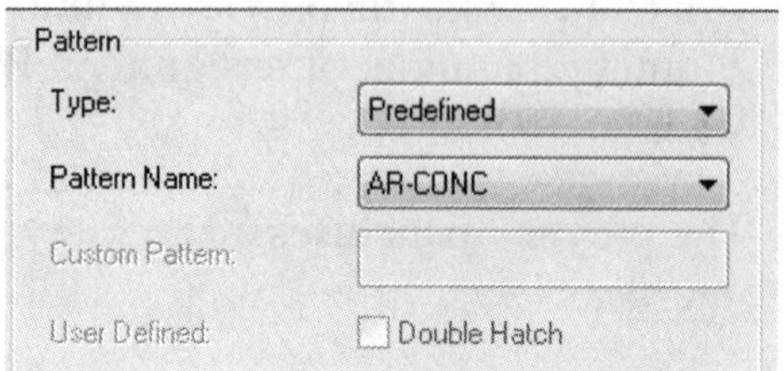

Select the **Hatching** tab.

Highlight **Plan Hatch** and select **Pattern**.

Under Type, select **Predefined**.

Under Pattern Name, select **AR-CONC**.

27. Assign the **AR-B88** Pattern to all the Display Components.

Set the Angles to **0**.

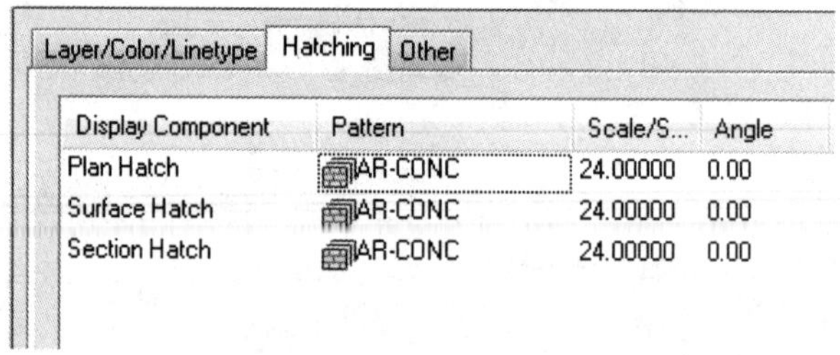

28. Press **OK** twice to return to the Materials tab of the Wall Properties dialog.

29.  Highlight **Insulation** and select the **Edit Material** tool.

30. Select the **Display Properties** tab.

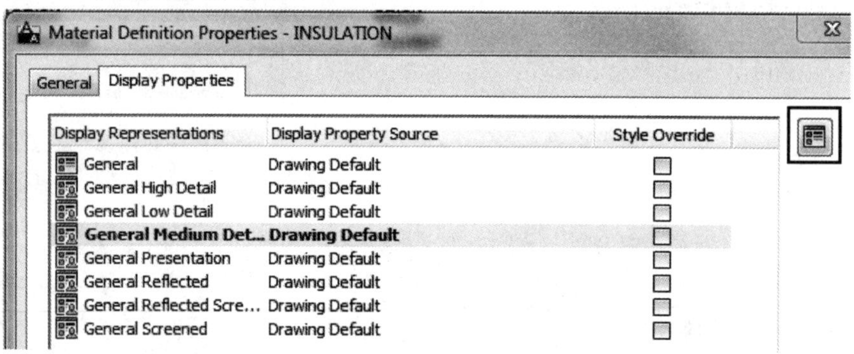

Highlight the **General Medium Detail** Display Property

Click on the **Style Override** button.

31. Select the **Hatching** tab.

Select all the Display Components so they all are highlighted.

32. 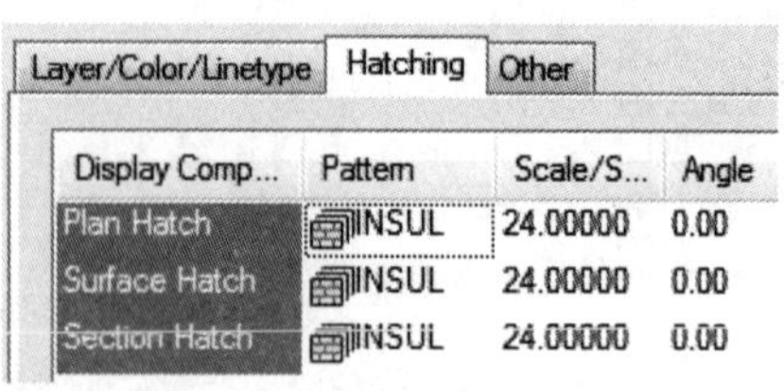

Set the Plan Hatch to the **INSUL** pattern under Predefined type.

Set the Angle to **0.00**.

33. 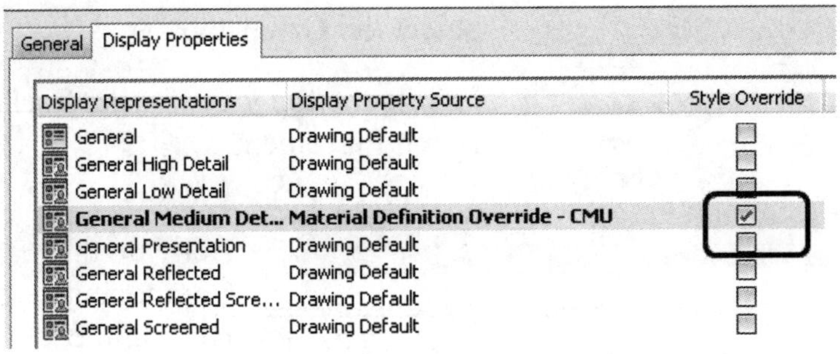

Verify that a check is placed in the Style Override button.

34. Press **OK** twice to return to the previous dialog.

35.  Highlight **Brick** and select the **Edit Material** tool.

36. 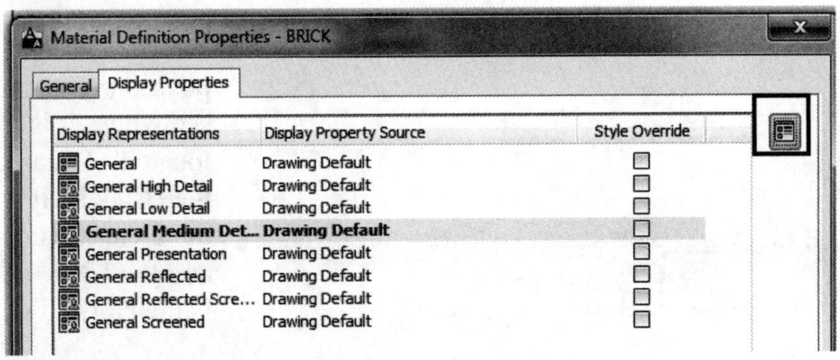

Select the **Display Properties** tab.

Highlight the **General Medium Detail** Display Representation.

Click on the **Style Override** button.

37. 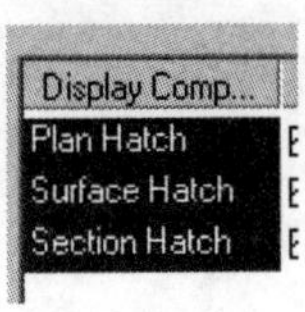

Select the **Hatching** tab.

Highlight the three display components.

Select the first pattern.

38. Set the Type to **Predefined**.

39. Select the **Browse** button.

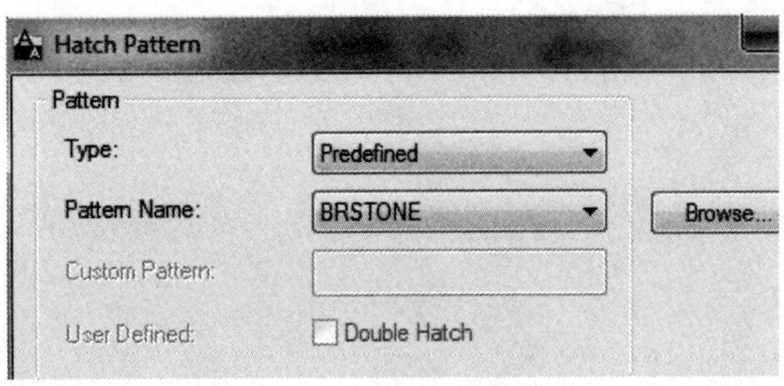

40. 

Select the **BRSTONE** pattern.

41. 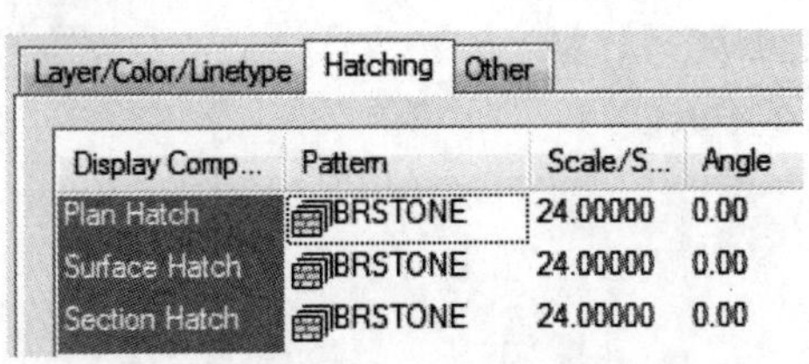

Set the Angle to 0 for all hatches.

Press **OK** twice.

42. 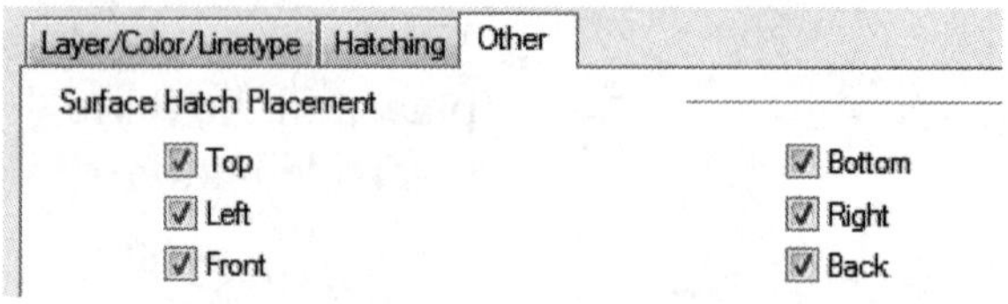

Select the **Other** tab.

Enable the top view for the Surface Hatch Placement.

43. 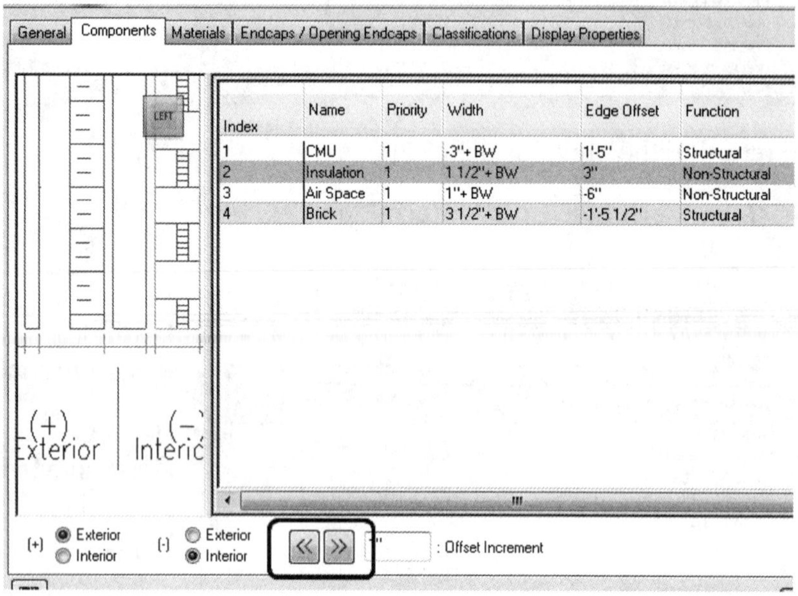

Activate the Components tab. Highlight each component and use the << >> arrows to position the component. By shifting each component position, you can see where it is located. Located the Brick so it is on the Exterior side and the CMU so it is interior.

44. 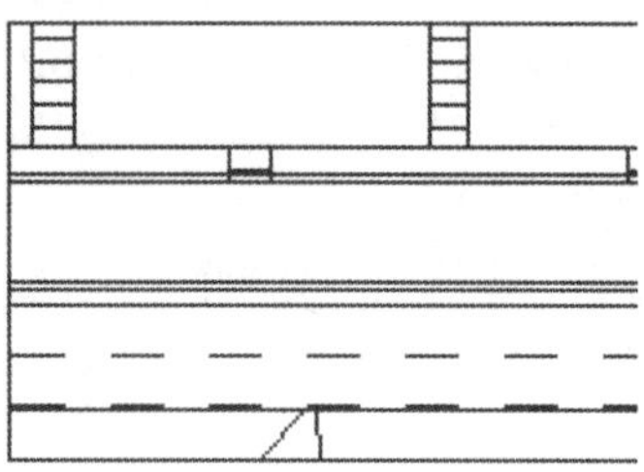

Close the Style Manager.

Press **OK** to exit the Edit dialog.
You can preview how the changes you made to the material display will appear when you create your wall.

45. Save as *ex1-5.dwg.*

Exercise 1-6:

Creating a Tool

Drawing Name: ex1-5.dwg
Estimated Time: 30 minutes

This exercise reinforces the following skills:

- ❑ Use of AEC Design Content
- ❑ Use of Wall Styles

1. Open or continue working in ***ex1-5.dwg***.

2. 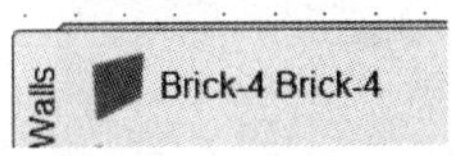

Verify that the tool palette is open with the Walls palette active.

3. 

Activate the **Manage** ribbon.

   Select the **Style Manager** tool.

4. 

Locate the Brick-Block wall style you created.

5. 

Drag and drop the wall style onto your Walls palette.

   Press **OK** to close the Style Manager.

6. 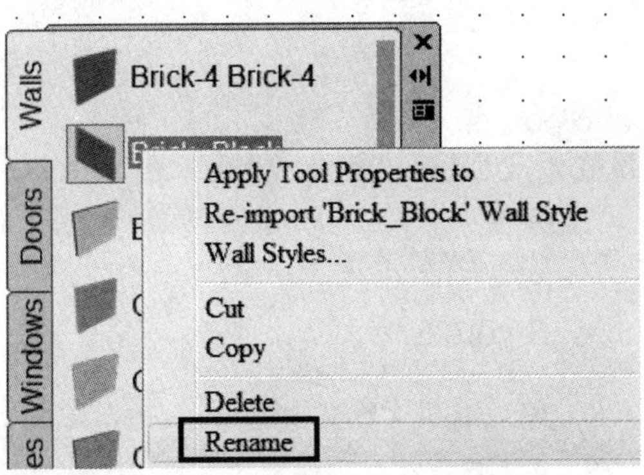

Highlight the Brick_Block tool.
Right click and select **Rename**.

7. 

Change the name to **8″ CMU- 3.5″ Brick [200 mm CMU – 90 mm]**.

8. 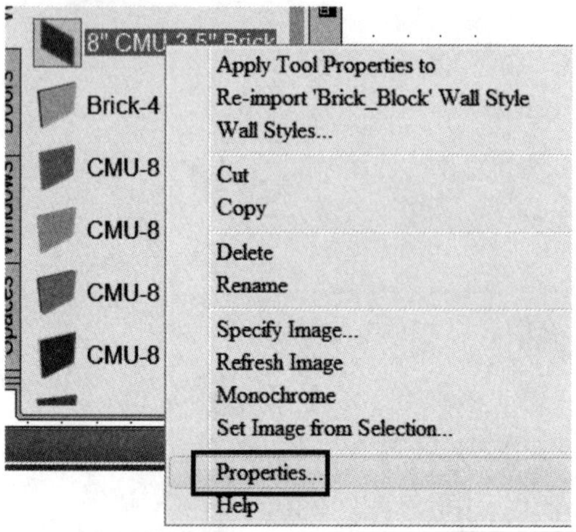

Highlight **8″ CMU- 3.5″ Brick** tool.

Right click and select **Properties**.

9. 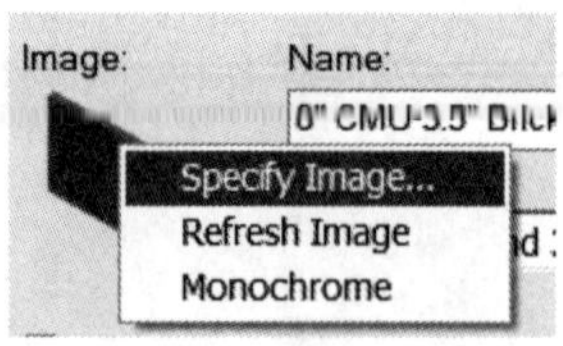

Highlight the image icon in the dialog.
Right click and select **Specify Image**.

10. Locate the file called **aecwall-CMU-8-Rigid-1.5 Air Brick-4.png**.

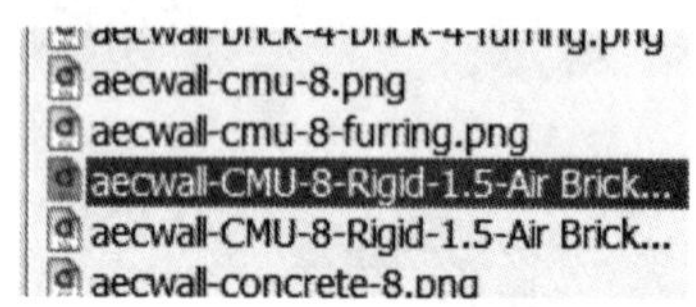

Press **Open**.

11. 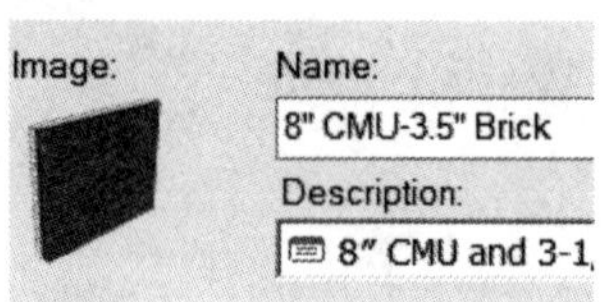

The image is reset.

Press **OK**.

12. Select the new tool and draw a wall.
You may draw a wall simply by picking two points.
If you enable the ORTHO button on the bottom of the screen, your wall will be straight.

13. 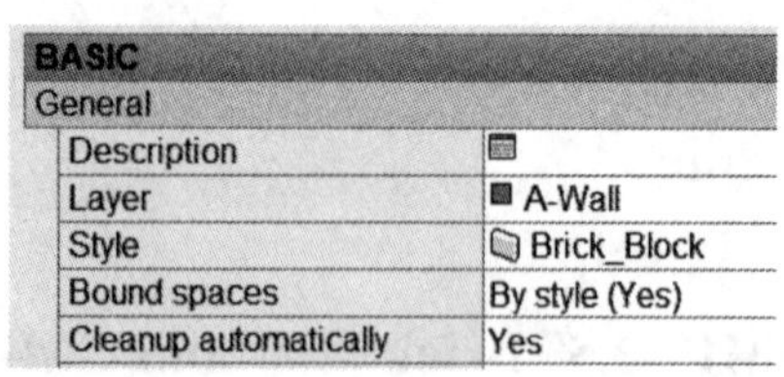

Select the wall you drew.

Right click and select **Properties**.

Note that the wall is placed on the A-Wall Layer and uses the Brick-Block Style you defined.

14. Save your file as ***Styles.dwg***.

TIP: The wall style you created will not be available in any new drawings unless you copy it over to the default template.

Exercise 1-7:

Copying a Style to a Template

Drawing Name: Styles1.dwg, Imperial (Metric).ctb.dwt
Estimated Time: 20 minutes

This exercise reinforces the following skills:

- Style Manager
- Use of Templates
- Properties dialog

1. 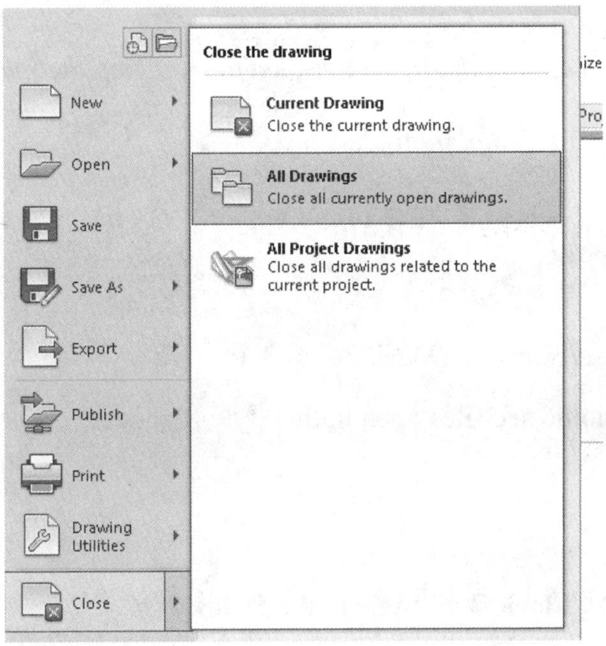

Close any open drawings.

2.  Open a New Drawing.

3. 

Activate the **Manage** ribbon.

Select the **Style Manager** tool.

4. 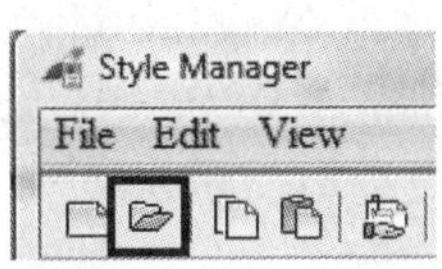

Select the **File Open** tool.

5. 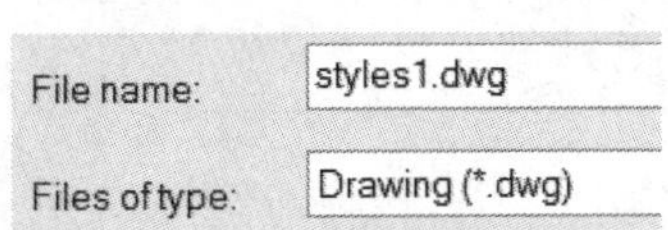

Locate the *styles.dwg* you created.
Select **Open**.

Note: Make sure the Files of type is set to dwg or you will not see your files.

6. 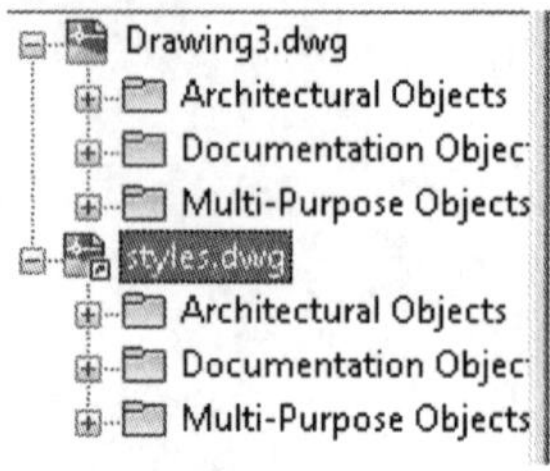

Styles is now listed in the Style Manager.

7. 

Select the **File Open** tool.

8. 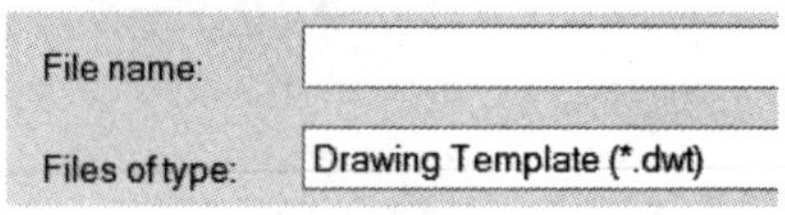

Set the Files of type to ***Drawing Template (*.dwt)***.

9 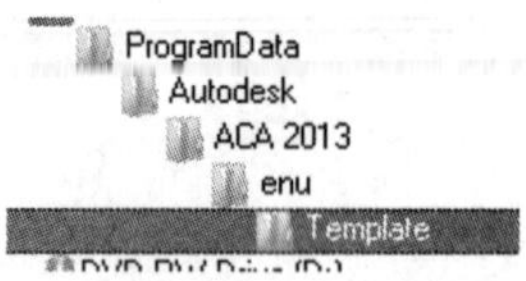

You should automatically be directed to the Template folder.

Browse to the *Template* folder.

10. 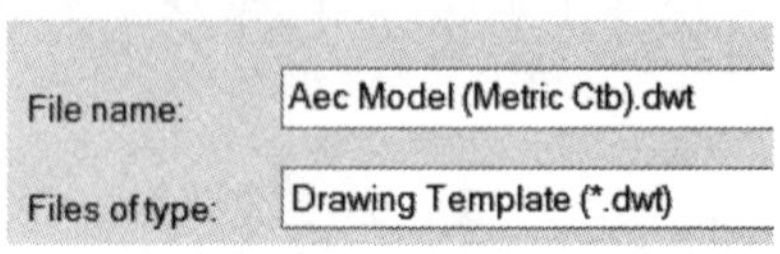

Locate the *AEC Model Imperial (Metric) Ctb.dwt* file.
Press **Open**.

This is the default template we selected for QNEW.

11. 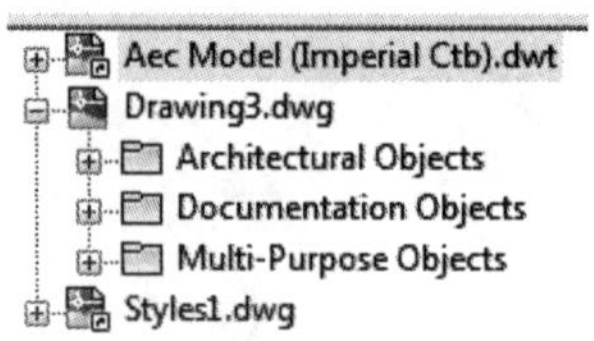

You should see files open in the Style Manager.

12. 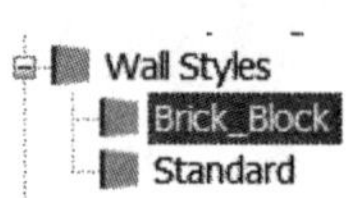

Locate the **Brick_Block** Wall Style in the *Styles.dwg*.

13. 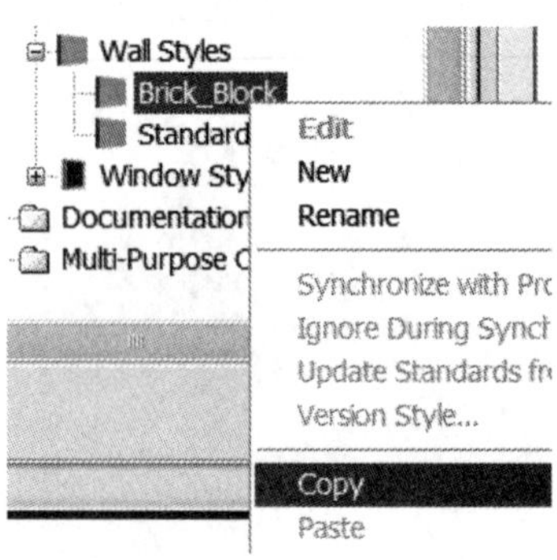

Right click and select **Copy**.

14. 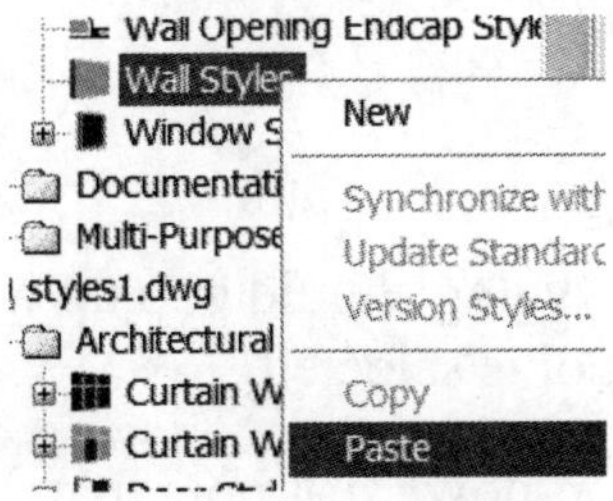

Locate Wall Styles under the template drawing.

Highlight, right click and select **Paste**.

15. 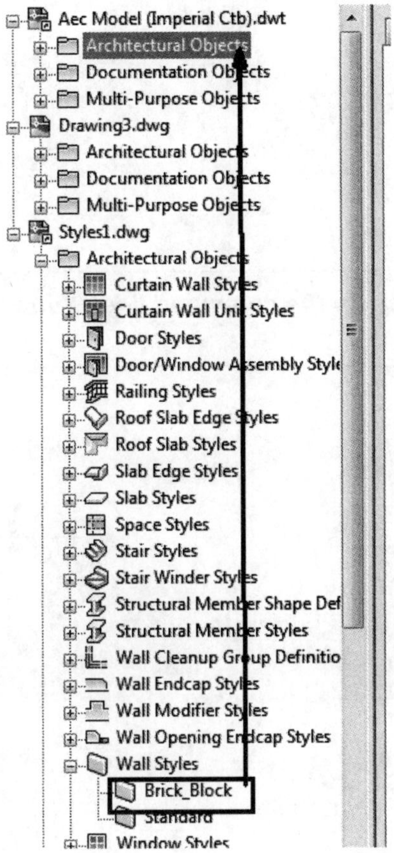

You could also just drag and drop the Brick_block style from the Styles file to the template.

16. 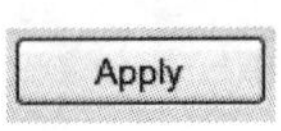

Press **Apply**.

17. 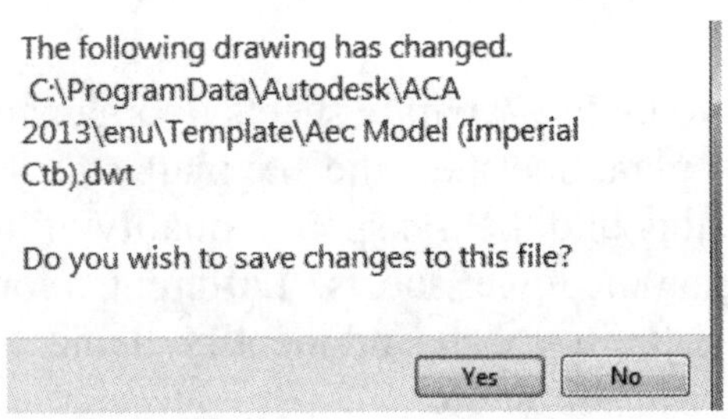

Press **Yes**.

18. Close the Style Manager.

19. 

If you go to Windows and look to see what drawings are open, you won't see Styles.dwg or the template drawing listed. These are only open in the Style Manager.

20. 

Select the **QNEW** tool.

21. 

Activate the Home ribbon.
Select the **Wall** tool.

22. 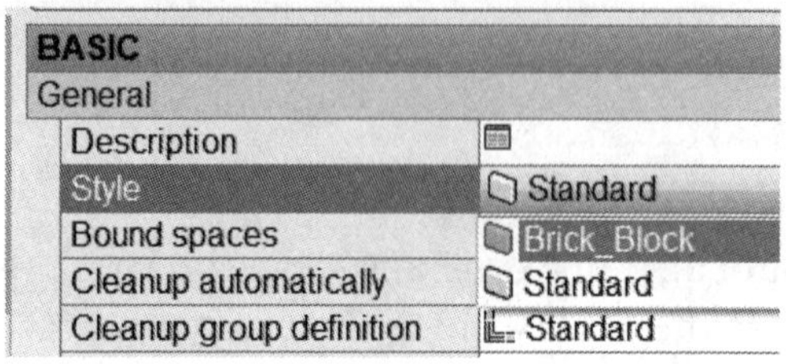

The Properties dialog should pop up when the WallAdd tool is selected.

In the Style drop-down list, note that Brick_Block is available.

23. Escape to end the WallAdd command.

24. Close all drawing files without saving.

A fast way to close all open files is to type CLOSEALL on the command line. You will be prompted to save any unsaved files.

Layer Manager

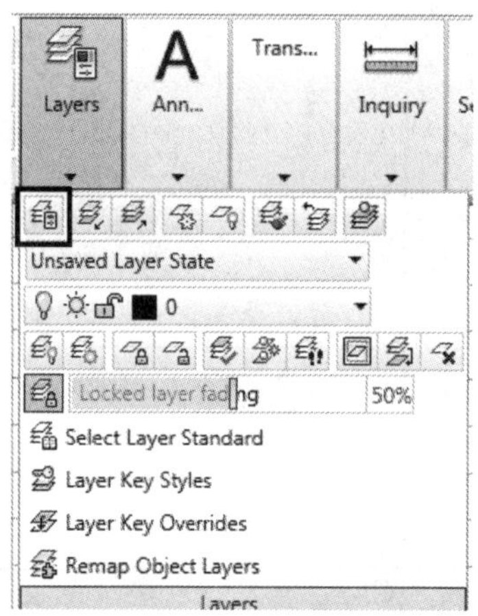

Back in the days of vellum and pencil, drafters would use separate sheets to organize their drawings, so one sheet might have the floor plan, one sheet the site plan, etc. The layers of paper would be placed on top of each other and the transparent quality of the vellum would allow the drafter to see the details on the lower sheets. Different colored pencils would be used to make it easier for the drafter to locate and identify elements of a drawing, such as dimensions, electrical outlets, water lines, etc.

When drafting moved to Computer Aided Design, the concept of sheets was transferred to the use of Layers. Drafters could assign a Layer Name, color, linetype, etc. and then place different elements on the appropriate layer.

AutoCAD Architecture has a Layer Management system to allow the user to implement AIA standards easily.

 *Layer Manager*

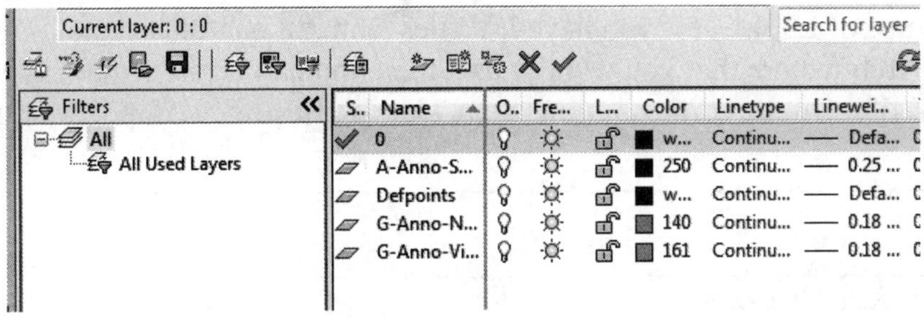

The Layer Manager helps you organize, sort, and group layers, as well as save and coordinate layering schemes. You can also use layering standards with the Layer Manager to better organize the layers in your drawings.

When you open the Layer Manager, all the layers in the current drawing are displayed in the right panel. You can work with individual layers to:

- Change layer properties by selecting the property icons
- Make a layer the current layer
- Create, rename, and delete layers

If you are working with drawings that contain large numbers of layers, you can improve the speed at which the Layer Manager loads layers when you open it by selecting the Layer Manager/Optimize for Speed option in your AEC Editor options.

The Layer Manager has a tool bar as shown.

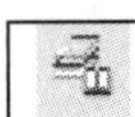	*Layer Standards* You can import Layer Standards from an existing drawing or Export Layer Standards using the current drawing. 
	*Layer Key Styles* – Brings up the Style Manager. A layer key is a map between the AEC object that you draw on screen and a defined layer. When you create an object, the layer key that is associated with the object automatically places that object on the layer to which the layer key is mapped. Using layer keys to automatically place objects on predefined layers is called *layer keying*.

TIP: The layer key styles in Autodesk AutoCAD Architecture, Release 3 and above replace the use of LY files. If you have LY files from S8 or Release 1 of AutoCAD AutoCAD Architecture that you want to use, then you can create a new layer key style from an LY file. On the command line enter **-AecLYImport** to import legacy LY files.

	Layer Key Overrides You can apply overrides to any layer keys within a layer key style that is based on a layer standard. The structure of the layer name of each layer that each layer key maps an object to is determined by the descriptive fields in the layer standard definition. You can override the information in each field according to the values set in the layer standard definition. You can allow overrides on all the layer keys within a layer key style, or you can select individual layer keys that you want to override. You can also choose to allow all of the descriptive fields that make up the layer name to be overridden, or you can specify which descriptive fields you want to override.
	Load Filter Groups This tool allows you to load a saved filter group.
	Save Filter Groups This tool allows you to save a defined filter group, so that you can use it in other drawings.
	New Property Filter A Property Filter displays only layers that meet a certain criteria, such as color, color, frozen/thawed, or names. You can specify more than one type of property for a filter.
	New Group Filter A Group Filter allows you to combine a set of layers together into a group. You can then turn on and off several layers by controlling the status of the group.
	New Standards Filter A Layer Standards filter contains layers that are assigned to a particular standard. For example, you can create a layer standards filter to only show layers associated with the AIA 2nd Edition standard.
	Layer States Manager The Layer States Manager allows you save your layer settings and restore them.
	New Layer Creates a new layer.
	New Layer from Standard Creates a new layer based on an existing layer standard.

	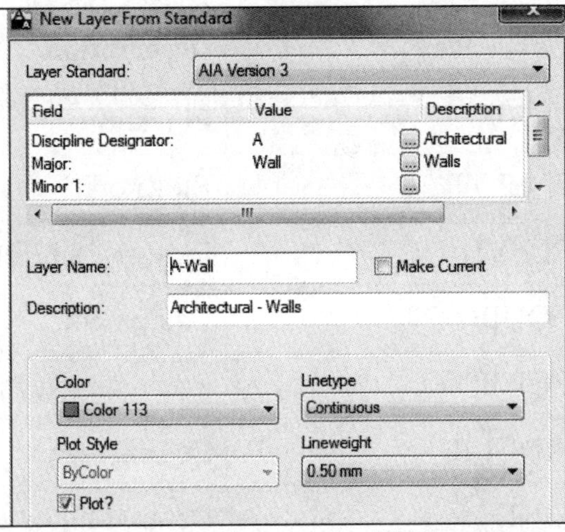
	*New Layer VP Frozen in All Viewports* Creates a new layer and automatically freezes it (makes it invisible).
	*Delete Layer* Highlight the layer(s) you wish to delete and select this tool.
	*Make selected layer current* Highlight a layer name in the list and press this button to set current.

The following are the default layer keys used by Autodesk AutoCAD Architecture when you create AEC objects.

Default layer keys for creating AEC objects			
Layer Key	**Description**	**Layer Key**	**Description**
ANNDTOBJ	Detail marks	COMMUN	Communication
ANNELKEY	Elevation Marks	CONTROL	Control systems
ANNELOBJ	Elevation objects	CWLAYOUT	Curtain walls
ANNMASK	Masking objects	CWUNIT	Curtain wall units
ANNMATCH	Match Lines	DIMLINE	Dimensions
ANNOBJ	Notes, leaders, etc.	DIMMAN	Dimensions (AutoCAD points)
ANNREV	Revisions	DOOR	Doors
ANNSXKEY	Section marks	DOORNO	Door tags
ANNSXOBJ	Section marks	DRAINAGE	Drainage
ANNSYMOBJ	Annotation marks	ELEC	Electric
APPL	Appliances	ELECNO	Electrical tags

Layer Key	Description	Layer Key	Description
AREA	Areas	ELEV	Elevations
AREAGRP	Area groups	ELEVAT	Elevators
AREAGRPNO	Area group tags	ELEVHIDE	Elevations (2D)
AREANO	Area tags	EQUIP	Equipment
CAMERA	Cameras	EQUIPNO	Equipment tags
CASE	Casework	FINCEIL	Ceiling tags
CASENO	Casework tags	FINE	Details- Fine lines
CEILGRID	Ceiling grids	FINFLOOR	Finish tags
CEILOBJ	Ceiling objects	FIRE	Fire system equip.
CHASE	Chases	FURN	Furniture
COGO	Control Points	FURNNO	Furniture tags
COLUMN	Columns	GRIDBUB	Plan grid bubbles
GRIDLINE	Column grids	SITE	Site
HATCH	Detail-Hatch lines	SLAB	Slabs
HIDDEN	Hidden Lines	SPACEBDRY	Space boundaries
LAYGRID	Layout grids	SPACENO	Space tags
LIGHTCLG	Ceiling lighting	SPACEOBJ	Space objects
LIGHTW	Wall lighting	STAIR	Stairs
MASSELEM	Massing elements	STAIRH	Stair handrails
MASSGRPS	Massing groups	STRUCTBEAM	Structural beams
MASSSLCE	Massing slices	STRUCTBEAMIDEN	Structural beam tags
MED	Medium Lines	STRUCTBRACE	Structural braces
OPENING	Wall openings	STRUCTBRACEIDEN	Structural brace tags
PEOPLE	People	STRUCTCOLS	Structural columns
PFIXT	Plumbing fixtures	STRUCTCOLSIDEN	Structural column tags
PLANTS	Plants - outdoor	SWITCH	Electrical switches
PLANTSI	Plants - indoor	TITTEXT	Border and title block

Layer Key	Description	Layer Key	Description
POLYGON	AEC Polygons	TOILACC	Arch. specialties
POWER	Electrical power	TOILNO	Toilet tags
PRCL	Property Line	UTIL	Site utilities
PRK-SYM	Parking symbols	VEHICLES	Vehicles
ROOF	Rooflines	WALL	Walls
ROOFSLAB	Roof slabs	WALLFIRE	Fire wall patterning
ROOMNO	Room tags	WALLNO	Wall tags
SCHEDOBJ	Schedule tables	WIND	Windows
SEATNO	Seating tags	WINDASSEM	Window assemblies
SECT	Miscellaneous sections	WINDNO	Window tags
SECTHIDE	Sections (2D)		

Desktop Display Manager

Exercise 1-8:

Exploring the Display Manager

Drawing Name: ex1-5.dwg
Estimated Time: 15 minutes

This exercise reinforces the following skills:

- ❑ Display Manager

1. Open *ex1-5.dwg*.

2. 

Access the **Display Manager** from the Manage ribbon.

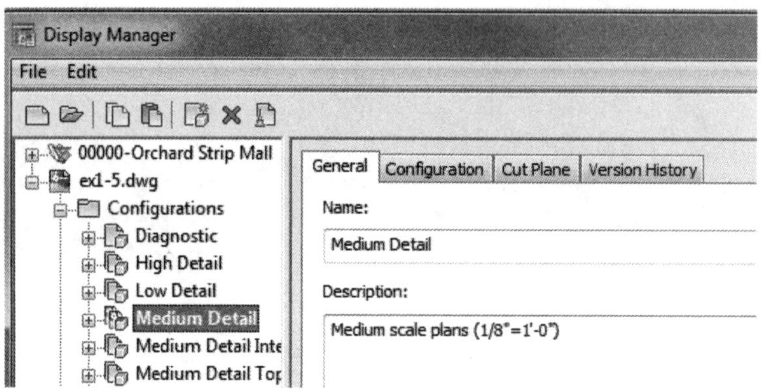

3. The display system in Autodesk® AutoCAD Architecture controls how AEC objects are displayed in a designated viewport. By specifying the AEC objects you want to display in a viewport and the direction from which you want to view them, you can produce different architectural displays, such as floor plans, reflected plans, elevations, 3D models, or schematic displays.

4. 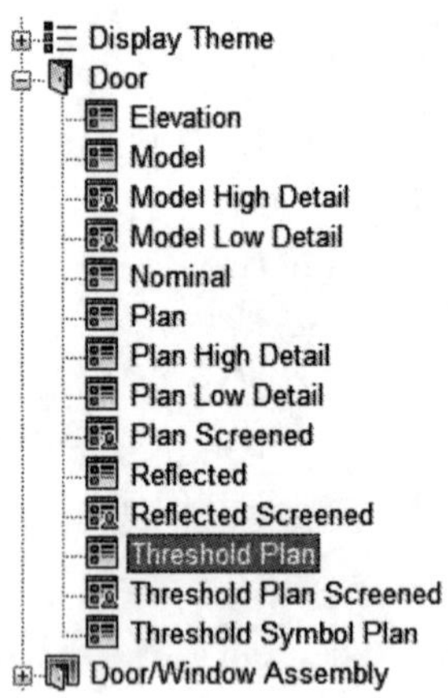

Expand the *Representations by Object* folder.

Locate Door.

You see that there are different ways a door will appear depending on the display configuration selected.

Highlight **Threshold Plan**.

5. 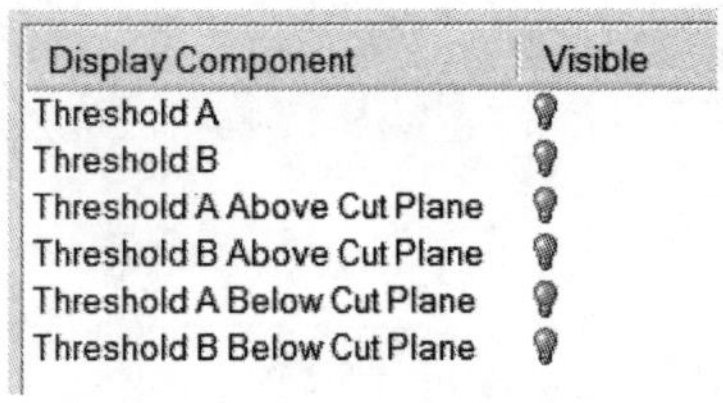

You see that the Threshold visibilities are turned off.

6. 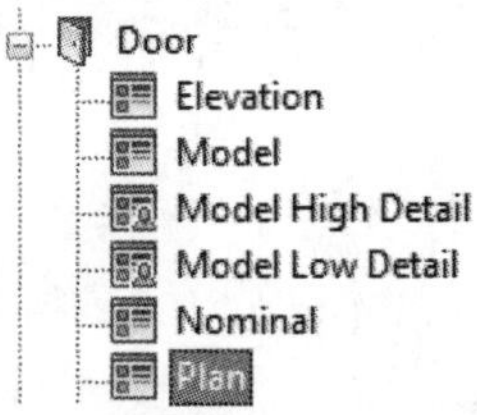

Highlight the **Plan** configuration.

7. 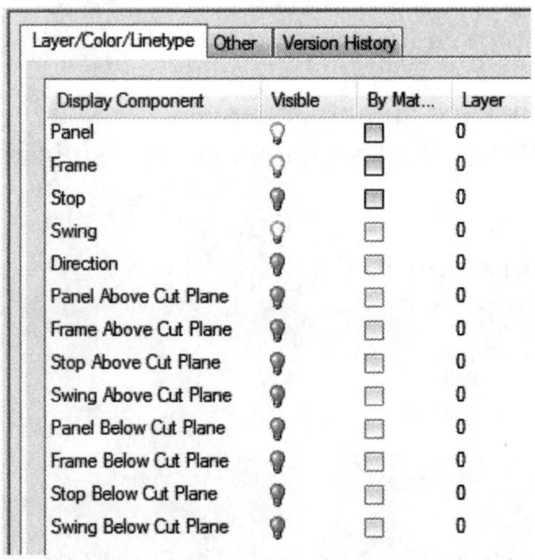

You see that some door components are turned on and others are turned off.

8. 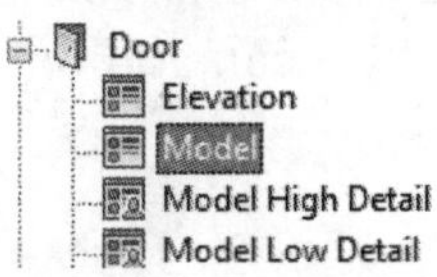

Highlight the Model configuration.

9. 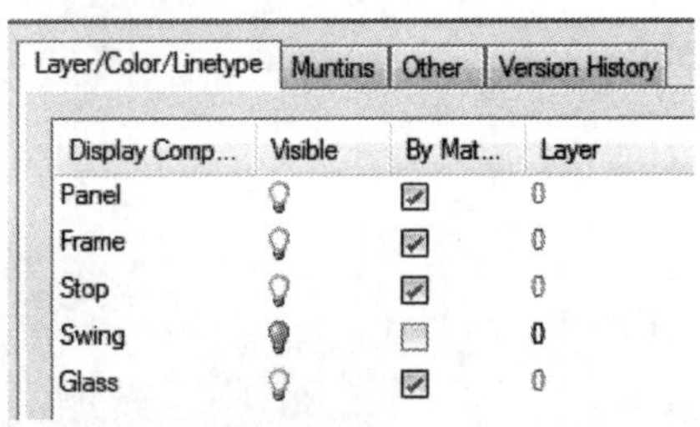

You see that some door components are turned on and others are turned off.

10. 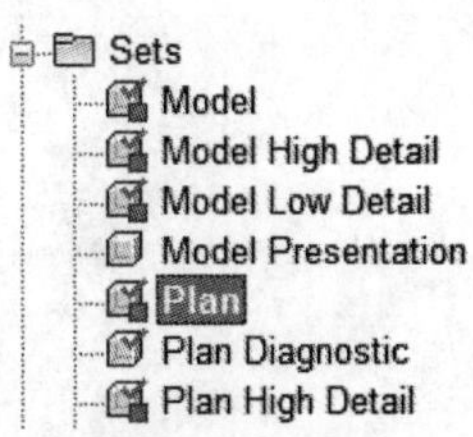

Go to the Sets folder. The Set highlighted in bold is the active Display Representation.

Highlight **Plan**.

11. 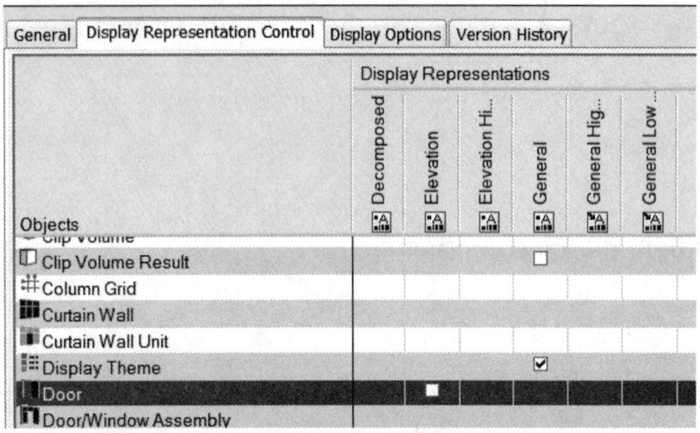

Select the Display Representation Control tab.
Locate **Door** under Objects.
Note that some display representations are checked and others are unchecked.
A check indicates that the door is visible. Which door components are visible is controlled under Representations by Object.

12. 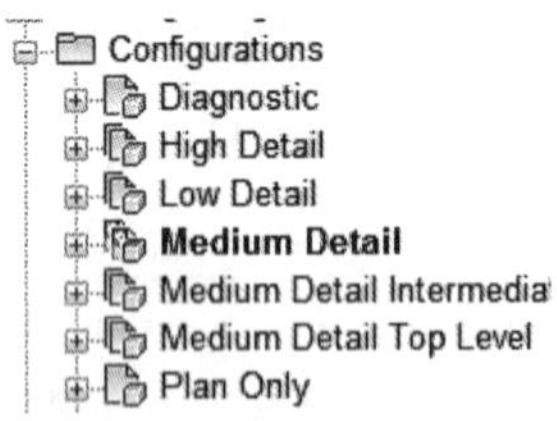

Expand the **Configurations** folder.

13. 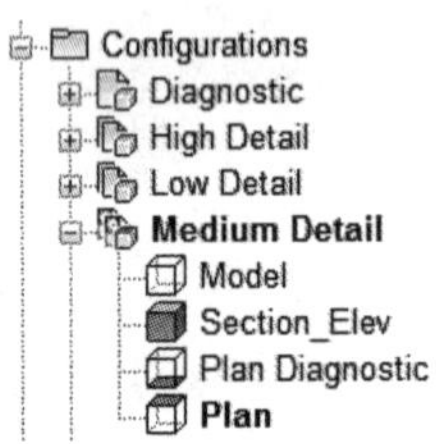

Expand Medium Detail.
You see the different display sets. Note that Medium Detail does not hold all the different display sets. You can add or remove display sets.
Close the Display Manager.

14. Close the drawing without saving.

Exercise 1-9:

Adding a Ribbon Tab

Drawing Name: new
Estimated Time: 15 minutes

This exercise reinforces the following skills:

- ❑ CUI – Custom User Interface
- ❑ Ribbon
- ❑ Panel
- ❑ Tab

1.  Start a new drawing.

2. 

Activate the **Manage** ribbon.

   Select the **User Interface** tool.

3. 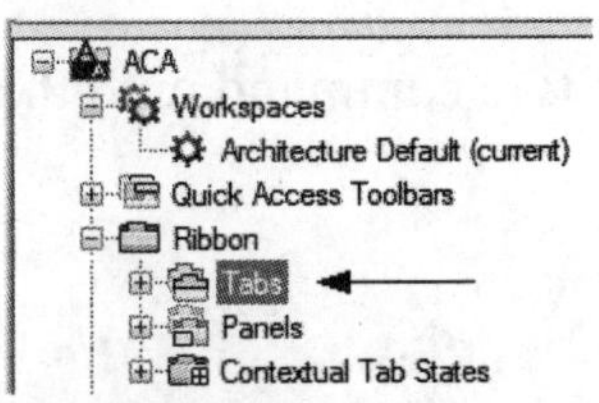

Locate the **Tabs** category under Ribbon.

4. 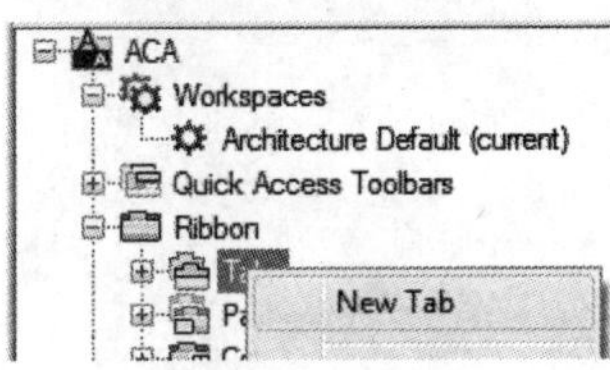

Highlight Tab.
Right click and select **New Tab**.

5. 

Rename it **Format – ACA**.

6. 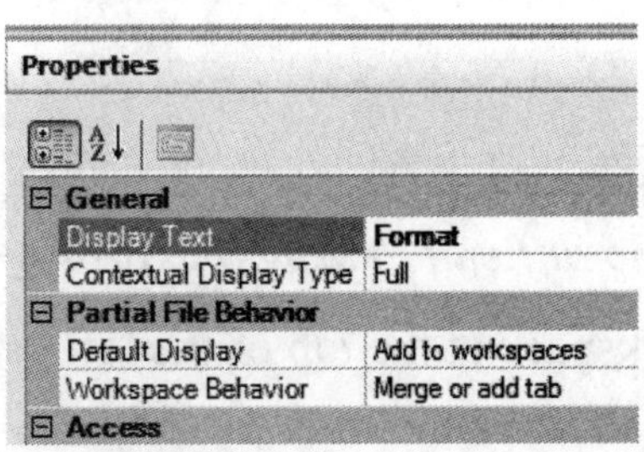

Under Properties, have the Display Text show only Format.

7. 

Highlight Panel.
Right click and select **New Panel**.

8. 

Rename the New Panel **Styles**.

9. 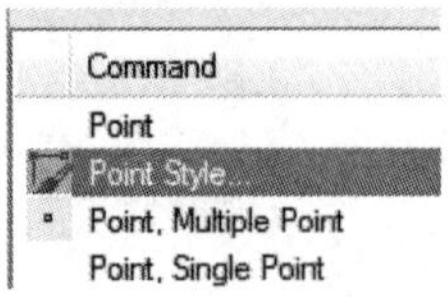

Locate the Point Style Command in the lower left pane.

10. 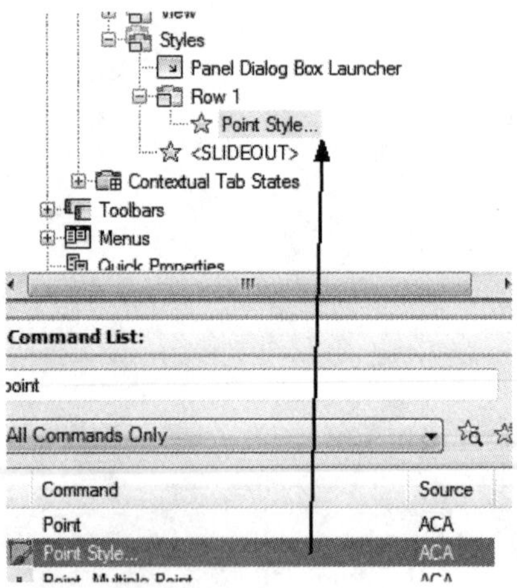

Drag and drop it into the Styles Panel you created.

11. 

Locate the **Text Style** command.

12. 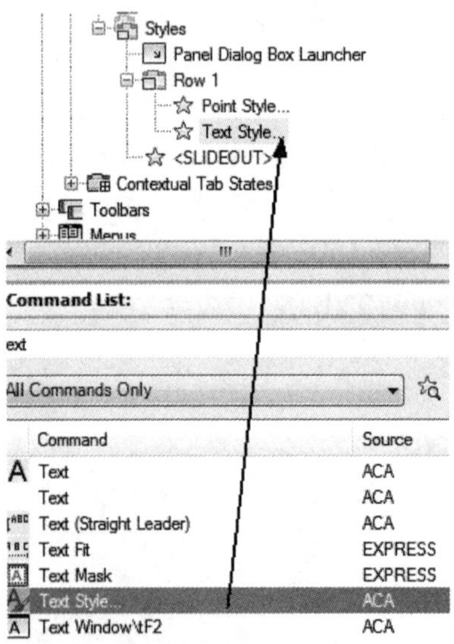

Drag and drop the Text Style command onto the new Styles Panel.

13. 

Drag and drop the Styles panel onto the Format tab.
You can also Copy and Paste if it is too difficult to drag and drop.

14. 

Highlight the current workspace at the top of the left pane.

15. 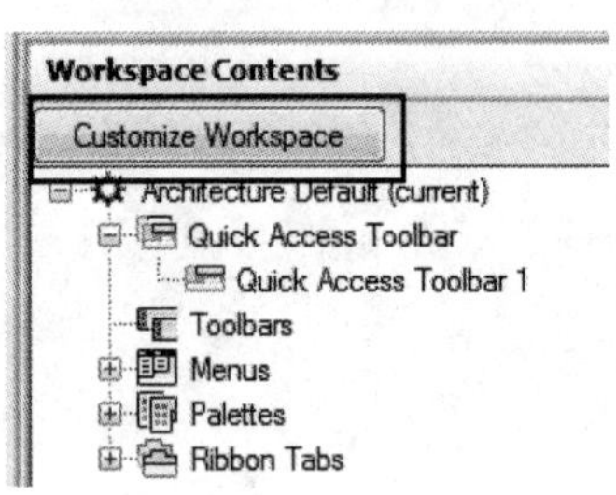

Select **Customize Workspace** on the upper right pane.

16. 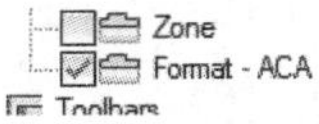

Place a check next to the Format tab you just created in the upper left pane.

17. 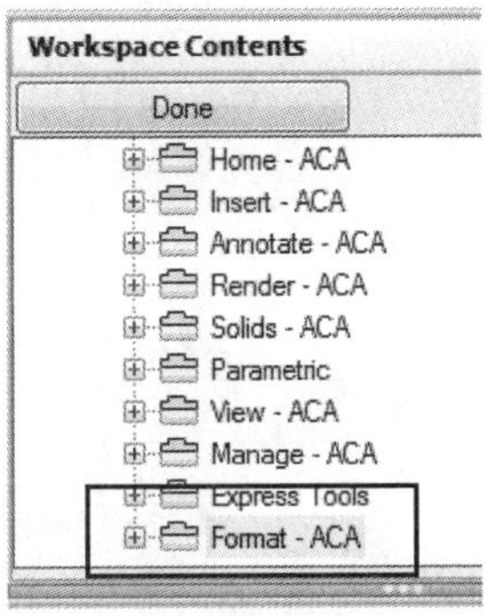

The Format tab will now appear in the Workspace on the upper right pane.

18. 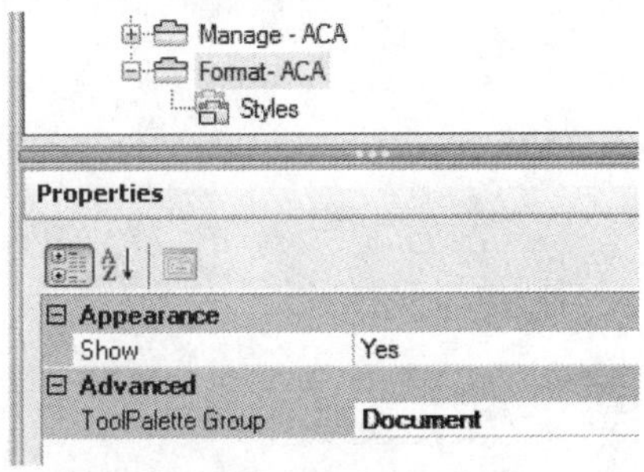

Highlight the **Format** tab.
Verify that Show is set to **Yes**.

Assign the Format tab to the **Document** ToolPalette group.

19. 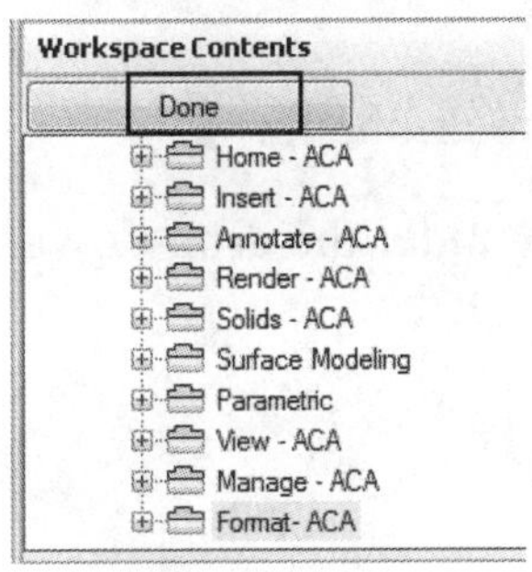

Press the **Done** button on the right pane.

20. 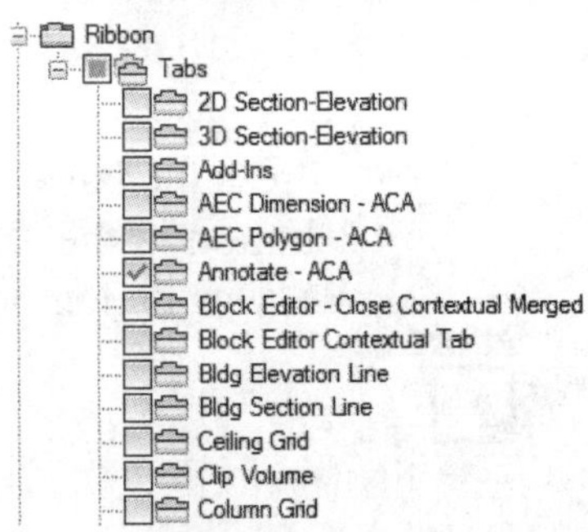

Checks indicate what is currently available in the workspace.

You can create different workspaces with different ribbon configurations.

21. 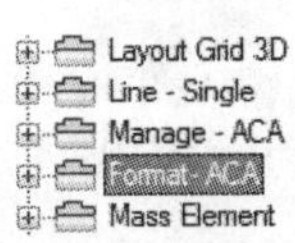

Move the new Format Tab so it is positioned below the Manage. This is done simply by dragging it into position.

22. Press **Apply** and **OK** to close the dialog.

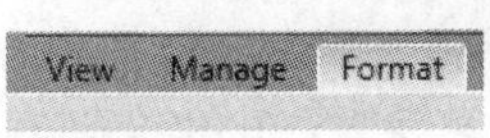

The Format tab now appears on the ribbon.

23. 

If you select the Format tab, you see the tools that were added.

As you find tools you need, you can add them to this ribbon.

24. Close the drawing without saving.

Exercise 1-10:

Creating a Text Style

Drawing Name: new
Estimated Time: 15 minutes

This exercise reinforces the following skills:

- CUI – Custom User Interface
- Ribbon
- Panel
- Tab

1. 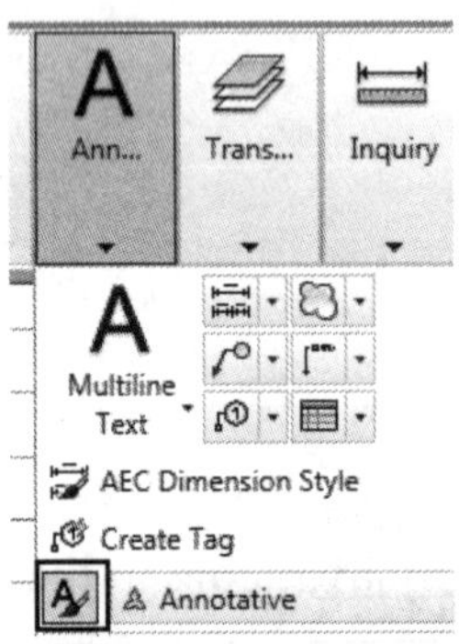

Select the Text Style tool on the Home ribbon.

It is located on the Annotation panel under the drop-down.

2. 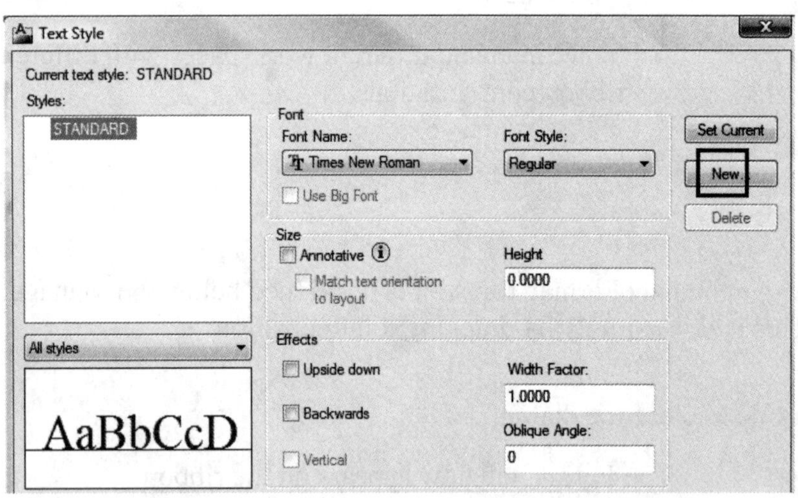

Press the **New** button in the Text Styles dialog box.

3. 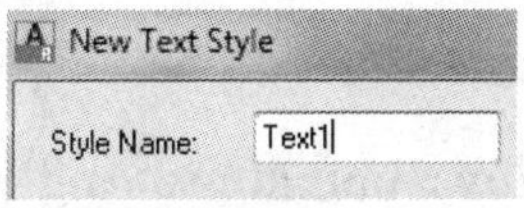

In the New Text Style dialog box, enter **TEXT1** for the name of the new text style and press **OK**.

4. 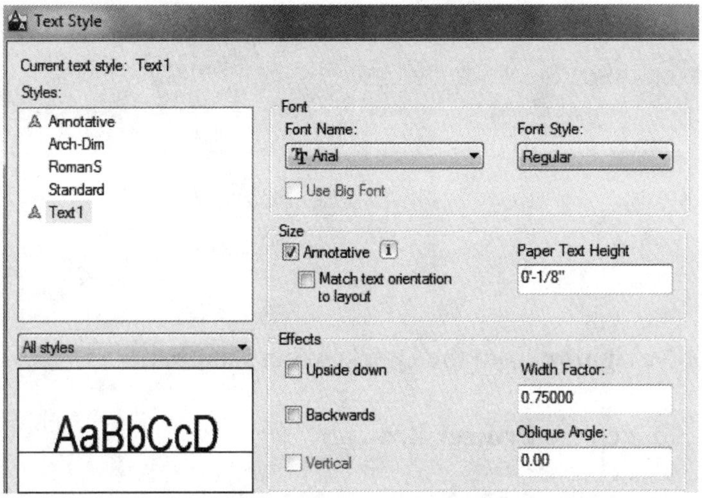

Fill in the remaining information in the Text Style dialog box as shown.
Set the Font Name to **Arial**.
Set the Font Style to **Regular**.
Set the Paper Text Height to **1/8″**.

5. Press the Apply button first and then the Close button to apply the changes to TEXT1 and then close the dialog box.

6. Save as *fonts.dwg*.

Tips & Tricks

- You can use PURGE to eliminate any unused text styles from your drawing.
- You can import text styles from one drawing to another using the Design Center.
- You can store text styles in your template for easier access.

Exercise 1-11

Project Settings

Drawing Name: new
Estimated Time: 5 minutes

This exercise reinforces the following skills:

- Project Navigator
- Project Path Options

In order for tags on windows, doors, etc. to work properly, you must assign your building model to a project.

1. Start a new drawing.

2. 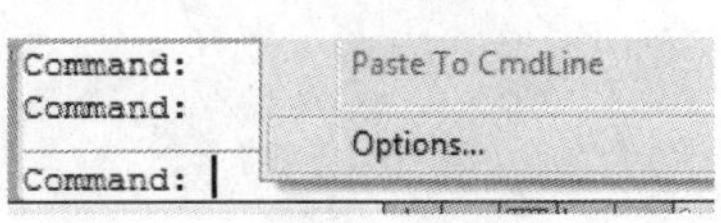

Right click in the command window and select **Options**.

3. 

Select the **AEC Project Defaults** tab.

4. Set the AEC Project Location Search Path to the location where you are saving your files.

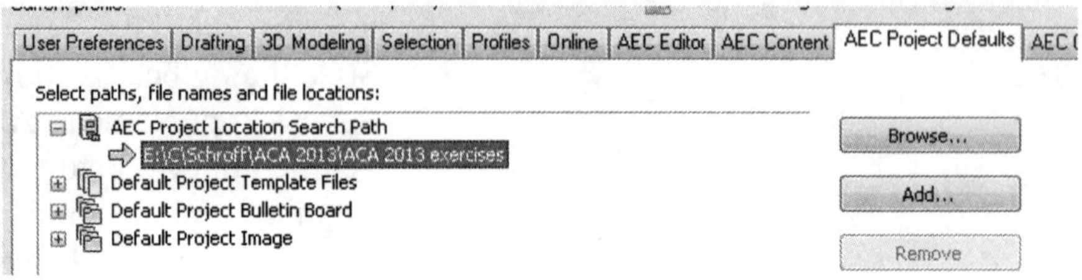

Close the dialog.

5.  Launch the **Project Navigator** from the Quick Access toolbar.

6.  Launch the **Project Browser**.

7.  Select the **New Project** tool.

8. 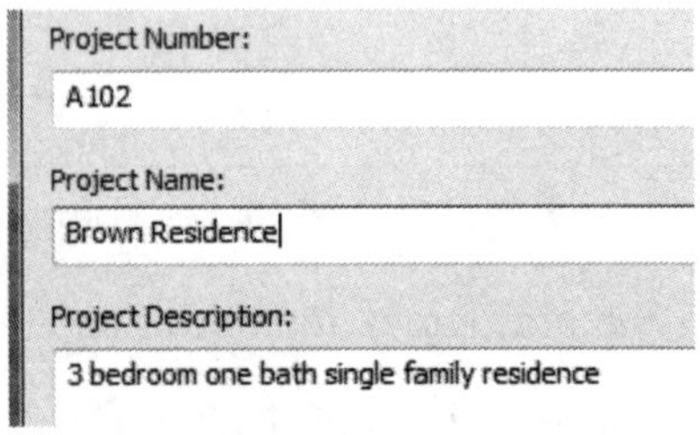

Type **A102** for the Project Number.

Type **Brown Residence** for the Project Name.

Enter a project description.

Press **OK**.

9. 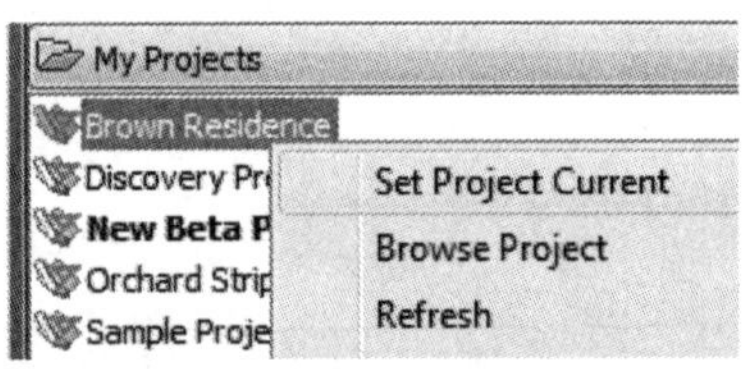

Highlight the **Brown Residence** project.

Right click and select **Set Project Current**.

10. Close the Project Browser.

11. Save as *ex1-11.dwg.*

Lesson 2:
Site Plans

Most architectural projects start with a site plan. The site plan indicates the property lines, the house location, a North symbol, any streets surrounding the property, topographical features, location of sewer, gas, and/or electrical lines (assuming they are below ground – above ground connections are not shown), and topographical features.

When laying out the floor plan for the house, many architects take into consideration the path of sun (to optimize natural light), street access (to locate the driveway), and any noise factors. AutoCAD Architecture includes the ability to perform sun studies on your models.

AutoCAD Architecture allows the user to simulate the natural path of the sun based on the longitude and latitude coordinates of the site, so you can test how natural light will affect various house orientations.

A plot plan must include the following features:

- ❑ Length and bearing of each property line
- ❑ Location, outline, and size of buildings on the site
- ❑ Contour of the land
- ❑ Elevation of property corners and contour lines
- ❑ North symbol
- ❑ Trees, shrubs, streams, and other topological items
- ❑ Streets, sidewalks, driveways, and patios
- ❑ Location of utilities
- ❑ Easements and drainages (if any)
- ❑ Well, septic, sewage line, and underground cables
- ❑ Fences and retaining walls
- ❑ Lot number and/or address of the site
- ❑ Scale of the drawing

The plot plan is drawn using information provided by the county/city and/or a licensed surveyor.

When drafting with pencil and vellum. you would draw to a scale, such as ⅛″ = 1′, but with AutoCAD Architecture, you draw full-size and then set up your layout to the proper scale. This insures that all items you draw will fit together properly. This also is important if you collaborate with outside firms. For example, if you want to send your files to a firm that does HVAC, you want their equipment to fit properly in your design. If everyone drafts 1:1 or full-size, then you can ensure there are no interferences or conflicts.

Exercise 2-1:

Installing the Express Tools

Drawing Name: None
Estimated Time: 15 minutes

This exercise reinforces the following skills:

- ❑ Modifying the Software Installation
- ❑ Customization
- ❑ Express Tools

The Express Tools are not installed using the default installation. If you did not install the Express Tools during your first installation, you can add them later. You will need your installation CD to complete the installation. To check if the Express Tools have been installed, type EXPRESSTOOLS in the command window.

1. Close all applications, including AutoCAD Architecture. Turn off any virus checking software, such as Norton.

2. Go to the **Control Panel→Programs and Features**.

3. 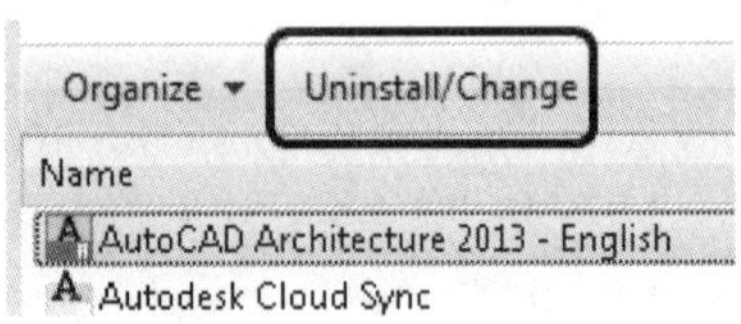

Locate the installation of Autodesk AutoCAD Architecture. Select **Uninstall/Change**.

4. 

Select **Add or Remove Features**.

5. 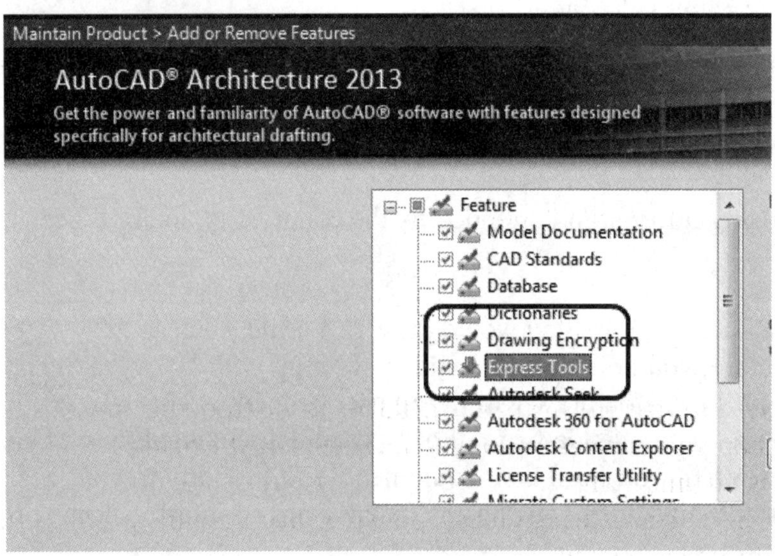

Press **Next**.

Locate the *Express Tools* and enable.

Press **Update**.

6. Press **Finish** to conclude the update.

Exercise 2-2:
Creating Custom Line Types

Drawing Name: New
Estimated Time: 15 minutes

This exercise reinforces the following skills:

- ❑ Creation of linetypes
- ❑ Customization

Architectural drafting requires a variety of custom linetypes in order to display specific features. The standard linetypes provided with AutoCAD Architecture are insufficient from an architectural point of view. You may find custom linetypes on Autodesk's website, www.cadalog.com, or any number of websites on the Internet. However, the ability to create linetypes as needed is an excellent skill for an architectural drafter.

It's a good idea to store any custom linetypes in a separate file. The standard file for storing linetypes is acad.lin. If you store any custom linetypes in acad.lin file, you will lose them the next time you upgrade your software.

1. Once the Express Tools are installed, you can start this exercise.

To verify that the Express Tools are installed, simply look at your ribbon headings.

2. Start a new drawing using **QNEW**.

3. ——————— ——— ——— ———————

Draw a property line.
This property line was created as follows:
Set ORTHO ON.
Draw a horizontal line 100 units long.

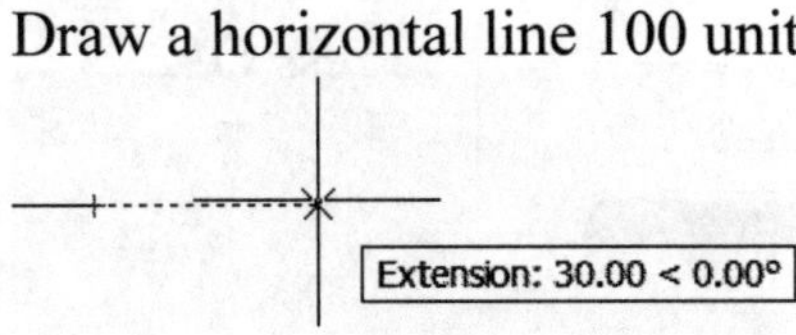

Use SNAP FROM to start the next line @30,0 distance from the previous line.
You can also simply use object tracking to locate the next line.
The short line is 60 units long.
Use SNAP FROM to start the next line @30,0 distance from the previous line.
The second short line is 60 units long.
Use SNAP FROM to start the next line @30,0 distance from the previous line.
Draw a second horizontal line 100 units long.

4. 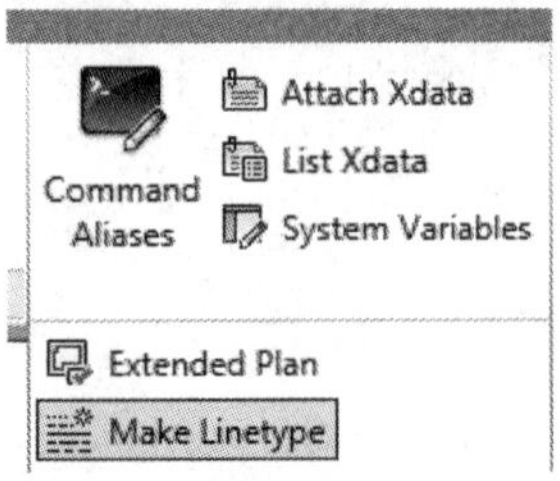

Activate the Express Tools ribbon.

Select the **Tools** drop-down.

Go to **Express→Tools→Make Linetype**.

5. Browse to the folder where you are storing your work.

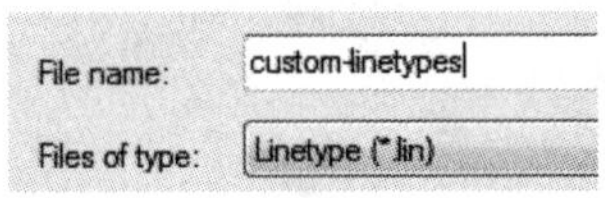

Create a file name called *custom-linetypes.lin* and press **Save**.

> **TIP:** Place all your custom linetypes in a single drawing file and then use the AutoCAD Design Center to help you locate and load the desired linetype.

6. When prompted for the linetype name, type: property-line.
When prompted for the linetype description, type: property-line.
Specify starting point for line definition; select the far left point of the line type.
Specify ending point for line definition; select the far right point of the line type.
When prompted to select the objects, start at the long line on the left and pick the line segments in order.

7. Type **linetype** to launch the Linetype Manager.

8. 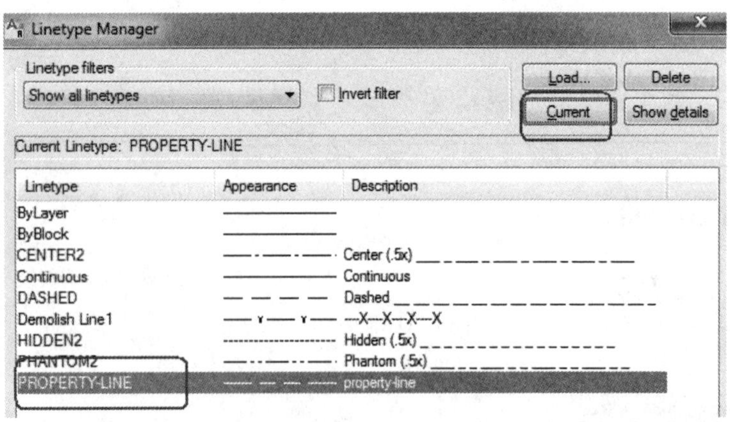

The linetype you created is listed.

Highlight the PROPERTY-LINE linetype and select CURRENT.

Press **OK**.

9. Draw some lines to see if they look OK. Make sure you make them long enough to see the dashes. If you don't see the dashes, adjust the linetype scale using Properties. Set the scale to 0.0125.

10. 

Locate the *custom-linetypes.lin* file you created.

Open it using NotePad.

11. 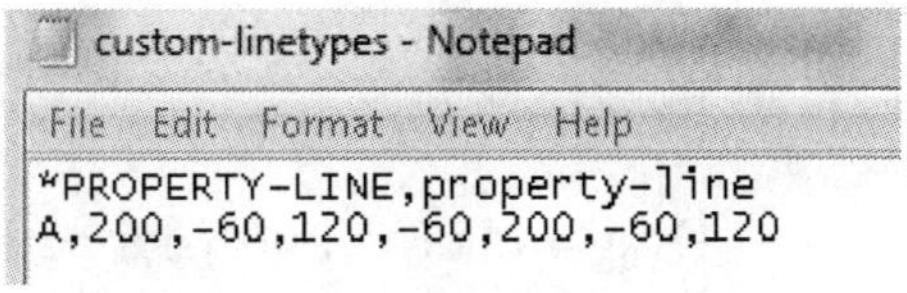

You see a description of the property-line.

12. Save as *ex2-2.dwg*.

Exercise 2-3:

Creating New Layers

Drawing Name: New, ex2-2.dwg
Estimated Time: 20 minutes

This exercise reinforces the following skills:

- Design Center
- Layer Manager
- Creating New Layers
- Loading Linetypes

1.  Start a new drawing using QNEW.

   Open Ex2-2.dwg.

2. Launch the Design Center.
   The Design Center is on the Insert ribbon in the Content section. It is located in the drop-down under the Content Browser. You can also launch using Ctl+2.

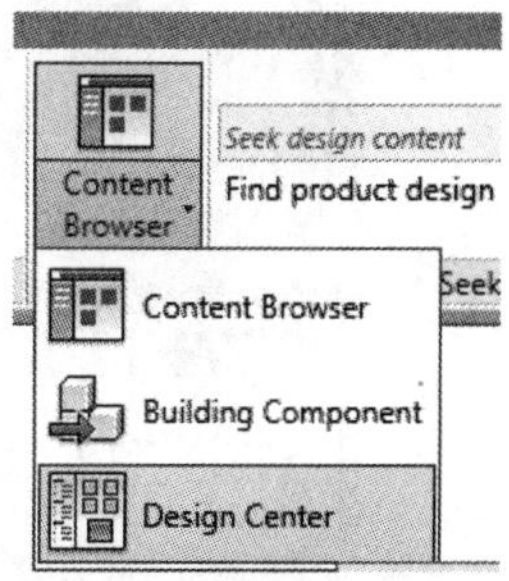

3. 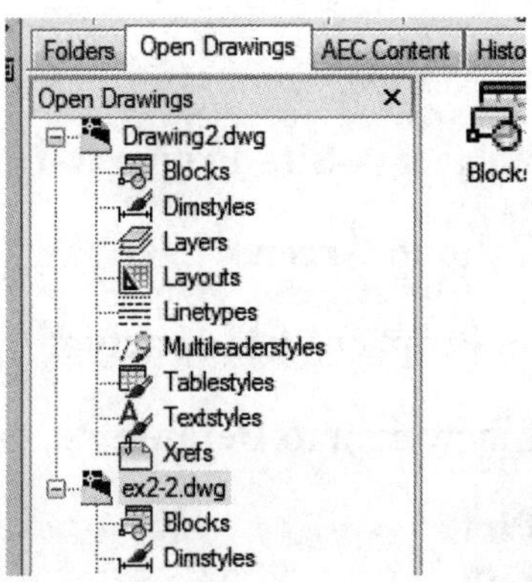

Select the **Open Drawings** tab.

Browse to the *Ex2-2.dwg* file.

Open the Linetypes folder.

Scroll to the **Property-line** linetype definition.

4. 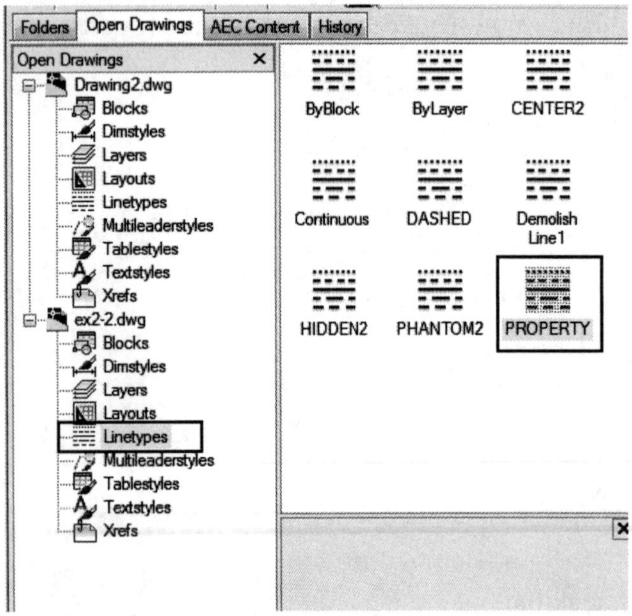

Highlight the PROPERTY-LINE linetype.

Drag and drop into your active window or simply drag it onto the open drawing listed.

5. Close the Design Center.

6. 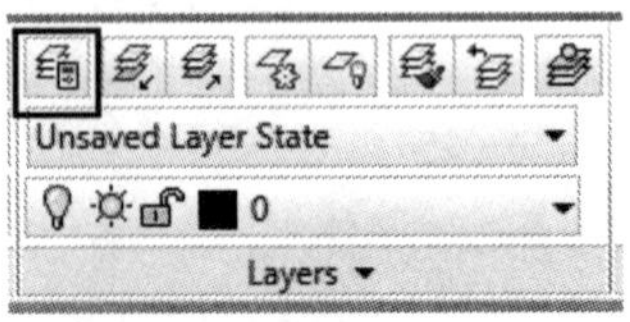

Activate the **Layer Manager** on the Home ribbon.

7. 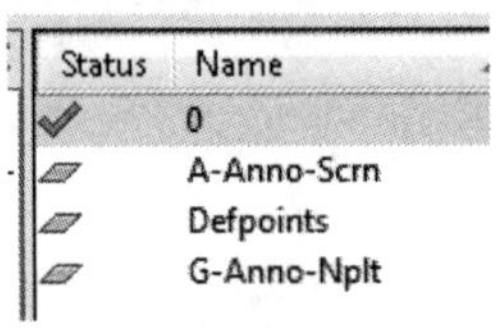

Note that several layers have already been created. The template automatically sets your Layer Standards to AIA.

8.  Select the New Layer from Standard tool.

9. 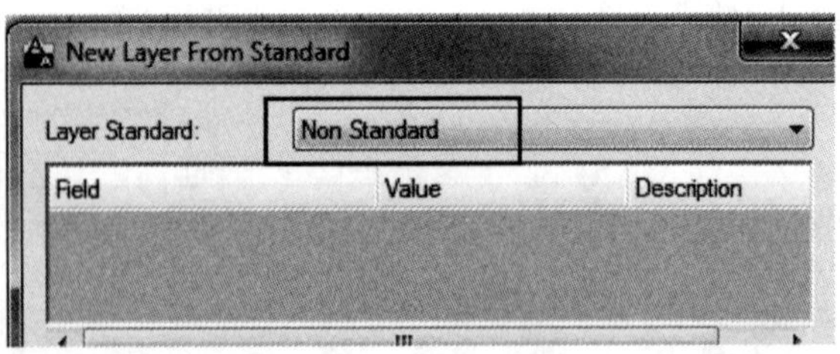

Under Layer Standard, select **Non Standard**.

10. 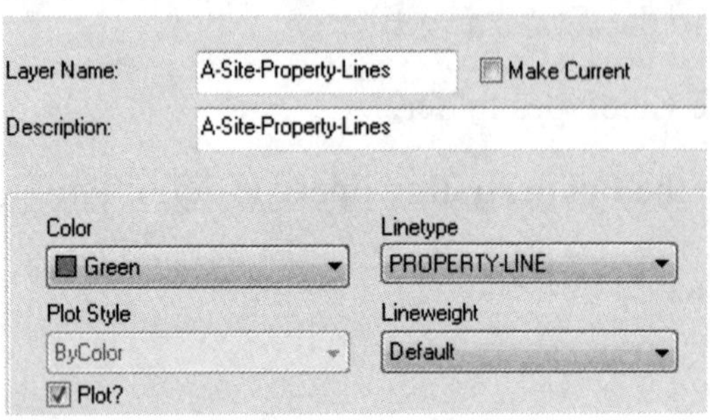

Name the layer **A-Site-Property-Lines**.

Set the Color to **Green**.

Select the **Property-Line** linetype.

Set the Lineweight to **Default**.

Enable **Plot**.
Press **Apply**.

11. 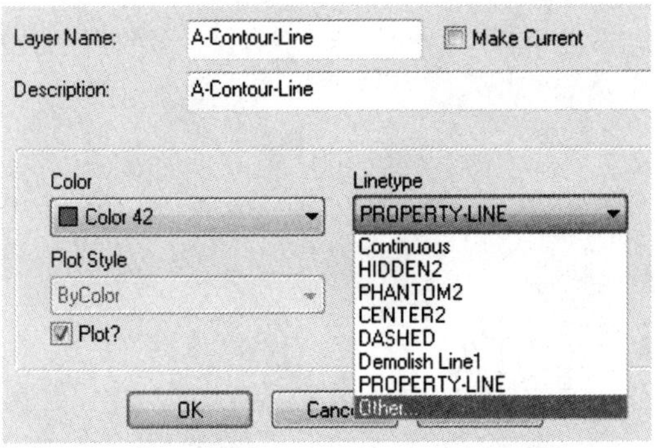

Create another layer.

Name the layer **A-Contour-Line**.

Set the color to **42**.

Select the linetype pane for the new linetype.

Press **Other**.

12. 

Enable **Show Linetypes in File.**

Highlight **DASHEDX2** and press **OK** to assign it to the selected layer name.

13. 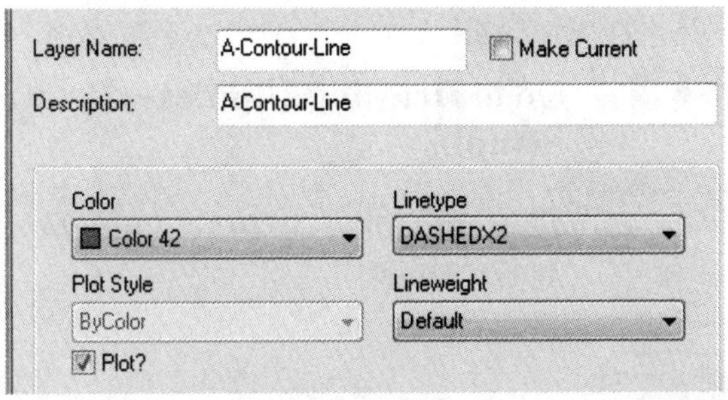

Note that the linetype was assigned properly.

Press **OK**.

14. 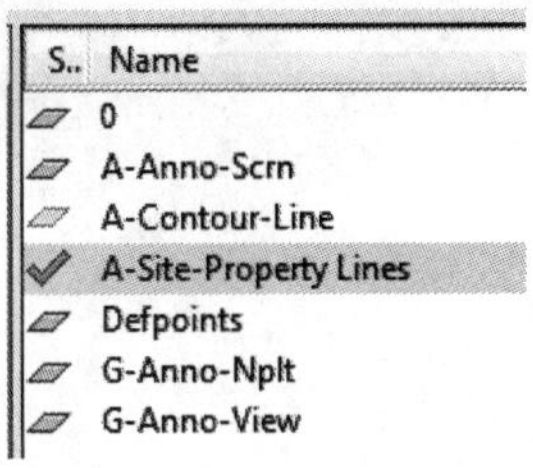

Set the A-Site-Property-Lines layer current.

Highlight the layer name then select the green check mark to set current.

You can also double left click to set the layer current.

15. Right click on the header bar and select **Maximize all columns** to see all the properties for each layer.

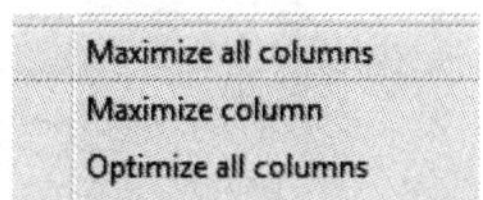

16. Use the X in the upper corner to close the Layer Manager.

17. Save as *Ex2-3.dwg.*

Exercise 2-4:

Creating a Site Plan

Drawing Name: Ex2-3.dwg
Estimated Time: 30 minutes

This exercise reinforces the following skills:

- Use of ribbons
- Documentation Tools
- Elevation Marks
- Surveyors' Angles

1.  Open or continue working in *ex-2-3.dwg*.

2. 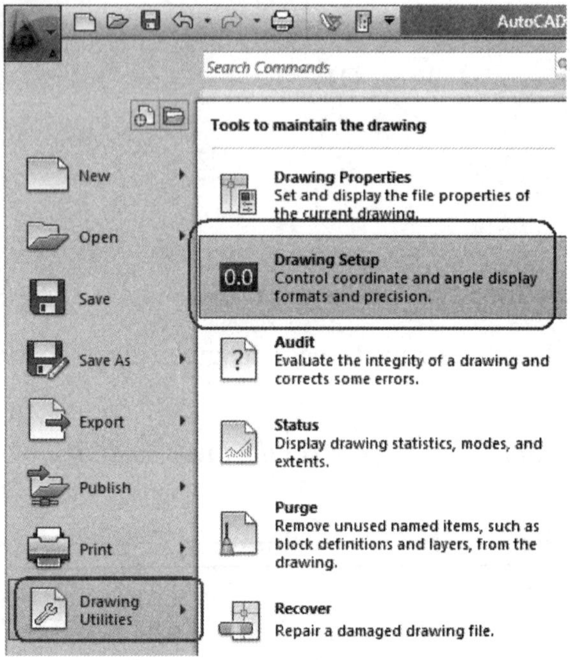

Go to **Drawing Utilities→Drawing Setup**.

This is located on the Applications Menu panel.

3. 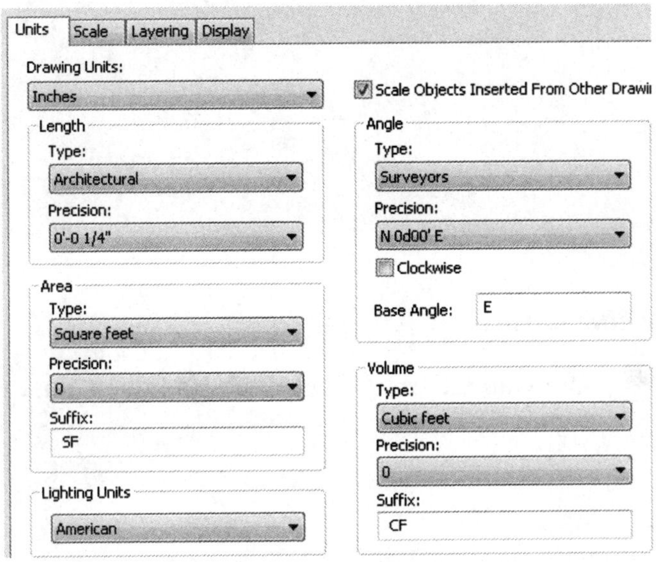

Select the **Units** tab.
Set the Drawing Units to **Inches**.
Set up the Length Type to **Architectural**.
Set the Precision to ¼″.
Set the Angle Type to **Surveyors**.
Set the Precision to **N 0d00′ E**.
Press **Apply** and **OK**.

TIP: You can set your units as desired and then enable **Save As Default** 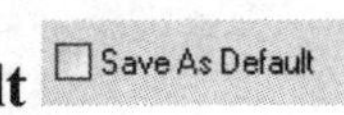

. Then, all future drawings will use your unit settings.

4. Draw the property line shown on the **A-Site-Property-Lines** layer.

Specify first point: 1′,5′
Specify next point: @186′ 11″ < s80de
Specify next point: @75′<n30de
Specify next point: @125′11″<n
Specify next point: @250′<180

Metric data entry using centimeters:

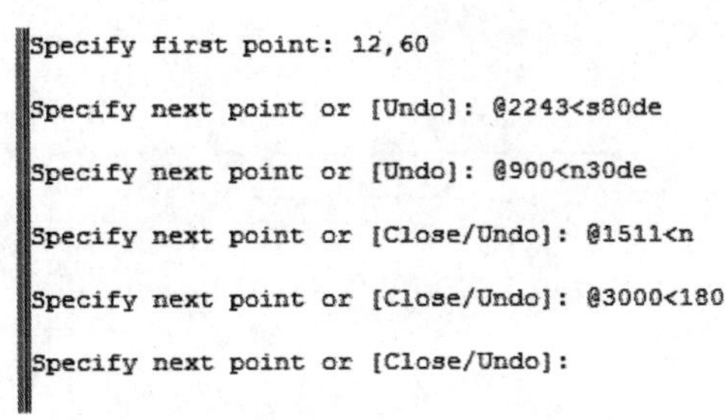

This command sequence uses Surveyor's Units.

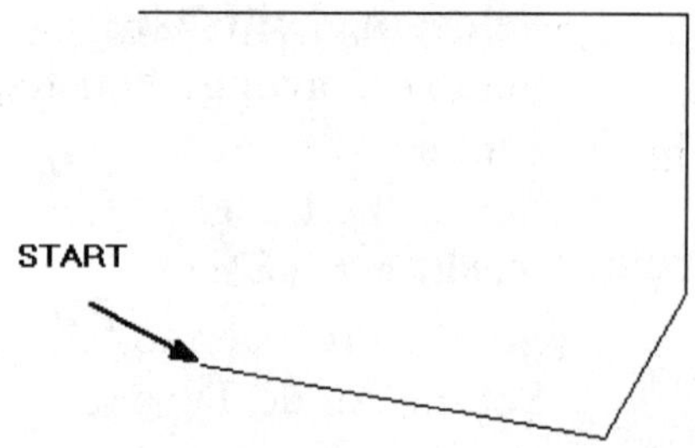

Turn ORTHO off before creating the arc.

5. 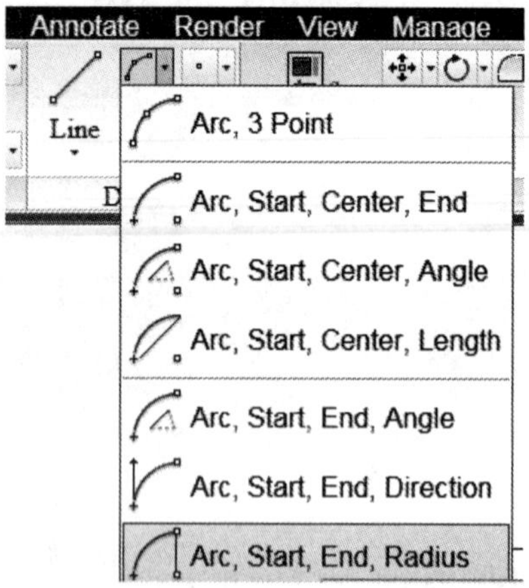

Draw an arc using Start, End, Radius to close the figure.

6. 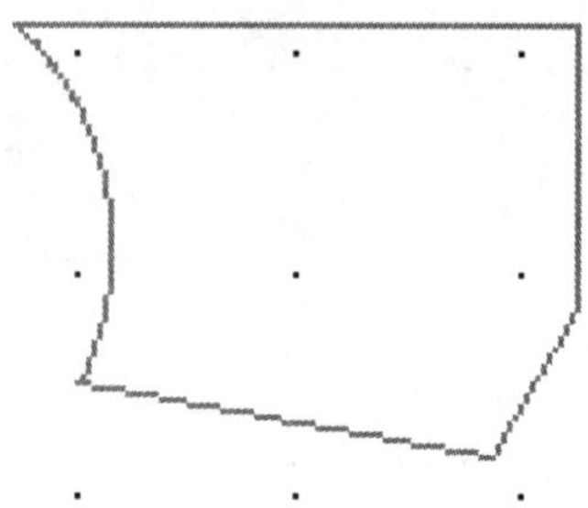

Select the bottom point as the Start point.
Right click and select the End option.
Select the top point at the End point.
Right click and select the Radius option.
The radius is 1584″ [4023.36 cm].

7. Set the **A-Contour-Line layer** current.

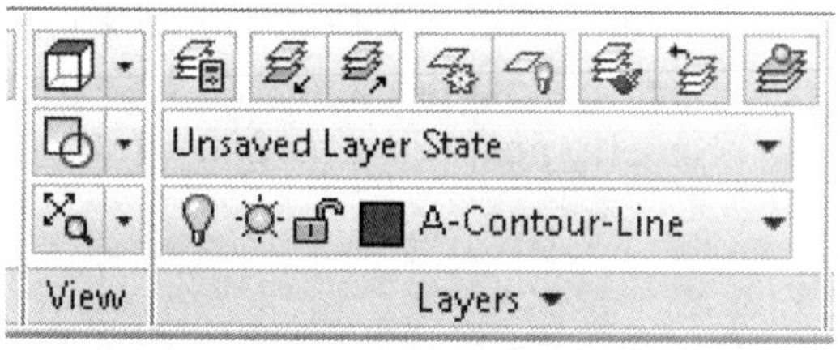

8. 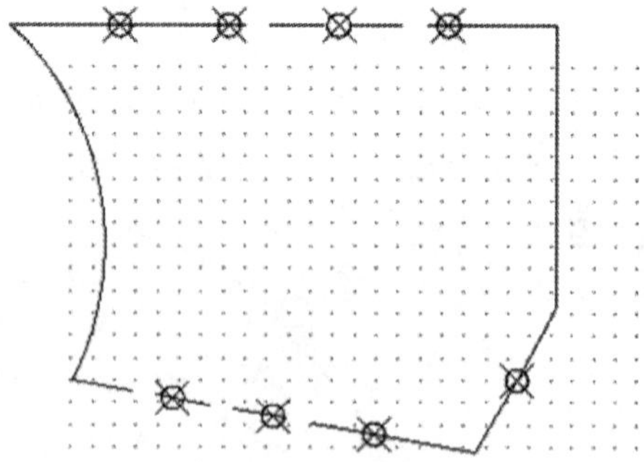

Use the **DIVIDE** command to place points as shown.
The top line is divided into five equal segments.
The bottom-angled line is divided into four equal segments.
The small angled line is divided into two equal segments.

9. 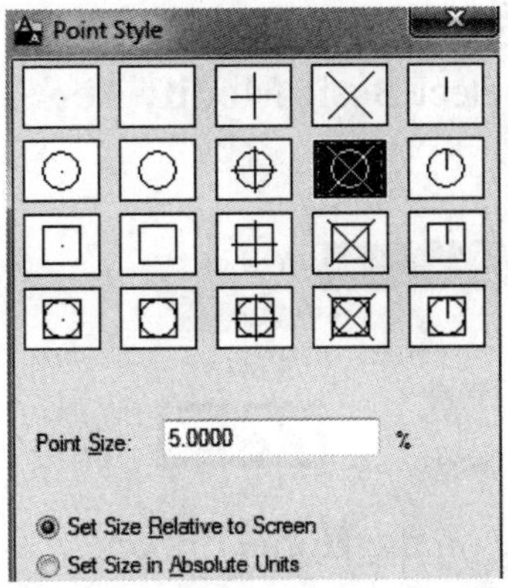

Type **DDPTYPE** to access the Point Style dialog or use the Point Style tool that was added to the Format tab on the ribbon in Lesson 1.

Go to **Format→Point Style** to set the points so they are visible.

Select the Point Style indicated.

Press **OK**.

10. Draw contour lines using **Pline** and **NODE** Osnaps as shown.

Be sure to put the contour lines on the contour line layer.

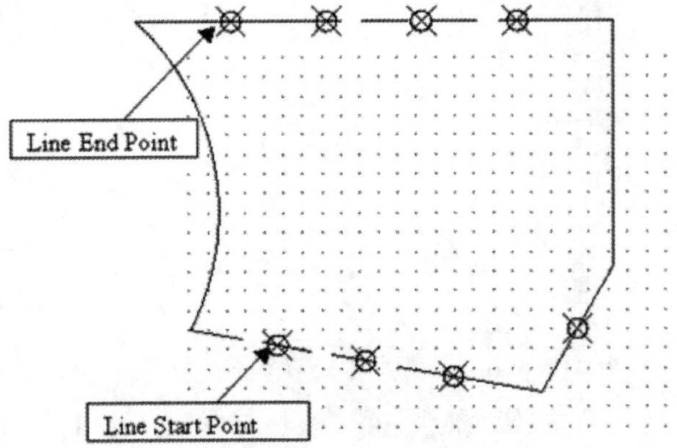

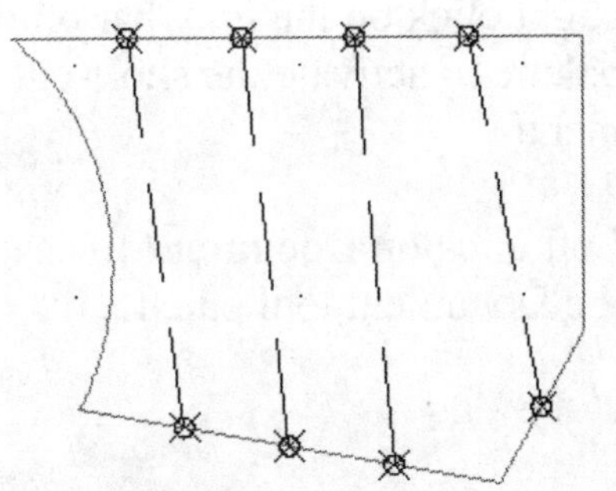

11. Type **qselect** on the *Command* line.

12. 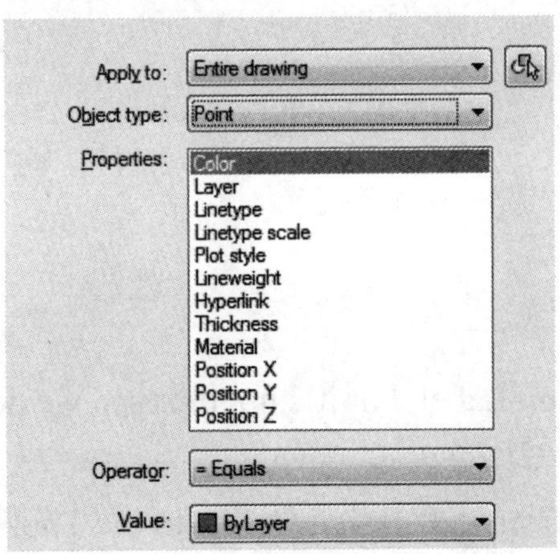

Set the Object Type to **Point**.
Set the Color = Equals **ByLayer**.

Press **OK**.

13. 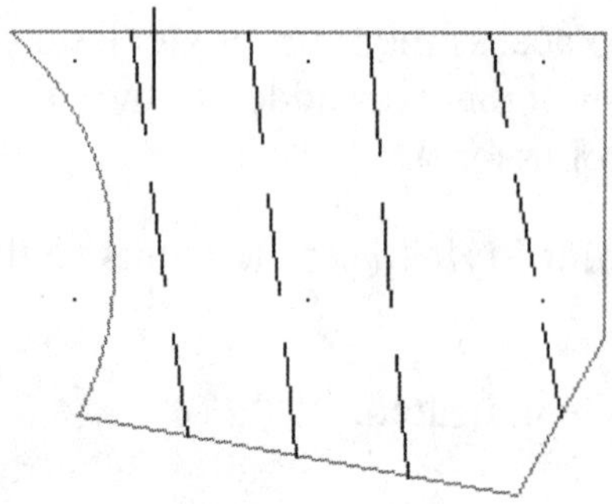

All the points are selected.
Right click and select **Basic Modify Tools→ Delete**.

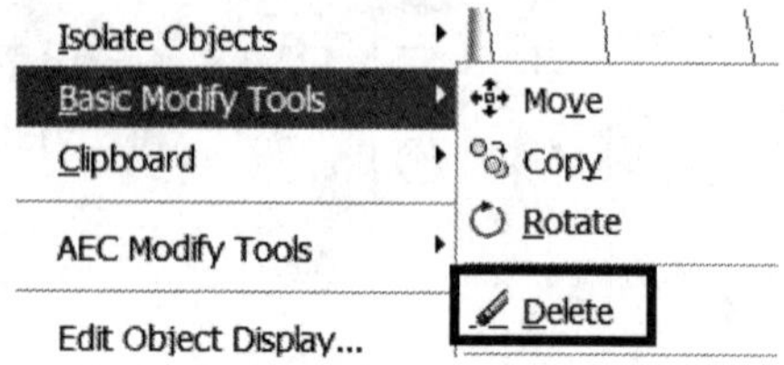

14. 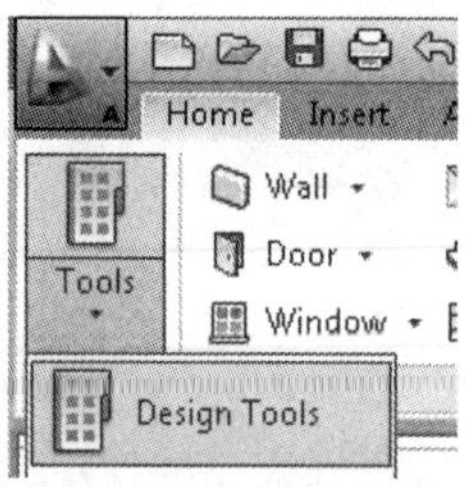

Activate the Design Tools palette on the Home ribbon.

15. 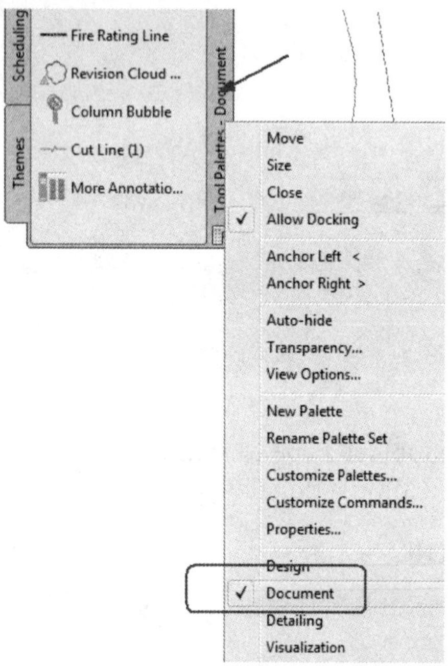

Right click on the gray bar on the palette to activate the short-cut menu.

Left click on **Document** to enable the Document tool palette.

16. Activate the Annotation tab on the palette.

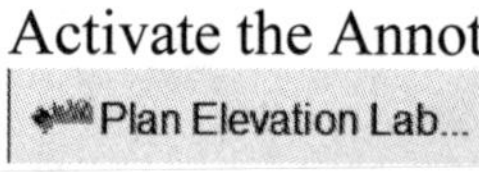

Locate the Plan Elevation Label, but it's not the type we need for a site plan.

17. Instead we'll have to add an elevation label from the Design Center to the Tool Palette.

18. 

Type **Ctl+2** to launch the Design Center.
Or:
Activate the **Insert** ribbon.
Select the **Design Center** tool under Content
Or:
Type **ADC**.

19. 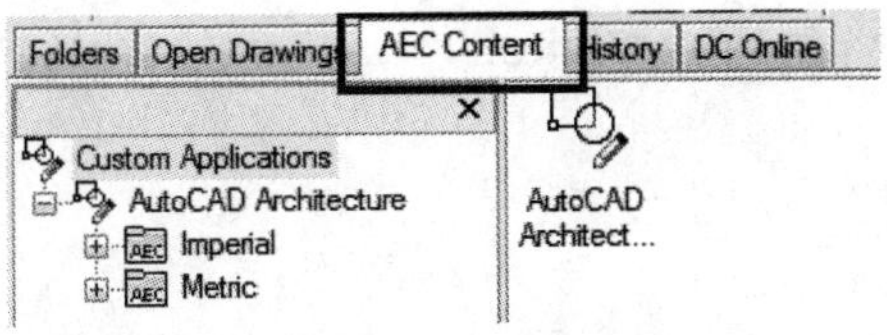

Select the **AEC Content** tab.

20. Browse to *Imperial/Documentation/Elevation Labels/ 2D Section.* [*Metric/Documentation/Elevation Labels/2D Section*].

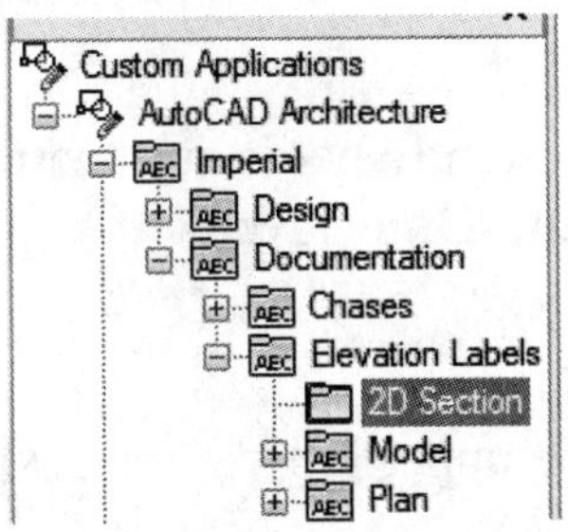

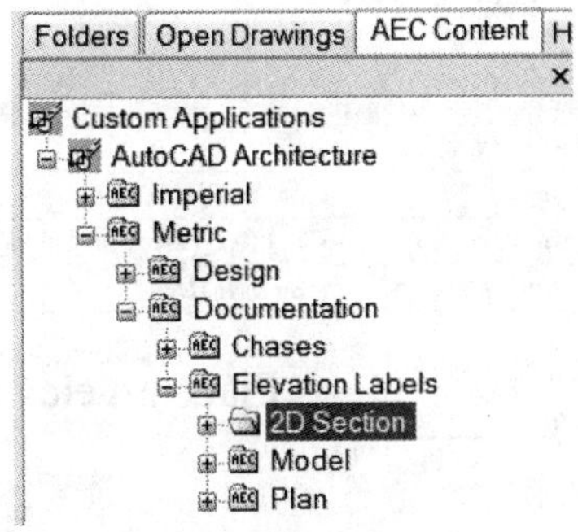

21. 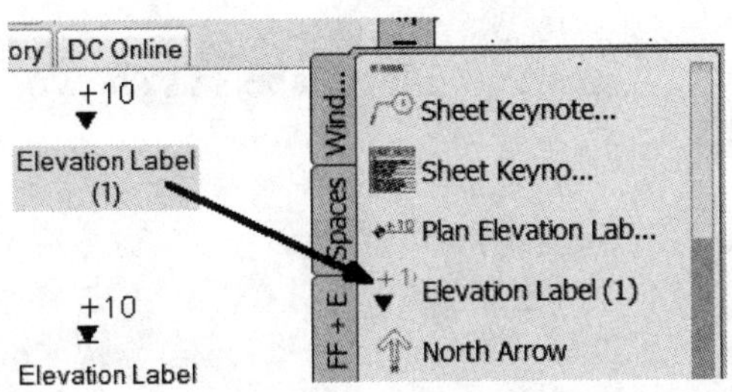

Locate the Elevation Label (1) file.

Highlight the elevation label.

Drag and drop onto the Tool Palette.

Close the Design Center.

22. 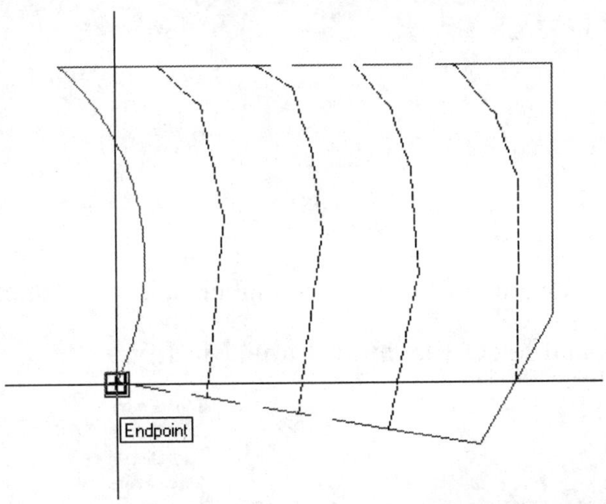

Select the Elevation Label on the Tool Palette.

Select the Endpoint shown.

23. Set the Elevation to **0″** [**0.00**].
Set the Prefix to **EL**.
Press **OK**.

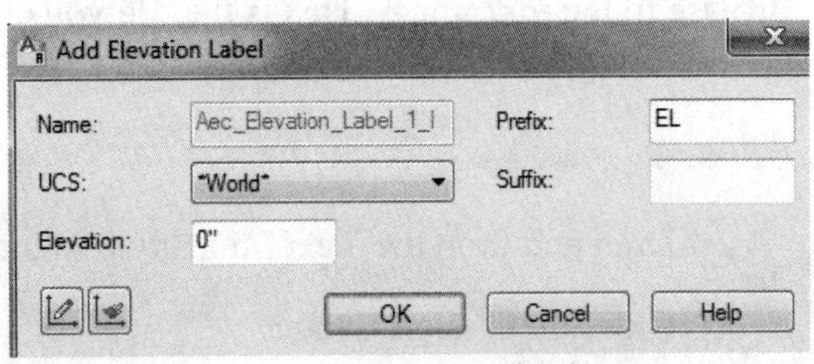

24. 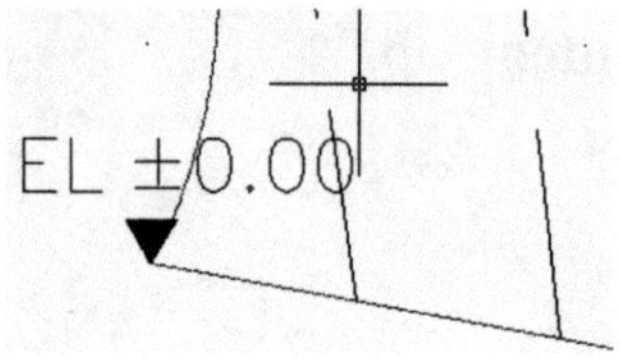

Zoom in to see the elevation label.

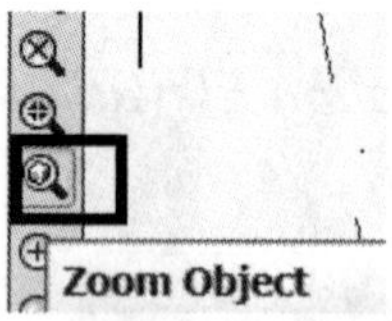

You can use the **Zoom Object** tool to zoom in quickly.

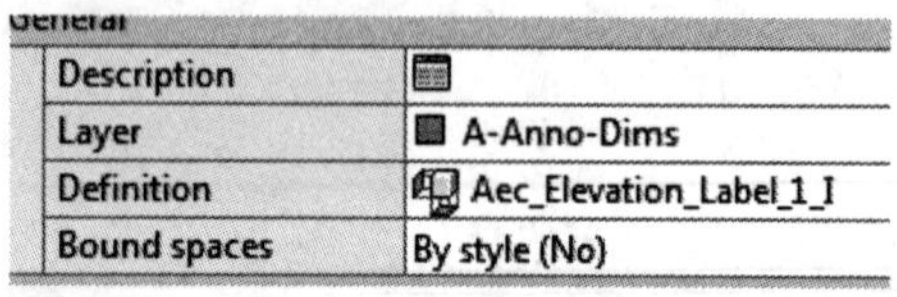

General	
Description	
Layer	A-Anno-Dims
Definition	Aec_Elevation_Label_1_I
Bound spaces	By style (No)

The Elevation Label is automatically placed on the A-Anno-Dims layer.

25. 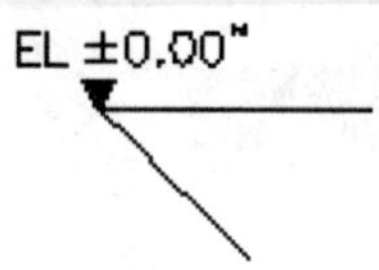

Place an elevation label on the upper left vertex as shown.

26. 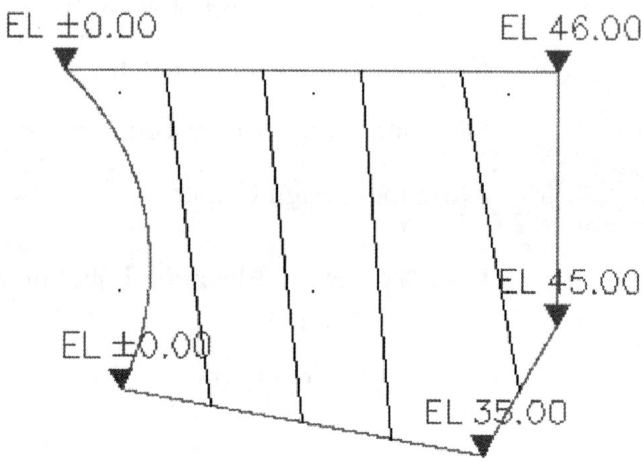

Place labels as shown.

27. 

To modify the value of the elevation label, select the label.

Right click and select **Elevation Label Modify**.

28. Type **Ctl+2** to launch the Design Center.

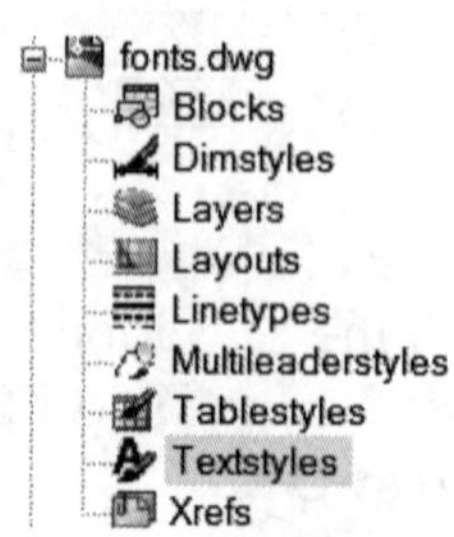

Select the Folders tab.
Browse to the *fonts.dwg*. This is the file you created in a previous exercise.

29. 

Drag and drop the **Text1** text style into the drawing.

Close the Design Center.

30. 

Use the **TEXT** command to create the text.

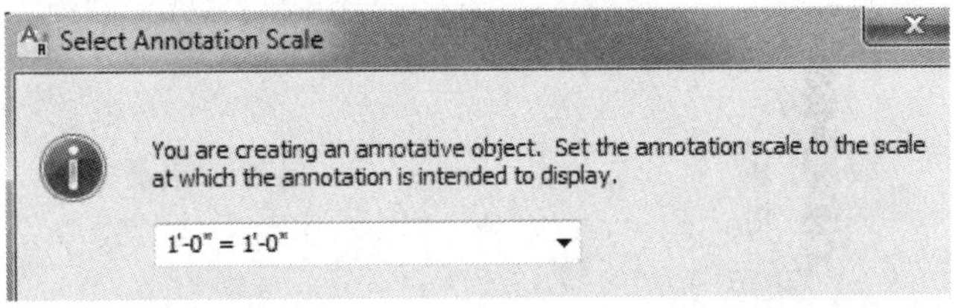

If this dialog appears, set the scale to the same scale as the current view.

Select the midpoint of the line as the insertion point.
Right click and select **Style**.
Set the current style to **Text1**.
Right click and select **Justify**.
Set the Justification to **Center**.
Set the rotation angle to **–10** degrees
Use %%d to create the degree symbol.

31. 

To create the S60… note, use the **TEXT** command.

Use a rotation angle of 60 degrees.

When you are creating the text, it will preview horizontally. However, once you left click or hit ESCAPE to place it, it will automatically rotate to the correct position.

32. 

Create the **Due South 125′ 11″ [Due South 3840.48]**, with a rotation angle of 90 degrees.

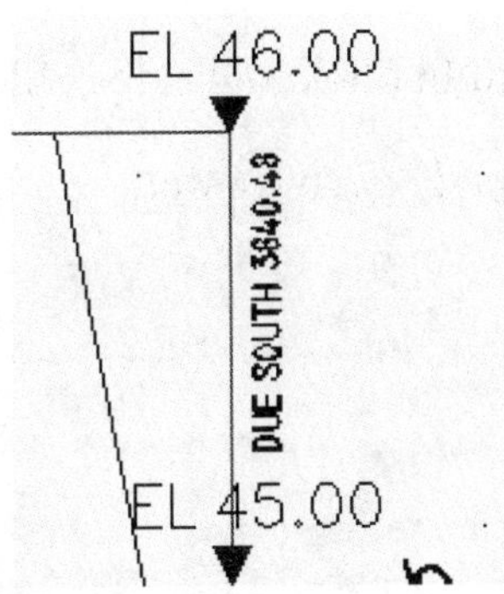

Add the text shown on the top horizontal property line.

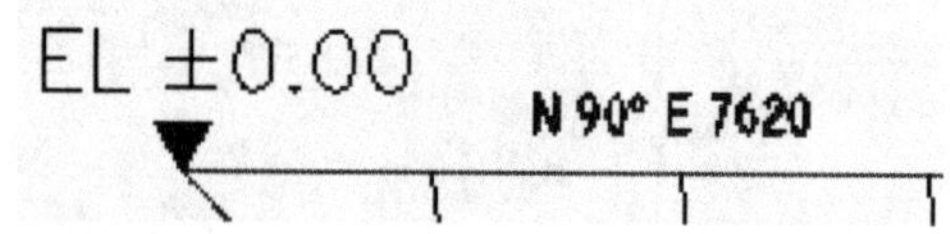

33. Add the Chord note shown. Rotation angle is 90 degrees.

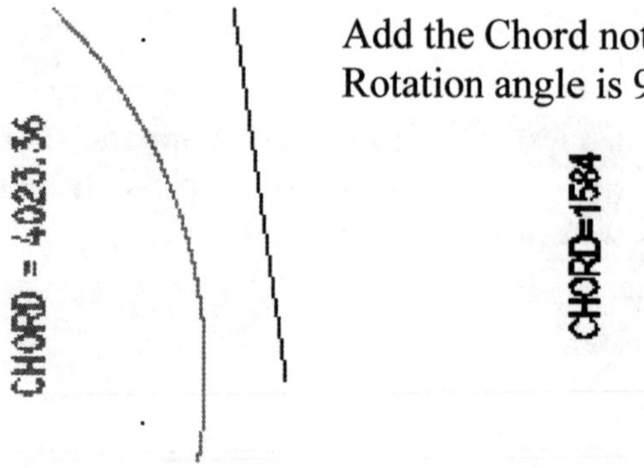

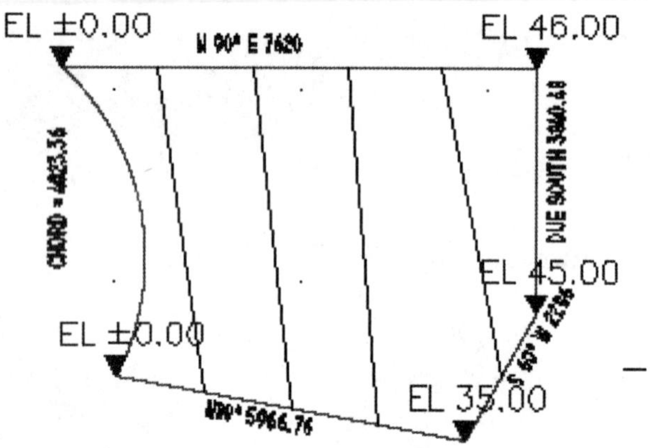

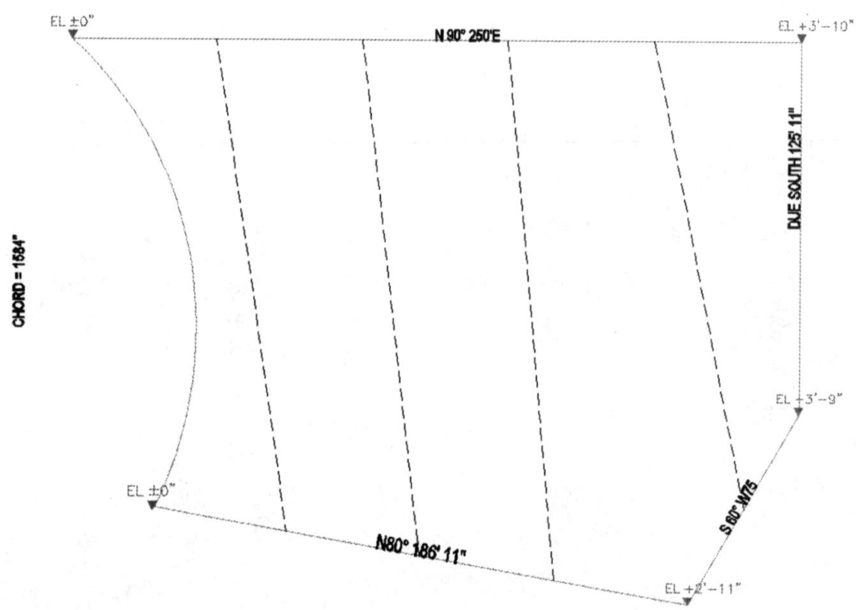

34. Save the file as *ex2-4.dwg*.

Exercise 2-5:

Creating a Layer User Group

Drawing Name: Ex 2-4.dwg
Estimated Time: 15 minutes

This exercise reinforces the following skills:

- Use of toolbars
- Layer Manager
- Layer User Group

A Layer User Group allows you to group your layers, so you can quickly freeze/thaw them, turn them ON/OFF, etc.

> **TIP:** The difference between FREEZING a Layer and turning it OFF is that entities on FROZEN Layers are not included in REGENS. Speed up your processing time by FREEZING layers.

We can create a group of layers that are just used for the site plan and then freeze them when we don't need to see them.

1.  Open *ex2-4.dwg*.

2.  Select the **Layer Manager** tool.

3. 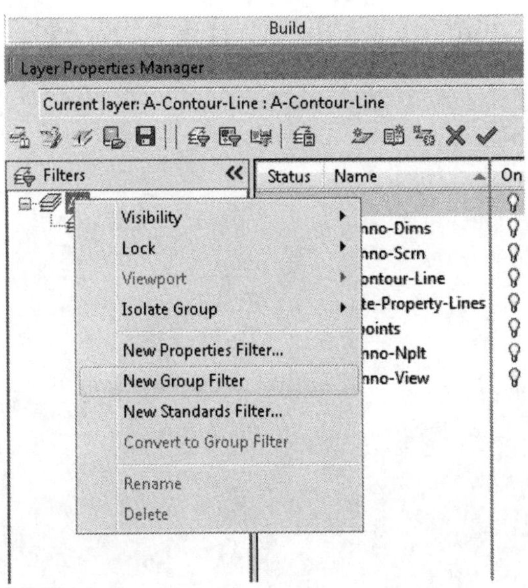

Highlight the word **All** in the Filters pane.

Right click and select the **New Group Filter**.

4. 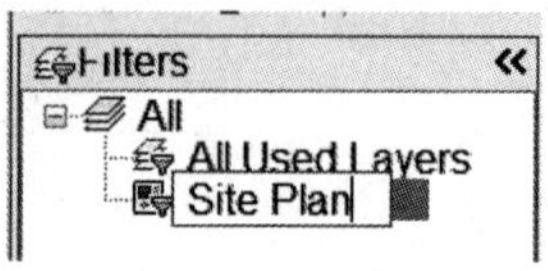

Name the group **Site Plan**.

5. 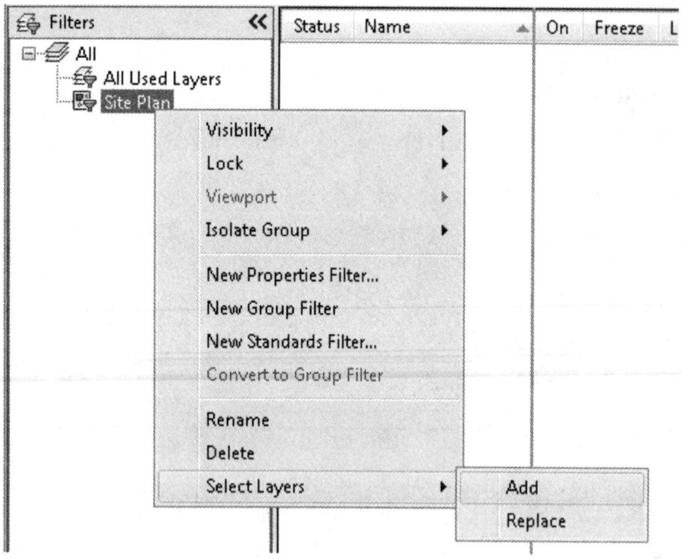

Highlight the Site Plan group.
Right click and select **Select Layers→Add**.

6. Type **ALL** on the command line.
This selects all the items in the drawing.
Press **ENTER** to finish the selection.
The layers are now listed in the Layer Manager under the Site Plan group.

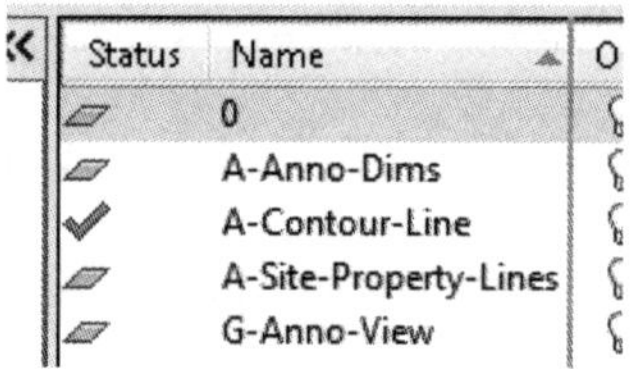

Close the Layer Manager.

7. We can use this group to quickly freeze, turn off, etc. the layers in the Site Plan group.

Save the drawing as *ex2-5.dwg* and close.

QUIZ 1

True or False

1. Doors, windows, and walls are inserted into the drawing as objects.
2. The Architectural Toolbars are loaded from the ACA Menu Group.
3. To set the template used by the QNEW tool, use Options.

4. If you start a New Drawing using the 'QNew' tool shown above, the Start-Up dialog will appear unless you assign a template.
5. Mass elements are used to create Mass Models.
6. The Layer Manager is used to organize, sort, and group layers.
7. Layer Standards are set using the Layer Manager.
8. You must load a custom linetype before you can assign it to a layer.

Multiple Choice
Select the best answer.

9. If you start a drawing using one of the standard templates, AutoCAD Architecture will automatically create ___________ layouts.

   A. A work layout plus Model Space
   B. Four layouts, plus Model Space
   C. Ten layouts, plus Model Space
   D. Eleven layouts, plus Model Space

10. Options are set through:

   A. Options
   B. Desktop
   C. User Settings
   D. Template

11. The Display Manager controls:

   A. How AEC objects are displayed in the graphics window
   B. The number of viewports
   C. The number of layout tabs
   D. Layers

12. Mass Elements are created using the _____ Tool Palette.

    A. Massing
    B. Concept
    C. General Drafting
    D. Documentation

13. Wall Styles are created by:

    A. Highlighting a Wall on the Wall tab of the Tool Palette, right click and select Wall Styles
    B. Type **WallStyle** on the command line
    C. Go to **Format→Style Manager**
    D. All of the above

14. To create a New Layer, use:

    A. Type **LayerManager** at the command line
    B. Type **Layer** at the command line
    C. Use **Format→Layer Management→Layer Manager**
    D. All of the above

15. You can change the way AEC objects are displayed by using:

    A. Edit Object Display
    B. Edit Display Properties
    C. Edit Entity Properties
    D. Edit AEC Properties

ANSWERS:

1) T; 2) T; 3) T; 4) F; 5) T; 6) T; 7) T; 8) T; 9) A; 10) A; 11) A; 12) A; 13) D; 14) D; 15) A

Lesson 3
Floor Plans

The floor plan is central to any architectural drawing. We start by placing the exterior walls, then the interior walls, then doors, and finally windows.

Exercise 3-1:
Creating Walls

Drawing Name: New
Estimated Time: 10 minutes

This exercise reinforces the following skills:

- Create Walls
- Wall Properties
- Wall Styles
- Model and Work space

1.  Start a new drawing using QNEW.

2. 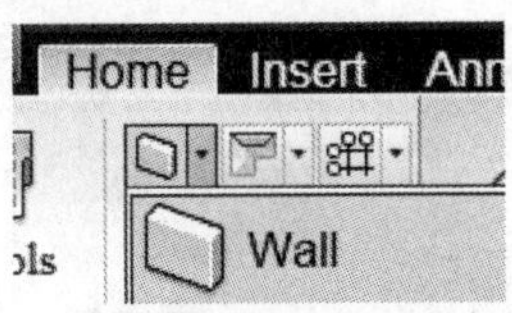

Select the **Wall** tool from the Home ribbon.

3. 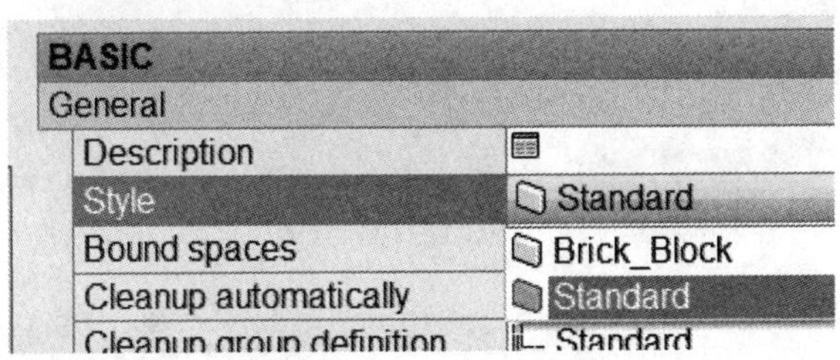

In the Properties dialog, check under the Style drop-down list.

   Only the Brick_Block and Standard styles are available.

   These are the wall styles that are loaded in the template.

4. Exit out of the command by pressing ESC.

5. 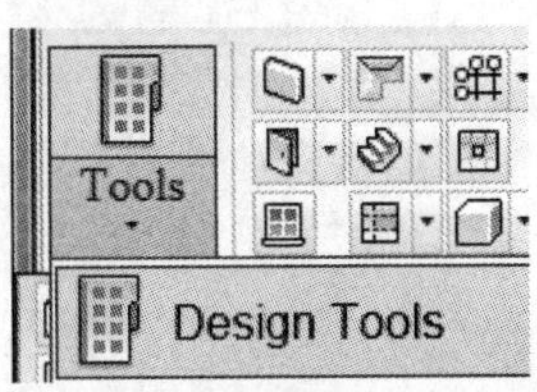

Launch the Design Tools palette from the Home ribbon.

6. 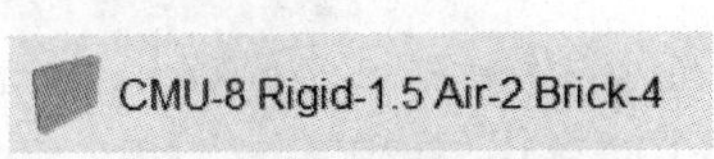

Activate the Walls tab on the palette.
Select the CMU-8 Rigid-1.5 Air 2 Brick-4

[CMU 190 Rigid-038 Air – 050 Brick -090].

7. 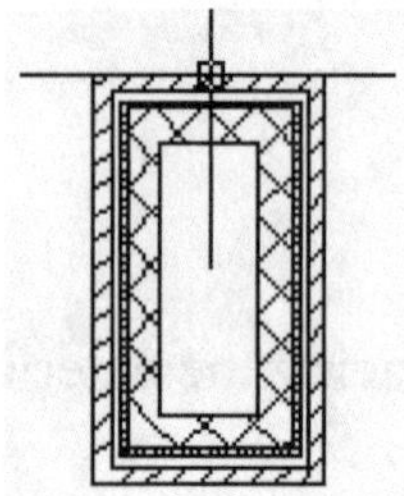

Toggle **ORTHO** ON.

Start the wall at 0,0.
Create a rectangle 72 inches [1830 mm] tall and 36 inches [914 mm] wide.

8. Select the **Work** tab.

9. 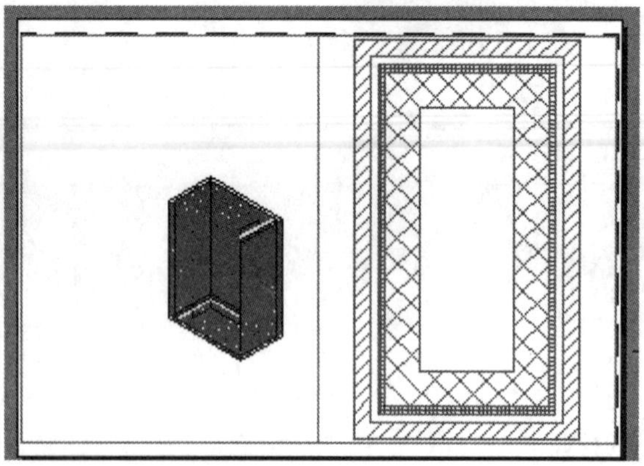

You see that the walls you placed are really 3-dimensional.

10. 

Switch back to the Model space tab.

11. 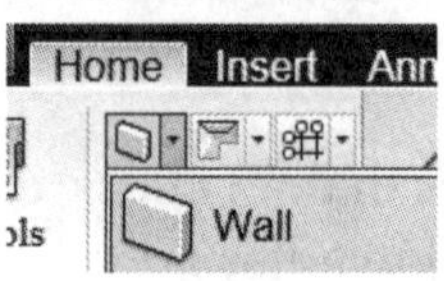

Select the **Wall** tool from the Home ribbon.

12. 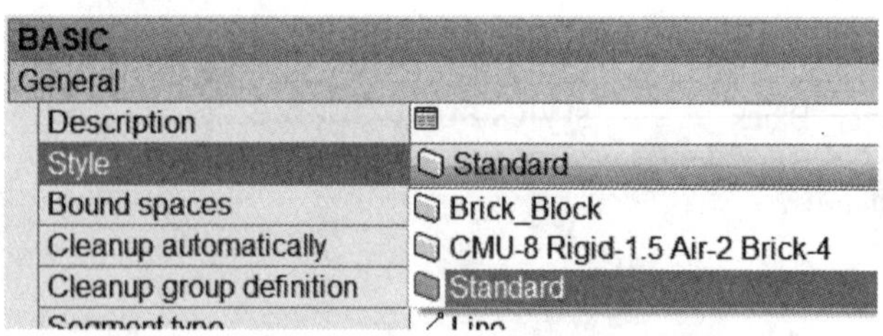

In the Properties dialog, check under the Style drop-down list.

Note that the CMU wall style is now available under the drop-down list.

13. Exit out of the command by pressing ESC.

14. Save your drawing as *Ex3-1.dwg.*

TIP: If you draw a wall and the materials composing the wall are on the wrong side, you can reverse the direction of the wall. Simply select the wall, right click and select the Reverse option from the menu.

Exercise 3-2:

Inserting a Drawing Reference

Drawing Name: new
Estimated Time: 60 minutes

This exercise reinforces the following skills:

- Drawing references (previously known as external references or Xrefs)

1.  Start a new drawing using **QNEW**.

2. 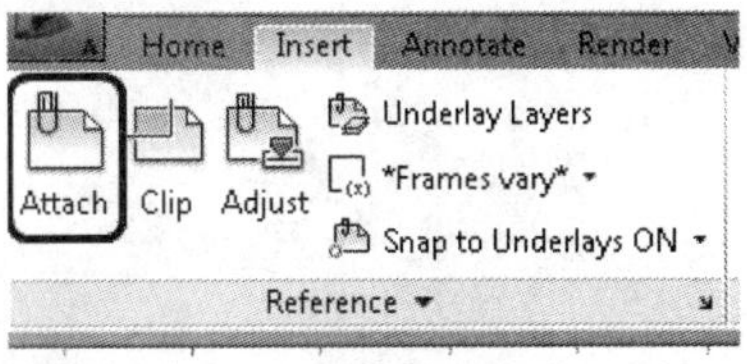

Activate the Insert ribbon.

Select **Attach** on the Reference panel.

3. 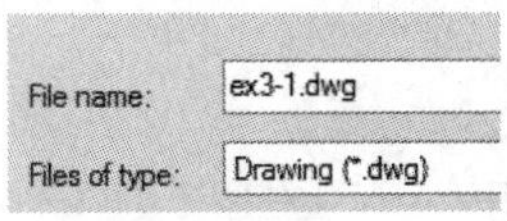

Set the Files of type to **.dwg*. 

Locate *ex3-1.dwg*.

Press **Open**.

> **TIP:** Many architects use external drawing references to organize their projects. That way teams of architects can concentrate just on their portions of a building. External references also use less system resources.

4. 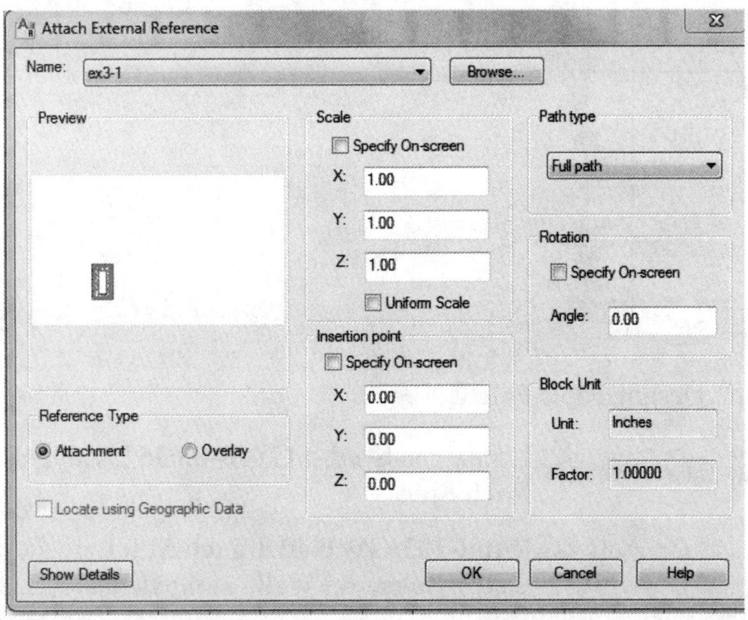

Uncheck **Specify On-Screen** under Insertion point, scale, and rotation.

Press **OK**.
This will insert the file as an external reference at 0,0,0.

5. Save the file as *ex3-2*.

> **TIP:** You can convert lines, arcs, circles, or polylines to walls. If you have created a floor plan in AutoCAD and want to convert it to 3D, open the floor plan drawing inside of AutoCAD Architecture. Use the Convert to Walls tool to transform your floor plan into walls.

Exercise 3-3

Convert to Walls

Drawing Name: floor plan.dwg
Estimated Time: 10 minutes

This exercise reinforces the following skills:

- ❑ Convert to Walls

1.

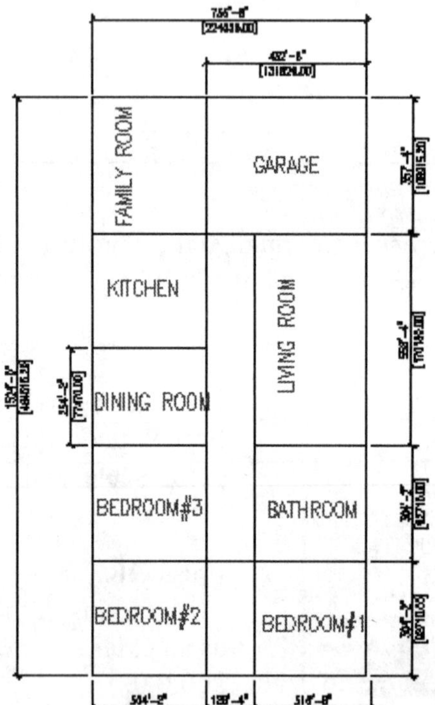

Open *floor plan.dwg*.
This file can be downloaded from the book's detail page on www.SDCpublications.com.

This floor plan has both architectural and metric units shown.

2. On the Walls tab of the Design Tools Palette:

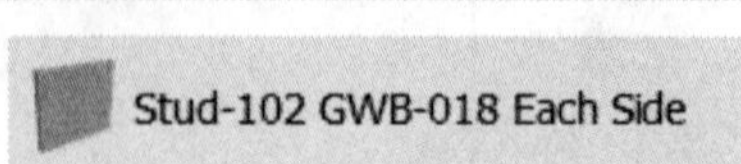

Locate the **Stud-4 GWB-0.625 2 Layers Each Side**

[Stud-102 GWB-018 Each Side] wall style on the Walls tool palette.

3. Highlight the wall tool.

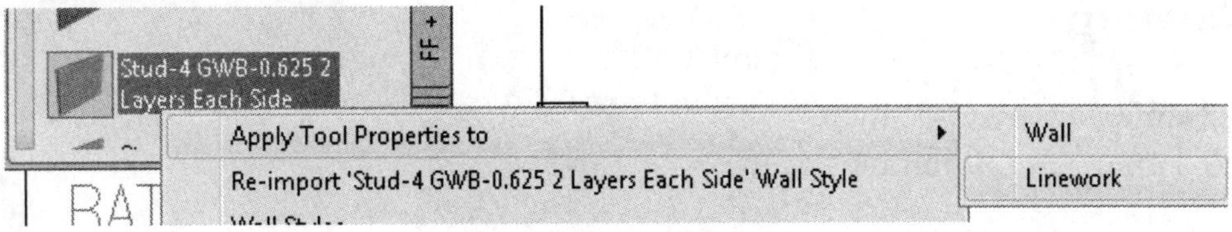

Right click and select
Apply Tool Properties to →Linework.

4. Select all the interior lines.

Press **ENTER** when you are done selecting.

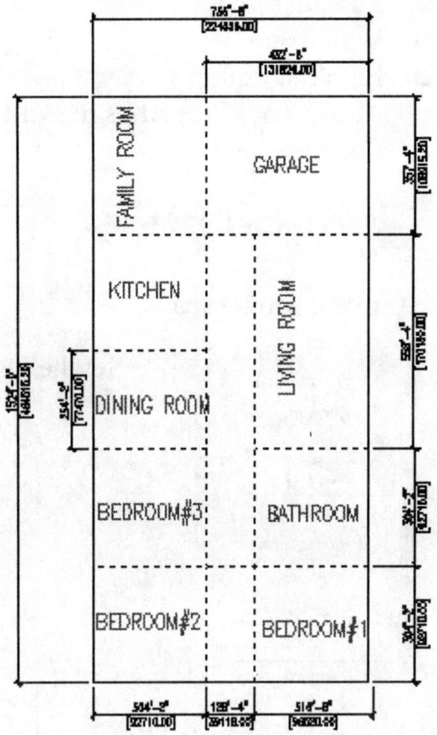

You are prompted if you want to erase the layout geometry. Type **Y** for Yes.

5. Switch to the Work tab so you can see how your house looks in 3D.

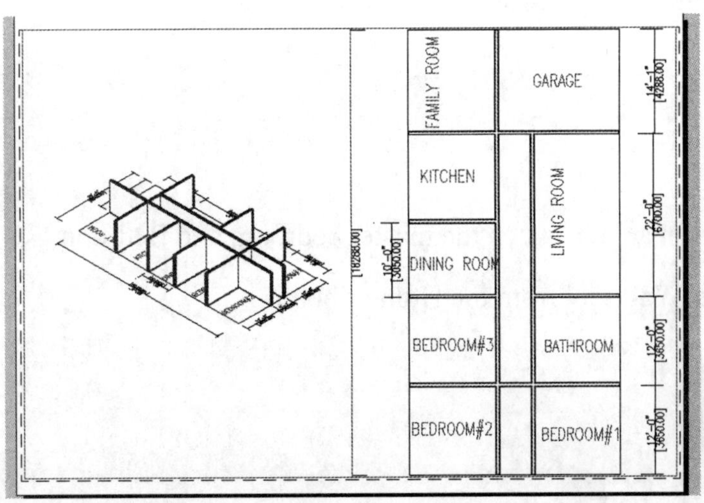

6. Save the file as *ex3-3.dwg.*

Exercise 3-4:
Wall Cleanup

Drawing Name: ex3-3.dwg
Estimated Time: 30 minutes

This exercise reinforces the following skills:

- Modifying Walls
- Edit Justification
- Wall Tools
- Break at Point
- Apply Tool Properties to Wall
- Cleanup Tools

1.  Open *ex3-3.dwg*.

2. Activate Model space.

3. 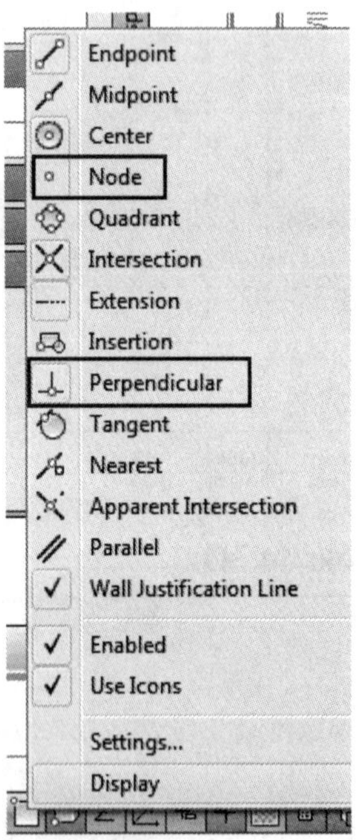

Set the Osnaps so that Node and Perpendicular are enabled.

4. 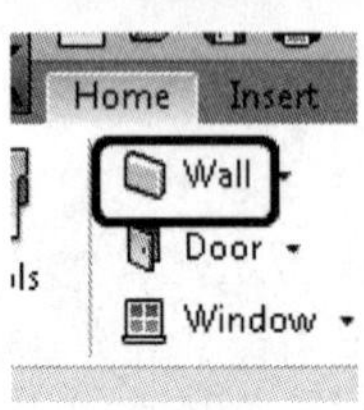

Add a closet area between the master bedroom and Bedroom #1.

Select the **Wall** tool from the Home ribbon.

5. 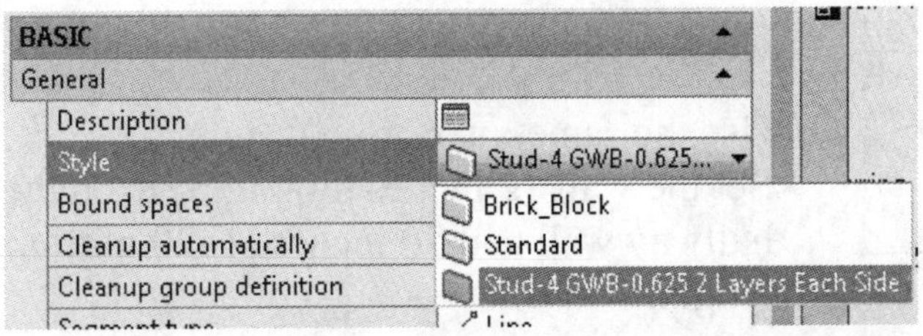

Verify that the Stud-4GWB is the selected as the active style.

6. 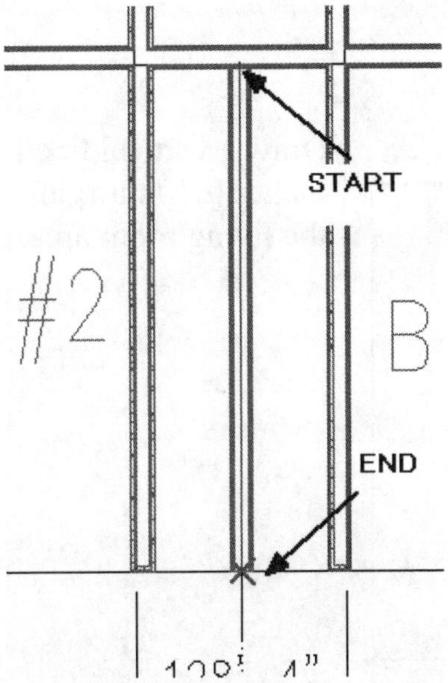

Pick the start point as shown.

You should see a node snap at the start point.

Select the endpoint shown using a perpendicular osnap.

7. 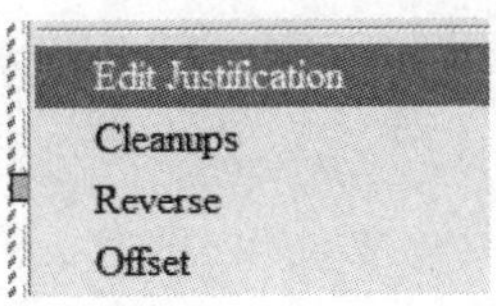

Select the wall just placed.

Right click and select **Edit Justification.**

8. 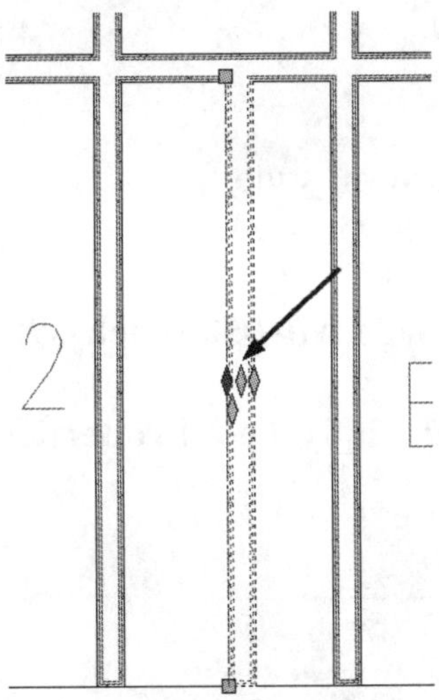

Diamond grips will appear to indicate different wall justification methods (Left/Right/Center).

The diamond on the top indicates the current justification.

Select the Center Diamond.

This will justify the wall to the center.

9. 

If you mouse over a diamond, you will see a tool tip to tell you what type of justification will be selected.

10. 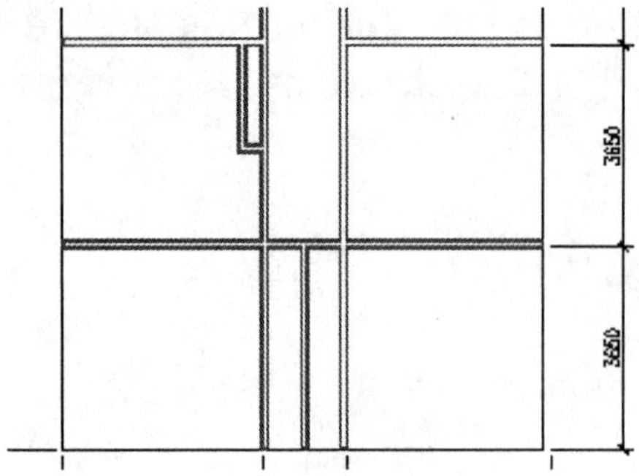

Draw a closet in Bedroom #2.

- Use the same interior wall style.
  Set the wall 12 inches [304 mm] from the hallway wall and 70 inches [1820 mm] in length.

11. 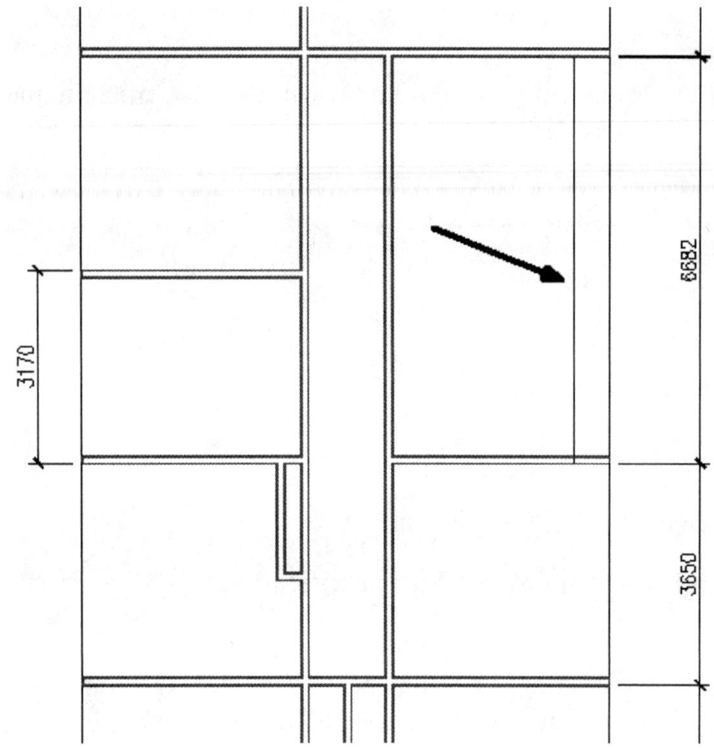

Draw a vertical line 24 inches [610 mm] inside the living room area.

12. 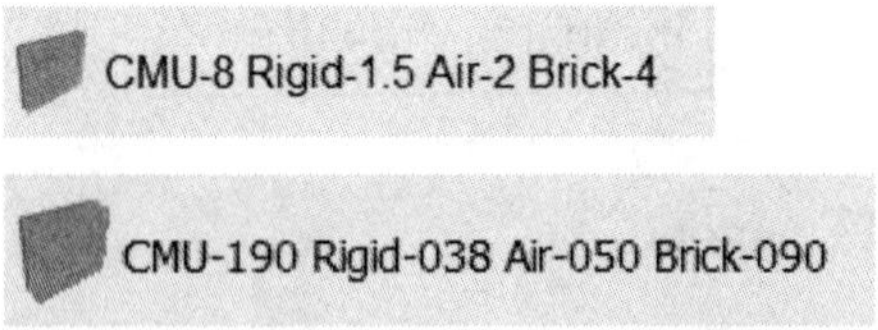

Locate the exterior wall style:
CMU-8 Rigid – 1.5 Air – 2 Brick -4

[CMU-190 Rigid-038 Air-050 Brick-090].

13. Convert the outside lines to the exterior wall style using **Apply Tool Properties to Linework**.

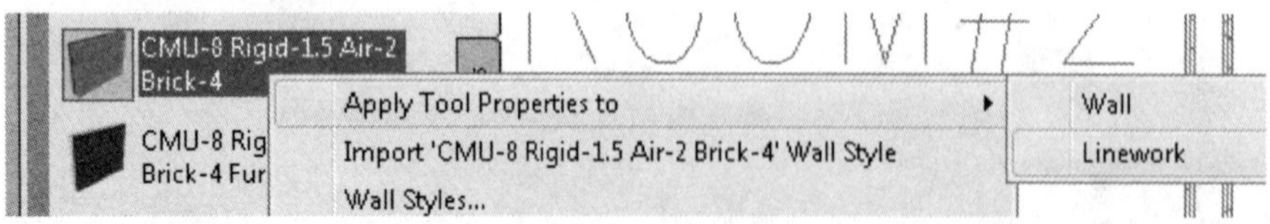

14. 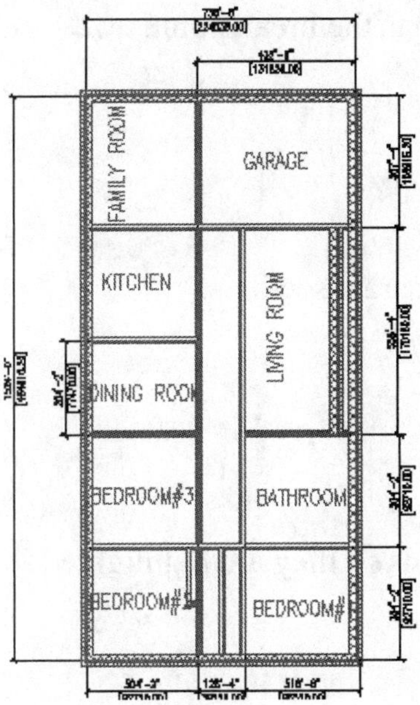

Our floor plan so far.

15. When prompted to erase layout geometry, enter **Yes**.

16. 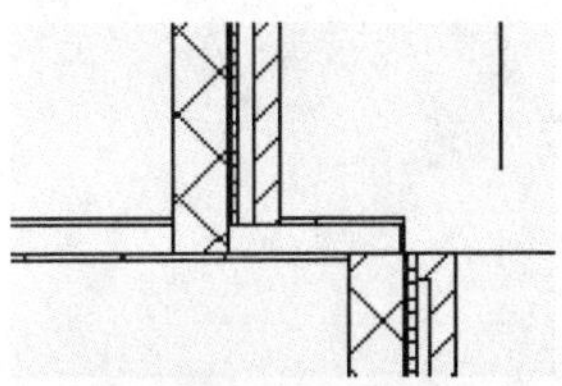

We have a small section of wall on the upper and lower right corners of the living room area that should be split so that it can be assigned the exterior wall style.

17. 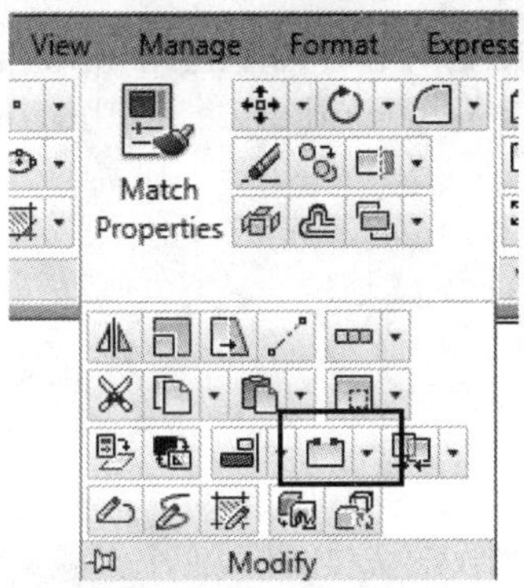

Locate the **Break** tool located on the Modify panel of the Home ribbon.

18. 

Select the **Break at Point** tool on the Break tool drop-down list to split the wall into two sections.

19. 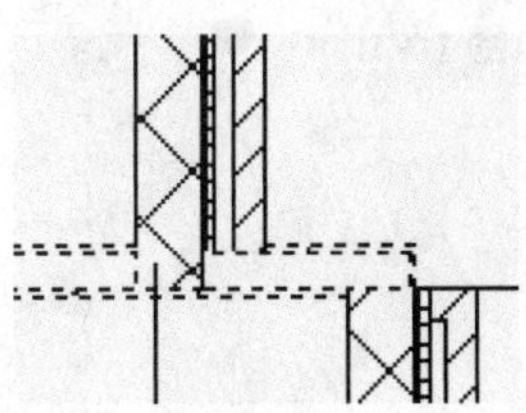

Select the wall.

It will highlight.

20. 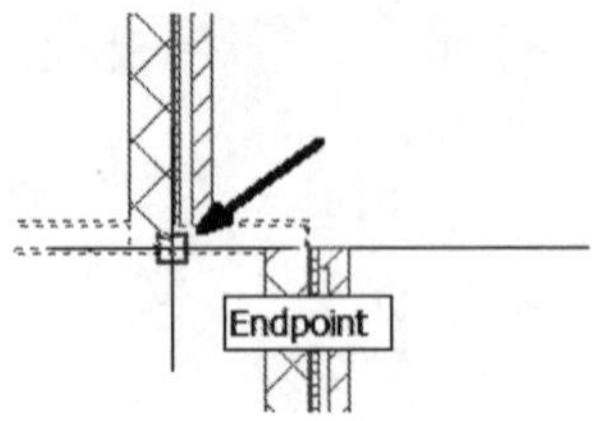

Select the point indicated as the break point.

21. 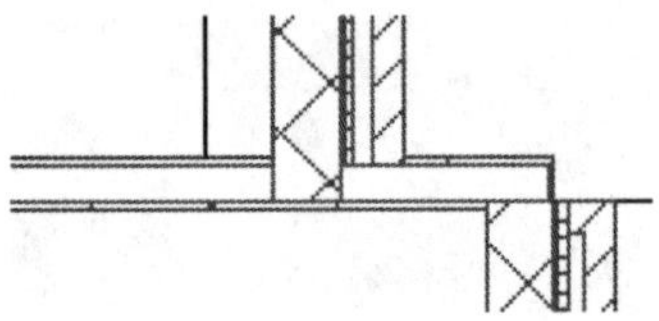

The wall is now two separate sections.

22. Repeat for the other side of the wall.

23. 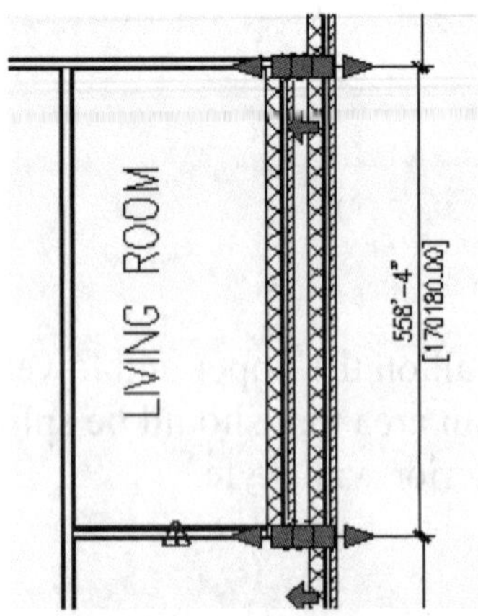

Select both wall sections so they are highlighted.

24. 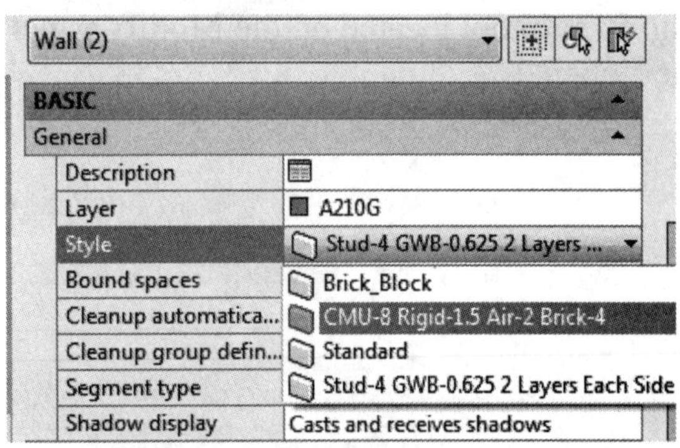

Locate the **CMU-190 Rigid-038 Air-050 Brick-090** wall style on the tool palette.

25. 

Right click and select **Apply Tool Properties to→Wall.**

The walls will be converted to the correct wall style.

26. Press ESC to deselect the walls.

27. 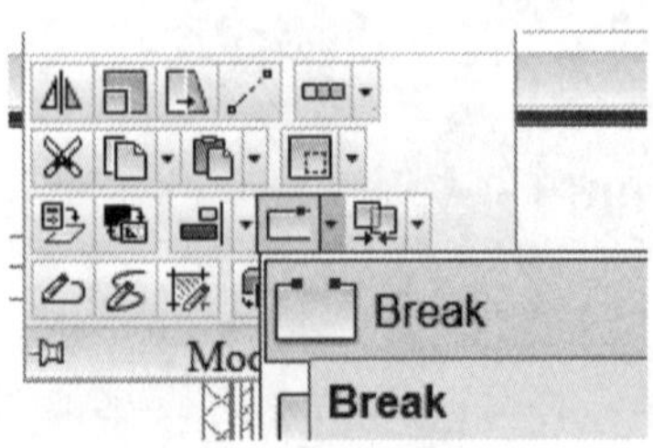

Select the **Break at two points** tool.

28. 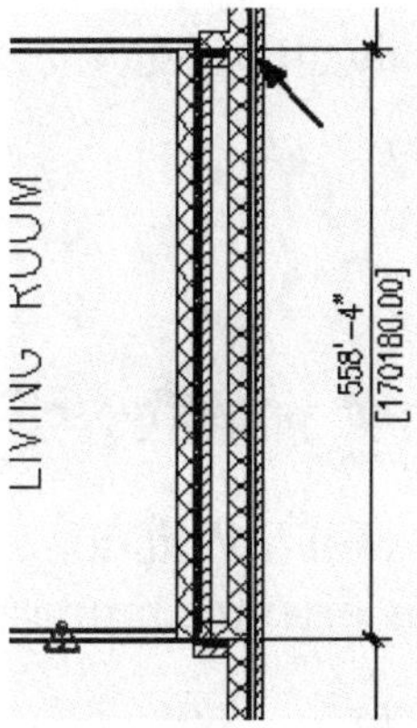

Select the point indicated to break the wall.

29. 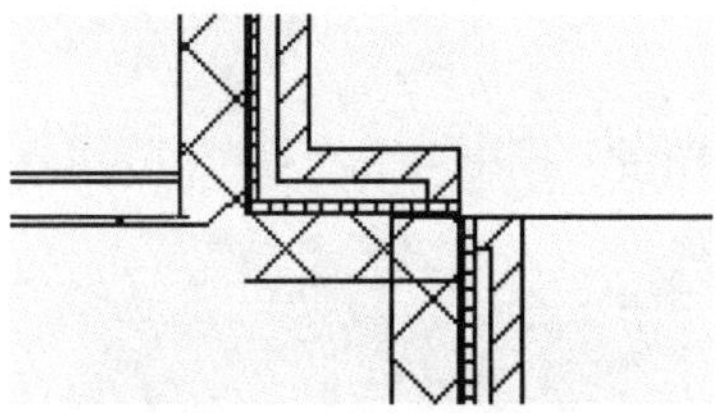
Select the small section of wall.

30. 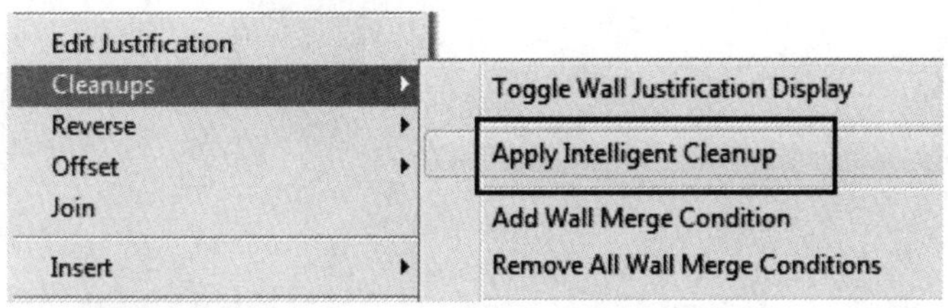

Right click and select **Cleanups→Apply Intelligent Cleanup**.

31. 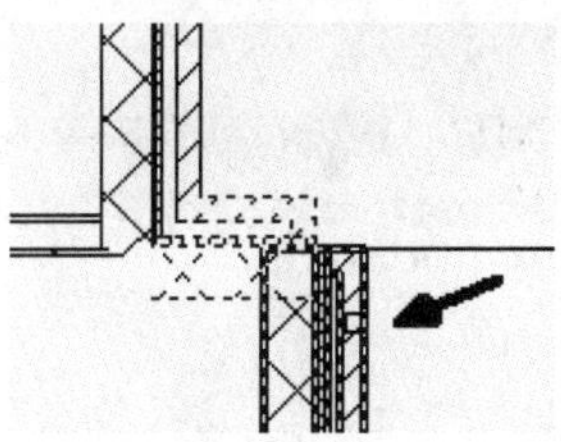
You'll be prompted to select the wall to cleanup with.

Select the wall indicated.

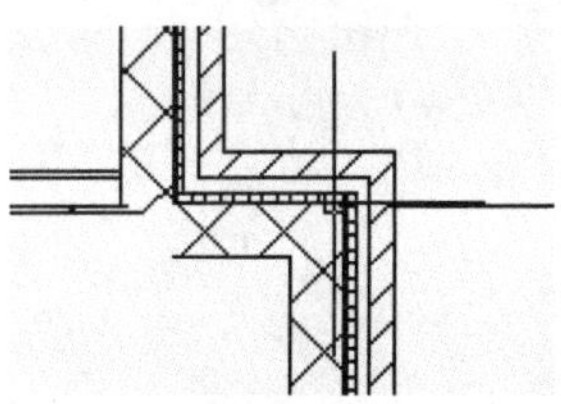
The corner is cleaned up.

32. 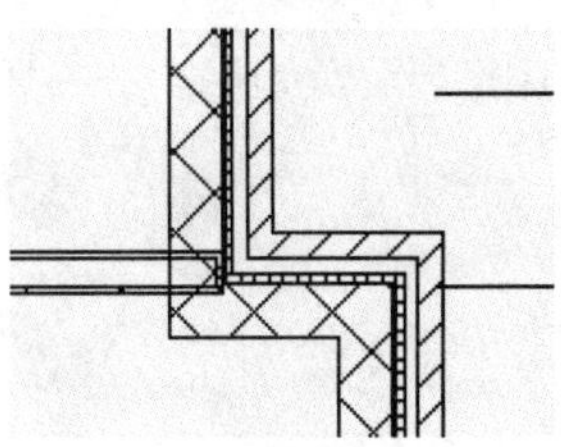
Repeat on the other corner.

33. 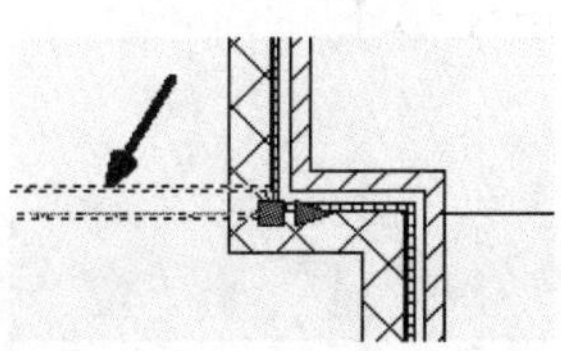
Select the interior wall.
Right click and select **Cleanups→Apply Intelligent Cleanup**.

34. 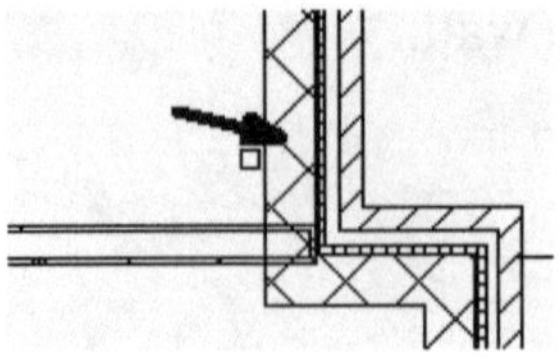

When prompted to select the boundary wall, select the wall indicated.

35. 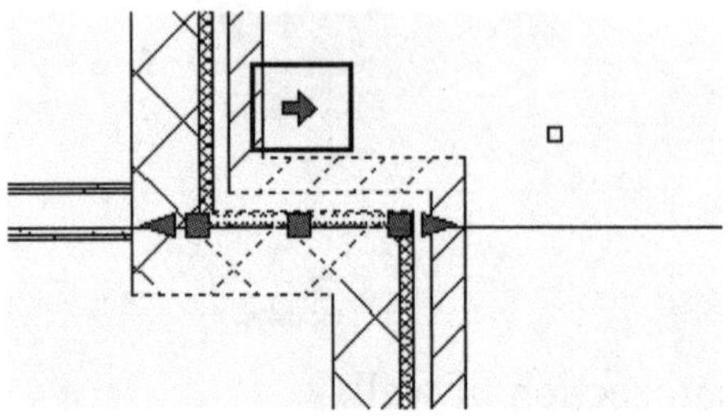

If the wall does not clean up properly, select the wall.
Use the arrow to flip the wall orientation so the exterior side of the wall is oriented properly.

Then try the Cleanup again.

36. 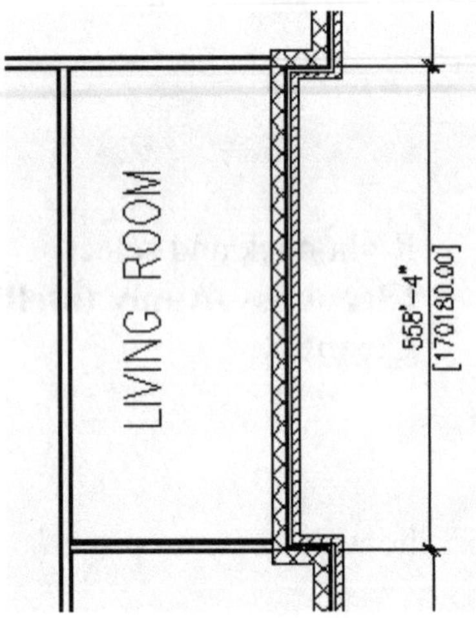

The walls appear cleaner.

37. 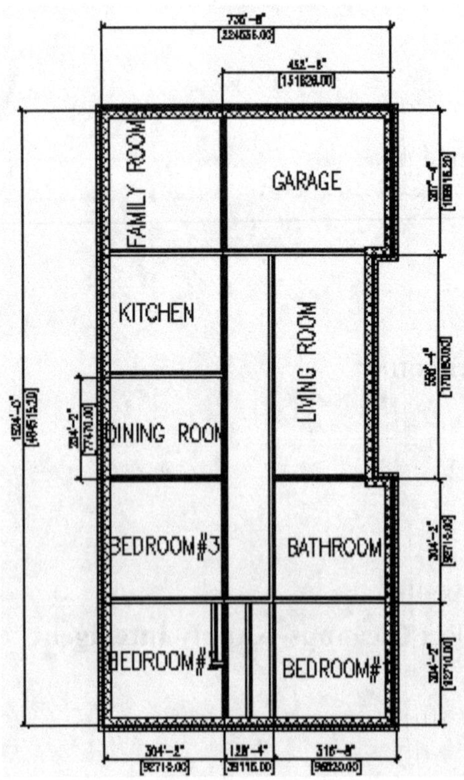

The drawing is now updated.

Save as *ex3-4.dwg*.

> **TIP:** To create a freestanding door, press the ENTER key when prompted to pick a wall. You can then use the grips on the door entity to move and place the door wherever you like.
>
> To move a door along a wall, use Door→Reposition→Along Wall. Use the OSNAP From option to locate a door a specific distance from an adjoining wall.

Exercise 3-5:

Adding Closet Doors

Drawing Name: Ex3-4.dwg
Estimated Time: 10 minutes

This exercise reinforces the following skills:

- Adding Doors
- Door Properties

1.  Open *ex3-4.dwg.*

2. 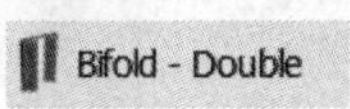

Locate the **Bifold-Double** door on the Doors tab of the Tool Palette.

3. 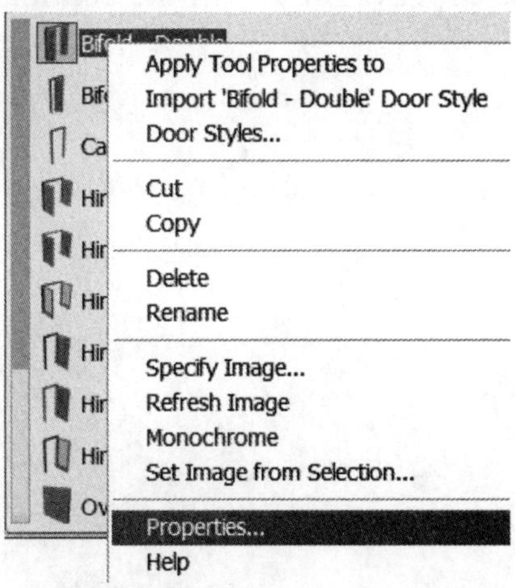

Highlight the **Bifold-Double** door.
Right click and select **Properties**.

4. 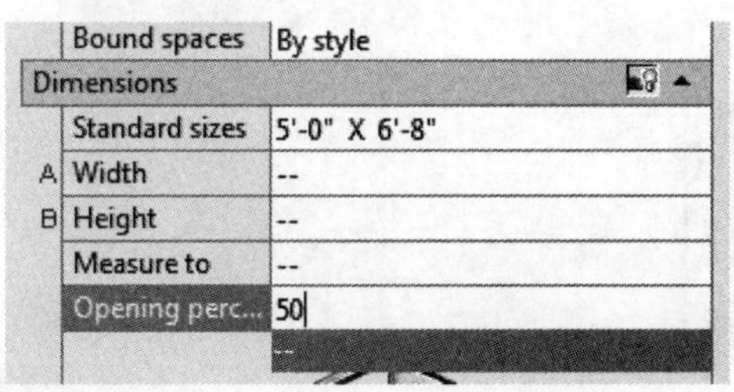

Expand the **Dimensions** section.
Set the Standard sizes to
5′-0″ x 6′-8″ [1500.00 x 2100.00].

Set the Opening percent to **50**.

TIP: If you left click in the field, a down arrow will appear…select the down arrow and you will get a list of standard sizes. Then, select the size you want.

A 25% opening will show a door swing at a 45-degree angle.
The value of the Opening percentage determines the angle of the arc swing.
A 50% value indicates the door will appear half-open at a 90-degree angle.

5. 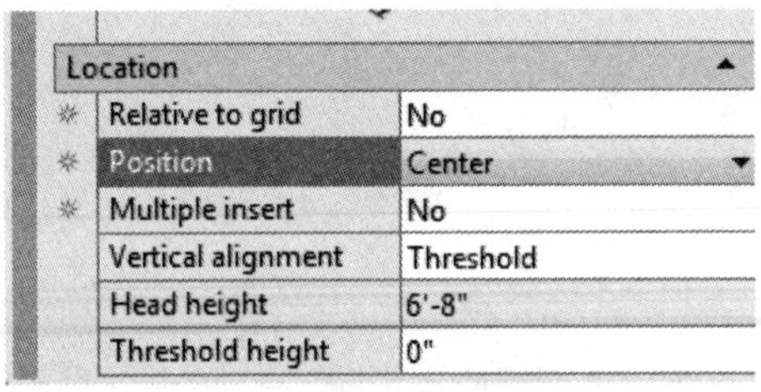

Expand the **Location** section.

Set Position along wall to **Center**.
This will center the closet doors along the wall.

6. Place the Bifold Double doors at the two closets.

The orientation of the door swing is determined by the wall side selected.

In both cases, you want to select the outside face of the wall.

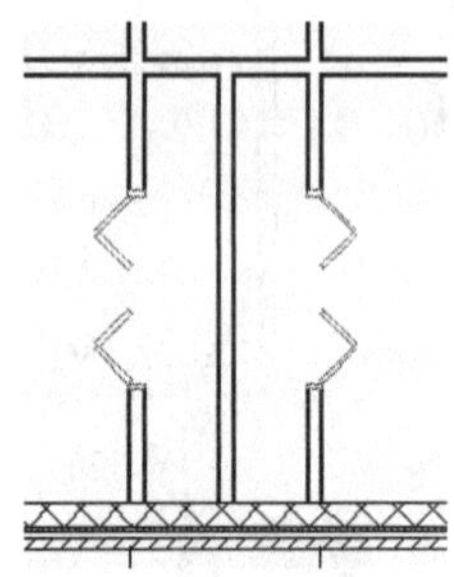

7. 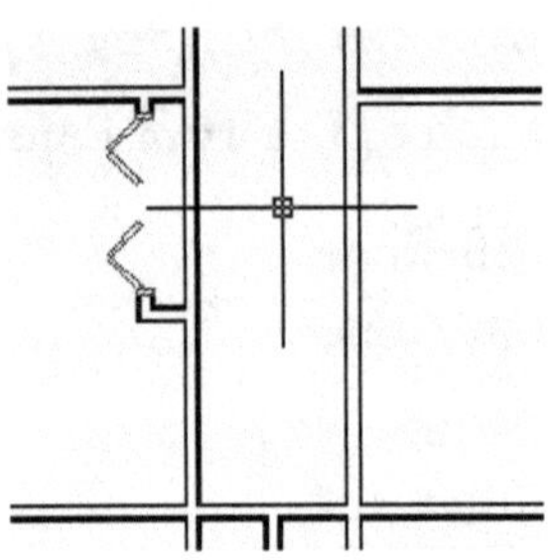

Place a Bi-fold Double door in the wall shown.

Right click and select ENTER to exit the command.

8. Save as *ex3-5.dwg*.

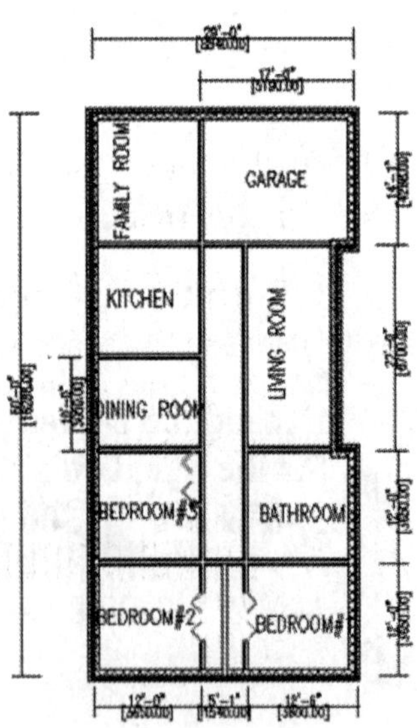

Exercise 3-6:
Adding Interior Doors

Drawing Name: ex3-5.dwg
Estimated Time: 10 minutes

This exercise reinforces the following skills:

- Adding Doors
- Door Properties

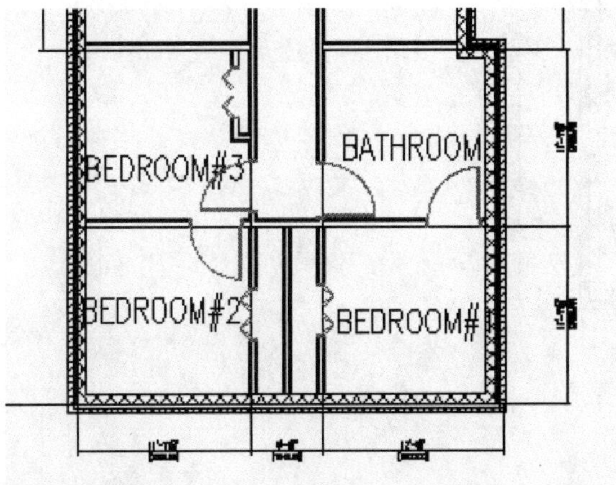

We will add single hinge doors in the areas shown.

You may need to do some wall cleanup to get the rooms to look proper.

Use AddWall, Extend, and Trim as needed.

Try to keep the walls so they line up to keep the floor plan looking clean.

1.  Open *ex3-5.dwg.*

2. 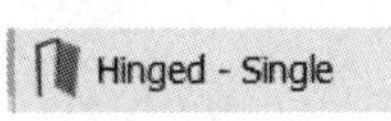

Locate the **Single Hinged** door on the Doors tab of the Tool Palette. Right click and select **Properties**.

3.

Dimensions		
	Standard sizes	3'-6" X 6'-8"
A	Width	3'-6"
B	Height	6'-8"
	Measure to	Inside of frame
	Swing angle	90

Expand the **Dimensions** section.
Set the Standard sizes to
3′6″ x 6′8″ [1000.00 X 2100.00].
Set the Swing angle to **90**.

Dimensions		
	Standard sizes	1000.00 X 2100.00
A	Width	1000.00
B	Height	2100.00
	Measure to	Inside of frame
	Swing angle	90

4.

Location	
Relative to grid	No
Position	Offset
Automatic offset	6"
Multiple insert	No
Vertical alignment	Threshold
Head height	7'-0"
Threshold height	0"

Set the Position along wall to **Offset**.
Set the Automatic offset to **6″ [150**].

Press **OK**.

5. Place the doors as indicated.

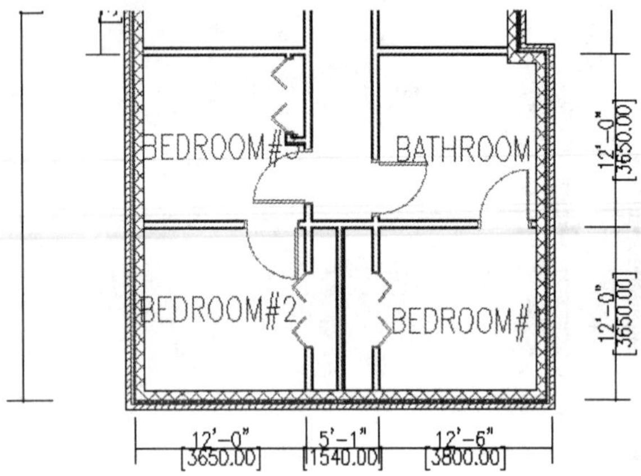

6. Save the file *ex3-6.dwg*.

Exercise 3-7:

Create an Arched Opening Tool

Drawing Name: ex3-6.dwg
Estimated Time: 10 minutes

This exercise reinforces the following skills:

- Copying Tools
- Tool Properties

1.  Open *ex3-6.dwg*.

2. 

Locate the **Cased Opening** tool on the Doors tab of the Tool Palette.

3. 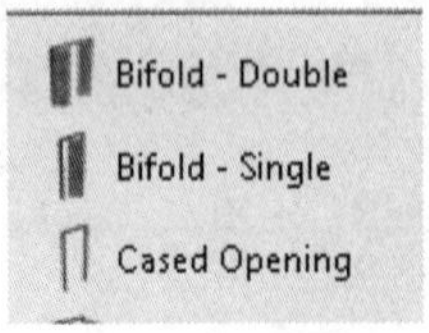

Right click and select **Copy**.

4. 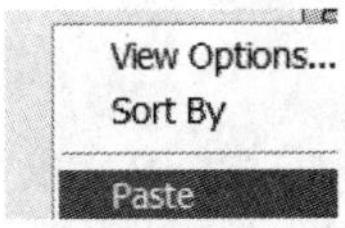

Select the **Doors** tab.
Right click and select **Paste**.

5. 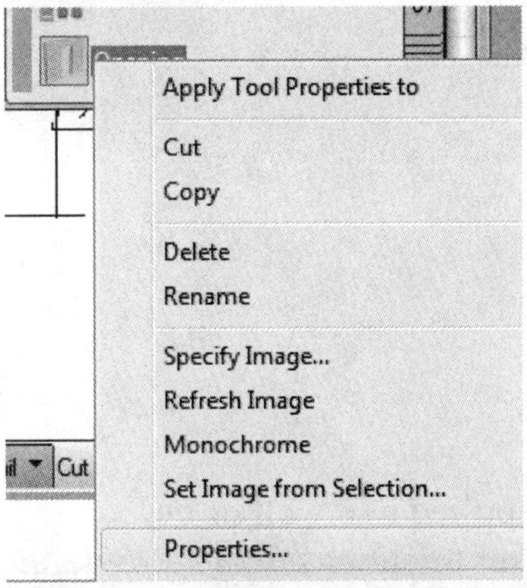

Highlight the copied tool.
Right click and select **Properties**.

6. 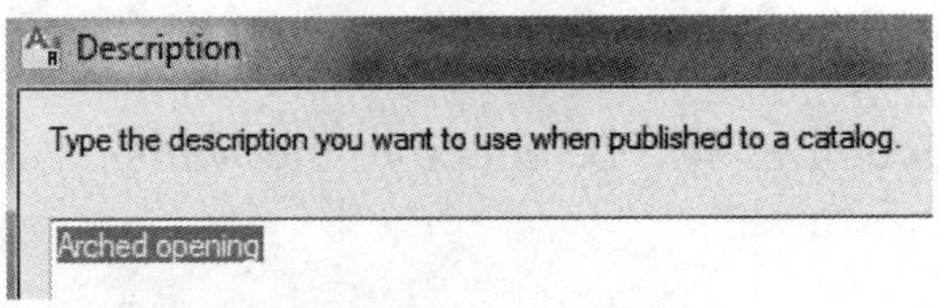

Change the Name to **Arched Opening**.
Change the Description to **Arched Opening**.
Press **OK**.

7. 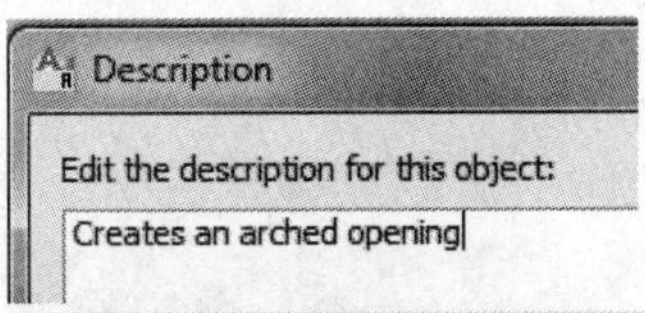

Expand the General section.
Set the Description to **Creates an Arched Opening**.

8. 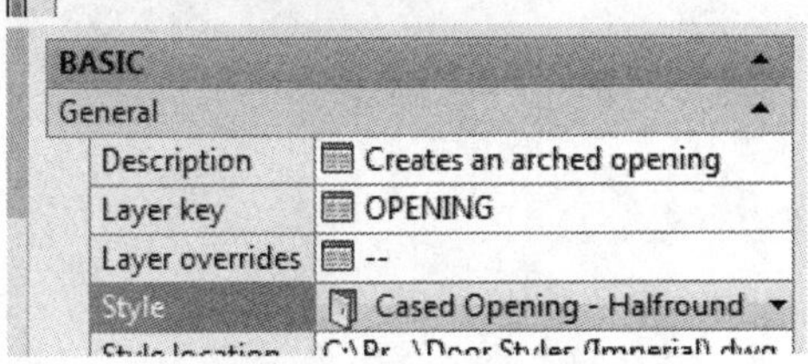

Set the Layer key to **OPENING**.
Set the Style to **Cased Opening-Half round**.

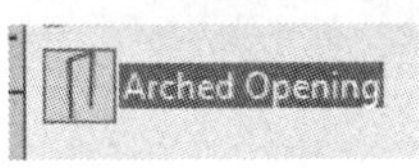

The tool is defined in the palette.

9. Save as *ex3-7.dwg*.

Exercise 3-8:
Adding an Opening

Drawing Name: ex3-7.dwg
Estimated Time: 10 minutes

This exercise reinforces the following skills:

- Adding Openings
- Opening Properties
- Copying Tools
- Set Image from Selection

Openings can be any size and elevation. They can be applied to a wall or be freestanding. The Add Opening Properties allow the user to either select a Pre-defined shape for the opening or use a custom shape.

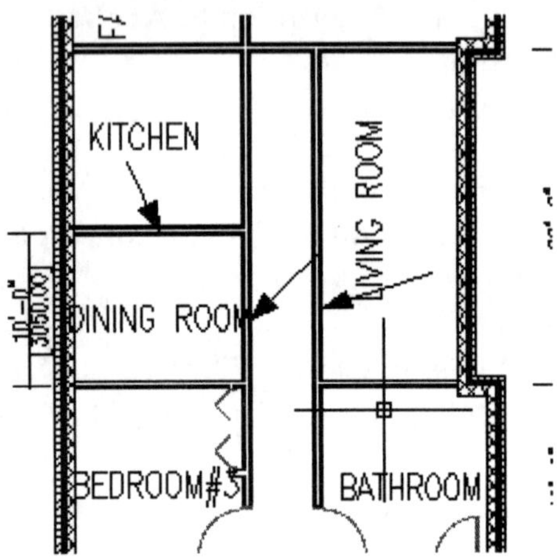

Openings will be added to the walls indicated.

1.  Open *ex3-7.dwg.*

2. 

Select the **Arched Opening** tool.

3. 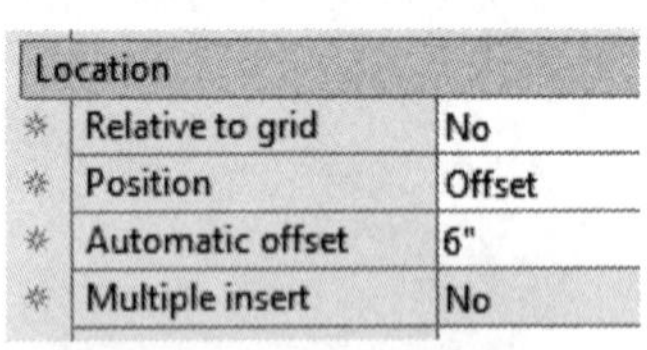

Expand the Location section.
Set the Position to **Offset**.
Set the Automatic offset to **6″ [300.00].**

4. 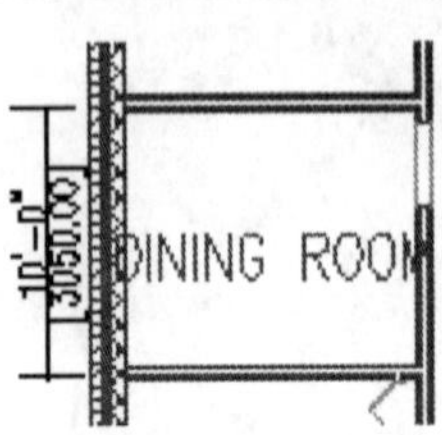

Place the arched opening in the dining room wall.

5. Use the View tools on the View ribbon **View→SW Isometric** and **3D orbit** to view the arched opening.

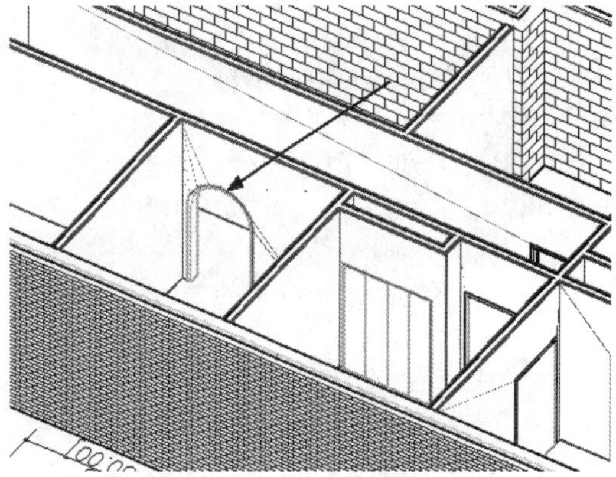

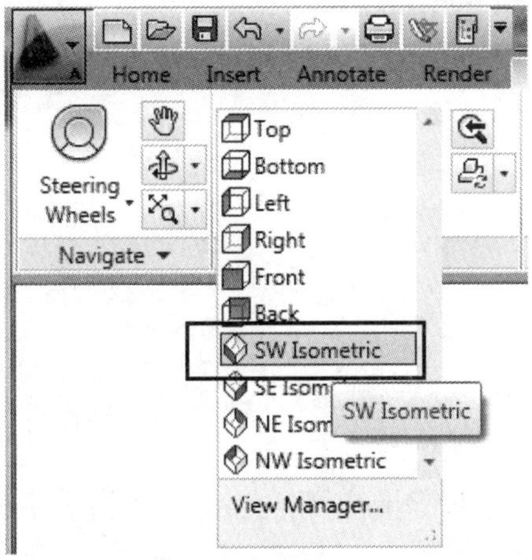

6. 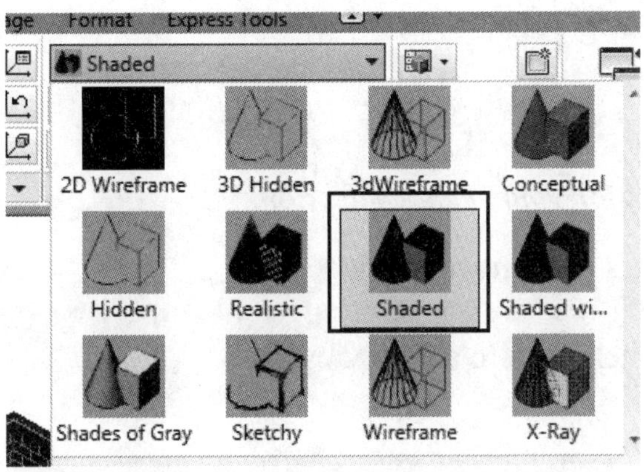

On the View ribbon:

Switch to a **Shaded** display.

If your walls are reversed, you can change the orientation in the plan/top view.

7. 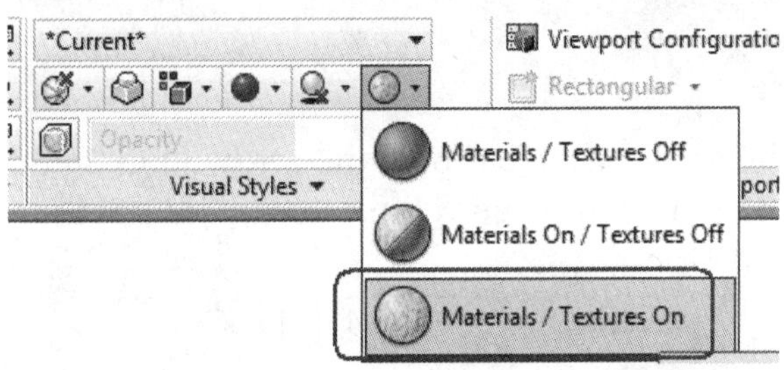

Set the **Materials/Textures On**.

8. 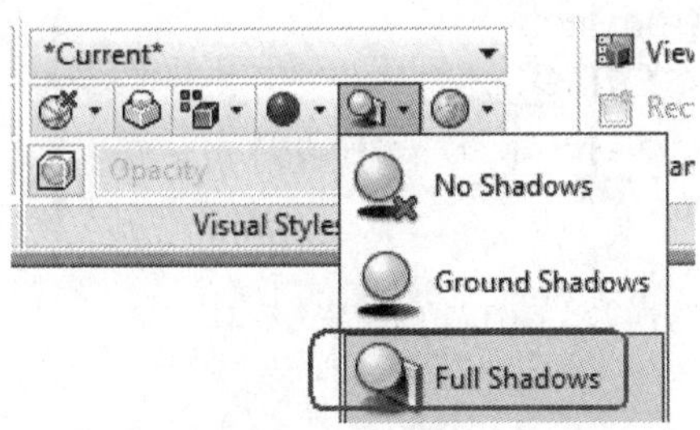

Set to **Full Shadows**.

Note how the display changes.

When materials, textures, and shadows are enabled, more memory resources are used.

9. 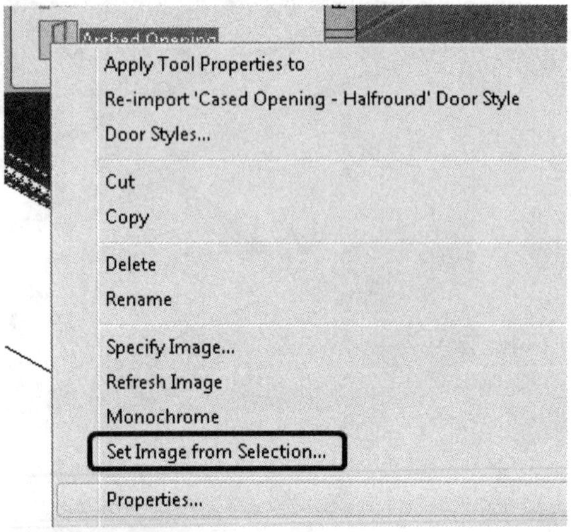

Select the **Arched Opening** icon on the tool palette.
Right click and select **Set Image from Selection…**
Pick the arched opening you created.

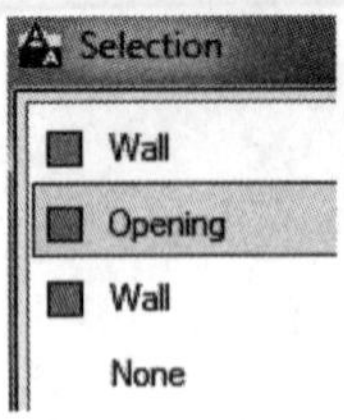

A dialog box allows you to choose which object to use for the image selection.

Select **Opening**.

Press **Enter**.

You can select more than one object for your image selection.

10. 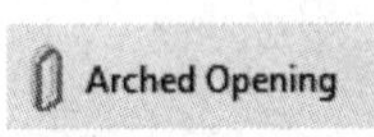

The tool icon updates with the new image.

11. 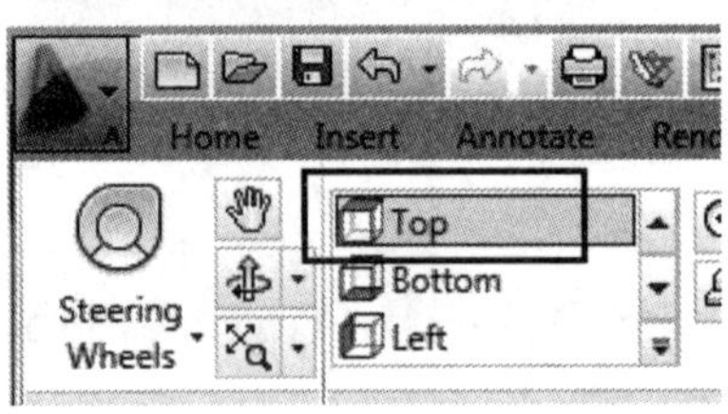

Switch back to a **Top** view.

To flip a wall orientation, simply select the wall and pick the arrow icon that appears in the center of the door. The arrow indicates the exterior side of the wall.

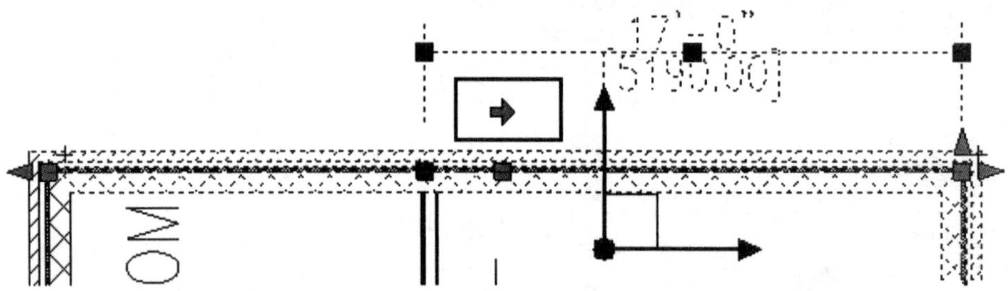

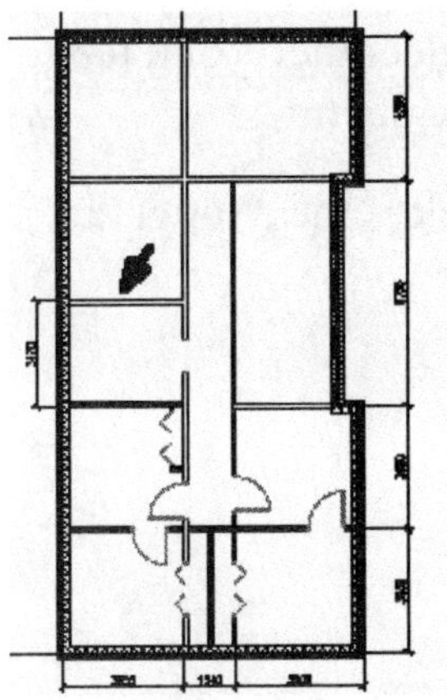

Next we place a rectangular opening in the location indicated.

12. Cased Opening — Select the **Cased Opening** tool from the Doors tool palette.

13.

Dimensions		
	Standard sizes	3'-6" X 6'-8"
A	Width	3'-6"
B	Height	6'-8"
	Measure to	Inside of frame
	Opening percent	50

Expand the Dimensions section.
Select the Standard sizes of **3′6″ x 6′8″**

Dimensions		
	Standard sizes	1000.00 X 2200.00
A	Width	1000.00
B	Height	2200.00
	Measure to	Inside of frame
	Opening percent	50

[1000.00 X 2200.00].

14.

Location	
Relative to grid	No
Position	Center
Multiple insert	No
Vertical alignment	Threshold
Head height	7'-0"
Threshold height	0"
Rotation	0.00

Expand the Location section.
Set the Position to **Center**.

15.

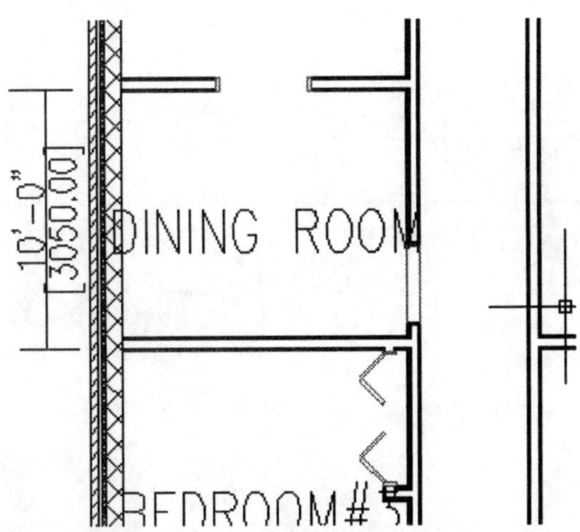

Place the opening in the wall between the kitchen and the dining room.

16. 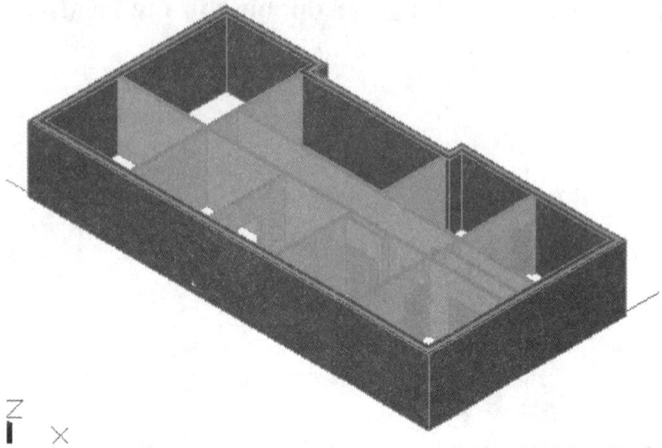

Select the **Work** tab to view the openings.

Select the **Model** tab.

17. 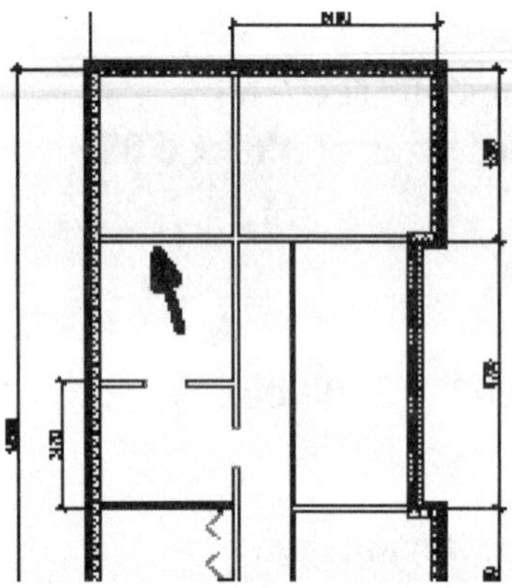

Place a rectangular opening between the kitchen and the family room.

18. 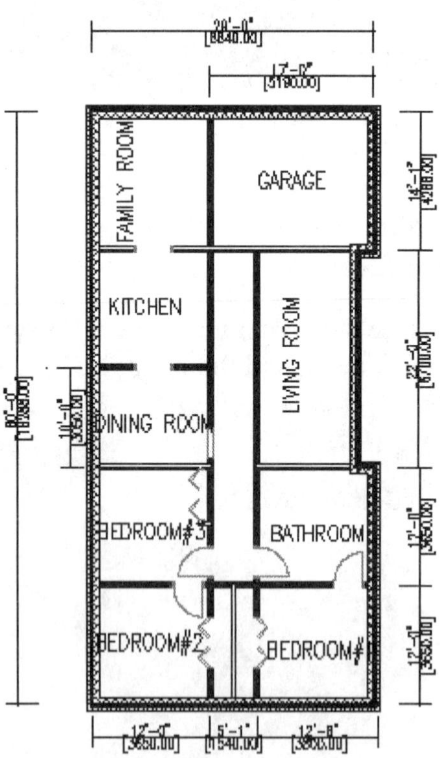

This is our floor plan so far.

Save the file as *ex3-8.dwg.*

Exercise 3-9:
Adding Doors

Drawing Name: ex3-8.dwg
Estimated Time: 20 minutes

This exercise reinforces the following skills:

- Adding Doors

1.  Open *ex3-8.dwg.*

2. 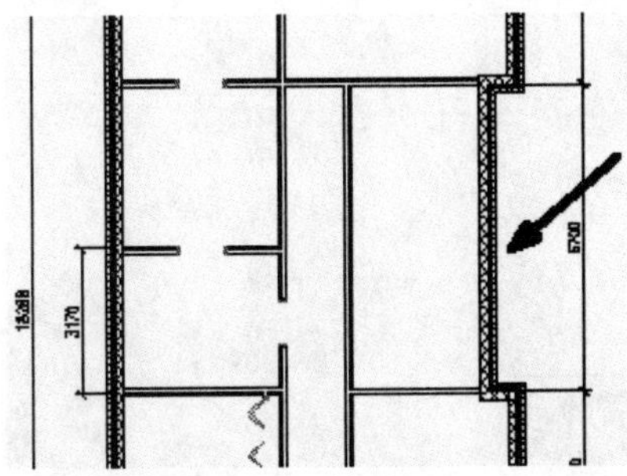 We will add an entry door on the wall indicated.

3. 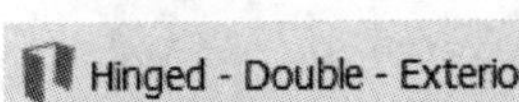

Select the **Hinged-Double-Exterior** door.

4. 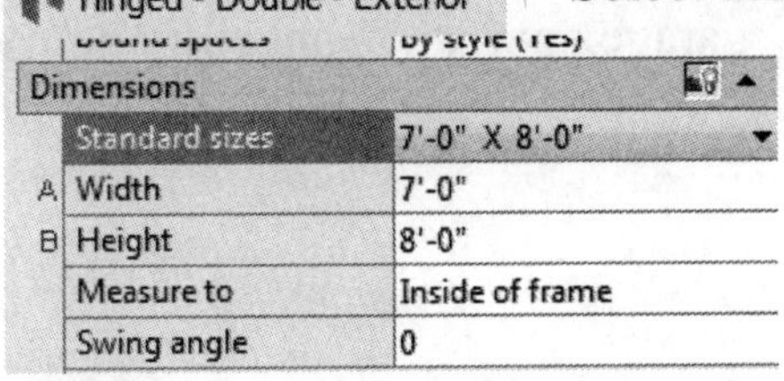

Expand the Dimensions section.
Set the Standard size to **7′-0" x 8′-0" [1800.00 x 2200.00]**.
Set the Swing angle to **0**.

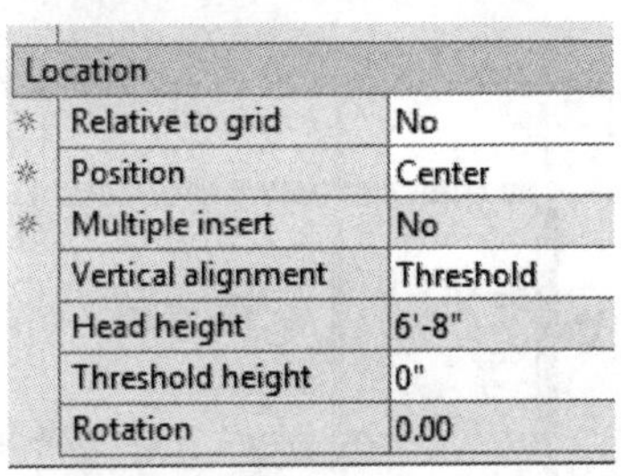

Expand the Location section.
Set the Position to **Center**.

5. 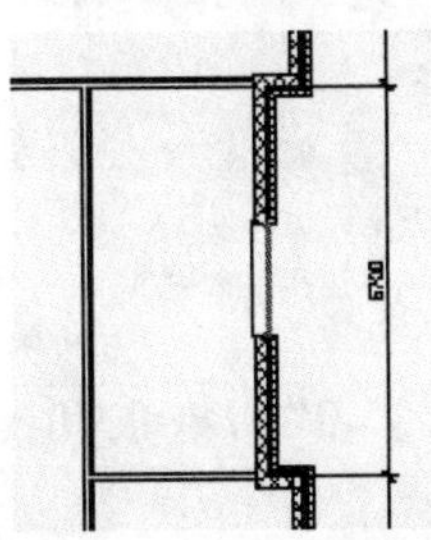 Place the door so it is centered in the wall.

6. 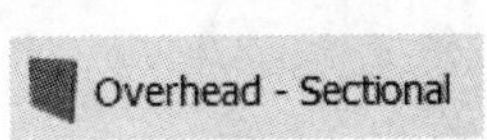

Select the **Overhead - Sectional** door.

7.

Dimensions		
	Standard sizes	8'-0" X 7'-0"
A	Width	8'-0"
B	Height	7'-0"
	Measure to	Inside of frame
	Opening percent	0

Expand the Dimensions section.
Set the Standard size to **8′ 0″ x 7′-0″ [2440.00 x 2134.00]**.
Set the Swing angle to **0**.

8.

Location		
*	Relative to grid	No
*	Position	Center
*	Multiple insert	No
	Vertical alignment	Threshold
	Head height	8'-0"
	Threshold height	0"
	Rotation	0.00

Set the Position along wall to **Center**.

9. 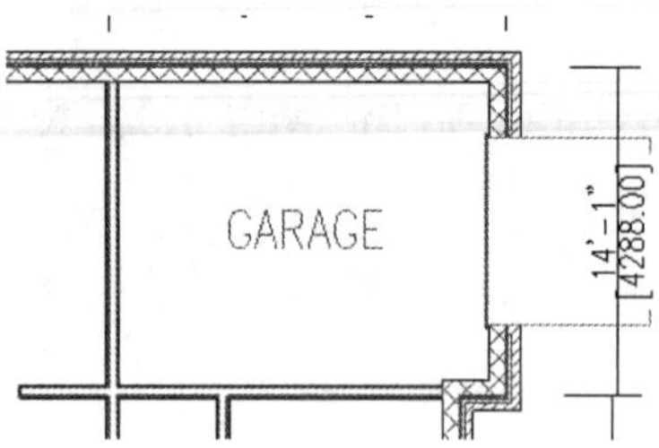

Place the door in the garage wall.

10. 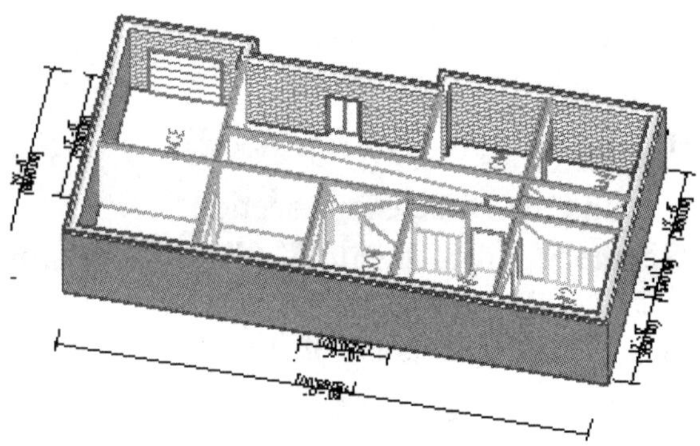

Switch to the Work tab to view the garage door and front entry door.

Switch back to the Model tab.

11. Next we add a sliding door to the family room wall indicated.

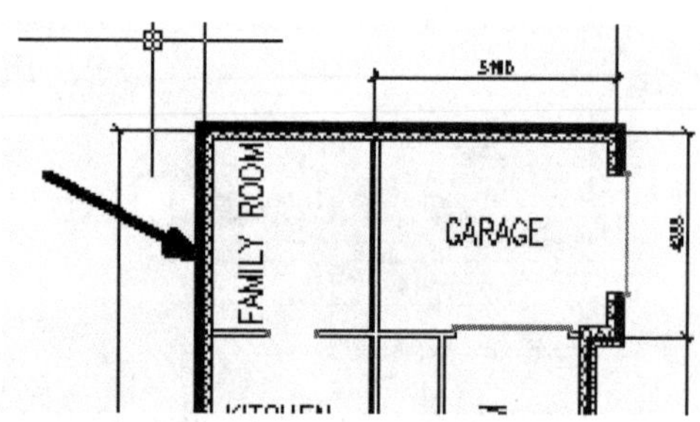

12. Select a **Sliding Door - Double - Full Lite** to add to the family room.

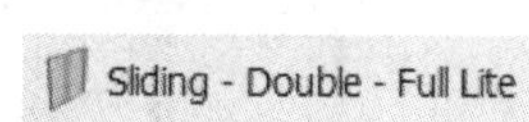

13.

Dimensions		
	Standard sizes	6'-0" X 7'-0"
A	Width	6'-0"
B	Height	7'-0"
	Measure to	Inside of frame
	Opening percent	0

Expand the Dimensions section.
Set the Standard size to **6′-0″ x 7′-0″ [1800.00 x 2200.00]**.
Set the Swing angle to **0**.

14. 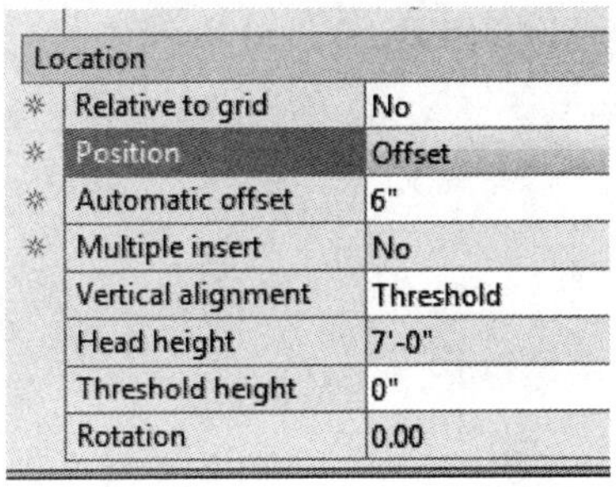

Expand the **Location** section.
Set the Position to **Offset**.
Set the Automatic offset to **6″ [300]**.

15. 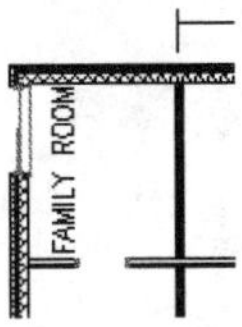

Place the sliding door.

16. 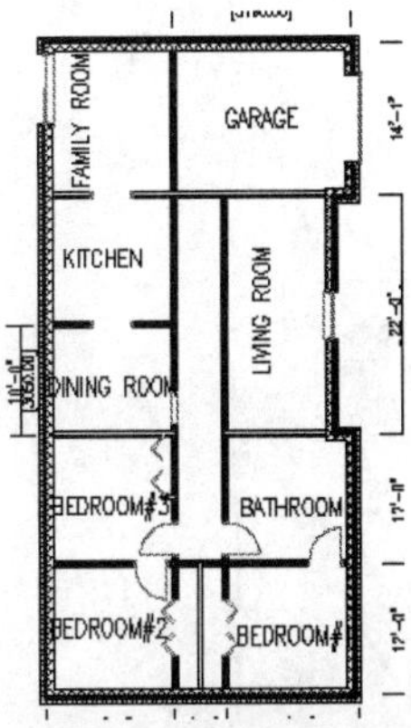

If your doors don't look proper, use the Display Manager to modify the appearance.

17. 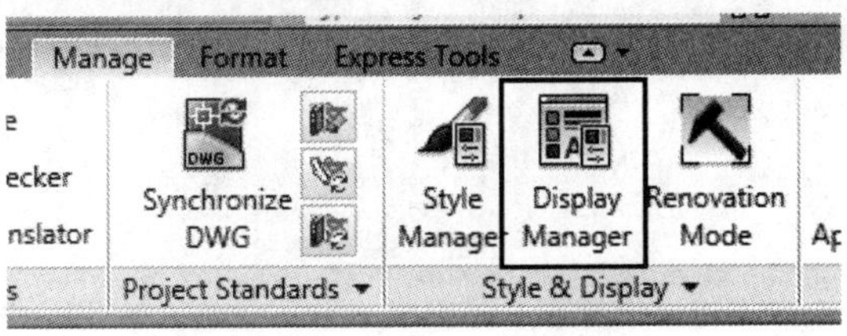

Activate the Manage ribbon.

Select **Display Manager**.

18. 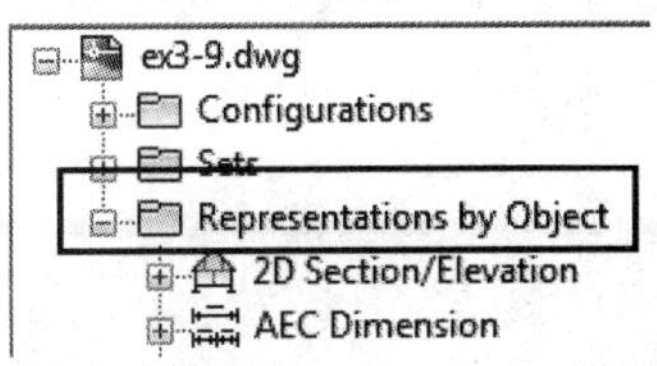

Expand the **Representations by Object** folder.

Scroll down to **Doors**.

19. 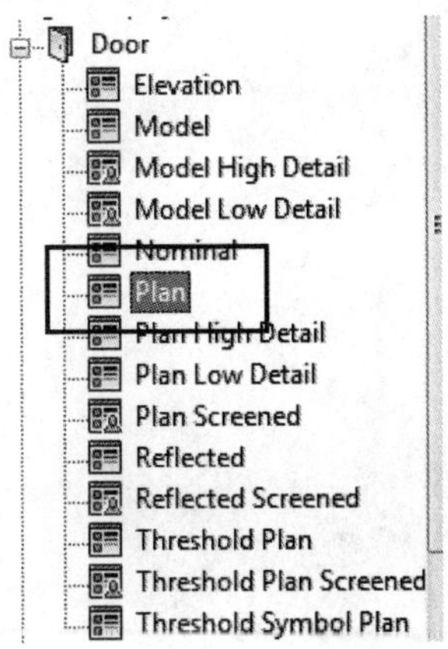

Highlight the **Plan** view.

Note you can control how doors appear in different views.

20. 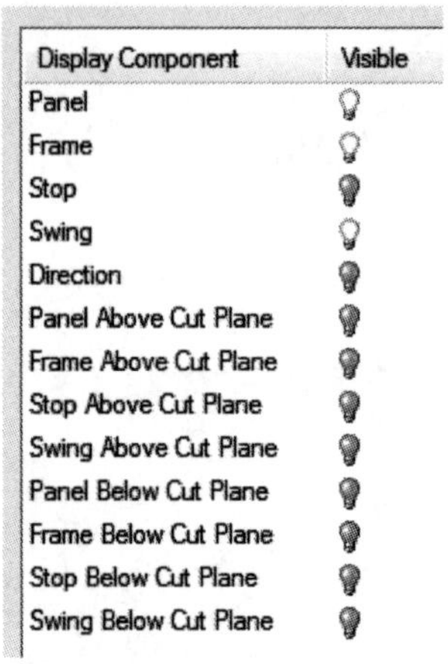

Note you can turn the visibility of different door components on or off.

21. Press **Apply** and **OK**.

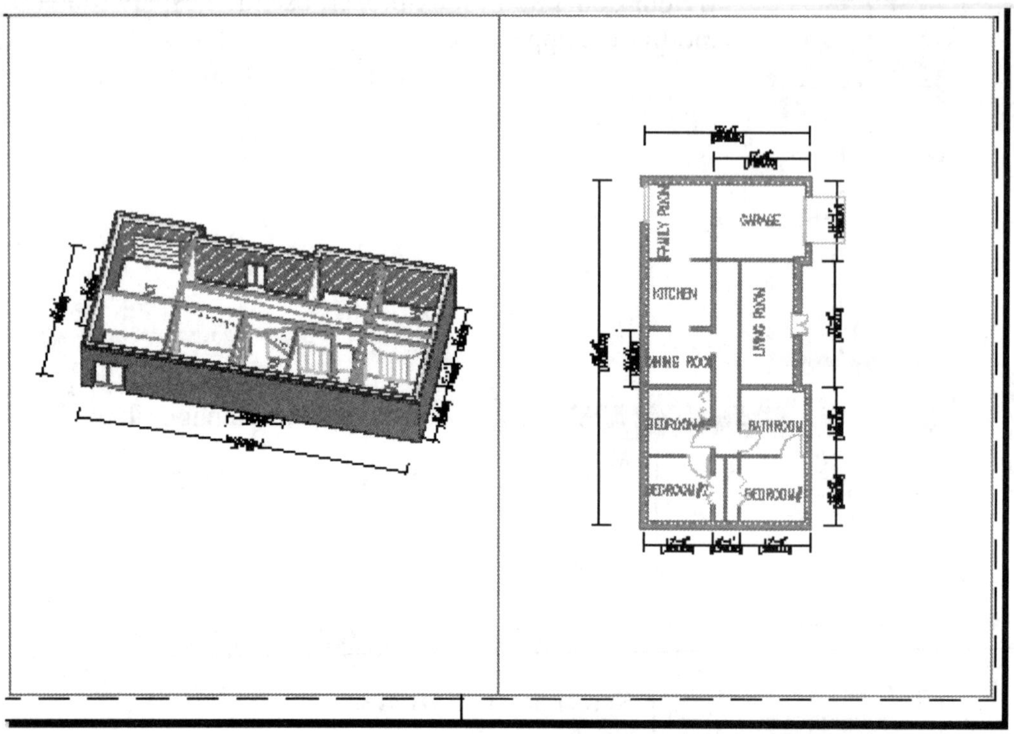

22. Select the Work tab to view your model. 

23. Save the file as *ex3-9.dwg.*

Exercise 3-10
Add Window Assemblies

Drawing Name: Lesson 3-9dwg
Estimated Time: 30 minutes

This exercise reinforces the following skills:

- Add Windows

1.  Open *ex3-9.dwg.*

2.  Select the Model tab.

3. 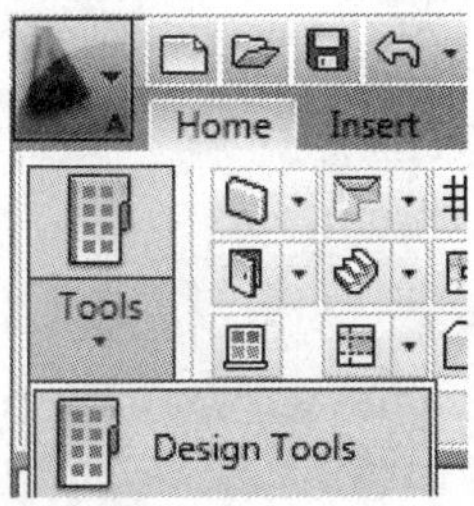

Activate the **Design Tools** from the Home ribbon, if they are not launched.

4. 

Select the Windows tab of the Tool Palette.

5. 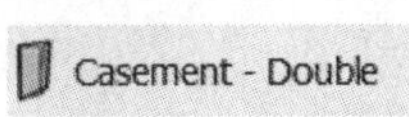

Select the **Casement-Double** window.

6. 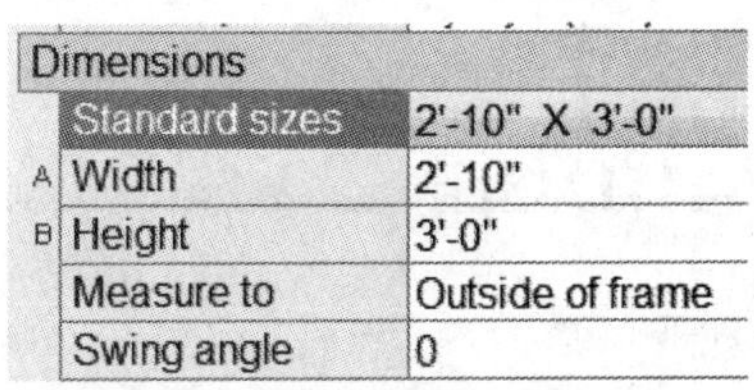

Expand the Dimensions section.
Set the size to **2′-10″ x 3′-0″ [600 x 900]**.

7. 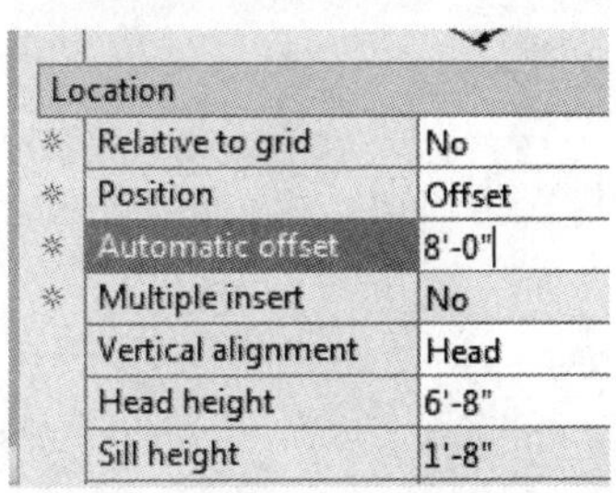

Expand the Location section.
Set the Position to **Offset**.
Set the Automatic Offset to **8′-0″ [2510.00]**.

8. 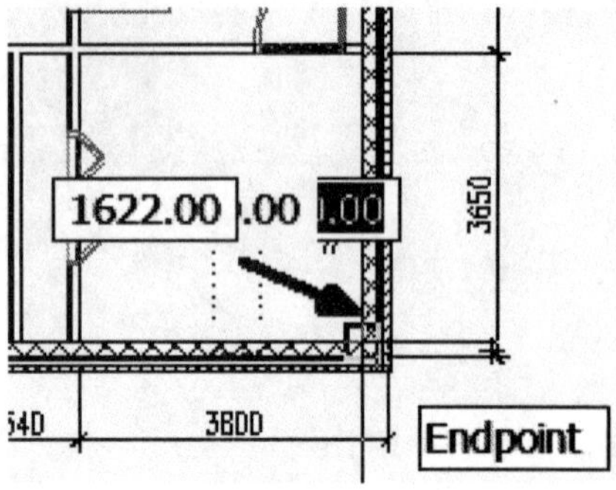

Select the wall shown and the endpoint indicated.

The endpoint is where the offset is calculated from.

9. Select the **Casement-Double** window again

10. 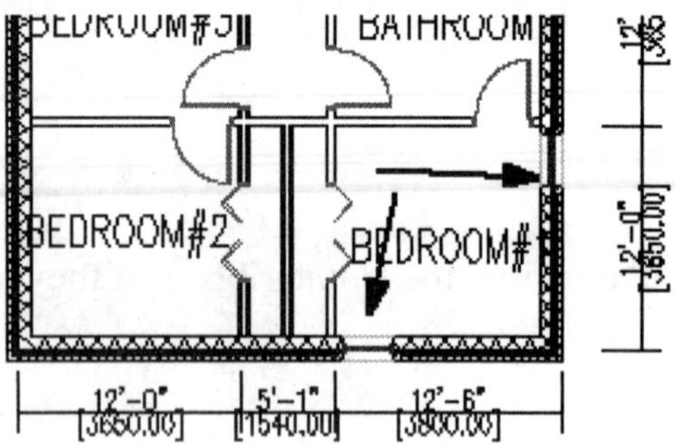

Place the window on the vertical bedroom wall.

Remember – if you don't like the position of any of the Windows, you can reposition them. Just select the window, right click, and select **Reposition Along Wall.**

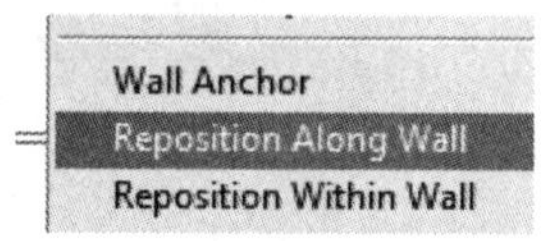

11. 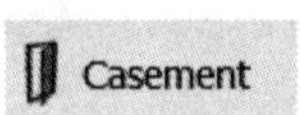

Select the **Casement** window from the Design Palette.

12. 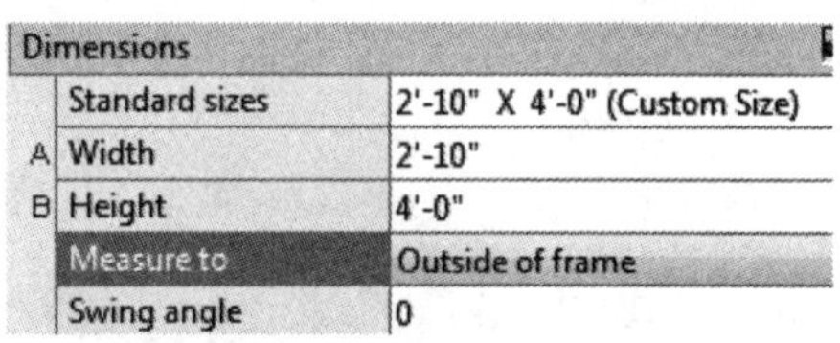

Expand the Dimensions section.
Set the size to **2′-10″ x 4′-0″ [600.00 x 1200.00]**.

13. 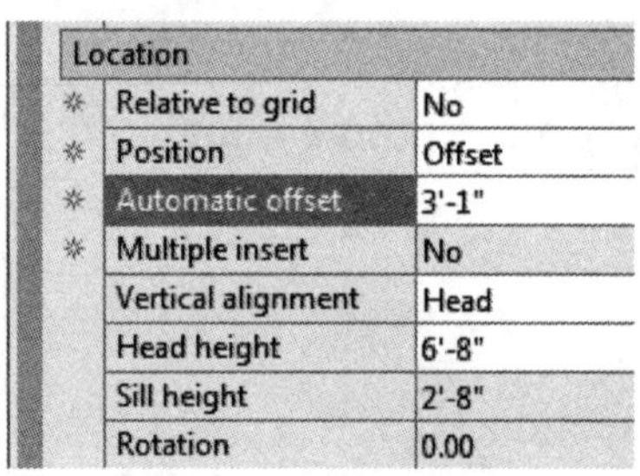

Expand the Location section.
Set the Position to **Offset**.
Set the Offset to **3′-1″ [1215]**.

14. 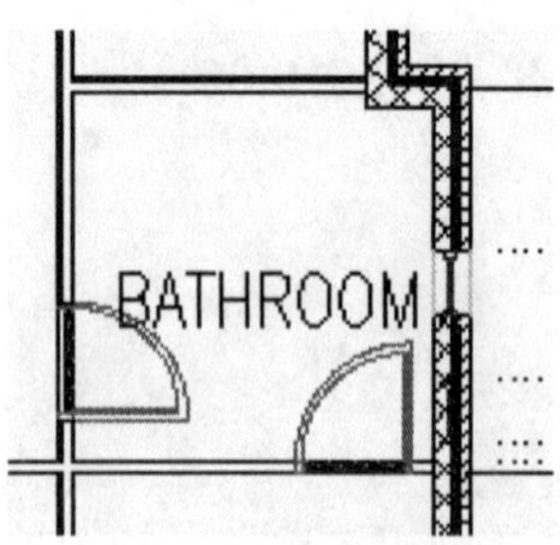

Place the window in the bath wall.

15. Place a Double Casement window in Bedroom #2.

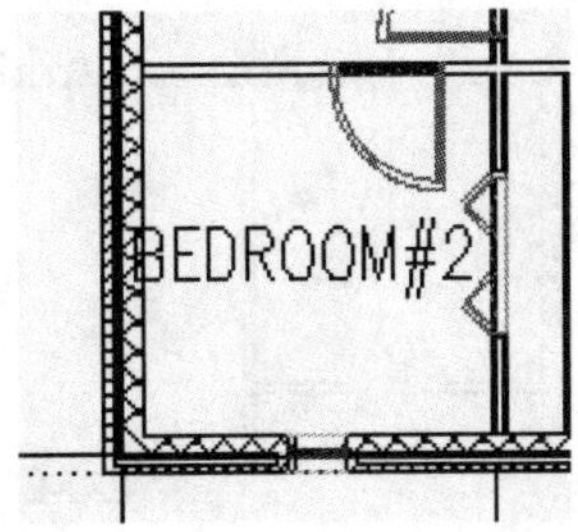

16. 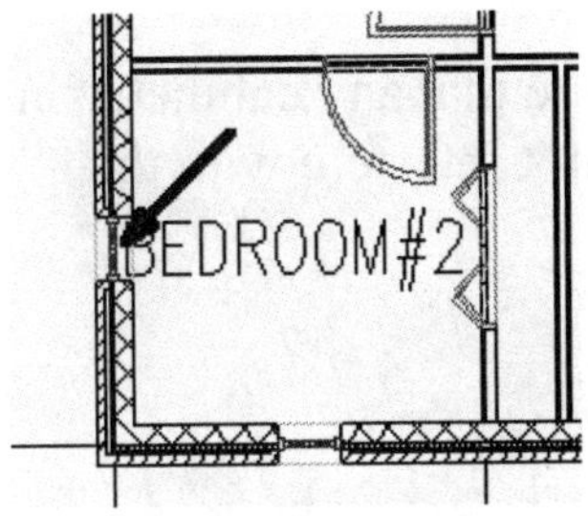

Place a Double Casement window in Bedroom #2 on the left vertical wall.

17. Place a Double Casement window in Bedroom #3 on the left vertical wall.

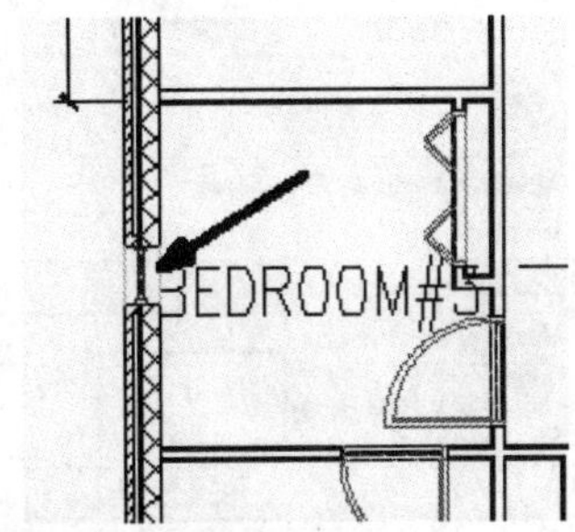

18. 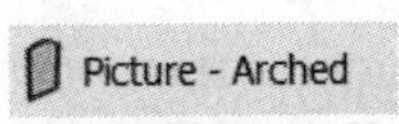

Locate the **Picture- Arched** to place in the left dining room wall.

19. 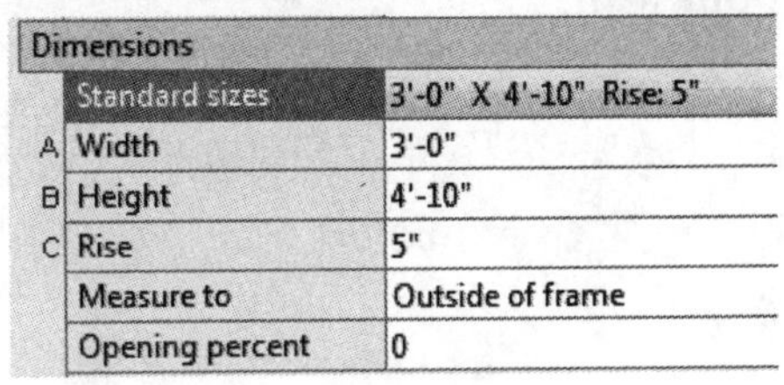

Dimensions		
	Standard sizes	3'-0" X 4'-10" Rise: 5"
A	Width	3'-0"
B	Height	4'-10"
C	Rise	5"
	Measure to	Outside of frame
	Opening percent	0

Expand the Dimensions section.
Set the size to **3′-0″ x 4′10″ Rise: 5″ [600.00 x 1500.00 Rise 300.00]**.

20. 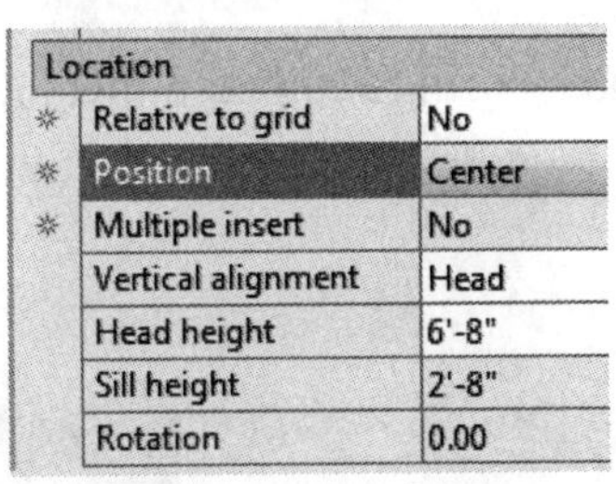

Location		
*	Relative to grid	No
*	Position	Center
*	Multiple insert	No
	Vertical alignment	Head
	Head height	6'-8"
	Sill height	2'-8"
	Rotation	0.00

Expand the Location section.
Set the Position to **Center**.
Set the Offset to **0″ [0.00]**.

21. 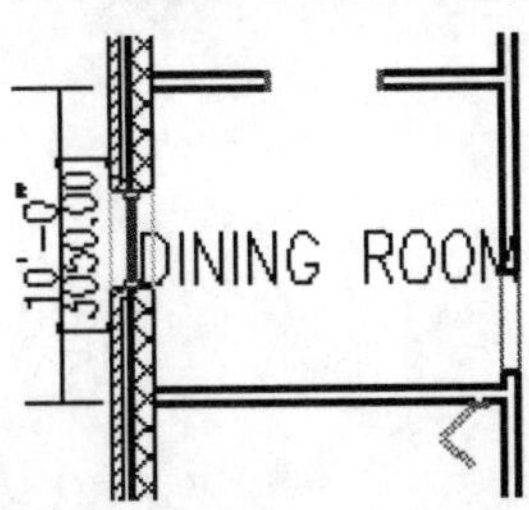

Place the window.

22. 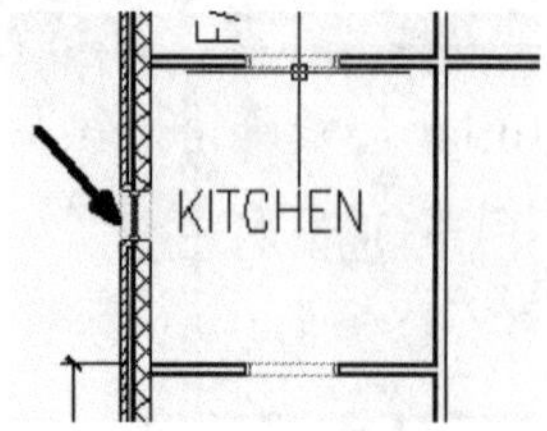

Add a **Casement: Single** window to the kitchen.

23. 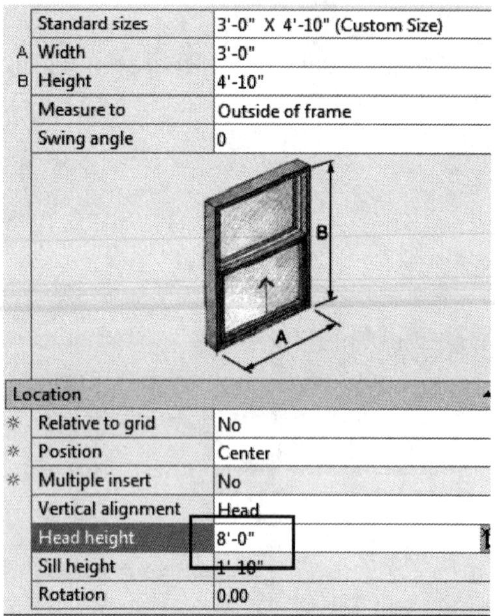

Set the Head height to **8′-0″ [2050]**.

This will ensure that any cabinetry in the kitchen does not interfere with the window.

24. 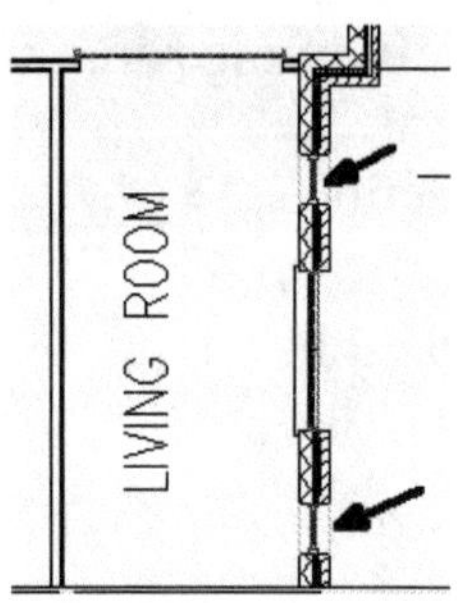

Place an **Arched Picture** window on each side of the entry door in the right living room wall.

25. 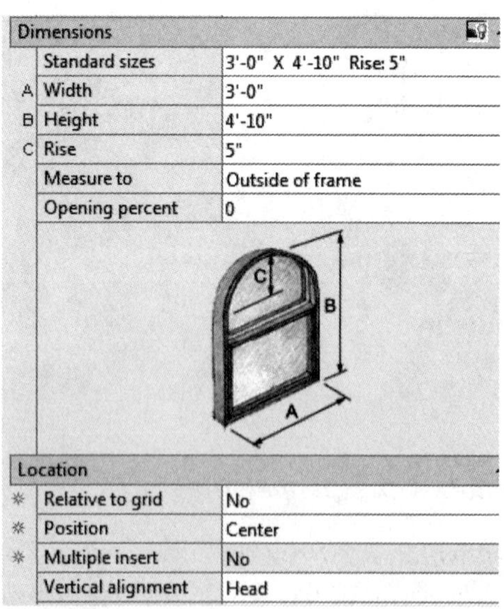

Use the previous settings to place the windows.

26. 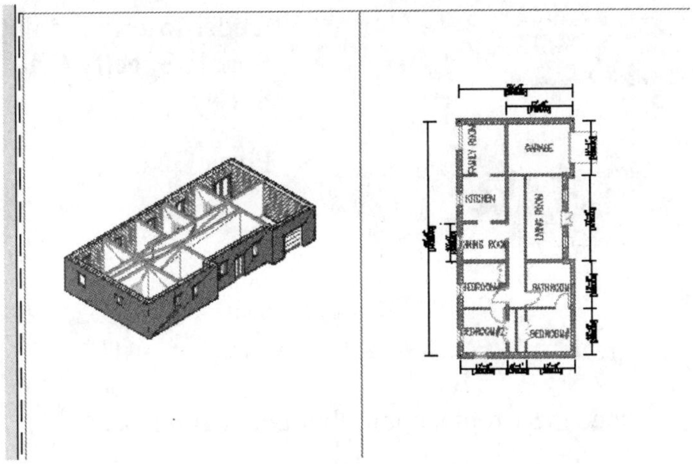

Your floor plan should look similar to the one shown here.

Save as *ex3-10.dwg*.

Exercise 3-11:

Adding a Fireplace

Drawing Name: ex3-10.dwg
Estimated Time: 20 minutes

This exercise reinforces the following skills:

- Using the Design Center
- Adding Openings

In this exercise, we add a fireplace to the family room. You can download the fireplace from the publisher's website.

1.  Open *ex3-10.dwg.*

   Select the Model tab.

2. 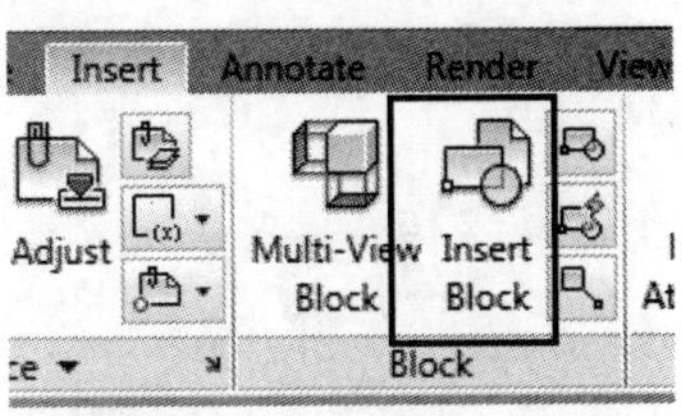

   Activate the **Insert** ribbon.

   Select **Insert Block.**

3. 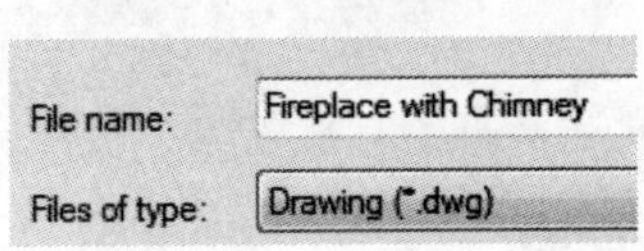

   Locate the *Fireplace with Chimney* file.

   This file can be downloaded from the book's detail page on the publisher's website at www.SDCpublications.com.

4. 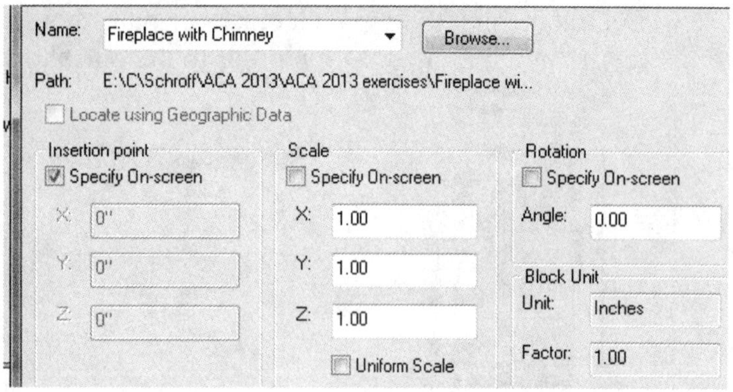

Under Insertion point: Enable **Specify On-Screen**.

Press **OK**.

5. 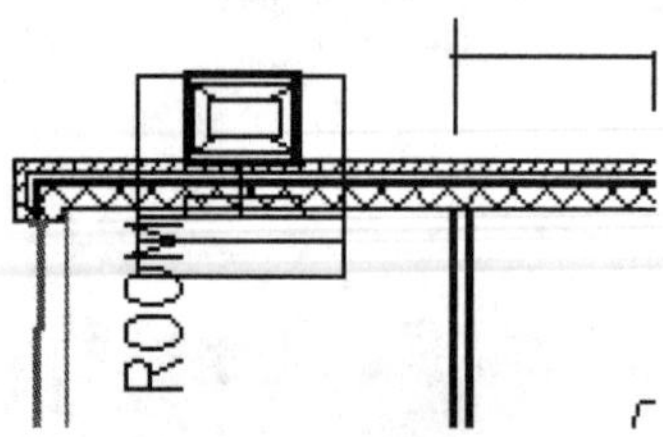

Place the fireplace into the family room wall.

Use a midpoint osnap to help place the fireplace. You can also Shift-right click to select a midpoint snap on the fly.

6. 

Set the display to **Shaded**.

7. 

Use the ViewCube tool to inspect your work so far.

8. 

Use the 3D Orbit tool to inspect how the fireplace appears.

We need to add an opening

Switch back to a plan view.

9. 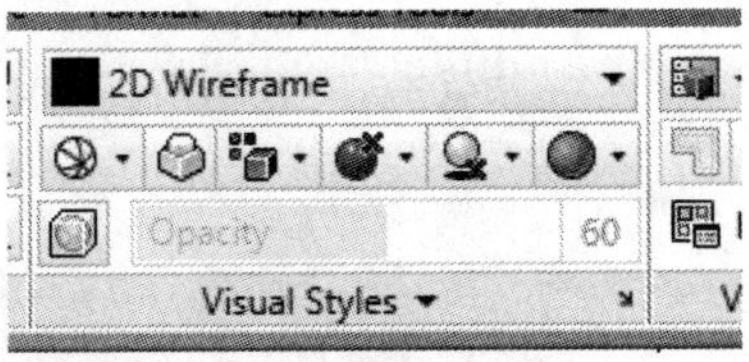

Set the display to **2D Wireframe**.

10. 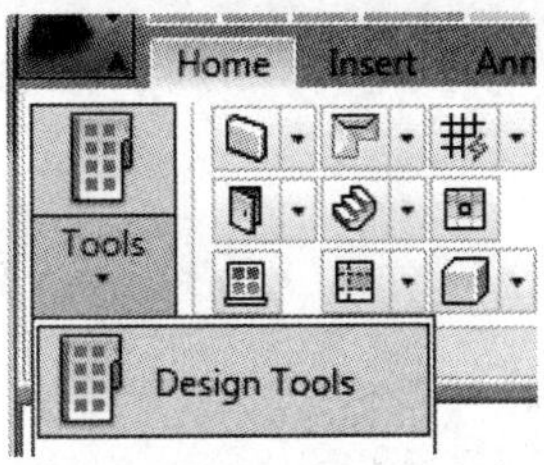

Activate the Home ribbon.

Launch the Design Tools palette.

11. 

Select the **Opening** tool from the Design Palette.

12. 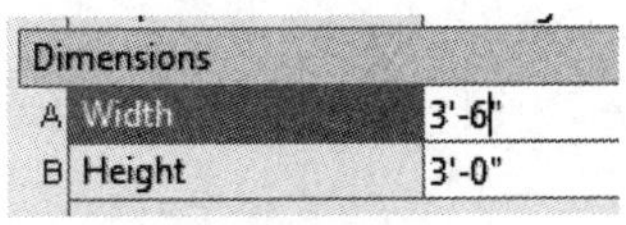

Change the Width to **3′-6″ [914.4]**.
Change the Height to **3′-0″ [862.6]**.

13. 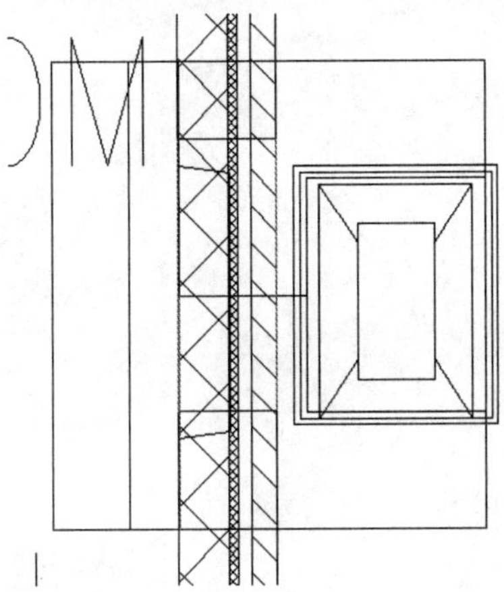

Place the opening in the wall.

14. 

Select the Home icon to switch to a 3D view.
Then use the ViewCube to inspect the opening in the fireplace.

Your finished fireplace and chimney should look similar to this.

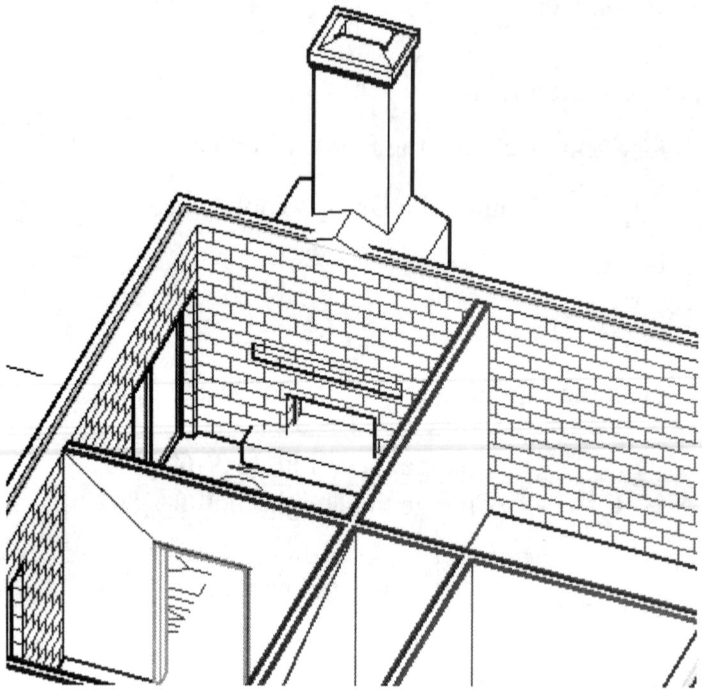

15. Save the file as *ex3-11.dwg*.

Close all open drawings.
You can do this by typing **CLOSEALL** on the command line.

Lesson 4
Space Planning

A residential structure is divided into three basic areas:

- Bedrooms: Used for Sleeping and Privacy
- Common Areas: Used for gathering and entertainment, such as family rooms and living rooms, and dining area
- Service Areas: Used to perform functions, such as the kitchen, laundry room, garage, and storage areas

When drawing your floor plan, you need to verify that enough space is provided to allow placement of items, such as beds, tables, entertainment equipment, cars, stoves, bathtubs, lavatories, etc.

AutoCAD Architecture comes with Design Content to allow designers to place furniture to test their space.

Exercise 4-1:
Creating AEC Content

Drawing Name: new
Estimated Time: 20 minutes

This lesson reinforces the following skills:

- Design Center
- AEC Content
- Customization

1.  Start a new drawing using **QNEW**.

2. 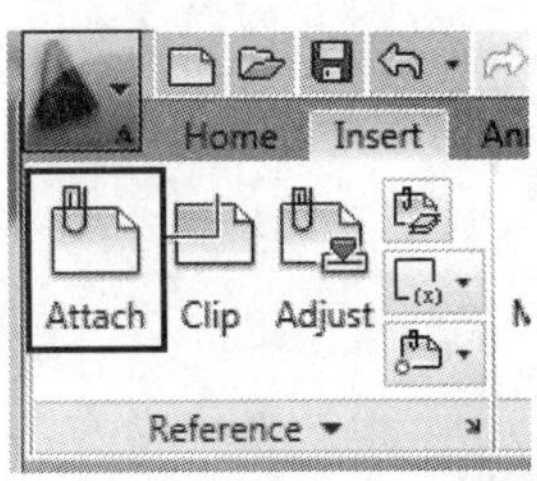

Activate the Insert ribbon.

   Select **Attach**.

3. 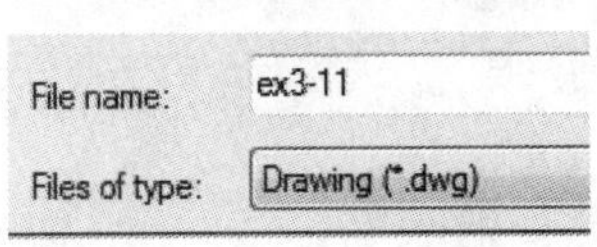

Browse for *ex3-11.dwg* and press **Open**.

4. 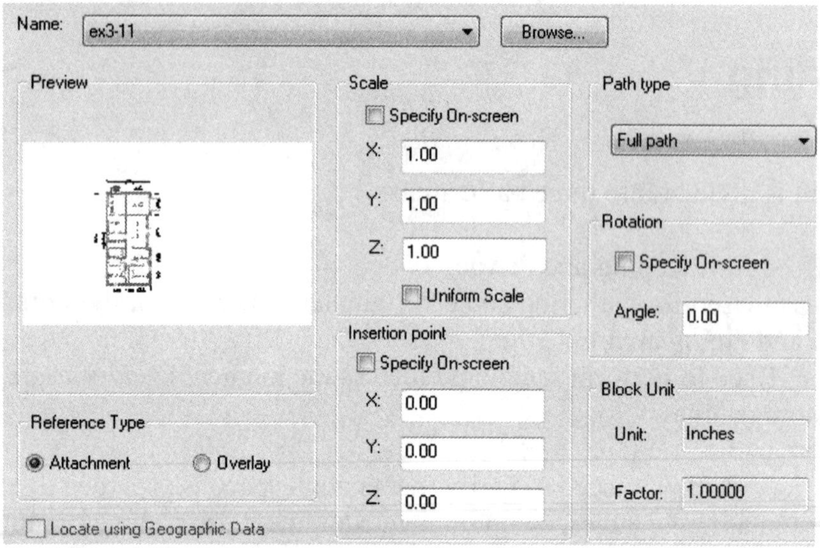

Accept the defaults.

Uncheck **Specify On-screen** for the insertion point.

Press **OK**.

5. 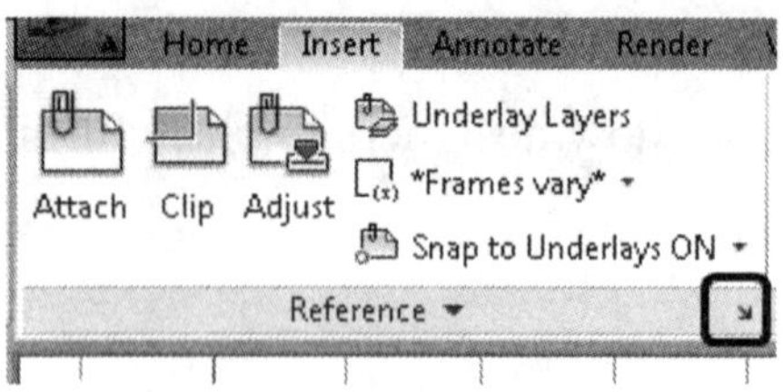

Launch the XREF Manager by selecting the small arrow in the Reference drop-down.

6. The palette lists the file references now loaded in the drawing.

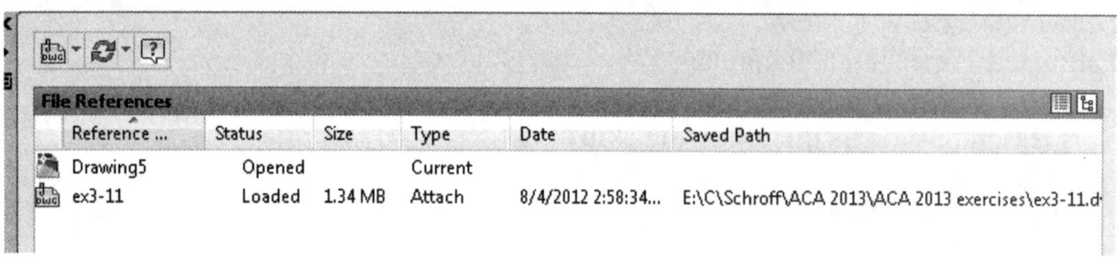

7. 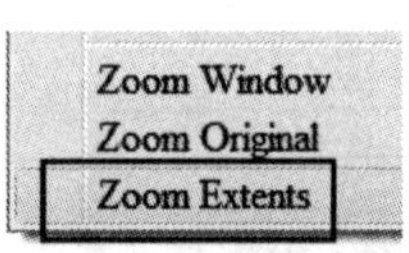

Zoom Extents

8. 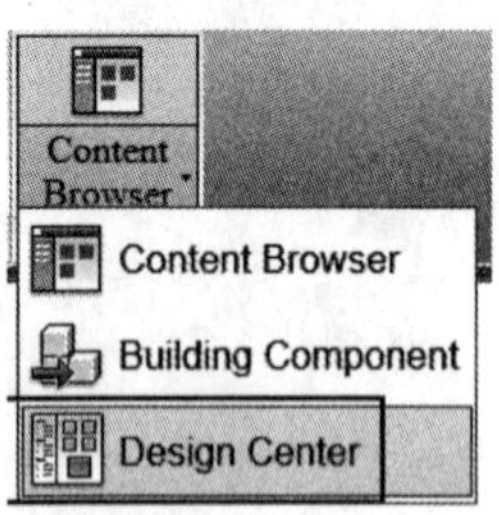

Launch the Design Center from the Insert ribbon or press Ctrl+2.

9. 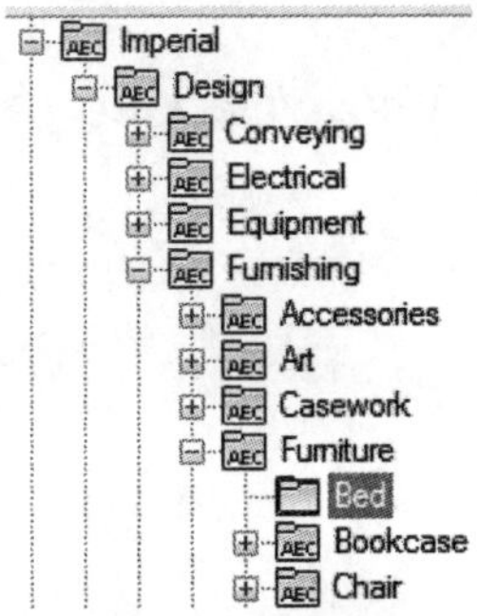

Select the AEC Content tab.

Browse to *AutoCAD Architecture/Imperial/Design/ Furnishing/ Furniture/Bed*

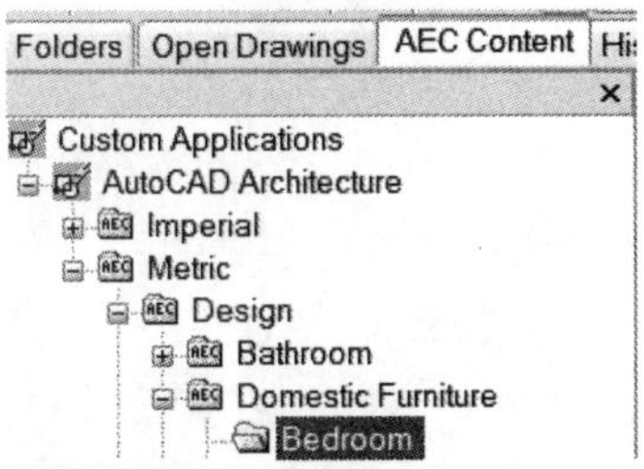

[AutoCAD Architecture/Metric/Design/Domestic Furniture/Bedroom].

10. 

Select the *Double [3D Double Bed].dwg* file.
Right click and select **Insert**.

11. 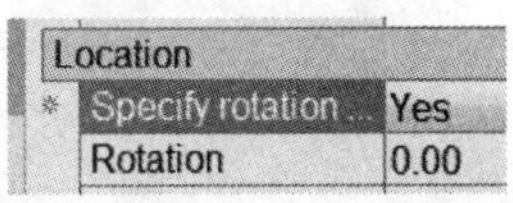

Set Specify rotation to **Yes** in the Properties dialog.

12. 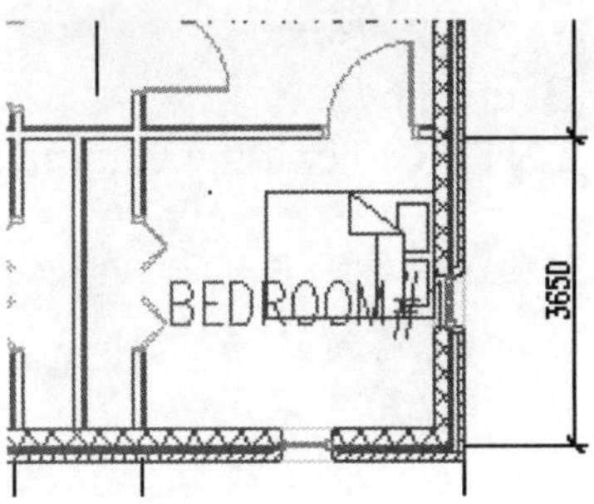

Place the bed in Bedroom #1.

Right click and select ENTER to exit the command.

13. 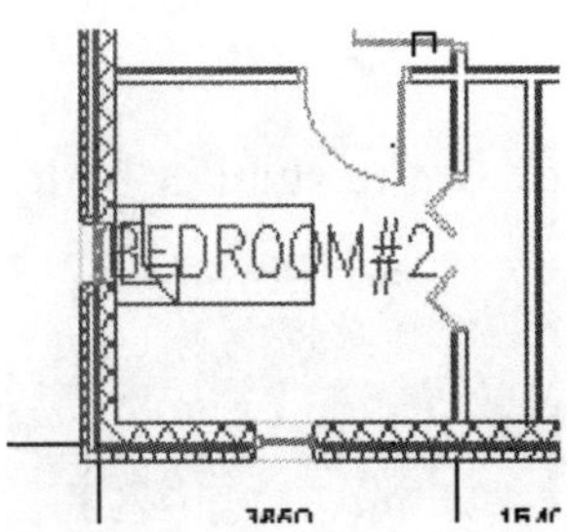

Locate the *Twin [3D Single Bed].dwg.*

Drag and drop it into Bedroom #2 as shown.

14. 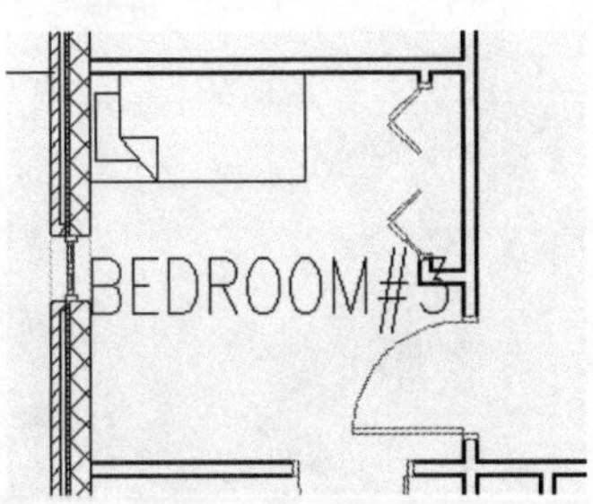

Place the *Twin* [*3D Single Bed.dwg]* in Bedroom#3.

Right click and select ENTER to exit the command.

15. 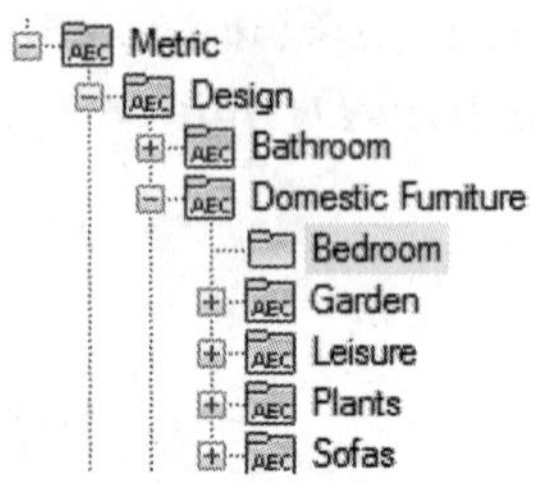

Browse to the *Bedroom* folder in the *Metric/Design/ Domestic Furniture* folder.

16. 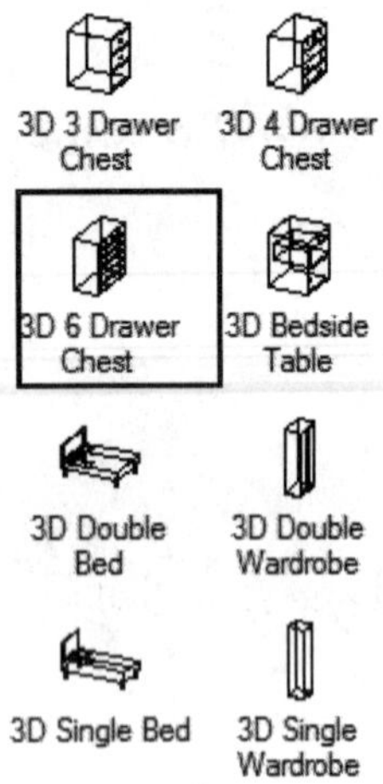

Locate the *3D 6 Drawer Chest.*

17. 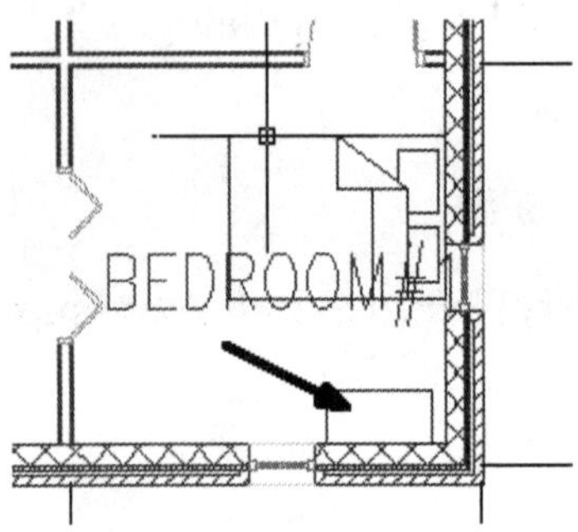

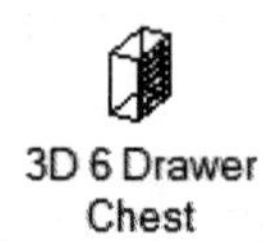

Place a Dresser in the Bedroom#1.
Right click and select ENTER to exit the command.

18. 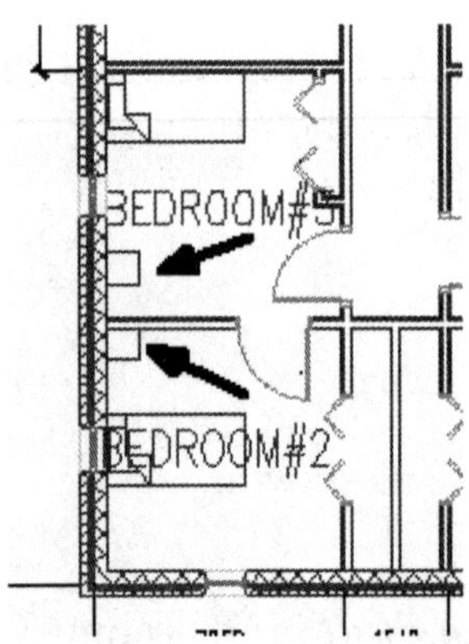

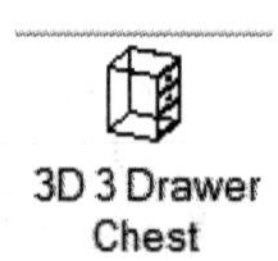

Add a 3D 3 Drawer Chest to each of the smaller bedrooms.

19. 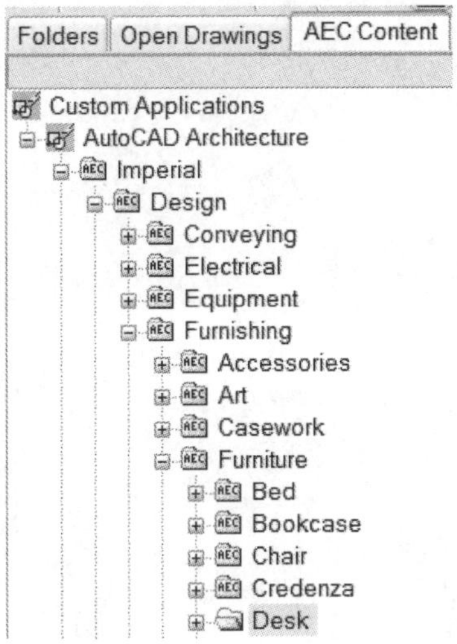

Browse to the *Desk* folder under *AutoCAD Architecture/Imperial/Design/Furnishing/Furniture/.*

20. 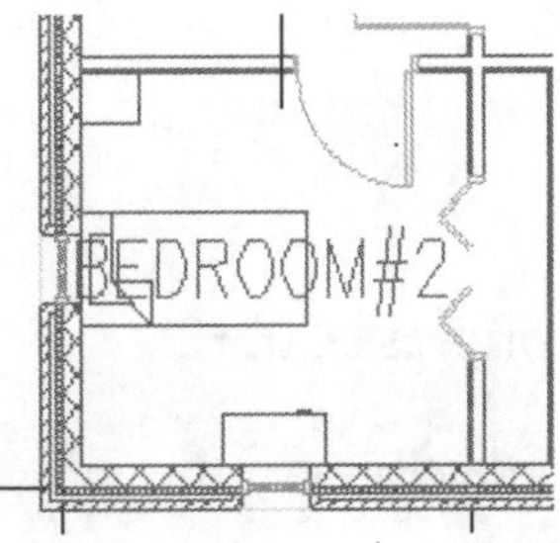

Locate the *36x18 Left.dwg* file under the *Desk* folder. Place into Bedroom #2.

21. 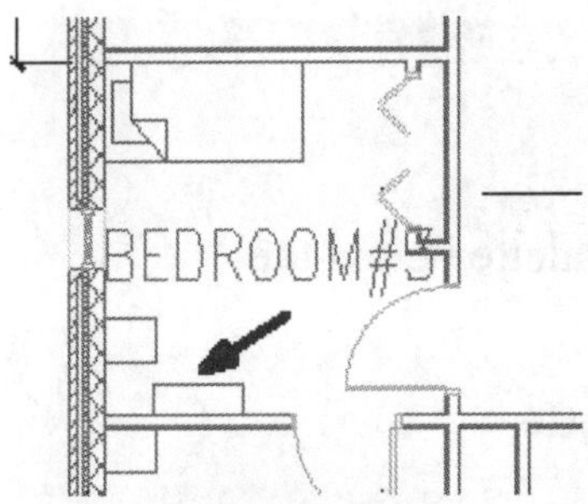

6 Shelves

Locate the *6 Shelves.dwg* bookcase in the *Bookcase* folder.
Place in Bedroom #3.

22. 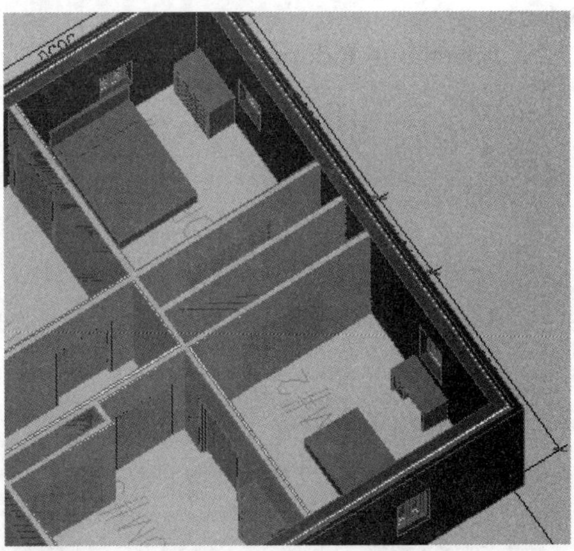

Switch to a 3D view and use 3D Orbit to view the furniture placement.

23. Save as *ex4-1.dwg.*

Exercise 4-2:

Create a Tool Palette

Drawing Name: Ex4-1.dwg
Estimated Time: 30 minutes

This lesson reinforces the following skills:

- Design Center
- Tool Palette
- Customization

1.  Open *ex4-1.dwg.*

2. Select the Model tab.
Switch to a top view.

3.  Launch the **Design Center** from the Insert ribbon or press Ctrl+2.

4. 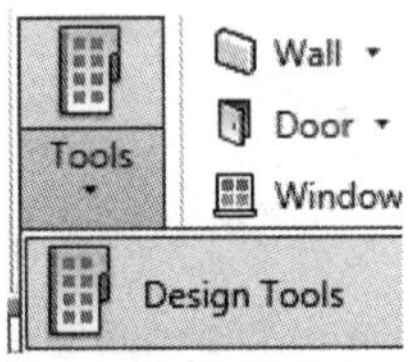

Launch the **Design Tools** from the Home ribbon.

5. 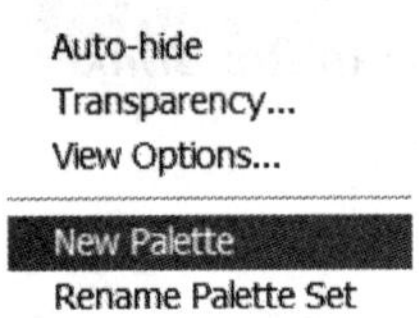

Select the title bar of the Tool Palette below the expand/contract arrows.

Right click and select **New Palette**.

6. 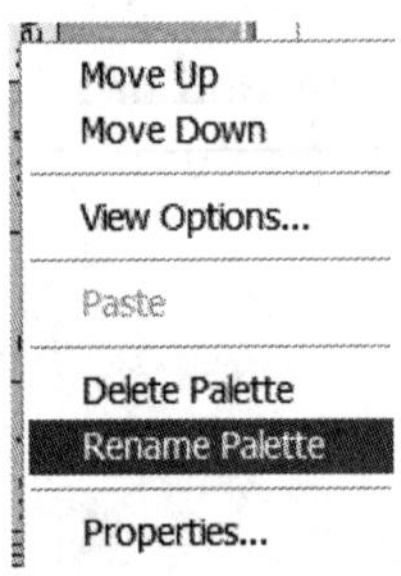

Pick the new palette tab.
Right click and select **Rename Palette**.

7. 

Type **Plumbing**.

8. 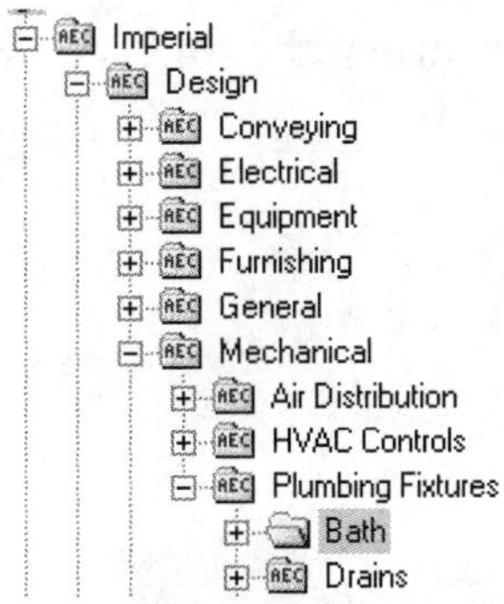

Locate the *Tub 32 x 66* file in the *Imperial/Design/ Mechanical/Plumbing Fixtures/Bath* folder.

9. 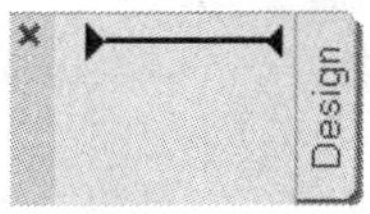

Drag and drop the *Tub 32 x 66* onto the Plumbing Palette. You can release when you see the bar as shown.

10. 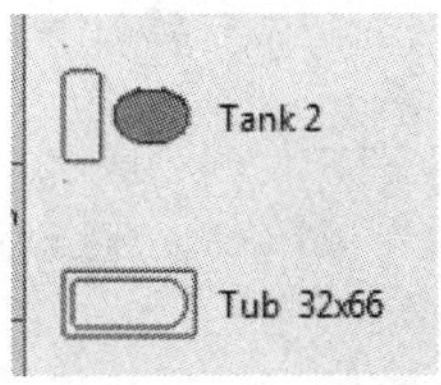

Locate *Tank 2* in the Toilet folder.
Drag and drop onto the Plumbing palette.

11. 

Locate the *32 x 34* shower in the shower folder.
Drag and drop onto the Plumbing palette.

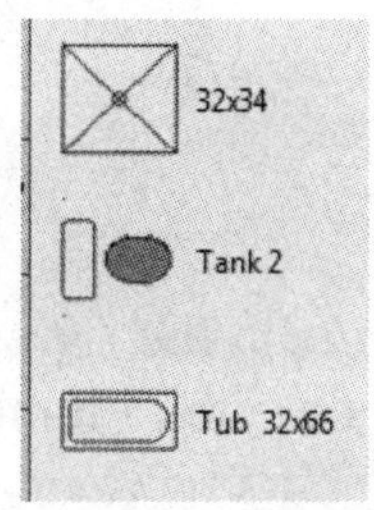

12. 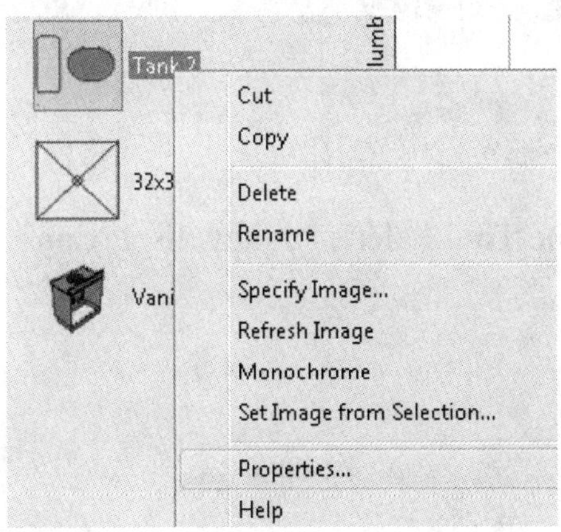

You change how icons appear on the tool palette by using the View options.

Highlight the icon for the Toilet.
Right click and select **Properties**.

13. 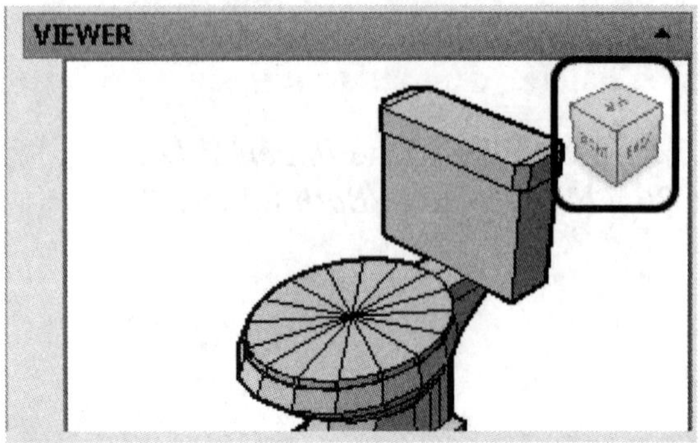

In the Viewer, orient the toilet to the desired view.

Press **OK**.

14. 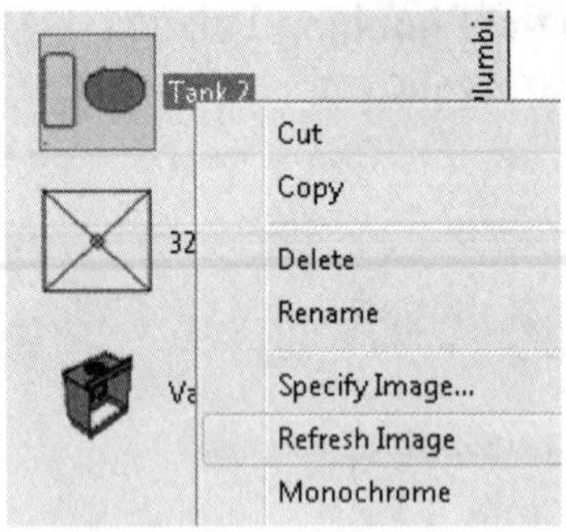

Highlight the toilet icon.

Right click and select **Refresh Image**.

15. 

The image will update.

16. 

Locate the *Vanity* in the *Lavatory* folder. Drag and drop onto the Plumbing palette.

Close the Design Center.

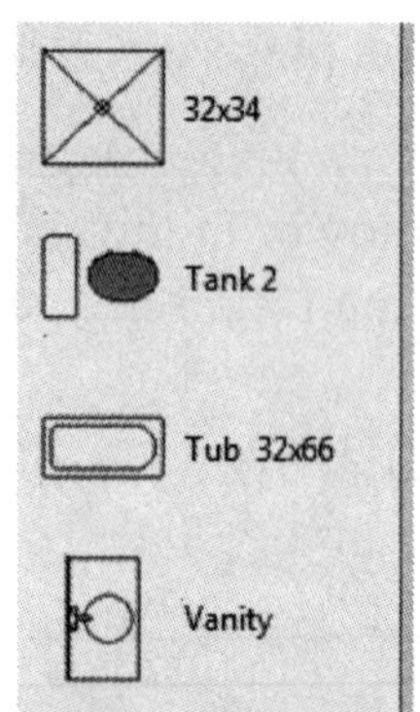

17. 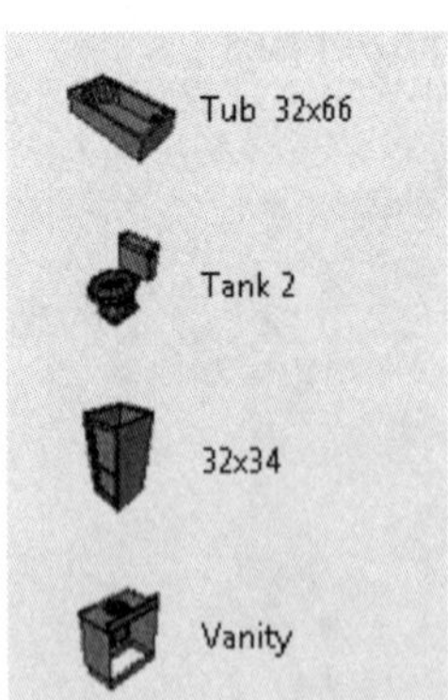

Adjust all the icons on the Tool Palette so they display an isometric view.

18. 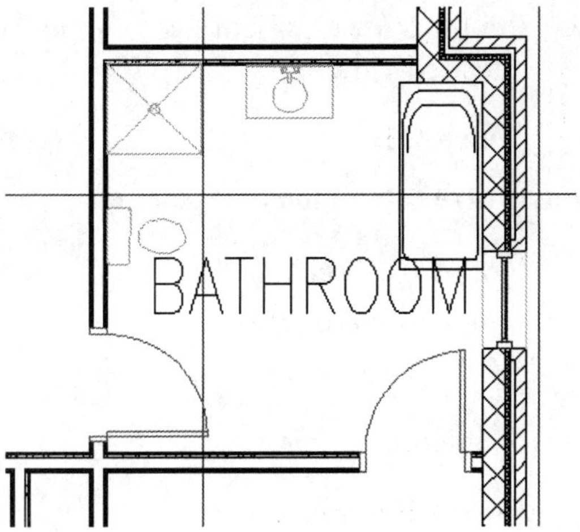

Using the tools on the new Plumbing Palette, equip the bathroom as shown.

19. Save as *ex4-2.dwg*.

TIP: The Space Planning process is not just to ensure that the rooms can hold the necessary equipment, but also requires the drafter to think about plumbing, wiring, and HVAC requirements based on where and how items are placed.

As an additional exercise, place towel bars, soap dishes and other items in the bathrooms.

Exercise 4-3:
Furnishing the Common Areas

Drawing Name: Ex4-2.dwg
Estimated Time: 30 minutes

Common areas are the Living Room, Dining Room, and Family Room.

This lesson reinforces the following skills:

- Design Center
- Tool Palette
- Customization

You will need Internet access in order to complete this exercise.

1. Open *ex4-2.dwg*.
Select the Model tab.
Switch to a top view.

2.  Launch the Design Center.

3.  Launch the Tool Palette

4. 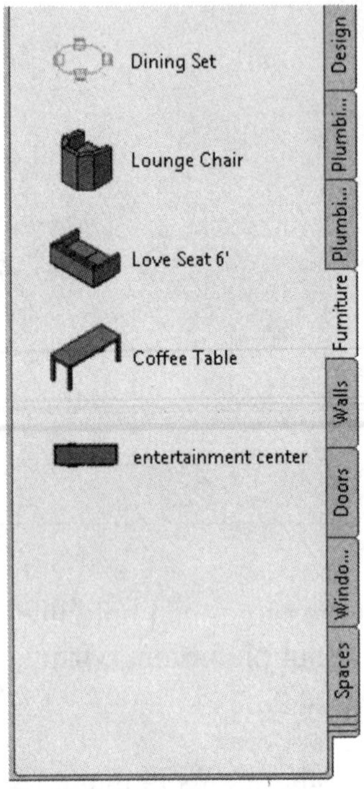

Activate the **Furniture tab** on the tool palette.

If you don't have a furniture tab, you can create one by using New Palette and renaming it.

5. 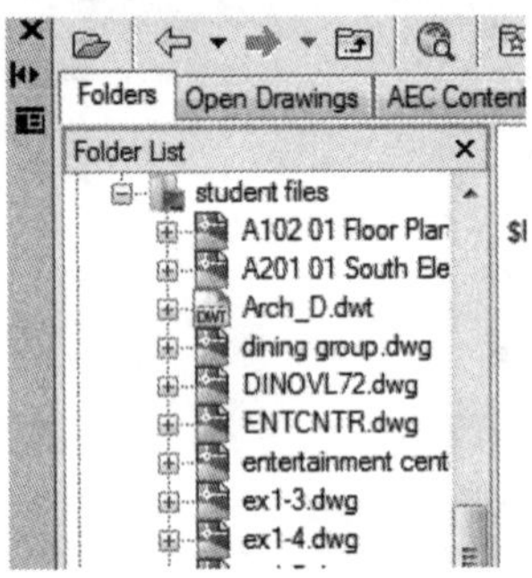

In the Design Center dialog, select the Folders tab.

Browse to the folder where you stored the files downloaded from the publisher.

6. 

Drag and drop the file called **dining group** onto the new palette.

7. Select the dining group tool.
Right click and select **Properties**.

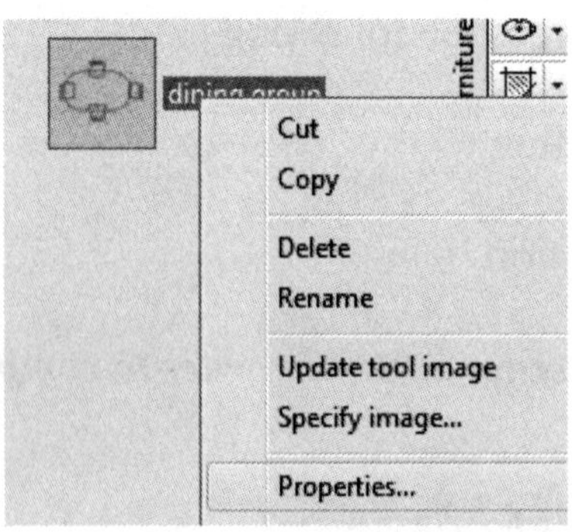

8. 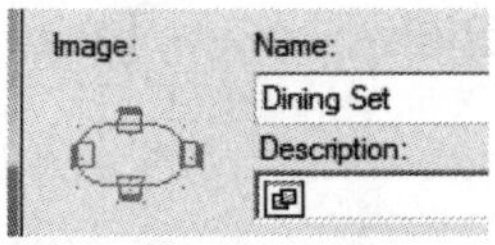

Change the name to **Dining Set**.

9. 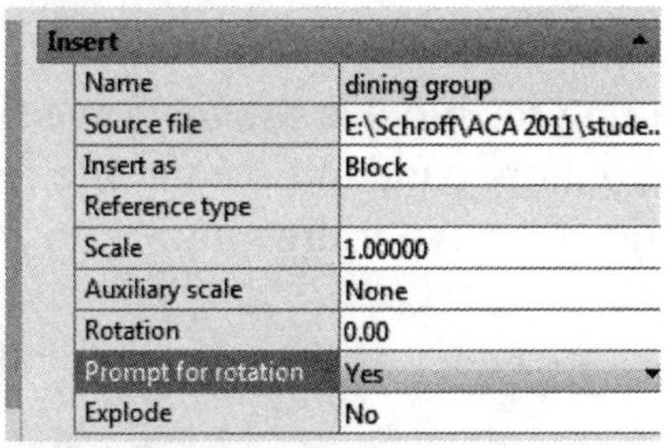

Set the Prompt for rotation to **Yes**.

10. 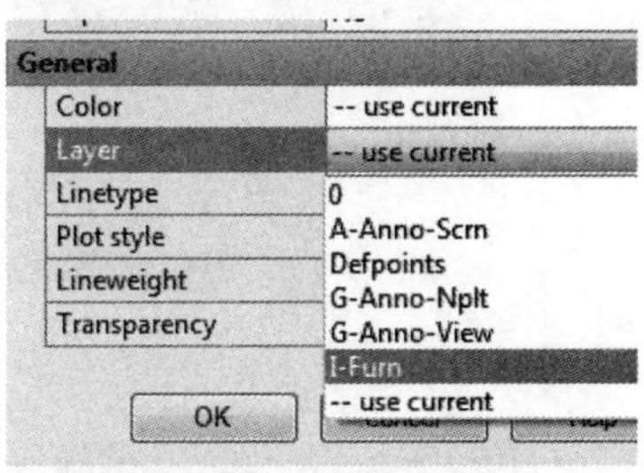

Set Layer **to I-Furn**.

This ensures that the block will be placed on the I-Furn layer regardless of what layer is current.

11. 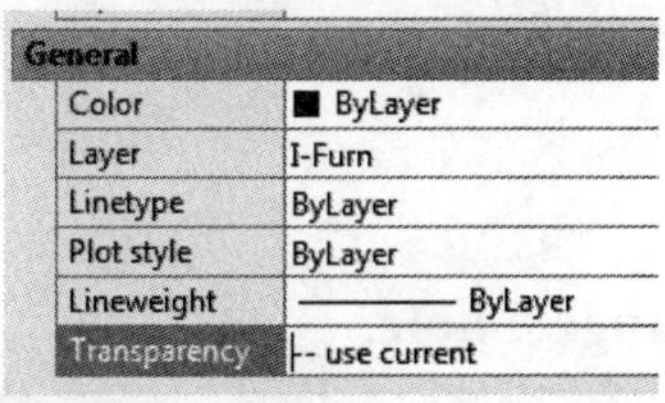

Set the Color, Linetype, Plot Style, and Lineweight to ByLayer.

This means that the I-Furn layer properties will control the display of color, linetype, plot style and lineweight.

Press **OK** to close the Properties dialog.

12. 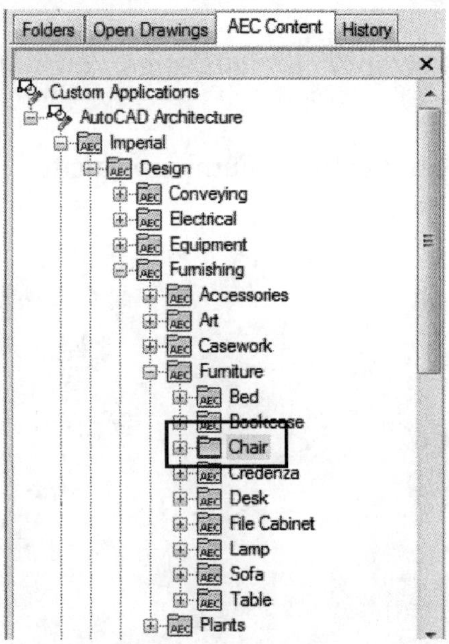

Activate the **AEC Content** tab on the Design Center.

Browse to *AutoCAD Architecture/Imperial/Design/Furnishing/ Furniture/Chair* folder.

13. 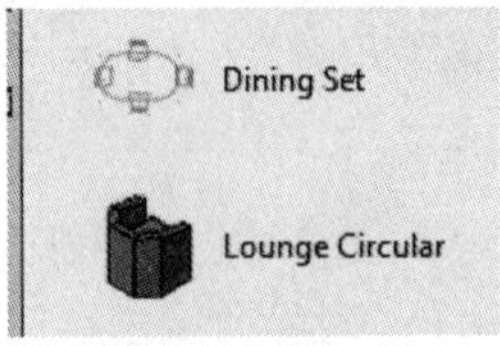

Drag and drop the **Lounge Circular** chair onto the Furniture palette.

14. 

If you have problems downloading the blocks, use the **Save this symbol as…**link located in the bottom pane to save the file to your work folder. Then, simply insert it into your drawing.

15. 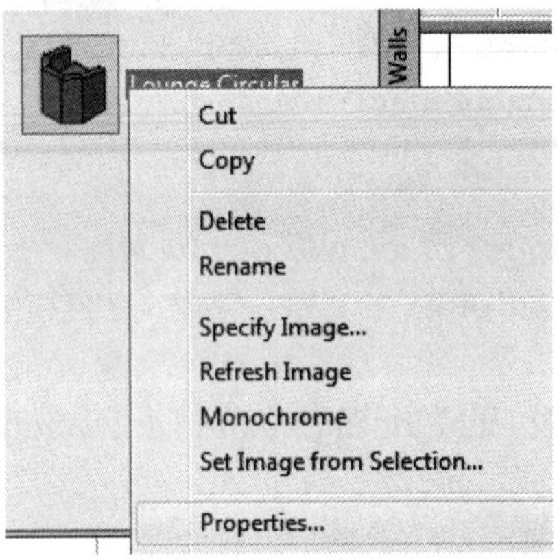

Select the **Lounge Circular** tool.

Right click and select **Properties**.

16. 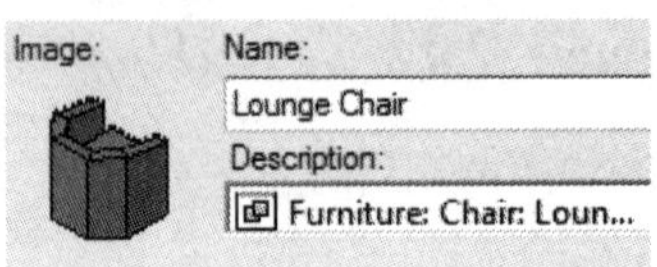

Change the name to **Lounge Chair**.

Press **OK** to close the Properties dialog.

18. 

Browse to *AutoCAD Architecture/Imperial/Design/Furnishing/Furniture/Sofa* folder.

Drag and drop the **Love Seat 2** onto the Furniture palette.

19. Select the **Love Seat 2** tool.
Right click and select **Properties**.

20. 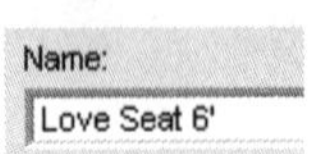

Change the Name to **Love Seat 6′**.

21. 

Browse to *AutoCAD Architecture/Imperial/Design/Furnishing /Furniture/Table* folder.

Drag and drop the **Coffee Table** onto the Furniture palette.

22. 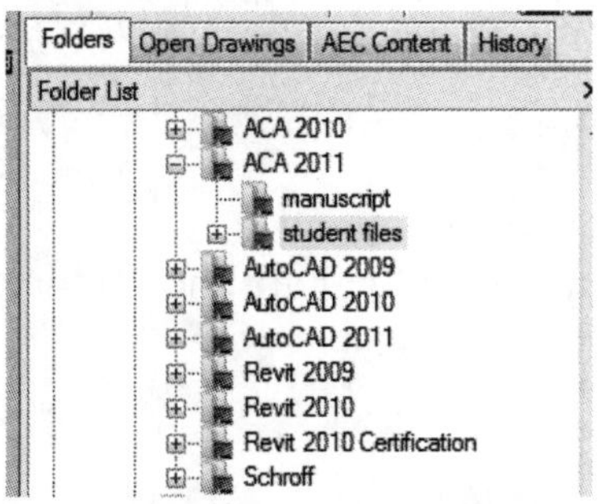

In the Design Center dialog, select the Folders tab.

Browse to the folder where you stored the files downloaded from the publisher.

23. 

Drag and drop the file called **entertainment center** onto the new palette.

24. Select the **entertainment center** tool. Right click and select **Properties**.

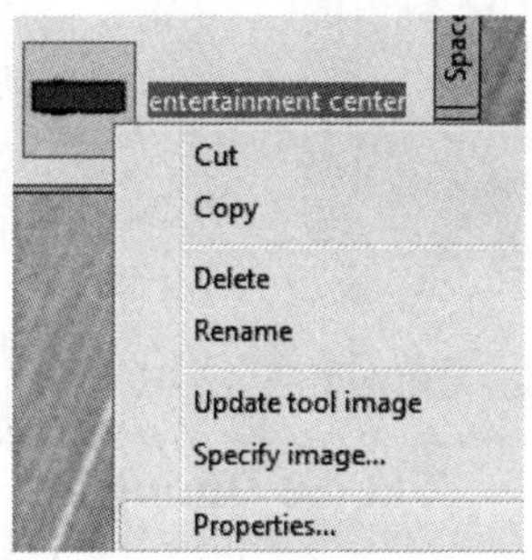

25. 

Change the name to **Entertainment Center**.

26. 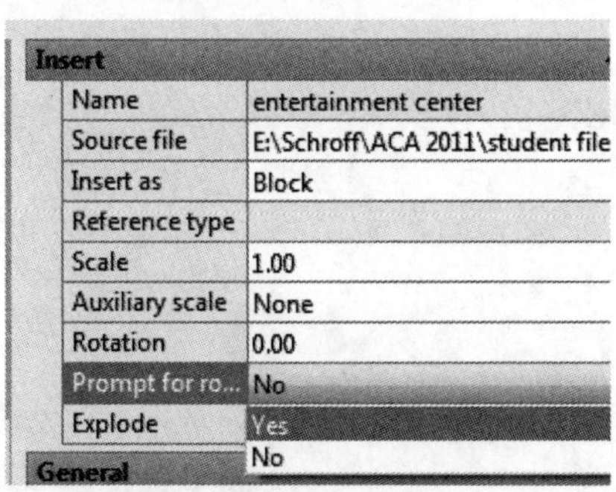

Set the Prompt for rotation to **Yes**.

27. 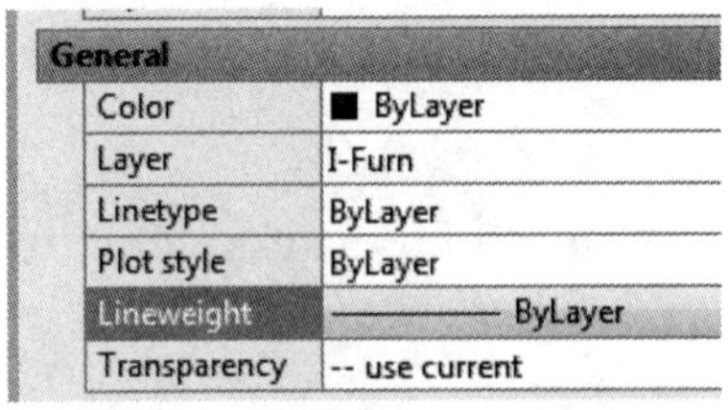

Set Layer **to I-Furn**.

This ensures that the block will be placed on the I-Furn layer regardless of what layer is current. The available layers are in the active drawing.

28. 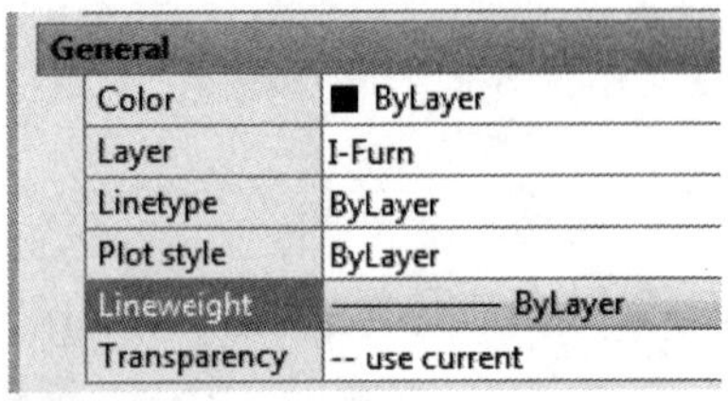

Set the Color, Linetype, Plot Style, and Lineweight to ByLayer.

This means that the I-Furn layer properties will control the display of color, linetype, plot style and lineweight.

Press **OK** to close the Properties dialog.

29. 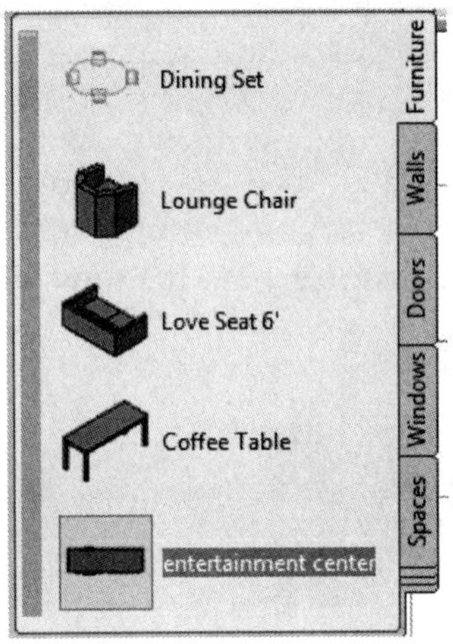

This is what your Furniture tool palette should look like.

30. Close the Design Center.

31. 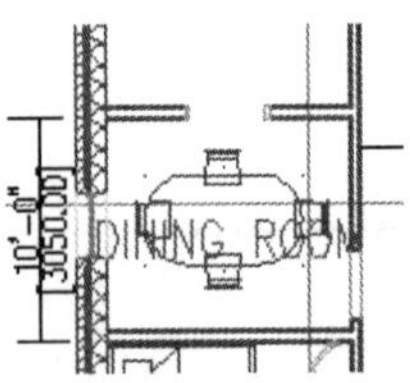

Add the **Dining Set** to the dining room.

32. 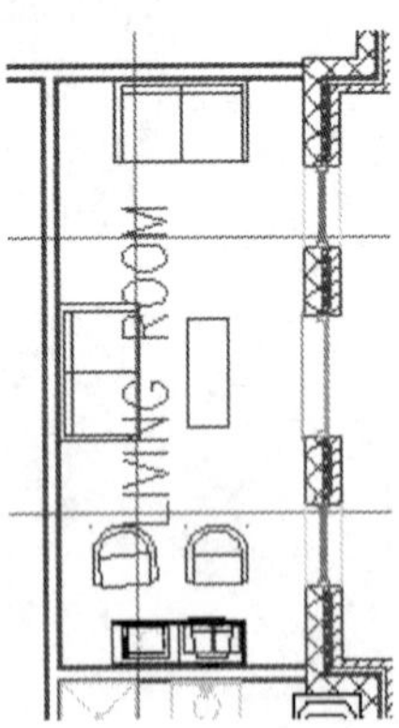

Furnish the living room with the lounge chair, sofa, coffee table, and entertainment center.

33. Add a sofa and coffee table to the family room.

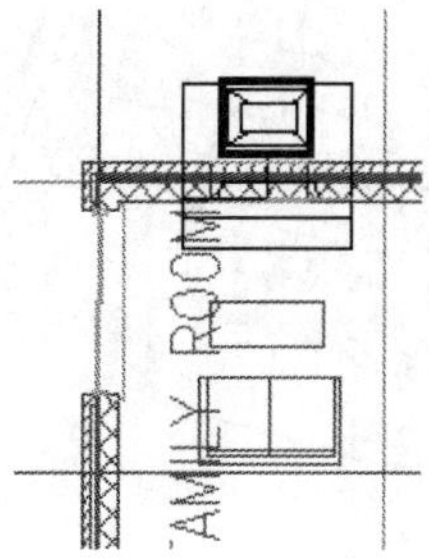

34. Save the file as *ex4-3.dwg.*

TIP: If the preview shown in the Design Center does not appear as a 3D object, then it is a 2D object. Don't select it for use in your model.

Exercise 4-4

Adding to the Service Areas

Drawing Name: Ex4-3.dwg
Estimated Time: 30 minutes

1.  Open *ex4-4.dwg.*
Select the Model tab.
Switch to a top view.

2.  Launch the Design Center.

3. 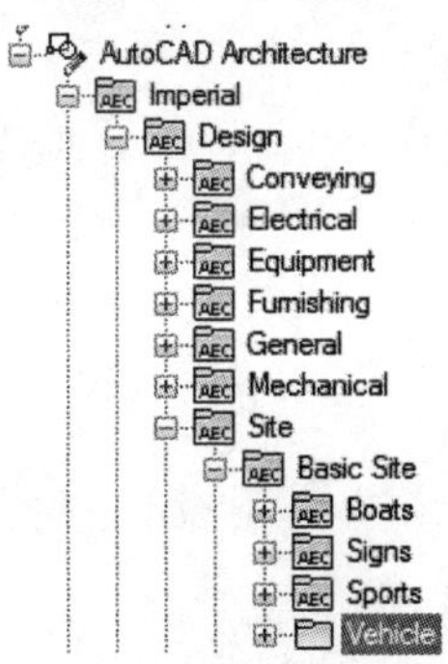

Select the AEC Content tab.
Browse to the *AutoCAD Architecture/Imperial/Design/Site/ Basic Site/Vehicles* folder.

4. 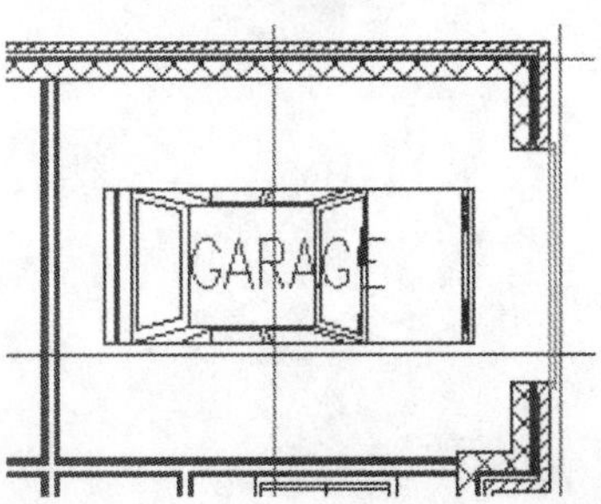

Drag and drop the *Sub-Compact* car into the garage.

All that remains is the kitchen area.

5. 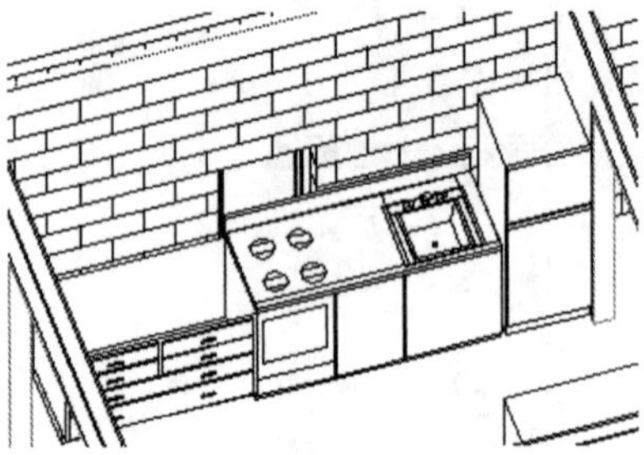

Use the Design Center to add casework, a kitchen sink, and an oven into the kitchen area.

We see now using our space planning that the window needs to be shifted up.

6. 

Add a refrigerator and additional cabinets to the other side of the kitchen.

Our completed floor plan.

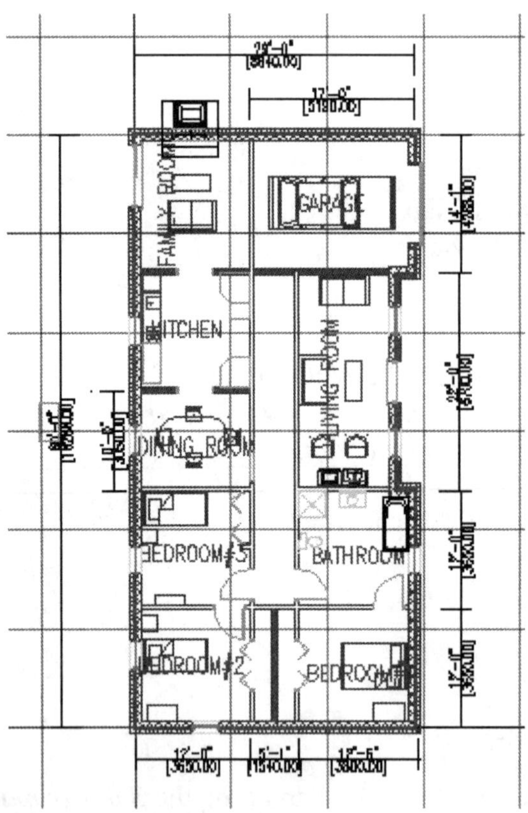

7. Save the file as *ex4-5.dwg*.

QUIZ 2

True or False

1. Once a door or window is placed, it can not be moved or modified.
2. Openings can be any size and any elevation.
3. The Offset value when placing a door/window/opening determines how far the door/window/opening is placed from a selected point.
4. Door, window and opening dimensions can be applied using the Design Center.

Multiple Choice

5. Select the entity type that can NOT be converted to a wall:

   A. Line
   B. Polyline
   C. Circle
   D. Spline

6. A HOT grip is indicated by this color:

   A. GREEN
   B. BLUE
   C. RED
   D. YELLOW

7. To assign an image to a tool on the tool palette using existing geometry, use

   A. Assign image
   B. Set Image from selection
   C. Insert
   D. Import

ANSWERS:

1) F; 2) T 3) T; 4) F; 5) C; 6) C; 7) A

Notes:

Lesson 5
Roofs

Roofs can be created with single or double slopes, with or without gable ends, and with or without overhangs. Once you input all your roof settings, you simply pick the points around the perimeter of the building to define your roof outline. If you make an error, you can easily modify or redefine your roof.

You need to pick three points before the roof will begin to preview in your graphics window. There is no limit to the number of points to select to define the perimeter.

To create a gable roof, uncheck the gable box in the Roof dialog. Pick the two end points for the sloped portion of the roof. Turn on the Gable box. Pick the end point for the gable side. Turn off the Gable box. Pick the end point for the sloped side. Turn the Gable box on. Pick the viewport and then press ENTER. A Gable cannot be defined with more than three consecutive edges.

Roofs can be created using two methods: ROOFADD places a roof based on points selected or ROOFCONVERT which converts a closed polyline or closed walls to develop a roof.

Tips & Tricks

- If you opt to use ROOFCONVERT and use existing closed walls, be sure that the walls are intersecting properly. If your walls are not properly cleaned up with each other, the roof conversion is unpredictable.
- The Plate Height of a roof should be set equal to the Wall Height.
- You can create a gable on a roof by gripping any ridgeline point and stretching it past the roof edge. You cannot make a gable into a hip using grips.

Shape – Select the Shape option on the command line by typing 'S.'	Single Slope – Extends a roof plane at an angle from the Plate Height.	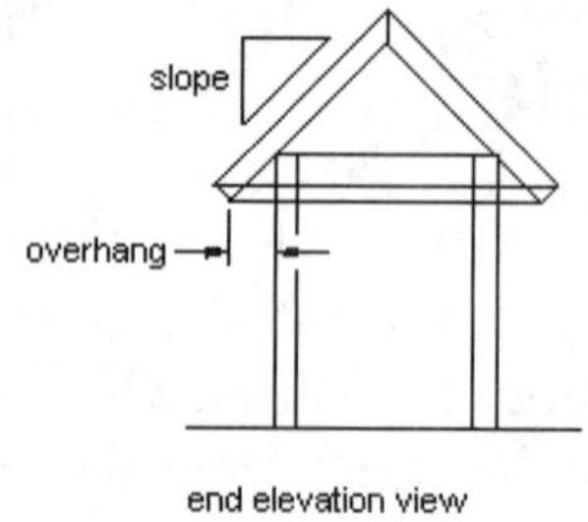
	Double Slope – Includes a single slope and adds another slope, which begins at the intersection of the first slope and the height specified for the first slope.	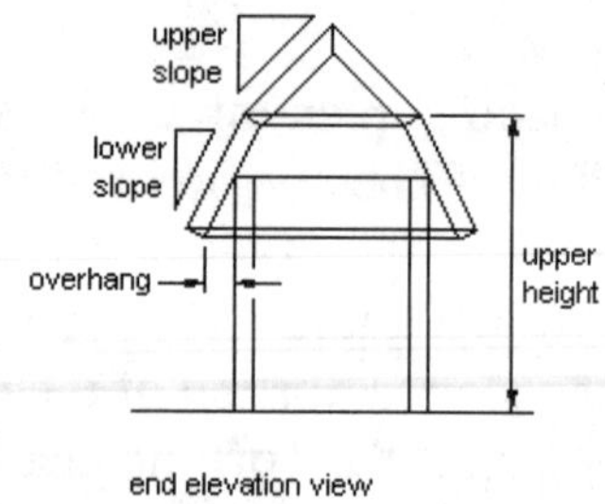
Gable – Select the Gable option on the command line by typing 'G.'	If this is enabled, turns off the slope of the roof place. To create a gable edge, select Gable prior to identifying the first corner of the gable end. Turn off gable to continue to create the roof.	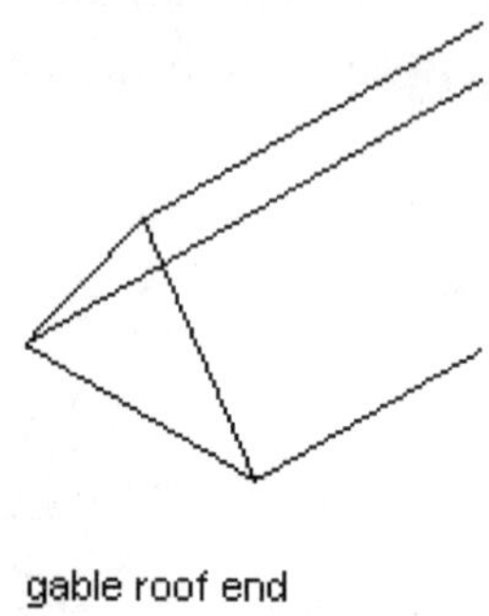
Plate Height – Set the Plate Height on the command line by typing 'PH.'	Specify the top plate from which the roof plane is projected. The height is relative to the XY plane with a Z coordinate of 0.	
Rise – Set the Rise on the command line by typing 'PR.'	Sets the angle of the roof based on a run value of 12.	A rise value of 5 creates a 5/12 roof, which forms a slope angle of 22.62 degrees.
Slope – Set the Slope on the command line by typing 'PS.'	Angle of the roof rise from the horizontal.	If slope angles are entered, then the rise will automatically be calculated.

Upper Height – Set the Upper Height on the command line by typing 'UH.'	This is only available if a Double Slope roof is being created. This is the height where the second slope will start.	
Rise (upper) – Set the Upper Rise on the command line by typing 'UR.'	This is only available if a Double Slope roof is being created. This is the slope angle for the second slope.	A rise value of 5 creates a 5/12 roof, which forms a slope angle of 22.62 degrees.
Slope (upper) – Set the Upper Slope on the command line by typing 'US.'	This is only available if a Double Slope roof is being created. Defines the slope angle for the second slope.	If an upper rise value is set, this is automatically calculated.
Overhang – To enable on the command line, type 'O.' To set the value of the Overhang, type 'V.'	If enabled, extends the roofline down from the plate height by the value set.	
	The Floating Viewer opens a viewer window displaying a preview of the roof.	
	The match button allows you to select an existing roof to match its properties.	
	The properties button opens the Roof Properties dialog.	
	The Undo button allows you to undo the last roof operation. You can step back as many operations as you like up to the start.	
	Opens the Roof Help file.	

Exercise 5-1:

Creating a Roof using Existing Walls

Drawing Name: ex3-1.dwg
Estimated Time: 10 minutes

This exercise reinforces the following skills:

- Roof
- Roof Properties
- Visual Styles

1.  Open *ex3-1.dwg.*

2. 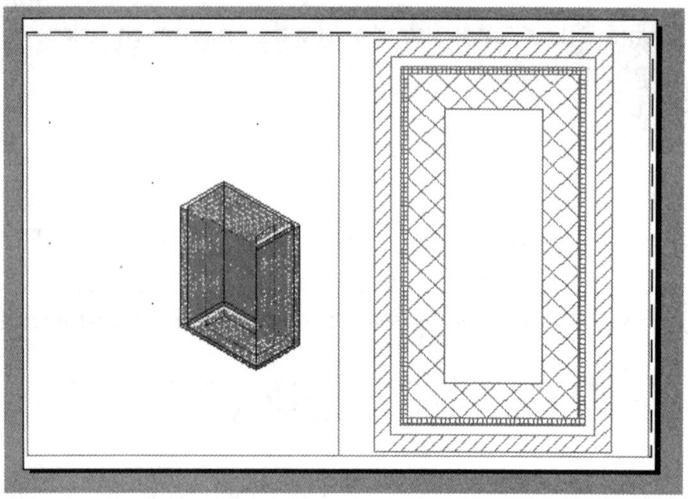

Select the Work icon.
Activate the right viewport that shows the top or plan view.

3. 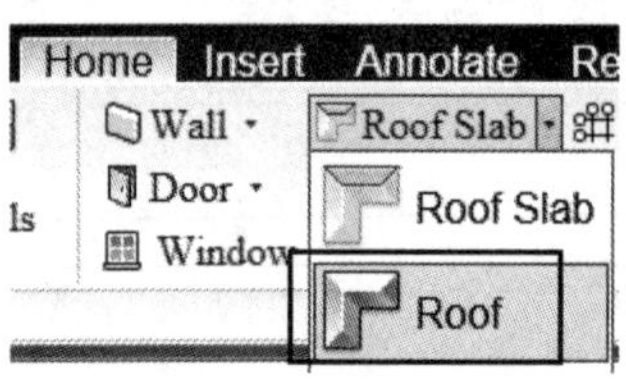

Select the **Roof** tool from the Home ribbon.

4. 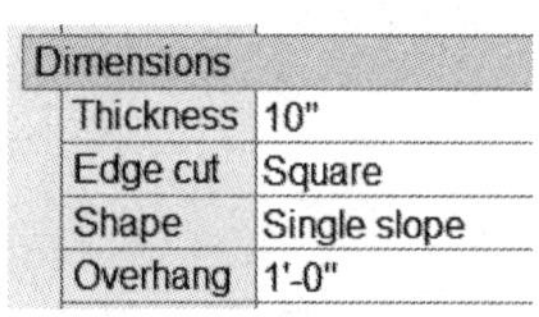

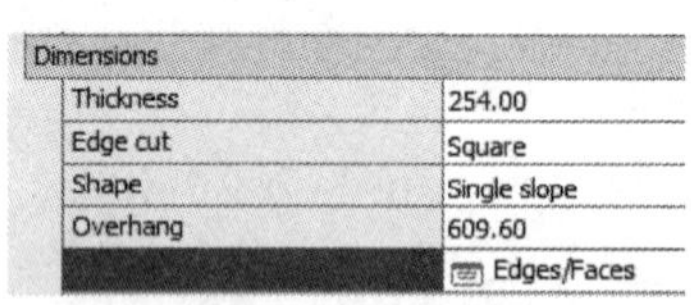

Expand the Dimensions section.
Set the Thickness to **10″ [254.00 mm]**.
Set the Shape to **Single slope**.
Set the Overhang to **1′-0″ [609.6 mm]**.

5. 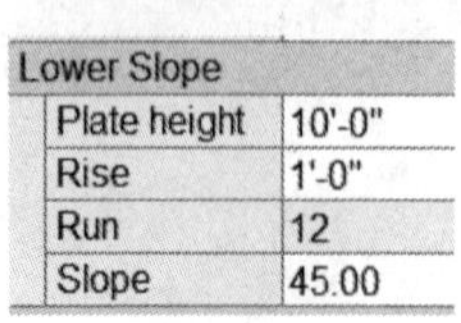

Expand the Lower Slope section.
Set the Plate height to **10′-0″ [3000 mm]**.

The plate height determines the level where the roof rests.

6. 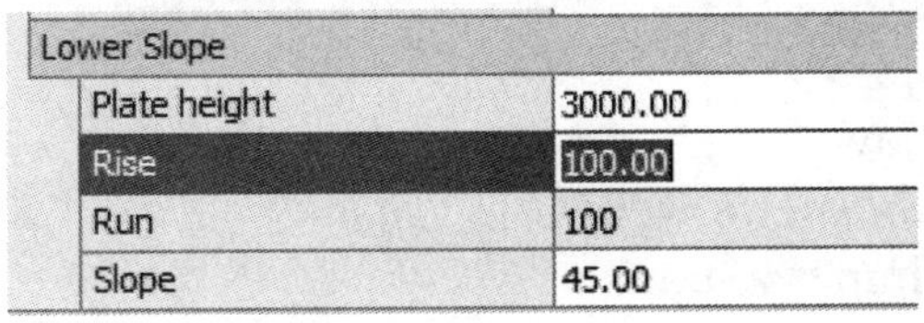

Set the Rise to **1′-0″ [100 mm]**.

7. 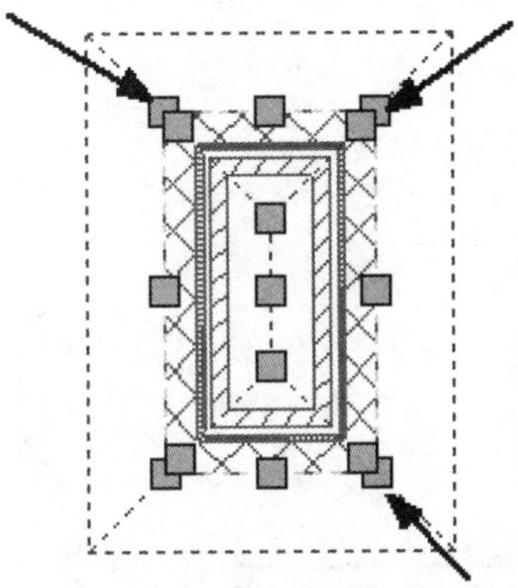
Pick the corners indicated to place the roof.

Press **Enter**.

8. 

Switch to the **Work** layout.

9. 

Activate the View ribbon.

Select the **Shades of Gray** under Visual Styles.

10. 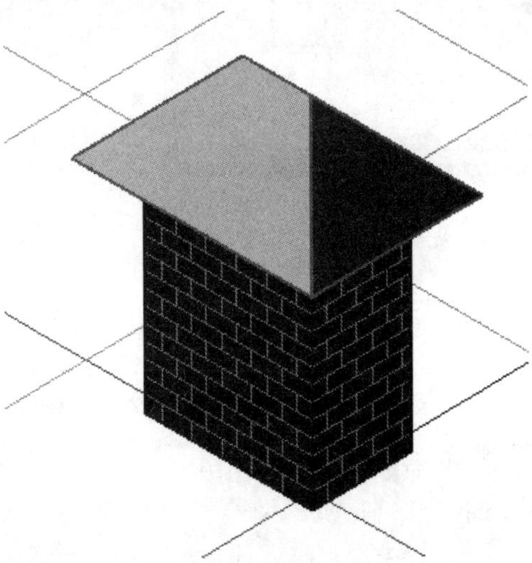
Save as *ex5-1.dwg*.

Our roof works, but strictly speaking we can make it better with a couple of changes around the chimney. AutoCAD Architecture allows us to cut holes through roofs (to allow for vents, chimneys and skylights), and to add other faces or subsidiary roofs such as dormers.

In order to edit a roof you have to convert it to Roof Slabs.

Exercise 5-2:
Roof Slabs

Drawing Name: i_ex5-2.dwg, m_ex5-2.dwg
(download from the publisher's website)
Use the i_ version for Imperial units.
Use the m_ version for Metric units.

Estimated Time: 15 minutes

This exercise reinforces the following skills:

- Convert to Roof
- Roof Slab Tools

1.  Open *i_ex5-2.dwg [m_ex5-2.dwg].*

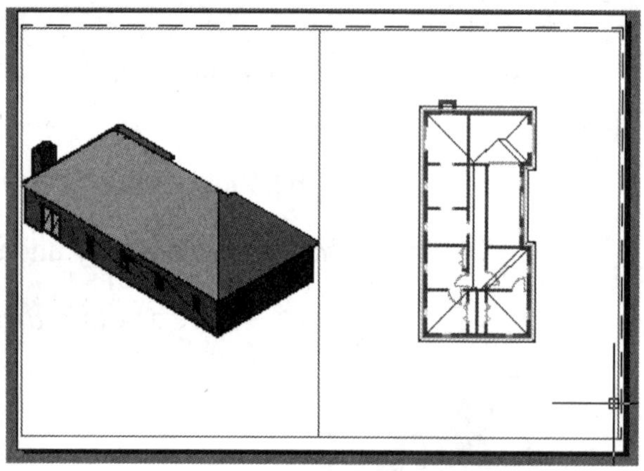

2. 

Select the Work icon.

3. 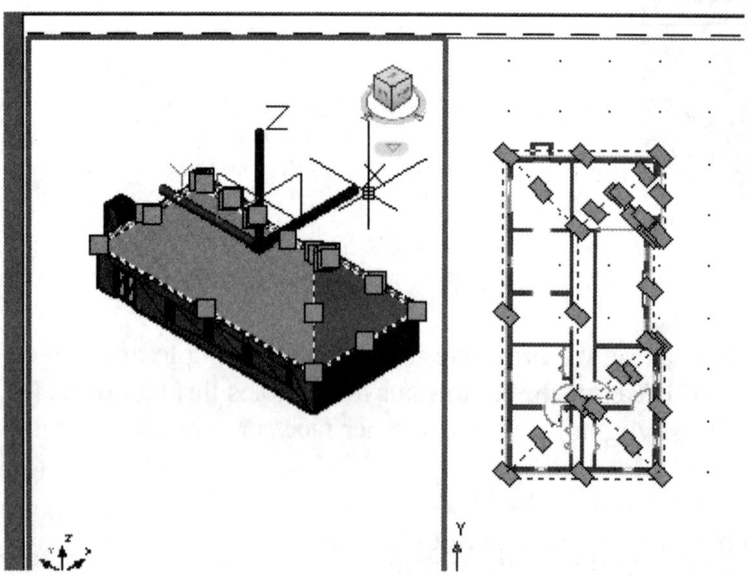

Activate the left viewport that shows the isometric view.

4. 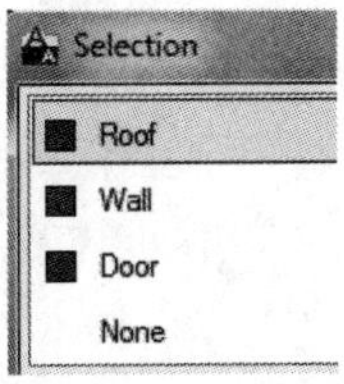

Select the **Roof** in the Selection dialog.

The roof will highlight.

5. 

Select **Convert** from the Roof ribbon.

6. 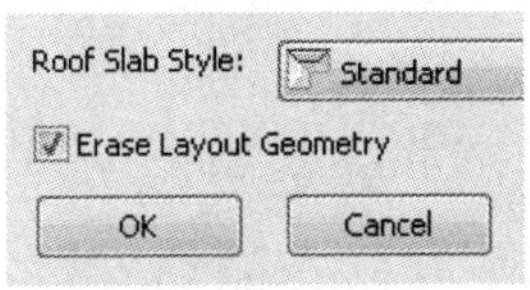

Enable the **Erase layout geometry** checkbox.

Press **OK**.

The Roof Slab Properties dialog appears.
Close it.

The roof will change appearance slightly. It now consists of individual slabs.

7. 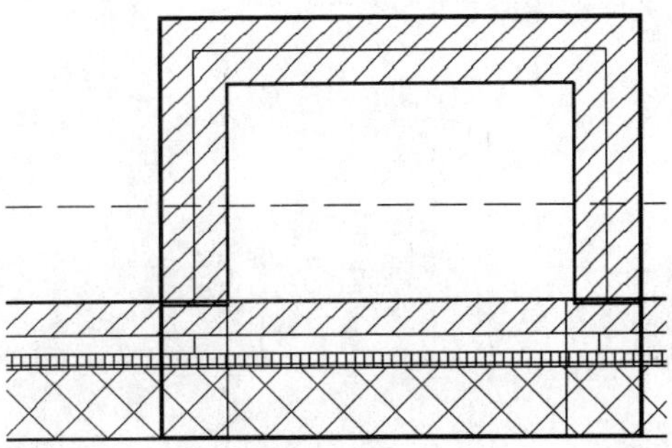

Activate the right viewport.
Zoom into the area where the chimney is located.

Activate the Home ribbon.
Draw a rectangle over the outline of the chimney. Make sure that the rectangle extends beyond the roof line.

8. 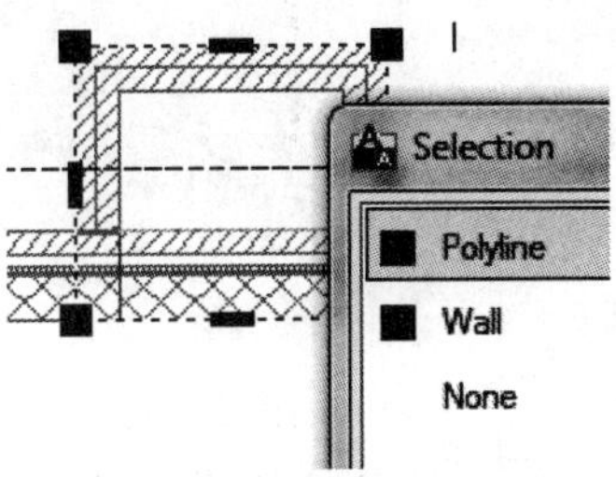

Select the rectangle.

Select the **Polyline** in the Selection dialog.

9. 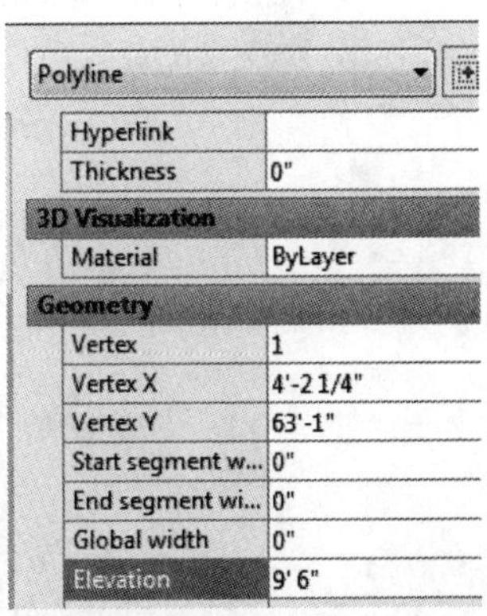

Right click and select **Properties**.

Set the Elevation to **9′-6″** **[3000]**.

This moves the rectangle to the same elevation as where the roof is placed.

Close the Properties dialog.
Deselect the rectangle by hitting the ESC key.

10. 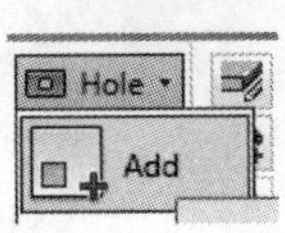

Select the roof slab located on top of the chimney.

Select **Hole→Add** from the ribbon.

11. 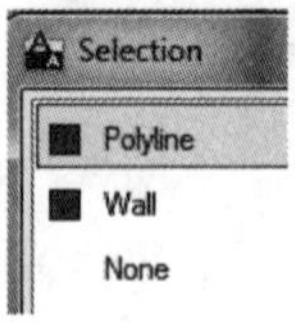

At the next prompt pick the rectangle.
Select the **Polyline** in the Selection dialog.

At the 'Erase Layout Geometry?' prompt hit, right click and select **Yes**.

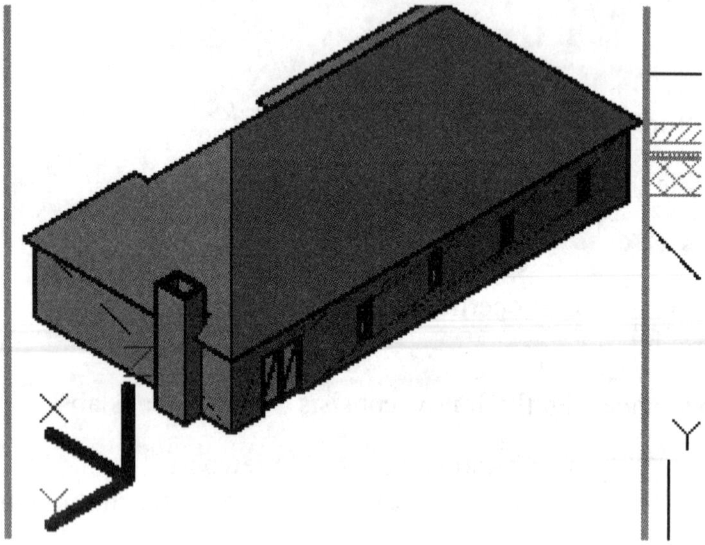

The hole will appear.

Use the Viewcube in the viewport to orient the view so you can see the chimney.

The chimney now appears OK.

12. Save as *i_ex5-2a.dwg*.

Lesson 6
Structural Members

Architectural documentation for residential construction will always include plans (top views) of each floor of a building, showing features and structural information of the floor platform itself. Walls are located on the plan but not shown in structural detail.

Wall sections and details are used to show:

- the elements within walls (exterior siding, sheathing, block, brick or wood studs, insulation, air cavities, interior sheathing, trim)
- how walls relate to floors, ceilings, roofs, eaves,
- openings within the walls (doors/windows with their associated sills and headers)
- how walls relate to openings in floors (stairs).

Stick-framed (stud) walls usually have their framing patterns determined by the carpenters on site. Once window and door openings are located on the plan, and stud spacing is specified by the designer (or the local building code), the specific arrangement of vertical members is usually left to the fabricators and not drafted, except where specific structural details require explanation.

The structural members in framed floors that have to hold themselves and/or other walls and floors up are usually drafted as framing plans. Designers must specify the size and spacing of joists or trusses, beams and columns. Plans show the orientation and relation of members, locate openings through the floor and show support information for openings and other specific conditions.

In the next exercises, we shall create a floor framing plan. Since the ground floor of our one-story lesson house has already been defined as a concrete slab, we'll assume that the ground level slopes down at the rear of the house and create a wood deck at the sliding door to the family room. The deck will need a railing for safety.

Autodesk AutoCAD Architecture includes a Structural Member Catalog that allows you to easily access industry-standard structural shapes. To create most standard column, brace, and beam styles, you can access the Structural Member Catalog, select a structural member shape, and create a style that contains the shape that you selected. The shape, similar to an AEC profile, is a 2D cross-section of a structural member. When you create a structural member with a style that you created from the Structural Member Catalog, you define the path to extrude the shape along.

You can create your own structural shapes that you can add to existing structural members, or use to create new structural members. The design rules in a structural member style allow you to add these custom shapes to a structural member, as well as create custom structural members from more than one shape.

All the columns, braces, and beams that you create are sub-types of a single Structural Member object type. The styles that you create for columns, braces, and beams have the same Structural Member Styles style type as well. When you change the display or style of a structural member, use the Structural Member object in the Display Manager and the Structural Member Styles style type in the Style Manager.

If you are operating with the AIA layering system as your current layer standard, when you create members or convert AutoCAD entities to structural members using the menu picks or toolbars, AutoCAD Architecture assigns the new members to layers: A-Cols, A-Cols-Brce or A-Beam, respectively. If Generic AutoCAD Architecture is your standard, the layers used are A_Columns, A_Beams and A_Braces. If your layer standard is Current Layer, new entities come in on the current layer, as in plain vanilla AutoCAD.

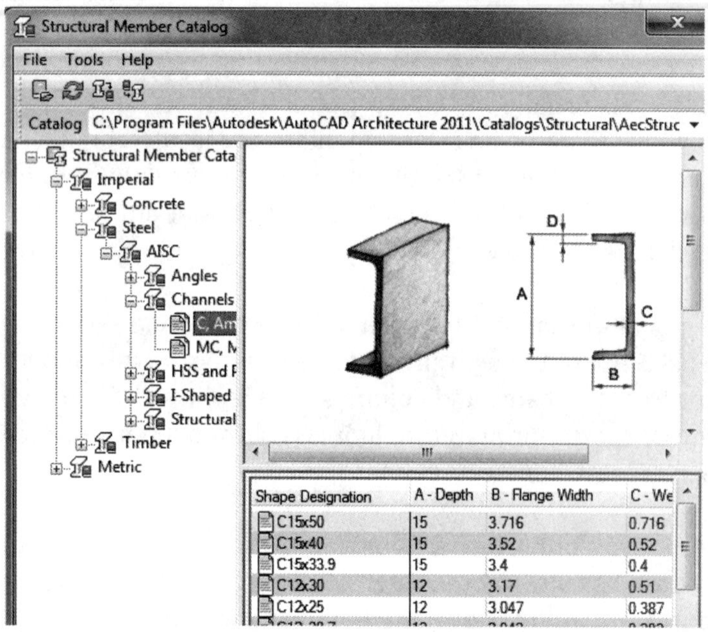

The Structural Member Catalog includes specifications for standard structural shapes. You can choose shapes from the Structural Member Catalog, and generate styles for structural members that you create in your drawings.

A style that contains the catalog shape that you selected is created. You can view the style in the Style Manager, create a new structural member from the style, or apply the style to an existing member.

When you add a structural member to your drawing, the shape inside the style that you created defines the shape of the member. You define the length, justification, roll or rise, and start and end offsets of the structural member when you draw it.

You cannot use the following special characters in your style names:

- less-than and greater-than symbols (< >)
- forward slashes and backslashes (/ \)
- quotation marks (")
- colons (:)
- semicolons (;)
- question marks (?)
- commas (,)
- asterisks (*)
- vertical bars (|)
- equal signs (=)
- backquotes (`)

The left pane of the Structural Member Catalog contains a hierarchical tree view. Several industry standard catalogs are organized in the tree, first by imperial or metric units, and then by material.

	Open a catalog file - The default is the catalog that comes with ADT, but you can create your own custom catalog. The default catalog is located in the following directory path: \\Program Files\Autodesk AutoCAD Architecture R3\Catalogs\catalogs.
	Refresh Data
	Locate Catalog item based on an existing member – allows you to select a member in a drawing and then locates it in your catalog.
	Generate Member Style – allows you to create a style to be used.

We will be adding a wood framed deck, 4000 mm x 2750 mm, to the back of the house. For purposes of this exercise we will assume that the ground level is 300 mm below the slab at the back of the house and falls away so that grade level below the edge of the deck away from the house is 2 meters below floor level: - 2 m a.f.f. (above finish floor) in architectural notation. We will place the top of the deck floorboards even with the top of the floor slab.

We will use support and rim joists as in standard wood floor framing, and they will all be at the same level, rather than joists crossing a support beam below. In practice this means the use of metal hangers, which will not be drawn. Once the floor system is drawn we will add support columns at the outside rim joist and braces at the columns.

Exercise 6-1:

Creating Member Styles

Drawing Name: i_ex6-1.dwg [m_ex6-1.dwg]
Estimated Time: 5 minutes

This exercise reinforces the following skills:

- Creating Member Styles
- Use of Structural Members tools

1.  Open *i_ex6-1.dwg [m_ex6-1.dwg].*

2. 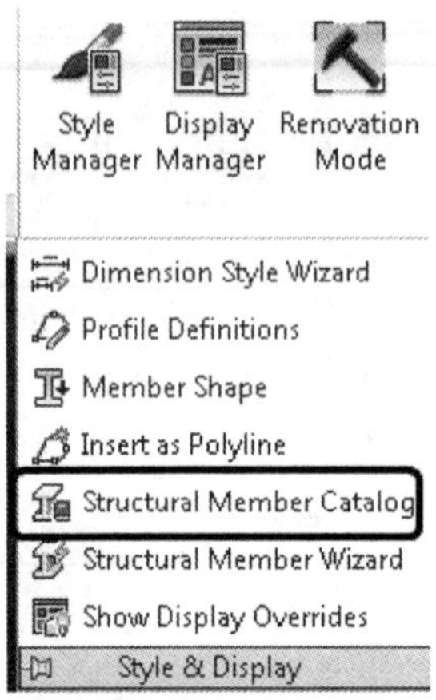

Activate the Manage ribbon.

Go to **Style & Display→Structural Member Catalog**.

3. 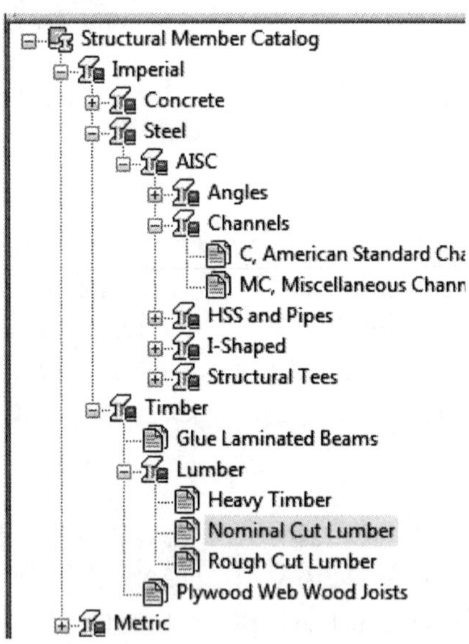

Browse to the **Imperial/Timber/Lumber/Nominal Cut Lumber [Metric/Timber/Lumber Metric]** folder.

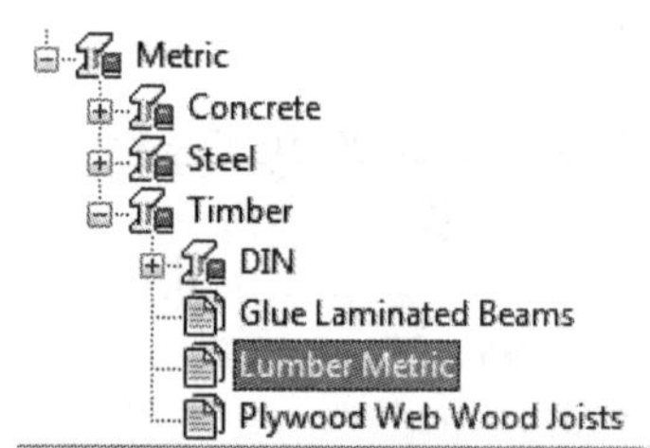

4. In the lower right pane:

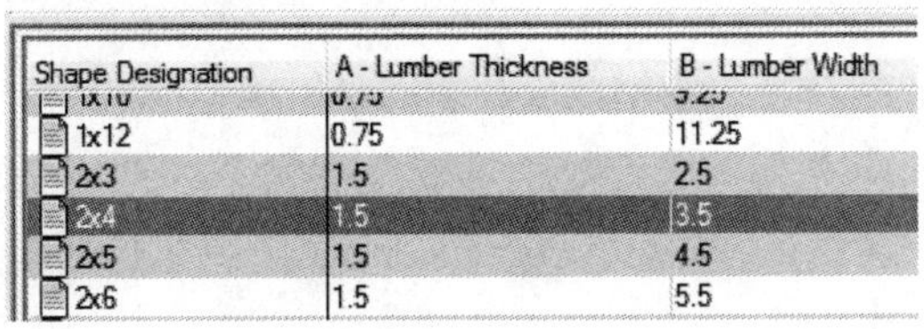

Locate the **2x4 [50mmx150mm]** shape designation.

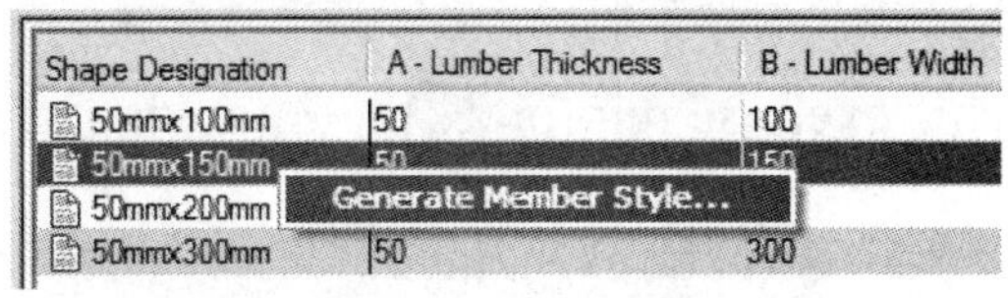

Right click and select **Generate Member Style**.

5. 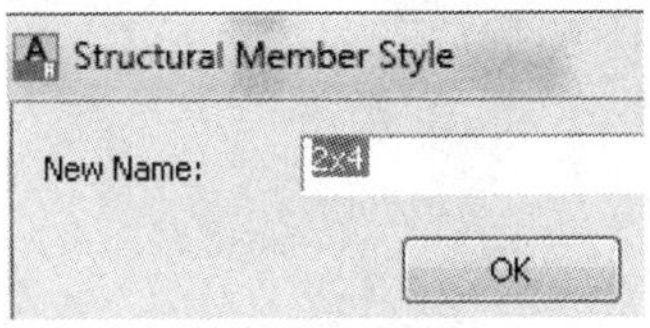

In the Structural Member Style dialog box, the name for your style automatically fills in.

Click **OK**.

6. In the lower right pane:

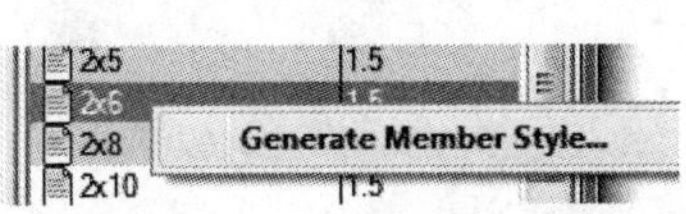

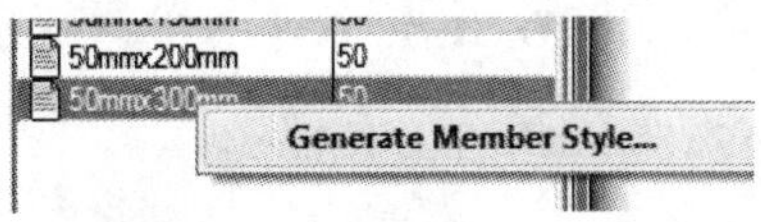

Locate the **2x6 [50mmx300mm]** shape designation.
Right click and select **Generate Member Style**.

7. 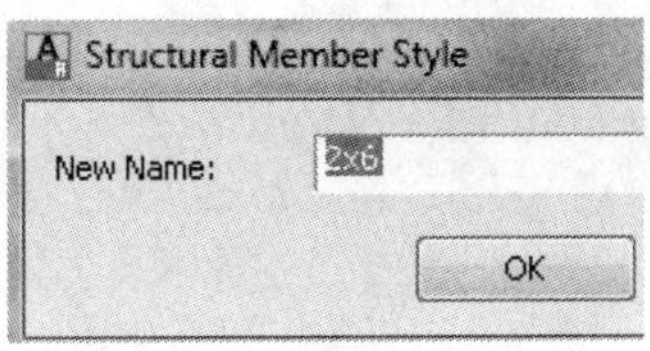

In the Structural Member Style dialog box, the name for your style is displayed.

Click **OK**.

8. Close the dialog.
Save as *i_ex6-1a.dwg*.

Exercise 6-2:
Creating Member Shapes

Drawing Name: i_ex6-1a.dwg
Estimated Time: 10 minutes

This exercise reinforces the following skills:

- Structural Member Wizard

1. 
   Open *i_ex6-1a.dwg.*
   Select the Work tab.
   Activate the right viewport.

2. 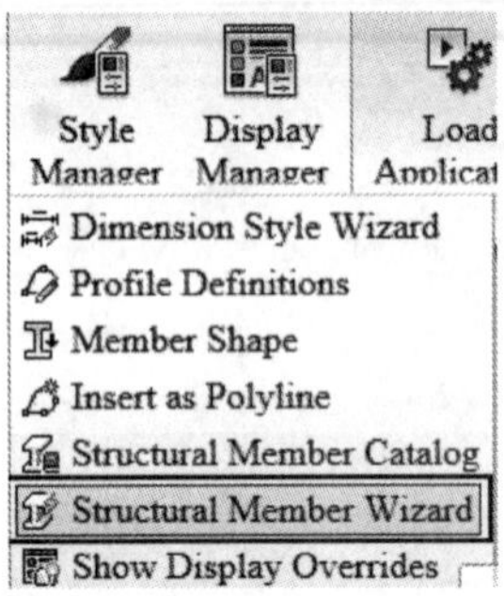

   Activate the **Manage** ribbon.

   Go to **Style & Display→Structural Member Wizard**.

3. 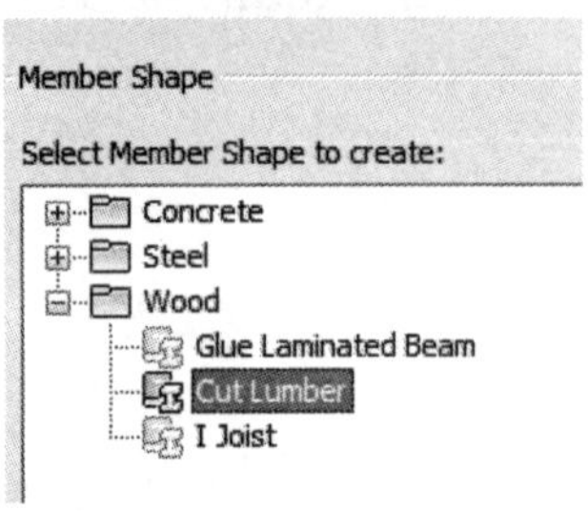

   Select the **Cut Lumber** category under Wood.

   Press **Next**.

4. 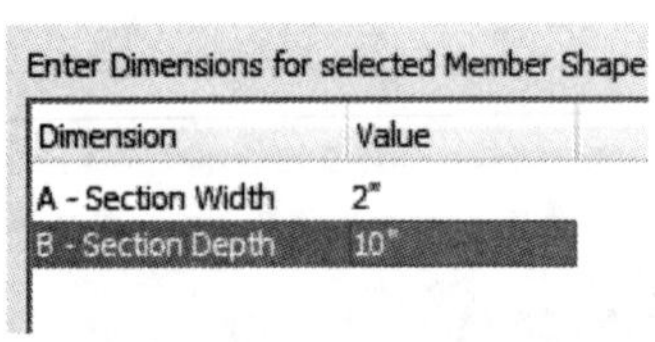

   Set the Section Width to **2″ [50.00]**.

   Set the Section Depth to **10″ [250.00]**.

   Press **Next**.

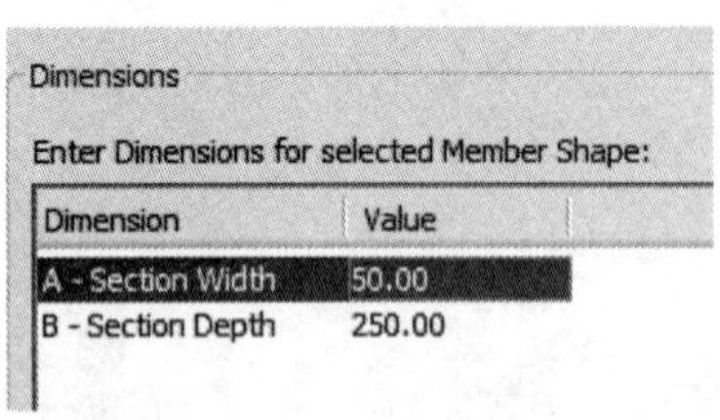

5. 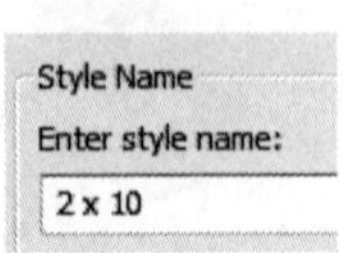

   Enter the style name as **2 x 10 [50mmx250mm]**.

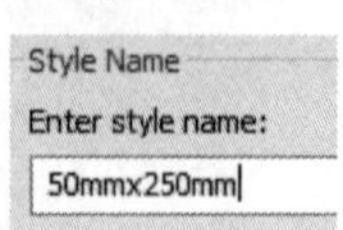

   Press **Finish**.

6. 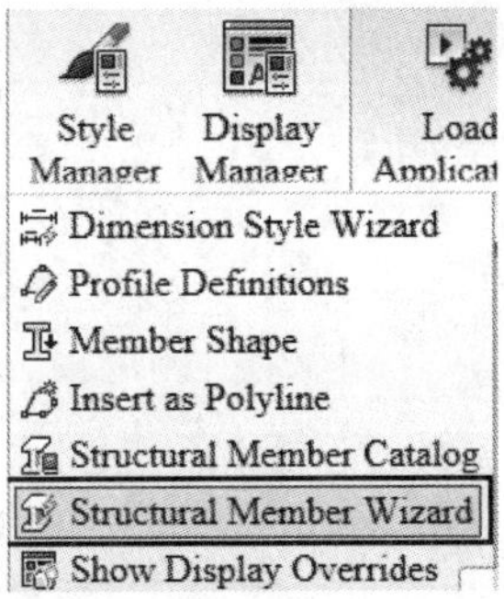

Activate the **Manage** ribbon.

Go to **Style & Display→Structural Member Wizard**.

7. 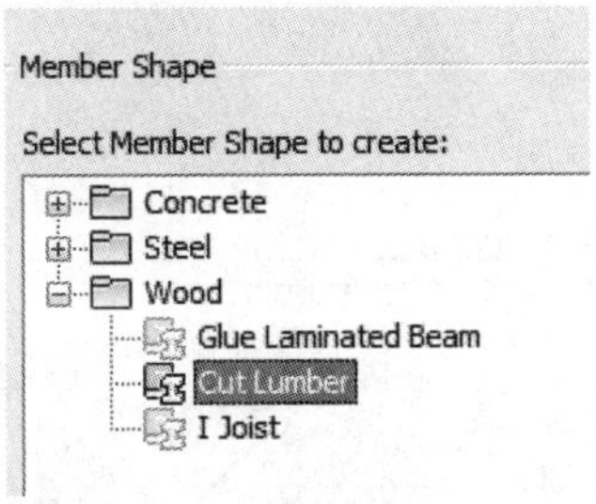

Select the **Cut Lumber** category under Wood.

Press **Next**.

8. 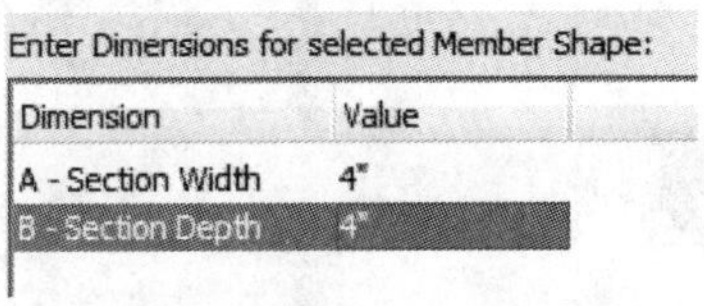

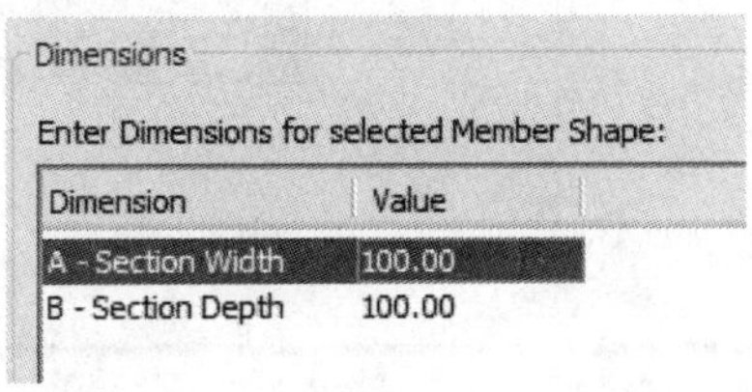

Set the Section Width to **4″ [100.00]**.

Set the Section Depth to **4″ [100.00]**.

Press **Next**.

9. 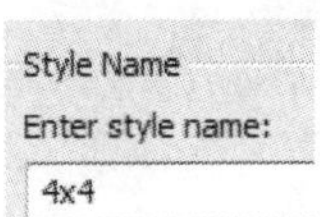

Enter the style name as **4x4 [100mmx100mm]**.

Press **Finish**.

10. Save as *ex6-2.dwg*.

Exercise 6-3:

Adding Structural Members

Drawing Name: ex6-2.dwg
Estimated Time: 25 minutes

This exercise reinforces the following skills:

- Creating Member Styles
- Use of Structural Members tools

1.  Open *ex6-2.dwg.*

2. Select the Work icon.
Activate the right viewport.

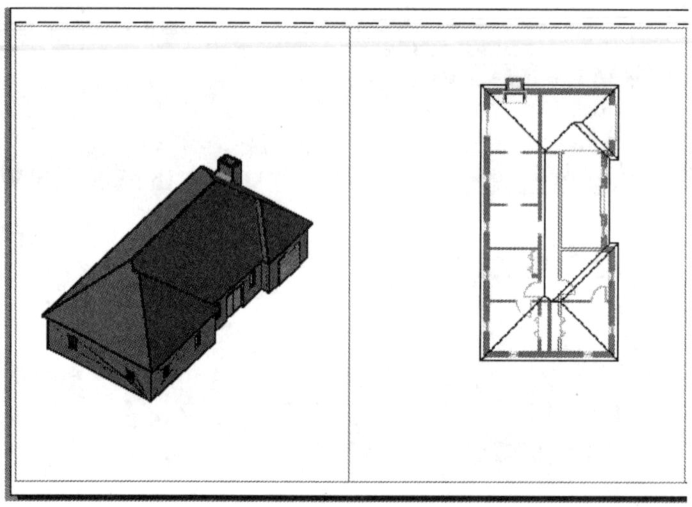

3. 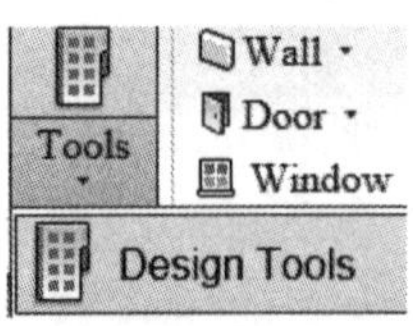

Activate the Tools palette if it is not available.

To activate, launch from the Home ribbon.

4. 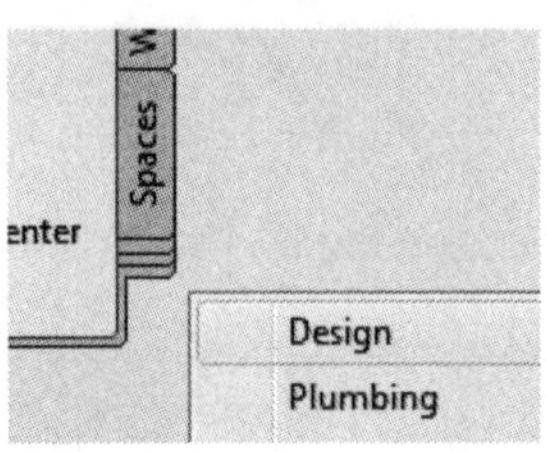

Activate the **Design** Palette.
To do this, right click on the palette and select **Design**.

5. 

Select the Structural **Beam** tool on the **Design** Tool Palette.

6. 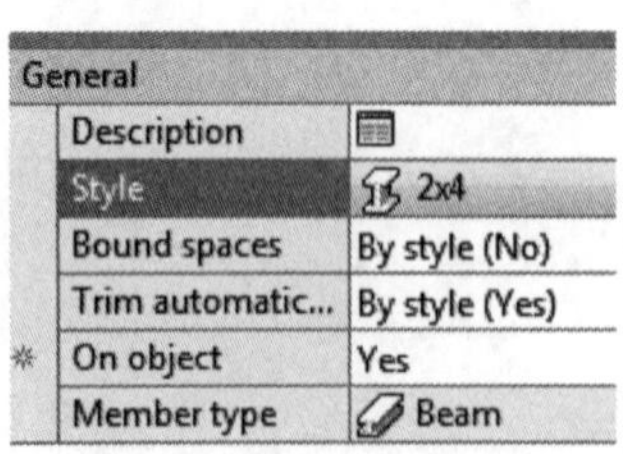

Select the **2x4 [50mmx250mm]** style from the Style drop-down on the Properties dialog.

7. 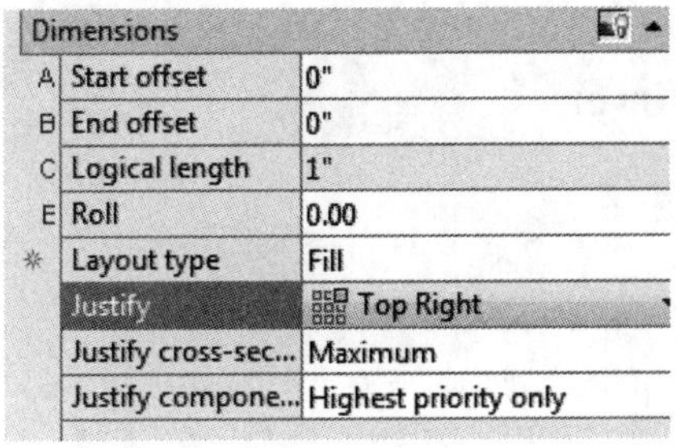

Set Justify to Top Right.
Set the Roll to 0.
Set the Start Offset to 0″.

8. Zoom into the family room area (the top left of the floor plan).

   Use the From Osnap, pick the upper left corner of the house wall, and type **@14′-0″ <90 [@4250<90]** for the Offset; press ENTER. This shifts the first beam slightly below the wall.

   Pull the cursor down at a 270° angle, and type in **14′-0″ [4250]** for the length. DO NOT EXIT THE COMMAND.

9. Change the Justification to Top Left.
   Pull the cursor to the left (180°) and enter **9′-0″ [2750]** for the length.

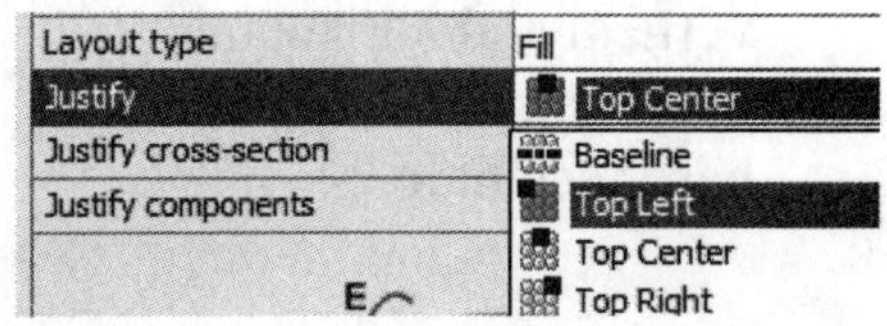

   Hit ENTER to terminate the command.

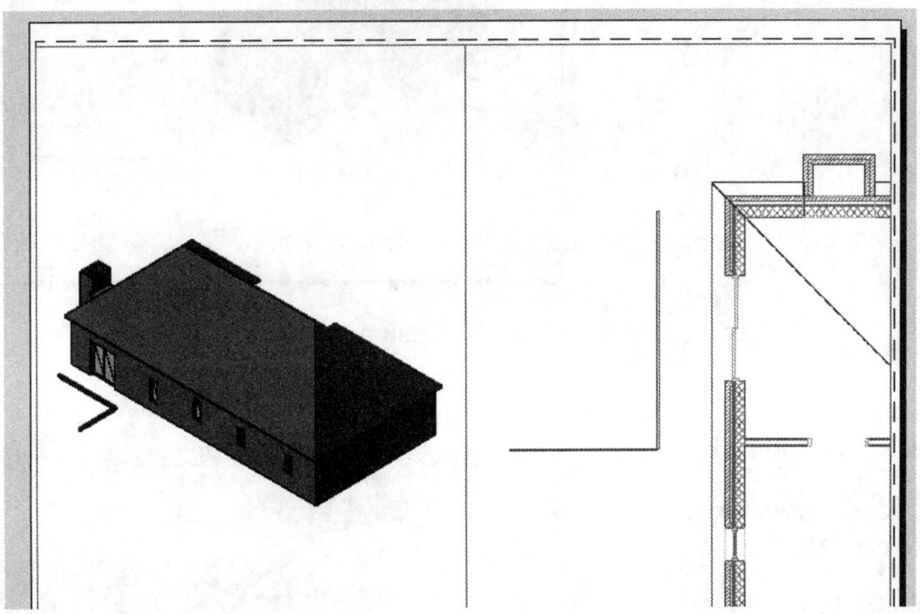

TIP: If you have difficulty starting the beam, draw the first two beams to the left of the building and then move them into position.

10. Select the first beam.
Right click and select **Basic Modify Tools→Mirror**.

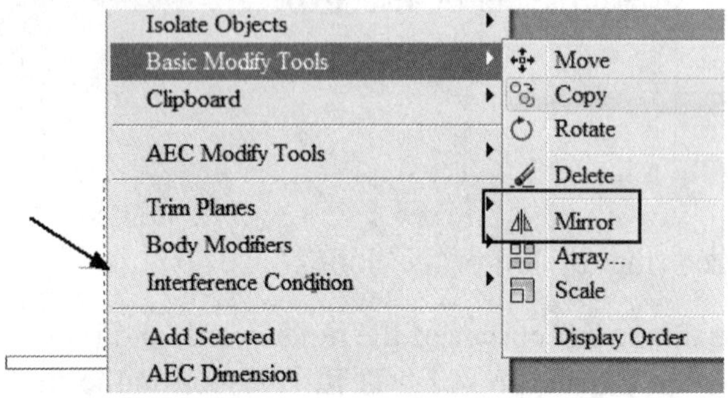

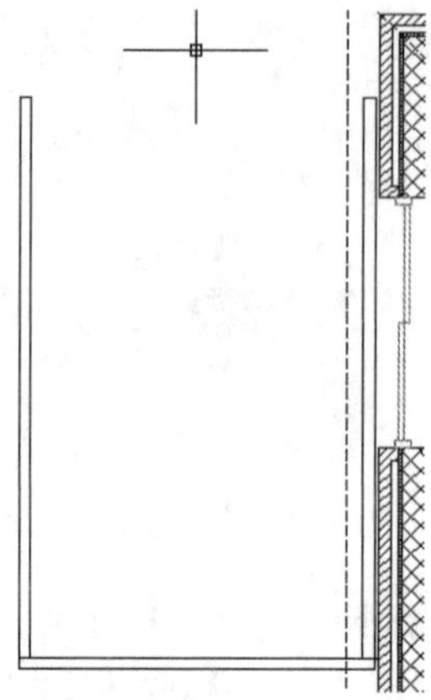

11. When prompted if you want to erase the source object, press ENTER to accept the default response of NO.

12. You should have the vertical and horizontal beam mirrored to create a base rectangle.

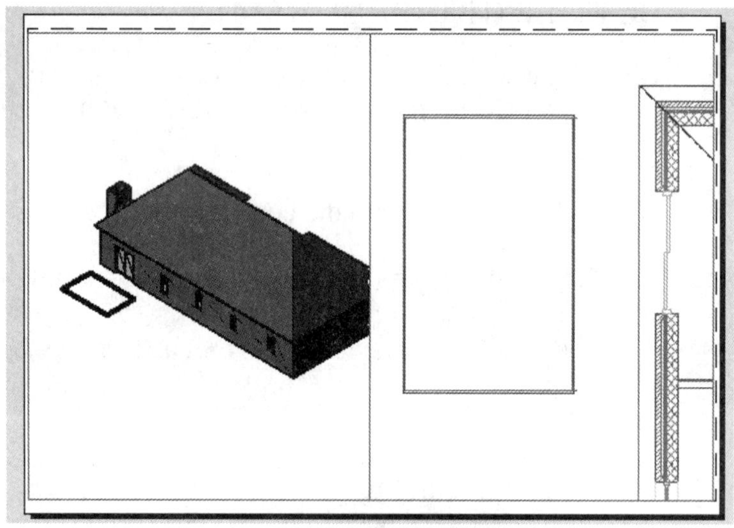

13. 

Select the **Beam** tool on the Design Palette.

14. Set the Style to **2″ x 10″ [50mmx250mm]**.

Under Layout type:
Select **Fill**.

Under Layout:
Set Array to **Yes**.
Set Layout Method to **Space evenly**.
Set Number of bays to **10**.

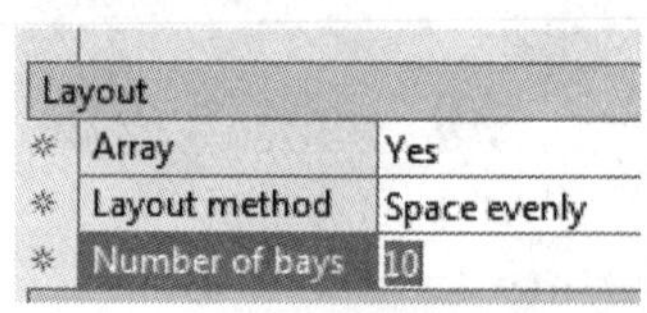

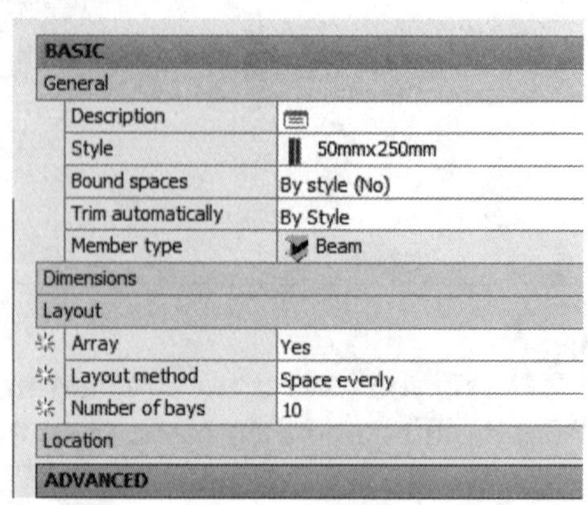

15. 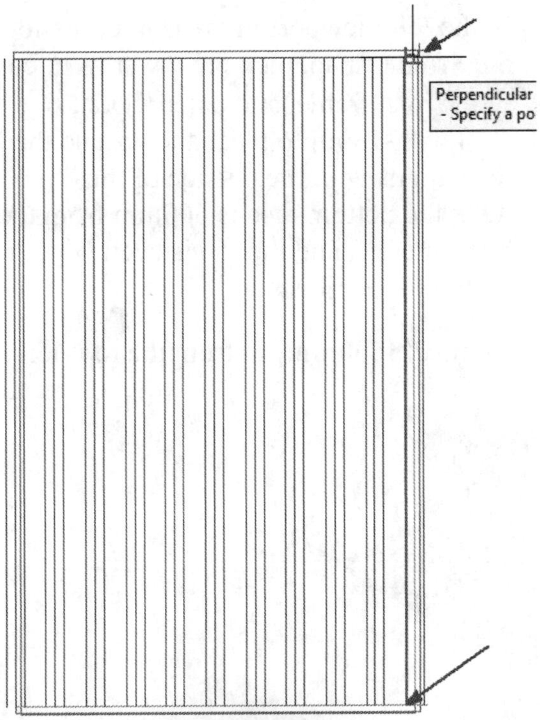

Select the start and end points for the beginning and end of the array.
Pick the bottom left side of the right vertical beam.
Pick the top left side of the right vertical beam.
You should see a preview image of the array that will be placed.

Press ENTER to accept the array placement.

16. 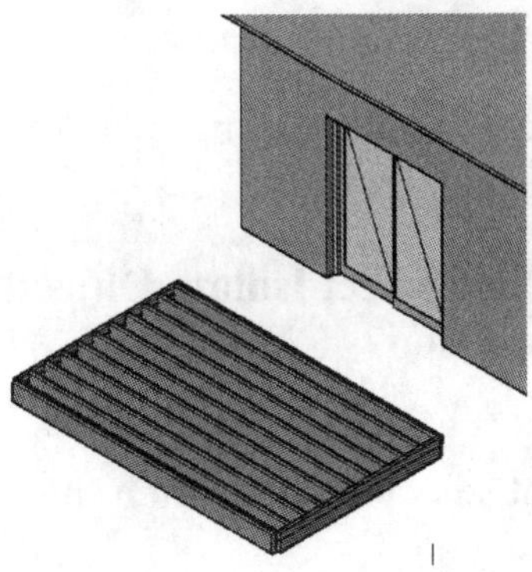

The array is placed.

If you are unable to create the array using the beam tool, verify that the UCS is set to view. Then, use the standard array command; select the horizontal beam and use a row spacing of 1′ 6″ [450 mm].

Some students may find it easier to construct this deck away from the house and then move it into position.

17. 

Select the **Column** tool from the Design Palette.

18. Set the Style to **4″ x 4″ [100mm x 100mm]**.
Set the Length to **5′ 9″ [1800]**.
Set Justify to **Bottom Left**.
Set the Roll to **0**.

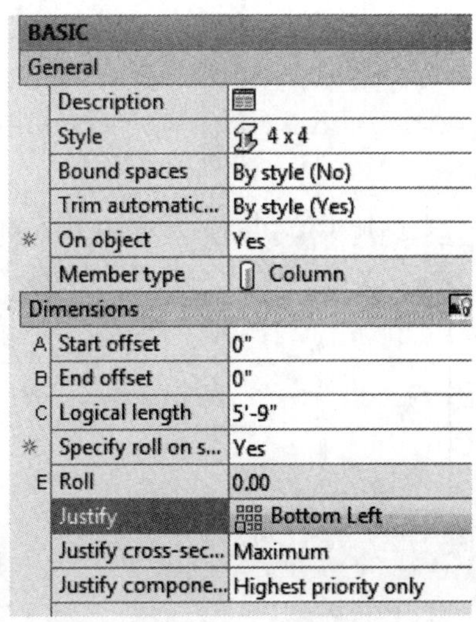

19. 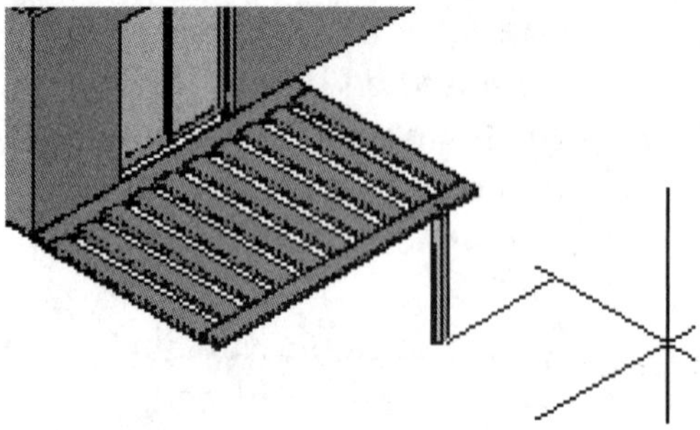

In the left viewport in the isometric view, use the From Osnap, pick the lower right corner of the joist frame, and enter **@0,2′,-6′ [@0,600,-1800]** to place the post so the left face aligns with the outside of the doubled joist, the bottom face is 600mm from the bottom edge, and the top is even with the bottom of the joists.

20.  Mirror the post to place another column **2′ [600mm]** in from the top (left side) of the frame.

21. Zoom in to the isometric view of the structure.

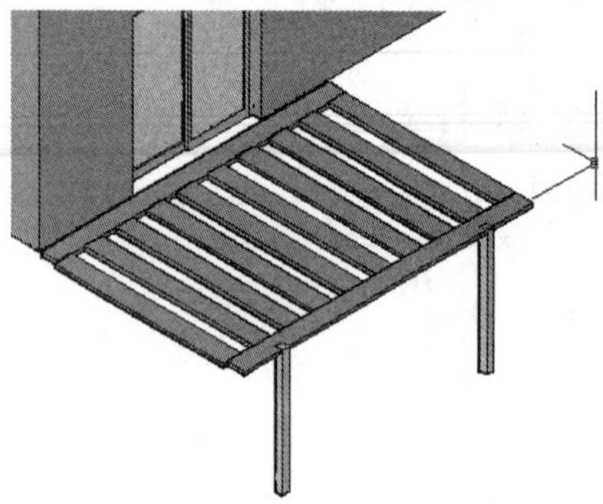

22. Select the front joist and the two posts. You may select using crossing, window, the control key, and de-select using the SHIFT key.

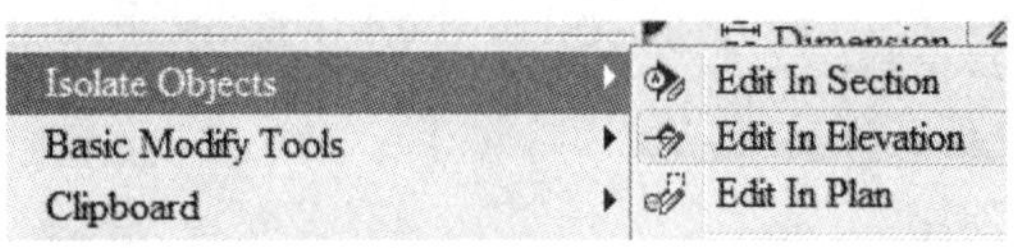

Right click and select **Isolate Objects→ Edit In Elevation**.

This will temporarily hide all the objects that were not selected and switch the display to an elevation view.

23. 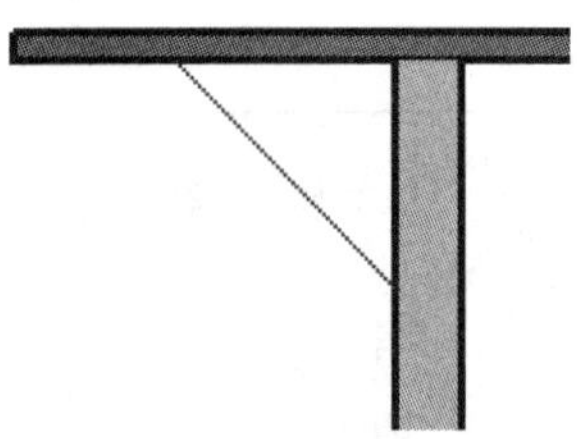

Draw a line to locate a brace in the elevation view.

24. 

In the plan view in the right viewport, adjust the line so it is straight and half-way into the front joist.

25. 

On the Design Palette:
Highlight the **Brace** tool.
Right click and **select Apply Tool Properties to→Linework.**

26. 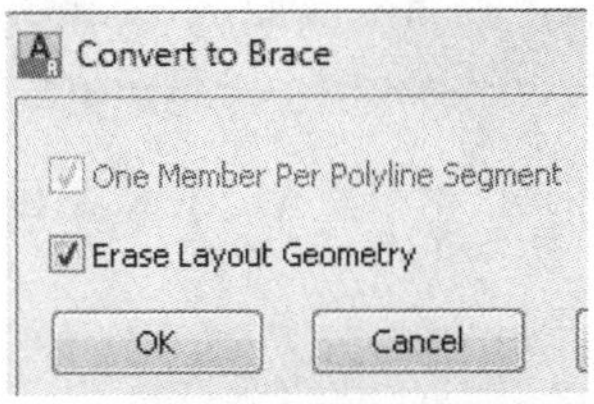

Select the line you just drew.

Place a check on **Erase Layout Geometry**.

Press **OK**.

27. 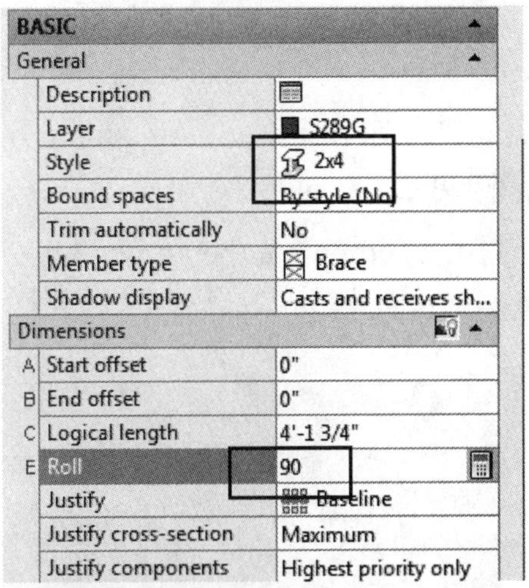

By default, the standard style brace is placed.

In the Properties dialog, select the **2 x 4** style.

Set the Roll to **90**.

28. 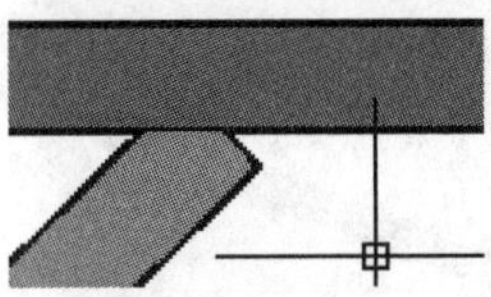

The brace needs to be trimmed.

29. 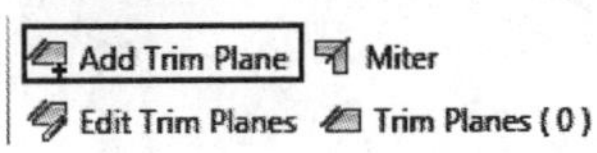

With the brace selected, select **Add Trim Plane** from the ribbon.

30. 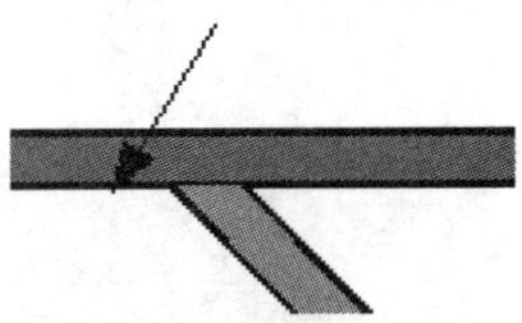

Select the bottom edge of the joist.

The brace will trim to the joist.

31. 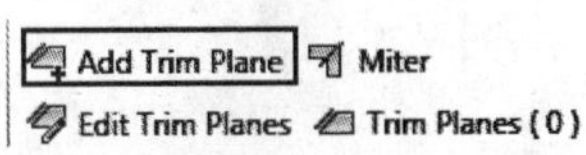

With the brace selected, select **Add Trim Plane**.

32. 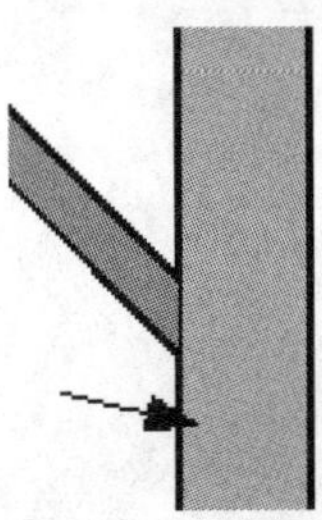

Select the side face of the joist.

The brace will trim to the joist.

Press ESC to release the selection.

33. 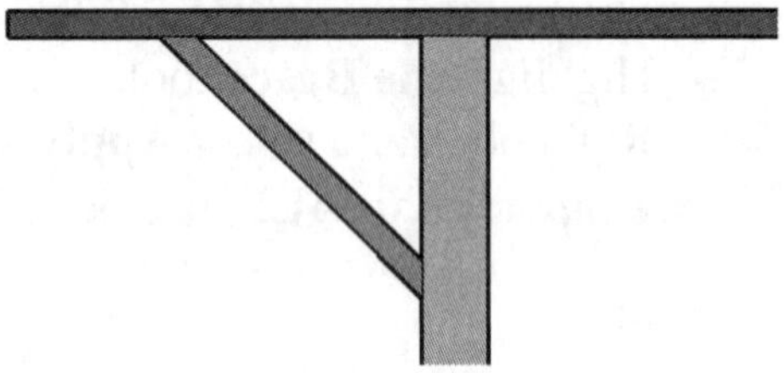
Select the brace and mirror it to the other side of the column.

34. 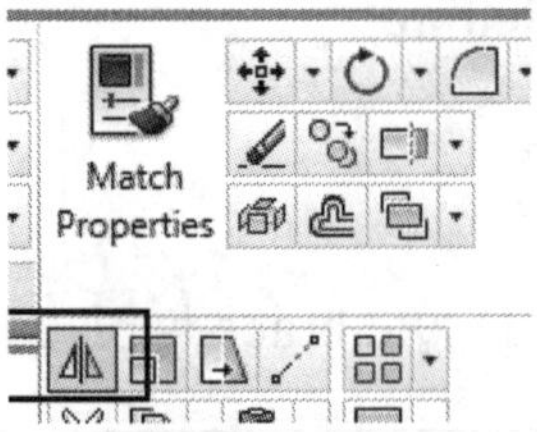

The Mirror tool is on the Home ribbon in the Modify drop-down.

35. 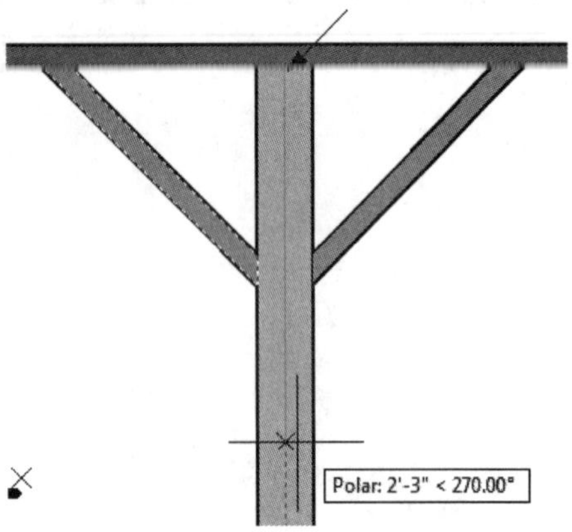

Select the midpoint of the column and move the cursor down at a 270° angle.

Press ENTER to complete the command.

36. Use Mirror to copy the brace to the other column.

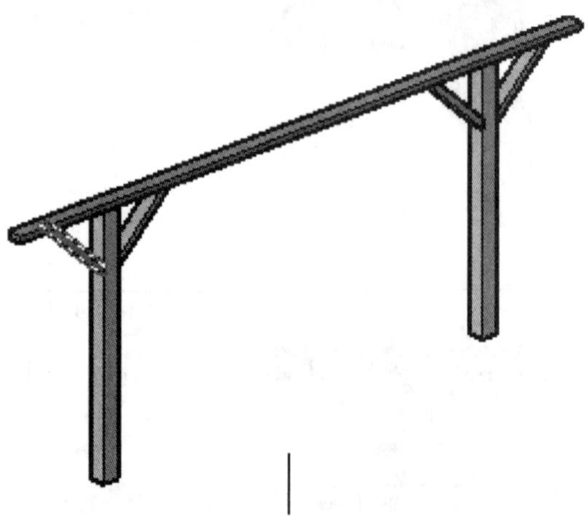

37. 

Locate the **Edit in View** window.

Click the X to end the isolate mode.

You may have to search for this window.

38. Save as *ex6-3.dwg*.

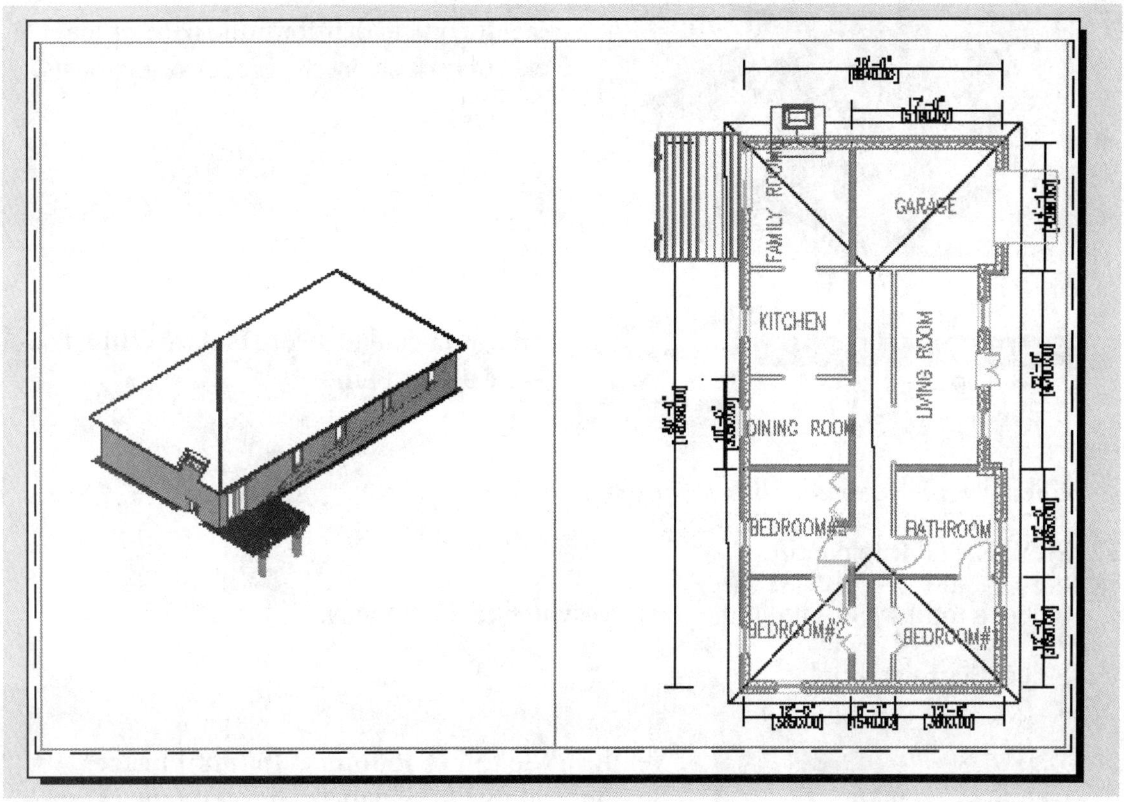

Exercise 6-4:

Add Floorboards

Drawing Name: ex6-3.dwg
Estimated Time: 20 minutes

This exercise reinforces the following skills:

- Structural Members
- Use of Structural Members tools

The top of the joist frame we created in the last exercise is sitting even with the top of the floor slab. It needs to be lowered to allow for nominal 2x6 deck boards.

1.  Open *ex6-3.dwg.*
Select the Work tab.
Activate the right viewport.

2. 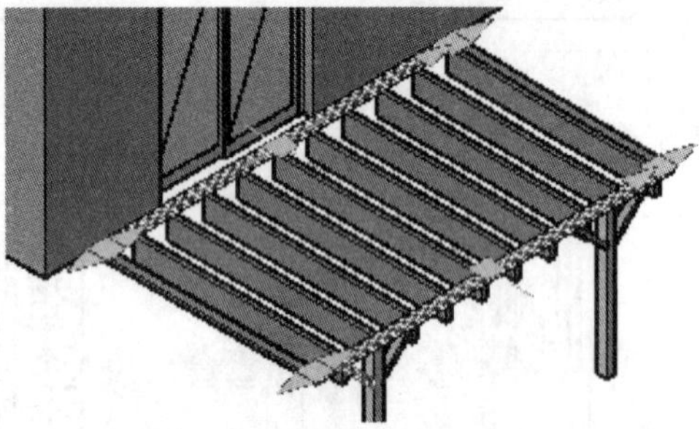

Select the joists that form the base of the deck. Do not select the braces or the posts.

3. 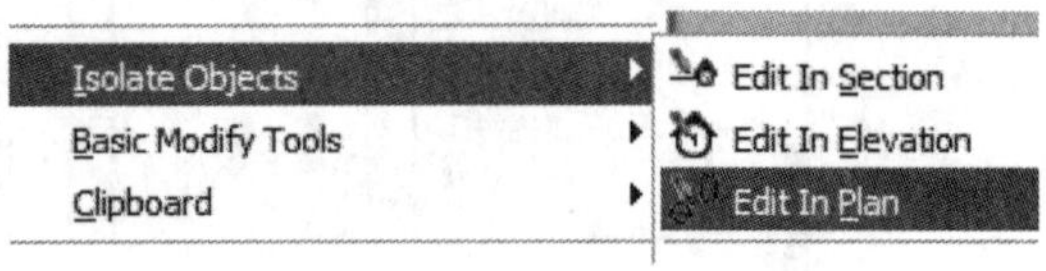

Right click and select **Isolate Objects →Edit In Plan**.

Check on the command line for prompts.

Press **ENTER** to continue.

4. Select a top face of one of the joists to switch to a plan view.

5. Select the **Beam** tool. 

6. 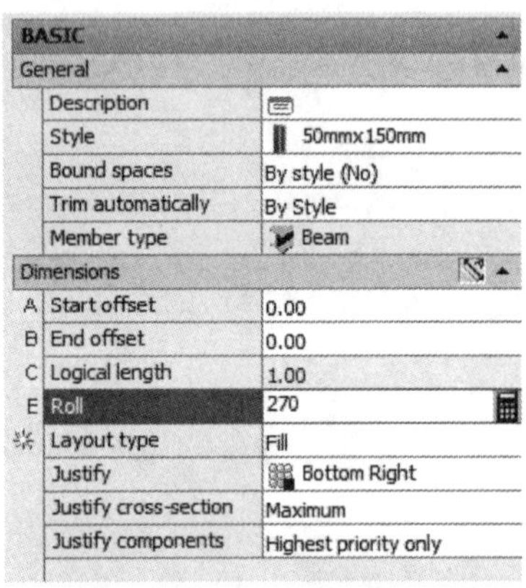

Set the Style to **2x6 [50mm x 150mm] brace**.
Set the Roll to **270°**, so that it lies flat rather than vertical.
Set the Justification to **Bottom Right**, so the board sits on top of the joists.

7. 

Pick the lower right corner of the joist at the house wall, drag the cursor up (90°), and give the board a length of 8′ [2430mm]. Drag the cursor up at 90° and add a second board of length 6′ [1820mm].

TIP: If you have difficulty starting the beam, draw the first beam to the left of the building and then move them into position.

8. 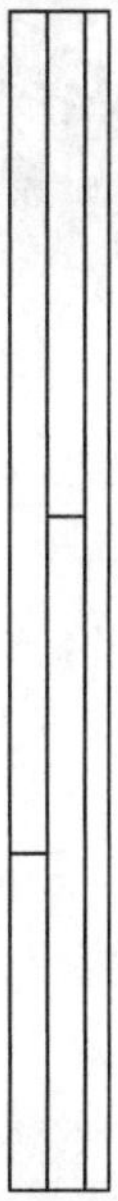

Enter twice to terminate and restart the command so you can pick a new starting point.

Pick the lower left corner of the first deck board you created, pull the cursor up at 90°, enter a distance of 4′ [1200mm], then pull the cursor up at 90° and enter a distance of 10′ [3050mm]. (Although not strictly necessary, we are providing suggested lengths of deck boards to minimize wastage.) Deck boards are laid with a nominal ⅜″ [10 mm] space between them to allow for drainage and board warping, so move the last two deck boards ⅜″ [10 mm] to the left.

9. 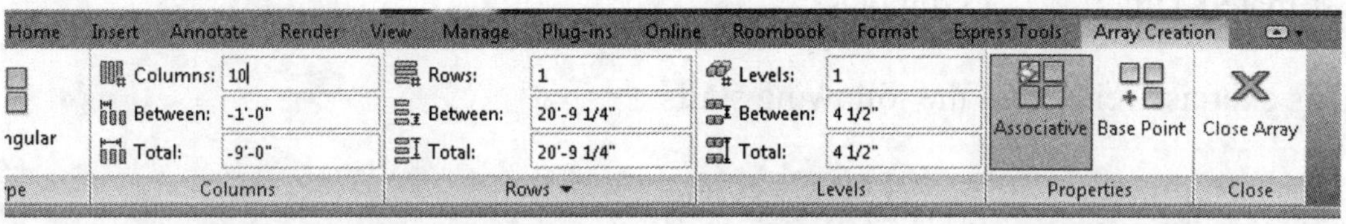

Array the 4 deck boards to fill the deck: 1 row, 10 columns with a column offset of **1′ [300mm]**.

10. 

Use the Preview option of the Array to check your array.

Right click the mouse to accept.

11. 

Select the **Exit Edit In View** button.

Note: You want a gap between the boards to allow for expansion and compression due to seasonal changes.

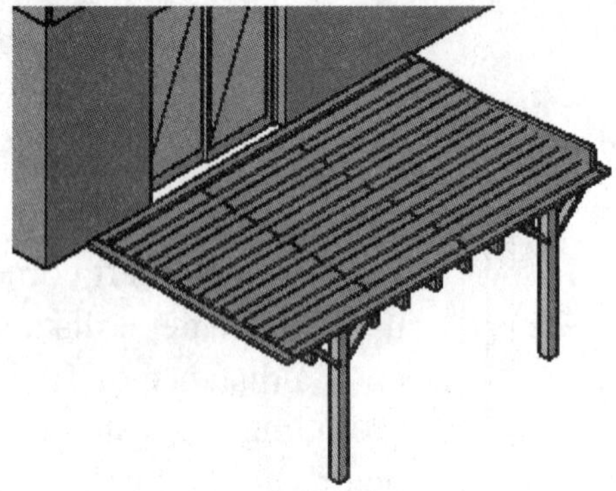

12. Save as *ex6-4.dwg*.

Exercise 6-5:

Add Railing

Drawing Name: Ex6-4.dwg
Estimated Time: 15 minutes

This exercise reinforces the following skills:

- Railings
- Railing Styles

1.  Open *ex6-4.dwg*.
Select the Work tab.
Activate the right viewport.

2. 

Select the **Railing** tool from the Design palette.

3. Create endpoints at 8′ 6″ [2620 mm] to the left (180°), then 13′ 6″ [4100 mm] up (90°), and 6′ 4″ [1900 mm] to the right (0°). This leaves an opening at the corner of the house.

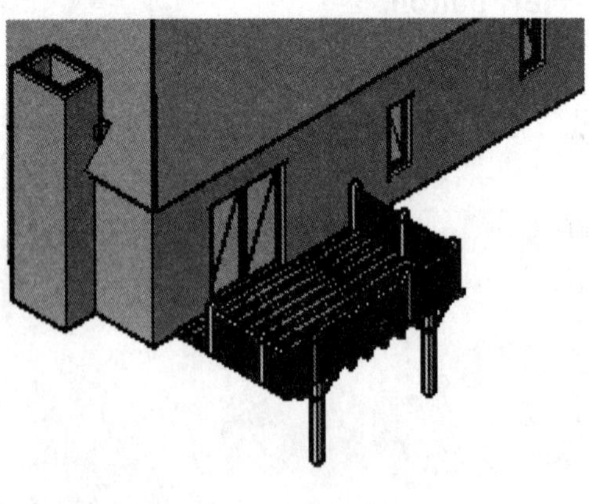

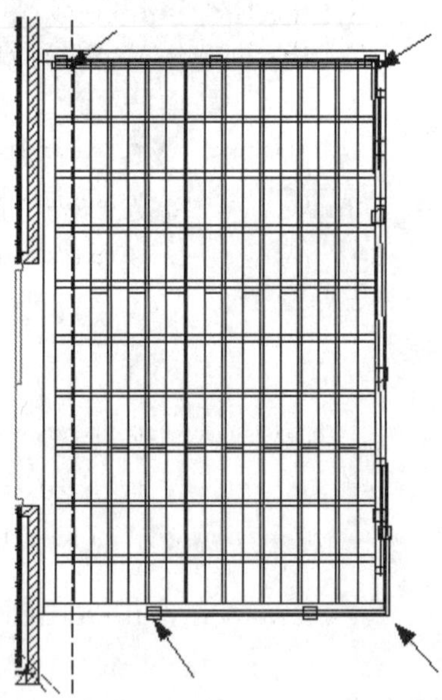

4. 

Select the **Railing** tool from the Design Palette.
Right click and select **Railing Styles**.

5. 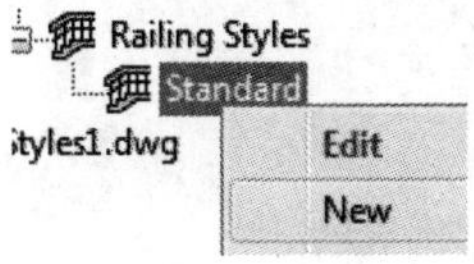

Select **Standard** under Railing Styles.
Right click and select **New**.

6. 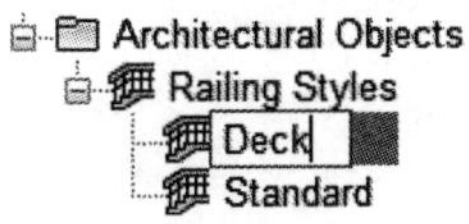

Name the new railing style **Deck**.

7. 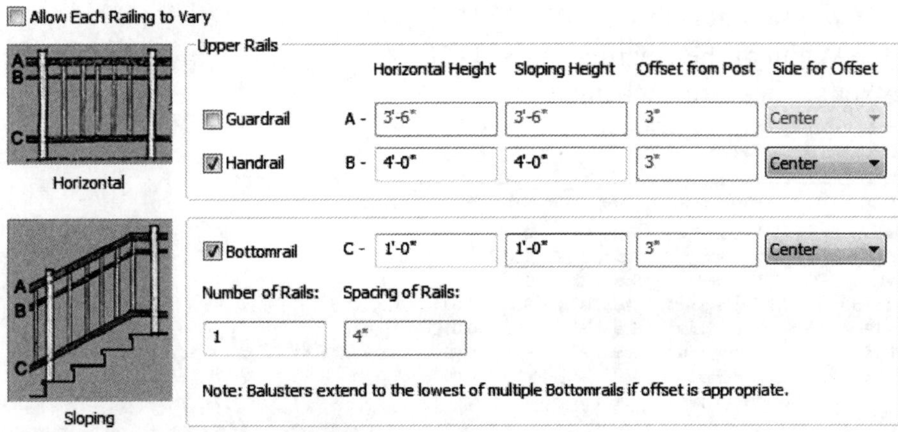

Select the **Rail Locations** tab.
Enable **Handrail** for the Upper Rails.
Set the Horizontal Height to **4′ [900]**.
Set the Sloping Height to **4′ [900]**.
Set the Side for Offset to **Center**.
Enable the **Bottom Rail**. (This adds a bottom rail)
Set the Horizontal Height to **1′-0″ [100]**.
Set the Sloping Height to **1′-0″ [150]**.
Set the Number of Rails to **1**.

8. 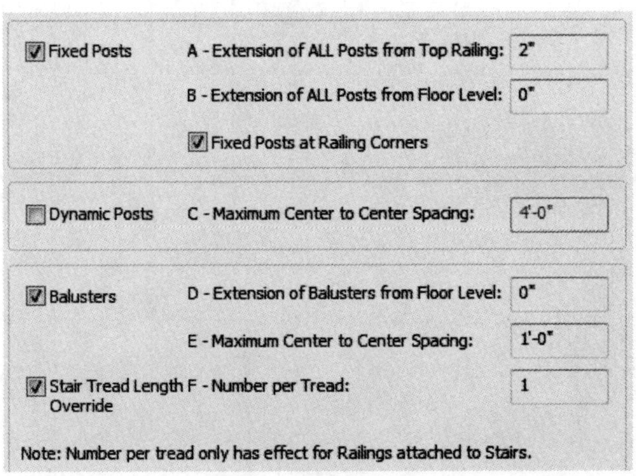

Select the **Post Locations** tab.
Enable **Fixed Posts.**
Enable **Fixed Posts at Railing Corners**. (This adds a post to each corner.)
Set the Extensions of ALL Posts from Top Railing to **2″ [50]**.
Enable **Dynamic Posts.**
Set the Maximum Center to Center Spacing to **4′ 0″ [1350]**.
Enable **Balusters.**
Set the Maximum Center to Center Spacing to **1′-0″ [100]**.
Enable the **Stair Tread Length Override.**
Set the Number per Tread to 1.

9. Select the **Components** tab.
Change the Width of the Guardrail to **3″ [75]**.
All the other settings are unchanged.

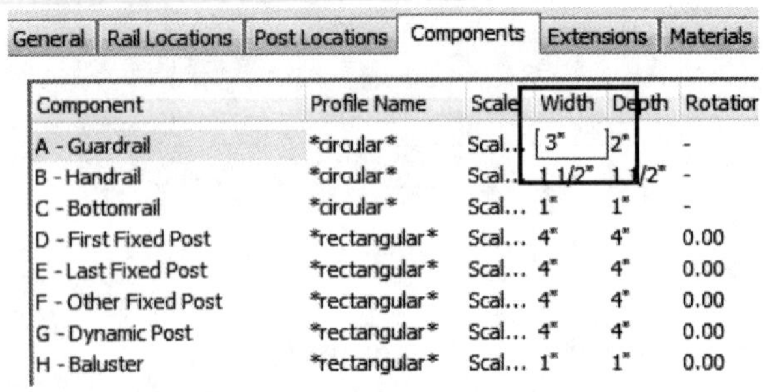

Component	Profile Name	Scale	Width	Depth	Rotatior
A - Guardrail	*circular*	Scal...	3"	2"	-
B - Handrail	*circular*	Scal...	1 1/2"	1 1/2"	-
C - Bottomrail	*circular*	Scal...	1"	1"	-
D - First Fixed Post	*rectangular*	Scal...	4"	4"	0.00
E - Last Fixed Post	*rectangular*	Scal...	4"	4"	0.00
F - Other Fixed Post	*rectangular*	Scal...	4"	4"	0.00
G - Dynamic Post	*rectangular*	Scal...	4"	4"	0.00
H - Baluster	*rectangular*	Scal...	1"	1"	0.00

Press **OK** to close the dialog box.

10. Select the Railing.
Right click and select **Properties**.

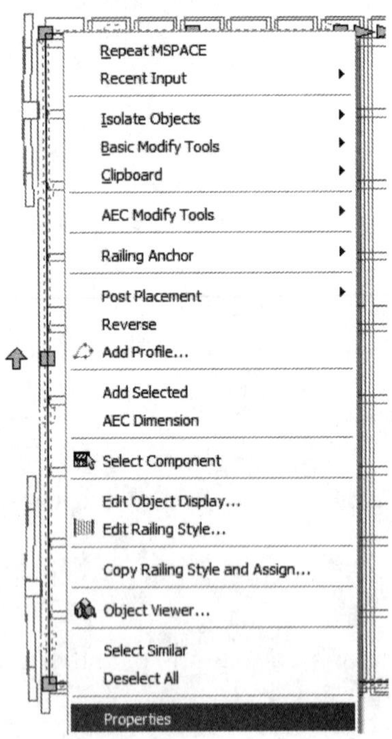

11. 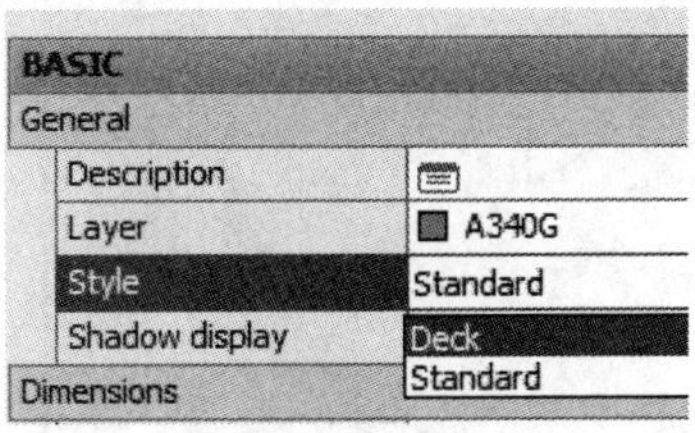

Change the Style to **Deck.**
Close the dialog.

12. Save as *ex6-5.dwg*.

Stairs

A house may have main stairs (from the first floor to the second floor) and/or a set of service stairs. Main stairs are usually constructed using pre-fabricated parts and are generally of better quality than service stairs. Service stairs are built on location. They are generally constructed of construction lumber.

There are six general types of stairs commonly used in residential construction. They are straight-run, L stairs, double-L stairs, U stairs, winder stairs and spiral stairs.

Straight run stairs are the most common. They are the least expensive to build, but they require a long open space.

Common terms associated with stairs include:

Balusters:	vertical members that support the handrail on open stairs
Enclosed stairs:	stairs that have a wall on both sides (also known as closed, housed, or box stairs). These can be stairs leading down to a basement or cellar.
Headroom:	The shortest clear vertical distance measured from the nosing of the tread and the ceiling.
Housed stringer:	A stringer that has been routed or grooved to accommodate the treads and risers.
Landing:	The floor area at either end of the stairs; also the area between a set of stairs, such as in an L stairs.
Newel:	The main posts of the handrail at the top and bottom or at points where the stairs change direction.
Nosing:	The rounded projection of the tread which extends past the face of the riser.

We will be adding service stairs to our deck.

Exercise 6-6:

Add Stairs

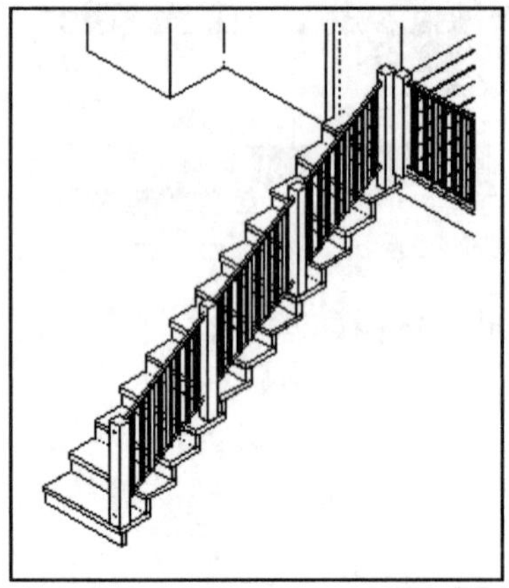

Drawing Name: Ex6-5.dwg
Estimated Time: 15 minutes

This exercise reinforces the following skills:

- Add Stairs
- Add Railing

1.  Open *ex6-5.dwg.*
   Select the Work tab.
   Activate the right viewport.

2. 

   Select the **Stair** tool from the Design Palette.

3. 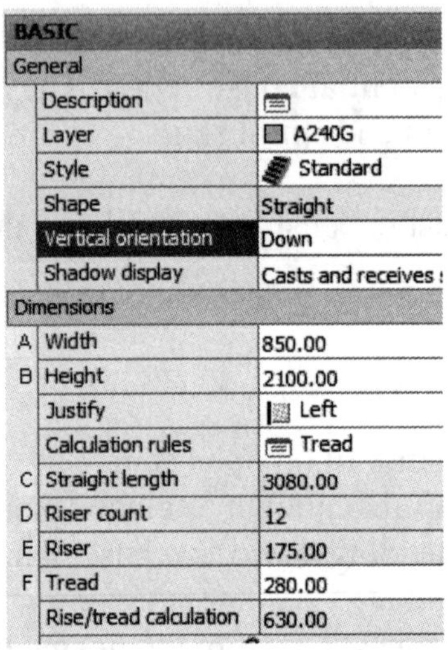

BASIC		
General		
	Description	
	Layer	A240G
	Style	Standard
	Shape	Straight
	Vertical orientation	Down
	Shadow display	Casts and receives
Dimensions		
A	Width	850.00
B	Height	2100.00
	Justify	Left
	Calculation rules	Tread
C	Straight length	3080.00
D	Riser count	12
E	Riser	175.00
F	Tread	280.00
	Rise/tread calculation	630.00

Set the Style to **Standard**.
Set the Shape to **Straight**.
Set the Vertical Orientation to **Down**.
Set the Width to **2′ 9″ [850]**.
Set the Height to **6′ 5″ [2100]**.
Set the Tread to **11″ [280]**.
Set Justify to **Left**.

Note that the Straight length is automatically calculated at **9′ 2″ [3080]**.

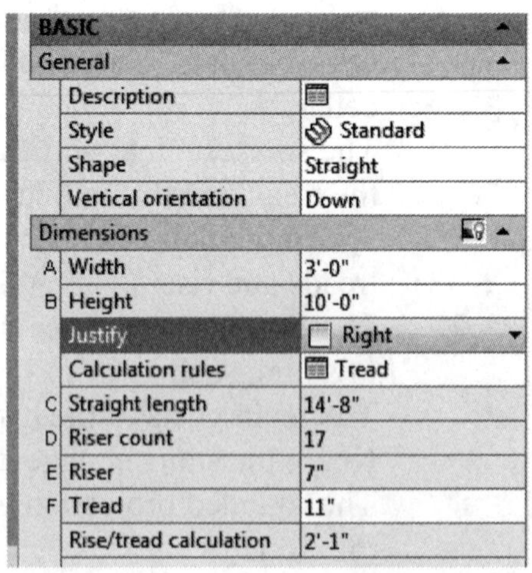

BASIC		
General		
	Description	
	Style	Standard
	Shape	Straight
	Vertical orientation	Down
Dimensions		
A	Width	3'-0"
B	Height	10'-0"
	Justify	Right
	Calculation rules	Tread
C	Straight length	14'-8"
D	Riser count	17
E	Riser	7"
F	Tread	11"
	Rise/tread calculation	2'-1"

4. 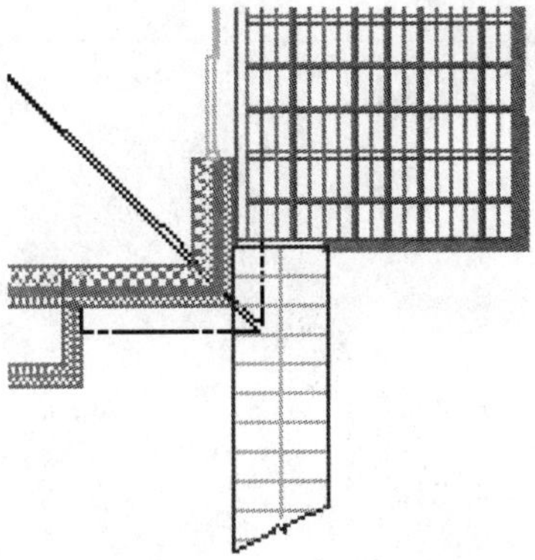

Pick an end point by the left side of the deck opening near the start of the railing.

Pick a point near the top of the deck for the end point of the stairs.

Close the dialog box.

5. We see the stair as a broken view.

6. 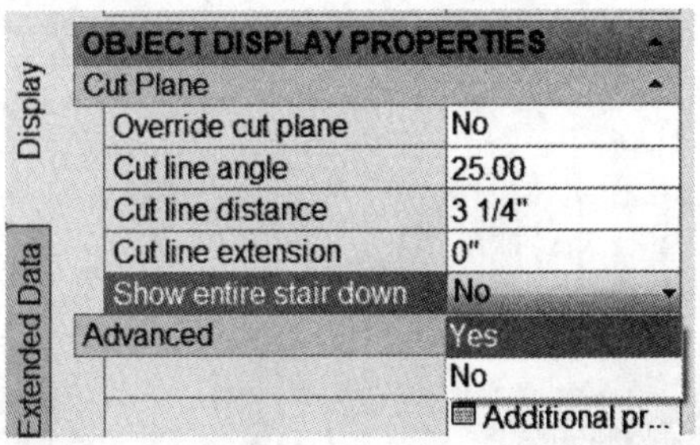

Select the stairs.
Right click and select Properties.
Select the Display tab.
Set Show entire stair down to **Yes**.

7. Type **Regen**.
The stairs now appear without a break mark.

Note: *If the view doesn't update, try switching to a different view and then switch back to Plan view.*

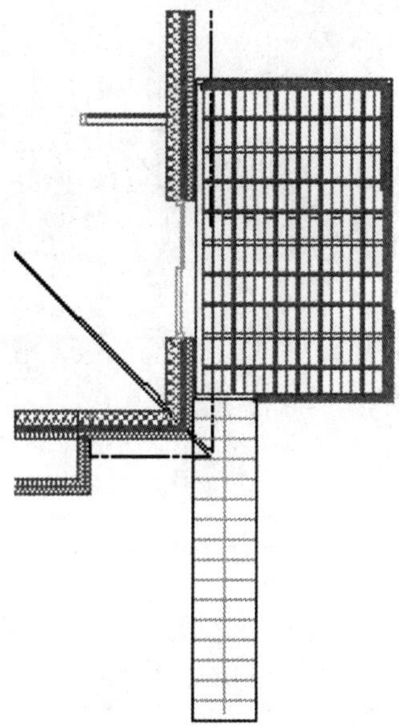

8. 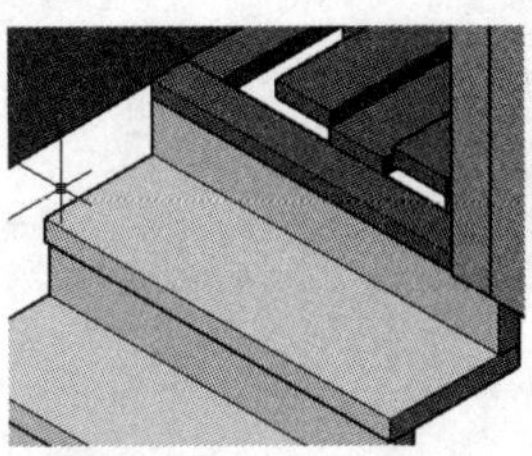

The stairs are placed, but they may need to be shifted slightly to fit with the deck.
Use the MOVE tool to position the stairs properly.
Safety regulations require a handrail down the stairs.

9. 

Select the **Railing** tool from the Design Palette.

10. 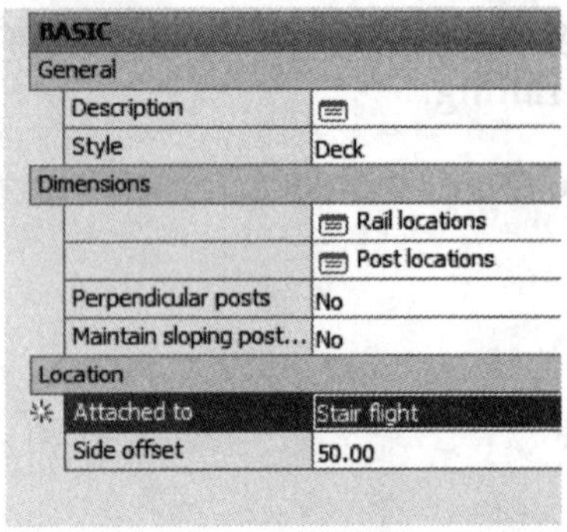

Set the Style to **Deck**.
Set Attached to: **Stair Flight**.
Set Offset to **2″ [50]**.

11. 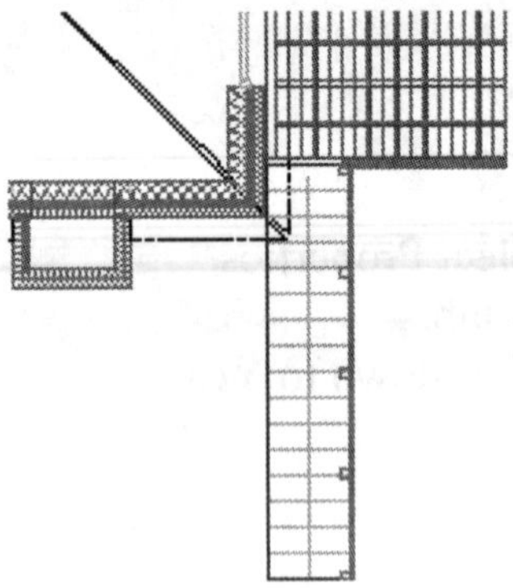

You will be prompted to select the stairs.
Pick the left side of the stair to place railing on the left side.

12. Save as *ex6-6.dwg*.

QUIZ 3

True or False

1. Custom content can be located in any subdirectory and still function properly.
2. The sole purpose of the Space Planning process is to arrange furniture in a floor plan.
3. The Design Center only has 3D objects stored in the Content area because ADT is strictly a 3D software.
4. Appliances are automatically placed on the APPLIANCE layer.
5. When you place a wall cabinet, it is automatically placed at the specified height.
6. You can create tools on a tool palette by dragging and dropping the objects from the Design Center onto the palette.

Multiple Choice

7. A residential structure is divided into:

    A. Four basic areas
    B. Three basic areas
    C. Two basic areas
    D. One basic area

8. Kitchen cabinets are located in the ______________ subfolder.

    A. Casework
    B. Cabinets
    C. Bookcases
    D. Furniture

9. Select the area type that is NOT part of a private residence:

    A. Bedrooms
    B. Common Areas
    C. Service Areas
    D. Public Areas

10. To set the layer properties of a tool on a tool palette:

    A. Use the Layer Manager
    B. Select the tool, right click and select Properties.
    C. Launch the Properties dialog
    D. All of the above

11. Vehicles placed from the Design Center are automatically placed on this layer:

   A. A-Site-Vhcl
   B. A-Vhcl
   C. C-Site Vhcl
   D. None of the above

12. The **Roof** tool is located on this tool palette:

   A. DESIGN
   B. GENERAL DRAFTING
   C. MASSING
   D. TOOLS

ANSWERS:

1) T; 2) F; 3) F; 4) F; 5) T; 6) T; 7) B; 8) A; 9) D; 10) B; 11) C; 12) A

Lesson 7
Documentation

Before we can create our construction drawings, we need to create layouts or views to present the design. AutoCAD Architecture is similar to AutoCAD in that the user can work in Model and Paper Space. Model Space is where we create the 3D model of our house. Paper Space is where we create or setup various views that can be used in our construction drawings. In each view, we can control what we see by turning off layers, zooming, panning, etc.

To understand paper space and model space, imagine a cardboard box. Inside the cardboard box is Model Space. This is where your 3D model is located. On each side of the cardboard box, tear out a small rectangular window. The windows are your viewports. You can look through the viewports to see your model. To reach inside the window so you can move your model around or modify it, you double-click inside the viewport. If your hand is not reaching through any of the windows and you are just looking from the outside, then you are in Paper Space or Layout mode.
You can create an elevation in your current drawing by first drawing an elevation line and mark, and then creating a 2D or 3D elevation based on that line. You can control the size and shape of the elevation that is generated. Unless you explode the elevation that you create, the elevation remains linked to the building model that you used to create it. Because of this link between the elevation and the building model, any changes to the building model can be made in the elevation as well.

When you create a 2D elevation, the elevation is created with hidden and overlapping lines removed. You can edit the 2D elevation that you created by changing its display properties. The 2D Section/Elevation style allows you to add your own display components to the display representation of the elevation, and create rules that assign different parts of the elevation to different display components. You can control the visibility, layer, color, linetype, lineweight, and linetype scale of each component. You can also use the line work editing commands to assign individual lines in your 2D elevation to display components, and merge geometry into your 2D elevation.

After you create a 2D elevation, you can use the AutoCAD BHATCH and AutoCAD DIMLINEAR commands to hatch and dimension the 2D elevation.

AutoCAD comes with standard title block templates. They are located in the Templates subdirectory under *Documents and Settings \<User Name>\Local Settings\Application Data\ Autodesk\ AutoCAD 2013\R18.2\enu \Template.*

If you are using VISTA or Windows 7, the templates are stored under *Users/<user name>/AppData/Local/ Autodesk/AutoCAD 2013/R18.2/enu/Template.*

Many companies will place their templates on the network so all users can access the same templates. In order to make this work properly, set the Options so that the templates folder is pointed to the correct path.

Exercise 7-1:
Creating a Custom Titleblock

Drawing Name: Architectural Title Block.dwg
Estimated Time: 30 minutes

This exercise reinforces the following skills:

- Title blocks
- Attributes
- Edit Block In-Place
- Insert Image
- Insert Hyperlink

1.  Select the **Open** tool.

2. Browse to
Documents and Settings\All Users\ Application Data\Autodesk\ACA 2013\enu\ Template\ AutoCAD Templates.

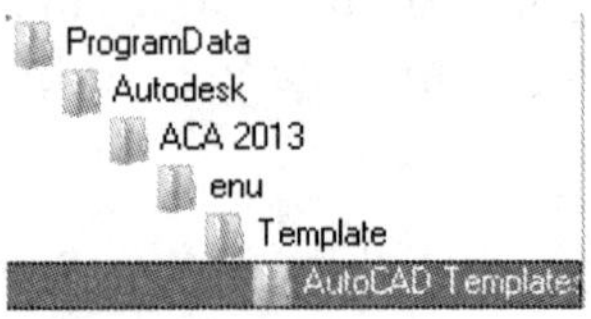

In Vista and Windows 7 machines, go to *Program Data/Autodesk/ACA 2013/enu/Template/AutoCAD Templates.*

3. 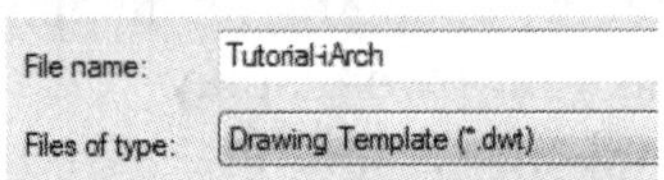

Open the *Tutorial-iArch.dwt.*
Verify that *Files of type* is set to Drawing Template or you won't see the file.

4. Perform a **File→Save as**.

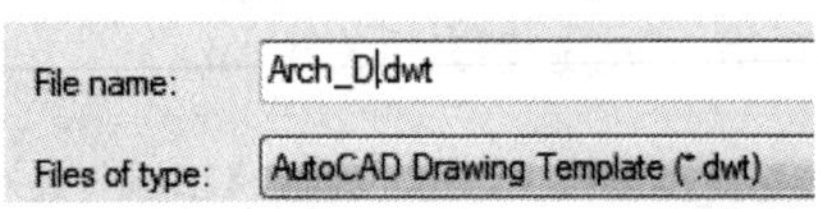

Save the file to your work folder.
Rename **Arch_D.dwt**.

5. 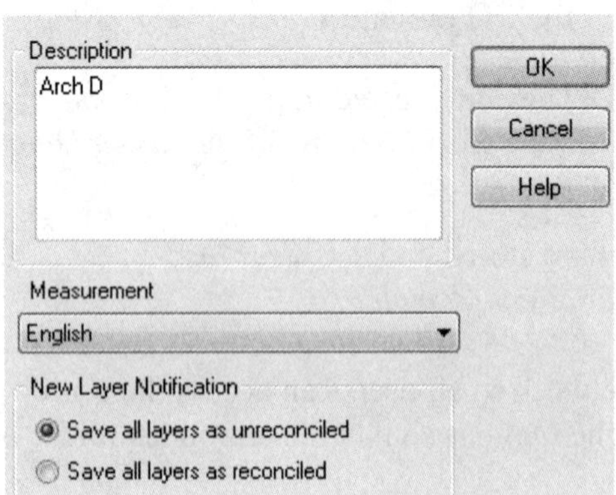

Enter a description and press **OK**.

6. 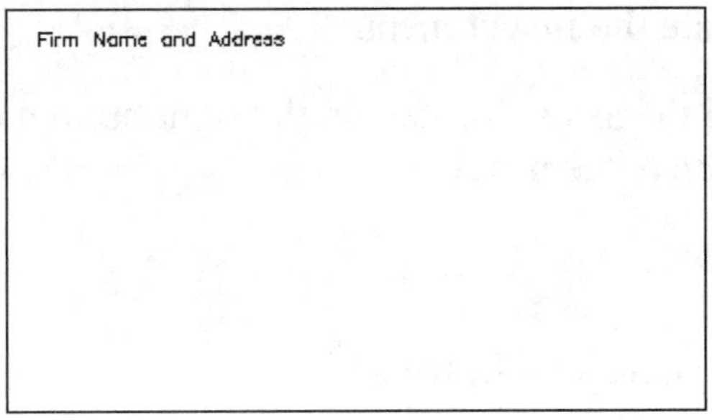

Zoom into the Firm Name and Address rectangle.

7. 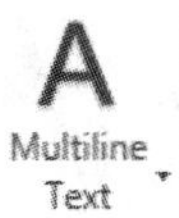

Select the **MTEXT** tool from the **Annotation** panel on the Home ribbon.

Draw a rectangle to place the text.

8. Set the Font to **Verdana**.

Hint: If you type the first letter of the font, the drop-down list will jump to fonts starting with that letter.

Set the text height to ⅛″.
Set the justification to **centered**.
Enter the name and address of your college.

9. 

Extend the ruler to change the width of your MTEXT box to fill the rectangle.

Press **OK**.

10. 

Use **MOVE** to locate the text properly, if needed.

11. 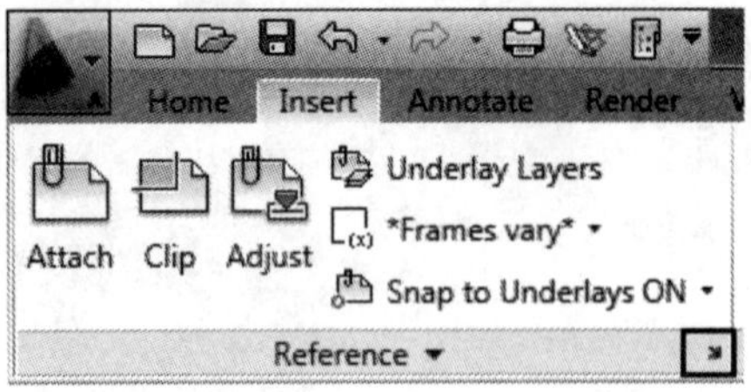

Activate the **Insert** menu.

Select the arrow located on the right bottom of the Reference panel.

12. 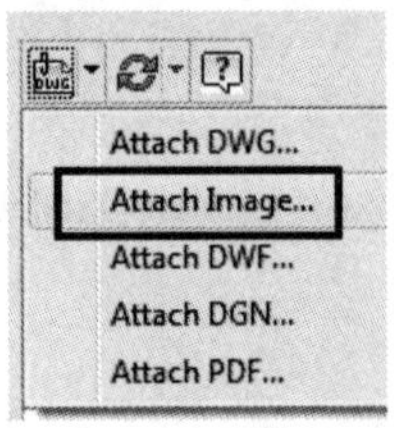

The External Reference Manager will launch.

Select **Attach Image** from the drop-down list.

13. 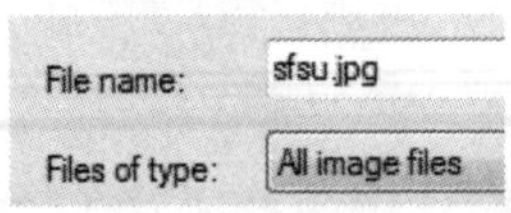

Locate the image file you wish to use.
There is an image file available for use from the publisher's website called *sfsu.jpg*.

14. 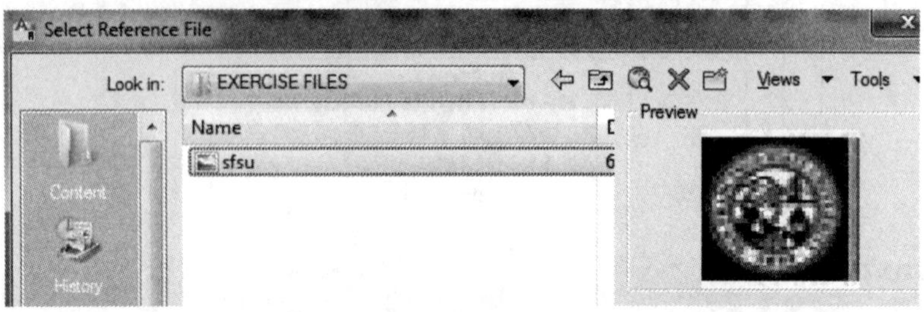

Press **Open**.

15. 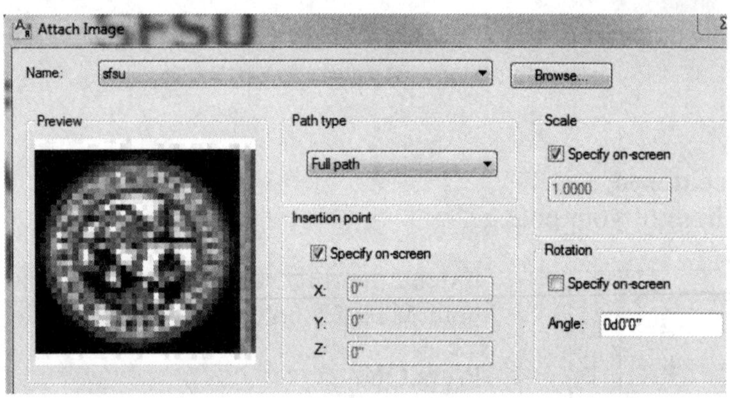

Press **OK**.

16. 

Place the image in the rectangle.

TIP: If you are concerned about losing the link to the image file (for example, if you plan to email this file to another person), you can use **INSERTOBJ** to embed the image into the drawing. Do not enable link to create an embedded object. The INSERTOBJ command is not available on the standard ribbon.

17. Select the image.
Right click and select **Properties**.

18. 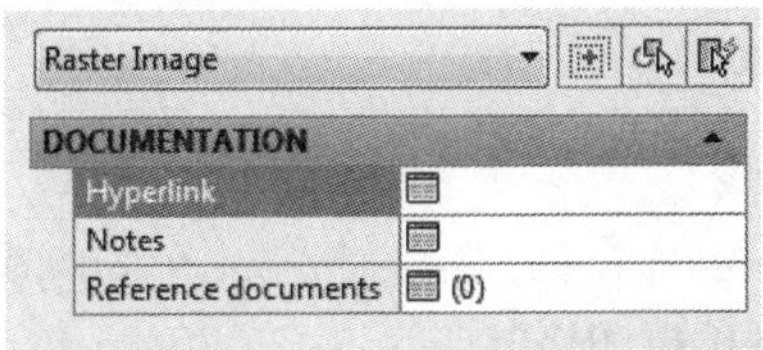

Select the **Extended** tab.
Pick the Hyperlink field.

19. 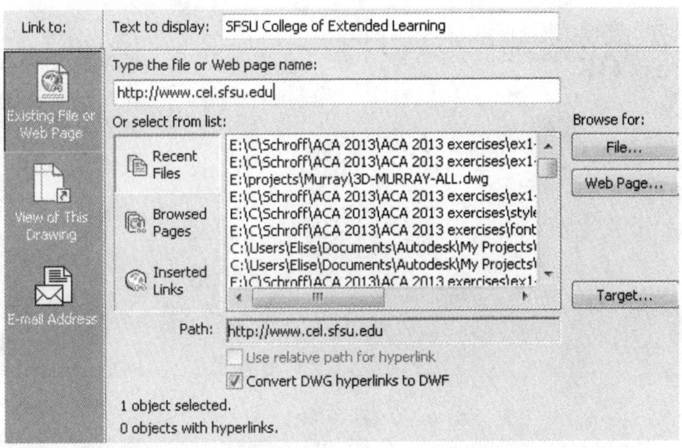

Type in the name of the school in the Text to display field.
Type in the website address in the *Type the file or Web page name* field.

Press **OK**.
Close the Properties dialog.

20. 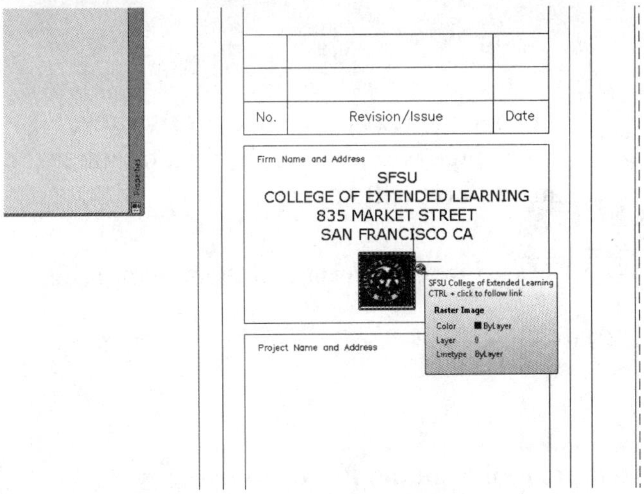

If you hover your mouse over the image, you will see a small World icon. This indicates there is a hyperlink attached to the image. To launch the webpage, simply hold down the CTRL key and left click on the icon.

TIP: If you are unsure of the web address of the website you wish to link, use the Browse for **Web Page** button.

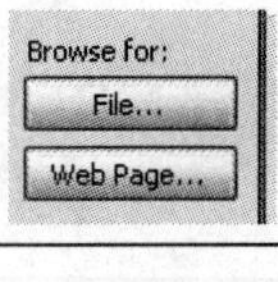

21. 

To turn off the image frame/boundary:

Type **IMAGEFRAME** at the command line.
Enter **0**.

> **TIP:** IMAGEFRAME has the following options:
> 0: Turns off the image frame and does not plot
> 1: Turns on the image frame and is plotted
> 2: Turns on the image frame, but does not plot

22. 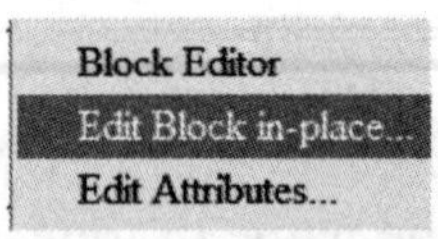

Select the titleblock.
Right click and select **Edit Block in-place**.

23. 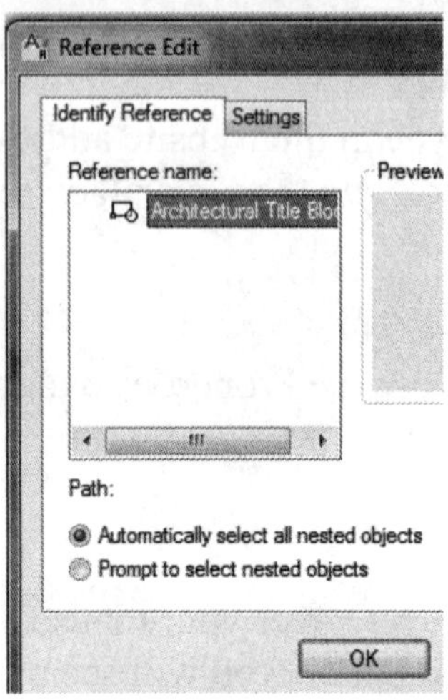

Press **OK**.

24. 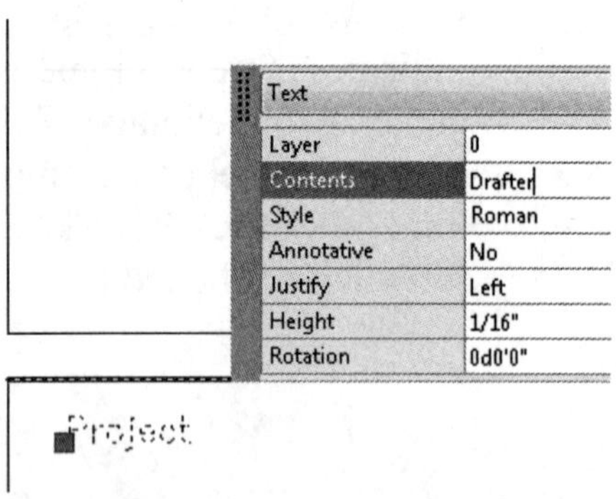

Change the text for Project to **Drafter**.
To change, simply double click on the text and an edit box will appear.

25. 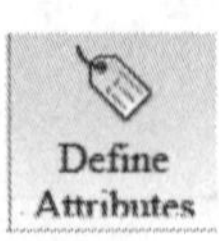

Select the **Define Attribute** tool from the Insert ribbon.

26. 

Select the **Field** tool.

27. 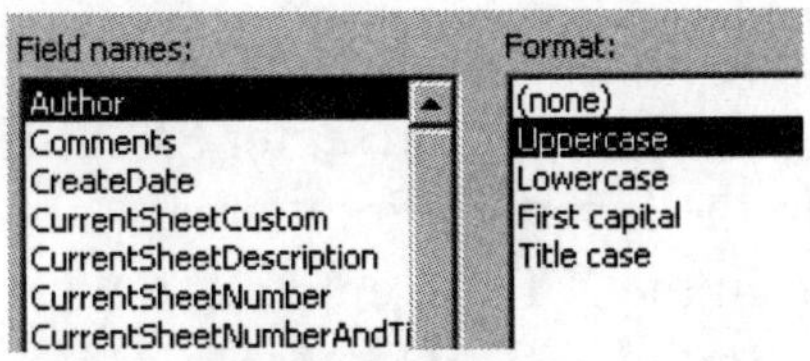

Highlight Author and Uppercase.

Press **OK**.

28. 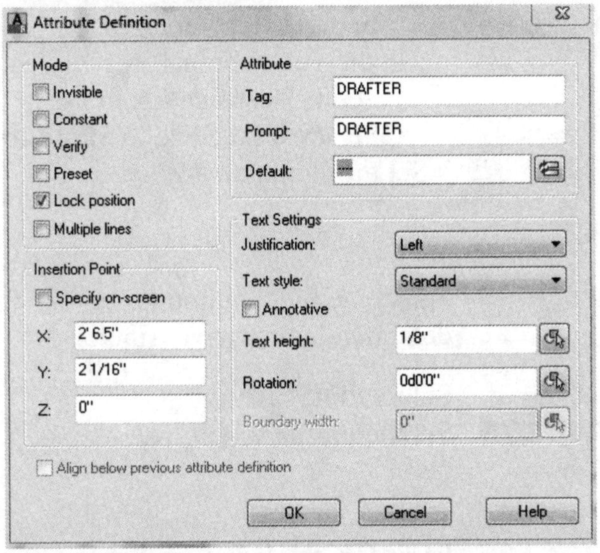

In the Tag field, enter **DRAFTER**.
In the Prompt field, enter **DRAFTER**.
The Value field is used by the FIELD property.
In the Insertion Point area:
In the X field, enter: **2′ 6.5″**.
In the Y field, enter: **2-1/16″**.
In the Z field, enter: **0″**.
In the Text Options area:
Set the Justification to **Left**.
Set the Text Style to **Standard**.
Set the Height to **1/8″**.

Press **OK**.

29. 

Select the **Define Attributes** tool.

30. 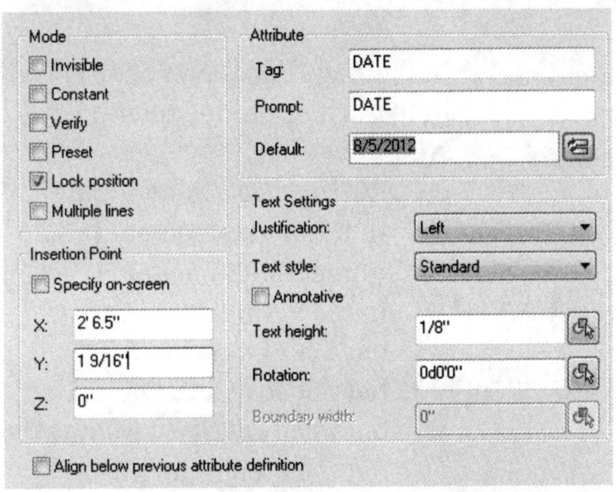

In the Tag field, enter **DATE**.
In the Prompt field, enter **DATE**.

In the Insertion Point area:
In the X field, enter: **2′ 6.5″**.
In the Y field, enter: **1-9/16″**.
In the Z field, enter: **0″**.
In the Text Options area:
Set the Justification to **Left**.
Set the Text Style to **Standard.**
Set the Height to **1/8″**.

31. Select the Field button to set the default value for the attribute.

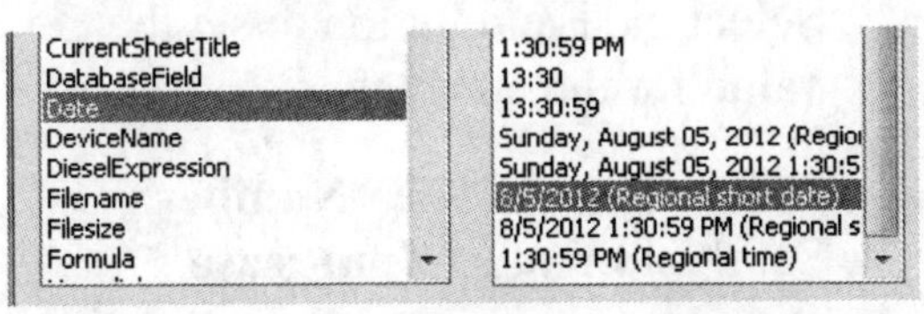

Select **Date**.
Set the Date format to **Regional short date**.

Press **OK**.

32. 

Select the **Define Attributes** tool.

33. 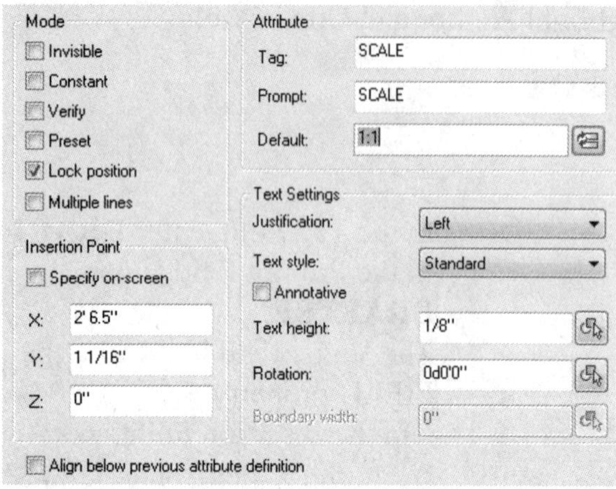

In the Tag field, enter **SCALE**.
In the Prompt field, enter **SCALE**.
In the Insertion Point area:
In the X field, enter: **2′ 6.5″**.
In the Y field, enter: **1-1/16″**.
In the Z field, enter: **0″**.
In the Text Options area:
Set the Justification to **Left**.
Set the Text Style to **Standard**.
Set the Height to **1/8″**.

34. 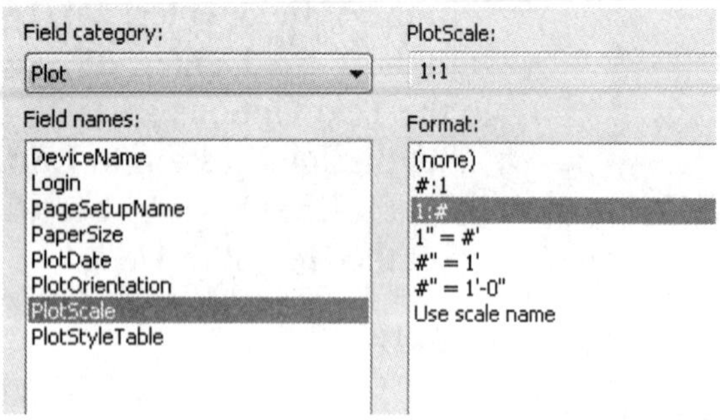

Select the Field button to set the default value for the attribute.

Select **PlotScale**.
Set the format to **1:#**.

Press **OK**.

Press **OK** to place the attribute.

35. 

Select the **Define Attributes** tool.

36. 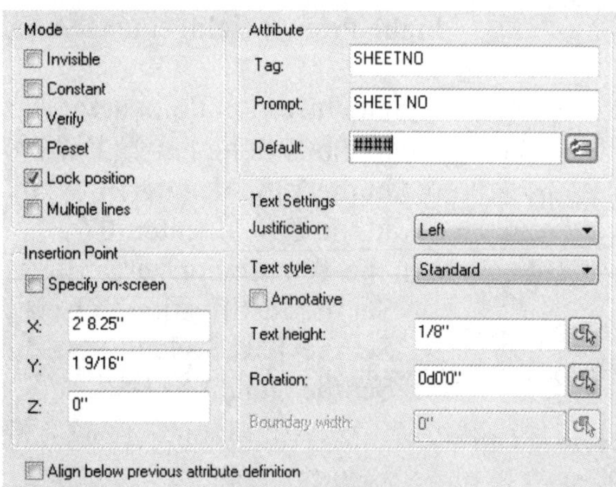

In the Tag field, enter **SHEETNO**.
In the Prompt field, enter **SHEET NO**.
In the Insertion Point area:
In the X field, enter: **2′ 8.25″**
In the Y field, enter: **1-9/16″**
In the Z field, enter: **0**
In the Text Options area:
Set the Justification to **Left**.
Set the Text Style to **Standard**.
Set the Height to **1/8″**.

37. 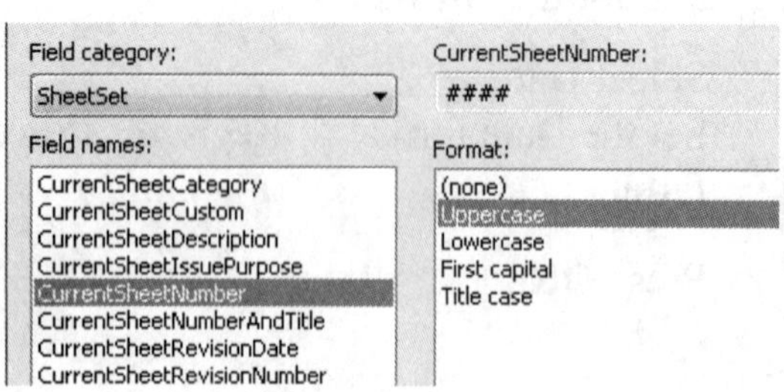

Select the Field button to set the default value for the attribute.

Select **CurrentSheetNumber**.
Set the format to **Uppercase**.

Press **OK**.

Press **OK** to place the attribute.

38. 

Select the **Define Attribute** tool.

39. 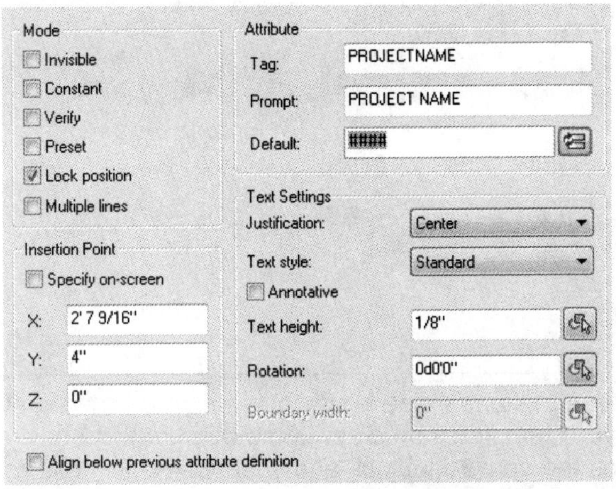

In the Tag field, enter **PROJECTNAME**
In the Prompt field, enter **PROJECT NAME**
In the Insertion Point area:
In the X field, enter: **2′ 7-9/16″**
In the Y field, enter: **4″**
In the Z field, enter: **0**
In the Text Options area:
Set the Justification to **Center**.
Set the Text Style to **Standard**.
Set the Height to **1/8″**.

40. Select the Field button to set the default value for the attribute.

Select **AEC Project** for the field category.
Set the Field Name to **Project Name**.
Set the format to **Uppercase**.

Press **OK**.

TIP: A common error for students is to forget to enter the insertion point. The default insertion point is set to 0,0,0. If you don't see your attributes, look for them at the lower left corner of your title block and use the MOVE tool to position them appropriately.

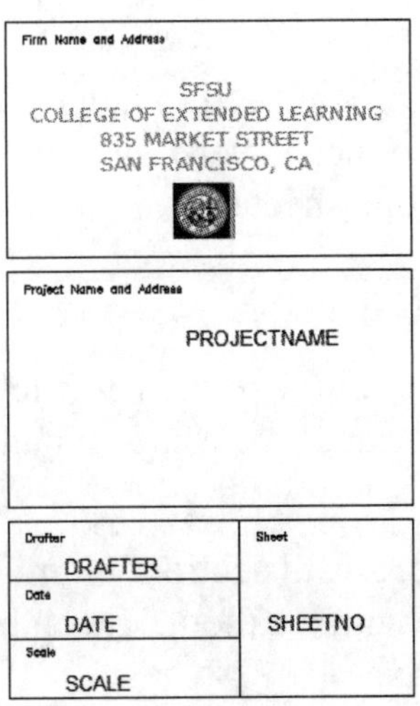

Your title block should look similar to the image shown.

If you like, you can use the MOVE tool to reposition any of the attributes to make them fit better.

41. 

Select **Save** on the ribbon to save the changes to the title block and exit the Edit Block In-Place mode.

42. 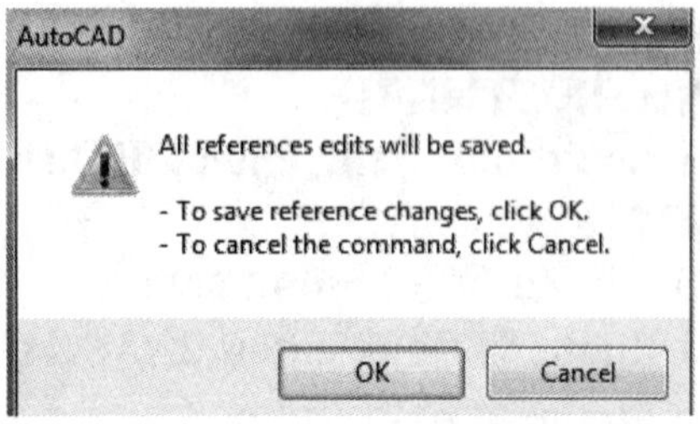

Press **OK**.

43. Save the file and go to **File→Close**.

➢ Use templates to standardize how you want your drawing sheets to look. Store your templates on a server so everyone in your department uses the same titleblock and sheet settings. You can also set up dimension styles and layer standards in your templates.

➢ ADT 2005 introduced a new tool available when you are in Paper Space that allows you to quickly switch to the model space of a viewport without messing up your scale. Simply select the **Maximize Viewport** button located on your task bar to switch to model space. To switch back to paper space, select the **Minimize Viewport** button.

You use the Project Navigator to create additional drawing files with the desired views for your model. The views are created on the Views tab of the Project Navigator. You then create a sheet set which gathers together all the necessary drawing files that are pertinent to your project.

Previously, you would use external references, which would be external drawing files that would be linked to a master drawing. You would then create several layout sheets in your master drawing that would show the various views. Some users placed all their data in a single drawing and then used layers to organize the data.

This shift in the way of organizing your drawings will mean that you need to have a better understanding of how to manage all the drawings. It also means you can leverage the drawings so you can reuse the same drawing in more than one sheet set.

You can create five different types of views using the Project Navigator:

- Model Space View – a portion that is displayed in its own viewport. This view can have a distinct name, display configuration, description, layer snapshot and drawing scale.
- Detail View – displays a small section of the model, i.e. a wall section, plumbing, or foundation. This type of view is usually associated with a callout. It can be placed in your current active drawing or in a new drawing.

- Section View – displays a building section, usually an interior view. This type of view is usually associated with a callout. It can be placed in your current active drawing or in a new drawing.
- Elevation View – displays a building elevation, usually an exterior view. This type of view is usually associated with a callout. It can be placed in your current active drawing or in a new drawing.
- Sheet View – this type of view is created when a model space view is dropped onto a layout sheet.

Note: Some classes have difficulty using the Project Navigator because they do not use the same work station each class, or the drawings are stored on a network server. In those cases, the links can be lost and the students get frustrated trying to get the correct results.

Exercise 7-2:

Verifying the Project Setting

Drawing Name: ex6-1.dwg
Estimated Time: 5 minutes

This exercise reinforces the following skills:

- Project Navigator
- Project Browser

1.  Open *ex6-1.dwg.*
2. 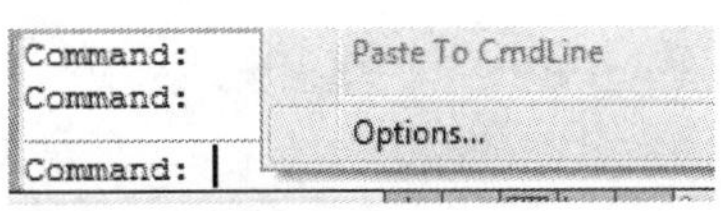

Right click in the command window and select **Options**.
3. 

Select the **AEC Project Defaults** tab.
4. 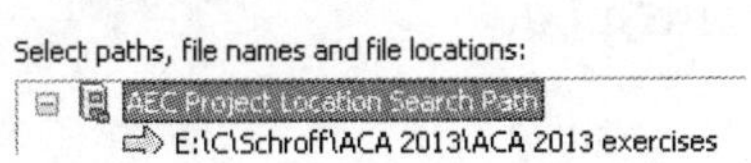

Verify that the AEC Project Location Search Path to the location where you are saving your files.
5. Press **OK** to close the Options dialog.
6.  Launch the **Project Navigator** from the Quick Access toolbar.
7. 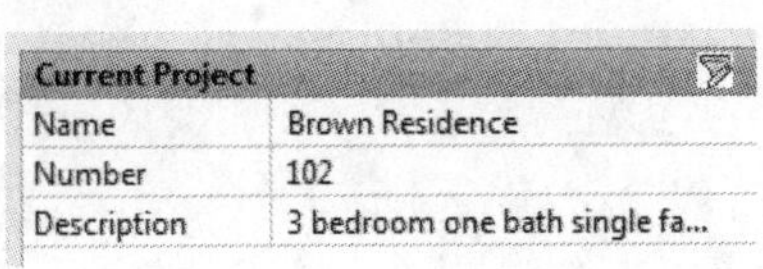

Verify that the Current Project is set to the Brown Residence project.

Tags and schedules use project information. If you do not have a current project defined, you may see some error messages when you tag elements.

Exercise 7-3:

Creating Elevation Views

Drawing Name: ex6-1.dwg
Estimated Time: 15 minutes

This exercise reinforces the following skills:

- Creating an Elevation View
- Adding a Callout
- Named Views

1.  Open *ex6-1.dwg.*

2. Switch to the Model tab.

3. 

Activate the **Top** view by clicking the top plane on the view cube.

4. 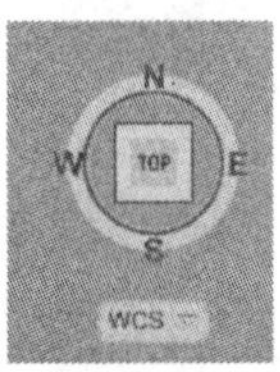

Spin the View cube so North is oriented on top.

5. 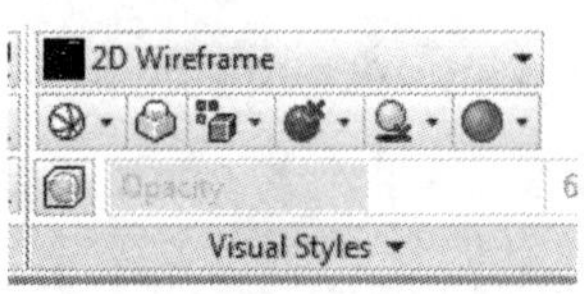

Set the view to **2D Wireframe** mode using the Visual Styles drop-down on the View ribbon.

6. 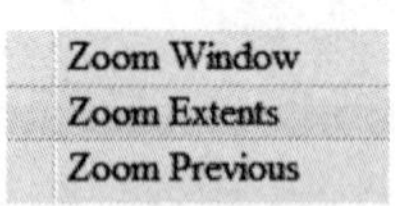

Use **Zoom Extents** to view the entire model.

7. 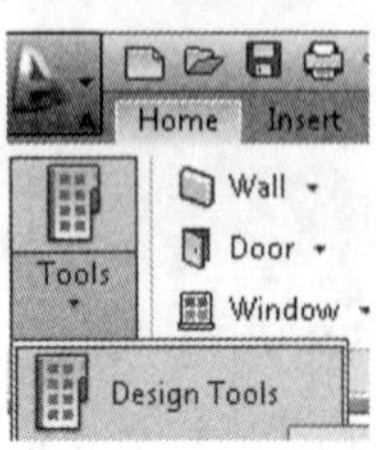

Launch the **Design Tools** palette.

8. 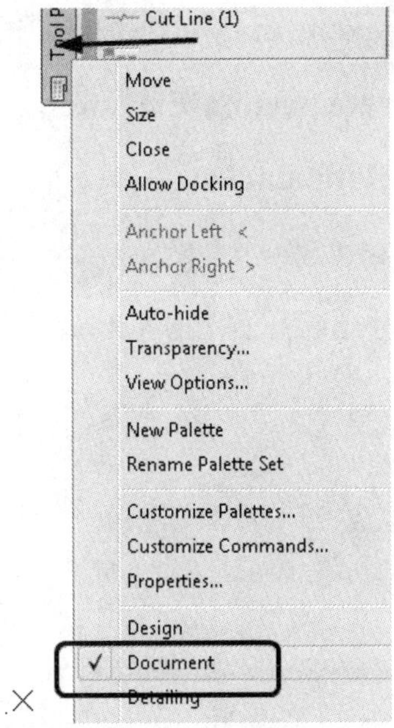

Right click on the grey bar on the left of the Design Palette.

Enable the **Document** palette.

9. 

Select the Callouts Palette on the Design Tools Palette.
Select the **Elevation Mark A2**.

10. 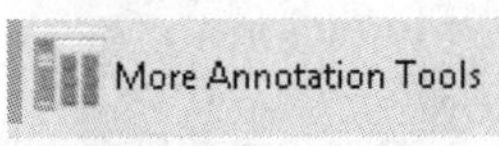

Select **More Annotation Tools**.

11. 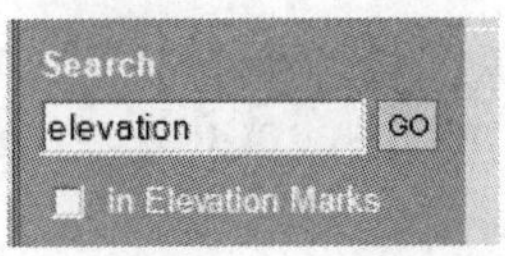

The Content Browser will launch.

Search for elevation.

12. 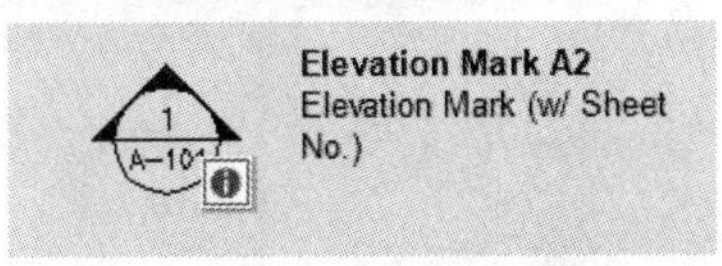

Locate **Elevation Mark A2**.

13. 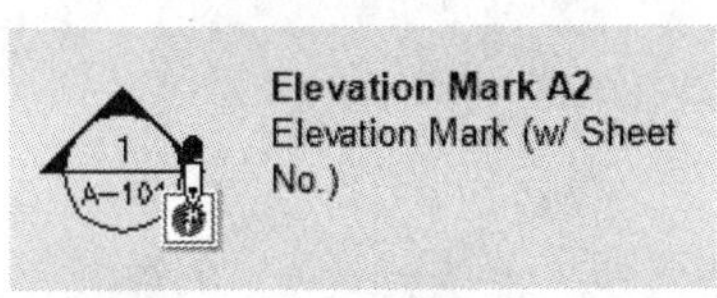

Hover the cursor over the **Elevation Mark A2** tool until you see an eyedropper.

14. 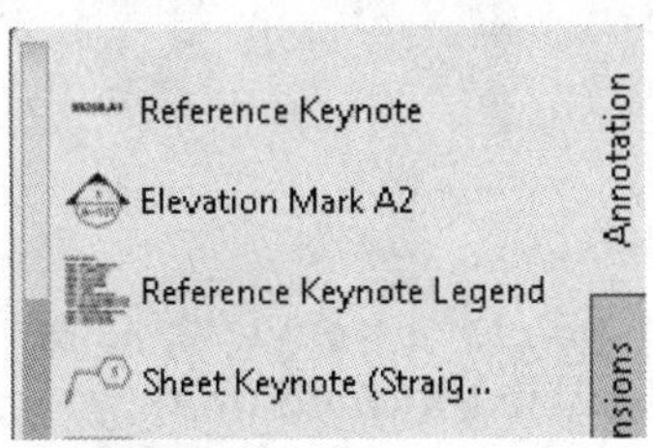

Hold down the left mouse button to drag and place the **Elevation Mark A2** on the Document Palette.

15. 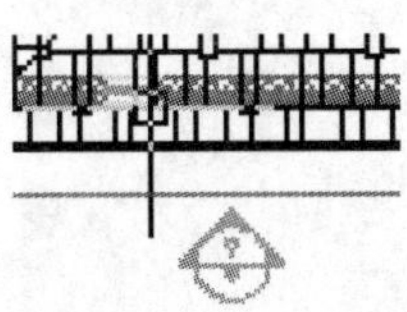

Place the elevation mark below the model.
Use your cursor to orient the arrow toward the building model.

16. 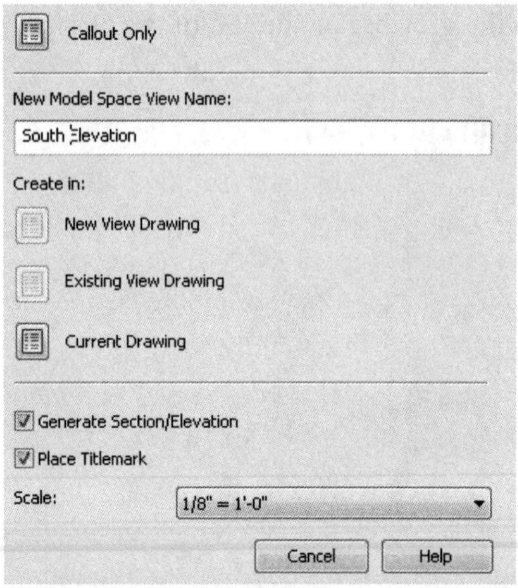

Set your view name to: **South Elevation**.

Enable **Generate Section/Elevation**.

Enable **Place Titlemark**.

Set the Scale to **1/8″ = 1′-0″**.

Press the **Current Drawing** button.

17. Window around the entire building to select it.
Select the upper left corner above the building and the lower right corner below the building.

18. 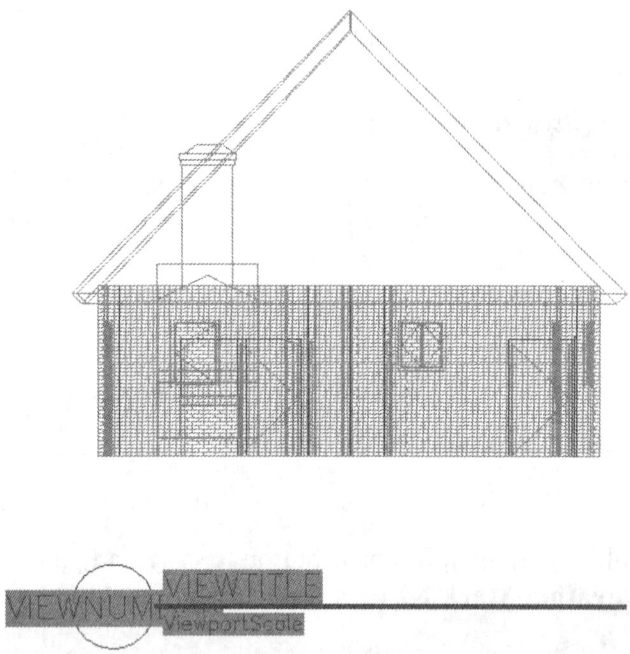

Place the elevation to the right of the view.

Zoom into the elevation view, so you can inspect it.

Zoom Extents.

19. 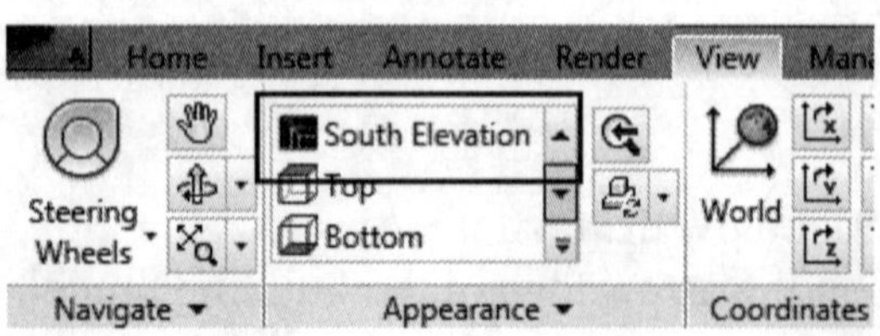

To activate the elevation view, select it from the View list located on the View ribbon.

20. Save as *ex7-3.dwg*

Exercise 7-4

Editing an Elevation View

Drawing Name: ex7-3.dwg
Estimated Time: 15 minutes

This exercise reinforces the following skills:

- Inserting a Titleblock
- Adding Keynotes
- Adding a Scale bar

1. Open *ex7-3.dwg*.

2. 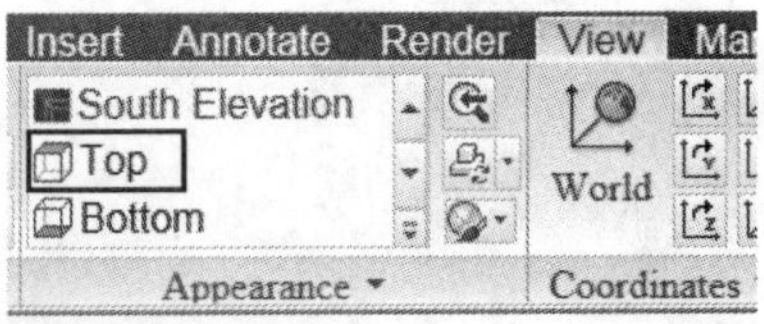

Activate the **Top** view from the View ribbon or using the View cube.

3. 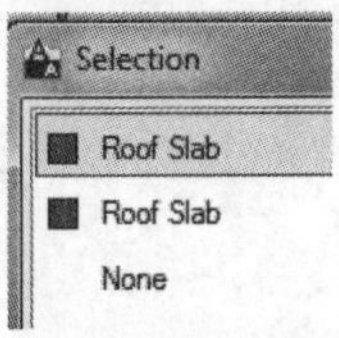

Select a roof slab.

   Select one of the slabs listed in the Selection dialog.

4. 

Select **Edit Style** from the ribbon.

5. 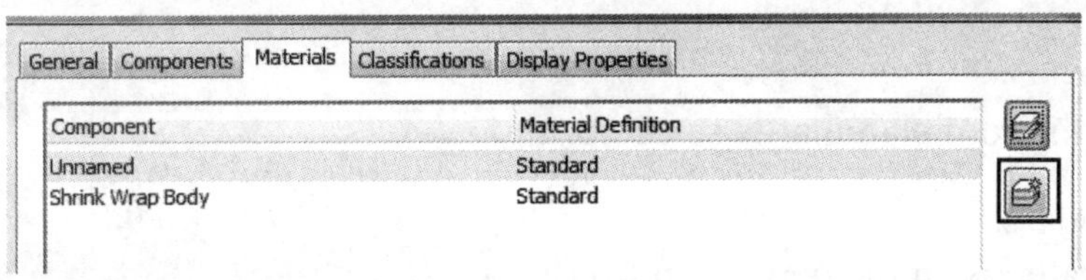

Select the Materials tab.

   Select the **Add Material** Button.

6. 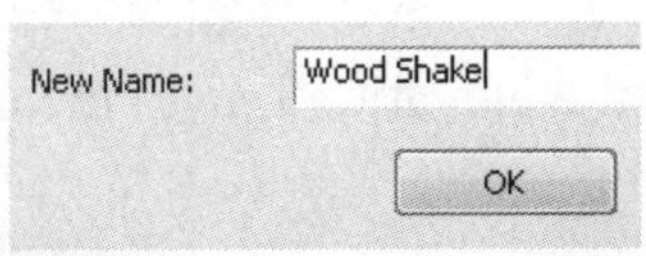

Name your new material **Wood Shake**. Press **OK**.

7. 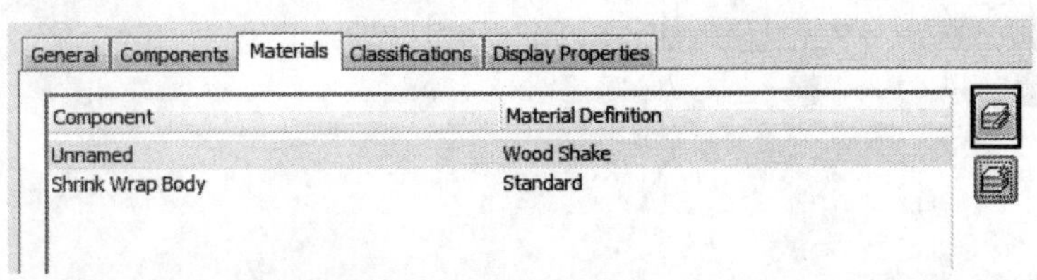

Select the **Edit Material** button.

8. 

Select the **Display Properties** tab.

9.  Select the **Properties** button.

10. 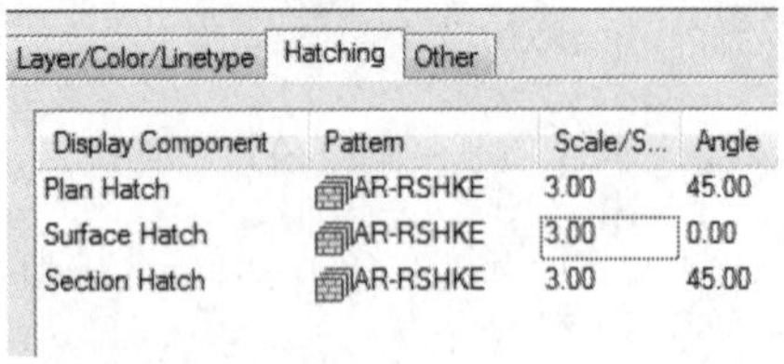

Select the **Hatching** tab.

Highlight all the Display Components.
Set the Hatch Pattern to **AR-RSHKE**.
Set the Scale to **3**.

11. 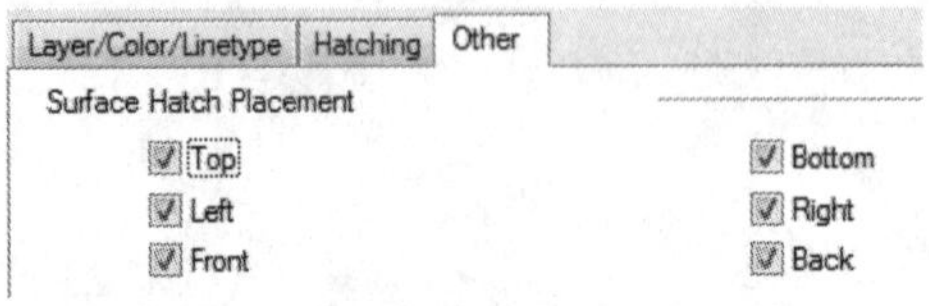

Select the Other tab.

Enable all the Surface Hatch Placement options.

12. 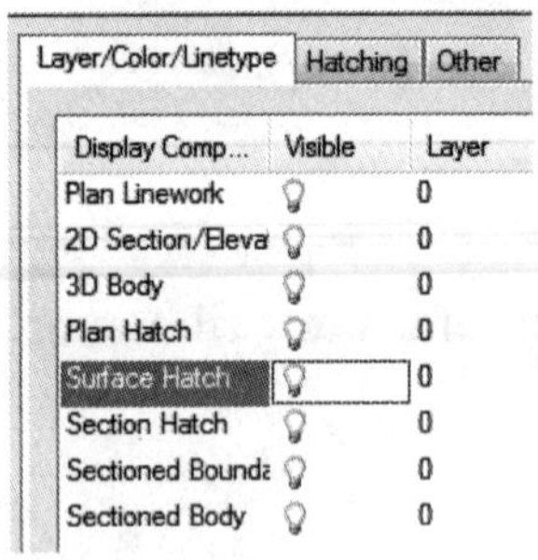

Select the Layer/Color/Linetype tab.

Turn on the layer for Plan Hatch, Surface Hatch, and Section Hatch.

13. Press **OK**.

14. 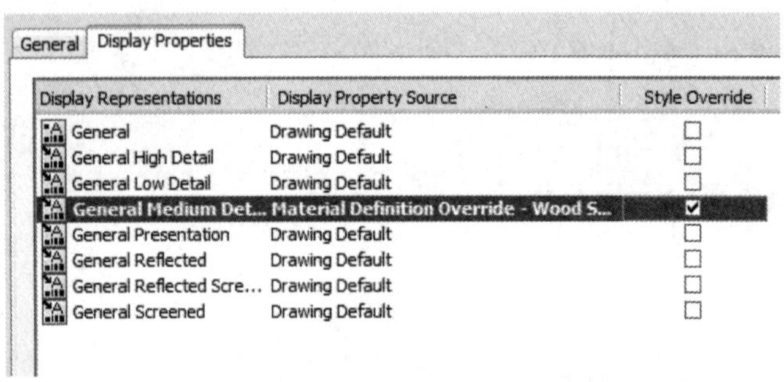

Verify that the Style Override is enabled.

15. Press **OK**.
Press ESC to release the roof slab that is selected.

The view does not update.
It needs to be regenerated with the new definition.

16. 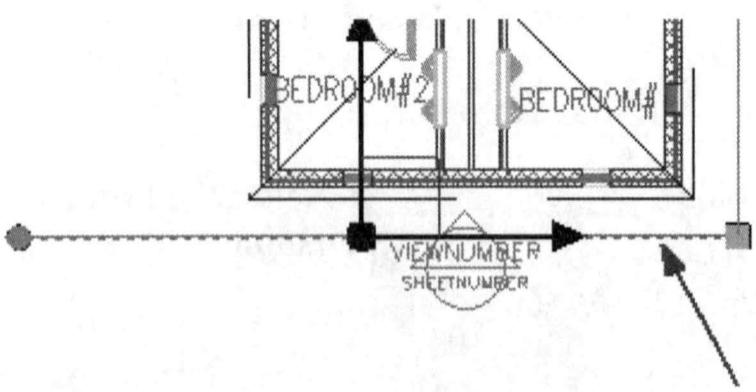

Select the elevation line in the top view.

17. 

Select **Generate Elevation** from the ribbon.

18. 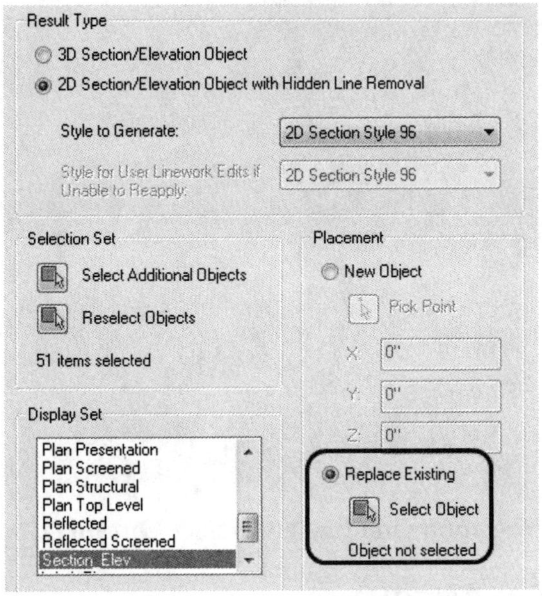

Enable **Replace Existing**.

Select the **Select Object** button.

Select the 2D Elevation placed in the previous exercise.

Press **OK**.

19. The elevation view updates.

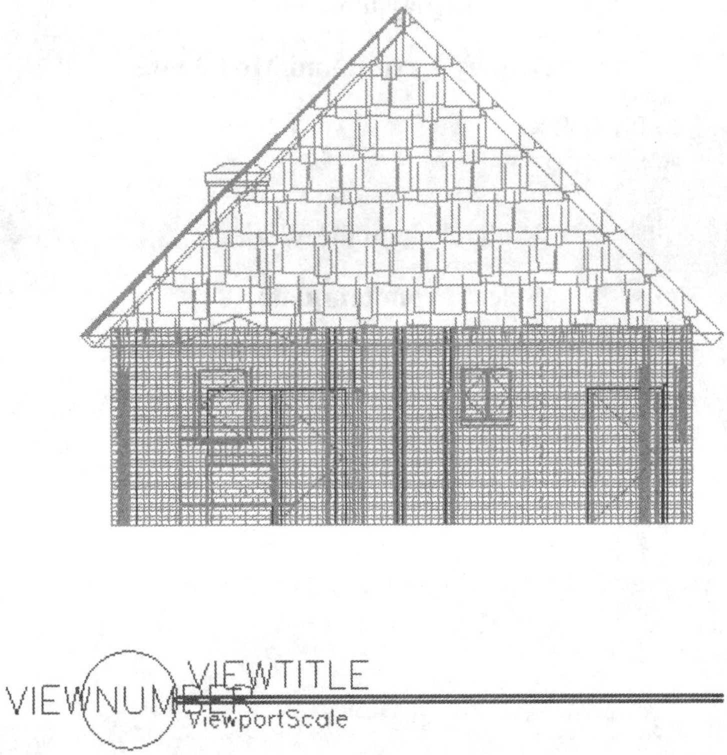

If you still do not see the shake hatch pattern, check the scale of the hatch pattern to ensure it is set low enough to be visible in the elevation view.

20. Save as *ex7-4.dwg*.

Exercise 7-5:
Creating Layouts

Drawing Name: ex7-4.dwg
Estimated Time: 25 minutes

This exercise reinforces the following skills:

- Create Layout
- Adding a View to a Layout
- Control Visibility of elements using Layers

1. Open *ex7-4.dwg*.

2. 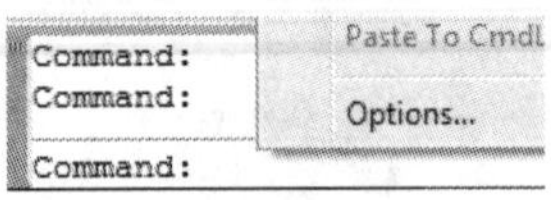

Right click on the command line and select **Options**.

   You can also type OPTIONS.

3. 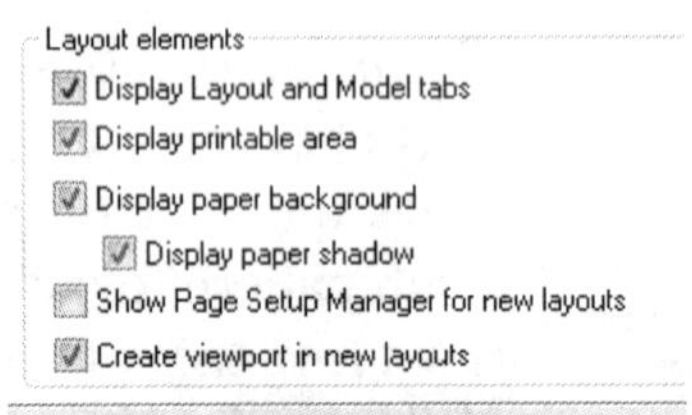

Activate the **Display** tab.

   Enable **Display Layout and Model tabs.**

   Press **OK.**

4. 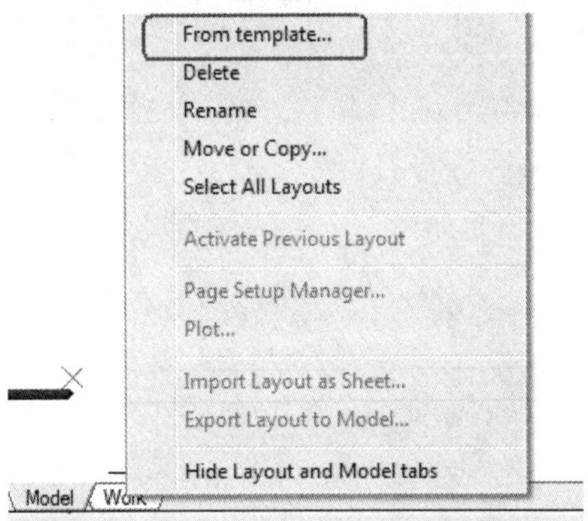

Right click on the Work tab.

   Select **From template**.

5. Browse to your exercise folder.

   Select the *Arch_D* template.
   Press **Open.**

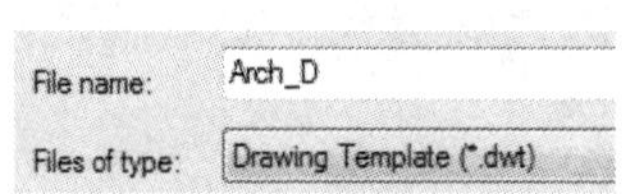

6. 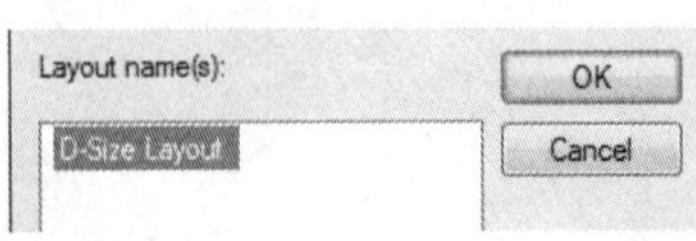

Press **OK.**

7. 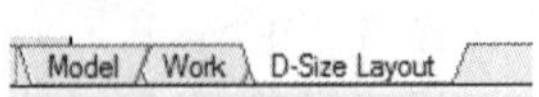

Activate the **D-Size Layout**.

8. 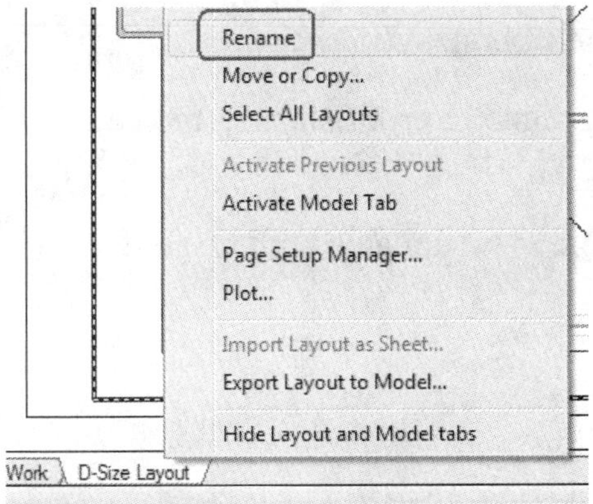

Right click on the **D-Size Layout** tab.

Select **Rename**.

9. 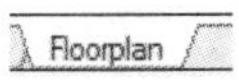

Rename Floorplan.

10. 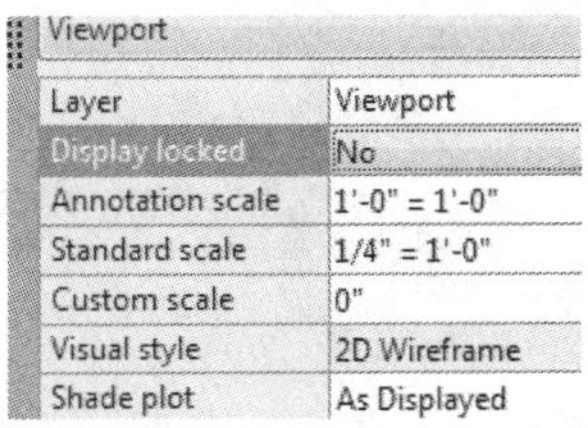

Select the viewport.

Set Display locked to **No**.

11. 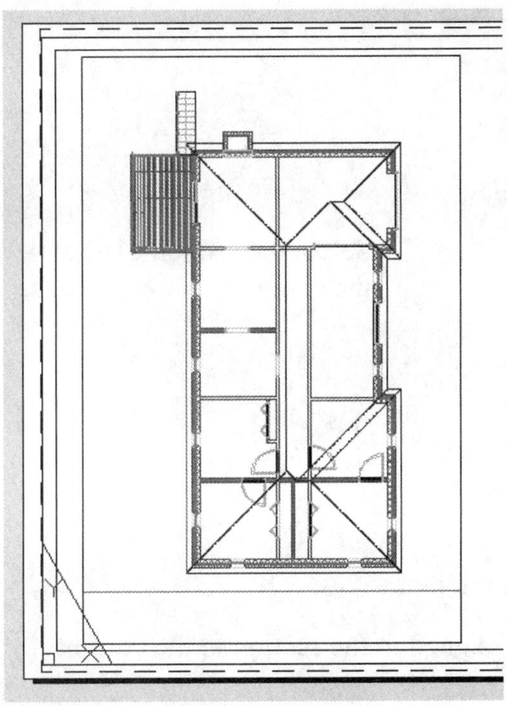

Resize the viewport to only show the floor plan.

Double click inside the viewport to activate model space.

Pan the model to position inside the viewport.

12. 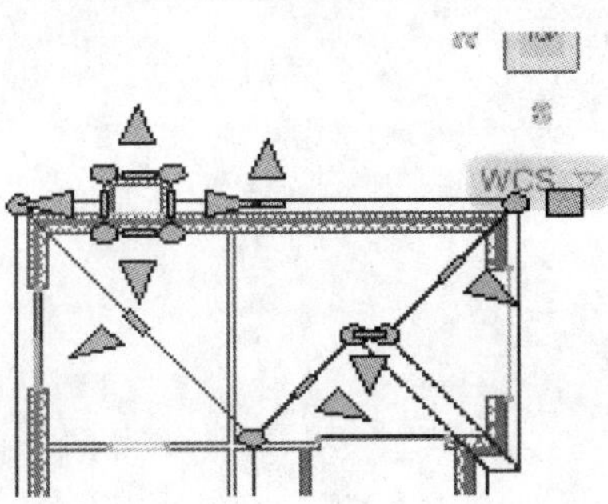

Select a roof slab.

13. 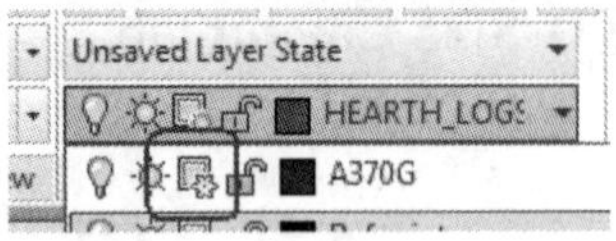

Activate the Home ribbon.

Freeze the layer assigned to roof slabs in the current viewport.

14. 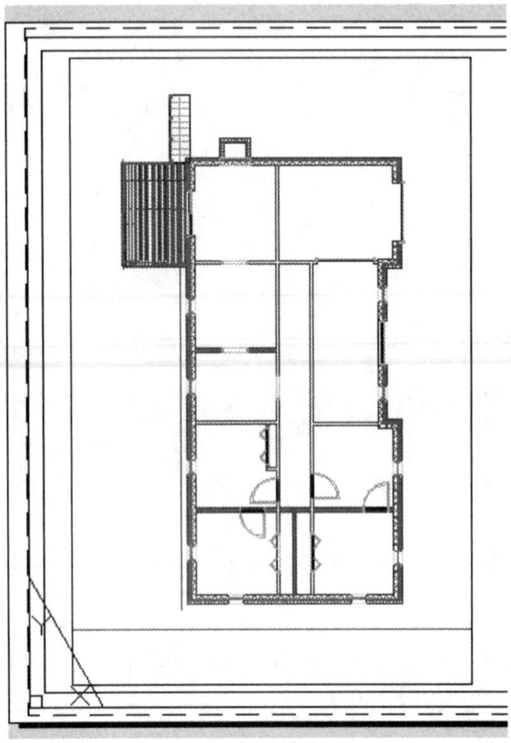

The view updates with no roof.

15. 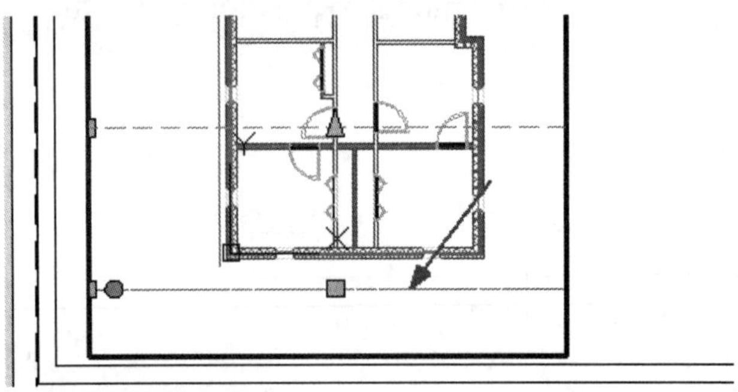

Select the section used to define the south elevation.

16. 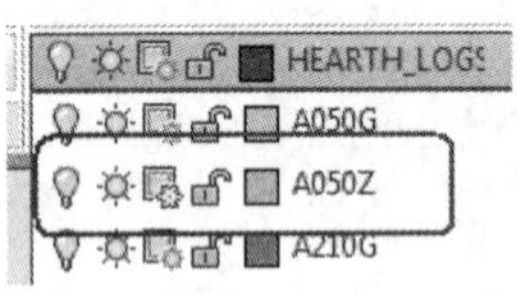

Activate the Home ribbon.

Freeze the layer assigned to the section in the current viewport.

17. 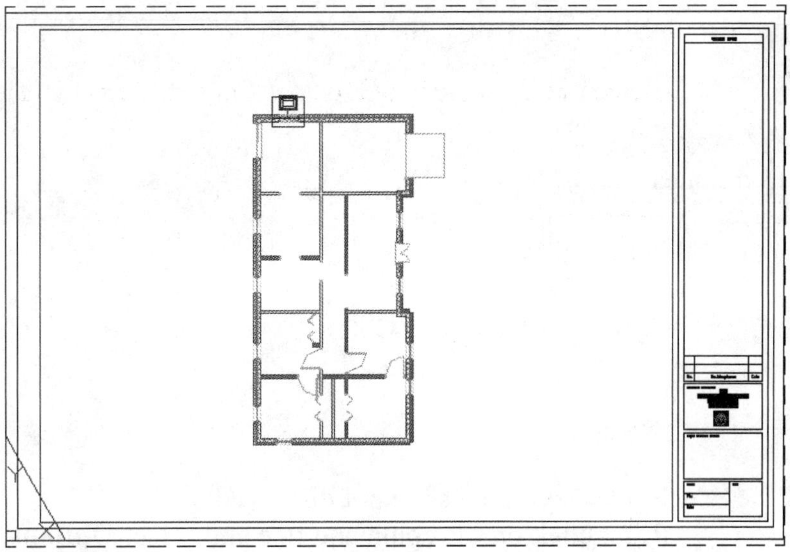

Double click outside the viewport to return to paper space.

Observe how the floor plan view has changed.

18. 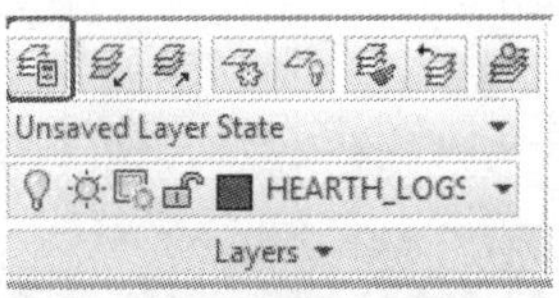

Activate the Home ribbon.

Launch the Layer Manager.

19. 

Scroll down to the Viewport layer.
Set the Viewport layer to DO NOT PLOT.

The viewports can be visible so you can adjust them but will not appear in prints.

Close the Layer Manager dialog.

20. 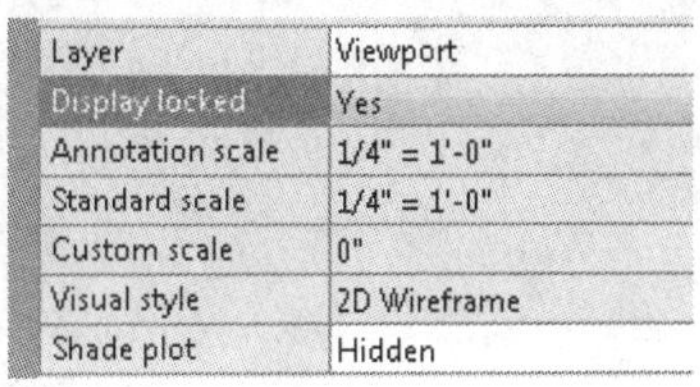

Layer	Viewport
Display locked	Yes
Annotation scale	1/4" = 1'-0"
Standard scale	1/4" = 1'-0"
Custom scale	0"
Visual style	2D Wireframe
Shade plot	Hidden

Select the viewport.
On the Properties palette:
Set the Annotation scale to **1/4″ = 1′-0″**.
Set the standard scale to **1/4″ = 1′-0″**.
Set the Shade plot to **Hidden**.
Set the Display locked to **Yes**.

21. Save as *ex7-5.dwg*.

Exercise 7-6:
Creating a Sheet

Drawing Name: ex7-5.dwg
Estimated Time: 15 minutes

This exercise reinforces the following skills:

- Layouts
- Viewports

1. Open *ex7-5.dwg*.

2. 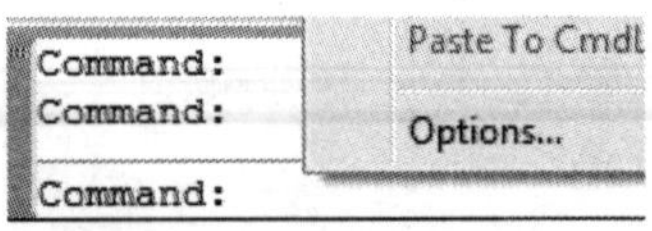

If your layout tabs are not displayed:
Right click on the command line and select **Options**.

You can also type OPTIONS.

3. 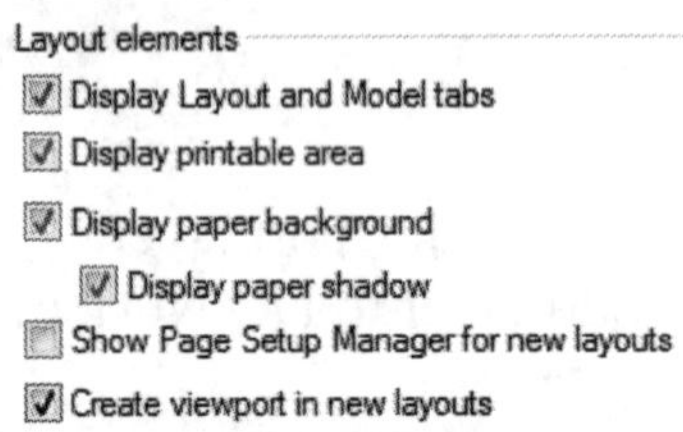

Activate the **Display** tab.

Enable **Display Layout and Model tabs.**

Press **OK**.

4. 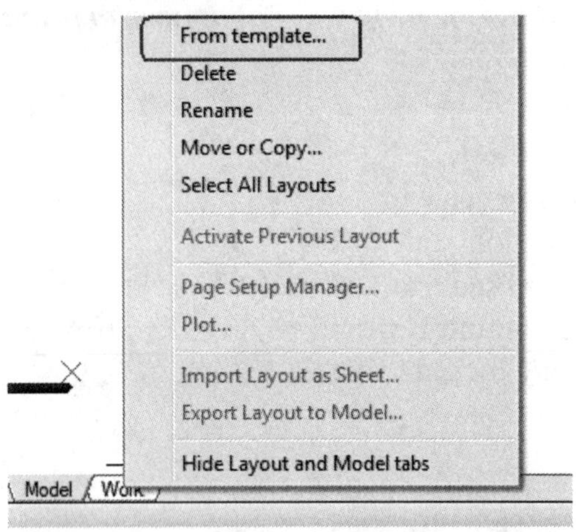

Right click on the Work tab.

Select **From template**.

5. 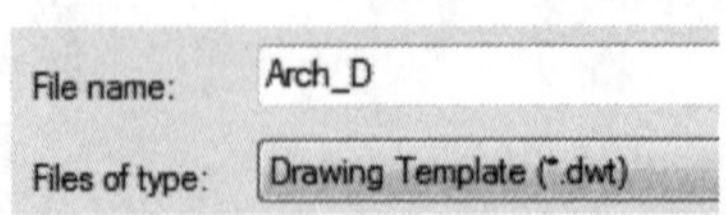

Browse to the folder where you are saving your work.
Select the *Arch_D* template.
Press **Open**.

6. 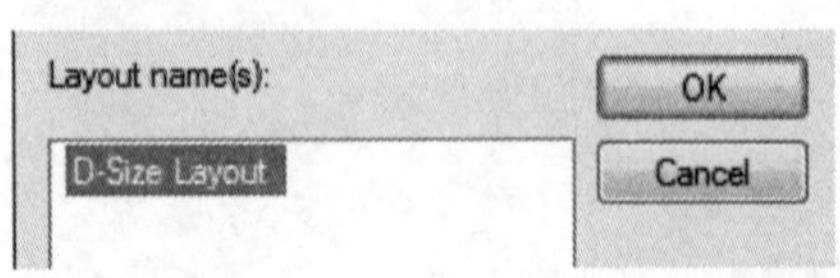

Press **OK**.

7. 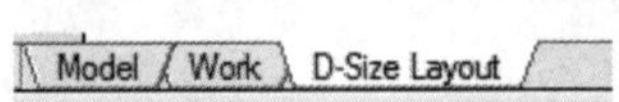

Activate the **D-Size Layout**.

8. 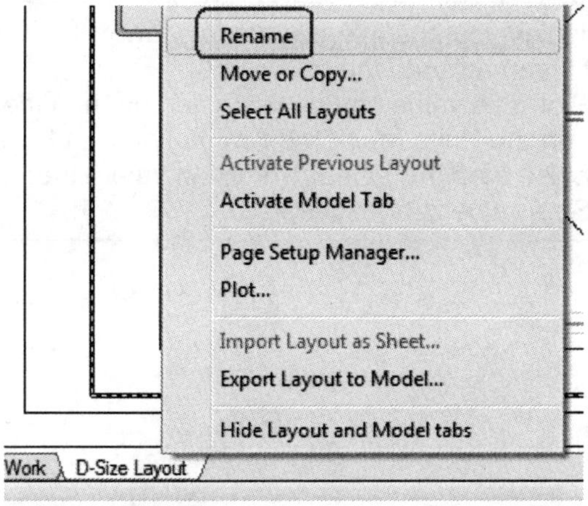

Right click on the **D-Size Layout** tab.

Select **Rename**.

9. 

Rename **South Elevation**.

10. 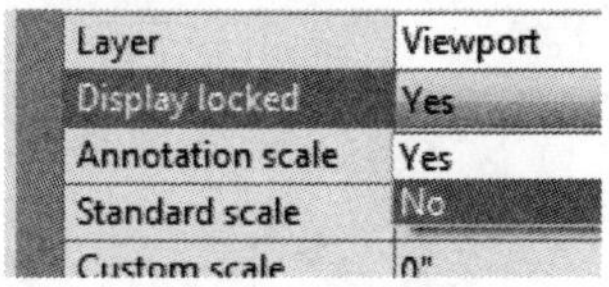

Select the viewport.
Right click and set the Display locked to **No**.

11. Double click inside the viewport to activate model space.

12. 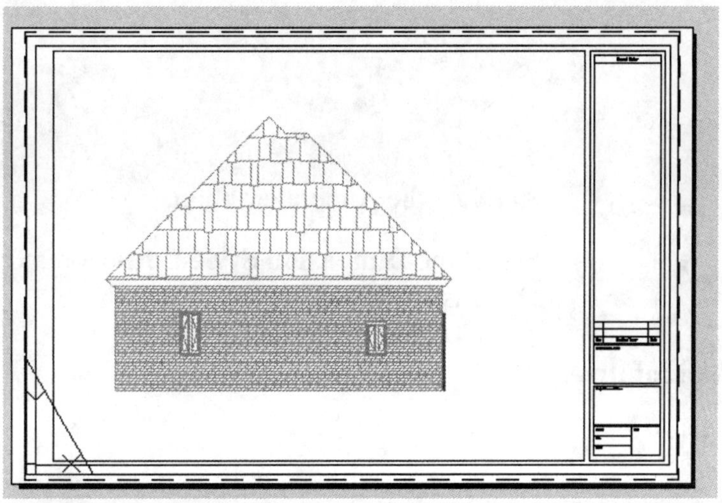

Left click inside the viewport and then position the elevation view inside the viewport.

13. 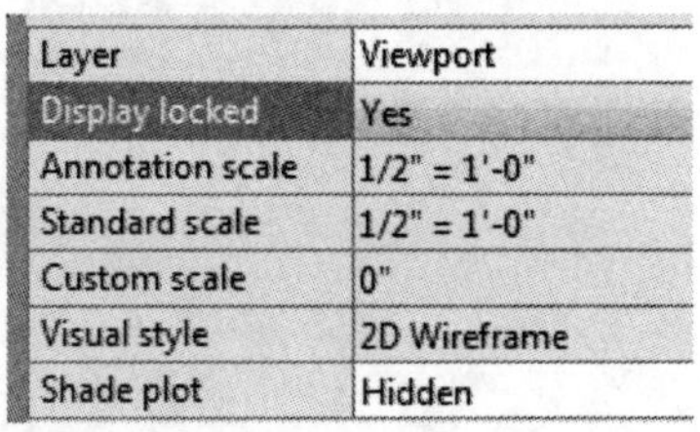

Select the viewport.
Set the Annotation scale to **½″ = 1′-0″ [1:100]**.
Set the Standard scale to **½″= 1′-0″ [1:100]**.

Set the Shade plot to **Hidden**.

You may need to re-center the view in the viewport after you change the scale. Use PAN to do this so the scale does not change.

Lock the display.

14. Save the file as *ex7-6.dwg*.

Tips & Tricks

- By locking the Display you ensure your model view will not accidentally shift if you activate the viewport.
- The Annotation Plot Size value can be restricted by the Linear Precision setting on the Units tab. If the Annotation Plot Size value is more precise than the Linear Precision value, then the Annotation Plot Size value is not accepted.

Exercise 7-7

Modify a Dimension Style

Drawing Name:	ex7-6.dwg
Estimated Time:	15 minutes

This exercise reinforces the following skills:

- Dimension Styles
- AEC Dimensions

1. Open *ex7-6.dwg*

2. 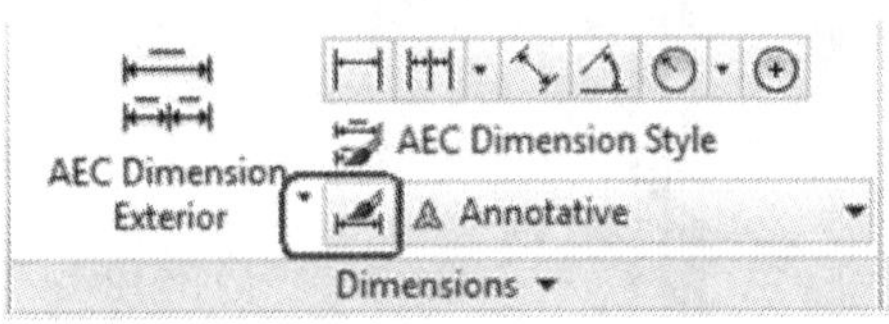

Activate the Annotate ribbon.

Select the **Dimension Style Editor** on the Dimensions panel.

3. 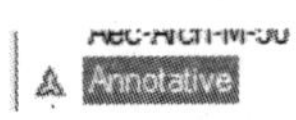

Highlight **Annotative**.

4. 

Select **Modify**.

5. 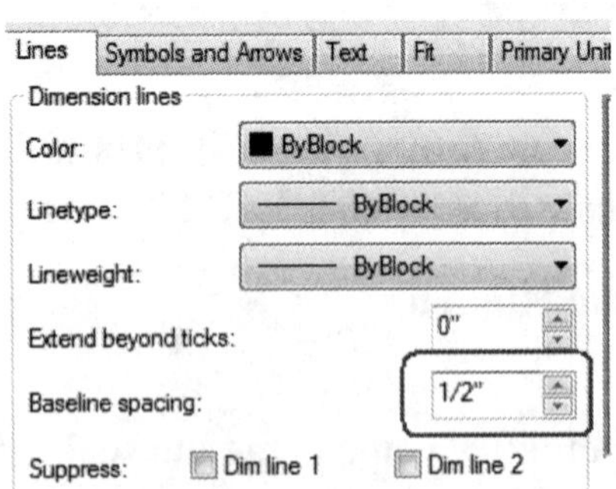

On the Lines tab:

Set the Baseline spacing to **1/2″**.

6. 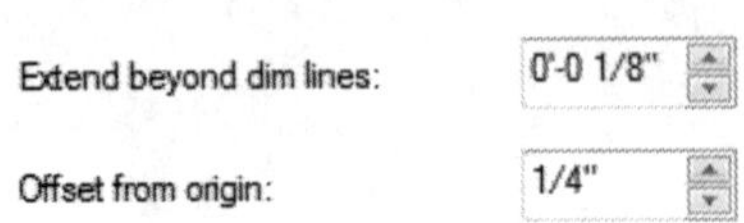

Set Extend beyond dim lines to **1/8″**.
Set Offset from origin to **1/4″**.

7. 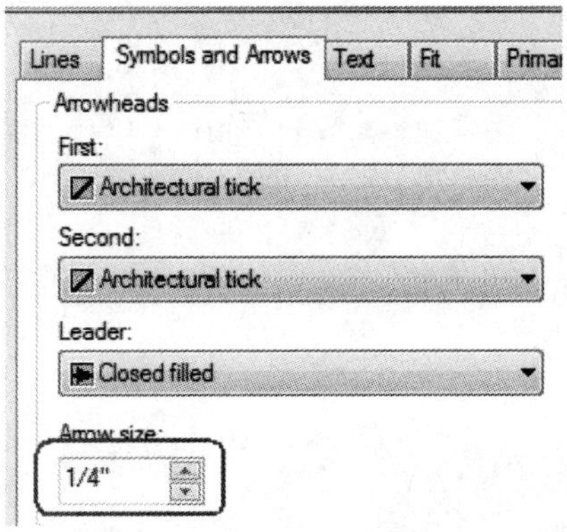

On the Symbols and Arrows tab:

Set the Arrow size to **1/4″**.

8. 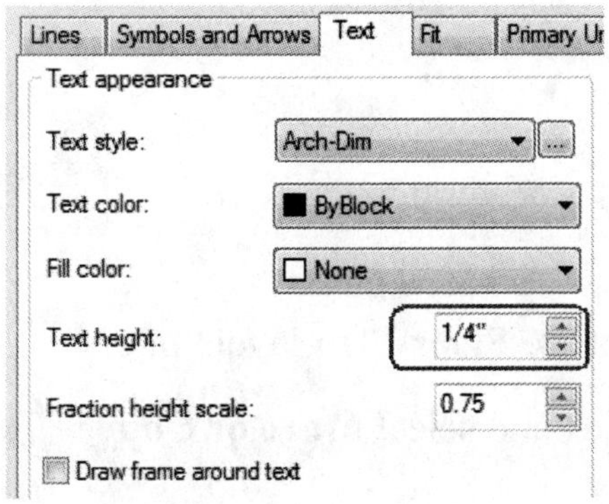

On the Text tab:

Set the Text height to **1/4″**.

9. 

Set the Offset from dim line to **1/8″**.

10. 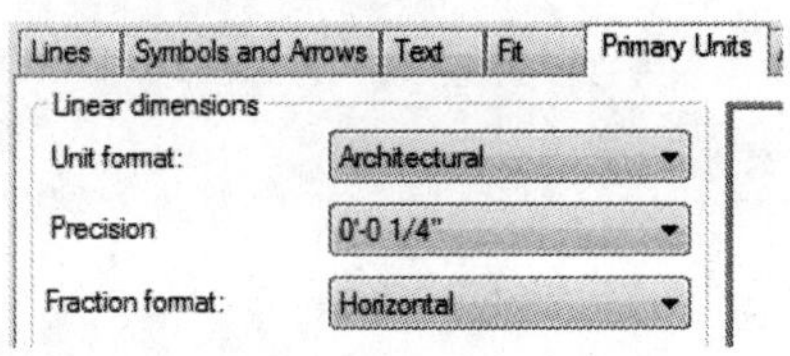

Activate the Primary Units tab.

Set the Unit format to **Architectural.**
Set the Precision to **1/4″**.

11. Press **OK** and **Close**.

12. Save as *ex7-7.dwg*.

Exercise 7-8
Dimensioning a Floor Plan

Drawing Name: ex7-7.dwg
Estimated Time: 30 minutes

This exercise reinforces the following skills:

- Drawing Setup
- AEC Dimensions
- Title Mark
- Attributes
- Layouts

1. Open *ex7-7.dwg*

2. 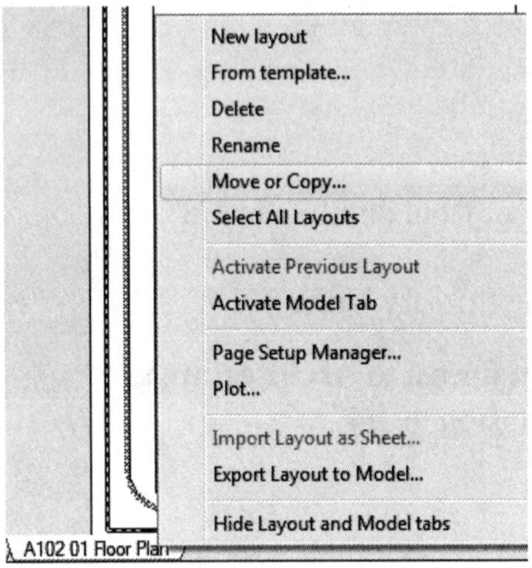

Highlight the **Floor Plan** layout tab.

Right click and select **Move or Copy**.

3. 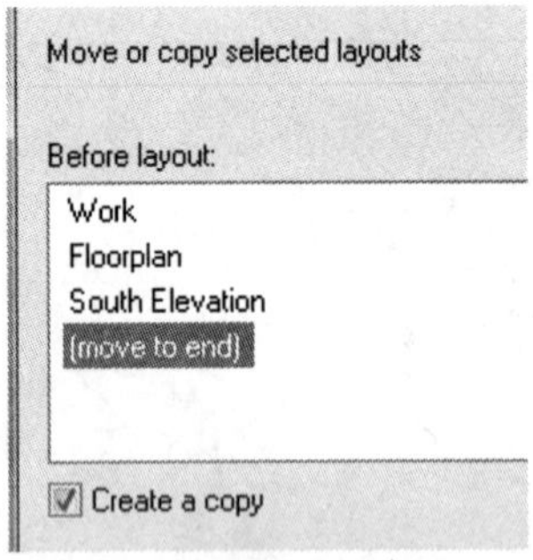

Enable **Create a copy**.

Highlight **(move to end)**.

Press **OK**.

4. 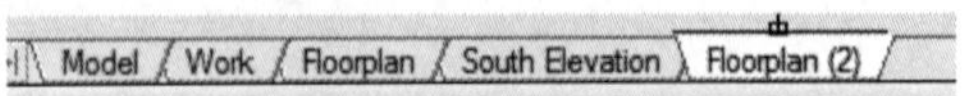

Select the second layout.

5. 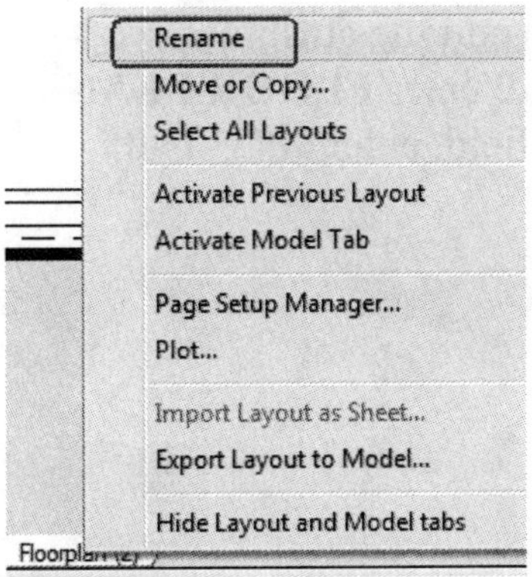

Highlight the second layout tab.

Right click and select **Rename**.

6. 

Modify the layout name to **A102 02 FLOOR PLAN**.

7. Launch the Tool Palette from the Home ribbon if it is not enabled.

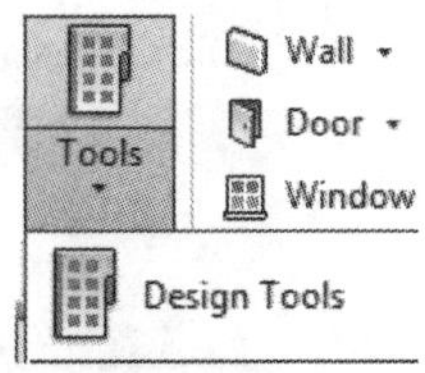

8. 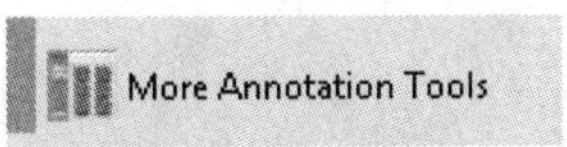

Select **More Annotation Tools** to launch the Content Browser.

9. 

Search for **title**.

10. 

Locate the **Title Mark** indicated.

11. 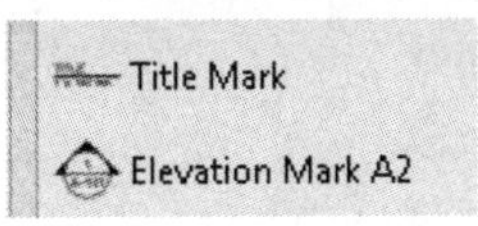

Drag and drop the Title Mark onto the Document Palette.

12. Double click inside the viewport to activate model space.

13. 

Select the **Title Mark** tool from the Callouts Palette.
Pick below the view to place the title mark.

14. 

Pick two points to indicate the start and end points of the title mark.

Place the title mark below the view.

15. 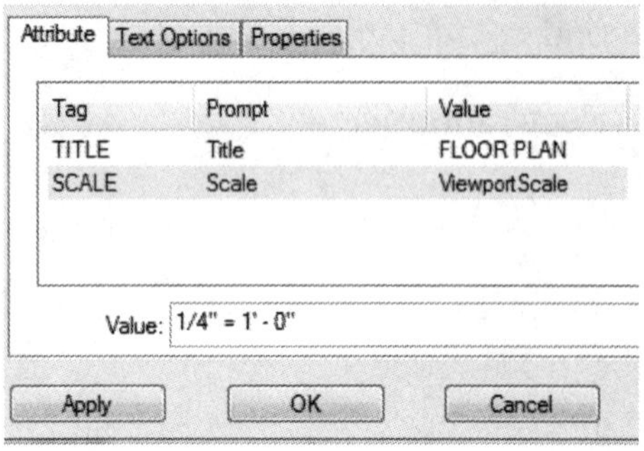

Double click to edit the attributes.
In the Title field, enter **FLOOR PLAN**.
In the SCALE field, enter **¼″ = 1′-0″**.

Press **OK**.

16. 

The view title updates.

17. 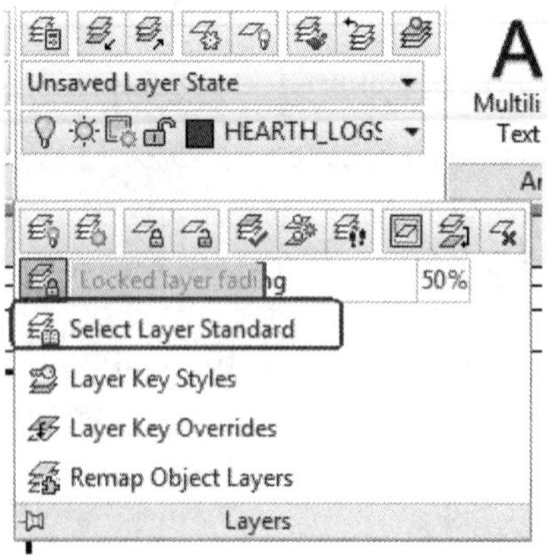

Activate the Home ribbon.

In the Layers panel drop-down:

Select **Select Layer Standard**.

18. 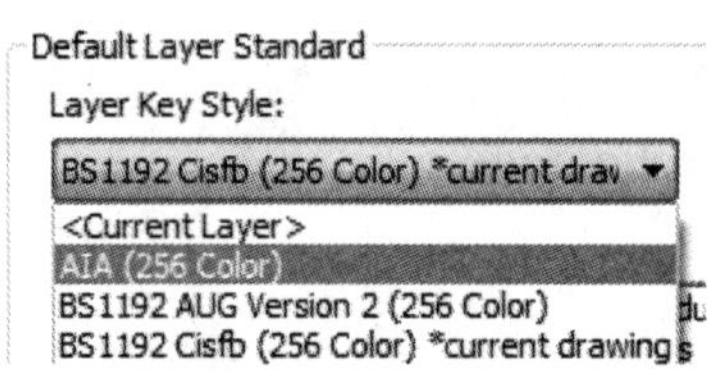

Set the Layer Key Style to **AIA (256 Color)**.

Press **OK**.

19. 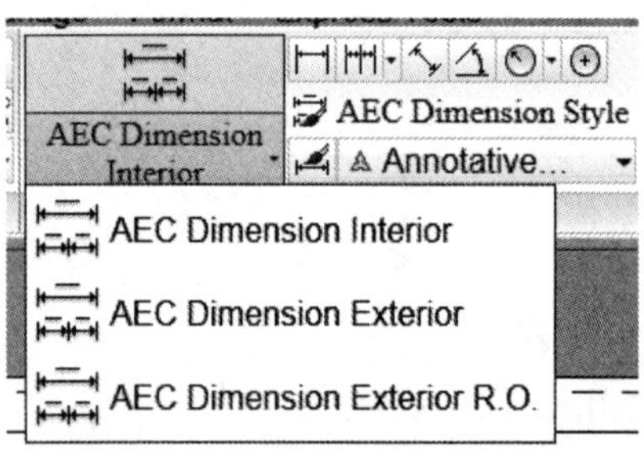

Select the **AEC Dimension - Exterior** tool on the Annotate ribbon.

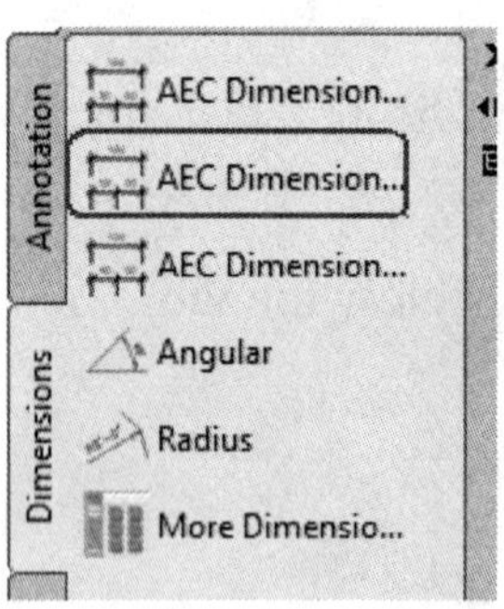

This tool is also available on the Documents tool palette on the Dimensions tab.

Add Wall Dimensions is only available in Model Space. Dimensions are automatically placed on A-Anno-Dim layer when the Layering Standard is set to AIA.

20. 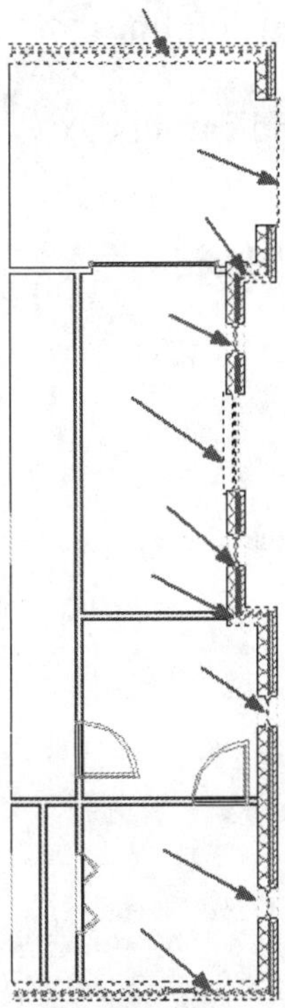

Select the walls, doors, and windows indicated on the right side of the building.

Press ENTER to complete the selection.

21. 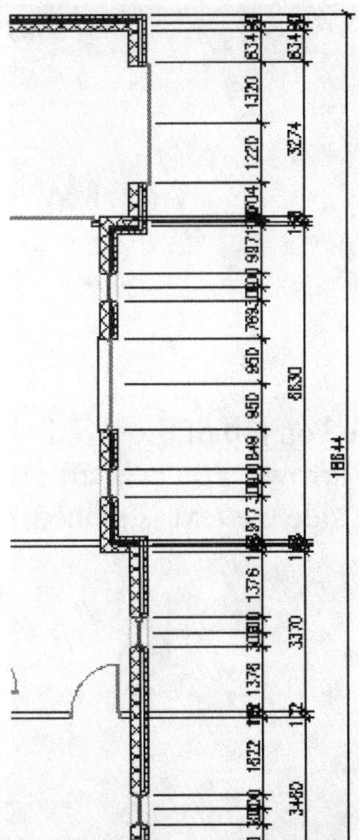

Pick to the right of the building to place the dimensions.

All dimensions relevant to the wall will be placed.

22. 

Select the Dimension you just placed.
Select **Remove Extension Lines** from the ribbon.

23. 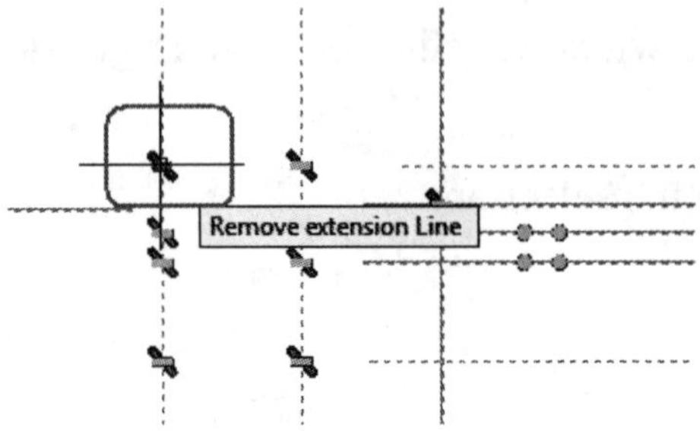

Select the grips on the extension lines that are not necessary.
You should see a tool tip indicating the extension line to remove.

The selected lines will be deleted.

24. To add an extension line:
Select the AEC Dimension.

Select the Add Extension Lines tool from the ribbon. 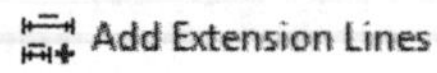

Then select the midpoint of the object to be dimensioned.
Then select the AEC Dimension.

25. 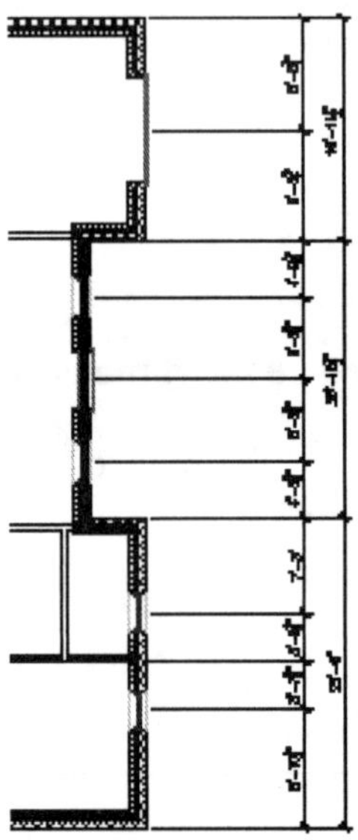
When you are done modifying the AEC Dimension, press ENTER to update the dimensions.

26. 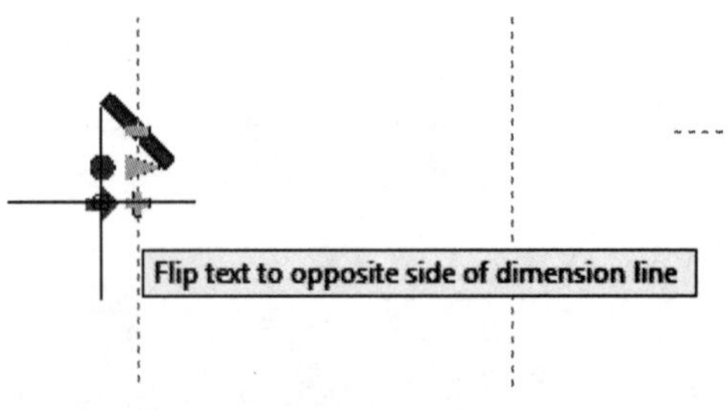

If the text landed on top of the building, look for a blue arrow. You can left click on it to flip the side the text is placed.

27. 

Select the dimension.

The dimension should automatically be placed on A-Anno-Dims because the Layer Standard was set to AIA.

28. Switch back to Paper space.

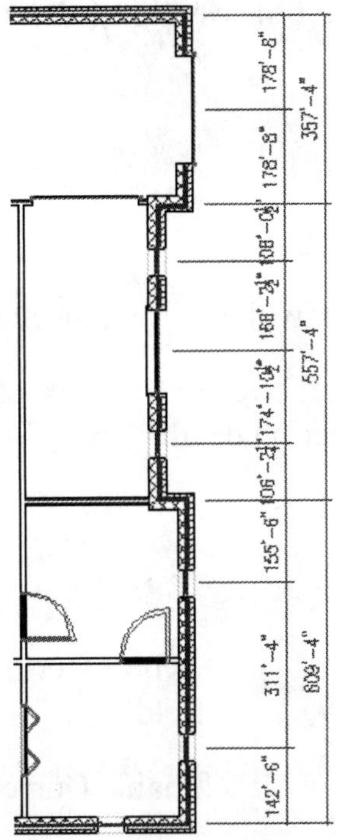

29. Save as *ex7-8.dwg.*

TIP: You can insert blocks into model or paper space. Note that you did not need to activate the viewport in order to place the Scale block.

Exercise 7-9

Create a Wall Section

Drawing Name: ex7-8.dwg
Estimated Time: 15 minutes

This exercise reinforces the following skills:

- Drawing Setup
- Dimension Styles
- AEC Dimensions
- Layouts

1. Open *ex7-8.dwg.*
2. 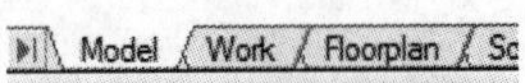

Activate the Model layout tab.

3. 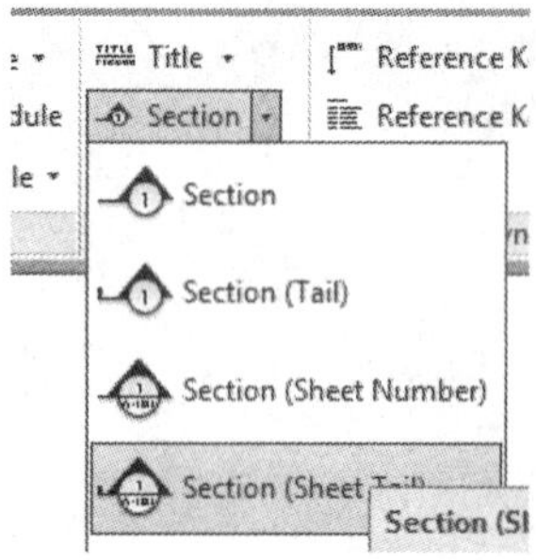

Activate the **Annotate** ribbon.

Select the **Section (Sheet Tail)** tool.

4. 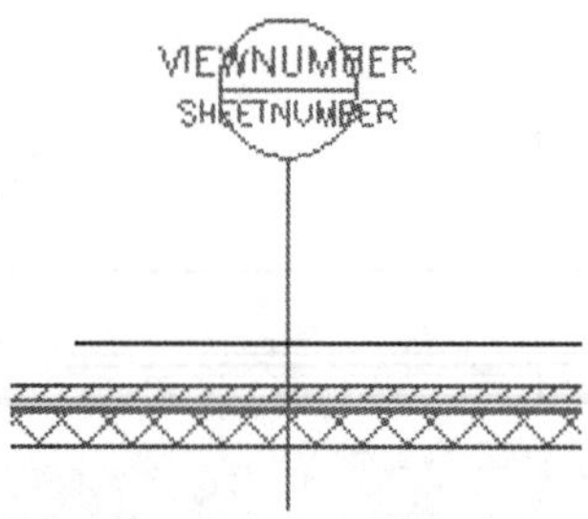

Draw the section through the north wall of the garage area.

Left click to the right of the section line to indicate the section depth.

5. 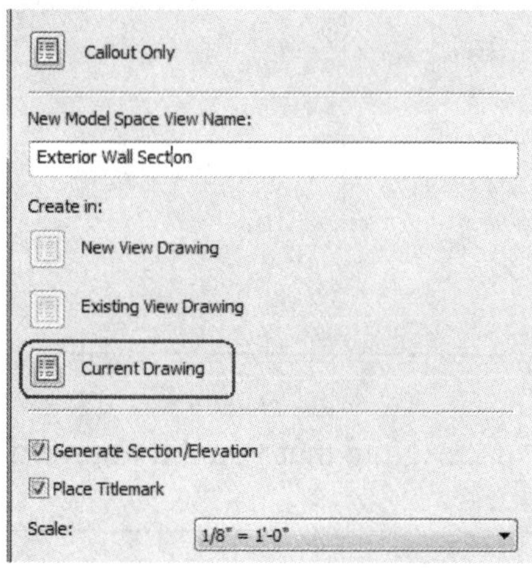

Type Exterior Wall Section in the View Name field.

Enable Current Drawing.

Enable Generate Section/Elevation.

Enable Place Title mark.
Set the Scale to 1/8″ = 1′-0″.

6. 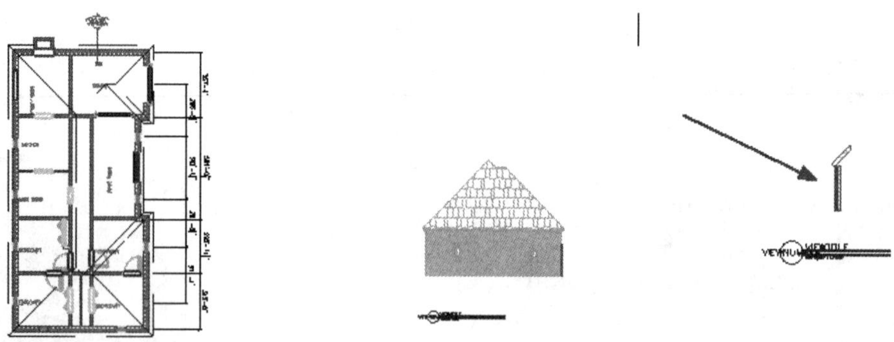

Place the view to the right of the South Elevation view.

7. 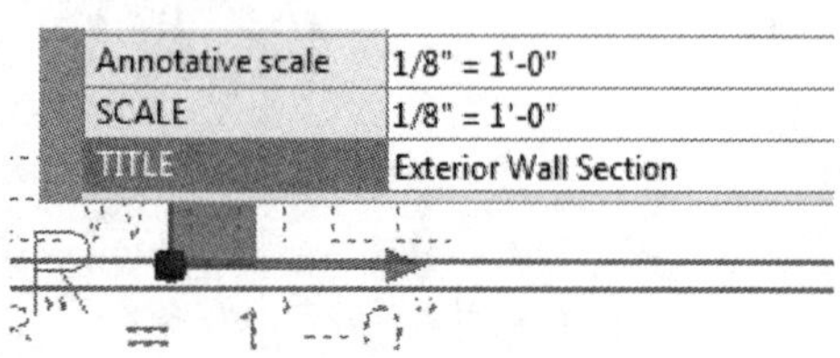

Select the view title for the wall section.

Type **1/8″ = 1′-0″** for the SCALE.

Type **Exterior Wall Section** for the TITLE.

Press ESC to release and update.

8. 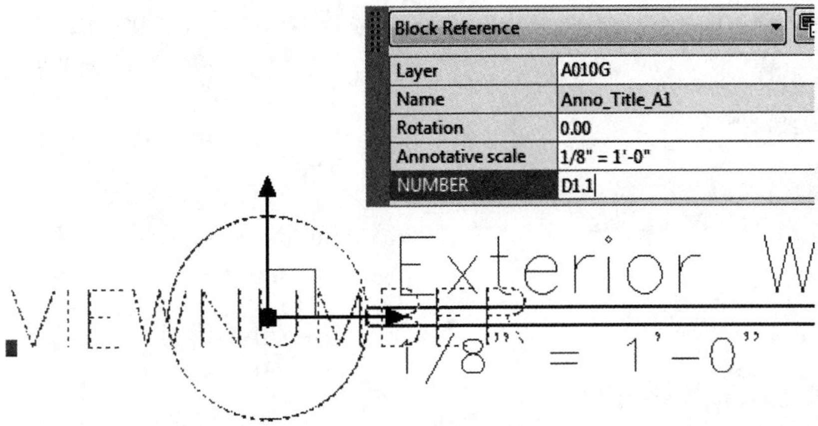

Select the View title bubble.

Type D1.1 for the NUMBER.

Press ESC to release and update.

9. 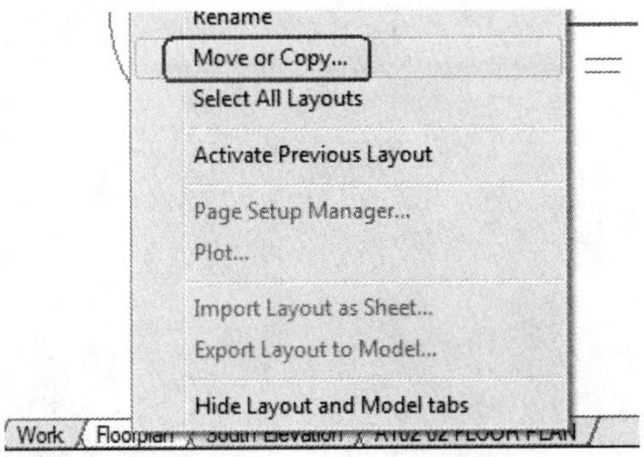

Highlight the **Floor Plan** layout tab.

Right click and select **Move or Copy**.

10. 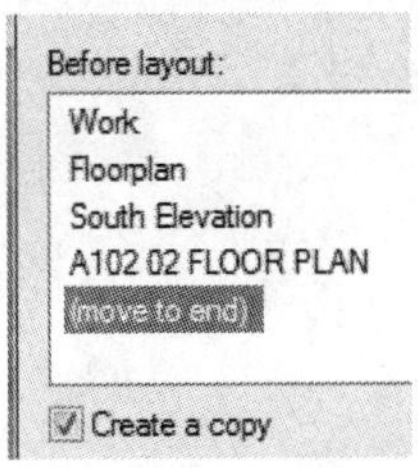

Enable **Create a copy**.

Highlight **(move to end)**.

Press **OK**.

11. 

Select the second layout.

12. 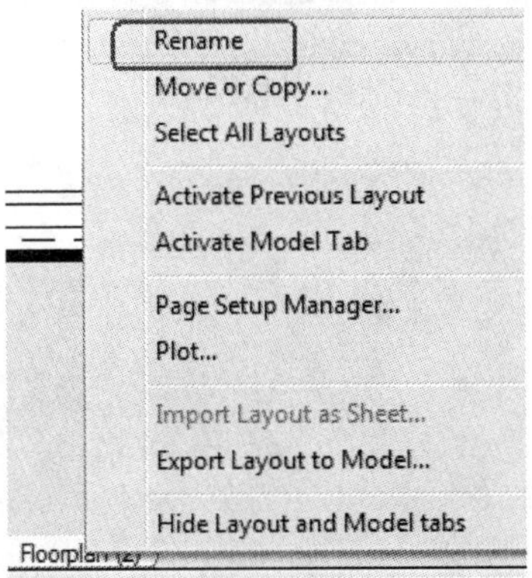

Highlight the second layout tab.

Right click and select **Rename**.

13. 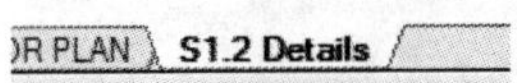

Modify the layout name to **S1.2 Details**.

14. Unlock the viewport.
Position the Exterior Wall Section in the viewport.
Adjust the size of the viewport.

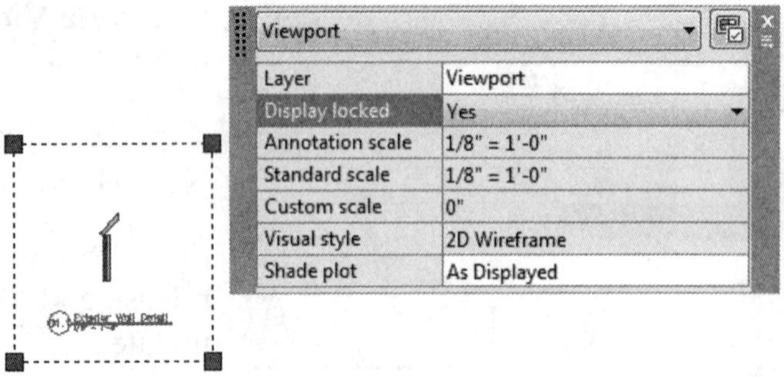

Select the viewport.
Set the Annotation scale to **1/8″ = 1′0″**.
Set the Standard scale to **1/8″ = 1′0″**.

Set the Shade plot to **As Displayed**.

Lock the display.

15. Press ESC to release the viewport.

16. Save as *ex7-9.dwg.*

Exercise 7-10

Create a Section View

Drawing Name: ex7-9.dwg
Estimated Time: 10 minutes

This exercise reinforces the following skills:

- Sections

1. Open *ex7-9.dwg.*

2. 

Activate the **Floorplan** layout tab.
Activate Model space.

3. 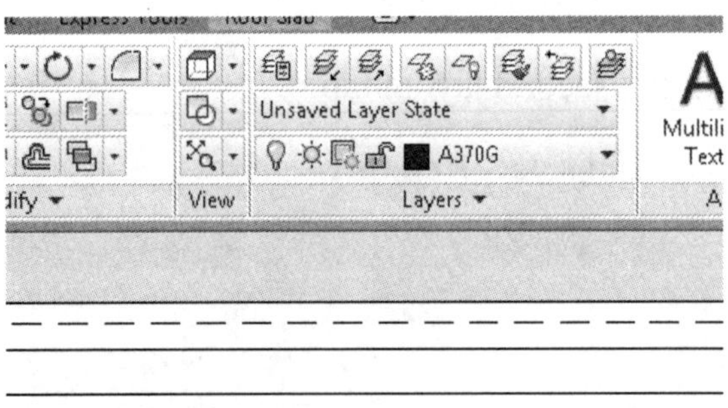

Thaw the roof slab layer.

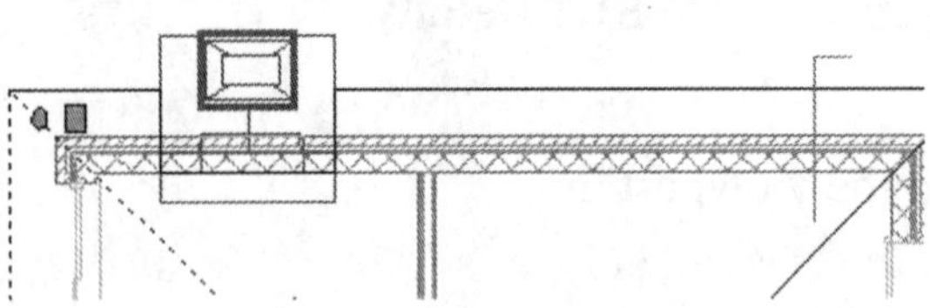

4. 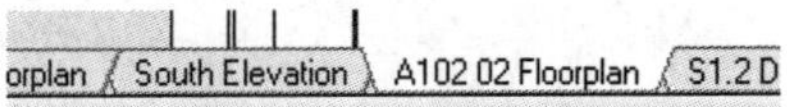

Activate the **A102 02 Floorplan** tab.

5. 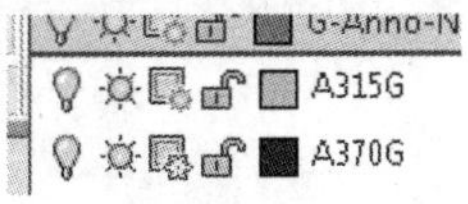

Freeze the roof slab layer in current viewport only.

6. 

Activate the **Floorplan** layout tab.
Activate Model space.

7. 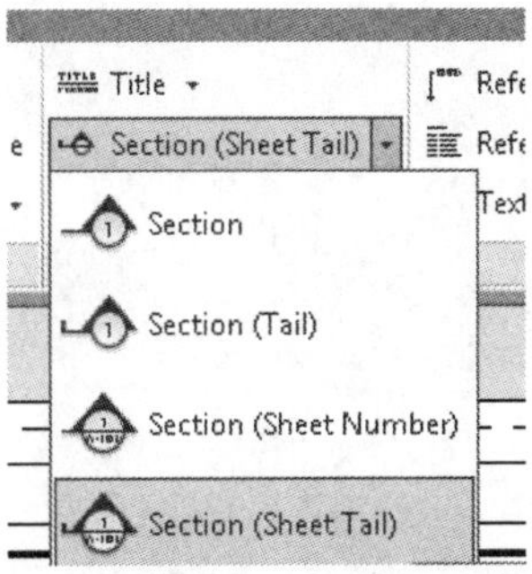

Activate the Annotate ribbon.

Select the **Section (Sheet Tail)** tool on the Callouts panel.

8. 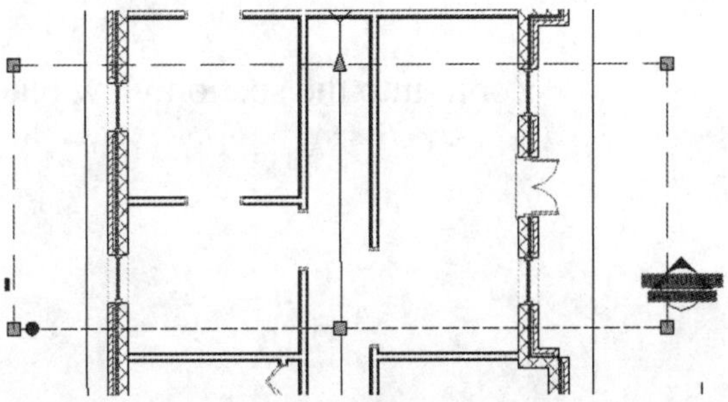
Draw a horizontal line through the walls as shown.

9. 

Name the View: South Section.
Enable Generate Section/Elevation.
Enable Place Titlemark.
Set the Scale to 1/2″ = 1′-0″.

Place the view in the current drawing to the right of the building.

10. 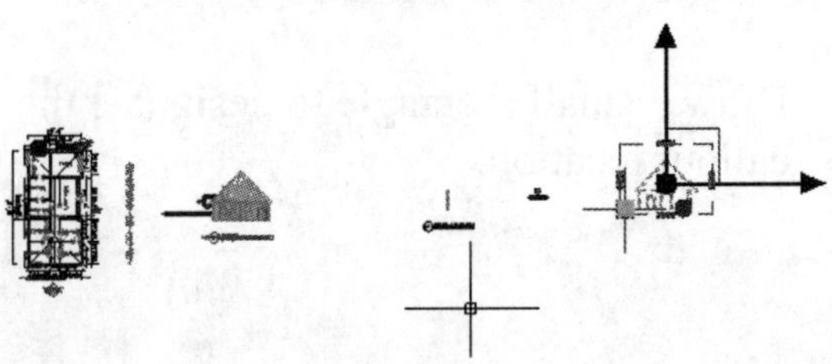
Switch to the Model tab and move the view to the right away from all the other views.

11. Save as *ex7-10.dwg*.

Exercise 7-11

Add a Callout

Drawing Name: ex7-10.dwg
Estimated Time: 45 minutes

This exercise reinforces the following skills:

- Callouts
- Wipeout
- Detail Elements
- Layouts

1. Open *ex7-10.dwg.*

2. 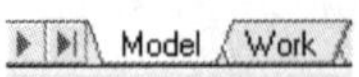

Activate the **Model** layout tab.

3. 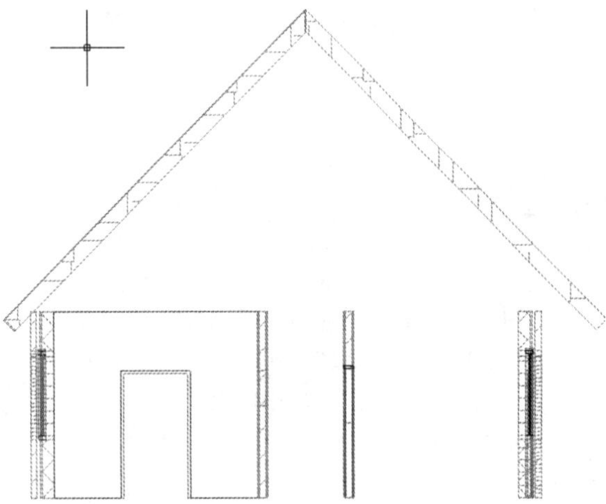
Zoom into the section view placed.

4. 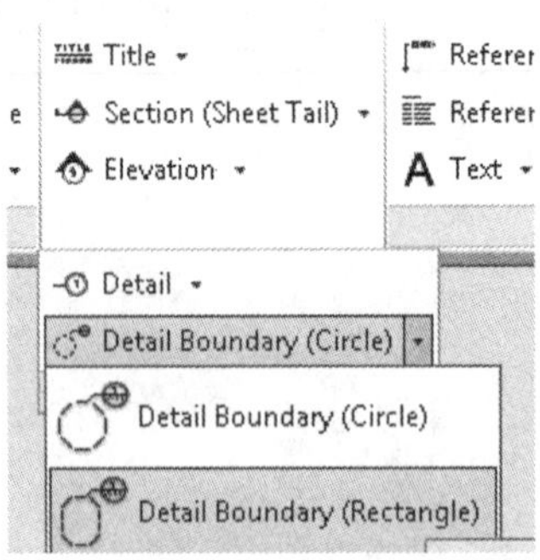

Activate the Annotate ribbon.

Select the **Detail Boundary (Rectangle)** callout tool on the Callouts panel.

5. 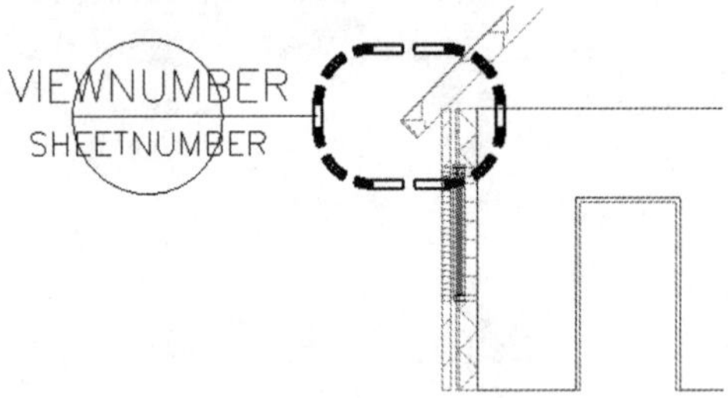

Draw a small rectangle to designate the callout location.

6.

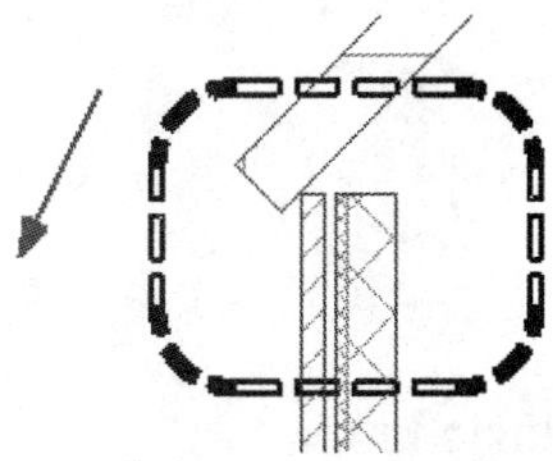

Left click to the left side of the wall section to place the label.

Press **ENTER** or right click to accept.

7.

Type **Detail of Exterior Wall Section** in the View Name field.

Enable **Current Drawing**.

Enable **Generate Section/Elevation**.

Enable **Place Titlemark**.

Set the Scale to **1/2″ = 1′-0″**.

8. Place the view to the right of the elevation.

9.

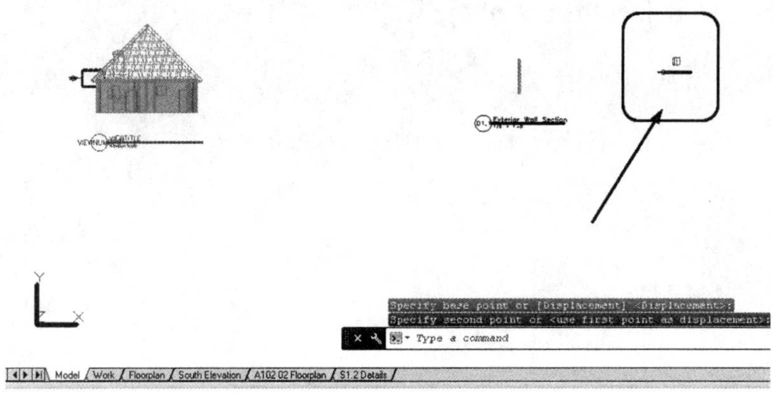

Switch to the Model tab and move the new callout view to the right of the wall section.

10.

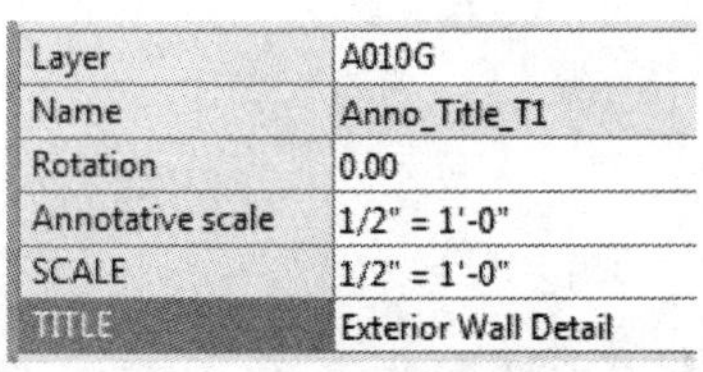

Select the view title for the wall section.

Type **1/2″ = 1′-0″** for the SCALE.

Type **Exterior Wall Detail** for the TITLE.

Press ESC to release and update.

11.

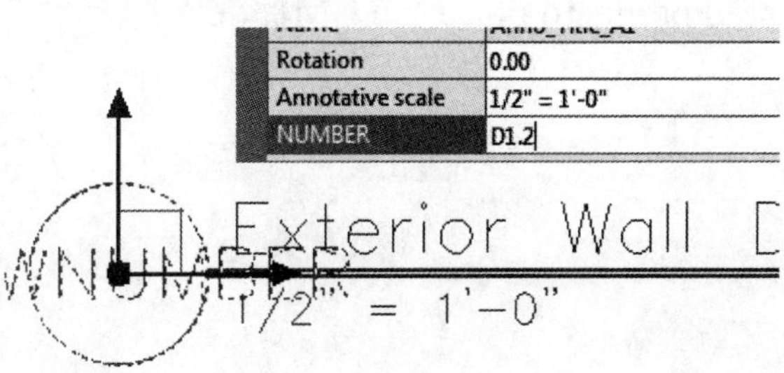

Select the View title bubble.

Type D1.2 for the NUMBER.

Press ESC to release and update.

12. 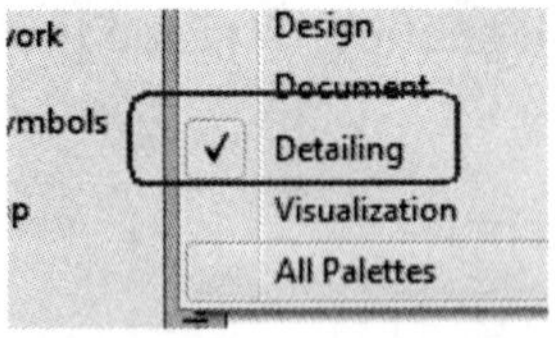

Right click on the Tool Palette's bar.

Enable the Detailing Palette.

13. 

Select the **04- Masonry** detail tool on the Basic tab.

14. 

Select the endpoint indicated to place the detail.

15. 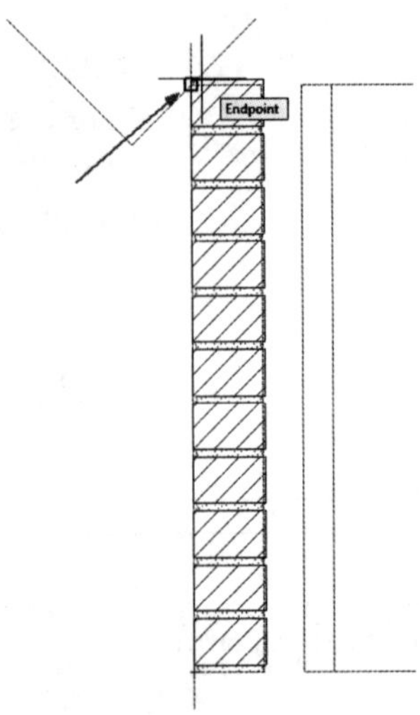

Select the top of the wall.

16. 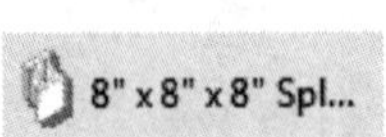

Select the Exterior tab.

Select the **8″ X 8″ X 8″ Split CMU** detail tool.

17. 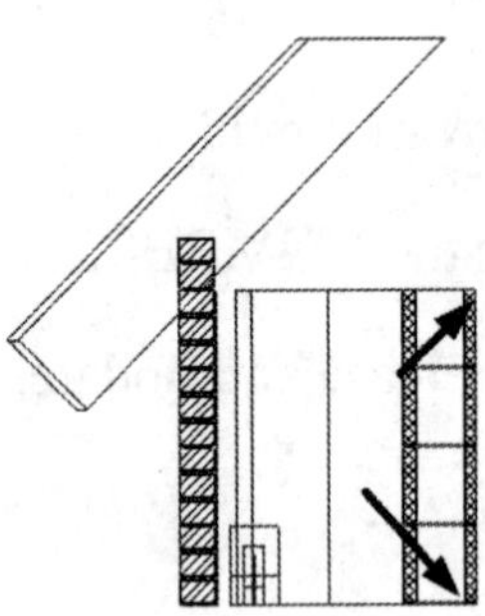
Pick the indicated points to place the CMU detail.

18. 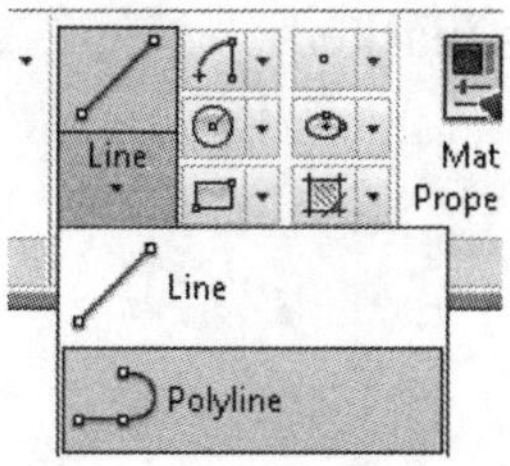

Select the **Polyline** tool from the Home ribbon.

19. 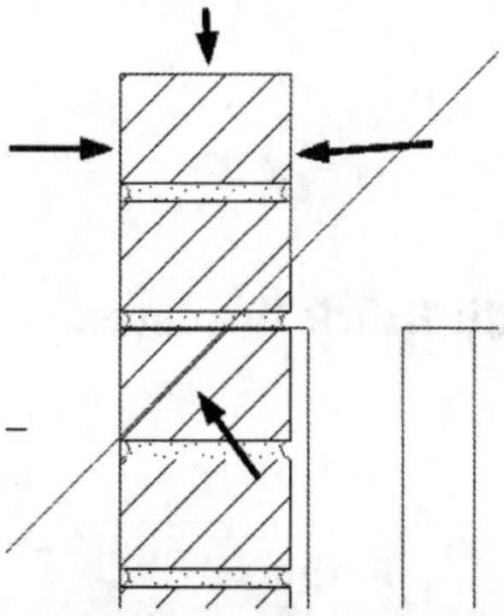

Trace around the masonry details to form a closed polygon.

20. 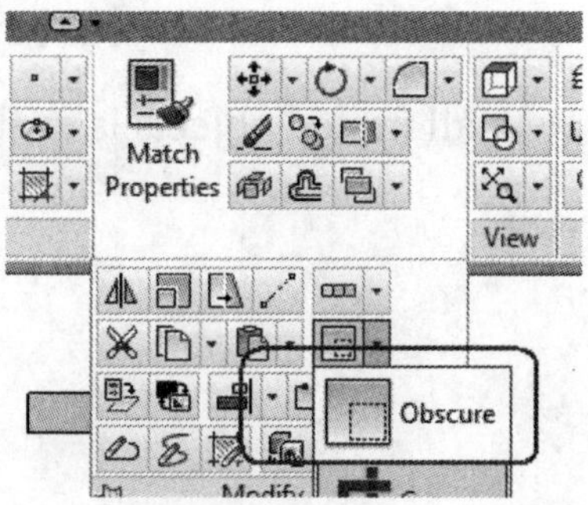

Activate the Home ribbon.

Select the **Obscure** tool on the Modify ribbon.

21. 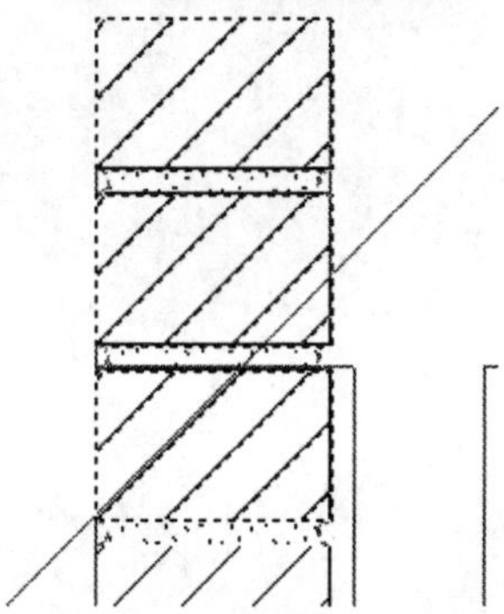

Select the details to be obscured.

Press ENTER.

22. 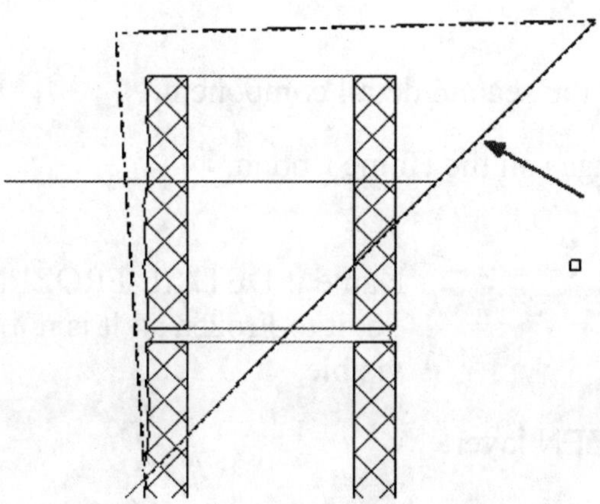

Select the polygon.

Press ENTER.

23. 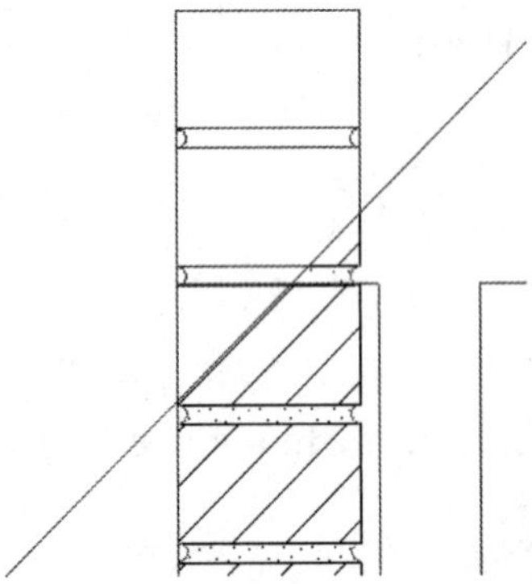
The hatch pattern on the detail is masked.

24. 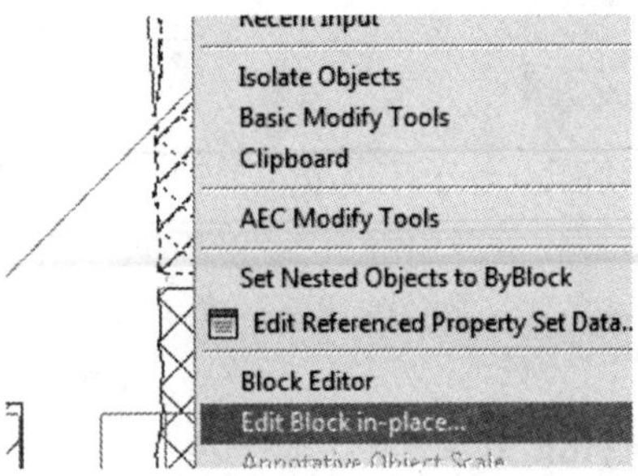

Select the detail.
Right click and select **Edit Block In-place...**

25. 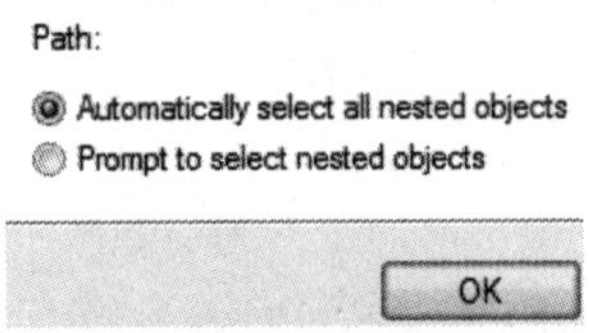

Verify that automatically select all nested objects is enabled.

Press **OK**.

26. 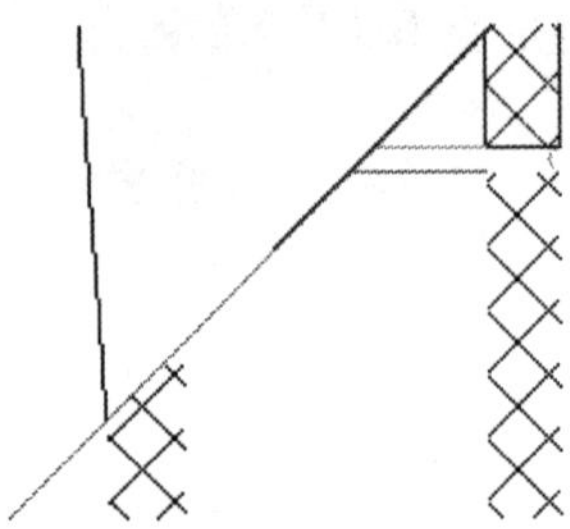
Delete the unwanted lines.

27. 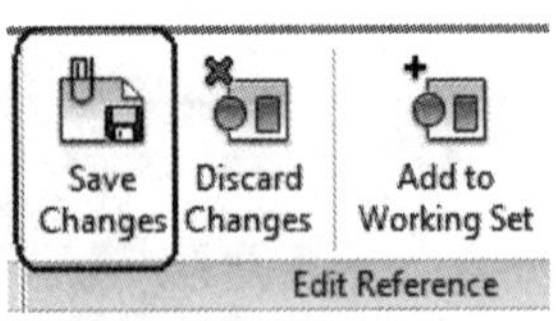

Select **Save Changes** on the ribbon.

28. 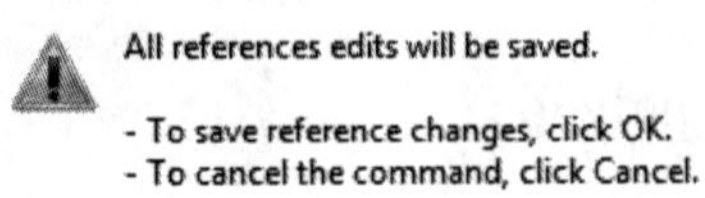

Press **OK**.

Repeat for the second detail component.

29. 
Activate the Layer Manager on the Home ribbon.
Create a new layer.

30. 

Name it DETAIL-FROZEN.
Set it to Frozen so it is not visible.

31. Place the polygon on the DETAIL FROZEN layer.

32. Our detail view so far.

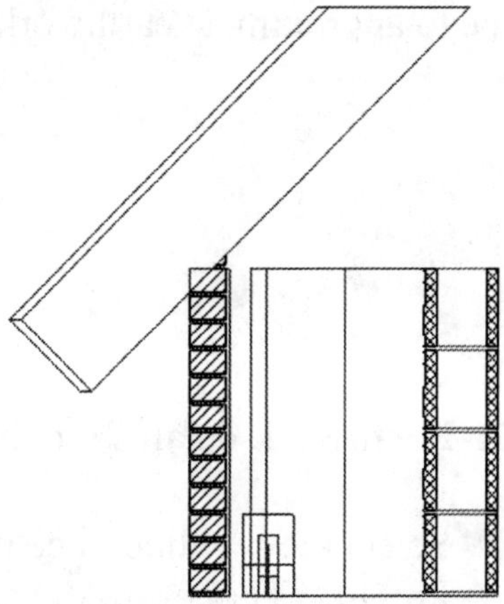

33. 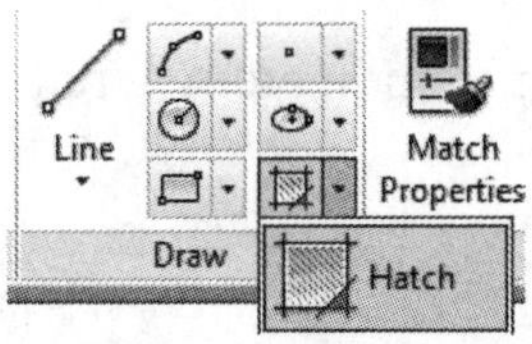

Select the Hatch tool from the Home ribbon.

34. 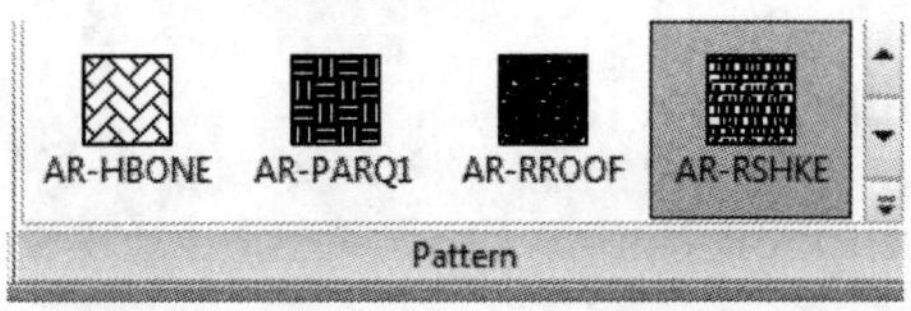

Select the **AR-RSHKE** hatch pattern.

35. 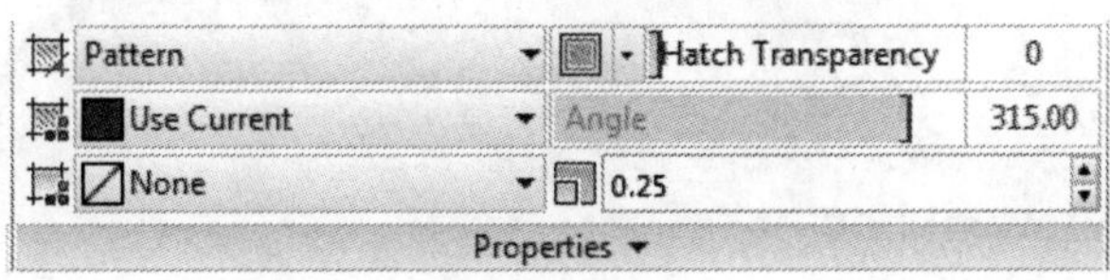

Set the angle to **315.00**.
Set the scale to **0.25**.

36. 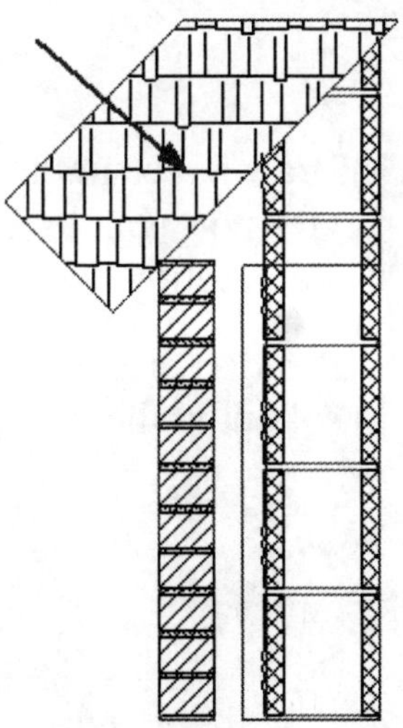
Pick a point inside the roof.

Press ENTER to place.

37. 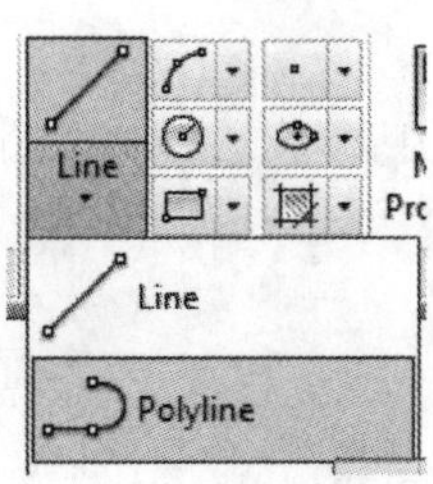

Select the **Polyline** tool from the Home ribbon.

38. 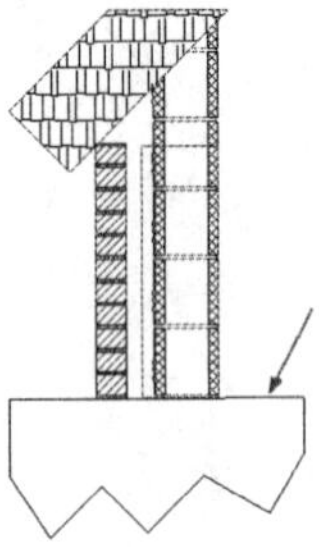

Draw a shape to approximate earthwork.

39. 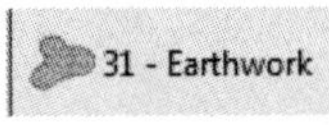

Select the **31-Earthwork** detail from the Basic tab on the Tool Palette.

40. 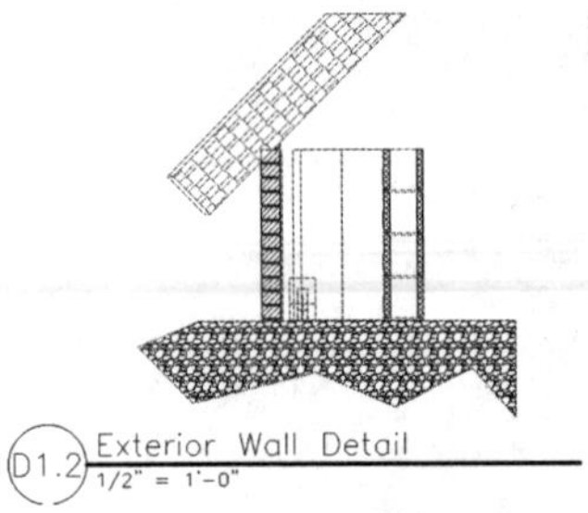

Select the polyline to be used as the boundary.
Press ENTER.

Select inside the polyline object to indicate where to place the hatch pattern.

Press ENTER.

41. 

Activate the **S1.2 Details layout** tab.

42. 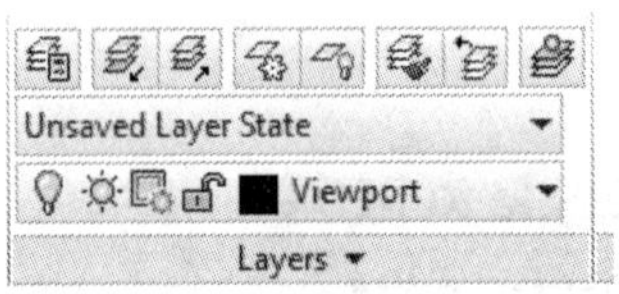

Set the current layer to Viewport.

43. 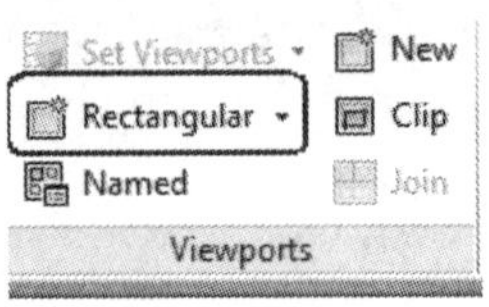

Activate the View ribbon.

Select the Rectangular viewport tool.

44. 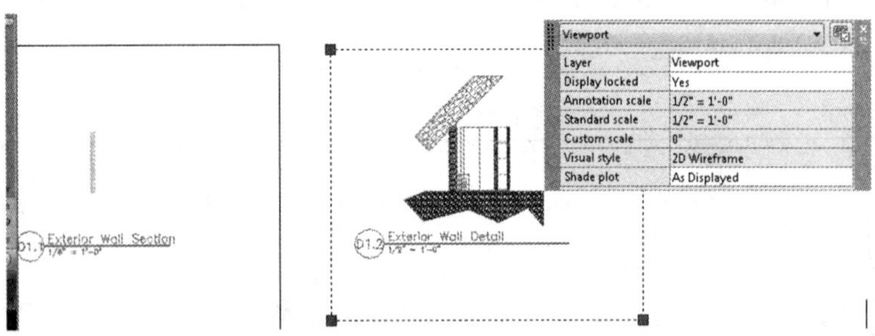

Draw a rectangular viewport next to the wall section detail.

Position the detail callout in the viewport.

45. Select the viewport.
Set the Annotation scale to **1/2″ = 1′0″**.
Set the Standard scale to **1/2″ = 1′0″**

Set the Shade plot to **As Displayed**.

Lock the display.

46. Press ESC to release the viewport.

47. Save as *ex7-11.dwg*.

Exercise 7-12
Creating Space Styles

Drawing Name: Ex7-11.dwg
Estimated Time: 10 minutes

1. Open *ex7-11.dwg.*

2. 

Activate the **Manage** ribbon.

Select the **Style Manager**.

3. 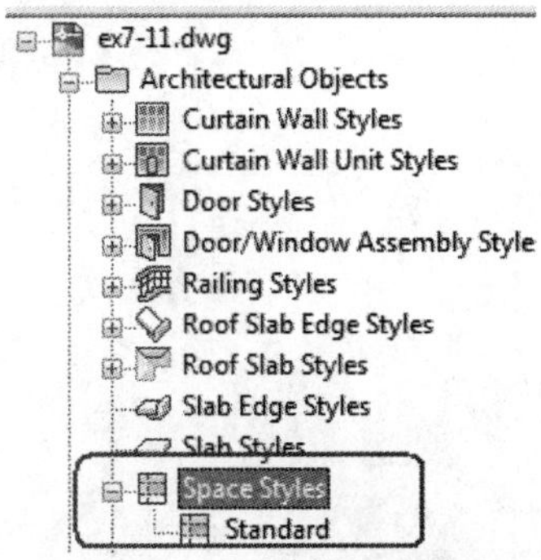

Locate the *Space Styles* drawing.

Make sure you set the Files of Type to dwg or you won't see it.

Note that there is only one space style currently available.

4. 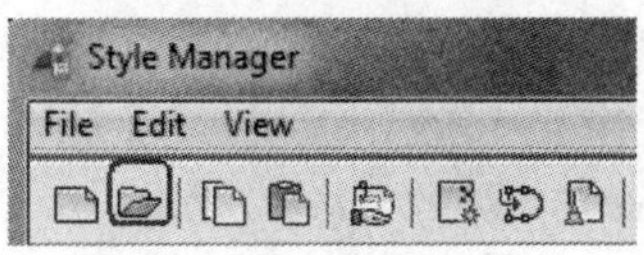

Select the **Open Drawing** tool.

5. 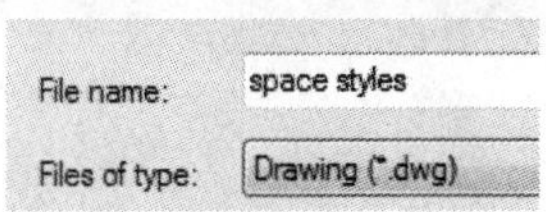

Browse to the exercise folders for this text.
Change the files of type to **Drawing (*.dwg).**
Open the *space styles.dwg*.

6. 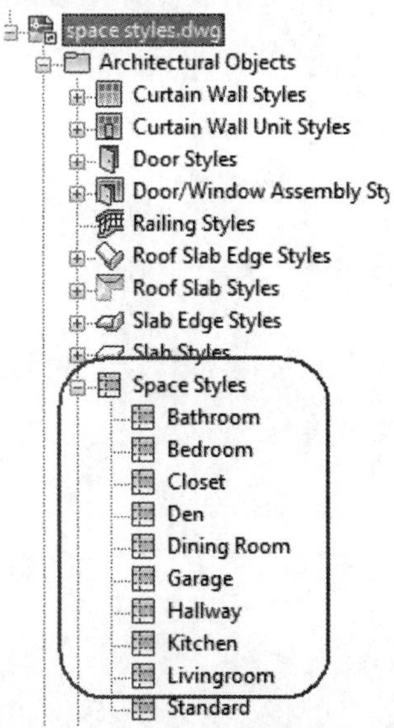

Expand the *space styles.dwg* in the Style Manager.

Note several space styles have been defined.

7. 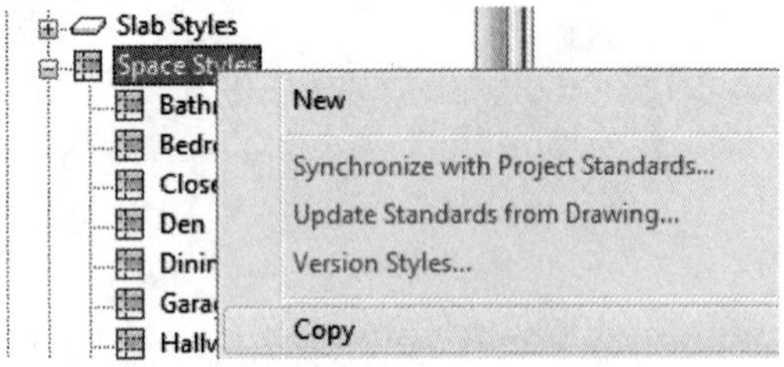

Highlight the **Space Styles** in the *space styles.dwg*.
Right click and select **Copy**.

8. 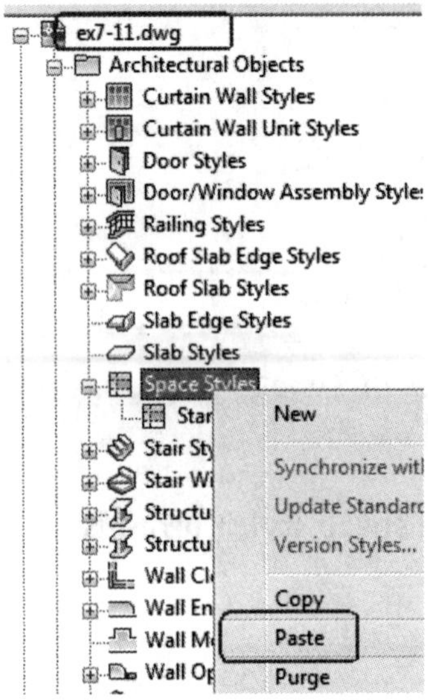

Scroll up to the *ex7-11.dwg*.

Highlight **Space Styles**.

Right click and select **Paste**.

9. 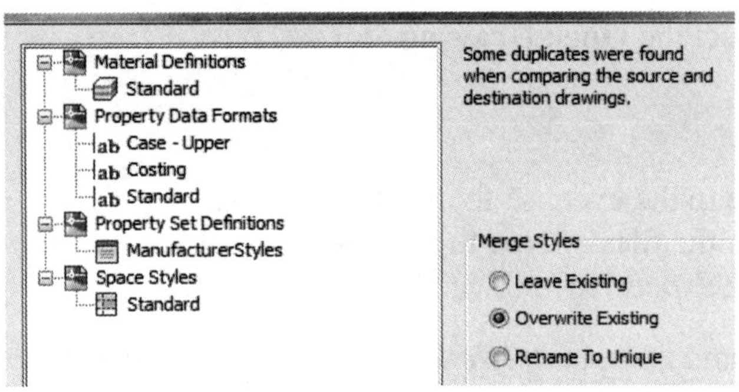

If this dialog appears advising of duplicate definitions:
Enable **Overwrite Existing**.
Press **OK**.

10. 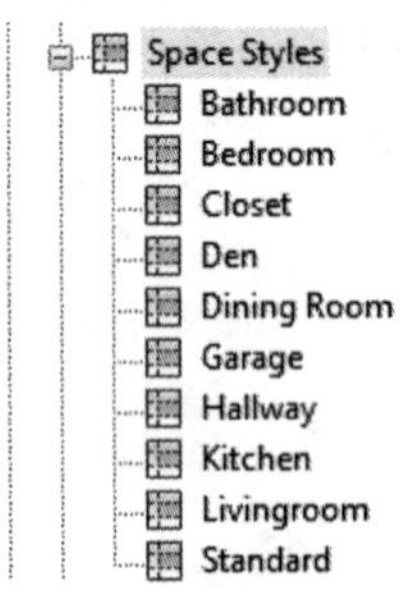

The space styles are now copied into your project.

Close the Style Manager.

11. Save as *ex7-12.dwg*.

Exercise 7-13

Adding Spaces

Drawing Name: Ex7-12.dwg
Estimated Time: 15 minutes

This exercise reinforces the following skills:

- Layouts
- Spaces

1. Open *ex7-12.dwg.*
2. Select the Model tab.
3. 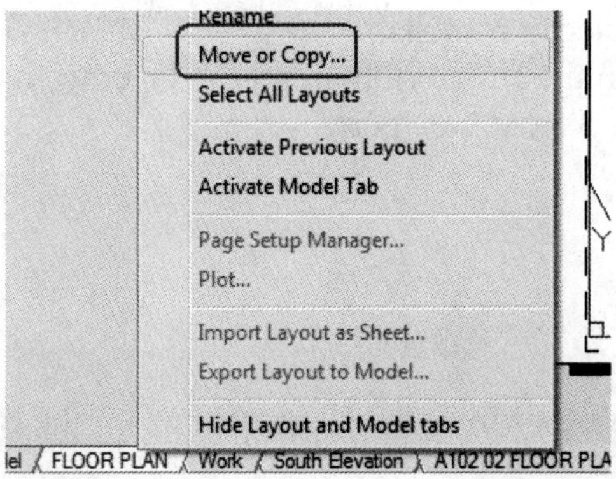

Highlight the **Floor Plan** layout tab.

Right click and select **Move or Copy**.

4. 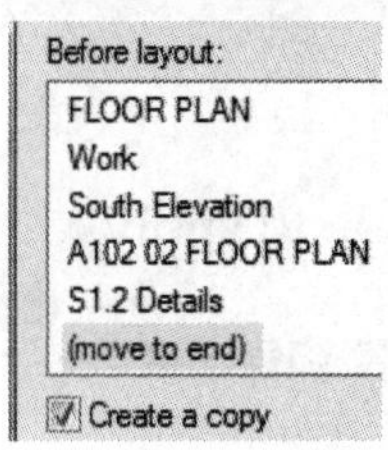

Enable **Create a copy**.

Highlight **(move to end)**.

Press **OK**.

5. 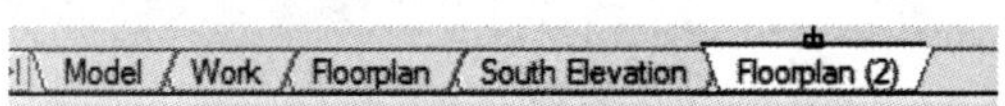

Select the second layout.

6. 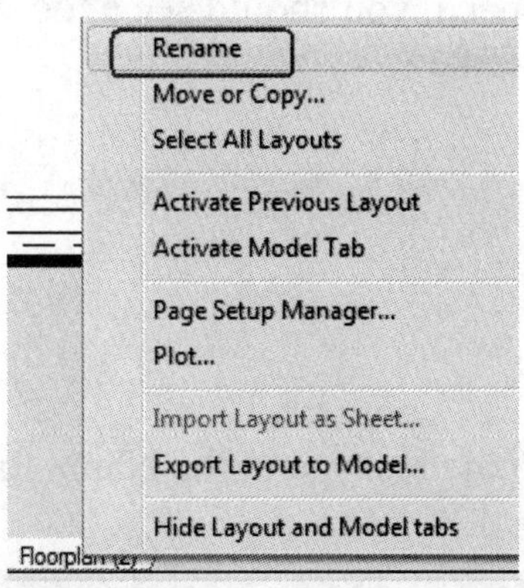

Highlight the second layout tab.

Right click and select **Rename**.

7. 

Modify the layout name to **A102 03 ROOM PLAN**.

8. 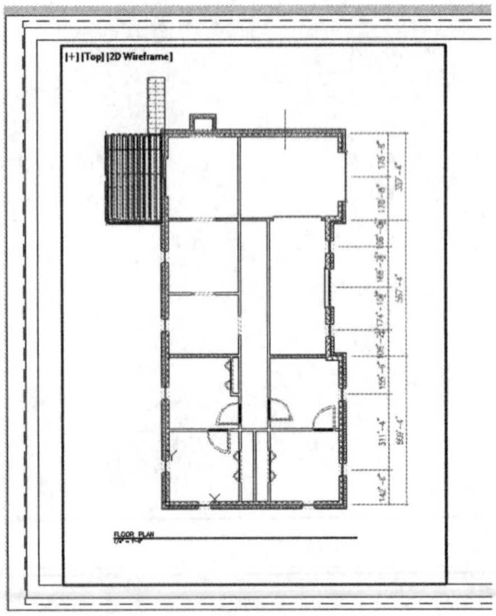

Double click inside the viewport to activate model space.

9. 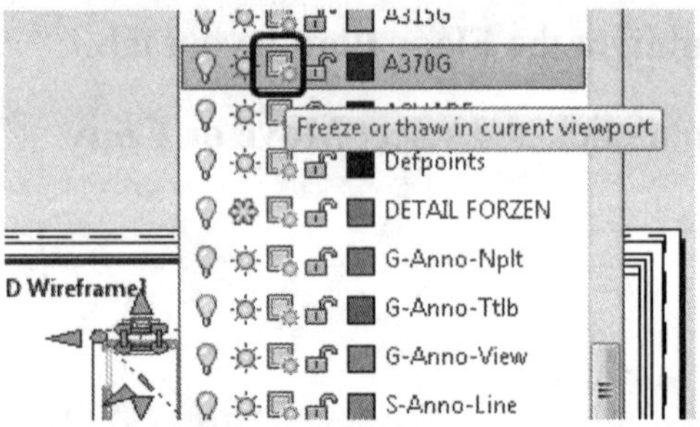

Select a roof slab.
On the Home ribbon, set the layer to freeze in current viewport.

10. 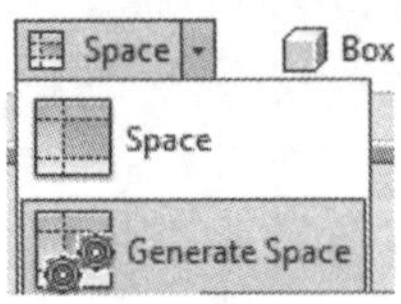

Select the **Generate Space** tool from the Home ribbon on the Build panel.

11. 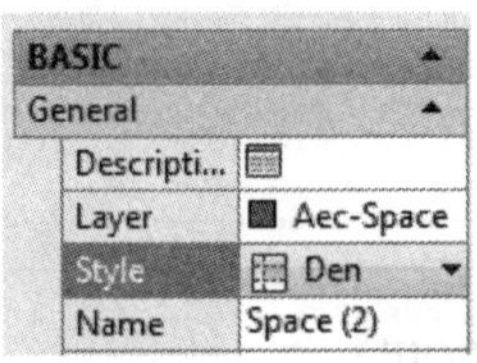

On the Properties palette, select the space style to apply.

Left click inside the designated space to place the space.

12. 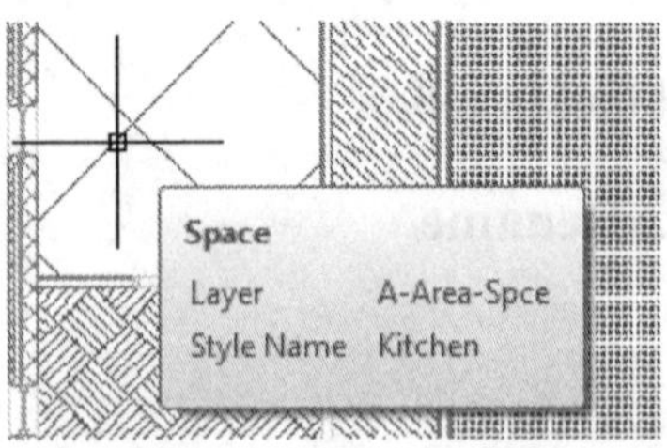

If you hover over a space, you should see a tool tip with the space style name.

13. 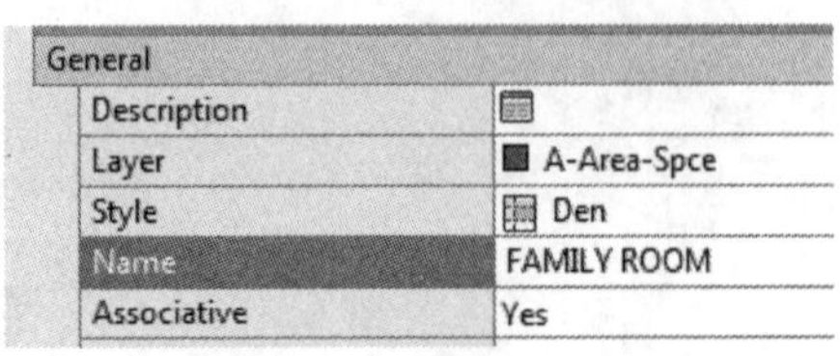

Select a space.

In the Properties palette: type in the Name for the SPACE.

This is the name that will appear on the room tag.

14. Repeat for all the spaces.
    Press ESC to release the selection of each space before moving on to the next space.

    Verify that only one space is selected to be renamed each time or you may assign a name to the wrong space unintentionally.

15. Save as *ex7-13.dwg*.

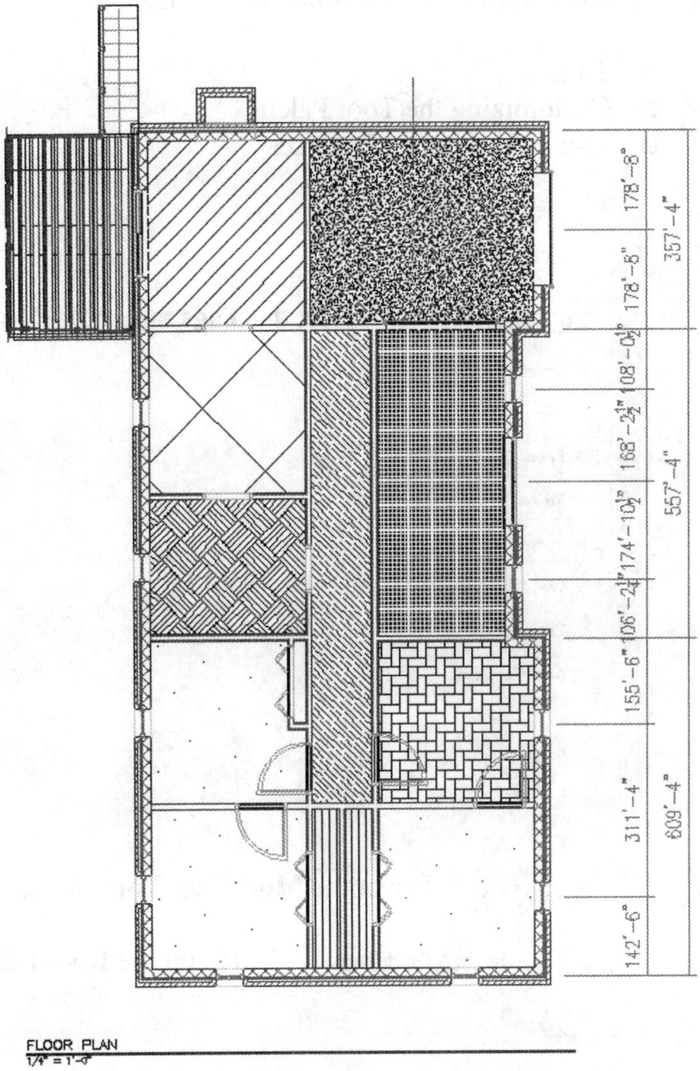

Exercise 7-14

Adding Room Tags

Drawing Name: ex7-13.dwg
Estimated Time: 15 minutes

This exercise reinforces the following skills:

- Tags
- Customizing the Tool Palette
- Using the Content Browser

1. Open *ex7-13.dwg.*

2. 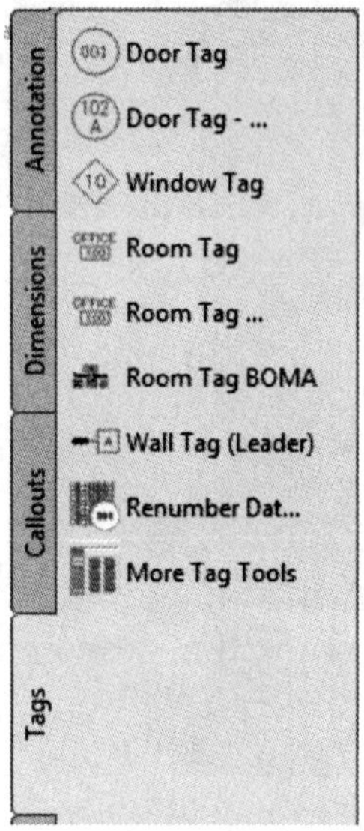

Select the **Tags** tab on the Document Tool Palette.

3. 

Select the **More Tag Tools** icon.

4. 

Click on the **Room & Finish Tags**.

5. 

Locate the **Room Tag (w/Dimensions)**.

6. 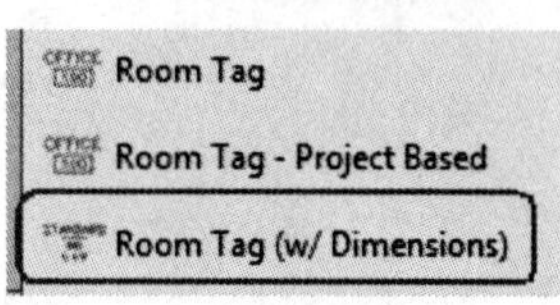

Drag and drop it onto the Tool Palette.

7. 

Select the **A102 03 ROOM PLAN** layout tab.
Double click in the viewport to activate model space.

8. 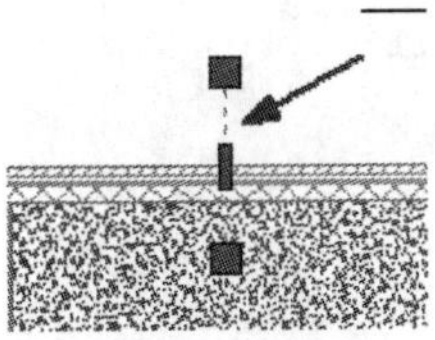
Select the section line on the north wall used to define the wall section.

9. 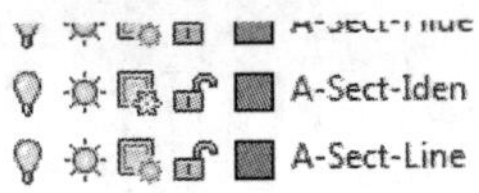

Set to **Hide in the current viewport** using the Layer drop-down on the Home ribbon.

10. 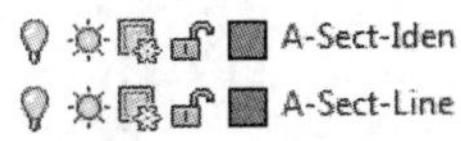

Set A-**Sect-Iden** to **Hide in the current viewport**.

11. 

Select the **Room Tag (w/Dimensions)**.

12. 

Select the family room space.
Press **ENTER** to place the tag centered in the room.

13. 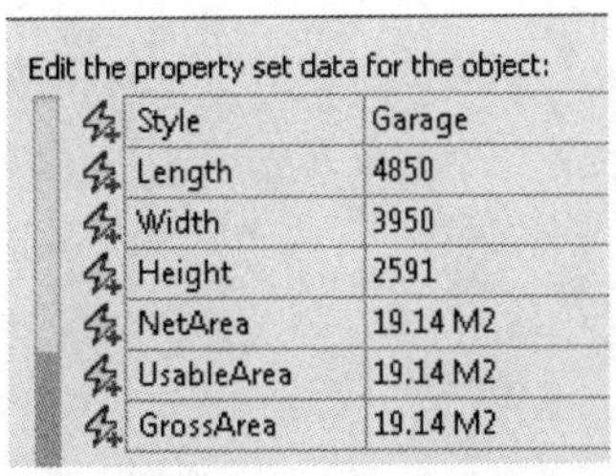

A small dialog will appear showing all the data attached to the space.

You can modify any field that is not grayed out.

Press **OK**.

14. 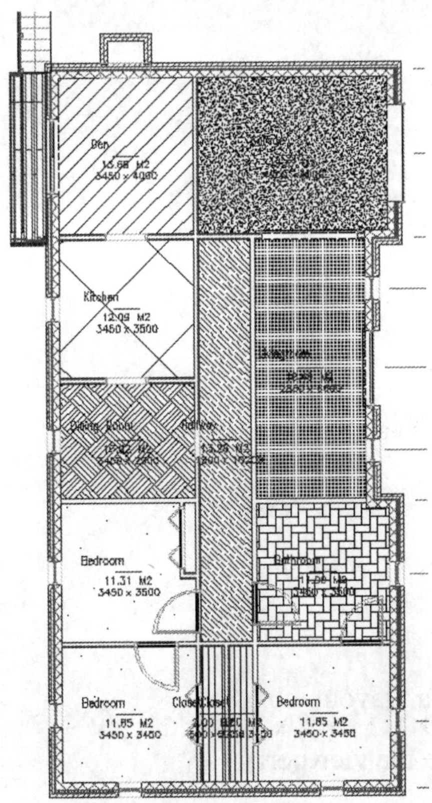

Repeat to tag all the spaces.

15. 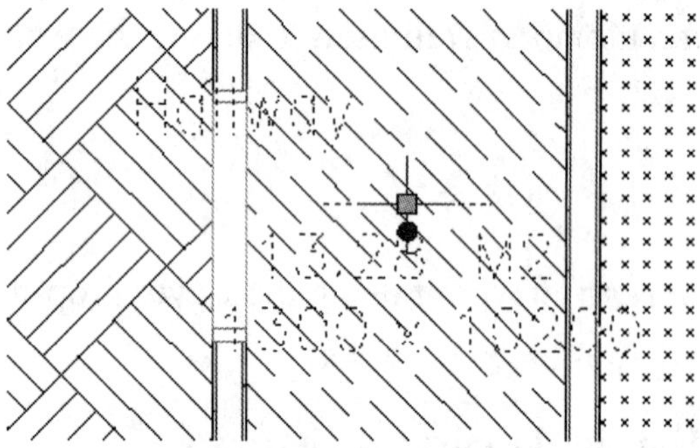 Select the Hallway tag.

16. 

On the Properties palette:
Select **Anchor**.

17. 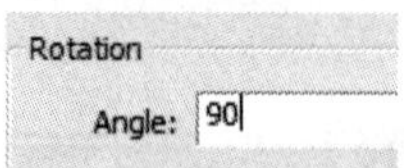

Set the Rotation angle to **90**.
Press **OK**.

18. Press ESC or left click outside the building model to release the selected tag.

19. 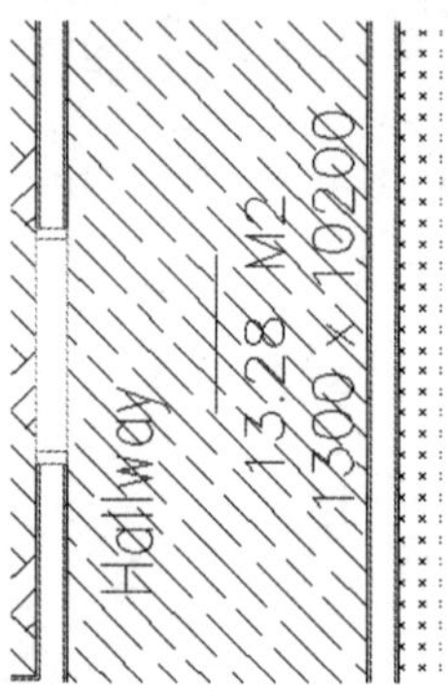

The tag is rotated 90 degrees.

20. Save as *ex7-14.dwg*.

Exercise 7-15

Adding Door Tags

Drawing Name: ex7-14.dwg
Estimated Time: 10 minutes

This exercise reinforces the following skills:

- Tags

1. Open *ex7-14.dwg.*

2. 

Activate the A102 02 Floor plan layout tab.

3. Activate model space by double-clicking inside the viewport.

4. 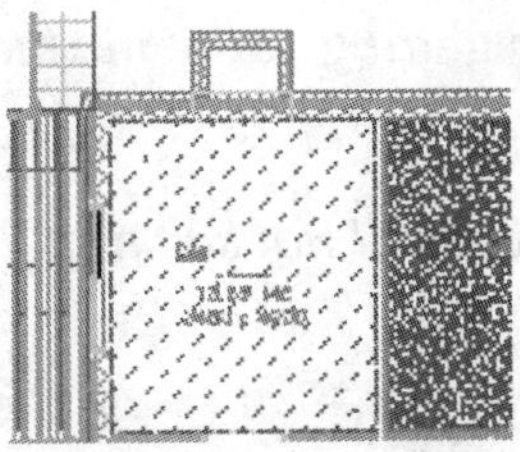

Select the DEN space so it is highlighted.

5. 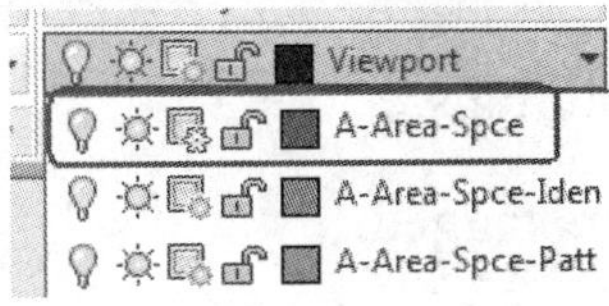

Activate the Home ribbon.
The A-Area-Spce layer should be shown.
Freeze the layer in the current viewport.

6. 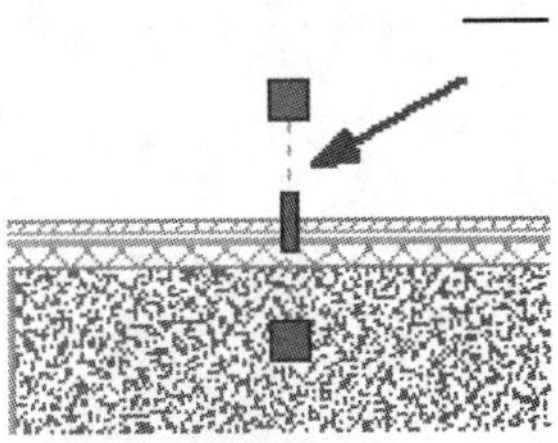

Select the section line on the north wall used to define the wall section.

7. 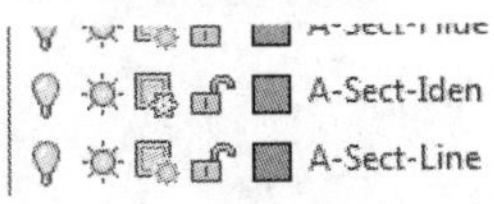

Set to **Hide in the current viewport** using the Layer drop-down on the Home ribbon.

8. 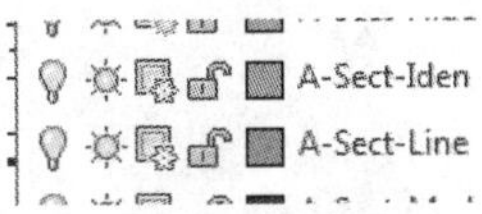

Set A-**Sect-Iden** to **Hide in the current viewport.**

9. Activate the Document palette.
Activate the Tags tab.

Select the Door Tag tool. 

10. 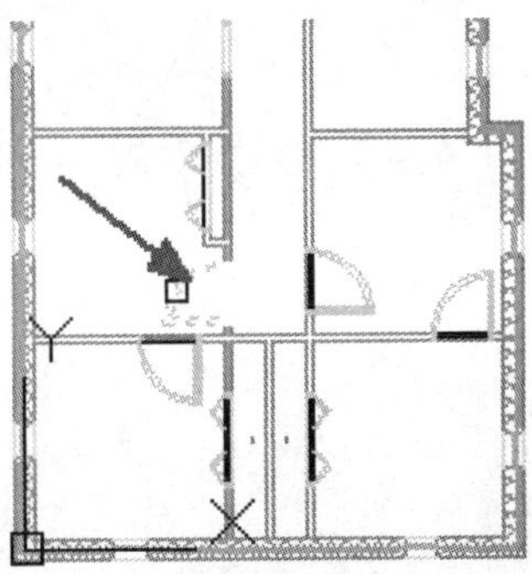

Select a door.

Press ENTER to center the tag on the door.

11. 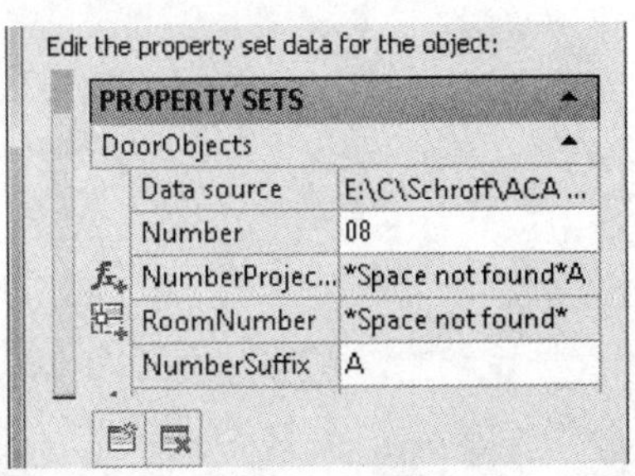

Press **OK**.

Some students may be concerned because they see the Error getting value next to the Room Number field.

If you tag the spaces with a room tag assigning a number, you will not see that error.

12. Right click and select **Multiple**.
    Type All.
    Select the remaining doors in the floor plan to add the door tags.

13. 

    There should be thirteen doors tagged.

    Save as *ex7-15.dwg*.

Exercise 7-16

Create a Door Schedule

Drawing Name: ex7-15.dwg
Estimated Time: 10 minutes

This exercise reinforces the following skills:

- Schedules

1. Open *ex7-15.dwg*.
2. 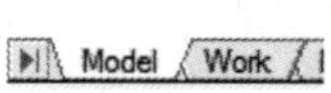

Activate the Model layout tab.
3. 

Select the Door Schedule tool.

The Door Schedule tool can be found on the Annotate ribbon or on the Document Tool Palette on the Scheduling tab.

4. Type **ALL** on the command line.

   ACA will automatically filter out any non-door entities and collect only doors.

   Press **ENTER**.

5. 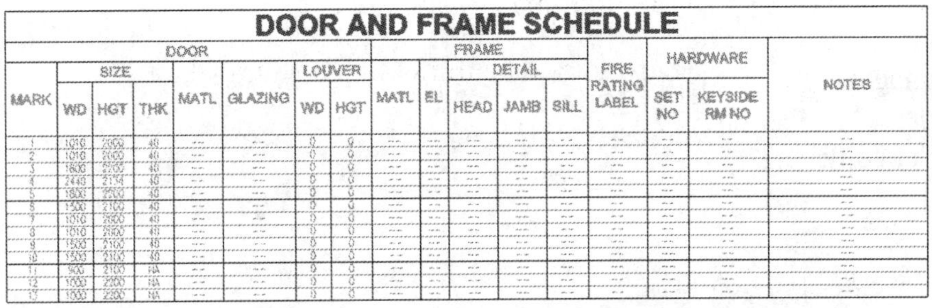

   Left click to place the schedule in the drawing window.

   Press **ENTER**.

6. 

   Activate the **A102 02 Floor Plan** layout tab.

7. 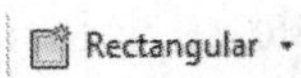

   Activate the View ribbon.
   Select the **Rectangular** viewport tool.

8. 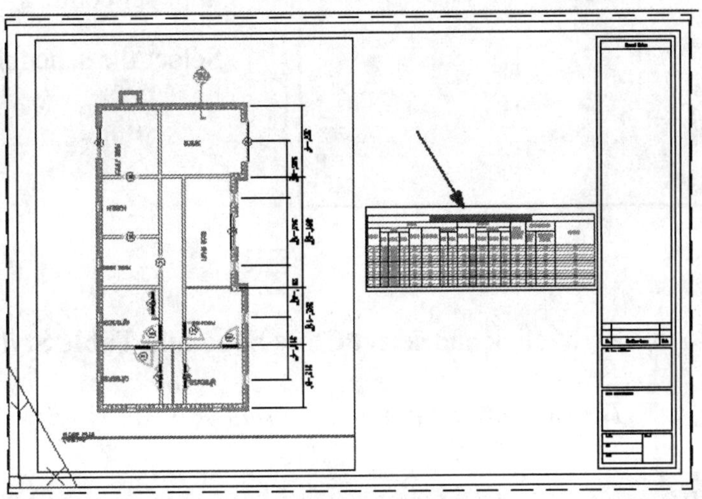

   Draw a rectangular viewport.

   Position the door schedule in the viewport.

9. 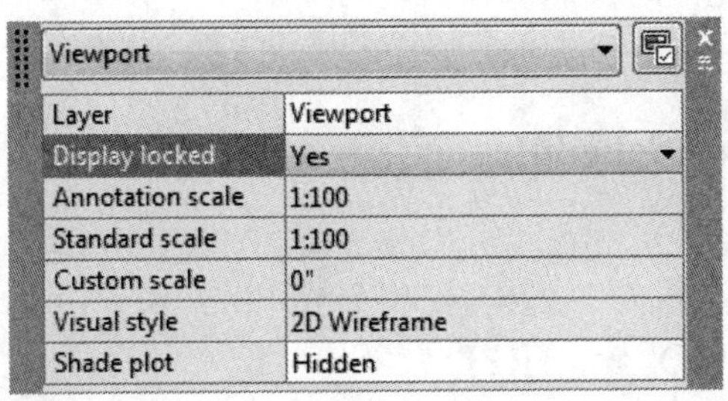

   Select the viewport.

   Verify that it is on the Viewport layer.

   Set the Standard scale to **1:100.**

   Set the Display locked to **Yes**.

10. Save as *ex7-16.dwg.*

Exercise 7-17

Create a Door Schedule Style

Drawing Name: ex7-16.dwg
Estimated Time: 30 minutes

This exercise reinforces the following skills:

- Schedules
- Style Manager
- Text Styles
- Update Schedule

1. Open *ex7-16.dwg.*
2. 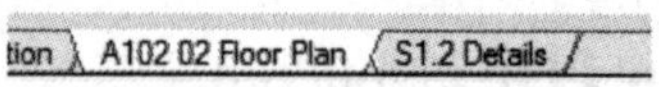

Activate the **A102 02 Floor Plan** layout tab.
3. 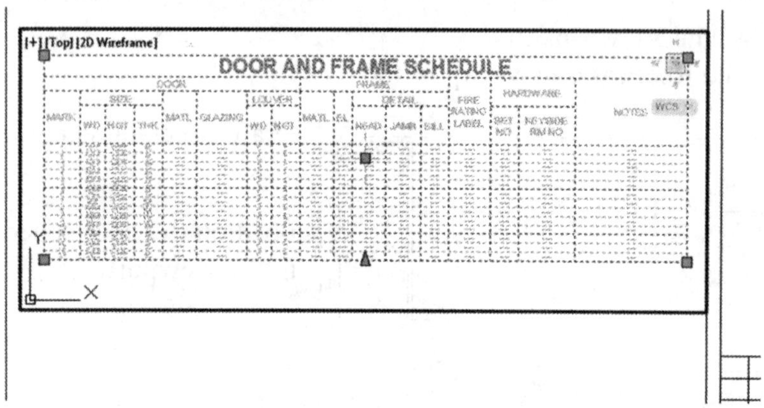

Double click inside the viewport with the door schedule.

   Select the schedule.
4. 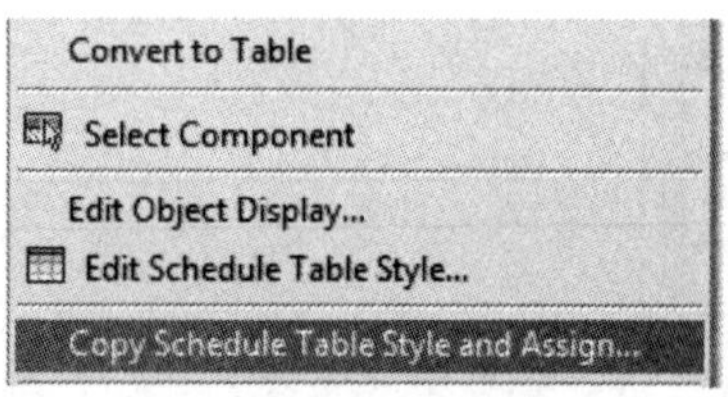

Right click and select **Copy Schedule Table Style**.

   This will create a new style that you can modify.
5. 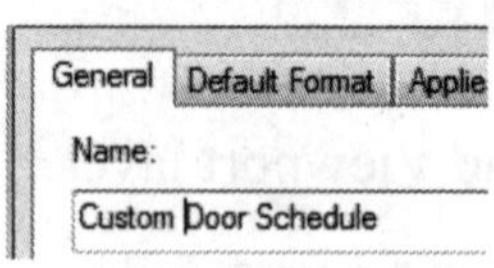

Select the **General** tab.

   Rename **Custom Door Schedule**.
6. 

Select the **Columns** tab.
7. 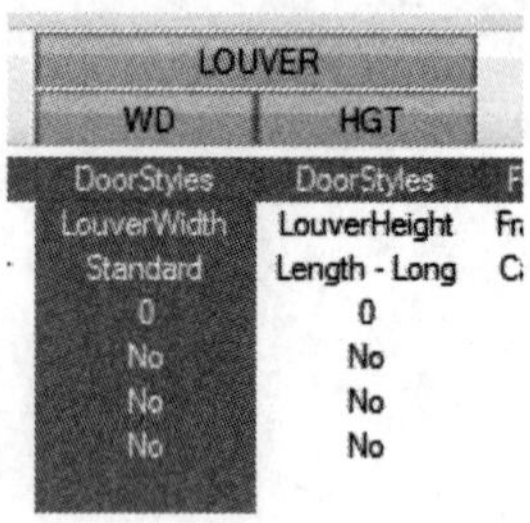

Highlight Louver, WD, and HGT.

8. 

Press **Delete**.

9. 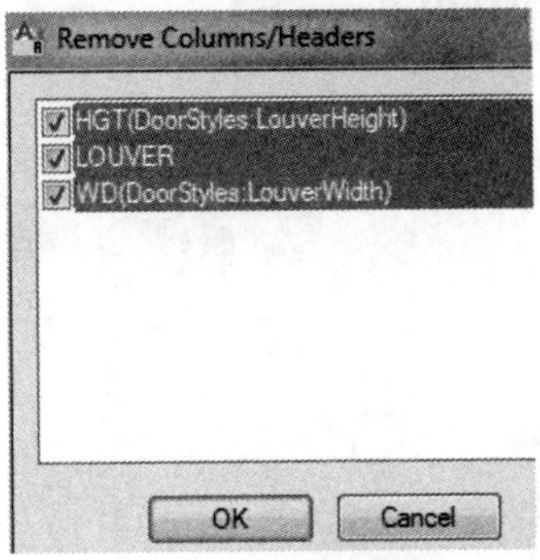

You will be asked to confirm the deletion.

Press **OK**.

10. 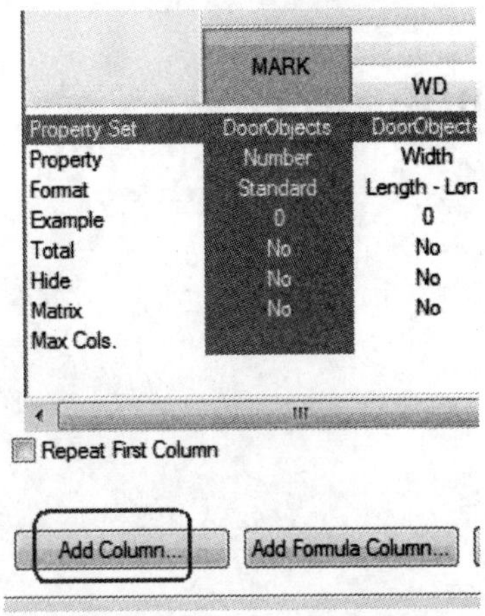

Highlight **MARK**.

Select the **Add Column** button.

11. 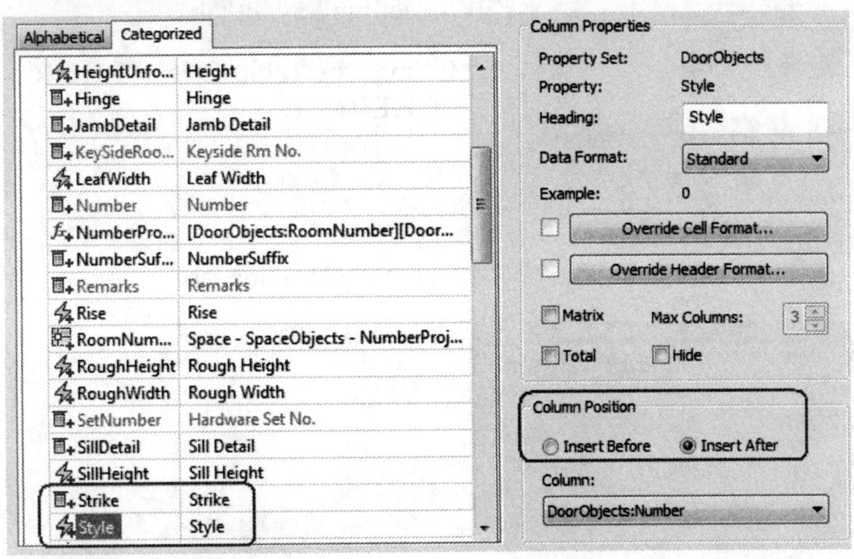

Scroll down until you see Style.

Highlight **Style**.

Confirm that the Column Position will be inserted after the DoorObjects: Number.

Press **OK**.

12. 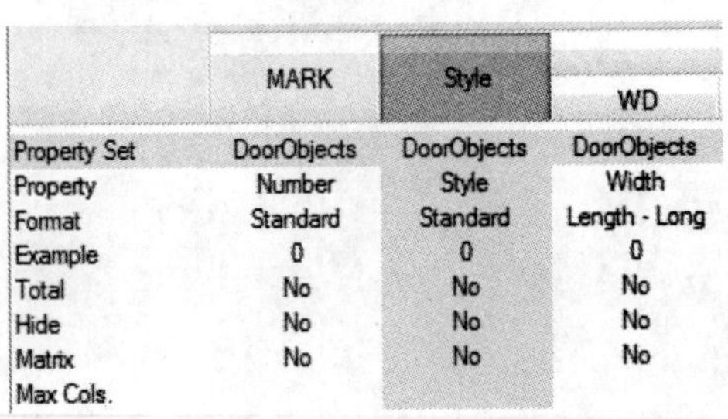

The new column is now inserted.

13. 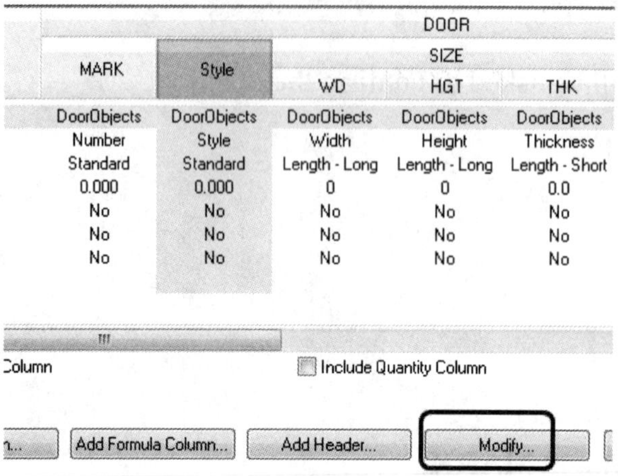

Highlight the **Style** Column and select **Modify**.

14. 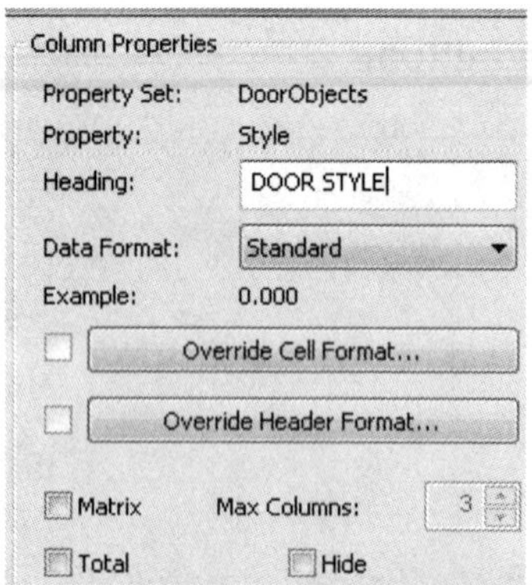

Change the Heading to **DOOR STYLE**.

Press **OK**.

15. 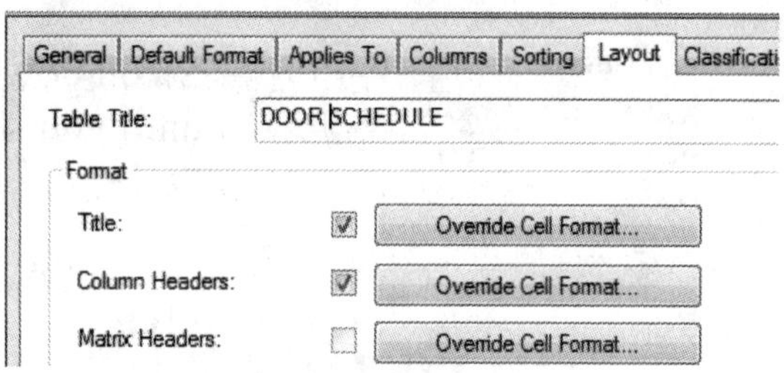

Select the Layout tab.

Change the Table Title to **DOOR SCHEDULE**.

16. 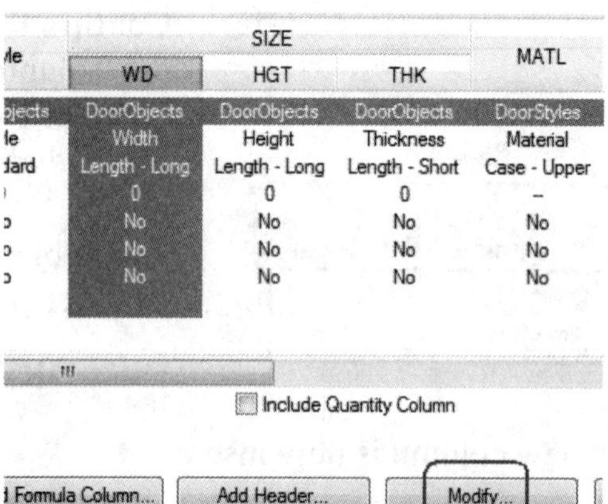

Activate the Columns tab.

Highlight the **WD** column.

Select **Modify**.

17. 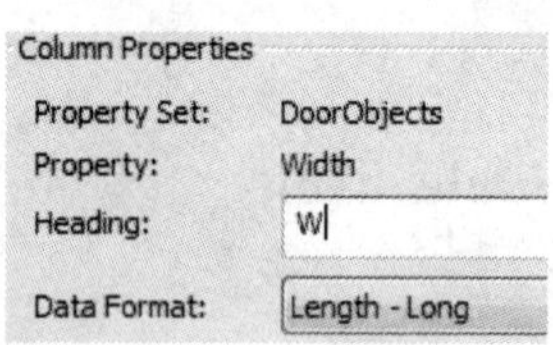

Change the Heading to **W**.

Press **OK**.

18. 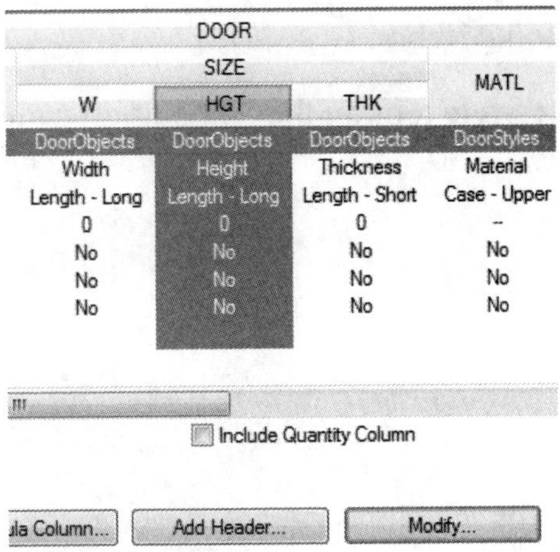

Highlight the **HGT** column.

Select **Modify**.

19. 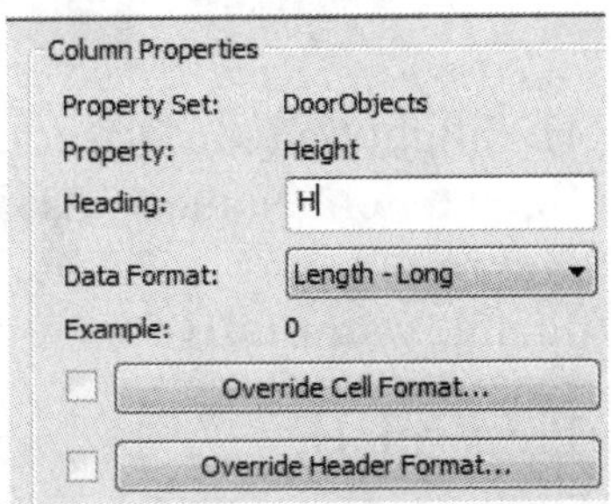

Change the Heading to **H**.

Press **OK**.

20. Press **OK** to close the dialog.

21. 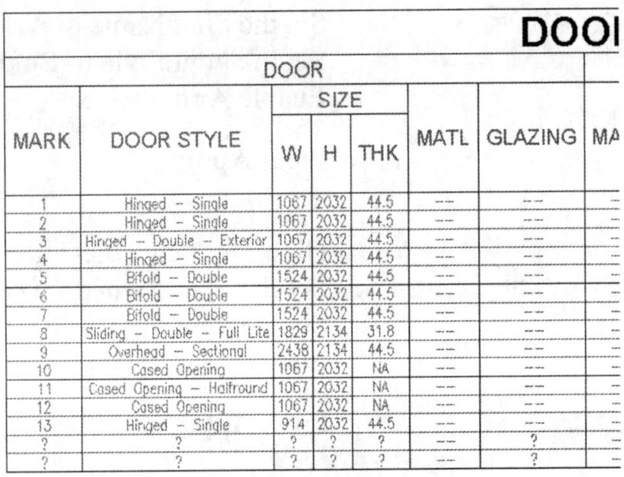

MARK	DOOR STYLE	W	H	THK	MATL	GLAZING
1	Hinged - Single	1067	2032	44.5	--	--
2	Hinged - Single	1067	2032	44.5	--	--
3	Hinged - Double - Exterior	1067	2032	44.5	--	--
4	Hinged - Single	1067	2032	44.5	--	--
5	Bifold - Double	1524	2032	44.5	--	--
6	Bifold - Double	1524	2032	44.5	--	--
7	Bifold - Double	1524	2032	44.5	--	--
8	Sliding - Double - Full Lite	1829	2134	31.8	--	--
9	Overhead - Sectional	2438	2134	44.5	--	--
10	Cased Opening	1067	2032	NA	--	--
11	Cased Opening - Halfround	1067	2032	NA	--	--
12	Cased Opening	1067	2032	NA	--	--
13	Hinged - Single	914	2032	44.5	--	--
?	?	?	?	?	--	?
?	?	?	?	?	--	?

The schedule updates.

If there are question marks in the schedule, that indicates doors which remain untagged.

22. 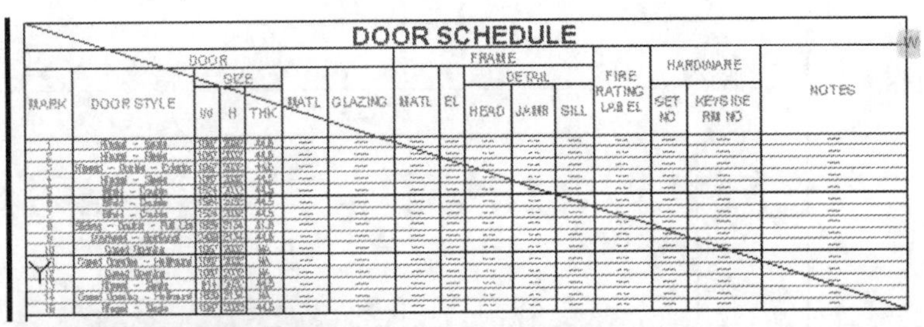

A diagonal line through the schedule indicates it requires updating.

23. 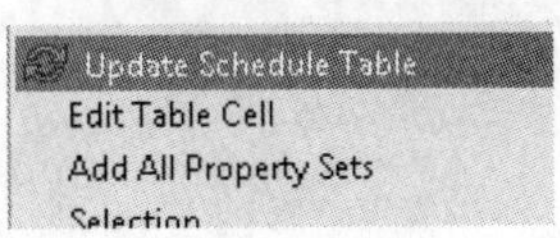

Select the schedule.
Right click and select **Update Schedule Table**.

24. 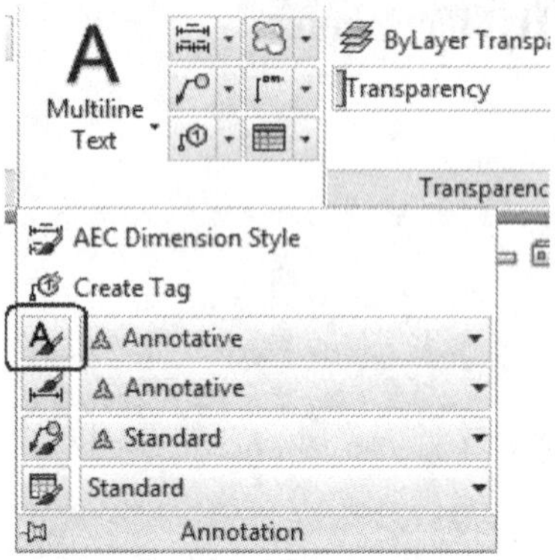

Activate the Home ribbon.

Select the **Text Style** tool on the Annotation panel.

25. 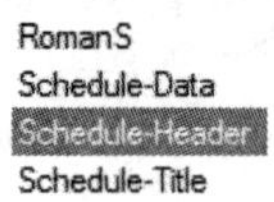

Notice there are text styles set up for schedules. Highlight each one to see their settings.

26. 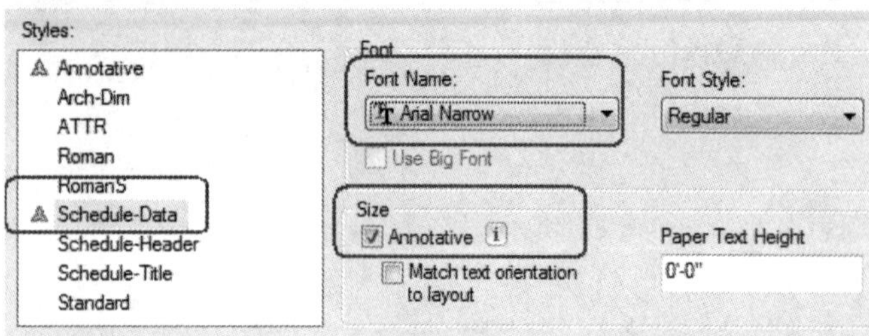

Highlight **Schedule-Data.**
Set the Font Name to **Arial Narrow**.
Enable **Annotative**.

Press **Apply**.

27. 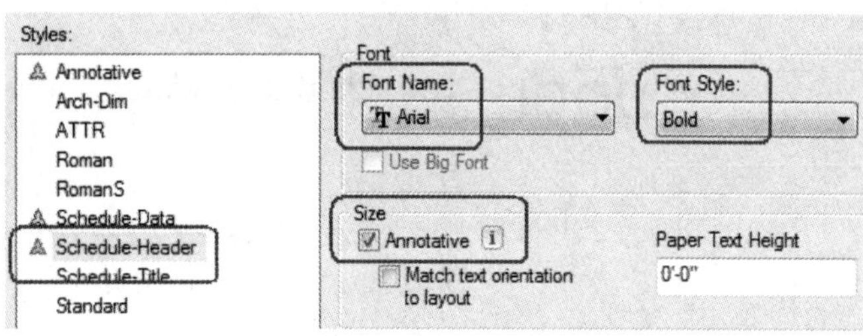

Highlight Schedule-Header.
Set the Font Name to **Arial**.
Set the Font Style to **Bold**.
Enable **Annotative**.

Press **Apply**.

28. 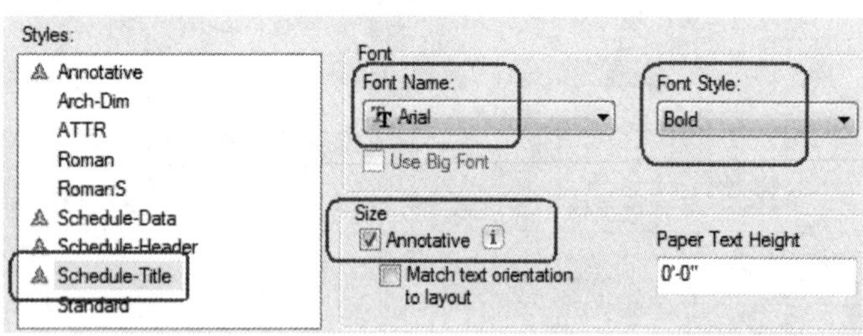

Highlight Schedule-Title.
Set the Font Name to **Arial**.
Set the Font Style to **Bold**.
Enable **Annotative**.

Press **Apply** and **Close**.

29. Note that the schedule automatically updates.

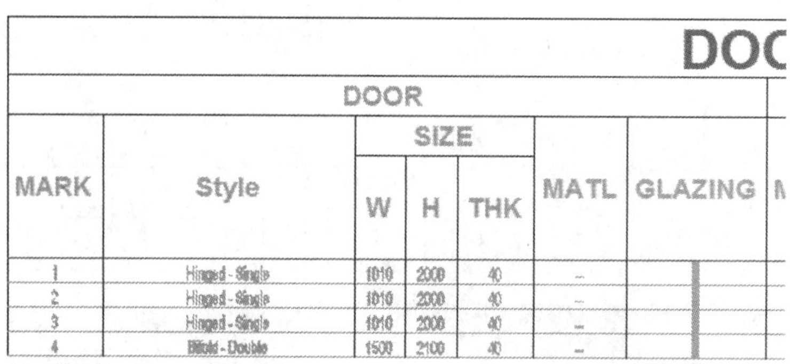

30. Save as *ex7-17.dwg*.

QUIZ 4

True or False

1. Columns, braces, and beams are created using Structural Members.
2. When you isolate a Layer User Group, you are freezing all the layers in that group.
3. You can isolate a Layer User Group in ALL Viewports, a Single Viewport, or a Selection Set of Viewports.
4. When placing beams, you can switch the justification in the middle of the command.
5. Standard AutoCAD commands, like COPY, MOVE, and ARRAY cannot be used in ACA.

Multiple Choice

6. Before you can place a beam or column, you must:

   A. Generate a Member Style
   B. Activate the Structural Member Catalog
   C. Select a structural member shape
   D. All of the above

7. Select the character that is OK to use when creating a Structural Member Style Name.

   A. -
   B. ?
   C. =
   D. /

8. Identify the tool shown.

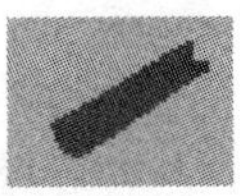

   A. Add Brace
   B. Add Beam
   C. Add Column
   D. Structural Member Catalog

9. Setting a Layer Key

   A. Controls which layer AEC objects will be placed on.
   B. Determines the layer names created.
   C. Sets layer properties.
   D. All of the above.

10. There are two types of stairs used in residential buildings:

    A. INSIDE and OUTSIDE
    B. METAL and WOOD
    C. MAIN and SERVICE
    D. FLOATING and STATIONARY

11. Select the stair type that does not exist from the list below:

    A. Straight-run
    B. M Stairs
    C. L Stairs
    D. U Stairs

12. The first point selected when placing a set of stairs is:

    A. The foot/bottom of the stairs.
    B. The head/top of the stairs
    C. The center point of the stairs
    D. Depends on the property settings

ANSWERS:

1) T; 2) F; 3) T; 4) T; 5) F; 6) D; 7) A; 8) A; 9) A; 10) C; 11) B; 12) D